Crisis in American Institutions

CRISIS IN AMERICAN INSTITUTIONS

Thirteenth Edition

JEROME H. SKOLNICK

New York University

ELLIOTT CURRIE

University of California, Irvine

Boston   New York   San Francisco
Mexico City   Montreal   Toronto   London   Madrid   Munich   Paris
Hong Kong   Singapore   Tokyo   Cape Town   Sydney

Senior Series Editor: Jeff Lasser
Series Editorial Assistant: Erikka Adams
Senior Marketing Manager: Kelly May
Editorial-Production Service: Omegatype Typography, Inc.
Composition Buyer: Linda Cox
Manufacturing Buyer: JoAnne Sweeney
Electronic Composition: Omegatype Typography, Inc.
Cover Administrator: Joel Gendron

For related titles and support materials, visit our online catalog at www.ablongman.com.

Between the time website information is gathered and then published, it is not unusual for some sites to have closed. Also, the transcription of URLs can result in typographical errors. The publisher would appreciate notification where these errors occur so that they may be corrected in subsequent editions.

Library of Congress Cataloging-in-Publication Data

Crisis in american institutions / [edited by] Jerome H. Skolnick, Elliott Currie — 13th ed.
    p.   cm.
    Includes bibliographical references.
    ISBN 0-205-47215-X
    1. United States—Social conditions—1980–   2. United States—Social conditions—1960–1980. 3. Social problems—United States. 4. United States—Social conditions. I. Skolnick, Jerome H. II. Currie, Elliott.

HN65.C684 2007
306'.0973—dc22

                                     2006043181

Printed in the United States of America
10 9 8 7 6 5 4 3 2 1   RRD-VA   11 10 09 08 07 06

Credits appear on pp. 447–449, which constitute an extension of the copyright page.

Contents

SYSTEMIC PROBLEMS

Preface

We are, as always, extremely gratified by the positive response to the previous edition of *Crisis in American Institutions*. But once again, we have made many changes for this new edition.

Though we've kept the basic structure of the 12th edition, we've added a great deal of new material—while dropping many articles that seemed to us to have become dated or less relevant. We have filled out our coverage of economic issues with new pieces on the erosion of retirement security and the rise in debt among the young. We have updated our treatment of corporate "wealthfare" with two new articles, and added a piece on the limits of social mobility in the United States to the section on inequality. We've strengthened our discussion of sexism with two new pieces on gender discrimination in the workplace, and modernized the section on the environment with new articles on global environmental threats and on environmental racism. We've added new pieces on global terrorism, immigration, racial disparities in the criminal justice system, and more. We've also moved one piece—Herbert Gans on the "Underclass Label"—to the section on work and welfare, and replaced another with a new, revised version—Edward Wolff's discussion of wealth inequality in America.

Each edition has provided an opportunity to review the best contemporary writing on social problems, and with each we've regretted having to drop old favorites and omit much promising new work. We invariably find more good writing than we can use—which isn't surprising, because we cover a range of issues, from corporate power to racism, from the family to the environment, each of which could profitably occupy a lifetime of study.

We are deeply grateful to the many people who have helped make this new edition a reality. We want particularly to thank Jeff Lasser and Heather McNally of Allyn and Bacon for their help, and patience, in facilitating this revision. We would also like to thank the reviewers for this edition: Hollis Beloat, College of the Abermarle; Boyd Bergeson, Portland State University; Russell P. D. Burton, Washburn University; Patrick Donnelly, University of Dayton; Judy Morelock, University of Tennessee; Gregg Robinson, Grossmont College; James Roth, Regis University; and Gregory Squires, George Washington University. We are indebted to our colleagues at New York University and the University of California, Irvine, for providing unfailingly supportive and stimulating environments. We are grateful to the many students and teachers who have continued to educate us about each edition's strengths and weaknesses. And we are grateful most of all to the authors of the works we've selected here—without whom, of course, the book would never have been possible.

Crisis in American Institutions

Introduction

Approaches to Social Problems

I n the early years of the twenty-first century, American society presents us with some striking paradoxes. We are now the world's only "superpower," and our economic might is admired (and sometimes feared) throughout the world. Yet we are also a nation wracked by widespread poverty on a scale that is unknown in other industrial societies—a paradox that was driven home for many Americans during 2005, when Hurricane Katrina revealed a level of deprivation in New Orleans that many people did not know existed outside of the Third World. We are a country of crowded shopping malls—and crowded prisons; a country of glittering cities inhabited by stubborn legions of homeless people. We are a nation that routinely produces new technological marvels, from Internet software to breakthroughs in genetic medicine. But we are also a nation in which more than 40 million citizens have no regular source of health care and some lack the most basic sanitation.

This book explores these paradoxes and others through a collection of some of today's best writing on social problems in America. Our contributors are social scientists, specialists in public health and the environment, and journalists skilled in reporting and analyzing social issues. We don't claim that these articles, by themselves, can resolve all of the complex issues surrounding the causes and consequences of social problems in the United States. We do believe that they challenge readers to think more clearly and more critically about a range of issues that affect us all—from violence against women to racial profiling by police, from homelessness to global warming.

In that sense, these writings fit well with the best traditions in the study of social problems in the United States. Social scientists and others have been studying these problems for a long time, and the study of social problems has never taken place in the antiseptic confines of a scientific laboratory. Social theorists, like everyone else, are deeply influenced by broader trends in the society, the economy, and the cultural and technological setting of social life. As a way of introducing the articles that follow and of placing today's debates in some historical and intellectual context, we want to spend a few pages outlining the way in which the study of social problems has developed over time and how those larger social changes have shaped its basic assumptions and guiding themes.

DEFECTIVES AND DELINQUENTS

The earliest writers on social problems in this country were straightforward moralists, staunch supporters of the virtues of thrift, hard work, sexual purity, and personal

1

discipline. Writing at the end of the nineteenth century, they sought ways of maintaining the values of an earlier, whiter, more Protestant, and more stable America in the face of the new challenges of industrialization, urbanization, and immigration.[1]

This early social science usually concentrated on the problems of what one nineteenth-century textbook described as the "defective, dependent, and delinquent classes."[2] The causes of social problems were located in the physical constitution or moral "character" of the poor, the criminal, the insane, and other "unfortunates." For these theorists, the solution to nineteenth-century social problems lay in developing means of transforming the character of these "defective" classes, in the hope of equipping them better to succeed within a competitive, hierarchical society whose basic assumptions were never questioned. Social reformers working from these theories created, in the last part of the nineteenth and the first part of the twentieth centuries, much of the modern apparatus of "social control" in the United States: reformatories, modern prisons, institutions for the mentally ill, and the beginnings of the modern welfare system.

THE RISE OF "VALUE-FREE" SOCIAL PROBLEMS

During the first decades of the twentieth century, this straightforward moralism was increasingly discarded in favor of a more subtle, ostensibly "neutral" approach to writing about social problems. By the 1930s, the idea that the social sciences were—or could be—purely "objective" or "value-free" had come to be widely accepted. From that point until the present, social problems theory has been characterized by a tortuous attempt to prove that theories and policies serving to support the status quo are actually scientific judgments arrived at objectively. In this view, social scientists do not try to impose their own values in deciding what kinds of things will be defined and dealt with as social problems. Instead, the "scientific" student of social problems simply accepts "society's" definition of what is a problem and what is not. This approach is apparent in these statements, taken from major textbooks and articles, on what constitutes a social problem:

> Any difficulty or misbehavior of a fairly large number of persons which we wish to remove or correct.[3]
>
> What people think they are.[4]
>
> Whenever people begin to say, isn't it awful! Why don't they do something about it?[5]
>
> Conditions which affect sizable proportions of the population, which are out of harmony with the values of a significant segment of the population, and which people feel can be improved or eliminated.[6]
>
> Any substantial discrepancy between socially shared standards and actual conditions of social life.[7]

These definitions share the common idea that social problems are popularly defined. No condition is a problem unless a certain number of people in a society say it is. Because we are merely taking, as our starting point, the definitions of the problem that "other people," "society," or "significant segments of the population" provide, we are no longer in the position of moralizing about objective conditions.

The basic flaw in this happy scheme is that it does not make clear *which* segments of the population to consult when defining problems or deciding between conflicting ideas about what is problematic and what is not. In the real world, societies are divided along class, racial, sexual, and other lines, and the sociologist who proposes to follow "people's" definitions of social problems in fact generally adopts one of several competing ideologies of social problems based on those divisions. In practice, the ideology adopted has usually been not too different from that of the "unscientific" social problems writers of the nineteenth century.

These points are not new; they were raised as early as 1936 in an unusually perceptive paper called "Social Problems and the Mores," by the sociologist Willard Waller. Waller noted, for example, that discussions of poverty in the social problems literature of the 1930s were shaped by the unquestioning acceptance of the ideology of competitive capitalism:

> A simpleton would suggest that the remedy for poverty in the midst of plenty is to redistribute income. We reject this solution at once because it would interfere with the institution of private property, would destroy the incentive for thrift and hard work and disjoint the entire economic system.[8]

Waller's question is fundamental: What has been left out in a writer's choice of what are to be considered problems? What features of society are going to be taken for granted as the framework *within* which problems will be defined and resolved? In this case, the taken-for-granted framework is the principle of private property and individual competition. In general, Waller argued, "social problems are not solved because people do not want to solve them";[9] they *are* problems mainly because of people's unwillingness to alter the basic conditions from which they arise. Thus:

> Venereal disease becomes a social problem in that it arises from our family institutions and also in that the medical means which could be used to prevent it, which would unquestionably be fairly effective, cannot be employed for fear of altering the mores of chastity.[10]

For Waller, the definition of social problems was, in the broadest sense, a political issue involving the opposed ideologies of conflicting groups.

Waller's points still ring true. Most social problems writers in the United States still tacitly accept the basic structure of American society and restrict their treatment of social problems to maladjustments *within* that structure.

SOCIAL PROBLEMS IN THE 1950s: GRADUALISM AND ANTICOMMUNISM

This is not to say that the literature on social problems since the 1930s has all been the same. Books on social problems, not surprisingly, tend to reflect the preoccupations of the time when they were written. Those conceived in the 1950s, for example, reflect social and political concerns that now seem bizarre. The shadow of Mc-Carthyism and the general national hysteria over the "Communist menace" pervaded this literature. Consider the discussion of "civil liberties and subversion" in Paul B. Horton and Gerald R. Leslie's textbook *The Sociology of Social Problems*.[11] Horton and Leslie saw the "American heritage of liberty" being attacked from both Left and Right, from both "monolithic communism" and overzealous attempts to defend "our" way of life from it. Their position was resolutely "moderate." They claimed a scientific objectivity; yet, they were quite capable of moral condemnation of people whose politics were "extreme," whether Right or Left:

> Most extremists are deviants. Most extremists show a fanatical preoccupation with their cause, a suspicious distrust of other people in general, a disinterest in normal pursuits, recreations, and small talk, and a strong tendency to divide other people into enemies and allies.[12]

The preference for "normal pursuits," even "small talk," over social criticism and action was common in an age noted for its "silent generation," but it was hardly "scientific." Among the other presumably objective features of the book were the authors' "rational proposals for preserving liberty and security," including these:

> *An adequate national defense* is, needless to say, necessary in a world where an international revolutionary movement is joined to an aggressive major power. This is a military problem, not a sociological problem, and is not discussed here.
>
> *Counterespionage is essential.* Highly trained professional agencies such as the FBI and the Central Intelligence Agency can do this efficiently and without endangering personal liberties of citizens. If headline-hunting congressmen, Legion officials, or other amateurs turn G-men, they merely scare off any real spies and destroy the counterespionage effort of the professionals.[13]

The military and intelligence services themselves were not considered to be problems relevant for social science. Questions about the operation of these agencies were viewed as internal and technical, military rather than sociological, issues.

In a section on "Questions and Projects," the authors asked, "How have conservatives or reactionaries sometimes given unintentional assistance to the Communists? How have liberals sometimes given unintentional assistance to the Communists?"[14]

In the introduction to their book, Horton and Leslie considered the possibilities of social change and the proper role of social scientists in promoting it. They carefully adopted a middle ground between conservatives, to whom social problems were primarily problems of individual character, and "extremists" hoping for sudden or radical changes in social structure. They argued that the resolution of social problems "nearly always involves sweeping institutional changes" but also that such changes are "costly" and "difficult," and that therefore

> it is unrealistic to expect that these problems will be solved easily or quickly. . . . Basic solutions of social problems will come slowly, if at all. Meanwhile, however, considerable amelioration or "improvement" may be possible.[15]

Social change, according to these authors, must be gradual and realistic; it must also be guided by experts. The authors insisted that their own role, and that of social experts in general, was merely to show the public how to get what they already valued. But in this role it was folly for the "layman" to question the expert. Horton and Leslie wrote that "when experts are *agreed* upon the futility of one policy or the soundness of another, it is sheer stupidity for the layman to disagree."[16]

An elitist, Cold War liberalism and gradualism, a fear of extremism and of an international Communist conspiracy—all these were presented not as moral and political positions but as fundamental social scientific truths. The sturdy entrepreneurial and Protestant values described in Waller's paper of the 1930s gave way, in Horton and Leslie's book of the 1950s, to a general preference for moderation, anticommunism, and "normal pursuits."

THE 1960s: AFFLUENCE AND OPTIMISM

A different imagery dominated the social problems literature of the next decade. Robert K. Merton and Robert A. Nisbet's *Contemporary Social Problems*[17] was a product of the beginning of the 1960s, the period of the "New Frontier," which saw a significant shift, at least on the surface, in the focus of social concern. Americans were becoming aware of an "underdeveloped" world abroad and a "disadvantaged" world at home, both unhappily excluded from the benefits of an age of general "affluence" and well-being. New agencies of social improvement were created at home and abroad. A critique of old-style welfare efforts began to develop, along with the notion of "helping people help themselves," whether in Latin America, Harlem, or Appalachia. The idea of inclusion, of participation, in the American way of life became a political metaphor for the age. From a slightly different vantage, the idea emerged as "development" or "modernization." The social problems of the 1960s would be solved by extending the technological and intellectual resources of established American institutions into excluded, deprived, or underdeveloped places and groups. An intervention-minded government combined with an energetic social science on a scale unprecedented in this country.

In this period—very brief, as it turned out—social problems were often seen as problems of being *left out* of the American mainstream: "left behind," as the people of Appalachia were described; "traditional," like the Mexican Americans; or "underdeveloped," like most Africans, Asians, and Latin Americans. In social problems theory, these ideas were manifested in a conservative ideology that celebrated American society as a whole, coupled with a liberal critique of the conditions hindering the extension of the American way to all.

One variant of this view was given in Nisbet's introduction to *Contemporary Social Problems*. For Nisbet, social facts become problematic when they "represent interruptions in the expected or desired scheme of things; violations of the right or the proper, as a society defines these qualities; dislocations in the social patterns and relationships that a society cherishes."[18]

Nisbet's assessment of the American situation was in keeping with the exaggerated optimism of the early 1960s:

> In America today we live in what is often called an affluent society. It is a society characterized by imposing command of physical resources, high standards of private consumption, effective maintenance of public order and security, freedom from most of the uncertainties of life that plagued our ancestors, and relatively high levels of humanitarianism. There are also, of course, squalid slums, both urban and rural; occasional epidemics of disease; sudden eruptions of violence or bigotry, even in the most civilized of communities; people for whom the struggle for food and shelter yet remains obsessing and precarious. Thus, we are not free of social problems, and some of them seem to grow almost in direct proportion to our affluence.[19]

Nisbet was aware that America had not yet solved all its problems; indeed, some seem to come with the generally glittering package that is America in the twentieth century. Yet the problems were viewed as peripheral, as occasional eruptions in the backwaters of society where modern institutions had not fully penetrated.

Like earlier theorists, Nisbet sharply separated the role of the scientific student of social problems from that of other concerned people. The social scientist, as a scientist, should not engage in moral exhortation or political action but instead concentrate on understanding. At the same time, the scientist is

> as interested as the next citizen in making the protection of society his first responsibility, in seeing society reach higher levels of moral decency, and when necessary, in promoting such legal actions as are necessary in the short run for protection or decency.[20]

Here the scientific stance masked a preference for vaguely defined values—"societal protection" and "moral decency"—that, in turn, determine what will be selected as social problems. In this instance, problems were selected according to whether they offended the values of social stability, that is, values associated with the conservative tradition in social thought.

Thus, problems were repeatedly equated with "dislocations and deviations";[21] they were problems of "dissensus," as if consensus might not also be a problem. Indeed, the entire book was divided into two sections, one dealing with "deviant behavior" and the other with "social disorganization." The articles in the text were not all of a piece. A paper by Robert S. Weiss and David Riesman on the problems of work took a different view on what constitutes a problem; the authors declared that "social forms which tend toward the suppression or frustration of meaning and purpose in life are inferior forms, whether or not they tend toward disorganization."[22] But many of the articles simply accepted the purposes of existing institutions and defined problems in terms of combating disorganization *within* those institutions. Perhaps the clearest illustration of this tendency appeared in an essay by Morris Janowitz addressing problems of the military establishment:

> It is self-evident that the military establishment, the armed forces, and their administrative organizations have become and will remain important institutions of United States society. The distinctive forms of military organization must be analyzed in order

to understand the typical sources of personal and social disorganization found in military life.[23]

The existence of a large military establishment was defined as outside the critical concern of the sociologist. The focus was not on the effect of the military on national or international life but on the problems of maladjustment within the military apparatus. The increasing scope of military activities was noted, but it was simply accepted as a fact of modern life:

> The armed forces have also become involved in a wide variety of logistical, research, and training activities. In the current international scene, they must take on many politico-military duties, including military assistance of allied powers.[24]

The implication was that the militarization of American society is not itself a problem for social analysis. And the acceptance of the place of the military in American society leads to the enlistment of social science in the service of military ends. Thus, in discussing changes in the requirements of military discipline, Janowitz noted that, in the 1960s, instead of employing "shock technique" to assimilate the recruit into the military, the problem had become how to foster "positive incentives and group loyalties through a team concept."[25] Janowitz didn't ask *what* the recruit is being assimilated *into*. The effect of primary-group relations on morale under Cold War conditions was extensively discussed, but the Cold War itself was not.

Robert Merton's epilogue to *Contemporary Social Problems,* called "Social Problems and Sociological Theory," represented a major attempt to give theoretical definition to the "field" of social problems. Merton was well aware that different interests are present in society and therefore that definitions of social problems were likely to be contested—"one group's problem will be another group's asset"— and more specifically that "those occupying strategic positions of authority and power of course carry more weight than others in deciding social policy and so, among other things, in identifying for the rest what are to be taken as significant departures from social standards."[26]

According to Merton, however, this diversity of perspectives does not mean that sociologists must succumb to relativism or abandon their position as scientific students of society's problems. The way out of the dilemma is to distinguish between "manifest" and "latent" social problems—the latter are problems also "at odds with the values of the group" but not recognized as such. The task of the sociologist is to uncover the "latent" problems, or unrecognized consequences of existing institutions and policies; in this way, "sociological inquiry does make men increasingly accountable for the outcome of their collective and institutionalized actions."[27]

The demand that social science make people accountable for their actions was a healthy departure from the false relativism of some earlier theorists. But the distinction between manifest and latent problems did not do what Merton claimed for it: It did not make the choice of problems a technical or neutral one. Actually, Merton's approach is best seen as providing a rationale for evaluating and criticizing particular policies and structures within a presumably consensual society whose basic values and institutions are not seen as problematic.

We could easily agree with Merton that "to confine the study of social problems to only those circumstances that are expressly defined as problems in the society is arbitrarily to discard a complement of conditions that are also dysfunctional to values held by people in that society."[28] But what about those values themselves? Shouldn't they be examined and, if necessary, criticized? It seems obvious to us, for example, that it is part of the sociologist's task to study and criticize the values held by people in German society during the Nazi era or by slaveholders in the antebellum American South, rather than to confine ourselves to studying conditions that might be "dysfunctional" in terms of those values. To do otherwise amounts to an acceptance by default; the social scientist becomes an expert at handling problems within the confines of an assumed consensus on basic goals and values.

The division of social problems into the two categories of *deviant behavior* and *social disorganization* reflected this acceptance, for both categories were defined as "disruptions" of an existing social order and did not question the adequacy of that social order itself. Thus:

> Whereas social disorganization refers to faults in the arrangement and working of social statuses and roles, deviant behavior refers to conduct that departs significantly from the norms set for people in their social statuses.[29]

It is not, as some critics have suggested, that this kind of analysis suggests that whatever is, is right. But it does imply that whatever *disturbs* the existing social system is the primary problem.

The sociologist's "expert" judgment, of course, may conflict with what people themselves feel to be their problems, and if so, according to Merton, the expert should prevail. Merton argued:

> We cannot take for granted a reasonably correct public imagery of social problems; of their scale, distribution, causation, consequences and persistence or change. . . . Popular perceptions are no safe guide to the magnitude of a social problem.[30]

The corollary, presumably, is that the sociologist's imagery of social problems is at least "reasonably correct," even, perhaps, where segments of the public strongly object to having their problems defined, or redefined, for them. We seem to have come back to the same condescending attitude toward the public expressed by Horton and Leslie and other sociologists of the 1950s.

This kind of attitude wasn't, of course, confined to writers on social problems. It was a major theme in the social thought and government policy of the 1960s, a decade characterized by an increasing detachment of governmental action from public knowledge and accountability—as exemplified in the growth of a vast intelligence apparatus, the repeated attempts to overthrow popularly elected governments overseas, and the whole conduct of the Vietnam War. This process was often excused on the ground that political decisions involved technical judgments that were out of the reach of ordinary people.

The conception of social problems as technical, rather than moral and political, issues was explicit in Merton and Nisbet's text. Thus, Merton suggested that "the kind of problem that is dominated by social disorganization results from instrumental and technical flaws in the social system. The system comes to operate less efficiently than it realistically might."[31]

If the problems are technical ones, then it was, of course, reasonable to view social scientists as technicians and to regard their intervention into social life as free from partisan interest. It is this, apparently, that renders the social scientist a responsible citizen, rather than a "mere" social critic or ideologue:

> Under the philosophy intrinsic to the distinction between manifest and latent social problems, the social scientist neither abdicates his intellectual and professional responsibilities nor usurps the position of sitting in judgment on his fellow men.[32]

It is apparent, however, that this kind of "philosophy" lends itself all too easily to an alignment of expertise and "professionalism" with dominant values and interests masquerading as societal consensus. This is apparent in the choice of topics offered in most textbooks. Merton and Nisbet—whose widely used textbook has gone through several editions—characteristically dealt with mental disorders, crime and delinquency, drug use, alcoholism, suicide, sexual behavior, the population crisis, race relations, family disorganization, work and automation, poverty, community disorganization, violence, and youth and politics. The book did not deal with (to take some examples from our own table of contents) corporate power, sexism, health care, the criminal justice system, and so on. The pattern of these differences is obvious: Merton and Nisbet focused most heavily on those who have, for one reason or another, failed to "make it" within the American system—delinquents, criminals, the mentally ill, drug users—and on disorganization *within* established institutions. Even when individual authors in their book attempted to analyze the system itself, the effort was usually relegated to a peripheral, or merely symbolic, place.

Despite its claim to political neutrality, the social science of the 1960s typically focused on the symptoms of social ills, rather than their sources: the culture of the poor, rather than the decisions of the rich; the "pathology" of the ghetto, rather than the problems of the economy. What "socially shared standards" dictated this choice of emphasis? In the introduction to a newer edition of *Contemporary Social Problems,* Nisbet tried to answer this question. "It may well be asked," he writes, "why these problems have been chosen by the editors," rather than other problems that "for some persons at least might be regarded as even more pressing to national policy."

> The answer is that this is a textbook in sociology. Sociology is a special science characterized by concepts and conclusions, which are based on analysis and research, yielding in turn perspectives on society and its central problems. For many decades now, sociologists have worked carefully and patiently on these problems. In other words this book is concerned not only with the presentation of major social problems but with the scientific concepts and procedures by which these problems have been, and continue to be, studied.[33]

Nisbet seems to be explaining that these problems were selected by the editors because sociologists have studied them, and not other problems, in the past. Such an argument is hardly compelling.

THE 1970s TO THE PRESENT:
A HARSHER VISION

Much of the thinking about social problems in the 1960s—and the public policies that flowed from it—tended to assume, at least implicitly, that most of the ills of American society were solvable; that a rich and technologically advanced society should be able to overcome problems like poverty, unemployment, and inadequate health care, if it had the will to do so. And so an active government launched a number of social programs and experiments designed to bring the American reality in closer harmony with the American ideal. In the 1980s, it became fashionable to say that the government attempted too much in those years, throwing vast amounts of money at social problems. In fact, though we did try a multitude of programs, the amounts we spent on them were never large. Our total federal spending on job training, public job creation, and schooling programs for low-income people, for example, never rose to as much as one-half of 1 percent of our gross national product during the 1960s.[34]

But the belief that government had taken on too big a role helped to usher in a harsher, more pessimistic perspective in the 1970s—a perspective that has dominated social policy in the United States ever since. In the context of a deeply troubled economy, the stubborn persistence of poverty and joblessness, and frightening levels of social disintegration in the cities, the moderate optimism of the 1960s began to give way to a new brand of scholarly pessimism arguing that many of these problems were due to "human nature" or defective "culture"—or even genetic deficiencies. The implication was that social concern of the 1960s variety couldn't have much positive impact on social problems—and, in the view of some writers, had probably made them worse.

Writers such as Arthur Jensen resurrected long-discredited hereditary theories of racial inferiority in intelligence to explain why blacks still remained at the bottom of the educational and economic ladder, despite all the equal opportunity programs of the 1960s. Others, such as Harvard's Edward Banfield, explained the persistence of poverty and urban crime as the reflection of a distinctive "lower-class culture" that prevented the poor from thinking ahead or delaying immediate gratification. By the 1980s, Charles Murray and other critics were explaining the stubbornness of poverty as the result of the demoralization of the poor by an overly generous welfare system. The growth of urban violence was similarly explained as the result of excessive leniency with criminals; in the 1980s, when years of "getting tough" with criminals left us with still-frightful levels of crime and violence, some writers began looking for the roots of crime—and of poverty and other social pathologies as well—in faulty physiology or defective genes.

By the 1980s, in other words, American thinking about social problems had just about come full circle; we had returned to something that looked very much like the focus on "defectives, dependents, and delinquents" that characterized late-nineteenth-century social science. And the harsh social policies that flowed from this attitude were also strikingly reminiscent of the Social Darwinism of the late nineteenth century. The belief that many of our social problems (from school failure to juvenile delinquency to welfare dependency) can be traced to deficiencies in the minds, cultures, or genetic makeup of a hard-core few—or to the folly of government intervention—a belief that was so comforting to the complacent thinkers of the nineteenth century, had returned with a vengeance.

As in the past, this outlook—still hugely influential today—serves to explain away some of the most troubling expressions of the crisis in American institutions, including many we address in this book: swollen prisons, the rapid descent of millions into the ranks of the poor, minority joblessness that persists at near-Depression levels through "good" economic times and bad. And it is used to justify sharp cutbacks in many of the programs created to address those problems—even successful programs in child health care, job training, and nutrition.

By now, however, this perspective has itself come under growing criticism. Its proponents, after all, have been arguing for a long time that the poor, the jobless, and the sick are largely responsible for their own problems and that they—along with the rest of us—would be better off with less help from government. We have, accordingly, been reducing government's role as well for a long time. But the problems haven't gone away; many have grown. The massive destruction wrought by Hurricane Katrina and the halting response to it by federal and state agencies sharply illustrated the consequences of the decades-long neglect of the most basic government fucntions. This was an especially stark example, but we see the results of that neglect across many American institutions—in crumbling schools, collapsing public facilities, decaying cities, and even in the lack of adequate armor for U.S. troops in Iraq. And so the job of developing a fresh and creative approach to social problems is once again on the agenda.

That task is certainly an urgent one. As many of the articles in this book suggest, we have reached what seems to be a crucial turning point in our policies toward social problems. Technological and economic changes are reshaping the conditions of American life with sometimes dizzying speed, and how we choose to deal with those changes will profoundly affect the character of life in the United States for many years to come.

Consider just one example: the rapidly shifting character of work in America. As suggested by several of the articles in this book (notably those by Barbara Ehrenreich, David Shipler, and William Julius Wilson), a combination of intense global economic competition and the continuing march of new workplace technology is dramatically affecting the pattern of jobs and incomes in the United States. Whether we can harness these changes to build a more sustaining and fulfilling society will depend on how our social and political institutions respond to them—whether, for example, we are willing to make a sufficient investment in worker retraining and job creation to offset the loss of many traditional jobs, and to provide adequate wages, child care, health care, and other benefits to those now at work in the lower levels of the new economy. And as American lives are more and more affected by the workings of a largely unregulated global economy, we will increasingly need to confront these issues on an international scale. More generally, the increasing interconnection between the United States and the rest of the world—dramatically revealed by the attacks on the World Trade Center in September 2001, and explored in a section at the end of this book—has given new urgency to questions of how we will manage our role as the only "superpower" in a world that is profoundly unstable and wracked by pervasive inequality and insecurity.

These are very big questions, and in this book we can only begin to explore them, not answer them once and for all. But we believe the articles that follow can provide a strong beginning. As in earlier editions, they represent a wide range of styles and perspectives. But most of them fit comfortably within a common overall vision: a critical, democratically inclined approach to social institutions that emphasizes the potential for constructive change.

Within this very broad perspective, there is plenty of room for controversy. Our authors don't necessarily share the same theoretical positions or social or political views. The editors, for that matter, don't always agree—and we think that's as it should be. We frequently argue about many of the issues covered in this book, and this debate has continued through thirteen editions. But we think this tension is fruitful, and we have tried to capture it in our selection of readings.

Our purpose is to raise issues, to provide students with the beginnings of a critical approach to the society they live in and will, we hope, help to improve. This book provides few definitive answers, and it leaves unresolved many basic theoretical and practical questions about the sources and solutions of American social problems. But its purpose will be accomplished if it helps students to begin their own process of confronting those questions.

ENDNOTES

1. C. Wright Mills, "The Professional Ideology of the Social Pathologists," in Irving L. Horowitz, ed., *Power, Politics, and People: The Collected Essays of C. Wright Mills* (New York: Ballantine, 1963).

2. Charles Richmond Henderson, *An Introduction to the Study of Defective, Dependent, and Delinquent Classes* (Boston: Heath, 1906).

3. Lawrence K. Frank, "Social Problems," *American Journal of Sociology,* 30 (January 1925), p. 463.

4. Richard C. Fuller and Richard R. Myers, "The Natural History of a Social Problem," *American Sociological Review,* 6 (June 1941), p. 320.

5. Paul B. Horton and Gerald R. Leslie, *The Sociology of Social Problems* (New York: Appleton-Century-Crofts, 1955), p. 6.

6. Arnold M. Rose, "Theory for the Study of Social Problems," *Social Problems,* 4 (January 1957), p. 190.

7. Robert K. Merton and Robert A. Nisbet, *Contemporary Social Problems* (New York: Harcourt, Brace, and World, 1961), p. 702.

8. Willard Waller, "Social Problems and the Mores," *American Sociological Review,* 1 (December 1936), p. 926.

9. *Ibid.,* p. 928.

10. *Ibid.,* p. 927.

11. Horton and Leslie, *The Sociology of Social Problems.* We refer here to the original edition in order to place the book in its historical context.

12. *Ibid.,* p. 517.

13. *Ibid.,* p. 520.

14. *Ibid.,* p. 523.

15. *Ibid.,* p. 12.

16. *Ibid.,* p. 19.

17. Merton and Nisbet, *Contemporary Social Problems.* Here, too, we refer to the first edition in order to consider the book in historical perspective. The general theoretical perspective in the book has changed little, if at all, as we will note later; there have been some substantive changes, however—for example, the chapter by Janowitz has been dropped and new chapters added.

18. Robert A. Nisbet, "The Study of Social Problems," in *ibid.,* p. 4.

19. *Ibid.,* p. 5. The reader might compare C. Wright Mills's notion, developed during the same period, that the United States should be seen as an "overdeveloped" society; see Irving L. Horowitz, "Introduction," in Horowitz, *Power, Politics, and People,* p. 8.

20. Nisbet, "The Study of Social Problems," p. 9.

21. *Ibid.,* p. 12.

22. Robert S. Weiss and David Riesman, "Social Problems and Disorganization in the World of Work," in Merton and Nisbet, *Contemporary Social Problems,* p. 464.

23. Morris Janowitz, "The Military Establishment: Organization and Disorganization," in Merton and Nisbet, *Contemporary Social Problems,* p. 515.

24. *Ibid.,* p. 516.

25. *Ibid.,* pp. 533–534.

26. Robert K. Merton, "Social Problems and Sociological Theory," in Merton and Nisbet, *Contemporary Social Problems,* p. 706.

27. *Ibid.,* p. 710.

28. *Ibid.,* p. 711.

29. *Ibid.,* p. 723.

30. *Ibid.,* pp. 712–713.

31. *Ibid.,* p. 723.

32. *Ibid.,* p. 712.

33. Robert M. Nisbet, "The Study of Social Problems," in *ibid.,* p. 2.

34. Gary L. Burtless, "Public Spending for the Poor," in Sheldon H. Danziger and Daniel H. Weinberg, *Fighting Poverty: What Works and What Doesn't* (Cambridge, MA: Harvard University Press, 1986), p. 37.

SYSTEMIC
PROBLEMS

PART ONE

Corporate Power

The myth of American capitalism is individual "free enterprise"—the vision of the hardworking, thrifty entrepreneur competing with others and constrained by the forces of the market. But the reality of American capitalism is what Ralph Nader once called "corporate collectivism": the domination of our economic life by a relative handful of large corporations.

The largest corporation in America, Wal-Mart, employs a number of people greater than the populations of San Diego, Dallas, or Philadelphia: if they were a city, indeed, they would be the fifth largest in the United States. Wal-Mart's 2004 revenue of more than a quarter of a trillion dollars is larger than the Gross Domestic Product of Sweden. The American corporation with the most assets—the Citigroup banking empire—has nearly one and one-half trillion dollars worth, or a sum comparable to the Gross Domestic Product of France.[1] The great size and power of these corporations influences virtually every aspect of life in America—and the world—today.

And as corporate business has become ever larger, it has also become much more entwined with—and dependent on—government. Part of our persistent myth of "free enterprise" is the belief that, unlike poor people on welfare or older people who receive Medicare or Social Security, private businesses must go it alone—earn their own way in the free market—or go under. But the reality is very different: as the articles here by Mark Zepezauer and Robert S. McIntyre show, corporations are the recipients of an enormous amount of "welfare" of their own, ultimately paid for by American taxpayers. Some of these giveaways come in the form of subsidies to various industries, which, as Zepezauer reveals, vastly overshadow what we spend, as a nation, on all forms of welfare for the poor. The selection we reprint here describes just one of those favored industries—agribusiness—which at this writing received more than $30 billion in subsidies, most of which went to the wealthiest farmers and agricultural corporations. Adding to the illogic, one of the beneficiaries of these government subsidies is the tobacco industry—just as the government is simultaneously trying to discourage smoking, a habit that costs the economy billions every year.

Another way in which government subsidizes corporate business is through an intricate set of tax breaks that are mostly unavailable to ordinary citizens. As Robert S. McIntyre shows, these tax giveaways are increasingly arcane and difficult for even experts to unravel. But they have resulted in a startling decline in the proportion of overall U.S. taxes that are contributed by big corporations. In recent years, indeed, many of the wealthiest corporations have managed to pay little or no federal or state taxes—a situation that is not only patently unfair, but that contributes mightily to the perennial budget crises that have forced repeated cutbacks in schools, public health care, and other critical services. In recent years, Congress has taken some steps to rein in spending on corporate welfare. But these have been far less effective than measures to cut back on public assistance for the poor or working Americans.

This is not surprising, since the poor, unlike large corporations, have little to contribute to the campaign coffers of elected officials. As Mark Green illustrates in his article on the "cost of money," the increasingly massive flow of money into the political process has drastically reshaped politics in America, in ways that have deeply undercut the principles of democracy on which the nation was founded. Most obviously, it costs ordinary Americans vast sums of money by influencing politicians to support legislation that benefits corporations to the detriment of everyone else. But there are also more subtle effects of the growing dominance of money in American politics. By forcing legislators to spend much of their time raising money in order to get elected, it reduces the amount of time and energy they can spend on actually governing. It renders many elections uncompetitive, since only those candidates with huge financial 'war chests'—often incumbents or the independently wealthy—have much of a chance in an increasingly expensive political arena. And it fuels political apathy and cynicism—helping to explain why half of American voters stay home during presidential elections—as potential voters become increasingly convinced that politicians are essentially 'bought' and that their own votes don't matter.

All of these articles suggest that the corporations enjoy an especially privileged position in American society today, supported by an array of special benefits that belie the traditional image of the "free market." The rise of that remarkable combination of private power and public support has been fueled, in part, by the widespread belief that the private sector can do a better job than government in addressing economic needs, and that it should be left alone by government, as much as possible, in order to get the job done most efficiently. The United States has gone much farther in this direction than most countries, with a relatively smaller role for government in economic life than in many other advanced industrial societies. And the dominance of the private sector has increased considerably in recent years, as private companies have moved in to take over many functions that used to be public ones—everything from running schools to operating prisons to providing water, one of the most basic needs of human life.

As John Luoma points out in "Water for Profit," the takeover of water systems in many cities—and countries—by a handful of large corporations was supposed to make the delivery of water more efficient. But in some places, especially in some developing countries, the results have been the opposite. Water, which had been taken for granted even by the poor, suddenly became too expensive for many to afford, and often became unhealthy as well. In the United States, most people still get their water from public utilities, but not for long, if some corporations have their way. Illustrating the reach and complexity of the modern large corporation, among the companies most prominent in the drive to privatize water is the French-based Vivendi Universal, which, among other enterprises, also owns the USA television network and the Universal motion picture studios. Luoma concludes that "If success is measured in terms of delivering an essential commodity to everyone who needs it, then the industry's record is less than encouraging." As we hear calls to turn more and more of our basic needs over to private corporations, we would do well to ponder this example.

ENDNOTE

1. Corporate figures from *Fortune* magazine, April 8, 2005, pp. F-1, F-33: country GDP and city populations from *Statistical Abstract of the United States,* 2004-2005.

CHAPTER 1

Take the Rich off Welfare

MARK ZEPEZAUER

Wealthfare—the money government gives away to corporations and wealthy individuals—costs us more than $815 billion a year. That's:

- 47% of what it costs to run the US government (which is about $1.73 trillion a year, not counting entitlement trust funds like Social Security and Medicare)[1]
- enough money to eliminate the federal debt in just over eight years (the total is now $6.6 trillion, accumulated over 200-plus years)[2]
- more than four times what we spend on welfare for the poor . . .

When agricultural subsidies began during the Great Depression, their main purpose was to keep farmers on the farm by enabling them to earn roughly what people in cities did. Of course, in those days, some 25% of the population lived and worked on farms. Today, only 2% of us do.[1] These days the average net worth of farm households is $564,000—nearly double the $283,000 for nonfarm households.[2] Farmers' household income from all sources (an average of $64,347 in 1999) has exceeded that of nonfarmers' income every year since 1986.[3]

Agricultural subsidies are particularly bizarre these days because they go mostly to relatively few states, for relatively few crops, to benefit relatively few farmers. The wealthiest 10% of subsidized farmers take 74% of the handouts, while the bottom four-fifths get 12% of the total. The bottom half? Just 2%. And 60% of US farmers get nothing at all.[4] Five crops—wheat, corn, rice, cotton, and soybeans—receive 90% of all federal subsidies.[5] Almost two-thirds of total US farm production—including most fruits and vegetables—remains unsubsidized.[6]

Concentrating the subsidies on certain crops also concentrates them geographically. Just 15 states receive 74% of the benefit from federal agriculture programs, while paying only 24% of the cost.[7] In California, the largest agricultural producer, only 9% of the farms received any subsidy at all. (These were mostly big cotton and rice farms, while the state's many orchards and vegetable farms didn't get a penny.)[8] The Northeast gets a particularly raw deal, paying for 30% of the cost of crop subsidies (that is, it contributes 30% of federal taxes), while receiving just 2.4% of the benefit.[9] In an effort to get in on the party, New York's congressional delegation helped create a new subsidy for its dairy farmers in the 2002 farm bill.[10]

Not surprisingly, many of the "luckiest" states are those that can help swing the results of national elections or that have powerful representatives in Congress who help to write farm legislation. The 2002 farm bill gave the most money to Iowa, and the largest increase to Texas. Iowa is the home of Senator Tom Harkin, then the chair of the Senate Agriculture Committee. And Texas sent Republican Larry Combest, chair of the House Agricultural Committee, and Democrat Charles Stenholm, a member of the same committee, to Washington, where they helped double the amount of subsidies for their home state.[11]

And just coincidentally, Representative Stenholm himself is a subsidized farmer, receiving more than $39,000 under the 1996 farm bill (from 1996 through 2002). At least ten of his colleagues, including Senators Grassley (R-IA), Lugar (R-IN), and Lincoln (D-AR), are also on the dole. Representative Marion Berry of Arkansas (not to be confused with the former mayor of Washington, DC) took in more than $750,000 in subsidies between 1996 and 2002. Perhaps you will not be surprised to hear that Berry feels that federal farm subsidy programs are "woefully underfunded."[12]

Not only is the US Department of Agriculture (USDA) generous in its handouts to farmers, it's also quite generous in who it calls a farmer. Making a complete mockery of the supposed aims of the farm subsidies (to help keep 'em down on the farm), the USDA doled out almost $3.5 billion to recipients in urban zip codes between 1996 and 2001.[13] Many recipients aren't even located in the same state as their farms. Among celebrity farmers (outside of Congress) are billionaire David Rockefeller, basketball star Scottie Pippen, broadcaster Sam Donaldson, tycoon Ted Turner, and corporate crime poster boy Kenneth Lay of Enron.[14] In fact, any land that produces $1,000 or more in agricultural products can be officially regarded as a farm.[15] So if you see the word "farmers" in quotes below, you'll know why.

Of course, it's not even necessary to be a human being to qualify as a farmer. One study found farm subsidies going to 413 municipal governments, 44 universities, and 14 prison systems.[16] And such Fortune 500 companies as Chevron Oil, John Hancock Life Insurance, Caterpillar Manufacturing, and Eli Lilly Pharmaceuticals are also quote, farmers, unquote—subsidized with your tax dollars.[17] . . .

One last thing before we dive into the details. Despite all the booty being siphoned off to the wealthy, these programs are routinely justified by the need to help combat rural poverty or save small family farms. But there's an alternative that would be a whole lot simpler and cheaper. We could bring the income of every full-time farmer in the United States up to at least 185% of the federal poverty level (about $33,000) for just $4 billion a year.[18] If the agribusiness subsidy's goal were to reduce rural poverty, we could simply write a check to every poor farmer. But of course that's not the goal anymore, is it?

Agribusiness subsidies take several forms:

- With price supports, quasi-governmental agencies or cooperatives buy up "excess" production of a crop to keep the price high. (It's like government-sanctioned price fixing.)
- Production quotas limit who can farm a particular crop (peanut and tobacco farmers, for example, must be licensed by the government).
- Market quotas control how much of a crop can be sold; the "excess" is warehoused (at taxpayer expense) or destroyed.
- Import restrictions limit how much of a crop can be imported into the United States.
- Crop insurance provides low-cost insurance against crop failures and disasters.
- Deficiency payments. . . .

THE "CHEAPER FOOD" RUSE

One rationale for agribusiness subsidies—to the extent that they have any—is that you get cheaper food prices out of the deal. Dream on.

First of all, we pay for many of these handouts with our income taxes, so you'd have to add a portion of those taxes to your food bill to come up with an accurate total. According to one estimate, the average household can tack on $1,805 over the next decade.[19] Besides that, there are indirect subsidies you pay for at the checkout counter without even realizing it.

Price supports, import restrictions, and market and production quotas keep the prices of sugar, dairy products, and peanuts higher in the United States than on the world market. They cost consumers $2 billion a year in higher sugar prices, $1.7 billion in higher dairy prices, and $500 million in higher peanut prices. That's $4.2 billion at the cash register right there.[20]

But crop subsidies actually help drive up the price of many other foods, because they help inflate the cost of rural real estate—by some 25% in 2000 alone.[21] Land that produces subsidized crops is worth more, thus bidding up the price of neighboring land. But more important, because subsidies are paid according to the number of acres planted (instead of farmer need), land becomes overvalued. Land prices are the single biggest contributor to the cost of food.

As a further illustration of the law of unintended consequences, the higher land prices are pushing more small family farms out of business and contributing to the dominance of corporate factory farms. Subsidies push up the price of land beyond what many poor farmers can afford. If they're tenant farmers, their rent goes up, and if they're owner-operators, their property taxes go up. Since neither group can afford to expand their operations, big corporations are able to gobble up more of the available land—which then makes the remaining land that much more valuable. On top of that, the larger agribusiness concerns bid up the price of land in competition with each other, leaving small family farms in the dust.[22]

Even when agribusiness subsidies actually do bring down the cost of food, you typically end up paying for them in other ways. For example, diverting productive salmon streams to grow potatoes in the desert may be great for fast-food outlets and the corporate farmers who supply them, but it's hell on fishermen and recreational workers. Their unemployment insurance is part of the cost of your cheaper meal.

The bottom line is that as agribusiness consolidation has increased, farm employment has declined. There have been jobs created in peripheral sectors, but not as many; employment in these sectors grew by 36,000 from 1975 to 1996, while farm employment dropped 667,000 jobs. More tellingly, the job "growth" in these sectors comes largely at the expense of the environment. Larger farms require more pesticides and machinery, leading to more pollution in our skies and streams as well as our food. So once again, we're subsidizing the deterioration of our environment, and we pay for it in health care costs as well as in taxes.

LIVESTOCK SUBSIDIES

Many Americans are cutting back on meat and dairy products for health reasons. But whatever your diet, you help pay for these products with your taxes (not to mention the Medicare costs for those who over-consume meat and dairy products).

While most farmers have to treat their profits as ordinary income, livestock profits are classified as capital gains and are taxed at a lower rate (now just 15%). But the costs of buying, breeding, and raising livestock are ordinary expenses that can be deducted immediately.[23] This best-of-both-worlds tax treatment encourages people to get into the livestock business, and there are nontax inducements as well.

Cattle ranchers graze their herds on public lands leased to them at about one-eighth of their market value—which works out to pennies per acre. In 2001, the Bureau of Land Management (BLM) took in $4.5 million from grazing leases and spent more than 17 times as much—$77 million—managing the lands. Note that even if the BLM had charged market value, we still would have lost more than $40 million on the deal.[24]

As far as I can tell, the main justification for this seems to be that ranchers are "cultural icons" who maintain a "way of life" that is worth preserving. (There may be a more sophisticated rationale, but I haven't come across it yet.) It's an emotional argument that ignores the facts about how little of the nation's livestock ranching is actually done on public lands—less than 0.1%, according to one study.[25] Besides, maintaining this lifestyle contributes to plenty of destruction.

Cattle trample native plants and grasses, foul local streams, and contribute to erosion. The BLM and the Forest Service have to deal with the effects on wildlife and watersheds in the lands they manage. Add in those environmental factors and the true cost of grazing leases comes to about *$500 million* a year, according to a study by the Center for Biological Diversity in Tucson, Arizona.[26]

Like most agribusiness handouts, cattle subsidies go disproportionately to the very rich—75% of the grazing land leased by the BLM is controlled by fewer than 10% of the lessees. Among these "welfare cowboys" are computer moguls Bill Hewlett and (the late) David Packard of Hewlett-Packard, as well as Jack Simplot, one of the 500 richest people in America. Other handouts go to Texaco, the Mormon Church, and Anheuser-Busch (which presumably grazes its famous Clydesdale horses at your expense). One study of Arizona's Prescott National Forest found that 64% of all leases were held by doctors, lawyers, art dealers, and other business owners—who are hardly dependent on ranching for their livelihoods and certainly aren't clinging to a bygone way of life.[27]

Amazingly, we are paying all this money—and subsidizing the destruction of our public lands—to benefit just 3% of all livestock producers in the United States.[28] This welfare ranching takes up 300 million acres of federally held land. That includes 90% of the BLM's land, 69% of the Forest Service's land, as well as various national parks, wildlife refuges, and nature preserves.[29] But other uses of federal lands contribute far more to local and regional economies. One study of the Kaibab Plateau in Arizona found that recreational activities and hunting licenses generated $1.5 million for the local economy, compared to $46,000 from federal grazing.[30]

Another handout to ranchers is the Western Livestock Protection Program, which spent $9.8 million in 1996 to protect livestock by exterminating predators—in the same year that livestock losses from predators totaled $5.8 million.

In 1998, Congress appropriated $28.8 million for this program, even though the House voted 229 to 193 for the Bass-DeFazio amendment, which would have killed the funding. Supporters of cowboy welfare forced a second vote the next day. As Taxpayers for Common Sense noted,

> After it passed, an inadvertent technical drafting error in the amendment was discovered. On June 24, the technical error was fixed by a unanimous consent request by the amendment's sponsor. Later that same day opponents of the original amendment sought a revote and inaccurately claimed that the error had not been fixed, even though House members were clearly told it had been fixed by Representative Bass. On June 24, the House rejected the amendment, 192–232.[31]

In fiscal year 2003, the program is budgeted at $68 million.

However, the Livestock Protection Program (LPP) is not to be confused with the Livestock Compensation Program (LCP), an emergency program with $750 million to cover drought losses, or the Livestock Assistance Program (LAP), which compensates ranchers for losses not covered by the LCP or the LPP. The LAP kicks in with another quarter billion for FY2003.[32] You'll be relieved to know, though, that nobody is allowed to collect from both the LCP and the LAP at the same time.

Of course, ordinary people have to buy their own insurance to cover losses from natural disasters. The ranchers seem unwilling to shoulder the risks inherent in their chosen business. And once again, it would actually be cheaper to simply write a check to each welfare cowboy for predator losses than to fund these programs.

SUBSIDIES FOR DRUG PEDDLERS

But at least beef and milk are edible. Tobacco, a drug that kills 48 Americans every hour, is also subsidized with a combination of price supports, import restrictions, and production and market quotas.[33]

By keeping foreign tobacco out and limiting domestic production, the government creates a lower supply for the same amount of demand, allowing domestic producers to charge more. There is no rational justification for this; tobacco does far more harm to the economy than any conceivable benefit that could be gained from government support. When the program started in 1933, the health effects of tobacco were not widely known, and there were far more farmers in need of assistance. The program survives today because of sheer political clout. While some tobacco farmers are definitely hurting because of industry outsourcing, the bulk of the subsidy goes to absentee landlords, not farmers. Then again, the mythical promise of a subsidy might keep these smaller farmers producing tobacco, rather than switching to a more useful, though unsubsidized, crop.

In 1996, then-Representative Richard Durbin (now a Democratic senator from Illinois) introduced a proposal to end tobacco subsidies, estimating their direct cost at about $41 million.[34] The price supports also generate higher costs to consumers, at an estimated $857 million. (This doesn't count the additional cost to taxpayers of dealing with smoking-related illnesses through Medicare, Medicaid, veterans hospitals, and government employees' health plans. That costs you an extra $38 billion a year.[35] And that doesn't count the money the Social Security Administration pays out in survivors' benefits to kids whose parents have died from smoking. That puts another $1.8 billion on the tally.[36])

In June 1996, the House of Representatives voted down Durbin's measure by a smoke-thin margin of 212 to 210. There hasn't been a serious effort to end the subsidies since. Usually the tobacco lobby does better than a two-vote margin. Its 13 PACs, among the most generous on Capitol Hill, handed out almost $9.5 million in the 2001–2002 election cycle alone.[37] This is quite a boost from the $10 million distributed between 1986 and 1995.[38] (When you kill off 400,000 of your customers every year, you need all the friends you can get.)

Although the tobacco lobby has made sure that some portion of the federal government supports tobacco farmers, public pressure has forced other parts of the government to discourage smoking. Seeing the writing on the wall, US tobacco manufacturers are making a big push for new customers overseas. US tobacco exports have risen 275% since 1985, when we started threatening countries like Japan, Thailand, South Korea, and Taiwan with trade sanctions unless they opened their markets to US cigarettes.[39]

Taiwan has been trying to restrict smoking in public areas, and to ban cigarette ads and vending machine sales. That should sound familiar, because the same efforts are being made here. But when they do it, we call it an unfair trade practice. If this hypocritical coercion of ours succeeds, the results will be as disastrous for Taiwan as they were for South Korea. One year after the US tobacco giants penetrated that market, the smoking rate for teenage boys had almost doubled (from 18% to

30%), while the rate for teenage girls had more than quintupled (from 1.6% to 8.7%).[40]

Meanwhile, as US tobacco companies have moved more production offshore to service foreign markets, they've also been importing more foreign tobacco to use in domestic cigarettes. This has put the squeeze on US tobacco farmers, the very people these subsidies are supposed to help. At the same time, the USDA has cut tobacco quotas in half in the past few years. To compensate for market losses, the USDA paid out $350 million in direct payments to tobacco farmers in FY2001. This amounts to eight times the previous annual subsidy.[41] (Of course, many of the beneficiaries are absentee landlords who don't farm tobacco but get rich selling their quotas to tenant farmers.) The big payout was not repeated in 2002, but a 2003 farm bill added a new $53 billion program to pay off the farmers again.[42] That brings the current total in tobacco subsidies to $96 million.

Editors' Note: *Notes for this reading can be found in the original source.*

CHAPTER 2

Tax Cheats and Their Enablers

ROBERT S. MCINTYRE

> You . . . can be a millionaire . . . and never pay taxes! You can be a millionaire . . . and never pay taxes!
>
> You say . . . "Steve . . . how can I be a millionaire . . . and never pay taxes?"
>
> First . . . get a million dollars.
>
> Now . . . you say, "Steve . . . what do I say to the tax man when he comes to my door and says, 'You . . . have never paid taxes'?"
>
> Two simple words. Two simple words in the English language: "I forgot!"
>
> —Steve Martin, *Saturday Night Live*, January 21, 1978

INTRODUCTION

Lots of unscrupulous big corporations and wealthy people are working hard to hide their profits and income from the tax collector. Their schemes are more complicated than Steve Martin's comic infomercial envisioned, but they're just as damaging to our country, and just as reprehensible. In fact, almost three decades after he delivered it, Martin's tax advice needs only minor updating. Add a few zeros to $1,000,000 and change the punch line to "Seven simple words . . . 'I have a note from my lawyer.'"

The culprits are many. The greedy tax dodgers, of course. Their unscrupulous tax advisers, including America's most prestigious accounting firms, biggest banks and many law firms—who make billions of dollars facilitating evasion and avoidance. But most of all, the blame lies with demagogic lawmakers in Washington, who have turned a blind eye to tax evasion, and have refused to give the Internal Revenue Service—the tax police—the resources to stop the abuses.

Tax dodging takes many forms. There are, of course, legal loopholes enacted by Congress in response to lobbying pressure. Generally termed "incentives," they purport to encourage people or companies to do something socially or economically useful. Then there are potentially legal (but often not) tax shelters—what might be called "roll your own" loopholes to cut taxes in ways that Congress never officially intended. And finally, there's outright cheating—simply failing to report your income or making up deductions.

Distinguishing one from the other isn't always easy. Taking a deduction for donating your old car to charity is perfectly legal, for instance. But making up an inflated value for the deduction is cheating. Moving your money offshore and failing to declare the income it earns is clearly cheating if you're a person. But it may be a legal—or at least quasi-legal—tax shelter if you're a multinational corporation. . . .

Far too many investors and business owners are tempted to understate their gross business receipts and/or overstate their expenses, move their investments offshore, fail to report their capital gains accurately, and so forth. Not all succumb, of course. Even for those who do, the actual alchemy of making income disappear for tax purposes is probably often a mystery. That doesn't in any way absolve the tax cheats and aggressive avoiders from blame: they're the demand side of the equation. But without the supply side, the lawyers, accountants and banks that set up the shelters, the demand would go unrequited.

The ethically-challenged tax advisers who are willing to help would-be tax evaders are well aware that the chances of their clients being audited by the IRS are extremely low, so long as a tax return doesn't raise obvious red flags. Their chief weapons to win this "audit lottery" are complexity and subterfuge.

In contrast, the vast majority of Americans who make almost all their money from wages have few opportunities for serious tax cheating. Taxes are withheld from paychecks, W-2 forms are easily matched against tax returns, and straightforward deductions for mortgage interest, state and local taxes, and (most) charitable donations are easily checked for accuracy.

So the majority of us who honestly pay our taxes have a major stake in getting the tax dodgers to ante up, too—hundreds of billions of dollars a year, in fact, although no one knows the exact amount for sure.

Taxes, as Supreme Court Justice Oliver Wendell Holmes noted a century ago, are "the price of civilization." Most of us are willing to pay our fair share of the cost of all the things we want and need our government to do—so long as we believe others are chipping in, too. But others—too often those who have gained the most from our society—prefer to shirk their responsibilities and pass the cost onto the rest of us. . . .

"Is it the right time to be migrating a corporation's headquarters to an offshore location? We are working through a lot of companies who feel that it is, that just the improvement on earnings is powerful enough that maybe the patriotism issue needs to take a back seat to that."
—Ernst & Young webcast advising its corporate clients to shelter their profits from U.S. taxes by reincorporating in Bermuda—issued in the fall of 2001 soon after the 9/11 terrorist attacks

"My father said all businessmen are S.O.B.s but I didn't believe it until now."
—John F. Kennedy, *The New York Times,* April 23, 1962

CORPORATE SHELTERS

Big corporations have an advantage over people in sheltering their income from tax. First of all, of course, they have tremendous lobbying power in Congress. So they can get special tax concessions enacted that ordinary citizens never could. In addition, unlike individuals, corporations are allowed to break themselves into pieces on paper and treat completely phony, non-existent transactions among those pieces as if they really happened. Because large corporations typically operate in many jurisdictions through multiple subsidiaries, they have lots of opportunities to move profits away from where they're actually earned and into places where they're not taxed.

Corporate America, outside of a few industries like oil, was a bit slow to get into the tax-avoidance game. That's why as recently as the 1950s, corporate taxes paid for about a third of the federal government. Indeed, in the early sixties, much of Big Business actually opposed the Kennedy administration's "investment tax credit" as an unwise interference in the marketplace. But by the time that loophole had been repealed in 1969 on grounds of cost and general uselessness, big American companies had gotten a taste of tax dodging and wanted more.

President Nixon was happy to oblige, with expanded depreciation write-offs, tax breaks for exporters and a number of other giveaways. There was a brief tax reform moment in 1976, but it was soon followed by the "supply-side" period that began in 1978 and continued through 1981. Ronald Reagan in his first term was particularly devoted to loopholes. By his second term, however, Reagan (or at least his staff) had come to his senses, and presided over the 1986 Tax Reform Act, which repealed most of the 1981-enacted tax breaks, along with many others, in exchange for lower tax rates.

But tax reform didn't last. Due to enacted loopholes, new tax-dodging schemes and insufficient enforcement, corporate tax sheltering has run amuck. Some of the shelters that corporations use are identical to the tax-avoiding schemes that wealthy people engage in. But corporations can do much more.

For example, a company may make products in one place and sell them in others. If the place it makes the products has low taxes, it may charge its selling subsidiaries, on paper, a lot for the products. That means high profits in the low tax country where the products are made, and low or no profits in the places where the products are sold. Conversely, if the place products are made has the high taxes, then the company will "sell" its products cheaply to its selling subsidiaries, and shift profits to the places where the products are sold.

Or a company may borrow from one of its subsidiaries in a low-tax place. The interest will be deductible against income that would otherwise be taxable in a higher-tax place, and taxed little, if at all by the low-tax place.

Or a company may have a very valuable asset, such as a trade name. If it transfers the ownership of that name to a low-tax place and then charges its taxable operations large royalties to use the name, it can avoid huge amounts in taxes.

One of the more blatant corporate tax shelter schemes that we know about involves a foreign company, the Yukos Oil Company, until recently Russia's biggest oil producer. After the break-up of the Soviet Union, many of Russia's previously state-owned businesses were transferred into private hands, typically at bargain basement prices. Some of the new owners became instant billionaires, and their corruption didn't stop there.

The new Russian tax code was drafted with the help of major American accounting firms, and was, on its face, as full of holes as Swiss cheese. One oddity of the Russian corporate income tax is that its revenues are dedicated to the Russian republics (the rough equivalent of our states), and those republics are authorized to give tax "incentives" to corporations, ostensibly to encourage economic development.

The republics where Yukos pumped and refined its oil weren't about to offer Yukos tax breaks. After all, they didn't need to. They already had the oil and the refineries trapped within their boundaries. But on the advice of its accountants, who included PricewaterhouseCoopers, Ernst & Young and KPMG, Yukos found what it thought was a way around that problem. Yukos went to one of the Russian republics, Mordovia, and sought a tax break for its oil profits. This probably seemed pretty weird at first to Mordovian officials. After all, Mordovia's official website notes:

> "There are no large deposits of natural resources except building materials on the territory of Mordovia. However . . . there are some parts of the Moksha, the Vad and the Sura rivers with deposits of the unique type of resources that is stained oak."

One can imagine the conversation between Yukos and Mordovian officials going something like this:

YUKOS: We'd like a tax exemption for our Mordovian oil profits.
MORDOVIA: But you don't have any oil profits here in Mordovia.
Y: Maybe not yet, but we will soon.
M: What's in it for us?
Y: We'll make it worth your while.
M: And if we say no?
Y: Don't even ask.

Once Yukos got its tax exemption in Mordovia it simply transferred its profits, on paper, to that republic, and slashed its Russian income taxes down to near zero.

Unfortunately for Yukos, its thuggish billionaire chief executive, Mikail Khodorkovsky, decided to get involved in Russian politics and television. Russian President Vladimir Putin didn't like the competition and charged Khodorkovsky and Yukos with billions of dollars in tax evasion. Although the Russian tax authorities had previously ignored this misbehavior and the Russian tax code was vague at best, it wasn't a hard case to make.

Yukos's inside-Russia tax shelter was particularly crude, but American companies do much the same thing inside the United States to avoid their state income taxes, with only a patina of added sophistication. Toys "R" Us, for example, transferred the ownership of its trade name to Delaware, which doesn't tax royalties, and then charged its stores around the country hefty fees to use the name. From 2001 through 2003, Toys "R" Us paid no state income tax on its $549 million in reported pretax U.S. profits. Similarly, many Wisconsin banks have avoided taxes by transferring ownership of their income-producing loans to subsidiaries located in

Nevada, which has no income tax. Texas-based corporations such as Dell and SBC Communications have shifted the nominal ownership of their companies to partnerships located in Delaware to avoid Texas income taxes. And on and on.

This February, my group, Citizens for Tax Justice, released a study of the state income taxes of 252 of America's largest and most profitable corporations. We found that from 2001 to 2003, these companies avoided paying state income taxes on almost two-thirds of their U.S. profits—at a cost to state governments of $42 billion. Overall, corporate state tax avoidance has led to a 40 percent drop in state corporate income tax collections as a share of the economy from 1989 to 2003.

Shifting profits to no-tax states is just the intramural version of the much larger international tax sheltering that America's big corporations also engage in. The infamous Enron, which paid no federal income tax at all in four of five years from 1996 through 2000, had 881 subsidiaries in foreign tax-haven countries, 692 of them in the Cayman Islands alone, which it used for both tax evasion and financial shenanigans. Halliburton has hundreds of such offshore entities. Famous American logos, such as "Ford" and "Coca Cola," are now being held by offshore affiliates in the Cayman Islands, in an international version of Toys "R" Us's state tax dodge. Most other big corporations have tax-haven subsidiaries, too, all for the purpose of hiding profits from tax.

To be sure, there are some rules against companies shifting otherwise taxable profits out of the U.S. and into tax-haven countries. Indeed, a major section of the tax code, called "Subpart F," is devoted to curbing such behavior. These rules are full of loopholes, hard to enforce and in need of reform, but they do have some salutary effect. In fact, the reason that Ernst & Young advised its corporate clients in the fall of 2001 to renounce their U.S. citizenship and reincorporate in Bermuda was that it would help get around these restrictions, since the Subpart F rules are harder to enforce or don't apply to "foreign" companies.

Some of the tax schemes that multinational corporations engage in look downright wacky on their face, but they're very lucrative. For example, one of our biggest banks, Wachovia, used a leasing tax shelter in which it pretended to own a German town's sewer system. That strange scheme allowed Wachovia to eliminate all of its U.S. federal income taxes in 2002.

The list of complicated corporate tax avoidance activities is almost endless, but the effects on federal corporate tax collections is easy to understand.

When Citizens for Tax Justice examined the federal taxes of 275 of the largest U.S. corporations last September, we found that in 2003 these companies, on average, paid only 17.3 percent of their U.S. profits in federal income taxes—less than half the 35 percent rate that the tax code purportedly requires. From 2001 to 2003, 82 of the 275 corporations enjoyed at least one year in which they paid nothing at all in federal income tax, despite pretax U.S. profits in those no-tax years totaling $102 billion.

In 1965, federal and state corporate income taxes in the U.S. equaled 4.0 percent of our GDP, much more than the 2.4 percent average in the other major developed countries. By 2001, the latest year available for international statistics, corporate taxes in those other countries had risen to 3.2 percent of GDP. But American corporate taxes in 2003 had plummeted to only 1.6 percent of GDP. (European countries are becoming increasingly worried, however, about growing corporate tax sheltering in their jurisdictions, too.)

The bottom line is this: Due to enacted corporate tax breaks, rate reductions and tax sheltering, U.S. corporate tax collections at the federal level alone have fallen from 4.8 percent of the gross domestic product in the 1950s to only 1.6 percent in 2004—a drop of two-thirds. To put that in perspective, if corporations paid the same effective tax rate now that they paid in the fifties, corporate tax payments to the U.S. Treasury would be $380 billion a year higher than they actually are.

Some of that decline in federal corporate tax payments since the 1950s reflects a drop in the corporate tax rate from 52 percent to 35 percent. So cracking down on corporate tax evasion and tax sheltering wouldn't restore all of the lost revenue. But it would be a major step toward reducing the budget deficit, maintaining essential government services and protecting honest taxpayers.

CHAPTER 3

The Cost of Money

MARK GREEN

> The day may come when we'll reject the money of the rich as tainted, but it hadn't come when I left Tammany Hall at 11:25 today.
>
> —George Washington Plunkitt, 1905

> I don't think we buy votes. What we do is we buy a candidate's stance on issues.
>
> —Allen Pross, executive director of the California Medical Association's PAC, 1989

> I got $3500 over 10 years [from Enron]. Heck, I'm the chairman of the committee. That wasn't a contribution. That was an insult.
>
> —Senator Ernest F. Hollings (D–SC), 2002

In April 2002, when President George W. Bush's approval rating—bolstered by post–September 11 patriotism—stood at 74 percent, six out of ten Americans surveyed by Greenberg Quinlan Rosner Research agreed with the following statement: "When it comes to domestic policies, the Bush administration always seems to do what the big corporations want." President Bush wasn't alone. In other polls commissioned around the same time, large majorities believed that "special-interest groups own Congress" and have too much influence over elected officials. And while 29 percent of those polled by the University of Michigan's National Election Studies in 1964 felt the government was "run by a few big interests looking out for themselves," that number rose to 76 percent in 1994.

This growing belief that big interests run Washington parallels the growing donations that big interests have sent to Washington—and the perception that money gets results.

In a study conducted by Ellen Miller for the Center for Responsive Politics, 20 percent of the members of Congress *admitted* that campaign contributions affected their voting; only half claimed contributions had no effect, and 30 percent said they weren't sure. "Let's be clear," writes Fred Wertheimer, former president of Common Cause. "Though for many years it has been taboo in most Washington circles to use the word 'corruption' to portray the political money system in action, that is precisely what's going on."

Put yourself in the shoes of a candidate. If elections cost millions of dollars to win—and given the ego and the high stakes involved, you'd sure like to win—you'll need to get the money from somewhere. Support from friends and family is a good start, but if you're like most people, it wouldn't be nearly enough to make you competitive. So whom do you count on when your personal network is exhausted? (Hint: It's not working people and advocacy groups.)

There's a huge cost involved when candidates engage in the primordial task of hunting and gathering monetary gifts from the 1 percent of wealthy Americans who do the vast majority of the contributing. And a huge cost when a Congress becomes in effect a pay-per-use system utilized only by those wealthy enough to afford the membership dues.

Most *current* incumbents try to explain away the inevitable reality that when Joe Citizen calls on line 1 and Marty the Millionaire on line 2, Marty's line is going to get picked up first. But most *former* elected officials complain about the wear and tear of the money chase on their time and their integrity.

The pay-to-play mentality has so seeped into our system that there now exist two classes of citizens. There are those for whom tax breaks, bailouts, and subsidies are granted; for whom running for and winning office is plausible; and with whom elected officials take time to meet. And then there are the rest of us—the non-donors for whom taxes go up, consumer prices rise, and influence evaporates.

In *The Godfather,* Marlon Brando's Don Corleone tells a man named Bonasera in the opening scene: "Someday, and that day may never come, I'll call upon you to do a service for me. But until that day, accept this justice as a gift on my daughter's wedding day." The only difference between Bonasera and a member of Congress is that, for the latter, that day will *surely* come.

Some lobbyists, and even some elected officials, will argue that industry campaign contributions reward a member's *past* performance, and have no implication for how he or she should behave in the *future.* But the past-future analysis is a distinction without a difference. For candidates and contributors aren't just mineral matter, with no sense of the future. Bribes are unnecessary when everyone involved in the money chase knows implicitly that gifts will keep coming if a candidate keeps supporting the industry.

Lobbyists themselves can be part of the problem. Of course, lobbyists—named for those in the 1800s who huddled in the lobbies off the floor of Congress waiting to pounce—are exercising their right to "petition government" and "redress grievances" under the First Amendment. And since members of Congress and their staffs can't know everything about everything, or even something about everything, they look to interested parties (discounting for bias) to bring key information to their attention. The problem occurs when an army of lobbyists for one interest—say, a lower capital gains rate, or bigger gas-guzzling cars—combines with big contributions from that interest to overwhelm a less vocal or invisible opposition. And 17,000 lobbyists in Washington overall—or more than 30 per member of Congress—is quite an army.

"Every day there's a cadre of special-interest lobbyists lined up outside the House chamber on the sidewalk," reports Matt Keller, legislative director of Common Cause, who's spent years lobbying on Capitol Hill. "It's like a caricature. You've got Mr. Oil Man, Mr. Gas Man, Mr. Tobacco Man. It's like something out of *The Simpsons.* These guys spend their days trying to defeat something so obviously in the best interests of the country and the planet, and they can't possibly believe in what they're doing—but money talks. It's bizarre and frightening to watch up close.". . .

THE MONEY CHASE DISCOURAGES VOTING AND CIVIC PARTICIPATION

As special-interest dollars in elections go up by the millions, voter participation goes down. While Israel reliably achieves over 80 percent turnout in its elections for prime minister, and France and the United Kingdom typically turn out about three quarters of their voting-age populations, the United States has not broken *60* percent since 1968 (see Table 3.1). The turnout for American elections is no higher today than it was in the 1930s—with roughly half of eligible voters staying home in presidential elections, and nearly two thirds in congressional elections.

The 1988 presidential race between George Bush and Michael Dukakis had the worst turnout (50.1 percent) in 64 years, but that dubious honor was not held long: two cycles later, 1996's Clinton-Dole contest yielded a limp 49.1 percent. And four years after that, not even the tightness of 2000's Bush-Gore fight could inspire many more than half of registered voters to turn out. On the local level, the trends are similar: In a May 2002 Nebraska primary, a microscopic 20 percent of registered voters went to the polls, shattering the previous low mark of 36 percent.

TABLE 3.1   Turnout of Eligible Voters in Presidential Elections since 1960

Year	Percent	Year	Percent
1960	63.1	1984	53.1
1964	61.9	1988	50.1
1968	60.8	1992	55.1
1972	55.2	1996	49.1
1976	53.6	2000	51.2
1980	52.6		

Source: Federal Election Commission.

When right-wing extremist Jean-Marie Le Pen took second place in France's 2002 presidential race, legions of press attributed the accused racist's surprise finish to the large number of so-called absent voters. Soberingly, the 72 percent turnout for that race—France's lowest in nearly four decades—is higher than any U.S. turnout in the twentieth century. "The nation that prides itself on being the best example of government of, for, and by the people," notes Curtis Gans, director of the nonpartisan Committee for the Study of the American Electorate, "is rapidly becoming a nation whose participation is limited to the interested or zealous few."

Consider these regressive trends, as reflected in Robert Putnam's much discussed *Bowling Alone: The Collapse and Revival of American Community:*

- Just 11 percent of eighteen- and nineteen-year-olds eligible to vote for the first time in 1998 actually did so.
- Beyond a 25 percent decline in voting, there has been a 50 percent dip in political involvement (measured by campaign activities) over the last forty years. In 1973, a majority of Americans wrote an article, signed a petition, made a speech, or sent a letter to an elected official; twenty-one years later, most Americans did none of these.
- In 1973, two-thirds of Americans attended at least one organization or club meeting a year; in 1994, the reverse was true. Over the same time span, membership in social and civic organizations fell 16 percent, while active participation in these same groups dropped by 50 percent.
- Volunteering has diminished among nearly every age group, churchgoing has gone down 10 percent, and active involvement in church activities has plummeted by 25 to 50 percent.

"There is now a lower level of trust toward our government than at any time perhaps since the 1920s, perhaps ever," explains Gans. One reason, he says, is "the media's increasingly cynical portrayal of politics, aided by thousands of deaths in Vietnam, the Iran-Contra affair, George [H. W.] Bush's 'Read My Lips, No New Taxes' vow, and impeachment."

Gans believes that citizens watching six hours a day of TV are left with little time to do much else but work, eat, and sleep; their civic information base is unvaried and limited because it's filtered nearly exclusively through the TV screen. He points also to the increasingly stressful lives people lead today: more Americans are single, divorced, commuting, generally anxious, and therefore less likely to participate in civic affairs—including voting—when faced with a crude cost-benefit decision. Also, Gans notes, although "leaders" like Newt Gingrich and Tom DeLay call government the enemy, demagoguing against the government isn't likely to encourage participation in government.

Beyond the campaign finance arena, however, in recent years a number of plausible and promising ideas have been proposed to boost voting. One idea is the nationwide adoption of election day registration (EDR). Currently practiced by six states, EDR reduces barriers to participation by enabling voters who mistakenly think they are already registered to do so on election day. This would also solve the additional problems of voters being turned away because their registration hasn't been processed in a timely manner, or because they've been wrongly purged from voter lists. According to a report by the nonpartisan research group Demos, states using EDR in the 2000 presidential election had turnout rates nearly 12 percent higher than the national average—63.2 percent versus 51.3 percent.

Another pro-turnout initiative is 1993's "Motor Voter" Act, or the National Voter Registration Act. This historic bill, aimed at increasing participation, enabled voters to register at their department of motor vehicles, public assistance offices, or other state agencies while applying for driver's licenses or government assistance. The legislation also provided for mail-in voter registration. The results have been modest but encouraging: from 1992 to 2000, registration went up 5.2 percent.

In Oregon, voting by mail has proven to boost participation. In addition to being cost-effective (between 1995 and 1997, Oregon counties saved over $1 million in three voting-by-mail special elections), the system is obviously more convenient for voters than driving to the polls. In the 1996 Republican and Democratic presidential primaries, Oregon led the nation in turnout, with over 53.7 percent of voters mailing in their ballots. New Hampshire ranked second, with a 45 percent turnout.

Despite these signs of improvement, turnout and registration remain low among many demographic groups, including persons of low income (less than half of those making under $50,000 annually are registered, compared with 77 percent of those making $75,000 or more), communities of color (Latinos, for instance, register at approximately half the rate whites do), and young people (only 44 percent of citizens eighteen to twenty-four were registered in 1998, compared with a rate of over three fourths among senior citizens).

While from 1992 to 2000 soft money contributions increased five-fold, hard money nearly doubled, and party fund-raising tripled, voting in federal elections went *down* four percentage points overall. Obviously nothing can be done to change the statistical fact that one person's vote is highly unlikely to sway an election (although the tightness of Bush-Gore should make voters think twice). But with the combination of incumbency and money apparently predetermining election results, many voters rationally assume their vote can't really matter.

This problem is of concern not just to liberals but to all small-d democrats. "We're perilously close to not having democracy," said Paul Weyrich, a prominent conservative who heads the Free Congress Foundation. "Non-voters are voting against the system, and if we get a bit more than that, the system won't work."

THE MONEY CHASE DISCOURAGES COMPETITIVE ELECTIONS

In an age when incumbency and money are mutually reinforcing and "redistricting" is little more than a synonym for "incumbent protecting," the realistic number of potentially competitive seats in this fall's general elections can be counted on one's fingers and toes. In fact, getting reelected has become so automatic that a member of Congress is almost more likely to vacate his or her seat by *dying* than by losing.

In both 1998 and 2000, more than 98 percent of House incumbents who sought reelection won their races. (Senate challengers fared slightly better, winning 10 percent and 18 percent, respectively.) In 1996, every single one of the 113 Congress members first elected in the 1980s won his or her race for reelection. All but 4 won by 10 percent or more, and 75 won by a whopping 30 percent or more. While 142 incumbents were defeated in the 1960s, that number fell to just 97 in the 1970s, to 88 in the 1980s, and to 102 in the 1990s. . . .

The incumbent's advantage is largely predicated on money. Of course, the fact that incumbents can gerrymander districts once a decade also helps their bids for reelection but is marginal when compared with the potent mixture of money and incumbency. In 1988, incumbents ended up with twice as much in *leftover* funds as their challengers *spent.* In 2000, House incumbents outspent their challengers by better than 4 to 1 ($408.5 million to $89 million), enjoyed an 8-to-1 edge in PAC money, and by the end of October had a 13-to-1 advantage in cash on hand. Senate incumbents in 2000 raised $155.9 million, compared with $63 million by their challengers, and held a 6-to-1 edge in both PAC funds and cash on hand. . . . One can't help but conclude that the two distinct political parties in Washington have given way to one monolithic alternative: the incumbent party.

Carrying over war chests is one of the great time-honored traditions of the incumbency protection program. Amass as much cash as you possibly can—even if you have no known opponent—and then use it to intimidate potential challengers, who will drop out or never even run to begin with. Once reelection is achieved, the member of Congress carries over the war chest into the next campaign and the next and the next. In a very real sense rolling over such treasuries violates the spirit of the campaign finance contribution limits, since a John Donor may give Challenger X only $2000 for a particular campaign in a particular year but may have given Congressman Z a total of $8000 for a campaign against Challenger X ($2000 in each of four election cycles).

In Public Citizen's Congress Watch study *House Insurance: How the Permanent Congress Hoards Campaign Cash,* members of the 101st Congress were found to have over $67 million stowed away in campaign war chests *the month they took office,* "virtually assur[ing] reelection [and] certainly discourag[ing] qualified candidates from challenging the financially stronger representatives." According to the same Congress Watch report, 89 percent of House incumbents faced financially noncompetitive races in 2000, meaning they faced either no opposition or challengers with less than half their campaign resources.

The only ways to crack open this continuing "unfair advantage" are serious campaign finance reform or congressional term limits. And we'll get reform only when members of Congress start fearing limits on their terms more than they fear limits on their money.

THE MONEY CHASE CREATES "PART-TIME LEGISLATORS, FULL-TIME FUND-RAISERS"

On any given workday, you can see streams of Congress members leaving their Capitol Hill offices to go to small campaign cubicles in order to dial for dollars. "The problem is much worse than portrayed," says Senator Ron Wyden (D–OR). "The money chase is so time-consuming that people should wonder how we have time to get anything done. Yes, the day after an election, people sleep in on Wednesday. But then the money chase starts in again, day after day, year in and year out.

"In an election year," he continued, "members have cards or Blackberrys that say '8–9 Grange; 9–10 Hearing on Technology; 10–4 money calls at DCCC.' For that much of the day, a significant number of public officials are sitting in a dank office away from their public office with their tin cup out instead of thinking about how to help their constituents."

Ask anyone involved in the game, and, if they're honest, the refrain will be the same. In his autobiography, Bill Bradley wrote that, despite his fame and popularity, he had to spend 40 percent of his freshman Senate term fund-raising for reelection. One New York congressman, well known for raising tons of special-interest money, confided at a fund-raiser in early 2002, "I spend almost half my time raising money." When asked if his job performance would change if he didn't have to fund-raise incessantly, the representative didn't hesitate. "Oh yes, I'd be much more independent and effective."

Even Senator Dick Durbin (D–IL), among the hardest working of the new senators, is candid enough to admit in an interview, "Of course I won't miss votes, but after that, fund-raising has to take precedence. We'll schedule fund-raisers and then build around them." Representative Sherrod Brown (D–OH) confides that he has three full-time jobs: "Congressman, campaigner, fund-raiser."

Senator Robert C. Byrd, the longest-serving member of either chamber, put it best, calling his colleagues "part-time legislators and full-time fund-raisers." Senator Byrd told Mark Shields that during his tenure as Senate majority leader he often had to delay votes because of fund-raising conflicts. He mocked the parade of requests he endured for years: "Please, no votes Monday . . . no votes after four on Thursday . . . I've got a fund-raiser scheduled in Los Angeles . . . in New York . . . in my home state." Senator John Kerry, who refuses to take PAC money and has 55,000 donors averaging $36 each, said in the early 1990s, "A few months ago, I was out in Columbus, Ohio. And the same day I was there, across the hall was Tom Harkin of Iowa, and the next morning there was a room reserved downstairs for Bill Bradley of New Jersey. Now, that is Columbus, Ohio. That is ridiculous."

Stanley Sheinbaum, a prominent Democratic donor and activist in California, grew so frustrated with members of Congress calling to ask for money that he told a high-ranking senator he would accept his request for a meeting only "on the proviso that money not be discussed." But given the rules of engagement, is it really a surprise that incumbents regard donors more as ATMs than as people, and that donors come to resent it?

THE MONEY CHASE DETERS TALENT FROM SEEKING OFFICE

Challengers know they must make it through a "money primary" first if they ever want to reach the "voters' primary"—and the polling place of donors can turn away anyone without secure financing, which of course deters potential contenders who have more talent than funds. "At some point," argues Joshua Rosenkranz of the

Brennan Center for Justice, "the spending of money is less an exercise in speech, and more an exercise in raw power—the power to dominate the conversation and to scare away all potential challengers." Of course it's impossible to calculate how many good women and men decide not to seek office because of the prohibitive costs, but most astute observers assume that it's many. As Senator Paul Wellstone (D–MN) laments, "People are giving up and not running for senator or governor because the money chase is too much."

When Elizabeth Dole aborted her run for president in October 1999, money was the single reason she cited. She pointed to the 80-to-1 fund-raising edge George W. Bush held over her. "I hoped to compensate by attracting new people to the political process, by emphasizing experience and advocating substantive issues," she told a roomful of tearful supporters. "But as important as these things may be, the bottom line remains money."

Perhaps most alarming is the case of Reubin Askew. So vast and disquieting were the demands for money in Askew's 1988 Florida Senate race that the former governor abruptly dropped out—despite opinion polls showing him with a 4-to-1 lead in the primary and a 2-to-1 advantage in the general election. "Something is seriously wrong with our system," Askew explained, "when many candidates for the Senate need to spend 75 percent of their time raising money." As Askew's issues director for the campaign, Dexter Filkins, wrote, "The need to raise so much cash so fast limited Askew's contact with the average voter—that is, one who did not donate money. We simply didn't have time for them." If Askew, a popular elected official, couldn't handle the incessant demands of fund-raising, how do you suppose an unwealthy, unfamous, and unsubsidized workingman or -woman might make out?

Of course, there's no formal "money primary" in the law or Constitution. All potential candidates are allowed to raise up to $1000 a donor per election or give themselves as much of their personal wealth as they can. "The law, in its majestic equality, permits the rich as well as the poor to sleep under bridges, to beg in the streets and steal bread," wrote Anatole France, which inspired this extrapolation from the late U.S. Appellate Court Judge J. Skelly Wright: "The law, in its majestic equality, allows the poor as well as the rich to form political action committees, to purchase the most sophisticated polling, media and direct mail techniques and to drown out each other's voices by overwhelming expenditures in political campaigns. Financial inequities . . . undermine the political proposition to which this nation is dedicated—that all men are created equal."

These financial disparities account in part for why there are so few blue-collar workers in Congress. "Do you honestly think that a butcher could get elected to the Senate today?" Senator Byrd rhetorically asked. "A garbage collector? A small grocery man? A welder?"

THE MONEY CHASE FAVORS MULTIMILLIONAIRES

When soliciting funds from individuals and PACs turns out to be inadequate to cover the costs of campaigning, candidates will often supply the requisite funds by drawing from their personal finances. In 2000, twenty-seven House and Senate candidates spent at least $500,000 of their own money on their own campaigns. Self-financing is especially pronounced for challengers and for candidates in open-seat races. Challengers in the 1996 House elections spent an average of over $40,000 of their own money, one sixth of their total campaign costs; candidates in open-seat races spent over $90,000. The average Senate challenger that year spent $645,000— one quarter of his/her total campaign costs—out of his/her own pocket.

Already, more than a third of Senate members are millionaires—and the number keeps growing. At least 50 members of the two houses are multimillionaires, among them the following senators: John Kerry, with a net worth of $675 million; Jon Corzine, $400 million; Herbert Kohl (D–WI), $300 million; Jay Rockefeller IV (D–WV), $200 million; Peter Fitzgerald (R–IL), $50 million; Mark Dayton (D–MN), $20 million; and Bill Frist (R–TN), $20 million.

Asked why so many of the deep-pocketed senators are, surprisingly, Democrats, Senator Carl Levin laughs. "It's a growing solution to Republican money. Since we can't raise as much special-interest money, we look more for candidates who can spend their own." Corzine, a former Goldman Sachs CEO, agrees. "Democratic leaders more eagerly recruited [wealthy self-financers] to relieve financial pressure on the party and because more such Democrats [than Republicans] run believing that government does good things," New Jersey's junior senator explains. "There's a tradition from FDR to JFK of Democrats who do it to fix the world and level the playing field of society."

Indeed, party leaders acknowledge that they explicitly try to recruit self-financing candidates, not necessarily the best candidates, to run. But since *Buckley v. Valeo* permits the wealthy to contribute as much to their own campaigns as they like—because the Court reasoned a person can't corrupt *himself*, never considering how such spending could corrupt the *process*—the strategy is legal, and often a winning one. Think about the thousands of hours of fund-raising that can be used for other things, like wooing party officials and opinion leaders, reaching out to voters, studying up on issues, and making news. Or the bottomless budget for television advertising that enables the candidate to flood the airwaves with her message.

Those who counter that advertisements don't force voters to vote for their candidates are correct, at least in a narrow sense. There's probably no amount of money that could persuade a majority to vote for Pat Buchanan, or to buy an Edsel. But advertising is a $600-billion-a-year industry for a reason—and the reason is that, overall, the more advertising a candidate does, the more likely he is to make the sale. Or to raise doubts about an opponent who can't afford to rebut. Put it another way: Suppose the New York Yankees are the best team in baseball; who would you bet on if the Yankees could bat in only two innings while their opponent, the worst major-league team, could bat in nine?

That said, being a multimillionaire certainly doesn't guarantee victory. Sometimes a candidate does something so self-immolating, or is found so untenable, that not even money can glide him into office. Jay Rockefeller and Jon Corzine—and even publishing magnate William Randolph Hearst, whose newspaper empire helped fund winning campaigns for Congress in 1902 and 1904—may have been successful, but Michael Huffington and Al Checchi are two examples of wealthy self-financing candidates in California who lost. Huffington, in his $30 million campaign for U.S. Senate in 1994, lost the election after attacking the immigrants flooding the state while, it was revealed, he himself had hired an illegal alien in his household. Checchi, the past head of American Airlines, lost his $40 million Democratic gubernatorial primary in 1998 after he ran a barrage of ads so brutally harsh that people began to resent *him*. Both candidates also faced opponents who were well financed and able to spend at least half their amounts—incumbent Senator Dianne Feinstein against Huffington, and now-Governor Gray Davis against Checchi.

But self-financers are starting to win major races now, which encourages other very wealthy people to try to do the same. As I mentioned earlier, multimillionaires Tony Sanchez in Texas and Douglas Forrester in New Jersey won competitive primaries in 2002. Following the success of Michael Bloomberg in New York City, five multimillionaires ran in statewide races in New York in 2002: Jane S. Hoffman (who later dropped out due to health) and Dennis Mehiel for lieutenant governor, William Mulrow for comptroller, and Tom Golisano for governor. Eliot Spitzer, the incumbent Attorney General, also significantly self-financed his initial victory in 1998.

Mark Schmitt of the Open Society Institute wrote, "The self-financed Democrats of most recent vintage . . . have all shown themselves to be as capable, liberal, and brave as their older counterparts like Jay Rockefeller. But there is no getting around the fact that the advantage of self-financed candidates has created a political plutocracy that looks less like America, economically, than at any time since before the direct election of senators."

If something doesn't change soon, there will be only three types of people running for and holding office in the future: super-fund-raisers, celebrities, and multimillionaires.

THE MONEY CHASE CORRUPTS LEGISLATION— "BUYING SHARP'S SILENCE"

Of course, much of the $3 billion contributed to candidates in 2000 came because donors knew the candidate, believed in the candidate's philosophy, liked his/her personality, looks, religion, or race. The problem, however, is that the system is also flooded with a Niagara of contributions from economic interests seeking a return. And getting one.

A dozen years ago, the Democracy Project, a policy institute I founded, published a study attempting to analyze the costs of the private financing of elections. *Public Funding vs. Private Funding: Two Case Studies of the Benefits of Campaign Finance Reform* was an early attempt to quantify a significant and largely immeasurable problem. We started by examining how special-interest-inspired legislation can increase a product's cost to consumers, how tax breaks due to PACs increase the burden to taxpayers generally, and how legislation needed but forestalled by PACs can impose additional health and other costs on taxpayers.

The results, similar to estimates conducted more recently by groups like Public Citizen, were staggering. In *taxpayer* costs alone, the bailout of failed S&Ls cost $25 billion a year, the deregulation of tobacco (plus a farm bill authorizing manufacturers to buy stored tobacco at 90 percent discounts) cost Americans $2.1 billion a year, and loopholes won by Chicago's commodities traders hit taxpayers with a $300 million tab.

Then add new *consumer* costs. Sugar price supports (delivered to repay seventeen major sugar PACs who doled out $3.3 million to Senate and House members) cost consumers $3 billion a year. Similarly, dairy and milk price supports milked consumers by tacking an additional $9 billion onto the $45 billion shoppers already were spending on dairy.* Add to that an additional $2 billion a year on utilities, $10 billion a year on beer and wine, and $4.3 billion on health costs stemming from the passage of a much weaker version of the Clean Air Act, and the impact of PACs on American families is, in effect, a political corruption tax.

In all, the rough cost to Americans of the *private* system of financing elections was $50 billion annually. By contrast, the costs of *public* financing are modest and transparent; no serious proposals for public funding of elections have exceeded $500 million to $1 billion.

"I think most people assume—I do, certainly—that someone making an extraordinarily large contribution is going to get some kind of an extraordinary return for it," said Supreme Court Justice David H. Souter. "I think that is a pervasive assumption. And . . . there is certainly an appearance of, call it an attenuated corruption, if you will, that large contributors are simply going to get better service, whatever that service may be, from a politician than the average contributor, let alone no contributor."

*To put this in perspective, the market wholesale price of a gallon of milk at the time was 61 cents worldwide versus 87 cents in the United States.

CHAPTER 4

Water for Profit

JOHN LUOMA

Even before the water turned brown, Gordon Certain had plenty to worry about. With his north Atlanta neighborhood in the middle of a growth boom, the president of the North Buckhead Civic Association had been busy fielding complaints about traffic, a sewer tunnel being built near a nature preserve, and developers razing tidy postwar ranch homes to make room for mansions. But nothing compared to the volume of calls and emails that flooded Certain's home office in May, when Georgia's environmental protection agency issued an alert to North Buckhead residents: Their tap water, the agency warned, wasn't safe to drink unless they boiled it first. Some neighbors, Certain recalls, had just fed formula to their baby when they heard the alert. "I had parents calling me in tears," he says. "The things that have happened to the water here have sure scared the hell out of a lot of people." A month later, another "boil water" alert came; this time, when Certain turned on his own tap, the liquid that gushed out was the color of rust, with bits of debris floating in it.

Atlanta's water service had never been without its critics; there had always been complaints about slow repairs and erroneous water bills. But the problems intensified three years ago, says Certain, after one of the world's largest private water companies took over the municipal system and promised to turn it into an "international showcase" for public-private partnerships. Instead of ushering in a new era of trouble-free drinking water, Atlanta's experiment with privatization has brought a host of new problems. This year there have been five boil-water alerts, indicating unsafe contaminants might be present. Fire hydrants have been useless for months. Leaking water mains have gone unrepaired for weeks. Despite all of this, the city's contractor—United Water, a subsidiary of French-based multinational Suez—has lobbied the City Council to add millions more to its $21-million-a-year contract.

Atlanta's experience has become Exhibit A in a heated controversy over the push by a rapidly growing global water industry to take over public water systems. At the heart of the debate are two questions: Should water, a basic necessity for human survival, be controlled by for-profit interests? And can multinational companies actually deliver on what they promise—better service and safe, affordable water?

Already, the two largest players in the industry, French-based conglomerates Suez and Vivendi Universal, manage water for 230 million people, mostly in Europe and the developing world. Now they are seeking access to a vast and relatively untapped market: the United States, where 85 percent of people still get their water from public utilities. Private water providers have positioned themselves as the solution to the developing world's water problems, notes Hugh Jackson, a policy analyst at the advocacy group Public Citizen. "But it's a lot harder for them to make the case when here, in the world's center of capitalism, cities are delivering tremendous amounts of high-quality, clean, inexpensive water to people."

Yet over the past decade, hundreds of U.S. cities and counties, including Indianapolis and Milwaukee, have hired private companies to manage their waterworks. Currently New Orleans; Stockton, California; and Laredo, Texas, are in the process of going private, although opposition has sprung up in all three cities. Water companies have been conducting annual "fly ins" to Washington, D.C., to press their legislative agenda, lobbying for laws that would protect companies from lawsuits over contaminated water and block municipalities from taking back troubled privatized systems. Most recently, a bipartisan group in Congress has been pushing a federal waterworks funding bill, advocated by the National Association of Water Companies, which would require cities to "consider" privatization before they can tap federal funds for upgrading or expanding public utilities and would also subsidize such privatization deals.

At the municipal level the lobbying pressure is equally intense, with water companies actively courting local officials (the U.S. Conference of Mayors' website features a large ad from Vivendi subsidiary U.S. Filter) and spending hundreds of thousands of dollars supporting privatization in local referendums. "It's hard for local guys to turn these companies away," Massachusetts' former water commissioner Douglas MacDonald has said. "They're everywhere, with arms like an octopus."

The argument behind privatization is that only corporate efficiency can rescue the nation's aging waterworks. But if success is measured in terms of delivering an essential commodity to everyone who needs it, then the industry's record is less than encouraging. Around the world, cities with private water-management companies have been plagued by lapses in service, soaring costs, and corruption. In Manila—where the water system is controlled by Suez, San Francisco-based Bechtel, and the prominent Ayala family—water is only reliably available for two hours a day and rates have increased so dramatically that the poorest families must choose each month between either paying for water or two days' worth of food. In the Bolivian city of Cochabamba, rate increases that followed privatization sparked rioting in 2000 that left six people dead. And in Atlanta, city officials are considering canceling United Water's contract as early as this winter.

"Atlanta was going to be the industry's shining example of how great privatization is," says Public Citizen's Jackson. "And now it's turned into our shining example about how it maybe isn't so great an idea after all."

On a cloudy August day that brought a welcome bit of drizzle to drought-parched Atlanta, Mayor Shirley Franklin lugged a seven-pound bound volume off a shelf and heaved it onto a table in her office. The report, prepared by a committee she appointed shortly after taking office last January, contained the city's case against United Water. It detailed violations of federal drinking water standards, including one instance in which levels of chlorine rose to six times the level the company agreed to in its contract.

The report also listed a string of maintenance problems ranging from broken security cameras and gates to open manholes and water-main leaks that went unrepaired for weeks. Some residents had to wait months for basic repairs, even though the company's contract specifies that some repairs must be made within 15 days. In fact, United failed to complete more than half of all required repairs in 2001, and it allowed rust and debris to build up, so that when the boil-water alerts forced the company to flush the system, brown water flowed from the taps. Finally, the report noted, instead of improving collections of unpaid water bills as promised, United actually allowed collection rates to drop from 98 to 94 percent, costing the city millions of dollars.

United has succeeded at one thing, according to the city: cutting its own operating costs, chiefly by reducing the waterworks staff by 25 percent even as demand for water in burgeoning Atlanta keeps rising. Staff reductions were partly responsible for the company's service troubles, the report indicated, as were higher-than-expected repair expenses: Last year United demanded that the city provide an additional $80 million for unanticipated maintenance costs. The increase was blocked when a lone City Council member refused to sign the revised contract.

In mid-August, Mayor Franklin announced that "United Water has not lived up to its responsibility" and formally notified the company that it had 90 days to fix the problems or the city would terminate its contract. "They keep telling me they are part of a world-class corporation that can bring us world-class service," she says, offering a small smile. "So I'm giving them a chance to prove it." United has offered to spend $1 million on outside inspectors to reassure city officials that it isn't, as Franklin puts it, "cutting any corners."

It wasn't supposed to turn out this way. In 1998, when Atlanta's City Council voted to contract out its water filtration and delivery system, city officials insisted that corporate management would stave off a budget crisis and drastic rate increases, and would lower costs by more than 40 percent while improving service. (Franklin herself, then a management consultant, lobbied for one of the companies bidding on the contract.) It was the largest water-privatization program ever attempted in the United States and was expected to prompt a wave of similar contracts around the country.

Water privatization has been gaining steam since the early 1990s, when market advocates began touting it as the next logical step after deregulating electricity. Many city waterworks that were built or expanded in the 1970s are now decaying, and the cost of needed repairs is staggering. The U.S. Environmental Protection Agency estimates that U.S. cities will have to spend nearly $151 billion to upgrade or replace pipes, filters, storage tanks, and other infrastructure over the next two decades. Cities will have to spend an additional $460 billion on sewage systems—another area where the corporate water giants are making inroads.

The prospect of skyrocketing infrastructure costs prompted U.S. officials to look overseas, where privatization is already a booming business. Multinational companies now run water systems for 7 percent of the world's population, and analysts say

BOX **4.1**

Water's Big Three

A handful of global companies have come to dominate the water industry by buying up dozens of smaller competitors. The three top players are based in Europe, but San Francisco-based Bechtel is a close fourth, and Enron's water division, Azurix, was muscling its way into water contracts from Ghana to India before it collapsed. A quick sketch of the Big Three:

SUEZ

- **Number of customers:** 120 million
- **Does business in:** 130 countries, including France, U.K., Argentina, Indonesia, Philippines, and Cameroon; runs water systems in dozens of cities, including Buenos Aires, Casablanca, and Amman, Jordan
- **U.S. activity:** Owns United Water, which manages systems in Atlanta, Puerto Rico, Milwaukee, and Washington, D.C., and is bidding to take over New Orleans' sewer system
- **Also owns:** Waste disposal, electricity, and gas operations; built the Suez Canal in 1858
- **Trouble spots: Nkonkobe, South Africa.** The city went to court late last year to get out of its contract with a Suez subsidiary, arguing that it could save $1.8 million by returning the water system to municipal control.
- **Buenos Aires, Argentina.** In 1992, Suez won a 30-year contract to manage the city's water and sewage systems. But because it failed to install wastewater lines fast enough, sewage has been flooding streets and basements, posing a threat to public health.

VIVENDI UNIVERSAL

- **Number of customers:** 110 million

- **Does business in:** 100 countries, including Hungary, China, South Korea, Kazakhstan, Lebanon, Chad, Romania, and Colombia
- **U.S. activity:** Owns U.S. Filter, the second-largest U.S. water company, best known for its Culligan filters; runs water systems in more than 500 communities
- **Also owns:** Universal Studios, the USA television network, and Houghton Mifflin, as well as waste disposal, energy, and telecommunications operations
- **Trouble spot: Tucuman, Argentina.** Water prices more than doubled after Vivendi took over management of local water systems throughout the province in 1995. Residents protested, and in 1998 the company withdrew from its 30-year contract.

RWE/THAMES WATER

- **Number of customers:** 51 million
- **Does business in:** 44 countries, including U.K., Germany, Turkey, and Japan
- **U.S. activity:** Acquiring American Water Works, which runs water systems in 27 states; the company also owns E'town, a water and sewage company that serves more than 50 communities in New Jersey
- **Also owns:** Electric utilities in Germany, wastewater, gas, recycling, and oil operations
- **Trouble spot: Lexington, Kentucky.** When American Water Works announced its merger with RWE/Thames in September 2001, Lexington indicated that it might try to buy out the conglomerate's local subsidiary, Kentucky-American Water. In response, the company sent letters to each of its 104,000 customers, asking them to fight a "forced government takeover." At present, the utility is still under RWE/Thames' control.

that figure could more than double, to 17 percent, by 2015. Private water management is estimated to be a $200 billion business, and the World Bank—which has encouraged governments to sell off their utilities to reduce public debt—projects it could reach $1 trillion by 2021. *Fortune* has called water "one of the world's great business opportunities," noting that it "promises to be to the 21st century what oil was to the 20th."

The biggest contenders for this emerging market are Suez, a corporate descendant of the company that built the Suez Canal, and the media conglomerate Vivendi Universal, which owns the USA network and Universal Studios. Together, the two companies now control about 70 percent of the world's private water-delivery systems and take in a combined $60 billion in revenues. Both have spent billions in recent years expanding in the United States: In 1999, Suez bought United Water for $1 billion, and Vivendi acquired the then-largest American company, U.S. Filter, for more than $6 billion. RWE/Thames Water, a German/British conglomerate, is currently completing its merger with the biggest remaining domestic company, American Water Works.

The water companies have been expanding even more dramatically in the developing world, where antiquated, often colonial-era, water systems are no match for rapidly increasing populations. More than 1 billion people lack access to clean drinking water, notes Peter Gleick, president of the Pacific Institute for Studies in Development, Environment and Security; a recent report he co-authored points out that "half the world's people fail to receive the level of water services available in many of the cities of ancient Greece and Rome."

Yet corporate water's record in fixing those problems—or even maintaining the industrialized world's systems—has been mixed at best. In 1989 Prime Minister Margaret Thatcher pushed through a program to privatize the United Kingdom's water supply; costs to consumers soared over the following decade, despite billions in government subsidies to the water companies. In some cities, water bills rose by as much as 141 percent in the '90s, while thousands of public-sector jobs were lost. Even the conservative *Daily Mail* declared that "Britain's top ten water companies have been able to use their position as monopoly suppliers to pull off the greatest act of licensed robbery in our history."

Last year the Ghanaian government agreed to privatize local water systems as a condition for an International Monetary Fund loan. To attract investors, the government doubled water rates, setting off protests in a country where the average annual income is less than $400 a year and the water bill—for those fortunate enough to have running water—can run upwards of $110.

In Bolivia's third largest city, Cochabamba, water rates shot up 35 percent after a consortium led by Bechtel took over the city's water system in 1999; some residents found themselves paying 20 percent of their income for water. Street protests led to riots in which six people were killed; eventually, the Bolivian government voided Bechtel's contract and told company officials it could not guarantee their safety if they stayed in town.

Privatization has also spawned protests and, in some cases, dominated elections in several other countries, including Paraguay—where police last summer turned water cannons on anti-privatization protesters—Panama, Brazil, Peru, Colombia, India, Pakistan, Hungary, and South Africa.

Here in the United States, some municipalities that initially jumped on the privatization bandwagon are now having second thoughts. In Milwaukee, which turned its sewage system over to United Water in 1998, an audit released in July found that a sewer tunnel was dumping raw sewage into local waterways, including Lake Michigan. Vivendi managed Puerto Rico's water and wastewater treatment for seven years, but after a territorial commission cited inaccurate billing and poor maintenance this year, its contract wasn't renewed.

Companies scrambling for lucrative municipal water contracts have also been caught up in corruption scandals. In June, Katherine Maraldo, a New Orleans Sewer and Water Board member, and Michael Stump, the former president of Professional Services Group, which ran the city's wastewater system, were convicted on bribery charges. PSG is now part of Vivendi, which is bidding to take over New Orleans' drinking-water system. And in 2001, two associates of Bridgeport, Connecticut, Mayor Joseph Ganim pled guilty to racketeering, mail fraud, and falsifying tax returns in connection with a $806,000 payment from PSG, which was negotiating for the city's $183 million water contract.

Such incidents point to a fundamental problem with allowing private companies to take over public water systems, says the Pacific Institute's Gleick. In attempting to make attractive bids for long-term contracts, companies often underestimate the cost of maintaining a water system, and so are forced to either skimp on staffing or demand more money to keep turning a profit. "At least when you have public utilities, the money they take in stays in the community," Gleick says. "With the private companies, the profits are going to go out of your community, out of your state, and probably out of your country."

Nevertheless, Troy Henry, the southern regional manager of United Water, is convinced that private water providers can do a better job than public utilities. He readily admits that his company and Atlanta city managers have had problems "dealing with the complexities of the system" in Atlanta and says the company is spending "multiple millions of dollars [to] win back the citizens' and mayor's confidence." A biomedical and electrical engineer and former manager at IBM, Henry argues that private companies can do for water delivery what Big Blue did for computing—revolutionize technology and attract "the best and the brightest and most talented people."

Perhaps Henry can mend fences in Atlanta, which he insists is United Water's—and corporate parent Suez's—"No. 1 priority." But Clair Muller, chair of the City Council's utility committee, contends that even if United Water ends up saving its Atlanta contract, it will merely have proved that privatization can work only under tight city supervision. And if tight supervision is possible, why privatize? "If government is run correctly—and that's always a big *if*—there's no profit motive," she says. "So if this is about saving money, we should always be able to do it cheaper."

In the end, the debate is about more than money. Taking responsibility for a community's water, Muller argues, is simply not the same as running a sports stadium or a cable franchise. "Water is the worst thing to privatize," she says. "It's what we need to live. I think that's key to the whole debate—are we going to lose control over functions that are essential to life?"

PART TWO

Economic Crisis

The United States is the largest economic power in the world: measured in terms of sheer output, we tower over every other country. And when we look around us it is easy to see evidence of the marvels of American productivity: an ever-changing array of high-tech devices, new medical breakthroughs, an economy transformed by computers and the Internet. We are able to communicate almost instantaneously with people around the world. No one would doubt that our economy displays enormous wealth and potential.

But at the same time, we have not been able to translate that economic power and potential into security and well-being for all Americans. Our economy remains volatile and unstable, producing recurring cycles of good times and bad. A long burst of prosperity in the 1990s was followed by a hard fall as the new century began. And even in good times, great numbers of people in the United States have been unable to make a living. The articles in this part explore some of the dimensions, consequences, and causes of America's ongoing economic crisis.

One of the most troubling, and enduring, aspects of that crisis is the inability of our economy to ensure a decent standard of living to everyone who works in it. There was a time in our history when Americans assumed that they could attain the "good life" if they got a regular job and stuck with it. But despite our tremendous economic growth, that ideal has never materialized. To be sure, the American economy has produced vast numbers of jobs, and indeed it is sometimes described as a "job machine." But many of these jobs are found in the rapidly growing "service" economy of restaurants, hotels, and other low-paying employers. For people with few skills, these jobs—many paying little more than the minimum wage—may be the only ones they will ever hold. But can they provide a decent and dignified living? Journalist Barbara Ehrenreich spent several weeks working in a restaurant job in order to find out: and her answer is no. The mathematics of the new service economy are simple and harsh: it is virtually impossible to work solely at these low-wage jobs and make enough money to pay the rent and to afford life's basic necessities. As more and more of the jobs we create fit this description, and as we steadily cut back on other sources of income support for poor people—especially poor women—these stark realities should give us pause.

Ehrenreich's article focuses on people at the lower end of the spectrum of jobs and income in America. But they are not the only ones facing difficult economic conditions. Indeed, one of the most troubling changes in twenty-first century America is that economic supports and protections that were once taken for granted have been sharply eroded, even for the middle class and the well-educated. As the next two articles illustrate, economic stress and uncertainty have increased for Americans at every stage of life.

It will probably come as no surprise to many readers of this book, for example, that debt is a growing problem among young adults. But how sharply this burden has risen for young Americans in recent years is startling. As Tamara Draut and Javier Silva point out, credit card debt alone doubled among people aged 18–24 during the last decade of the twentieth century, leaving many students and college graduates "indebted from the start." Rising debt has been driven by many factors, including low wages, unstable jobs, and rising costs for such basics as housing, health and child care, and college tuition (see Chapter 35 for more details on this issue); without systematic efforts to address these underlying issues, the situation is unlikely to improve.

At the other end of the age spectrum, the recent economic shifts are even more momentous. During the long period of economic expansion that began with World War II, many Americans came to expect that they would be well taken care of in their retirement—through some combination of employer pensions, Social Security, and personal savings. That was especially true for workers in the big manufacturing industries that drove the economy in those years of affluence and growth. But today far fewer Americans work in those industries—and even when they do, the companies have often whittled down retirement benefits to a fraction of what they were. As *Washington Post* reporter Dale Russakoff shows, this has led to the odd and disturbing paradox that today's young workers cannot look forward to the kind of secure life after retirement that their grandparents now enjoy. Somehow, in a society of unprecedented wealth, the future prospects of many "ordinary" Americans have moved backward, not forward.

These articles describe an economy that is increasingly insecure—even for those who, in former president Bill Clinton's phrase, "work hard and play by the rules": an economy that routinely fails to meet the basic needs of many Americans. But if our present economic policies seem to work so poorly for so many people, why do they continue? In "The Limits of Markets," Robert Kuttner suggests one part of the answer. For many years, economic policy in the United States has been guided by the belief that economic decisions are best left to the unimpeded workings of the "market." Accordingly, we tend to reject any degree of government intervention to rectify the injustices and imbalances that the market economy creates. But the result of that one-sided reliance on the market is a society that is both unjust and, in many ways, inefficient. Some degree of balance between market and government is necessary, Kuttner argues, if we want to create an economy that maximizes both our economic well-being and our human values.

CHAPTER 5

Nickel-and-Dimed

On (Not) Getting by in America

BARBARA EHRENREICH

At the beginning of June 1998 I leave behind everything that normally soothes the ego and sustains the body—home, career, companion, reputation, ATM card—for a plunge into the low-wage workforce. There, I become another, occupationally much diminished "Barbara Ehrenreich"—depicted on job-application forms as a divorced homemaker whose sole work experience consists of housekeeping in a few private homes. I am terrified, at the beginning, of being unmasked for what I am: a middle class journalist setting out to explore the world that welfare mothers are entering, at the rate of approximately 50,000 a month, as welfare reform kicks in. Happily, though, my fears turn out to be entirely unwarranted: during a month of poverty and toil, my name goes unnoticed and for the most part unuttered. In this parallel universe where my father never got out of the mines and I never got through college, I am "baby," "honey," "blondie," and, most commonly, "girl."

My first task is to find a place to live. I figure that if I can earn $7 an hour—which, from the want ads, seems doable—I can afford to spend $500 on rent, or maybe, with severe economies, $600. In the Key West area, where I live, this pretty much confines me to flophouses and trailer homes—like the one, a pleasing fifteen-minute drive from town, that has no air-conditioning, no screens, no fans, no television, and, by way of diversion, only the challenge of evading the landlord's Doberman pinscher. The big problem with this place, though, is the rent, which at $675 a month is well beyond my reach. All right, Key West is expensive. But so is New York City, or the Bay Area, or Jackson Hole, or Telluride, or Boston, or any other place where tourists and the wealthy compete for living space with the people who clean their toilets and fry their hash browns.[1] Still, it is a shock to realize that "trailer trash" has become, for me, a demographic category to aspire to.

So I decide to make the common trade-off between affordability and convenience, and go for a $500-a-month efficiency thirty miles up a two-lane highway from the employment opportunities of Key West, meaning forty-five minutes if there's no road construction and I don't get caught behind some sun-dazed Canadian tourists. I hate the drive, along a roadside studded with white crosses commemorating the more effective head-on collisions, but it's a sweet little place—a cabin, more or less, set in the swampy back yard of the converted mobile home where my landlord, an affable TV repairman, lives with his bartender girlfriend. Anthropologically speaking, a bustling trailer park would be preferable, but here I have a gleaming white floor and a firm mattress, and the few resident bugs are easily vanquished.

Besides, I am not doing this for the anthropology. My aim is nothing so mistily subjective as to "experience poverty" or find out how it "really feels" to be a long-term low-wage worker. I've had enough unchosen encounters with poverty and the world of low-wage work to know it's not a place you want to visit for touristic purposes; it just smells too much like fear. And with all my real-life assets—bank account, IRA, health insurance, multiroom home—waiting indulgently in the background, I am, of course, thoroughly insulated from the terrors that afflict the genuinely poor.

No, this is a purely objective, scientific sort of mission. The humanitarian rationale for welfare reform—as opposed to the more punitive and stingy impulses that may actually have motivated it—is that work will lift poor women out of poverty while simultaneously inflating their self-esteem and hence their future value in the labor market. Thus, whatever the hassles involved in finding child care, transportation, etc., the transition from welfare to work will end happily, in greater prosperity for all. Now there are many problems with this comforting prediction, such as the fact that the economy will inevitably undergo a downturn, eliminating many jobs. Even without a downturn, the influx of a million former welfare recipients into the low-wage labor market could depress wages by as much as 11.9 percent, according to the Economic Policy Institute (EPI) in Washington, D.C.

But is it really possible to make a living on the kinds of jobs currently available to unskilled people? Mathematically, the answer is no, as can be shown by taking $6 to $7 an hour, perhaps subtracting a dollar or two an hour for child care, multiplying by 160 hours a month, and comparing the result to the prevailing rents. According to the National Coalition for the Homeless, for example, in 1998 it took, on average nationwide, an hourly wage of $8.89 to afford a one-bedroom apartment, and the Preamble Center for Public Policy estimates that the odds against a typical welfare recipient's landing a job at such a "living wage" are about 97 to 1. If these numbers are right, low-wage work is not a solution to poverty and possibly not even to homelessness.

It may seem excessive to put this proposition to an experimental test. As certain family members keep unhelpfully reminding me, the viability of low-wage work could be tested, after a fashion, without ever leaving my study. I could just pay myself $7 an hour for eight hours a day, charge myself for room and board, and total up the numbers after a month. Why leave the people and work that I love? But I am an experimental scientist by training. In that business, you don't just sit at a desk and theorize; you plunge into the everyday chaos of nature, where surprises lurk in the most mundane measurements. Maybe, when I got into it, I would discover some hidden economies in the world of the low-wage worker. After all, if 30 percent of the workforce toils for less than $8 an hour, according to the EPI, they may have found some tricks as yet unknown to me. Maybe—who knows?—I would even be able to detect in myself the bracing psychological effects of getting out of the house, as promised by the welfare wonks at places like the Heritage Foundation. Or, on the other hand, maybe there would be unexpected costs—physical, mental, or financial—to throw off all my calculations. Ideally, I should do this with two small children in tow, that being the welfare average, but mine are grown and no one is willing to lend me theirs for a month-long vacation in penury. So this is not the perfect experiment, just a test of the best possible case: an unencumbered woman, smart and even strong, attempting to live more or less off the land.

On the morning of my first full day of job searching, I take a red pen to the want ads, which are auspiciously numerous. Everyone in Key West's booming "hospitality industry" seems to be looking for someone like me—trainable, flexible, and with suitably humble expectations as to pay. I know I possess certain traits that might be advantageous—I'm white and, I like to think, well-spoken and poised—but I decide on two rules: One, I cannot use any skills derived from my education or usual work— not that there are a lot of want ads for satirical essayists anyway. Two, I have to take the best-paid job that is offered me and of course do my best to hold it; no Marxist rants or sneaking off to read novels in the ladies' room. In addition, I rule out various occupations for one reason or another: Hotel front-desk clerk, for example, which to my surprise is regarded as unskilled and pays around $7 an hour, gets eliminated because it involves standing in one spot for eight hours a day. Waitressing is similarly something I'd like to avoid, because I remember it leaving me bone tired when I was eighteen, and I'm decades of varicosities and back pain beyond that now. Telemarketing, one of the first refuges of the suddenly indigent, can be dismissed on grounds of personality. This leaves certain supermarket jobs, such as deli clerk, or housekeeping in Key West's thousands of hotel and guest rooms. Housekeeping is especially appealing, for reasons both atavistic and practical: it's what my mother did before I came along, and it can't be too different from what I've been doing part-time, in my own home, all my life.

So I put on what I take to be a respectful-looking outfit of ironed Bermuda shorts and scooped-neck T-shirt and set out for a tour of the local hotels and supermarkets. Best Western, Econo Lodge, and HoJo's all let me fill out application forms, and these are, to my relief, interested in little more than whether I am a legal resident of the United States and have committed any felonies. My next stop is Winn-Dixie, the supermarket, which turns out to have a particularly onerous application process, featuring a fifteen-minute "interview" by computer since, apparently, no human on the premises is deemed capable of representing the corporate point of view. I am conducted to a large room decorated with posters illustrating how to look "professional" (it helps to be white and, if female, permed) and warning of the slick promises that union organizers might try to tempt me with. The interview is multiple choice: Do I have anything, such as child-care problems, that might make it hard for me to get to work on time? Do I think safety on the job is the responsibility of management? Then, popping up cunningly out of the blue: How many dollars' worth of stolen goods have I purchased in the last year? Would I turn in a fellow employee if I caught him stealing? Finally, "Are you an honest person?"

Apparently, I ace the interview, because I am told that all I have to do is show up in some doctor's office tomorrow for a urine test. This seems to be a fairly general rule: if you want to stack Cheerio boxes or vacuum hotel rooms in chemically fascist America, you have to be willing to squat down and pee in front of some health worker (who has no doubt had to do the same thing herself). The wages Winn-Dixie is offering—$6 and a couple of dimes to start with—are not enough, I decide, to compensate for this indignity.[2]

I lunch at Wendy's, where $4.99 gets you unlimited refills at the Mexican part of the Superbar, a comforting surfeit of refried beans and "cheese sauce." A teenage employee, seeing me studying the want ads, kindly offers me an application form, which I fill out, though here, too, the pay is just $6 and change an hour. Then it's off for a round of the locally owned inns and guesthouses. At "The Palms," let's call it, a bouncy manager actually takes me around to see the rooms and meet the existing housekeepers, who, I note with satisfaction, look pretty much like me—faded ex-hippie types in shorts with long hair pulled back in braids. Mostly, though, no one speaks to me or even looks at me except to proffer an application form. At my last stop, a palatial B&B, I wait twenty minutes to meet "Max," only to be told that there are no jobs now but there should be one soon, since "nobody lasts more than a couple weeks." (Because none of the people I talked to knew I was a reporter, I have changed their names to protect their privacy and, in some cases perhaps, their jobs.)

Three days go by like this, and, to my chagrin, no one out of the approximately twenty places I've applied calls me for an interview. I had been vain enough to worry about coming across as too educated for the jobs I sought, but no one even seems interested in finding out how overqualified I am. Only later will I realize that the want ads are not a reliable measure of the actual jobs available at any particular time. They are, as I should have guessed from Max's comment, the employers' insurance policy against the relentless turnover of the low-wage workforce. Most of the big hotels run ads almost continually, just to build a supply of applicants to replace the current workers as they drift away or are fired, so finding a job is just a matter of being at the right place at the right time and flexible enough to take whatever is being offered that day. This finally happens to me at a one of the big discount hotel chains, where I go, as usual, for housekeeping and am sent, instead, to try out as a waitress at the attached "family restaurant," a dismal spot with a counter and about thirty tables that looks out on a parking garage and features such tempting fare as "Pollish [sic] sausage and BBQ sauce" on 95-degree days. Phillip, the dapper young West Indian who introduces himself as the manager, interviews me with about as much enthusiasm as if he were a clerk processing me for Medicare, the principal questions being what shifts can I work and when can I start. I mutter something about being woefully out of practice as a waitress, but he's already on to the uniform:

I'm to show up tomorrow wearing black slacks and black shoes; he'll provide the rust-colored polo shirt with HEARTHSIDE embroidered on it, though I might want to wear my own shirt to get to work, ha ha. At the word "tomorrow," something between fear and indignation rises in my chest. I want to say, "Thank you for your time, sir, but this is just an experiment, you know, not my actual life."

So begins my career at the Hearthside, I shall call it, one small profit center within a global discount hotel chain, where for two weeks I work from 2:00 till 10:00 P.M. for $2.43 an hour plus tips.[3] In some futile bid for gentility, the management has barred employees from using the front door, so my first day I enter through the kitchen, where a red-faced man with shoulder-length blond hair is throwing frozen steaks against the wall and yelling, "Fuck this shit!" "That's just Jack," explains Gail, the wiry middle-aged waitress who is assigned to train me. "He's on the rag again"—a condition occasioned, in this instance, by the fact that the cook on the morning shift had forgotten to thaw out the steaks. For the next eight hours, I run after the agile Gail, absorbing bits of instruction along with fragments of personal tragedy. All food must be trayed, and the reason she's so tired today is that she woke up in a cold sweat thinking of her boyfriend, who killed himself recently in an upstate prison. No refills on lemonade. And the reason he was in prison is that a few DUIs caught up with him, that's all, could have happened to anyone. Carry the creamers to the table in a monkey bowl, never in your hand. And after he was gone she spent several months living in her truck, peeing in a plastic pee bottle and reading by candlelight at night, but you can't live in a truck in the summer, since you need to have the windows down, which means anything can get in, from mosquitoes on up.

At least Gail puts to rest any fears I had of appearing overqualified. From the first day on, I find that of all the things I have left behind, such as home and identity, what I miss the most is competence. Not that I have ever felt utterly competent in the writing business, in which one day's success augurs nothing at all for the next. But in my writing life, I at least have some notion of procedure: do the research, make the outline, rough out a draft, etc. As a server, though, I am beset by requests like bees: more iced tea here, ketchup over there, a to go box for table fourteen, and where are the high chairs, anyway? Of the twenty-seven tables, up to six are usually mine at any time, though on slow afternoons or if Gail is off, I sometimes have the whole place to myself. There is the touch-screen computer-ordering system to master, which is, I suppose, meant to minimize server-cook contact, but in practice requires constant verbal fine-tuning: "That's gravy on the mashed, okay? None on the meatloaf," and so forth—while the cook scowls as if I were inventing these refinements just to torment him. Plus, something I had forgotten in the years since I was eighteen: about a third of a server's job is "side work" that's invisible to customers—sweeping, scrubbing, slicing, refilling, and restocking. If it isn't all done, every little bit of it, you're going to face the 6:00 P.M. dinner rush defenseless and probably go down in flames. I screw up dozens of times at the beginning, sustained in my shame entirely by Gail's support—"It's okay, baby, everyone does that sometime"—because, to my total surprise and despite the scientific detachment I am doing my best to maintain, I care.

The whole thing would be a lot easier if I could just skate through it as Lily Tomlin in one of her waitress skits, but I was raised by the absurd Booker T. Washingtonian precept that says: If you're going to do something, do it well. In fact, "well" isn't good enough by half. Do it better than anyone has ever done it before. Or so said my father, who must have known what he was talking about because he managed to pull himself, and us with him, up from the mile-deep copper mines of Butte to the leafy suburbs of the Northeast, ascending from boilermakers to martinis before booze beat out ambition. As in most endeavors I have encountered in my life, doing it "better than anyone" is not a reasonable goal. Still, when I wake up at 4:00 A.M. in my own cold sweat, I am not thinking about the writing deadlines I'm neglecting; I'm thinking about the table whose order I screwed up so that one of the boys didn't get his kiddie meal until the rest of the family had moved on to their Key Lime pies. That's the other powerful motivation I hadn't expected—the customers, or "patients," as I can't help thinking of them on account of the mysterious vulnerability that seems to have left them temporarily unable to feed themselves. After a few days at the Hearthside, I feel the service ethic kick in like a shot of oxytocin, the nurturance hormone. The plurality of my customers are hard-working locals—truck drivers, construction workers, even housekeepers from the attached hotel—and I want them to have the closest to a "fine dining" experience that the grubby circumstances will allow. No "you guys" for me; everyone over twelve is "sir" or "ma'am." I ply them with iced tea and coffee refills; I return, mid-meal, to inquire how everything is; I doll up their salads with chopped raw mushrooms, summer squash slices, or whatever bits of produce I can find that have survived their sojourn in the cold-storage room mold-free.

There is Benny, for example, a short, tight-muscled sewer repairman, who cannot even think of eating until he has absorbed a half hour of air-conditioning and ice water. We chat about hyperthermia and electrolytes until he is ready to order some finicky combination like soup of the day, garden salad, and a side of grits. There are the German tourists who are so touched by my pidgin "Willkommen" and "Ist alles gut?" that they actually tip. (Europeans, spoiled by their trade-union-ridden, high-wage welfare states, generally do not know that they are supposed to tip. Some restaurants, the Hearthside included, allow servers to "grat" their foreign customers, or add a tip to the bill. Since this amount is added before the customers have a chance to tip or not tip, the practice amounts to an automatic penalty for imperfect English.) There are the two dirt-smudged lesbians, just off their construction shift, who are impressed enough by my suave handling of the fly in the pina colada that they take the time to praise me to Stu, the assistant manager. There's Sam, the kindly retired cop, who has to plug up his tracheotomy hole with one finger in order to force the cigarette smoke into his lungs.

Sometimes I play with the fantasy that I am a princess who, in penance for some tiny transgression, has undertaken to feed each of her subjects by hand. But the non-princesses working with me are just as indulgent, even when this means flouting management rules—concerning, for example, the number of croutons that can go on a salad (six). "Put on all you want," Gail whispers, "as long as Stu isn't looking." She dips into her own tip money to buy biscuits and gravy for an out-of-work mechanic who's used up all his money on dental surgery, inspiring me to pick up the tab for his milk and pie. Maybe the same high levels of agape can be found throughout the "hospitality industry." I remember the poster decorating one of the apartments I looked at, which said "If you seek happiness for yourself you will never find it. Only when you seek happiness for others will it come to you," or words to that effect—an odd sentiment, it seemed to me at the time, to find in the dank one-room basement apartment of a bellhop at the Best Western. At the Hearthside, we utilize whatever bits of autonomy we have to ply our customers with the illicit calories that signal our love. It is our job as servers to assemble the salads and desserts, pouring the dressings and squirting the whipped cream. We also control the number of butter patties our customers get and the amount of sour cream on their baked potatoes. So if you wonder why Americans are so obese, consider the fact that waitresses both express their humanity and earn their tips through the covert distribution of fats.

Ten days into it, this is beginning to look like a livable lifestyle. I like Gail, who is "looking at fifty" but moves so fast she can alight in one place and then another without apparently being anywhere between them. I clown around with Lionel, the teenage Haitian busboy, and catch a few fragments of conversation with Joan, the svelte fortyish hostess and militant feminist who is the only one of us who dares to tell Jack to shut the fuck up. I even warm up to Jack when, on a slow night and to make up for a particularly unwarranted attack on my abilities, or so I imagine, he tells me about his glory days as a young man at "coronary school"—or do you say "culinary"?—in Brooklyn, where he dated a knock-out Puerto Rican chick and learned everything there is to know about food. I finish up at 10:00 or 10:30, depending on how much side work I've been able to get done during the shift, and cruise home to the tapes I snatched up at random when I left my real home—Marianne Faithfull, Tracy Chapman, Enigma, King Sunny Ade, the Violent Femmes—just drained enough for the music to set my cranium resonating but hardly dead. Midnight snack is Wheat Thins and Monterey Jack, accompanied by cheap white wine on ice and whatever AMC has to offer. To bed by 1:30 or 2:00, up at 9:00 or 10:00, read for an hour while my uniform whirls around in the landlord's washing machine, and then it's another eight hours spent following Mao's central instruction, as laid out in the Little Red Book, which was: Serve the people.

I could drift along like this, in some dreamy proletarian idyll, except for two things. One is management. If I have kept this subject on the margins thus far it is because I still flinch to think that I spent all those weeks under the surveillance of men (and later women) whose job it was to monitor my behavior for signs of sloth, theft, drug abuse, or worse. Not that managers and especially "assistant managers" in low-wage settings like this are exactly the class enemy. In the restaurant business, they are mostly former cooks or servers, still capable of pinch-hitting in the kitchen or on the floor, just as in hotels they are likely to be former clerks, and paid a salary of only about $400 a week. But everyone knows they have crossed over to the other side, which is, crudely put, corporate as opposed to human. Cooks want to prepare tasty meals; servers want to serve them graciously; but managers are there for only one reason—to make sure that money is made for some theoretical entity that exists far away in Chicago or New York, if a corporation can be said to have a physical existence at all. Reflecting on her career, Gail tells me ruefully that she had sworn, years ago, never to work for a corporation again. "They don't cut you no slack. You give and you give, and they take."

Managers can sit—for hours at a time if they want—but it's their job to see that no one else ever does, even when there's nothing to do, and this is why, for servers, slow times can be as exhausting as rushes. You start dragging out each little chore, because if the manager on duty catches you in an idle moment, he will give you something far nastier to do. So I wipe, I clean, I consolidate ketchup bottles and recheck the cheesecake supply, even tour the tables to make sure the customer evaluation forms are all standing perkily in their places—wondering all the time how many calories I burn in these strictly theatrical exercises. When, on a particularly dead afternoon, Stu finds me glancing at a *USA Today* a customer has left behind, he assigns me to vacuum the entire floor with the broken vacuum cleaner that has a handle only two feet long, and the only way to do that without incurring orthopedic damage is to proceed from spot to spot on your knees.

On my first Friday at the Hearthside there is a "mandatory meeting for all restaurant employees," which I attend, eager for insight into our overall marketing strategy and the niche (your basic Ohio cuisine with a tropical twist?) we aim to inhabit. But there is no "we" at this meeting. Phillip, our top manager except for an occasional "consultant" sent out by corporate headquarters, opens it with a sneer: "The break room—it's disgusting. Butts in the ashtrays, newspapers lying around, crumbs." This windowless little room, which also houses the time clock for the entire hotel, is where we stash our bags and civilian clothes and take our half-hour meal breaks. But a break room is not a right, he tells us. It can be taken away. We should also know that the lockers in the break room and whatever is in them can be searched at any time. Then comes gossip; there has been gossip; gossip (which seems to mean employees talking among themselves) must stop. Off-duty employees are henceforth barred from eating at the restaurant, because "other servers gather around them and gossip." When Phillip has exhausted his agenda of rebukes, Joan complains about the condition of the ladies' room and I throw in my two bits about the vacuum cleaner. But I don't see any backup coming from my fellow servers, each of whom has subsided into her own personal funk; Gail, my role model, stares sorrowfully at a point six inches from her nose. The meeting ends when Andy, one of the cooks, gets up, muttering about breaking up his day off for this almighty bullshit.

Just four days later we are suddenly summoned into the kitchen at 3:30 P.M., even though there are live tables on the floor. We all—about ten of us—stand around Phillip, who announces grimly that there has been a report of some "drug activity" on the night shift and that, as a result, we are now to be a "drug-free" workplace, meaning that all new hires will be tested, as will possibly current employees on a random basis. I am glad that this part of the kitchen is so dark, because I find myself blushing as hard as if I had been caught toking up in the ladies' room myself. I haven't been treated this way—lined up in the corridor, threatened with locker searches, peppered with carelessly aimed accusations—since junior high school. Back on the floor, Joan cracks, "Next they'll be telling us we can't have sex on the job." When I ask Stu what happened to inspire the crackdown, he just mutters about "management decisions" and takes the opportunity to upbraid Gail and me for being too generous with the rolls. From now on there's to be only one per customer, and it goes out with the dinner, not with the salad. He's also been riding the cooks, prompting Andy to come out of the kitchen and observe—with the serenity of a man whose customary implement is a butcher knife—that "Stu has a death wish today."

Later in the evening, the gossip crystallizes around the theory that Stu is himself the drug culprit, that he uses the restaurant phone to order up marijuana and sends one of the late servers out to fetch it for him. The server was caught, and she may have ratted Stu out or at least said enough to cast some suspicion on him, thus accounting for his pissy behavior. Who knows? Lionel, the busboy, entertains us for the rest of the shift by standing just behind Stu's back and sucking deliriously on an imaginary joint.

The other problem, in addition to the less-than-nurturing management style, is that this job shows no sign of being financially viable. You might imagine, from a comfortable distance, that people who live, year in and year out, on $6 to $10 an hour have discovered some survival stratagems unknown to the middle class. But no. It's not hard to get my co-workers to talk about their living situations, because housing, in almost every case, is the principal source of disruption in their lives, the first thing they fill you in on when they arrive for their shifts. After a week, I have compiled the following survey:

- Gail is sharing a room in a well-known downtown flophouse for which she and a roommate pay about $250 a week. Her roommate, a male friend, has begun hitting on her, driving her nuts, but the rent would be impossible alone.
- Claude, the Haitian cook, is desperate to get out of the two-room apartment he shares with his girlfriend and two other, unrelated, people. As far as I can determine, the other Haitian men (most of whom only speak Creole) live in similarly crowded situations.
- Annette, a twenty-year-old server who is six months pregnant and has been abandoned by her boyfriend, lives with her mother, a postal clerk.
- Marianne and her boyfriend are paying $170 a week for a one-person trailer.
- Jack, who is, at $10 an hour, the wealthiest of us, lives in the trailer he owns, paying only the $400-a-month lot fee.
- The other white cook, Andy, lives on his dry-docked boat, which, as far as I can tell from his loving descriptions, can't be more than twenty feet long. He offers to take me out on it, once it's repaired, but the offer comes with inquiries as to my marital status, so I do not follow up on it.
- Tina and her husband are paying $60 a night for a double room in a Days Inn. This is because they have no car and the Days Inn is within walking distance of the Hearthside. When Marianne, one of the breakfast servers, is tossed out of her trailer for subletting (which is against the trailer-park rules), she leaves her boyfriend and moves in with Tina and her husband.

- Joan, who had fooled me with her numerous and tasteful outfits (hostesses wear their own clothes), lives in a van she parks behind a shopping center at night and showers in Tina's motel room. The clothes are from thrift shops.[4]

It strikes me, in my middle-class solipsism, that there is gross improvidence in some of these arrangements. When Gail and I are wrapping silverware in napkins—the only task for which we are permitted to sit—she tells me she is thinking of escaping from her roommate by moving into the Days Inn herself. I am astounded: How can she even think of paying between $40 and $60 a day? But if I was afraid of sounding like a social worker, I come out just sounding like a fool. She squints at me in disbelief, "And where am I supposed to get a month's rent and a month's deposit for an apartment?" I'd been feeling pretty smug about my $500 efficiency, but of course it was made possible only by the $1,300 I had allotted myself for start-up costs when I began my low-wage life: $1,000 for the first month's rent and deposit, $100 for initial groceries and cash in my pocket, $200 stuffed away for emergencies. In poverty, as in certain propositions in physics, starting conditions are everything.

There are no secret economies that nourish the poor; on the contrary, there are a host of special costs. If you can't put up the two months' rent you need to secure an apartment, you end up paying through the nose for a room by the week. If you have only a room, with a hot plate at best, you can't save by cooking up huge lentil stews that can be frozen for the week ahead. You eat fast food, or the hot dogs and styrofoam cups of soup that can be microwaved in a convenience store. If you have no money for health insurance—and the Hearthside's niggardly plan kicks in only after three months—you go without routine care or prescription drugs and end up paying the price. Gail, for example, was fine until she ran out of money for estrogen pills. She is supposed to be on the company plan by now, but they claim to have lost her application form and need to begin the paperwork all over again. So she spends $9 per migraine pill to control the headaches she wouldn't have, she insists, if her estrogen supplements were covered. Similarly, Marianne's boyfriend lost his job as a roofer because he missed so much time after getting a cut on his foot for which he couldn't afford the prescribed antibiotic.

My own situation, when I sit down to assess it after two weeks of work, would not be much better if this were my actual life. The seductive thing about waitressing is that you don't have to wait for payday to feel a few bills in your pocket, and my tips usually cover meals and gas, plus something left over to stuff into the kitchen drawer I use as a bank. But as the tourist business slows in the summer heat, I sometimes leave work with only $20 in tips (the gross is higher, but servers share about 15 percent of their tips with the busboys and bartenders). With wages included, this amounts to about the minimum wage of $5.15 an hour. Although the sum in the drawer is piling up, at the present rare of accumulation it will be more than a hundred dollars short of my rent when the end of the month comes around. Nor can I see any expenses to cut. True, I haven't gone the lentil stew route yet, but that's because I don't have a large cooking pot, pot holders, or a ladle to stir with (which cost about $30 at Kmart, less at thrift stores), not to mention onions, carrots, and the indispensable bay leaf. I do make my lunch almost every day—usually some slow-burning, high-protein combo like frozen chicken patties with melted cheese on top and canned pinto beans on the side. Dinner is at the Hearthside, which offers its employees a choice of BLT, fish sandwich, or hamburger for only $2. The burger lasts longest, especially if it's heaped with gut-puckering jalapeños, but by midnight my stomach is growling again. . . .

How former welfare recipients and single mothers will (and do) survive in the low-wage workforce, I cannot imagine. Maybe they will figure out how to condense their lives—including child-raising, laundry, romance, and meals—into the couple of hours between full-time jobs. Maybe they will take up residence in their vehicles, if they have one. All I know is that I couldn't hold two jobs and I couldn't make enough money to live on with one. And I had advantages unthinkable to many of the long-term poor—health, stamina, a working car, and no children to care for and support. Certainly nothing in my experience contradicts the conclusion of Kathryn Edin and Laura Lein, in their recent book *Making Ends Meet: How Single Mothers Survive Welfare and Low-Wage Work,* that low-wage work actually involves more hardship and deprivation than life at the mercy of the welfare state. In the coming months and years, economic conditions for the working poor are bound to worsen, even without the almost inevitable recession. As mentioned earlier, the influx of former welfare recipients into the low-skilled workforce will have a depressing effect on both wages and the number of jobs available. A general economic downturn will only enhance these effects, and the working poor will of course be facing it without the slight, but nonetheless often saving, protection of welfare as a backup.

The thinking behind welfare reform was that even the humblest jobs are morally uplifting and psychologically buoying. In reality they are likely to be fraught with insult and stress. But I did discover one redeeming feature of the most abject low-wage work—the camaraderie of people who are, in almost all cases, far too smart and funny and caring for the work they do and the wages they're paid. The hope, of course, is that someday these people will come to know what they're worth, and take appropriate action.

ENDNOTES

1. According to the Department of Housing and Urban Development, the "fair-market rent" for an efficiency is $551 here in Monroe County, Florida. A comparable rent in the five boroughs of New York City is $704; in San Francisco, $713; and in the heart of Silicon Valley, $808. The fair-market rent for an area is defined as the amount that would be needed to pay rent plus utilities for "privately owned, decent, safe, and sanitary rental housing of a modest (non-luxury) nature with suitable amenities."

2. According to the *Monthly Labor Review* (November 1996), 28 percent of work sites surveyed in the service industry conduct drug tests (corporate workplaces have much higher rates), and the incidence of testing has risen markedly since the Eighties. The rate of testing is highest in the South (56 percent of work sites polled), with the Midwest in second place (50 percent). The drug most likely to be detected—marijuana, which can be detected in urine for weeks—is also the most innocuous, while heroin and cocaine are generally undetectable

three days after use. Prospective employees sometimes try to cheat the tests by consuming excess amounts of liquids and taking diuretics and even masking substances available through the Internet.

3. According to the Fair Labor Standards Act, employers are not required to pay "tipped employees," such as restaurant servers, more than $2.13 an hour in direct wages. However, if the sum of tips plus $2.13 an hour falls below the minimum wage, or $5.15 an hour, the employer is required to make up the difference. This fact was not mentioned by managers or otherwise publicized at either of the restaurants where I worked.

4. I could find no statistics on the number of employed people living in cars or vans, but according to the National Coalition for the Homeless's 1997 report "Myths and Facts About Homelessness," nearly one in five homeless people (in twenty-nine cities across the nation) is employed in a full- or part-time job.

CHAPTER 6

Generation Broke

The Growth of Debt among Young Americans

TAMARA DRAUT

JAVIER SILVA

INTRODUCTION

The average credit card debt of Americans aged 25 to 34 years old increased by 55 percent between 1992 and 2001, to a self-reported household average of $4,088. Estimates of card debt based on aggregate data put the dollar amount as much as three times higher.[2] This age group's bankruptcy rate grew by 19 percent over the same period—so that by 2001 nearly 12 out of every 1,000 young adults were filing for bankruptcy.[3] Young adults now have the second highest rate of bankruptcy, just after those aged 35 to 44. Their rate of bankruptcy is higher than it was for young Boomers who were 25–34 years old in 1991.

Why are today's young adults going into debt and going broke? During the boom of the 1990s, the popular media showered attention on the rising fortunes of Generation X, who appeared to be riding the tech boom to great heights. However, in 2001 adults aged 25 to 34 were showing signs that the path to adulthood had become more financially perilous than it was for the previous generation of late Baby Boomers in 1992. The major adult costs that begin to mount between the ages of 25 and 34—housing, child care, and health care—have all increased dramatically over the past decade. And the rising unemployment, slow real wage growth, and skyrocketing tuition and resulting student loan debts have combined to erode the economic security of today's young adults. Additionally, just at this time the newly-deregulated credit industry began aggressively marketing to young people on college campuses. Deregulation also brought higher rates and fees, making it increasingly difficult for young Americans to get out of debt. . . .

DEMOS' FINDINGS ON CREDIT CARD DEBT AMONG YOUNGER AMERICANS, 1992–2001

Prevalence of Credit Cards and Indebtedness.   Nearly 7 out of 10 young Americans aged 25 to 34 have one or more credit cards, a level basically unchanged since 1992. Compared to the population as a whole, however, young adult cardholders are much more likely to be in debt: 71 percent of young adult cardholders revolve their balances, compared to 55 percent of all cardholders.

Higher Balances.   Credit card debt among young adults has increased significantly since 1992, outpacing the rise among the population as a whole (Table 6.1). The average credit card debt among indebted 25 to 34 year olds increased by 55 percent, to $4,088.

Debt by Income Level.   All but the lowest-income young households experienced dramatic increases in credit card debt over the decade. Middle-income young adults experienced the fastest growth of any income group. Credit card debt rose 37 percent among moderate-income young adults earning between $10,000 and $24,999 (Figure 6.1). Middle-income young adults—those with incomes between $25,000 and $49,999—experienced a 65 percent increase in credit card debt. Upper middle-income young adults with incomes between $50,000 and $74,999 experienced a 55 percent increase in debt (Figure 6.2).

Debt Service-to-Income Ratio.   The true financial impact of debt is best understood by examining the percentage of income young adults must devote to debt payments, which is typically called the debt service-to-income ratio. Debt service-to-income ratios have been steadily rising for young Americans since 1992, when the average ratio for indebted young adults was 19. By 2001, the average debt service-to-income ratio for 25 to 34 year olds had risen to 24 percent—meaning that the average indebted young American spends nearly a quarter of every dollar earned servicing debt. However, the debt service-to-income ratio severely underestimates

TABLE 6.1   Average Credit Card Debt among Young Households with Credit Card Debt (2001 dollars)

	1992	2001	% Change 1992–2001
All households	$2,991	$4,126	38%
Aged 25–34	$2,640	$4,088	55%

Source: Demos' Calculations from the 1992 and 2001 Survey of Consumer Finances

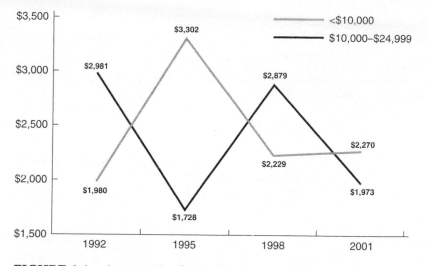

FIGURE 6.1   Average Credit Card Debt among Low- and
Moderate-Income Adults Aged 25 to 34 (in 2001 dollars)

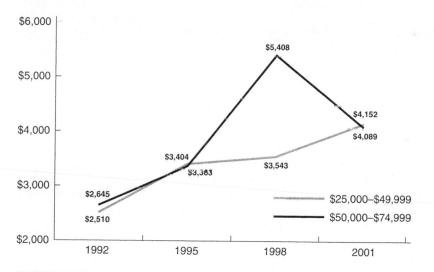

FIGURE 6.2   Average Credit Card Debt among Middle- and
Upper-Middle-Income Adults Aged 25 to 34

the financial burdens facing young Americans in several ways. First, the ratio only
measures outstanding mortgage and consumer debt, such as credit cards and auto
loans—excluding what is often a young household's largest expense: rent. Second,
since the figure doesn't include auto lease payments, the cost of a car may not be
reflected in the ratio. Finally, the ratio significantly underestimates credit card debt

TABLE 6.2   Percent of Credit Card Indebted Young Americans Aged 25 to 34 in Debt Hardship (Debt Payment to Income Ratio > 40%)

Income Group (25–34)	1992	2001
Overall	7.9%	13.3%
Income Group		
Under $10,000	37.1%	57.6%
$10,000–$24,999	8.4	22.3
$25,000–$49,999	6.7	13.4
$50,000–$74999	7.8	5.2

Source: Demos' Calculations from the 1992 and 2001 Survey of Consumer Finances

burden because it can only measure the minimum payment burden—which is typically 2½ percent of the total outstanding balance. That means that a credit card debt of $10,000 is counted as $250 in debt service. But the key to paying off credit card debt is making more than the minimum payment. If a young American were to only pay the minimum on a $10,000 balance with a 15% APR, it would take them more than 39 years and cost them over $16,000 in interest charges.

Debt Hardship.   A family spending more than 40 percent of their income on debt payments, including mortgages and student loan debt, is traditionally considered in a state of *debt hardship*. Overall, 13 percent of indebted young Americans experience debt hardship—nearly double the percentage in 1992. Lowest income households are the most likely to be in debt hardship, but middle-income young adults are also experiencing higher levels of debt hardship. About 13 percent of indebted young adults with incomes between $10,000 and $75,000 are in debt hardship (see Table 6.2). Young adults are having a harder time making payments, too. Nearly 1 out of 5 . . . reported being late or missing payments within the last year on any loan, up from 1 out of every 6 in 1992.

WHAT IS DRIVING DEBT?

Several factors may be driving the rise in credit card debt among young adults. In many ways, young families are just like other households—often their paychecks are just enough to cover the rent, groceries and car payment, so that any additional or unexpected expense is financed through credit. But there are unique economic circumstances that may contribute to young adults' greater reliance on credit cards to make ends meet. Young adults are often still servicing student loan debt, have higher unemployment rates and earn lower, entry-level wages. Likewise, today's young adults have come of financial age during an era of banking deregulation that has dramatically increased the availability and cost of credit.

Slow Real Wage Growth.   The earnings of 25 to 34 year olds have not kept up with inflation or the costs of basic necessities including housing, healthcare and student loan repayment obligations. Between 1992 and 2001, the median annual earnings of all male workers grew by 5 percent in real terms (see Table 6.3). Female workers made greater gains in their annual earnings, which rose by 6.7 percent in real terms. Both male and female workers with bachelor's degrees made greater gains than their non-degree holding counterparts. However, given the higher amounts of debt borrowed by those attending college in the 1990s, much of the annual earnings advantage by young college workers is diminished by debt service.

In 2001, the average starting salary for college grads was about $36,000, with wide variations among different fields.[4] Salaries in marketing started at $34,000; advertising jobs started at $28,000, and education majors got on average $39,000 out of the gate. It would be valuable to break down the budget for a typical college grad in 2001 (see Figure 6.3).

The sample budget . . . is for an average college graduate earning about $36,000. The budget makes conservative estimates and does not include expenses for entertainment, clothing, furniture or even household cleaning supplies or toiletries. At the end of the month, our average college grad has just $34 unaccounted for by monthly bills. That money must cover any additional expenses, such as car repairs, new work clothes or even a movie.

Under- and Un-Employment.   Today's young adults are entering a labor market radically different from that of their parents. Many young adults are part of the new contingent labor force, working in temporary jobs that pay less than full-time permanent positions and don't offer health or pension benefits. In 1999, one out of four

TABLE 6.3   Median Annual Earnings of All Wage and Salary Workers Age 25 to 34 (in 2002 dollars)

	Males			Females		
	All Males	Some College	Bachelor's Degree or Higher	All Females	Some College	Bachelor's Degree or Higher
1992	$34,051	$34,024	$45,756	$27,834	$27,134	$36,177
2001	35,778	35,598	48,782	29,723	26,769	38,331
2002	35,487	35,552	48,955	30,093	26,828	40,021

Source: National Center for Education Statistics, based on data from US Department of Commerce, Bureau of the Census. March Current Population Surveys, 1972–2003.

$2,058	Monthly Take Home Pay *($36,000 a year, average starting salary of college grads in 2001, minus taxes and a monthly health care contribution of $42)*

Absolute Expenses

$182	Student Loan Monthly Payment *(average monthly student loan payment reported by undergraduate borrowers)*
$797	Rent and Utilities *(median monthly rent for single, college educated adults in 2000)*
$456	Food and Groceries *(average monthly amount spent on food by 25–34 year olds, 2001)*
$464	Transportation *(average monthly amount for car, auto repairs, insurance and gas)*
$125	Credit Card Minimum Payment *(average credit card debt of 25–34 year olds; $4,008 balance at 16% APR)*
= $1,933	Total Monthly Expenses

Money Left Over for Everything Else

$34	For child care, entertainment, clothing, furniture, Internet access, etc.

FIGURE 6.3   Sample Budget for Recent College Graduate

contingent workers* was between the ages of 25 and 34, a higher percentage than any other age group.[6] College graduates make up the largest percentage of contingent workers, with nearly 38 percent holding bachelor's degrees or higher. Young adults under 24 tend to prefer their contingent arrangement to a full-time job, usually because they're balancing work and school. But the large majority of contingent workers over age 25 would prefer a full-time job.[7]

Not only are young adults frequently *under*-employed, they are also more likely to be unemployed, because young workers have less job tenure. The recent recession has been particularly bad for younger workers, as their unemployment rate rose faster than that of older workers. Almost one in ten young workers were unemployed in mid-2003.[8] Young adults of color face particularly dim prospects in the job market. In 2003, the unemployment rate was 17.9 percent for young African Americans; 9.6 percent for young Latinos and 7.6 percent for young whites.[9] Even

*The findings presented here are based on the Bureau of Labor Statistics definition of contingent worker: individuals who hold jobs that are temporary and not expected to continue.

during the boom year of 2000, young African Americans' unemployment rate was more than double that of young whites.

Workers with college degrees—who are typically more secure in jobs than those without—have been hit hard since the 2001 recession. In March 2004, the number of unemployed college graduates reached 1.17 million, higher than the number of unemployed high school dropouts. While statistics indicate that college education pays-off over the long term, over the short-term many young college grads are finding it difficult to secure jobs.

Student Loan Debt.   This generation is also the first to shoulder the costs of their college primarily through interest-bearing loans rather than grants. Most of the 25 to 34 year olds in the 2001 sample went to college in the 1990s—when college costs increased by an average of 38 percent, borrowing became more common among students, and the amount borrowed grew rapidly.[10] For example, in the 1992–1993 school year, 42 percent of students borrowed money for college. By the end of the decade, almost two-thirds of students had borrowed.[11] A survey of college borrowers conducted by Nellie Mae found that the average college senior graduated with $18,900 in student loans in 2002—taking a big $182 monthly bite out of their paychecks each month.[12] That's more than double the just over $9,000 average loan amount carried by young adults in the previous generation in 1992.[13] For young adults who pursued graduate degrees, the student loan burdens are even higher: the average combined student loan debt for grad school students is $45,900.[14] Young adults who went to grad school pay an average of $388 per month for student loans, amounting to nearly 13.5 percent of their income.

The average undergraduate student loan debt represents about 9 percent of young adults' income today.[15] The commonly accepted rule, used by credit counselors and lenders, is that total monthly debt payments should not exceed 36 percent of gross income. The debt included would be the rent or mortgage, credit cards, student loans, car leases and any other revolving type of loan. With student loan debt taking up 9 percent of young adults' income on average, that leaves just 27 percent of their paychecks to allocate to rent or a car loan without risking financial hardship—not to mention a damaged credit rating. With one out of every five young adults reporting that they have been late on or missed a loan payment in the past year, it is clear that servicing debt has become increasingly risky, and at a time when credit scores are growing more relevant for employment, housing, and even cell phones.

Aggressive Marketing to College Students.   While many younger Americans are going into debt to make ends meet, aggressive marketing tactics by the credit card industry have helped fuel the use of credit cards. Across college and university campuses at the beginning of each semester, credit card companies engage in "tabling" offering free t-shirts, mugs, pizza, and other incentives for students to fill out credit card applications. These tactics work exceedingly well—a recent study found that 96 percent of college seniors had a credit card. With little or no financial literacy training, many students fall victim to the aggressive marketing tactics offered by credit card companies.

Rising Housing and Transportation Costs.   During the last decade, both home prices and rents have grown faster than inflation. In 2001, 3.2 million households earning between $17,500 and $50,000—which includes the median earnings of today's 25 to 34 year olds—spent more than half their incomes on housing.[16] Compared to the late Boomers in 1992, Generation Xers were spending considerably more on average for rent and transportation, according to Consumer Expenditure Survey data.[17] On average, Gen X renters spent $6,815 annually on rent, about 10 percent more than Boomers of the same age spent in 1992. Young adult households are also spending more on getting around: $8,423 on average for transportation in 2002 compared to $6,820 in 1992 (inflation adjusted dollars).

The Cost of Being Uninsured.   Young adults are much more likely to be uninsured than older workers, putting many young adults at both physical and financial risk. Contrary to popular perception, young adults are not uninsured because they decline coverage from their employer. Only 3 percent of uninsured young workers were offered but declined insurance coverage.[18]

Young adults are more likely to work in jobs that don't offer health care benefits. Nearly half of full-time workers aged 19 to 29 lack job-based health benefits, compared to less than one-third percent of all workers under 65.[19] As a result, young adults are more likely to be uninsured than the population as a whole: approximately 1 in 3 young adults lacks health insurance compared to 1 in 6 Americans overall.[20] Not having health insurance exerts a physical and financial cost on young adults. About half of young adults aged 19 to 29 without health insurance reported having problems paying medical bills.[21]

Child Care Costs.   The ages of 25 to 34 are the prime years when young adults begin to start families. Today, the average woman will have her first child around the age of 25.[22] But unlike three decades ago, today's young families are more likely to have two parents working full-time. Today, mothers with infants are more likely to be working full-time than part-time—adding the expense of child care to the family budget.[23] According to the U.S. Census Bureau, 59 percent of mothers with a child under age 1, and 64 percent of mothers with a child under age 6, are in the workforce. Nationwide, about half of all working families with children under age 13 pay for child care, spending an average of $303 per month, or 9 percent of their earnings.[24] With full-day care ranging from $4,000 to $10,000 a year per child, the cost of child care is a major strain on young families' already tight budgets.

THE YOUNGEST ADULTS: INDEBTED FROM THE START

Today's 18 to 24 year olds are experiencing the pinnacle of two trends fueling the rise in debt: dramatic increases in the cost of college and aggressive marketing of credit cards on college campuses. In this section, we take a closer look at the debt among the youngest adults, those aged 18 to 24.

Randy Carter, Communications Professional, Age 28

Randy Carter got his first credit card from a mail solicitation at age 18. He didn't have to prove any source of income for the $800 credit line, just that he was a student at the University of Wisconsin in Madison. A combination of student loans and a part-time job at a hardware store weren't enough to meet the cost of going to school full-time, so the new Citibank credit card helped make up the difference. After six months of small, steady charges for things like books and meals, Citibank more than doubled Randy's limit to $2,000. Randy then took a new job more in line with his career ambitions that required him to drive around the state. Unfortunately, the non-profit employee didn't reimburse gasoline expenses, so he filled up his tank regularly on his card. "It was clear to the bank that I'd use just about as much credit as they gave me, and that I would make the minimum payment," he realized now. So Citibank doubled his limit again, to $4,000. More offers poured in the mail, and by his senior year, Randy had four cards and was $7,500 in debt. The minimum payments grew to be more than he could handle, so he began using the cash advance checks MBNA sent him to pay Citibank, and vice-versa. These checks carried immediate interest charges in the high twenty percent range, and the result was rapidly rising balances, even when he slowed his purchases. When Randy's older brother learned how deep in debt he was, he took out a low-interest personal loan and paid off most of his debt. "I sent the cards back to be cut up, except for the Citibank card, with a couple thousand dollars on it, because I wanted to take some responsibility for some of my debt," Randy explains.

His first job out of school was with a public television station that could only pay him $9 an hour for 20 hours of work a week, although he put in more than 50 hours a week. "I was committed to the job, and was hoping to translate my effort into a full-time job, which happened, finally, after two years of making under $15,000 a year." Credit continued to fill the gap between his salary and his living expenses, which were low by most standards. His rent in the college town was only $300, but his student loan payments were over $400. He eventually had to put his college loans in forbearance. When Randy finally got his full-time position, the salary was $27,000—lower than expected and with no raise in sight due to a Wisconsin state budget salary freeze.

In September of 2001, Randy decided he needed to take control of his career and his finances and follow a job lead in New York. Taking stock of $18,000 in credit card debt, he paid a $778 establishment fee for a debt settlement company to take $389 a month with the promise of using the savings to settle his debts in three years. Randy's new job at a New York dot com documentary company paid him $650 a week with no benefits, but he was able to live on his brother's couch rent-free. But the city's economy was in a tailspin, and he was laid off four months later. Randy cashed out his retirement savings, taking a substantial penalty to access only a few thousand dollars. He needed the money and couldn't get unemployment benefits for nearly two months because he'd worked in two different states. "I started to have to pay rent, which was a bargain in New York at $500, but with the $389 debt payment, I was left with less than $100 a month to live on. I applied for over 300 jobs and got nothing." When his unemployment ran out, he cobbled together a work week of odd jobs—babysitting, filing, light construction—until finally a temp agency took him on. "By this time, I was severely depressed. I had gone to college and worked hard and had so little to show for it."

After almost a year, he finally got a full-time job in his field, and is now doing better. "It still doesn't pay a fair or sustainable wage for New York, but it is stable and has advanced my career." Randy's bad credit has made getting an apartment of his own nearly impossible. "I've been told to pay the full year's rent up front. If I could do that, would I be so deep in debt?" He's also been told that he would be better off filing for bankruptcy. "I always thought it would be better for me to pay, to honor my debts even when I was unemployed and underemployed. But I've spent over $14,000 in the past 3 years, servicing my debt instead of going to the doctor. I'm 28 years old, and I'm worse than broke."

TABLE 6.4 Average Credit Card Debt among Young Households with Credit Card Debt (2001 dollars)

	1992	2001	% Change 1992–2001
Aged 18–24	$1,461	$2,985	104%

Source: Demos' Calculations from the 1992 and 2001 Survey of Consumer Finances

Credit card debt among 18 to 24 year olds rose sharply over the decade, by 104 percent, to an average of $2,985 in 2001 (see Table 6.4). Although the Survey of Consumer Finances does not survey current students, it is dear that the youngest adults' increased debt loads are to some extent a result of rising credit card debt among college students. On-campus credit card marketing exploded during the 1990s, as creditors sought to saturate the youth market for the first time.[25] The co-branded college cards and student-conscious advertising and rewards programs were successful: in 2001, fully 83 percent of all undergraduates had at least one credit card. By their senior year, 96 percent of all students have credit cards, carrying an average of six cards. Balances among college students have risen sharply over the last decade. Between 1990 and 1995, one survey found credit debt had shot up 134 percent, from $900 to $2,100.[26] In 2001, college seniors graduated with an average of $3,262 in credit card debt.[27]

Editors' Note: *Notes for this reading can be found in the original source.*

CHAPTER 7

Retirement's Unraveling Safety Net

DALE RUSSAKOFF

If it's a clear morning, you can count on seeing 80-year-old Junior K. Paugh strolling streets that tell his life story: Propeller Drive, Fuselage Avenue, Cockpit Street, Compass Road. He's been here more than 60 years, ever since aviation pioneer Glenn L. Martin put him to work making seaplanes and bombers at the defense plant down the road. Franklin D. Roosevelt was president and Martin himself walked the factory floor, urging on workers as the nation went to war.

Out of that perilous time came Paugh's now predictable world. He never is short of money, thanks to Social Security and his company pension that will last as long as he does. Health care costs him next to nothing, thanks to Medicare and retiree health insurance. His Baltimore County home is long paid for, thanks in part to a below-market price of $4,400, a result of wartime subsidies for defense-related housing construction.

"I feel completely secure," says Paugh, no small triumph for the third of 13 children born to farmers in Depression-era Appalachia. The triumph is not only his but also the country's—the fulfillment of a New Deal vision of cradle-to-grave security, underwritten by the federal government and large industrial employers.

That vision is being supplanted by one President Bush calls the Ownership Society, in which the burdens of economic security—and, the president hopes, the rewards—shift back to individuals. Social Security is only one aspect of the shift. The safety net big companies wove for Paugh's generation—long-term employment, pension security, retiree health insurance—has been giving way for so long that its unraveling is mere background accompaniment to Washington's noisy debate over Social Security. But in the lives of most middle-class families, it stays in the foreground, inseparable from the Social Security discussion.

This becomes clear in the company of Junior Paugh, his three children, all in their fifties, and five grandchildren, ages 18 to 35. Their three-generation journey has taken them from Appalachia to suburbia, from government relief to an assembly line to a management track at Sears. Yet, despite the apparent progress, their expectations are sinking: The grandchildren, all three generations agree, have it worse than their parents and grandparents—most dramatically in their prospects for retirement, when all gains and losses come home to roost.

Until now, financial planners have likened retirement security to a three-legged stool: employee pensions, personal savings and Social Security.

For the Paugh grandchildren, the savings leg is effectively gone, reflecting a plunging personal savings rate nationally. In place of Junior Paugh's pension, they have 401(k) plans, under which they—not employers—bear the risk and responsibility of investing enough for retirement. And under Bush's Social Security proposal, their promised benefit could drop significantly.

This is a new order with new givens. Paugh and his co-workers came of age as Democrats who felt protected by their union, their party and their government. His grandchildren are all registered Republicans who feel largely on their own in a world full of risks and responsibilities, and no guarantees. They are willing to give Bush's Ownership Society a try, saying they have no hope that government or employers can or will protect them.

The president is counting on the Ownership Society to do for the Republican Party what the New Deal did for the Democrats—that is, make it the nation's majority party. For now, it is easier to measure what has been lost in security than has been gained in opportunity. But the grandchildren's story is only beginning.

THE WAR GENERATION

If childhood in Western Maryland's Deer Park community during the Depression exposed Paugh early and often to life's hardships, adulthood became one encounter after another with protections government and businesses were erecting against risks his parents had battled on their own.

Paugh got his first job through Uncle Sam, driving a truck for the Civilian Conservation Corps, the New Deal agency that put unemployed people to work preserving natural resources. By the time he went to Glenn L. Martin Co. in 1942, wartime wage controls had led most industrial employers to provide pensions and health insurance—in part to secure their workers' loyalty in an exceptionally tight labor market.

Paugh's job even came with a home. The entrepreneur built whole communities to house his burgeoning workforce, which topped 52,000 in 1942 as military orders soared during World War II. The government subsidized the construction as part of the war effort, and Martin passed on the savings in cheap rent and later, low sales prices.

Initially, Paugh paid $19 a month—including water and electricity—for the house where he still lives at 108 Glider Dr. in Aero Acres, a subdivision built on a former strawberry field. Martin named every street for an airplane part (Left Wing and Right Wing drives had no larger connotation), and everyone lived in an identical 24-by-48-foot bungalow with a hallway, two bedrooms, a bathroom and a spacious living room.

Paugh went off to war in 1943, returning with a Purple Heart for shrapnel wounds in the Battle of Okinawa. He remained faithful to Martin, spurning other offers, including one from the Baltimore Orioles in the 1950s. A lanky lefty, Paugh was a star pitcher for the Martin Bombers, the company's standout industrial league team, but professional baseball had nothing on a factory job in his day. "No security," he explained.

Pitching for the Bombers was its own form of security. Martin was famously fanatical about baseball—he built a verdant field on Eastern Avenue and Wilson Point Road, watching Bombers practices from the wing of a strategically parked airplane. When layoffs began after the Korean War, the Bombers' entire roster was exempt.

In return for this security, Paugh traded away some flexibility. In his days as a "CCC Boy," as he still calls himself, he got $5 of his $30-a-month salary, and the CCC sent the rest home for his parents and 12 siblings.

And he would have received only a small fraction of his $920 monthly pension had he not spent his entire career, 41 years, with one employer—an arrangement dubbed the "invisible handshake." The pension is 40 percent of his retirement income; Social Security pays him $1,373.

Nor would Paugh have retired with lifetime health insurance, under which he pays only $2 for prescription drugs. Because of rising health care costs, retirement experts say, employers now pay as much or more for retiree health insurance—which supplements Medicare—as for pensions.

Another important feature of Junior Paugh's retirement security is his thrift, which was bred into him. "We saved and saved and saved," he said of himself and his wife, who died 10 years ago. Paugh is what his family calls "tight," and proud of it. He does not turn on lights until the afternoon sun all but disappears. "Hey, I'm paying for that," he cracked one day when son Doug stopped by after work and flipped on the living room light. He'd rather sweat than use air conditioning, turning it on only when his children and grandchildren visit. ("It was 110 degrees in the South Pacific and we still won the war," he said.)

In Paugh's day, only the wealthy invested in the stock market; Paugh put his trust in Uncle Sam through the "bond a week" savings plan. He also opened an individual retirement account in the early 1980s, with bank interest rates at 15 percent. Last year, the rate fell below 1 percent. His disappointment with IRAs makes him dubious of young people's faith in the stock market—what goes up, he warns, can come down.

At a recent monthly meeting of the Retirees Association of Martin Marietta, Paugh sat with seven former co-workers whose life experiences were almost identical to his: All 80 or older, all sitting pretty on three-legged retirement stools, and all worried about how their children and grandchildren will get by in old age.

"They spend their money before they make it," Ed Dorsey, 82, said of his children. "I say, 'What do you have for retirement?' They say it's a long way away. But they're all in their fifties!"

All said they regard Social Security as indispensable, and all said they know it cannot sustain their descendants in its current form.

"We're the generation that beat the system," said Elmer Sanders, 83. "Social Security didn't count on us living this long. I tell my wife if I have a stroke, and they put me on life supports, just don't unplug me. If I'm still breathing, the checks keep coming."

THE BOOMERS

For the children of Junior Paugh—Kay, 56, Doug, 54, and Dan, 50—the Social Security debate is only the latest reminder that nowadays few things keep coming.

Doug and Dan followed their father into the Martin Company, which became part of Martin Marietta and then Lockheed Martin until their division of about 700 workers was sold to General Electric Co. several years ago. Now named Middle River Aircraft Systems, still housed in the hangar where Junior Paugh worked, it manufactures thrust-reversers for commercial airplane engines. Dan is a senior buyer; Doug is a painter.

Unlike many who started out with them, the brothers have survived all the reorganizations, and still have the prospect of retiring with full pensions and lifetime health insurance, like their father. Typical of companies that still provide these plans, theirs conditions full benefits, which include health insurance for life, on more than 25 years of service—a tenure common in their father's generation, an anachronism in theirs.

"I know we're the fortunate ones," Doug said. "My kids definitely won't get anything like this."

It is not certain that they will either; they know of others who got caught short. Dan had a counterpart in purchasing at the Boeing Co. who had 20 years of service when her division recently was sold to a Canadian company. Her pension benefit was frozen, a 33 percent reduction from the full benefit, and she became ineligible for retiree health insurance. Dan's wife, Joyce, took the same hit in 2001 when her job at Lockheed Martin was eliminated after 21 years. She has since found work at a machine shop, but without a comfortable pension, she said, "It feels like I'll have to work till I die." Last week's news that United Airlines can terminate its pension plans in the largest corporate default in U.S. history sounded to them like more of the same.

So Social Security is hardly the biggest worry.

"As I understand it, people my age could end up getting less than we expect from Social Security, but not too much less, so I feel that it will be there in some form for me. It's not like the government will see you out," Dan Paugh said. "But a company could. As a middle-class person, this scares the daylights out of me."

Their dream, the brothers say, was to do as well as their father: a good job, good wages, a nice-enough house, a family trip now and then. And so far they have. They may even have a similarly secure retirement, buoyed in part by their ballooning home values. Dan's house in Essex has more than tripled in 20 years; Doug's in Cecil County has doubled in five.

Although they and their wives have been contributing to 401(k) plans for 20 years, the brothers say they would not have enough for a comfortable retirement if not for their homes. They may sell them and downsize.

They face a major savings challenge that Junior Paugh didn't: providing for grown-up children. While Junior had 15 years of peak earnings with no child-rearing expenses, Doug has three children, ages 18 to 24, still at home, along with one 4-year-old grandchild. And Junior's daughter, Kay Cody, at 56, is raising her 15-year-old grandson for her daughter, Pamela Cody, 35, a supervisor for a Towson answering service who says she barely can pay her own expenses.

Kay Cody knows the ownership society well, ever since her pension was converted to a 401(k) in the 1990s, forcing her to learn to manage her own retirement savings.

"Growing up, we didn't focus on stocks and mutual funds," she said. "But when they explained the 401(k) to me, I thought, 'That's a darned good idea.' I made sure I understood and kept track of it. Since then, I've taken finance classes, and now I'm on our committee here that monitors how we invest our funds."

In 1996, she suffered a much bigger blow to her security when her husband, a union construction contractor, died of Lou Gehrig's disease. In the process, Cody has learned to tolerate significantly more risk than her father had to. The 2001 stock market plunge following the Sept. 11 terrorist attacks posed no threat to Junior Paugh's pension check, for example, but it savaged his daughter's 401(k) balance. While her funds have mostly recovered, Cody said, "my biggest fear is what if we're hit again and go into another slide?"

Always frugal, she became even more so after her husband's death. Her home in Essex paid for, she put herself on a budget, with a goal of accumulating $5,000 in savings, "in case the washer broke, in case I needed new tires." She created a separate bank account, paying into it from each paycheck, even before buying groceries. When she reached $5,000, she said, $10,000 sounded safer. She passed that, and is still going. She also invested her husband's death benefit and insurance in mutual funds, and invests in a growth fund for her grandson. But she said that her 401(k) and savings amount to $114,000—far short of the $400,000 a financial adviser told her she will need to support herself in retirement.

Her job as an administrator in a medical practice reminds her daily of other risks. Unlike her brothers and her father, she has no expectation of retiring with lifetime health insurance. "I'd like to be like my father and never be sick or have medical needs, but if I'm not, I see every day that Medicare doesn't begin to pay for what health care costs," she said. Her father-in-law, a Bethlehem Steel Co. retiree, lost his retirement health insurance when the company declared bankruptcy, and he had to pay thousands of dollars when he needed a pacemaker, she said.

Amid these rough waters, Social Security represents an island of stability. At 56, Cody is not likely to face benefit reductions, since every proposal so far exempts people 55 and older. But while she supports Bush's call for private accounts, she said she worries more about the system's long-term solvency.

"It does give me huge peace of mind to know I won't have to think about what I have to live off when I'm a certain age," she said. "But of course I worry what will be there for my children and grandchildren. Sometimes I think things look as bleak for them as before Roosevelt started all this."

THE GRANDCHILDREN

One measure of the unraveling of old-fashioned retirement security is that the younger generation of Paughs does not even expect to find it. "Security to me is about having options in case something happens," says Jessica Paugh, 29, an assistant manager at Sears in the Harford Mall in Bel Air.

Daughter of Dan and Joyce, she says she lost confidence in the old order when her mother lost her job of 21 years. "It was heartbreaking," said Jessica, who is now a convert to the Ownership Society. "Now, every day a company is buying another company. So I figure if this works out, great! I love my job, but it could change, and I'll adapt."

Indeed, the Ownership Society looks much like a Sellership Society from the younger Paughs' encounters with it. Sears was sold last spring to Kmart, with potential implications for Jessica. Her cousin Pamela Cody took a cut in benefits when the locally owned answering service where she worked was sold to a national chain. And Jessica's father and uncle know only too well that GE could sell their division, just as Lockheed Martin sold it in the 1990s. Dan Paugh recalls the response of a Lockheed Martin official to workers' surprise about that sale: "For the right price, my best hunting dog is for sale."

In Junior Paugh's day, when experience was valued on the production line, cradle-to-grave security and loyalty to one employer made sense for companies and workers. But for the younger Paughs, who have watched jobs, capital and products cross borders ("Our payroll operation is in India!" Doug exclaimed), the invisible handshake can seem like handcuffs.

Doug's daughter Lindsay, 21, recently left a job as a bank teller to work for a rival bank that offered a raise and promotion, but she forfeited three years toward a pension. The pension was not a factor, she said, because if she hadn't left now, she was certain to leave later. This remark led her mother, Melanie Paugh, who has worked 13 years for BMW, to close her eyes momentarily, as if to steady her spinning head.

"Today, if kids see a $10 raise, they jump," she said. "We were raised to stay put."

Jessica accompanies Junior Paugh to Martin retirees' gatherings sometimes, and loves meeting his former co-workers, but cannot believe that all these years later these men still talk about their old company. "They still care about what goes on there—it's just really hard to imagine," she said. "For me, a job is where you work."

Retirement experts say the three-legged stool has only two legs for Paughs grandchildren's generation: Social Security and 401(k)s, which are like a merger of pensions and savings. Jessica's position at Sears comes with a 401(k) into which she tried to put 7 percent of her paycheck, although she said she recently cut back to 3 percent because she couldn't pay her expenses. "If I didn't use my credit card, I wouldn't have eaten some weeks," she said.

Jessica is the only descendant of Junior Paugh to go to college so far. Her parents didn't give her a choice. "They raised me to see college as inevitable, part of being prepared," she said. "Skills are the key. It's in the job description for my position—you need a college degree." Yet another child-rearing expense Junior Paugh did not face.

If Jessica's career goes well and the stock-market cooperates, she could end up as secure as her grandfather is in old age. But for now, even with her recent promotion to assistant manager (salary: $26,000), she and her parents are not counting on it. Her 401(k), now with a balance of $6,000, could reach $308,000 by retirement, according to a calculation provided by the plan, but this is well short of what economists say she would need. She said she hopes to invest more and see more gains.

"I check my balance online every other week," she said. "I have half the money in safe investments. With the rest I'm taking risks, just saying, 'Go! Go! Go!'"

Jessica said she believes firmly she never will be able to afford a house. Her cousin Pamela, who rents an apartment with her husband in Harford County, says the same. And her three younger cousins—Doug's children—have yet to move out on their own. As their parents see it, this is another wobble in the next generation's retirement security stool.

"We did as well and in some ways better than our parents," Melanie said. "I don't see how our kids will."

But Jessica and Lindsay, for their parts, are too optimistic to imagine things won't ultimately go their way, and too young to imagine ever being old.

"In my mind, right now, retirement is a myth. It may exist, but I can't see that far. I have my 401(k), so I'm preparing," Jessica said.

Pamela, the answering service supervisor, sees it differently. On a recent day, when Pamela's 11-year-old Ford Probe broke down, Junior Paugh made the hour-long drive to pick her up and take her to work. A starker contrast in two people's relationship to their government and employers would be hard to conjure.

Here was Junior Paugh at the wheel of his silver Buick LeSabre, having moved out of poverty, into the middle class, and now a secure retirement, with the help of one employer and his government. And here, only two generations behind him, sat Pamela Cody, feeling abandoned by everything her grandfather valued.

"I see how my grandparents were able to get by, but my husband and I just struggle from paycheck to paycheck," she said. "I don't have a pension and I'm not expecting Social Security to hold up long enough for me. Where is all the government's money going? Who is it benefiting? Nothing is benefiting me."

CHAPTER 8

The Limits of Markets

ROBERT KUTTNER

The claim that the freest market produces the best economic outcome is the centerpiece of the conservative political resurgence. If the state is deemed incompetent to balance the market's instability, temper its inequality, or correct its myopia, there is not much left of the mixed economy and the modern liberal project.

Yet while conservatives resolutely tout the superiority of free markets, many liberals are equivocal about defending the mixed economy. The last two Democratic presidents have mainly offered a more temperate call for the reining in of government and the liberation of the entrepreneur. The current vogue for deregulation began under Jimmy Carter. The insistence on budget balance was embraced by Bill Clinton, whose pledge to "reinvent government" was soon submerged in a shared commitment to shrink government. Much of the economics profession, after an era of embracing a managed form of capitalism, has also reverted to a new fundamentalism about the virtues of markets. So there is today a stunning imbalance of ideology, conviction, and institutional armor between right and left.

At bottom, three big things are wrong with the utopian claims about markets. First, they misdescribe the dynamics of human motivation. Second, they ignore the fact that civil society needs realms of political rights where some things are not for sale. And third, even in the economic realm, markets price many things wrong, which means that pure markets do not yield optimal economic outcomes.

There is at the core of the celebration of markets relentless tautology. If we begin by assuming that nearly everything can be understood as a market and that markets optimize outcomes, then everything leads back to the same conclusion—marketize! If, in the event, a particular market doesn't optimize, there is only one possible conclusion—it must be insufficiently market-like. This is a no-fail system for guaranteeing that theory trumps evidence. Should some human activity not, in fact, behave like an efficient market, it must logically be the result of some interference that should be removed. It does not occur that the theory mis-specifies human behavior.

The school of experimental economics, pioneered by psychologists Daniel Kahneman and Amos Tversky, has demonstrated that people do not behave the way the model specifies. People will typically charge more to give something up than to acquire the identical article; economic theory would predict a single "market-clearing" price. People help strangers, return wallets, leave generous tips in restaurants they will never visit again, give donations to public radio when theory would predict they would rationally "free-ride," and engage in other acts that suggest they value general norms of fairness. To conceive of altruism as a special form of selfishness misses the point utterly.

Although the market model imagines a rational individual, maximizing utility in an institutional vacuum, real people also have civic and social selves. The act of voting can be shown to be irrational by the lights of economic theory, because the "benefit" derived from the likelihood of one's vote affecting the outcome is not worth the "cost." But people vote as an act of faith in the civic process, as well as to influence outcomes.

In a market, everything is potentially for sale. In a political community, some things are beyond price. One's person, one's vote, one's basic democratic rights do not belong on the auction block. We no longer allow human beings to be bought and sold via slavery (though influential Chicago economists have argued that it would be efficient to treat adoptions as auction markets). While the market keeps trying to invade the polity, we do not permit the literal sale of public office. As James Tobin wrote, commenting on the myopia of his own profession, "Any good second-year graduate student in economics could write a short examination paper proving that voluntary transactions in votes would increase the welfare of the sellers as well as the buyers."

But the issue here is not just the defense of a civic realm beyond markets or of a socially bearable income distribution. History also demonstrates that in much of economic life, pure reliance on markets produces suboptimal outcomes. Market forces, left to their own devices, lead to avoidable financial panics and depressions, which in turn lead to political chaos. Historically, government has had to intervene, not only to redress the gross inequality of market-determined income and wealth, but to rescue the market from itself when it periodically goes haywire. The state also provides oases of solidarity for economic as well as social ends, in realms that markets cannot value properly, such as education, health, public infrastructure, and clean air and water. So the fact remains that the mixed economy—a strong private sector tempered and leavened by a democratic policy—is the essential instrument of both a decent society and an efficient economy.

The second coming of laissez faire has multiple causes. In part, it reflects the faltering of economic growth in the 1970s, on the Keynesian watch. It also reflects a relative weakening of the political forces that support a mixed economy—the declining influence of the labor movement, the erosion of working-class voting turnout, the suburbanization of the Democratic Party, and the restoration of the political sway of organized business—as well as the reversion of formal economics to preKeynesian verities.

Chicago-style economists have also colonized other academic disciplines. Public Choice theory, a very influential current in political science, essentially applies the market model to politics. Supposedly, self-seeking characterizes both economic man and political man. But in economics, competition converts individual selfishness into a general good, while in politics, selfishness creates little monopolies. Public Choice claims that office holders have as their paramount goal re-election, and that groups of voters are essentially "rent seekers" looking for a free ride at public expense, rather than legitimate members of a political collectivity expressing democratic voice. Ordinary citizens are drowned out by organized interest groups, so the mythic "people" never get what they want. Thus, since the democratic process is largely a sham, as well as a drag on economic efficiency, it is best to entrust as little to the public realm as possible. Lately, nearly half the articles in major political science journals have reflected a broad Public Choice sensibility.

The Law and Economics movement, likewise, has made deep inroads into the law schools and courts, subsidized by tens of millions of dollars from right-wing foundations. The basic idea of Law and Economics is that the law, as a system of rules and rights, tends to undermine the efficiency of markets. It is the duty of judges, therefore, to make the law the servant of market efficiency rather than a realm of civic rights. Borrowing from Public Choice theory, Law and Economics scholars contend that since democratic deliberation and hence legislative intent are largely illusory, it is legitimate for courts to ignore legislative mandates—not to protect rights of minorities but to protect the efficiency of markets. Regulation is generally held to be a deadweight cost, since it cannot improve upon the outcomes that free individuals would rationally negotiate.

These intellectual currents are strategically connected to the political arena. Take the journal titled *Regulation,* published for many years by the American Enterprise Institute, and currently published by the Cato Institute. Though it offers lively policy debates over particulars, virtually every article in *Regulation* is anti-regulation. Whether the subject is worker safety, telecommunications, the environment, electric power, health care—whatever—the invariable subtext is that government screws things up and markets are self-purifying. It is hardly surprising that the organized right publishes such a journal. What is more depressing, and revealing, is that there is no comparable journal with a predisposition in favor of a mixed economy. This intellectual apparatus has become the scaffolding for the proposition that governments should leave markets alone.

MARKETS, EFFICIENCY, AND JUSTICE

The moral claim of the free market is based on the interconnected premises that markets maximize liberty, justice, and efficiency. In a market economy, individuals are free to choose, as Milton Friedman famously wrote. They are free to decide what to buy, where to shop, what businesses or professions to pursue, where to live—subject "only" to the constraints of their individual income and wealth. The extremes of wealth and poverty seemingly mock the claim that markets epitomize human freedom—a poor man has only the paltry freedoms of a meager income. But the constraints of market-determined income are presumed defensible, because of the second claim—that the purchasing power awarded by markets is economically fair. If Bill Gates has several billion dollars to spend, that is only because he has added several billions of dollars of value to the economy, as validated by the free choices of millions of consumers. An unskilled high school dropout, in contrast, has little freedom to consume, because his labor offers little of value to an employer. There may be extenuating prior circumstances of birth or fortune, but each of us is ultimately responsible for our own economic destiny.

Linking these two premises is the third claim—that markets are roughly efficient. The prices set by supply and demand reflect how the economy values goods and services. So the resulting allocation of investment is efficient, in the sense that an alternative allocation mandated by extra-market forces would reduce total output. This is why professional economists who have liberal social values as citizens generally argue that if we don't like the social consequences of market income distribution, we should redistribute after the fact rather than tamper with the market's pricing mechanism.

Of course, each of these core claims is ultimately empirical. If in fact the freest market does not truly yield the optimal level of material output, then it follows that a pure market is neither just nor conducive of maximal liberty. A tour of the actual economy reveals that some sectors lend themselves to markets that look roughly like the market of the textbook model, while others do not.

Why would markets not be efficient? The most orthodox explanation is the prevalence of what economists call "externalities." These are costs or benefits not captured by the price set by the immediate transaction. The best-known negative externality is pollution. The polluter "externalizes" the true costs of his waste products onto society by dumping them, at no personal cost, into a nearby river or spewing them into the air. If the full social cost were internalized, the price would be higher.

Positive externalities include research and education. Individuals and business firms underinvest in education and research because the benefits are diffuse. The firm that trains a worker may not capture the full return on that investment, since the worker may take a job elsewhere; the fruits of technical invention, likewise, are partly appropriated by competitors. As economists put it, the private return does not equal the social return, so we cannot rely on profit-maximizing individuals for the optimal level of investment. By the same token, if we made the education of children dependent on the private resources of parents, society as a whole would underinvest in the schooling of the next generation. There is a social return on having a well-educated workforce and citizenry. As the bumper sticker sagely puts it, "If you think education is expensive, try ignorance."

Standard economics sees externalities as exceptions. But a tour of economic life suggests that in a very large fraction of the total economy, markets do not price things appropriately. When we add up health, education, research, public infrastructure, plus structurally imperfect sectors of the economy like telecommunications, they quickly add up to more than half of society's total product. The issue is not whether to temper market verdicts, but how.

SUPER MARKETS

Even realms that are close to textbook markets can actually be enhanced by extra-market interventions. Consider your local supermarket. The pricing and supply of retail food is mostly unregulated, and fiercely competitive. Somehow, the average consumer's lack of infinite time to go shopping, and less-than-perfect information about the relative prices of a thousand products in several local stores, exactly allows the supermarket to earn a normal profit.

Supermarkets connect the retail market to the agricultural one. The supermarket also provides part of the local market for labor and capital. Though cashiers and meat cutters are not the most glamorous of jobs, the supermarket manages to pay just enough to attract people who are just competent enough to perform the jobs acceptably. If supermarket profits are below par over time, the price of its shares will fall. That also operates as a powerful signal—on where investors should put their capital, and on how executives must supervise their managers and managers their employees.

Though there may be occasional missteps, and though some supermarkets go bankrupt, the interplay of supply and demand in all of these submarkets contributes to a dynamic equilibrium. It results in prices that are "right" most of the time. The supermarket stocks, displays, and prices thousands of different highly perishable products in response to shifting consumer tastes, with almost no price regulation. Supply and demand substitutes for elaborate systems of control that would be hopelessly cumbersome to administer. No wonder the champions of the market are almost religious in their enthusiasm.

But please note that supermarkets are not perfectly efficient. Retail grocers operate on thin profit margins, but the wholesale part of the food distribution chain is famous for enormous markups. A farmer is likely to get only 10 cents out of a box of corn flakes that retails for $3.99. Secondly, even supermarkets are far from perfectly free markets. Their hygiene is regulated by government inspectors, as is most of the food they sell. Government regulations mandate the format and content of nutritional labeling. They require clear, consistent unit pricing, to rule out a variety of temptations of deceptive marketing. Moreover, many occupations in the food industry, such as meat cutter and cashier, are substantially unionized; so the labor market is not a pure free market either. Much of the food produced in the United States is grown by farmers who benefit from a variety of interferences with a laissez-faire market, contrived by government to prevent ruinous fluctuations in prices. The government also subsidizes education and technical innovation in agriculture.

So even in this nearly perfect market, a modicum of regulation is entirely compatible with the basic discipline of supply and demand, and probably enhances its efficiency by making for better-informed consumers, less-opportunistic sellers, and by placing the market's most self-cannibalizing tendencies off-limits. Because of the imperfect information of consumers, it is improbable that repealing these regulations would enhance efficiency.

SICK MARKETS

Now, however, consider a very different sector—health care. Medical care is anything but a textbook free market, yet market forces and profit motives in the health industry are rife. On the supply side, the health industry violates several conditions of a free market. Unlike the supermarket business, there is not "free entry." You cannot simply open a hospital, or hang out your shingle as a doctor. This gives health providers a degree of market power that compromises the competitive model—and raises prices. On the demand side, consumers lack the special knowledge to shop for a doctor the way they buy a car and lack perfectly free choice of health insurer. And since society has decided that nobody shall perish for lack of medical care, demand is not constrained by private purchasing power, which is inflationary.

Health care also offers substantial "positive externalities." The value to society of mass vaccinations far exceeds the profits that can be captured by the doctor or drug company. If vaccinations and other public health measures were left to private supply and demand, society would seriously underinvest. Society invests in other public health measures that markets underprovide. The health care system also depends heavily on extra-market norms—the fact that physicians and nurses are guided by ethical constraints and professional values that limit the opportunism that their specialized knowledge and power might otherwise invite.

The fact that health care is a far cry from a perfect market sets up a chain of perverse incentives. A generation ago, fee-for-service medicine combined with insurance reimbursement to stimulate excessive treatment and drive up costs. Today many managed care companies reverse the process and create incentives to deny necessary care. In either case, this is no free market. Indeed, as long as society stipulates that nobody shall die for lack of private purchasing power, it will never be a free market. That is why it requires regulation as well as subsidy.

Here is the nub of the issue. Are most markets like supermarkets—or like health markets? The conundrum of the market for health care is a signal example of an oft-neglected insight known as the General Theory of the Second Best. The theory, propounded by the economists Richard Lipsey and Kelvin Lancaster in 1956, holds that when a particular market departs significantly from a pure market, attempts to marketize partially can leave us worse off.

A Second Best market (such as health care) is not fully accountable to the market discipline of supply and demand, so typically it has acquired second-best forms of accountability—professional norms, government supervision, regulation, and subsidy—to which market forces have adapted. If the health care system is already a far cry from a free market on both the demand side and the supply side, removing one regulation and thereby making the health system more superficially market-like may well simply increase opportunism and inefficiency. In many economic realms, the second-best outcome of some price distortion offset by regulation and extra-market norms may be the best outcome practically available.

Another good Second Best illustration is the banking industry. Until the early 1970s, banking in the United States was very highly regulated. Regulation limited both the price and the quantity of banking services. Bank charters were limited. So were interest rates. Banks were subject to a variety of other regulatory constraints. Of course, banks still competed fiercely for market share and profitability, based on how well they served customers and how astutely they analyzed credit risks. Partially deregulating the banking and savings and loan industries in the 1980s violated the Theory of the Second Best. It pursued greater efficiency, but led to speculative excess. Whatever gains to the efficiency of allocation were swamped by the ensuing costs of the bailout.

THE THREE EFFICIENCIES

The saga of banking regulation raises the question of contending conceptions of efficiency. The efficiency prized by market enthusiasts is "allocative." That is, the free play of supply and demand via price signals will steer resources to the uses that provide the greatest satisfaction and the highest return. Regulation interferes with this discipline, and presumably worsens outcomes. But in markets like health care and banking, the market is far from free to begin with. Moreover, "allocative" efficiency leaves out the issues that concerned John Maynard Keynes—whether the economy as a whole has lower rates of growth and higher unemployment than it might achieve. Nor does allocative efficiency deal with the question of technical advance, which is the source of improved economic performance over time. Technical progress is the issue that concerned the other great dissenting economic theorist of the early twentieth century, Joseph Schumpeter. Standard market theory lacks a common metric to assess these three contending conceptions of efficiency.

Countermanding the allocative mechanism of the price system may depress efficiency on Adam Smith's sense. But if the result is to increase Keynesian efficiency of high growth and full employment, or the Schumpeterian efficiency of technical advance, there may well be a net economic gain. Increasing allocative efficiency when unemployment is high doesn't help. It may even hurt—to the extent that intensified competition in a depressed economy may throw more people out of work, reduce overall purchasing power, and deepen the shortfall of aggregate demand.

By the same token, if private market forces underinvest in technical innovation, then public investment and regulation can improve on market outcomes. Patents, trademarks, and copyrights are among the oldest regulatory interventions acknowledging market failure, and creating artificial property rights in innovation. As technology evolves, so necessarily does the regime of intellectual property regulation.

In my recent book, *Everything For Sale,* I examined diverse sectors of the economy. Only a minority of them operated efficiently with no regulatory interference.

Some sectors, such as banking and stock markets, entail both fiduciary responsibilities and systemic risks. In the absence of financial regulation, conflicts of interest and the tendency of money markets to speculative excess could bring down the entire economy, as financial panics periodically did in the era before regulation.

Other sectors, such as telecommunications, are necessarily a blend of monopoly power and competition. New competitors now have the right to challenge large incumbents, but often necessarily piggyback on the infrastructure of established companies that they are trying to displace. Without regulation mandating fair play, they would be crushed. The breakup of the old AT&T monopoly allows greater innovation and competition, but if the new competition is to benefit consumers it requires careful ground rules. The 1996 Telecommunications Act, complex legislation specifying terms of fair engagement, is testament for the ongoing need for discerning regulation in big, oligopolistic industries.

Similarly, in the electric power industry, where new technologies allow for new forms of competition, the old forms of regulation no longer apply. Once, a public utility was granted a monopoly; a regulatory agency guaranteed it a fair rate of return. Today, the system is evolving into one in which residential consumers and business customers will be able to choose among multiple suppliers. Yet because of the need to assure that all customers will have electric power on demand, and that incumbents will not be able to drive out new competitors, the new system still depends on regulation. A regime of regulated competition is replacing the old form of regulation of entry and price—but it is regulation nonetheless.

Regulation, of course, requires regulators. But if democratic accountability is a charade, if regulators are hopeless captives of "rent-seeking" interest groups, if public-mindedness cannot be cultivated, then the regulatory impulse is doomed. Yet because capitalism requires ground rules, it is wrong to insist that the best remedy is no regulation at all. The choice is between good regulation and bad regulation.

In the 1970s, many economists, including many relative liberals such as Charles Schultze, began attacking "command-and-control" regulation for overriding the market's pricing mechanism. Instead, they commended "incentive regulation," in which public goals would take advantage of the pricing system. What Schultze proposed in the area of pollution control, Alfred Kahn commended for electric power regulation and Alain Enthoven proposed for health insurance. But what all three, and others in this vein, tended to overlook is that incentive regulation is still regulation. It still requires competent, public-minded regulators. And because technology continues to evolve, regulation is not merely transitional.

The 1990 Clean Air Act created an innovative acid rain program that supplanted "command-and-control" regulation of sulphur dioxide emissions with a new, "market-like" system of tradable emission permits. But before this system could operate, myriad regulatory determinations were necessary. Public policy had to specify the total permissible volume of pollutants, how the new market was to be structured, and how emissions were to be monitored. This was entirely a contrived market. So was the decision to auction off portions of the broadcast spectrum. Though hailed as more "market-like" than the previous system of administrative broadcast licensing, the creation of auctions required innumerable regulatory determinations.

Unlike airline deregulation, in which the supervisory agency, the Civil Aeronautics Board, was put out of business, the Federal Communications Commission and the Environmental Protection Agency remain to monitor these experiments in incentive regulation and to make necessary course corrections. Airline deregulation has been at best a mixed success, because there is no government agency to police the results and to intervene to prevent collusive or predatory practices.

Similarly, if we are to use incentives in sectors that have previously been seen as public goods, such as education, issues of distribution inevitably arise. How public policy allocates, say, vouchers, and how it structures incentives, cannot help affecting who gets the service. The ideal of a pure market solution to a public good is a mirage.

The basic competitive discipline of a capitalist economy can coexist nicely with diverse extramarket forces; the market can even be rendered more efficient by them. These include both explicit regulatory interventions and the cultivation of extramarket norms, most notably trust, civility, and long-term reciprocity. Richard Vietor of the Harvard Business School observes in his 1994 book, *Contrived Competition,* that imperfect, partly regulated markets still are highly responsive to competitive discipline. The market turns out to be rather more resilient and adaptive than its champions admit. In markets as varied as banking, public utilities, and health care, entrepreneurs do not sicken and expire when faced with regulated competition; they simply revise their competitive strategy and go right on competing. Norms that commit society to resist short-term opportunism can make both the market and the society a healthier place. Pure markets, in contrast, commend and invite opportunism, and depress trust.

THE INEVITABILITY OF POLITICS

A review of the virtues and limits of markets necessarily takes us back to politics. Even a fervently capitalist society, it turns out, requires prior rules. Rules govern everything from basic property rights to the fair terms of engagement in complex mixed markets such as health care and telecommunications. Even the proponents of market-like incentives—managed competition in health care, tradable emissions permits for clean air, supervised deregulation of telecommunications, compensation mandates to deter unsafe workplace practices—depend, paradoxically, on discerning, public-minded regulation to make their incentive schemes work. As new, unimagined dilemmas arise, there is no fixed constitution that governs all future cases. As new products and business strategies appear and markets evolve, so necessarily does the regime of rules.

The patterns of market failure are more pervasive than most market enthusiasts acknowledge. Generally, they are the result of immutable structural characteristics of certain markets and the ubiquity of both positive and negative spillovers. In markets where the consumer is not effectively sovereign (telecommunications, public utilities, banking, airlines, pure food and drugs), or where the reliance on market verdicts would lead to socially intolerable outcomes (health care, pollution, education, gross income inequality, the buying of office or purchase of professions), a recourse purely to ineffectual market discipline would leave both consumer and society worse off than the alternative of a mix of market forces and regulatory interventions. While advocates of laissez faire presume that the regulation characteristic of an earlier stage of capitalism has been mooted by technology, competition, and better-informed consumers, they forget that the more mannered capitalism of our own era is precisely the fruit of regulation, and that the predatory tendencies persist.

Contrary to the theory of perfect markets, much of economic life is not the mechanical satisfaction of preferences or the pursuit of a single best equilibrium. On the contrary, many paths are possible—many blends of different values, many mixes of market and social, many possible distributions of income and wealth—all compatible with tolerably efficient getting and spending. The grail of a perfect market, purged of illegitimate and inefficient distortions, is a fantasy.

The real world displays a very broad spectrum of actual markets with diverse structural characteristics, and different degrees of separation from the textbook ideal. Some need little regulation, some a great deal—either to make the market mechanism work efficiently or to solve problems that the market cannot fix. Someone has to make such determinations, or we end up in a world very far from even the available set of Second Bests. In short, rules require rule setters. In a democracy, that enterprise entails democratic politics.

The market solution does not moot politics. It only alters the dynamics of influence and the mix of winners and losers. The attempt to relegate economic issues to "nonpolitical" bodies, such as the Federal Reserve, does not rise above politics either. It only removes key financial decisions from popular debate to financial elites, and lets others take the political blame. A decision to allow markets, warts and all, free rein is just one political choice among many. There is no escape from politics.

QUIS CUSTODET?

The issue of how precisely to govern markets arises in libertarian, democratic nations like the United States, and deferential, authoritarian ones like Singapore. It arises whether the welfare state is large or small, and whether the polity is expansive or restrained in its aspirations. Rule setting and the correction of market excess are necessarily public issues in social-democratic Sweden, in Christian Democratic Germany, in feudal-capitalist Japan, and in Tory Britain. The highly charged question of the proper rules undergirding a capitalist society pervaded political discourse and conflict throughout nineteenth-century America, even though the public sector then consumed less than 5 percent of the gross domestic product.

The political process, of course, can produce good sets of rules for the market, or bad ones. Thus, the quality of political life is itself a public good—perhaps the most fundamental public good. A public good, please recall, is something that markets are not capable of valuing correctly. Trust, civility, long-term commitment, and the art of consensual deliberation are the antitheses of pure markets, and the essence of effective politics.

As the economic historian Douglass North, the 1993 Nobel laureate in economics, has observed, competent public administration and governance are a source of competitive advantage for nation-states. Third-world nations and postcommunist regimes are notably disadvantaged not just by the absence of functioning markets but by the weakness of legitimate states. A vacuum of legitimate state authority does not yield efficient laissez faire; it yields mafias and militias, with whose arbitrary power would-be entrepreneurs must reckon. The marketizers advising post-Soviet Russia imagined that their challenge was to dismantle a state in order to create a market. In fact, the more difficult challenge was to constitute a state to create a market.

Norms that encourage informed civic engagement increase the likelihood of competent, responsive politics and public administration, which in turn yield a more efficient mixed economy. North writes:

> The evolution of government from its medieval, Mafia-like character to that embodying modern legal institutions and instruments is a major part of the history of freedom. It is a part that tends to be obscured or ignored because of the myopic vision of many economists, who persist in modeling government as nothing more than a gigantic form of theft and income redistribution.

Here, North is echoing Jefferson, who pointed out that property and liberty, as we know and value them, are not intrinsic to the state of nature but are fruits of effective government.

The more that complex mixed markets require a blend of evolving rules, the more competent and responsive a public administration the enterprise requires. Strong civic institutions help constitute the state, and also serve as counterweights against excesses of both state and market. Lately, the real menace to a sustainable society has been the market's invasion of the polity, not vice versa. Big money has crowded out authentic participation. Commercial values have encroached on civic values.

Unless we are to leave society to the tender mercies of laissez faire, we need a mixed economy. Even laissez faire, for that matter, requires rules to define property rights. Either way, capitalism entails public policies, which in turn are creatures of democratic politics. The grail of a market economy untainted by politics is the most dangerous illusion of our age.

PART THREE

Inequality

There is no doubt that the United States is an extremely prosperous society, but that prosperity has not been shared by everyone. One of the most striking features of American society today, indeed, is the stark coexistence of great wealth and widespread poverty. In many respects, economic inequality is more glaring today than ever before in our recent history. But a wide gap between "haves" and "have-nots" has been with us from the beginning, and has stubbornly persisted even during good economic times.

In the 1950s and 1960s, for example, many social scientists described the United States as an "affluent" society—one in which most people could expect a steady improvement in their standard of living, great disparities in income and wealth were fast disappearing, and true poverty was soon to be a thing of the past. These perceptions were based on some undeniable facts. On average, Americans' incomes did rise substantially after World War II, and during the 1960s millions of the poor were lifted above the official poverty line. It was natural to believe that these trends would continue.

But even in the expanding economy of the 1950s and 1960s, there were important limits to what some believed was a steady march toward greater equality. For one thing, the progress in raising the overall standard of living had virtually no impact on the *distribution* of income and wealth in America—the gap between rich and poor. Throughout most of the period since World War II, the upper one-fifth of income earners received roughly 40 percent of the country's total personal income; the bottom fifth, about 5 percent. And although poverty was sharply reduced in many rural areas, it proved to be much more stubborn in the inner cities.

More recently, the trends have become much more discouraging: The limited postwar progress toward economic equality has been reversed. By the early 1980s, the spread of income inequality in the United States had begun to increase as the share of the most affluent rose while the share of the poor fell. In the 1990s, income inequality reached its most extreme level since World War II. By the turn of the new century, the top fifth of income earners took home half the nation's total income.

As Edward Wolff points out in his article on the distribution of wealth in America, the growth of inequality is actually understated if we look only at the gap in *income*—that is, the flow of cash that families and individuals receive over a given period. At least equally important is the widening gap in Americans' *wealth*—stocks and bonds, businesses, homes, and other assets. Even with a high income, a family without significant assets is vulnerable to economic insecurity. Wealth, moreover, confers a degree of economic and political influence that those without it cannot share. It's especially troubling, therefore, that the wealth gap is wider now than at any time since before the Great Depression of the 1930s, with the top 1 percent of American households cornering almost two-fifths of the country's entire net wealth.

As the economic fortunes of the richest Americans have shot upward, those of low-income Americans have deteriorated. At last count, close to 36 million Americans had incomes below the federal government's official "poverty line," calculated as slightly over $19,000 for a family of four in 2005. Today more than one American child in six lives in poverty—a far higher proportion, as the next article shows, than in most other industrial nations.

Many people are aware that poverty among children is widespread in America, but fewer realize that it is *much* more prevalent here than in other developed societies. Using data from the Luxembourg Income Study, an international comparison of levels of inequality and poverty begun in the 1980s, Lee Rainwater and Timothy Smeeding illustrate just how stark those differences are. Poor children are worse off in the United States—one of the world's most affluent countries—than in all but the poorest industrial societies. And the economic gap between affluent and poor children is wider—sometimes *much* wider—in the United States than in any other Western industrial country.

Poverty is more than a matter of income alone. One of the most devastating, and most visible, consequences of rising poverty (among other causes) has been the growth of homelessness in the United States. Elliot Liebow, an anthropologist, spent several years closely observing homeless women in and around Washington, D.C., and his article paints a compelling picture of what life is really like at the bottom of the American system of inequality. Being homeless, he reveals, means having to struggle every day for the bare essentials of life most of us take for granted—from a place to sleep to somewhere to store our belongings.

Why, when they seem so unfair, do we allow such harsh disparities between rich and poor to persist? One reason is that, as a nation, we have historically believed that, whatever one's present position on the economic ladder, it is always possible to move up—through hard work, pluck, and persistence. The idea that the United States is a unique land of virtually unlimited opportunity, where who your parents were is far less important than what you achieve on your own, has profoundly shaped our social policies from the beginning—helping to create a society that, in comparison with other advanced industrial nations, has done remarkably little to cushion the impact of inequalities in income and wealth. But as the article we reprint from the business-oriented *Wall Street Journal* suggests, the reality is more complicated. There was probably never as much opportunity to move up in America as we once believed, and the possibilities of moving upward out of poverty have stagnated, or even declined, in recent decades. That doesn't, of course, mean that this kind of upward mobility never happens; it does mean that the wealth and educational level of one's parents matters far more than the myth of unlimited opportunity implies.

CHAPTER 9

Top Heavy

EDWARD N. WOLFF

Before exploring more closely the facts and policies surrounding wealth inequality, a review of the central concepts is helpful. Family wealth refers to the
net dollar value of the stock of assets less liabilities (or debt) held by a household at one point in time.[1] Income, in contrast, refers to a flow of dollars over a period of time, usually a year. Though certain forms of income are derived from wealth,
such as interest from savings accounts and bonds, dividends from stock shares, and
rent from real estate, income and wealth are by no means identical. Many kinds of
income—wages and salaries, food stamps and other transfer payments—are not derived from household wealth, and many forms of wealth, such as owner-occupied
housing, produce no corresponding cash income flow.

Most people think of family income as a measure of well being, but family
wealth is also a source of well-being, independent of the direct income it provides.
There are both narrowly economic and broader reasons for the importance of
wealth. Some assets, particularly owner-occupied housing, provide services directly
to the owner. This is also true for consumer durables, such as automobiles. Such
assets can substitute for financial income in satisfying economic needs. Families receiving the same financial income but differing in their stocks of housing and consumer durables will experience different levels of well-being.

More important, perhaps, than its role as a source of income is the security that
wealth brings to its owners, who know that their consumption can be sustained even
if income fluctuates. Most assets can be sold for cash or used as collateral for loans,
thus providing for unanticipated consumption needs. In times of economic stress,
occasioned by such crises as unemployment, sickness, or family breakup, wealth is
an important cushion. The very knowledge that wealth is at hand is a source of comfort for many families.

In the political arena, large fortunes can be a source of economic power and
social influence that is not directly captured in the measure of annual income. Large
accumulations of financial and business assets can confer special privileges on their
holders. Such fortunes are often transmitted to succeeding generations, thus creating family "dynasties.". . .

FIGURE 9.1   Share of Wealth Owned by the Top 1 Percent of Households in the United States, 1922–1998

Wealth inequality in the United States was at a seventy-year high in 1998 (the latest date available), with the top 1 percent of wealth holders controlling 38 percent of total household wealth. If we focus more narrowly, on financial wealth, the richest 1 percent of households owned 47 percent of the total. How did this come to pass? After the stock market crash of 1929, there ensued a gradual if somewhat erratic reduction in wealth inequality, which seems to have lasted until the late 1970s. Since then, inequality of wealth holdings, like that of income, has risen sharply (see Figure 9.1).[1] If Social Security and other types of pension wealth ("augmented wealth") are included, the improvement between 1929 and 1979 appears greater, but the increase in inequality since 1980 is still sharply in evidence.

The rise in wealth inequality from 1983 to 1998 (a period for which there is comparable detailed household survey information) is particularly striking. The share of the top 1 percent of wealth holders rose by 5 percent. The wealth of the bottom 40 percent showed an absolute decline. Almost all the absolute gains in real wealth accrued to the top 20 percent of wealth holders.

CHANGES IN AVERAGE WEALTH HOLDINGS

Look first at trends in real wealth over the period from 1962 to 1998 (all in 1998 dollars).[2] As Figure 9.2 shows, average wealth grew at a respectable pace from 1962 to 1983 and even faster from 1983 to 1989. By 1989, the average wealth of households was $244,000 (in 1998 dollars), almost two-thirds higher than in 1962. From 1989 to 1998, wealth grew more slowly. In fact, mean marketable wealth grew only about

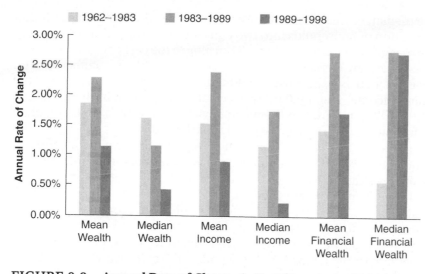

FIGURE 9.2 Annual Rate of Change in Real Income and Wealth 1962–1983, 1983–1989, and 1989–1998

Source: 1962, from the Survey of Financial Characteristics of Consumers; 1983, 1989, and 1998, from the Survey of Consumer Finances

half as fast between 1989 and 1998 as between 1983 and 1989 (1.2 percent per year versus 2.3 percent). Still, by 1998, average wealth had reached $270,000.

Average financial wealth grew faster than marketable wealth in the 1983–89 period (2.7 versus 2.3 percent per year), reflecting the increased importance of bank deposits, financial assets, equities, and small businesses in the overall household portfolio over this period. This reversed the relationship of the 1962–83 period, when financial wealth grew more slowly than marketable wealth (1.4 versus 1.8 percent per year). In the 1989–98 period, the gain in average financial wealth again outstripped net worth (1.7 versus 1.2 percent per year).

Average household income also grew faster in the 1983–89 period than in the 1962–83 period. Its annual growth accelerated from 1.5 percent to 2.4. Whereas in the first of the two periods, average income grew more slowly than average wealth (a difference of 0.3 percentage points per year), in the latter it grew slightly faster (a difference of 0.1 percentage points per year). However, in the 1989–98 period, income growth plummeted to 0.9 percent per year (0.2 percentage points per year lower than wealth growth).

The robust growth of average wealth disguises some changes in the distribution of that wealth. This becomes clear after examination of median rather than mean wealth. Mean wealth is simply the average: total wealth divided by total number of households. If the wealth of only the top 20 percent of households increases (with nothing else changing), then mean wealth increases because total wealth increases.[3]

In contrast, the median of wealth distribution is defined as the level of wealth that divides the population of households into two equal-sized groups (those with more wealth than the median and those with less). Returning to the earlier example, if only the top quintile enjoys an increase in wealth, median wealth is unaffected even though mean wealth increases, because all additional wealth accrues to people well above the median income. The median tracks what is happening in the middle of wealth distribution.[4] When trends in the mean deviate from trends in the median, this is a signal that gains and losses are unevenly distributed.

The trend in median household wealth in the United States gives a contrasting picture to the growth of mean wealth. Unlike mean marketable wealth, median marketable wealth grew faster in the 1962–83 period than in the 1983–89 period (1.6 percent versus 1.1 percent per year). Median wealth also grew much more slowly than mean wealth in the latter period (a difference of 0.8 percentage points per year). Overall, from 1983 to 1989, while mean wealth increased by 15 percent, median wealth grew by only 7 percent. The fact that mean wealth grew much faster than median wealth after 1983 implies that the bulk of the gains were concentrated at the top of the distribution—a finding that implies rising wealth inequality. The 1989–98 period was a repeat of the preceding one. While mean wealth grew by 11 percent, median wealth increased by only 4 percent.[5]

RISING WEALTH INEQUALITY IN THE 1980s

The rising level of wealth inequality between 1983 and 1989 is illustrated in Figure 9.3. The most telling finding is that the share of marketable net worth held by the top 1 percent, which had fallen 10 percentage points between 1945 and 1976, rose to 37 percent in 1989, compared with 34 percent in 1983. Meanwhile, the share of wealth held by the bottom 80 percent fell from 19 to 16 percent. Between 1989 and 1998, inequality continued to rise, though at a more moderate pace. The share of wealth held by the top 1 percent increased by another percentage point (to 38 percent), though the share of the bottom 80 percent stabilized.

These trends are mirrored in financial net worth, which is distributed even more unequally than total household wealth. In 1998, the top 1 percent of families as ranked by financial wealth owned 47 percent of the total (in contrast to 38 percent of total net worth). The top quintile accounted for 91 percent of total financial wealth, and the second quintile accounted for nearly all the remainder.

The concentration of financial wealth increased to the same degree as that of marketable wealth between 1983 and 1989. The share of the top 1 percent of financial wealth holders increased by 4 percentage points, from 43 to 47 percent of total financial wealth. The share of the next 19 percent fell from 48 to 46 percent, while that of the bottom 80 percent declined from 9 to 7 percent. Between 1989 and 1998, the share of total financial wealth of the top 1 percent increased a bit more (by 0.4 percentage points) but the share of the bottom 80 percent recovered to where it was in 1983.

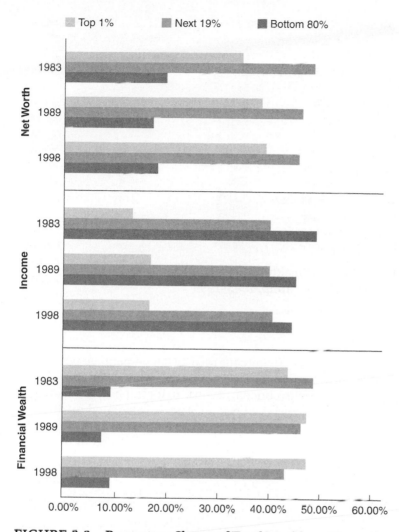

FIGURE 9.3   Percentage Shares of Total Wealth and Income of Percentile Groups in 1983, 1989, and 1998

Source: 1983 and 1989 Survey of Consumer Finances

Income distribution, too, became more concentrated between 1983 and 1989. As with wealth, most of the relative income gain accrued to the top 1 percent of recipients, whose share of total household income grew by 4 percentage points, from 13 to 17 percent.[6] The share of the next 19 percent remained unchanged at 39 percent. Almost all the (relative) loss in income was sustained by the bottom 80 percent of the income distribution, whose share fell from 48 to 44 percent. Between 1989 and 1998, income inequality increased a bit more. While the share of the top 1 percent

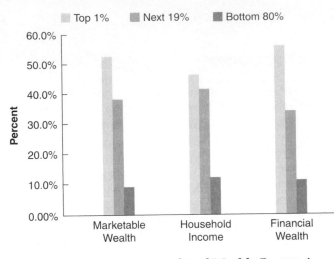

FIGURE 9.4   Percentage of Real Wealth (Income) Growth Accruing to Each Percentile Group, 1983–1998

Source: 1983 and 1998 Survey of Consumer Finances

remained stable, the share of the next 19 percent rose by 0.6 percentage points and that of the bottom 80 percent correspondingly fell by 0.6 percentage points.

Another way to view rising wealth concentration is to look at how the increases in total wealth were divided over a specified period. This is calculated by dividing the increase in wealth of each group by the total increase in household wealth.[7] The results for 1983–98, shown in Figure 9.4, indicate that the top 1 percent of wealth holders received 53 percent of the total gain in marketable wealth over the period. The next 19 percent received 38 percent, while the bottom 80 percent received only 9 percent. This pattern represents a distinct turnaround from the 1962–83 period, when every group enjoyed some share of the overall wealth growth and the gains were roughly in proportion to the share of wealth held by each in 1962. Over this period, the top 1 percent received 34 percent of the wealth gains, the next 19 percent claimed 48 percent, and the bottom 80 percent got 18 percent.

Gains in the overall growth in financial wealth were also distributed unevenly, with 56 percent of the growth accruing to the top 1 percent and 33 percent to the next 19 percent. The bottom 80 percent gained only 11 percent.

Finally, the changes in wealth distribution can be assessed by looking at the Gini coefficient. This indicator is used commonly to summarize data on the degree of inequality of income, wealth, or anything else of value. It ranges from 0 (exact equality) to 1 (one person owns everything); a higher Gini coefficient means greater inequality. This measure, like the others reviewed here, points to an increase in inequality: Between 1983 and 1989, the Gini coefficient increased from 0.80 to 0.84, between 1989 and 1998, the Gini coefficient remained at this high plateau.

TABLE 9.1   Number of Millionaires and Multimillionaires, 1983–1998 in 1,000s

Year	Total Number of Households	Number of Households with Net Worth Equal to or Exceeding[a]		
		$1,000,000	$5,000,000	$10,000,000
1983	83,893	2,411	247.0	66.5
1989	93,009	3,024	296.6	64.9
1992	95,462	3,104	277.4	41.6
1995	99,101	3,015	474.1	190.4
1998	102,547	4,783	755.5	239.4
Percent Change:				
1983–1989	10.9%	25.4%	20.1%	–2.4%
1989–1998	10.3%	58.2%	154.7%	269.1%

a. 1998 dollars.

Source: 1983, 1989, 1992, 1995, and 1998 Survey of Consumer Finances, Federal Reserve Board of Washington, D.C.

The increase in wealth inequality recorded over the 1983–98 period—particularly between 1983 and 1989—in the United States is almost unprecedented. The only other period in the twentieth century during which concentration of household wealth rose comparably was from 1922 to 1929. Then, inequality was buoyed primarily by the excessive increase in stock values, which eventually crashed in 1929, leading to the Great Depression of the 1930s.

Despite the seemingly modest increase in overall wealth inequality during the 1990s, the decade witnessed a near explosion in the number of very rich households (see Table 9.1). The number of millionaires climbed by 54 percent between 1989 and 1998, the number of "pentamillionaires" ($5,000,000 or more) more than doubled, and the number of "decamillionaires" ($10,000,000 or more) almost quadrupled. Much of the growth occurred between 1995 and 1998 and was directly related to the surge in stock prices. . . .

WHO HAS A STAKE IN THE STOCK MARKET?

There have been numerous reports in the media that stock ownership has substantially widened in the United States, particularly during the 1990s. There is some truth to these reports. The proportion of households owning some stock either outright or indirectly through mutual funds, trusts, or various pension accounts increased from 24.4 percent in 1983 to 48.2 percent in 1998 (see Table 9.2). Much of the increase was fueled by the growth in pension accounts like IRAs, Keogh plans,

TABLE 9.2   Percent of Households Owning Stock Directly or Indirectly, 1983–1989

	1983	1989	1992	1995	1998
Any stock holdings	24.4	31.7	37.2	40.4	48.2
Stock worth $5,000 or more[a]	14.5	22.6	27.3	29.5	36.3
Stock worth $10,000 or more[a]	10.8	18.5	21.8	23.9	31.8

a. 1998 dollars.

Source: 1983, 1989, 1992, 1995, and 1998 Survey of Consumer Finances, Federal Reserve Board of Washington, D.C. Figures include direct ownership of stock shares and indirect ownership through mutual funds, trusts, and IRAs, Keogh plans, 401(k) plans, and other retirement accounts.

and 401(k) plans. Indeed, between 1983 and 1989, direct stock ownership declined somewhat (from 13.7 to 13.1 percent)—likely a result of the 1987 stock market plunge. However, the share of households with pension accounts nearly doubled over this period, from 11 to 23 percent, accounting for the overall increase in stock ownership. Between 1989 and 1998, the direct ownership of stocks grew rather modestly, by 6 percentage points, while the share of households with a pension account again doubled, accounting for the bulk of the overall increase in stock ownership.

Despite the overall gains in stock ownership, less than half of all households had any stake in the stock market by 1998. Moreover, many of these families had only a minor stake. In 1998, while 48 percent of households owned some stock, only 36 percent had total stock holdings worth $5,000 or more and only 32 percent owned $10,000 or more of stock.

Stock ownership is also highly skewed by wealth and income class. As shown in Table 9.3, 93 percent of the very rich (the top 1 percent) reported owning stock either directly or indirectly in 1998, compared to 46 percent of the middle quintile and 19 percent of the poorest 20 percent. While over 91 percent of the very rich also reported stocks worth $10,000 or more, only 26 percent of the middle quintile and less than 2 percent of the bottom quintile did so. The top 1 percent of households owned 42 percent of all stocks, the top 5 percent two-thirds, the top 10 percent almost 80 percent, and the top quintile almost 90 percent.

Stock ownership also tails off by income class (see bottom panel of Table 9.3). Whereas 93 percent of households in the top income class (those who earned $250,000 or more) owned stock in 1998, 52 percent of the middle class (income between $25,000 and $50,000), 29 percent of the lower middle class (income between $15,000 and $25,000), and only 11 percent of poor households (income under $15,000) reported stock ownership. The comparable ownership figures for stock holdings of $10,000 or more are 92 percent for the top 1 percent, 27 percent for the middle class, 13 percent for the lower middle class, and 5 percent for the poor. Moreover, about three-quarters of all stocks were owned by the top 16 percent of house-

TABLE 9.3   Concentration of Stock Ownership by Wealth and Income Class, 1998

Category	Percent of Households Owning Stock Worth More Than			Percent of Stock Owned	
	$0	$4,999	$9,999	Shares	Cumulative
Wealth Class					
Top 1 percent	93.2	92.9	91.2	42.1	42.1
Next 4 percent	89.0	87.0	86.1	25.0	67.2
Next 5 percent	83.9	80.4	78.9	10.6	77.7
Next 10 percent	78.7	74.0	71.6	11.1	88.8
Second quintile	58.9	49.8	45.4	7.7	96.5
Third quintile	45.8	32.7	25.9	2.6	99.1
Fourth quintile	35.1	15.1	8.6	0.7	99.8
Bottom quintile	18.6	4.6	1.8	0.2	100.0
All	48.2	36.3	31.8	100.0	
Income Level					
$250,000 or more	93.3	92.7	91.9	36.1	36.1
$100,000–$249,999	89.0	85.5	82.8	27.7	63.9
$75,000–$99,999	80.7	70.4	66.5	10.8	74.7
$50,000–$74,999	70.9	55.6	48.8	13.1	87.8
$25,000–$49,999	52.0	34.3	27.4	8.5	96.3
$15,000–$24,999	29.2	16.9	12.9	2.6	98.9
Under $15,000	10.6	5.2	4.5	1.1	100.0
All	48.2	36.3	31.8	100.0	

Figures include direct ownership of stock shares and indirect ownership through mutual funds, trusts, IRAs, Keogh plans, 401(k) plans, and other retirement accounts.

Source: 1998 Survey of Consumer Finances, Federal Reserve Board of Washington, D.C.

holds (those earning $75,000 or more) and 88 percent were owned by the top third of households (by income).

Thus, in terms of wealth or income, substantial stock holdings have still not penetrated much beyond the reach of the rich and the upper middle class. The big winners from the stock market boom of the last few years have been these groups, while the middle class and the poor have not seen sizable benefits from the bull market. It is also apparent, therefore, which groups benefit from the preferential tax treatment of capital gains.

Editors' Note: *Notes for this reading can be found in the original source.*

CHAPTER 10

Doing Poorly

The Real Income of American Children in a Comparative Perspective

LEE RAINWATER

TIMOTHY M. SMEEDING

INTRODUCTION

Both poverty and inequality have increased in the United States since the late 1970s, particularly among families with children. By the official standard United States child poverty has risen steadily since the 1960s and has continued to rise in the 1990s. The question is whether these most recent increases in child poverty have been endemic in the rest of the industrial economies or whether they are unique to the United States. Cross-national comparisons of economic well-being are useful for learning how one nation is alike or different from other comparable nations, because countries which face similar economic and demographic issues may use different policy instruments to address these issues and may have very different outcomes. . . .

This paper compares the economic well-being of children in the 1980s and 1990s in 18 countries: 14 in Europe (Austria, Belgium, Denmark, Finland, France, Germany, Ireland, Italy, Luxembourg, Netherlands, Norway, Sweden, Switzerland, and the United Kingdom) and four elsewhere (Australia, Canada, Israel, and the

United States). The analysis is based on the Luxembourg Income Study (LIS) database (Smeeding, Rainwater and O'Higgns, 1990; LIS Users Guide, 1995). . . .

We compare the real spendable (disposable) incomes of well-off, average, and low income children in the United States with comparably situated children in 17 other nations. The average American child in a four person family in 1991 had a family income of $34,675.

In fact, American children who are in families in the upper 20 percent of the income distribution do very well indeed. They have much higher standards of living as measured by real spendable income than do similarly situated children in all countries, with only Switzerland and Canada being within 20 percent of the United States level. Scandinavia—e.g., Denmark, Sweden—has high-income children who live in families with three-quarters the income of the average American child. The only nations whose "rich" children live in households with incomes which are less than 60 percent of that found in the United States are Israeli and Irish children. Given that Israel and Ireland have, by far, the lowest overall real standards of living of the nations observed here, this is to be expected.

Focusing on children in the middle 20 percent we find that only in Denmark and in Canada are children as well off as are American children, although Swedish and Swiss children are almost as well off. The average child in Belgium, Germany, Norway, and Finland is only 90 percent as well off, and 80 percent or less as well off in countries like Austria, Italy, France. On the other hand, in only three countries is the average child less than three-quarters as well-off as in the United States—the United Kingdom at 72 percent, Israel at 52 percent, and Ireland at 43 percent.

At the lower end of the distribution we find a very different and surprising picture. Both national (U.S. Bureau of the Census, 1995) and international evidence suggests that the poverty rate of United States children is in the neighborhood of 20 percent. We compare the real spendable incomes of the typical poor American child—the one at the median of the bottom 10 percent—with that of comparable low-income children in other countries in Figure 10.1. We immediately see that in six countries low-income children have real standards of living at least 50 percent higher than in the United States—Switzerland, Sweden, Finland, Denmark, Belgium, and Norway. And in four other countries (Germany, Luxembourg, Netherlands, and Austria) low-income children are at least 30 percent better off than in the United States. Only in Israel and Ireland—the two nations with the lowest GDP per capita of those studied—do low-income children have a lower real standard of living than do children in the United States.

In other words, while the United States has a higher real level of income than most of our comparison countries it is the high- and middle-income children who reap the benefits (and much more the former than the latter). Low-income American children suffer in both absolute and relative terms. The average low-income child in the other 17 countries is at least one-third better off than is the average low-income American child.

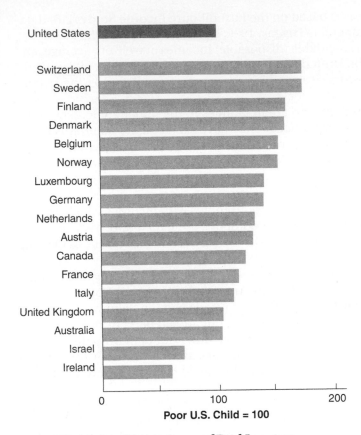

**FIGURE 10.1   Comparisons of Real Income:
Children in the Poorest Households**

Notes: Based on Table 10.1, Column 4. See note to Table 10.1 for explanation.

Source: Luxembourg Income Study.

EVIDENCE ON CHILD POVERTY: LEVEL AND TREND

We shift now to measures of relative income within each country to examine both the level and trend in child poverty across the 18 developed nations for which we have data. . . .

Child poverty rates throughout Western Europe are below 10 percent, with the exception of 12.0 percent in Ireland, also the poorest nation in real terms of the Western European nations observed here. And in the other Western nations, most recent child poverty rates range from 11.1 percent in Israel to 14.0 percent in Australia. Clearly the United States rate of 21.5 percent stands out as the largest percentage of children in poverty among the nations observed here (Figure 10.2).

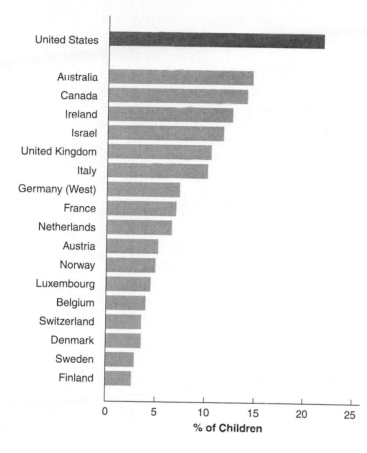

FIGURE 10.2   Child Poverty Rates in 18 Countries[a,b]

[a]Poverty is defined as percent of children living in families with adjusted disposable incomes less than 50 percent of adjusted median income for all persons. Income includes all transfers and tax benefits.

[b]Year for each estimate is most recent year in Table 10.1.

Trend

The 1980s was not a period in which the relative economic well-being of children in any of these countries was greatly improved. In two countries, there are hints of improvement from the 1970s through the 1980s to the 1990s (see Canada and Sweden in Table 10.1). But overall we have a picture of either stability or deterioration in the children's economic well-being. In the United States, Israel, and the United Kingdom there is a clear trend toward a worsening situation for children, though the most recent poverty rate for the United States suggests a leveling off of the previous increases. The 1990s results for Israel and the United Kingdom are not yet available.

TABLE 10.1   Level and Trend in Child Poverty Rates:[a] 1967–1992

Nation	Year of Survey	Period 1 <1971	Period 2 1972–1975	Period 3 1976–1981	Period 4 1982–1985	Period 5 1986–1988	Period 6 1989–
A. United States	69, 74, 79, 86, 91	13.1	17.3	18.5		22.9	21.5
B. West Europe:							
Austria	87					4.8	3.8
Belgium	85, 88, 92				3.4	3.1	2.5
Finland	87, 91					2.9	3.3
Denmark	87, 92					5.3	
France	79, 84			6.3	6.5		
Germany (West)	73, 78, 83/84, 89[b]		4.0	3.2	4.8/6.4	12.0	6.8
Ireland	87					10.8	9.6
Italy	86, 91					3.6	/6.2
Luxembourg	85				4.1		
The Netherlands	83, 87/91[c]				2.5	3.8	4.6
Norway	79, 86, 91			3.8		3.0	2.7
Sweden	67, 75, 81, 87, 92	3.5	1.9	3.9			
Switzerland	82				3.3		
United Kingdom	69, 74, 79, 86	5.3	7.0	8.5		9.9	
C. Other:							
Australia	82, 86, 90				13.1	13.6	14.0
Canada	71, 75, 81, 87, 91	15.2	14.6	13.9		11.1	13.5
Israel	79, 86			8.2			

[a] poverty is defined as percentage of children living in households with adjusted disposable minus less than 50 percent of median adjusted disposable income for all persons. Income includes all transfers and tax benefits.

[b] The slash (/) for Germany indicates that the German survey for 1973–1983 is different from that for 1984 and 1989, hence one cannot derive overall trend estimates from 1973 through 1989 from these figures.

[c] The slash (/) for The Netherlands indicates that the survey for 1983 and 1987 differs from the 1991 survey, hence one cannot derive trend estimates for 1983–1991 from these figures.

Source: Luxembourg Income Study.

Over an 18 year period, from 1969 to 1986, the child poverty rate increased from 5.3 percent to 9.9 percent in the United Kingdom and in the United States from 13.1 percent to 22.9 percent, before falling to 21.5 percent in 1991. In Israel, too, there was a deterioration during the first half of the 1980s. All of the Scandinavian countries have been able to keep child poverty below five percent, and many other European nations keep it in the 5 to 6 percent range over the 1980s and into the 1990s.

It needs to be emphasized that levels and trends in child poverty rates do not supply mirror levels and changes in overall income inequality in these nations. While the United States has the highest level of inequality among the nations observed here, Switzerland ranks third in overall inequality but very low in terms of child poverty (Gottschalk and Smeeding, 1995, Figure 3). And while patterns of increasing income inequality in the United States and in the United Kingdom are correlated with their rising child poverty rates over the longer term, the timing of increases in each nation are quite different. Inequality in the United States has continued to increase from the middle 1980s through the 1990s while child poverty has remained constant or has fallen slightly by our measure over this same period. Many nations observed here have sustained large increases in income inequality during the 1980s with no change in poverty, e.g., Sweden and Austria (Gottschalk and Smeeding, 1995, Tables 5 and 6). . . .

Differences between Two-Parent and Solo-Mother Families

A child's chance of being poor in the United States differs dramatically depending on whether he or she lives in a one- or two-parent family (Table 10.2). A child in a two-parent United States family has only about an 11 percent chance of being poor as compared to a 60 percent chance if the child lives with a lone parent who is a mother. In fact, in all countries studied, one's chance of being poor in a one-parent mother family is much higher than in two-parent families.

Because so few children in most countries live in solo-mother families the difference across countries in the percent of children living in solo-mother families has little to do with the difference in total child poverty rates. Only in the cases of Australia, Canada, and the United States would total poverty rates be noticeably lower if the proportion of solo-mother families was the average for these 17 countries. In other counties with greater than 10 percent of children in solo-mother families (Denmark, Norway, Sweden, United Kingdom), the poverty rates for single parent children are close enough to couples rates to not make a great deal of difference in the overall poverty rate. And demography is clearly not destiny; children in solo-mother families in Denmark, Finland (7 percent poverty rate), and Sweden (5 percent poverty rate) do better than children in two-parent families in many of the nations studied.

Comparing the poverty rates of children in two-parent families and in solo-mother families we note a group of countries with very low rates for both types— Sweden, Finland, Belgium, Denmark, and Luxembourg. Another group has child poverty rates in solo-mother families between roughly 20 and 40 percent but covers

TABLE 10.2   Poverty Rates for Children by Family Type[a]

Country (Year)	All Children	Children in Two-Parent Family[b]	Children in Single Parent/Solo Mother Family[c]	Percent of Children in Solo Mother Families[c,d]
United States (91)	21.5	11.1	59.5	21.2
Australia (90)	14.0	7.7	56.2	12.4
Belgium (92)	3.8	3.2	10.0	8.1
Canada (91)	13.5	7.4	50.2	13.4
Denmark (91)	3.3	2.5	7.3	14.3
Finland (91)	2.5	1.9	7.5	9.5
France (84)	6.5	5.4	22.6	6.5
Germany (89)	6.8	2.9	42.7	9.9
Ireland (97)	12.0	10.5	40.5	5.3
Israel (86)	11.1	10.3	27.5	5.1
Italy (91)	9.6	9.5	13.9	4.4
Luxembourg (85)	4.1	3.6	10.0	6.8
The Netherlands (91)	6.2	3.1	39.5	8.4
Norway (91)	4.6	1.9	18.4	15.4
Sweden (92)	2.7	2.2	5.2	14.6
Switzerland (82)	3.3	1.0	25.6	6.9
United Kingdom (86)	9.9	8.4	18.7	13.0

[a]Poverty is defined as in Table 10.1.

[b]Child poverty rates in two-parent families are for those children living in situations where there are only two adults who are married, or are living together as married.

[c]Single parent/solo-mother families are children living in those situations where one female adult resides in the household. Other adults (e.g., older children) may also occupy the residence.

[d]Because some children live in other types of situations, e.g., in multiple family unit households or in lone-father units, the weighted averages of children in solo-mother and two-parent households do not add to the "all children" total.

Source: Luxembourg Income Study database.

a wide range of rates in two-parent families—Germany, Switzerland, and Norway have quite low two-parent rates. France has a middling rate and Israel, Italy, and the United Kingdom higher rates for children in two-parent households.

The combination of difference in the poverty rates of children in two-parent compared to solo-mother families and the smaller differences in the percentage of children who live in solo-mother families has an important effect on the family type composition of the poor. In five countries more than half of poor children live in solo-mother families—the United States, Australia, Germany, Switzerland, and Norway with Canada coming close at around 40 percent. At the other extreme, fewer than 15 percent of poor children are in solo-mother families in the Netherlands, Belgium, Italy, and Israel. Children in solo-mother families make up between 15 and 30 percent of the poor in Luxembourg, Ireland, France, the United Kingdom, and Sweden. Thus, the rate of feminization of poverty varies dramatically across these countries based on both the poverty rate for children in single parent units and on the percentage of children living in each type of unit.

In summary, 1 of every 8 American children is a poor child living with a solo mother. Fewer than 1 in 100 children are in the same situation in Sweden, the Netherlands, Luxembourg, Italy, Finland, and Belgium. In the United States 1 of every 10 children is a poor child living in a two-parent family and this ratio is not too different in three other countries—Ireland, Israel, and Italy. In contrast the ratio is about 1 in 50 in Finland, Germany, Norway, Sweden, and Switzerland.

The results of this paper are striking. United States low-income children have a lower real standard of living than do their counterparts in almost every other nation studied. . . .

In contrast to our low-income children, our high-income children are better off than their counterparts in every nation studied. The wide variance in child well-being found in the United States mirrors the high level of overall income inequality in our nation. This pattern is not found in other nations. While their inequality is less than in the United States, children living in families at the bottom of the distribution enjoy living standards which are significantly above those found for similar children in the United States, even in nations where overall income inequality has increased during the 1980s. . . .

CONCLUSION

All nations begin with the issue of preventing severe poverty and disadvantage for at-risk children. The major difference we note is that other nations are able to produce lower levels of child poverty than in the United States. It follows that child poverty is neither intractable nor intransigent. The United States had an elder poverty problem in 1970 which it markedly reduced through increased social security spending and greater efforts on the part of the aged to save and invest. It now has a child poverty problem which produces an intolerably low real standard of living for a large number of American children. Our high-income children do very well in real terms compared to similar children in other nations. No one wants to take away these advantages for which the parents of these children work long and hard. What is needed is a reasonable response to the real needs of low-income American children. And as other nations have shown, there is an answer that we can find if we have the national will to face up to the sobering facts presented in this paper.

Editors' Note: *Notes for this reading can be found in the original source.*

CHAPTER 11

Day by Day

The Lives of Homeless Women

ELLIOT LIEBOW

On the street or in a shelter, homelessness is hard living. At first sight, one wonders why more homeless people do not kill themselves. How do they manage to slog through day after day, with no end in sight? How, in a world of unremitting grimness, do they manage to laugh, love, enjoy friends, even dance and play the fool? How, in short, do they stay fully human while body and soul are under continuous and grievous assault?

Simple physical survival is within the grasp of almost everyone willing and able to reach out for it.[1] As the women thrash about, awash in a sea of need, emergency shelters, along with public assistance in the form of cash, food stamps, and medical assistance, make it just possible for many of the women to keep their heads above water. Through the use of shelters, soup kitchens, and hospital emergency rooms, it is even possible for most homeless people who do not get public assistance to survive at some minimal level without benefit of a structured assistance program.

At their very best, however, these bare-boned elements of a life-support system merely make life possible, not necessarily tolerable or livable. Serious problems remain. Homelessness can transform what for others are little things into insurmountable hurdles. Indeed, homelessness in general puts a premium on "little things." Just as some homeless women seem to have learned (more than most of us, perhaps) to value a small gesture of friendship, a nice day, a bus token, or a little courtesy that others might take for granted or not notice at all, so too can events or circumstances that would be trivial irritants to others approach catastrophic proportions for the homeless person.[2]

For homeless women on the street, the struggle for subsistence begins at the animal level—for food, water, shelter, security, and safe sleep.[3] In contrast, homeless women in shelters usually have these things; their struggle begins at the level of human rather than animal needs—protection of one's property, health care, and avoidance of boredom. The struggle then moves rapidly to the search for companionship, modest measures of independence, dignity, and self-respect, and some hope and faith in the future. These needs are not particularly sequential or hierarchical. One can just as easily be immobilized by hopelessness and despair as by hunger and cold. Body and soul are equally in need of nurture and the women must grab whatever they can get when they can get it.[4]

* * *

For some of the women, day-by-day hardships began with the problem of getting enough sleep. A few women complained they could never get any sleep in a shelter. Grace was one of them. "There's no getting sleep in a shelter," she said. "Only rest."

There was indeed much night noise and movement. There was snoring, coughing, sneezing, wheezing, retching, farting, cries from bad dreams, occasional weeping or seizures, talking aloud to oneself or to someone else who may or may not have been present, and always movement to and from the bathroom. Grace was complaining about noise, and she found a partial remedy in ear plugs. But ear plugs could not help those women like Kathleen who were kept awake not by noise but by questions: Is this it for me? How did I end up here? How will I get out? But eventually, as the night wore on, there was a lot of snoring, and that meant that, Grace and Kathleen notwithstanding, there was a lot of sleeping, too.

Having to get up at 5:30 A.M. and be out of the shelter by 7:00 was a major hardship of shelter life. It was not simply the fact of having to get up and out, but rather that the women had to do this every day of the week, every day of the year (Thanksgiving and Christmas Day excepted), no matter what the weather or how they felt. On any given morning, as the women drifted onto the street, one might see two or three ailing women—this one with a fever or cough or headache, that one with a limp or stomach ache or other ailment—pick up their bags and walk silently into the weather.

The women especially missed Saturday and Sunday mornings, which looked just like Tuesday and Wednesday mornings. The occasional opportunity to stay in bed an extra hour or two was desperately missed. Not being able to sleep in, ever, especially on a weekend, was seen by many as a major deprivation that unfairly set them apart from the rest of the world. At 7:15, on a Sunday morning in the park, several women were looking for benches that offered some protection from the wind. The streets were empty of cars and people and the rest of the world seemed to be asleep. The women talked about how nice it would be to sleep in just one morning, just for the hell of it, or because you don't feel well, and how nice it would be to have *a* place—not even your own place, just a place—where you could go and lie down for a while without having anyone else around telling you to do this or do that.

One bitterly cold Sunday morning Betty announced she was going to the mayor's office the next day to tell him what it was like to live in a shelter and to ask him to order the county-funded shelters to allow people to remain there on Sundays, sleeping, resting, doing their nails or hair, watching TV, or whatever. "Everyone is entitled to a day of rest," she said. "Even homeless women." The women within ear-shot nodded agreement.

Some of the working women took motel rooms on weekends once or twice a month. Jane regularly disappeared on weekends. "She went to a motel for the weekend so she could sleep in," Judy explained to one of the women who asked about her. Samantha, who was working regularly, used the shelter for eating, washing, and socializing, but when the lights went out on Friday and Saturday nights, she left the shelter to sleep in a car so she could sleep late Saturday and Sunday mornings.

When Vicki learned she would be able to move into her own place in 10 days or so, she talked about her shelter experience as if it were already in the past. The hardest part of living in a shelter, she said, was having to get up every morning, no matter how you felt. The next worse thing was having to go out on the street and kill time—really kill time—until the shelter reopened in the evening.

* * *

Along with perennial fatigue, boredom was one of the great trials of homelessness. Killing time was not a major problem for everyone but it was high on most women's lists of hardships.* Betty could have been speaking for most of them when she talked about the problem. On a social visit to the state psychiatric hospital where, four years earlier, she had been an inpatient in an alcoholic program, Betty sought out a nurse named Lou. They embraced and Lou asked Betty what she was doing these days. Betty said she was living in a shelter. Lou said that was a shame, and asked Betty how she spent her time.

"I walk the streets," said Betty. "Twelve hours and 15 minutes a day, every day, I walk the streets. Is that what I got sober for? To walk the streets?" Betty went on to say that she sits on a lot of park benches looking for someone to talk to. Many times there is no one, so she talks to the birds. She and the birds have done a lot of talking in her day, she said.

Months later, Betty repeated much of this at her SSI (Supplemental Security Income) hearing. She told the hearing officer about being homeless and sleeping in the night shelter. He asked what her biggest problem was, and Betty said it was staying on the street for 12 hours and 15 minutes every day. She told him about the public library and park benches and the birds. Staying awake with nothing to do was a special problem, she added. You are not permitted to sleep in the library, she said, and she didn't dare fall asleep on a park bench for fear that someone would steal her bags or that a policeman would arrest her for vagrancy.

Some of the women with jobs also had trouble killing time. Like the others, Grace had to leave the shelter by 7:00 A.M. but she couldn't report to work much be-

---

*DIRECTOR: This world is a place for productive people. The idea of killing time, day after day, was an alien concept to the vigorous, enthusiastic staff. The Refuge volunteers would regularly suggest a plan of action which in a rational world would begin to solve a woman's problems. These solutions were offered with little understanding of the complexity of these women's lives.

fore 9:00, and her job was less than a 10-minute drive away. "Have you ever tried to kill two hours in the morning, every morning, with nowhere to go and nothing to do?" she asked. "I have some tapes I can listen to in the car—some Christmas carols and some Bible readings. But two hours? Every day?"

For Sara, leaving the shelter in the morning was by far the worst time of day. That was when being homeless hit her the hardest. You can't decide what to do because it doesn't matter what you do. You're not needed anywhere, not wanted anywhere, and not expected anywhere. Nobody cares what you do.

"I can't go on, walking the streets all day and coming here at night," announced Elsie one evening. "It's not my style. It's just not my style." Some women were better than others at finding relief in a book or TV program or jigsaw puzzle at the day shelter, or in conversation with others, but relief was typically short-lived. Sleeping may also have been tried as a remedy. In the parks, the lobbies of public buildings, and the day shelters, the women did a lot of sleeping. Some of this may have been because they did not sleep well at night, or because of medication, or depression perhaps, but some of it was also a way of killing time, a way of getting through the nothing-to-do present until it was time to do something—go to the soup kitchen, show up for a clinic appointment, or return to the night shelter.

Other kinds of behavior were also aimed at killing time or making it more bearable. Many of the women, for example, regularly appeared at the night shelter or the day shelter or the soup kitchen long before they opened, even when there were no lines to give advantage to early arrivals. It was as if the rush to get to the next "event" was a way of moving from a do-nothing to a do-something state.

For much the same reasons, the women might talk about and plan for an appointment with a doctor or a caseworker that was still several days away. In part, this may have been simply a matter of paying attention to what was most important to them at the moment, but this early anticipation may have also served to bring the event prematurely into present time, thereby giving the otherwise boring and undifferentiated present some sort of focus and direction.

Sometimes the women also made what looked like a deliberate effort to take apart a group of tasks and stretch them out over several days. At any given time, for example, a woman might need to make an appointment with a caseworker, visit a clinic, see a housing office representative, go to the unemployment office, or attend to some personal business. Any two of these tasks could normally be done in a day, one in the morning and one in the afternoon, and three in one day was not always out of the question.

Having a task to do, however, was a precious resource that gave point and structure to the day when it had to be done. To do two or three tasks on the same day would be a waste of resources, so the women often seemed to go out of their way to stretch their tasks over several days.* Thus, what often seemed to be procrastination or laziness or exasperating inefficiency to those looking in from the outside

---

*KIM: I think this is overstated. Service providers are spread out all over the county. It can take several bus transfers to reach Point B. Bus stop waits and waits in line add up to many hours. Filling out applications everywhere adds up to more. Particularly when dealing with Social Services, a great deal of time is wasted on the way to brick walls and dead ends.

may well have been, from the women's point of view, an attempt to distribute structure and meaning over as many days as possible.[5]

* * *

It is all too easy to think of homeless people as having few or no possessions ("How could a homeless person have anything of value?" sneered Kim), but one of the major and most talked-about problems was storage—how to keep one's clothing, essential documents, and other belongings secure and accessible. The preservation and protection of belongings could be a major consumer of one's time, energy, and resources. A principal difficulty was the fact that most emergency shelters had only limited space for individual storage—often space for only two bags or two small cardboard boxes.* And it was not uncommon to find shelters where one could not store anything at all.[6] Even where limited storage space was available, many women were reluctant to use it because there was no guarantee that their belongings would be intact when they returned. Stealing was believed to be common: "You've got to expect these things in shelters" was heard from staff and women alike. The end result was that many homeless women who would have left their belongings behind had they had a safe place to store them were forced to take most of their belongings with them. Some wore them in layers. Others carried them. They had become, in short, bag ladies.[7]

During a discussion of Luther Place, one of the best-run shelters in downtown Washington, one of the women said Luther Place was OK but she didn't like the women there—they were all bag ladies. One of the other women objected that the women at Luther Place were no different from women in other shelters. They were bag ladies, she said, because Luther Place had no storage space.

With some important exceptions, how much "stuff" one had was inversely proportional to the length of time one had been homeless. The longer a woman had been homeless, the more likely it was that she had had to jettison belongings, often stripping down to just what she could carry. For most women, this stripping-down process was a painful exercise in triage. Much of what they carried around in bags, boxes, or suitcases was clothing. Sometimes there was an emergency food ration. Along with toilet articles, some cosmetics, maybe a can opener, a bottle of aspirin or Tylenol or a prescription drug, almost everyone carried a birth certificate, pocket-size ID, varieties of legal documents or official papers, and perhaps some rent receipts or W-2's.

More important, however, were the other, more personal things. Often there were snapshots or framed photographs of children or other family members, personal letters, a color picture of Jesus, a Bible, and other religious and inspirational reading material. There may also have been a teddy bear or a bronzed baby shoe, a

---

*DIRECTOR: Without question, dealing with the "stuff" of these women was a great source of consternation. There was absolutely no room for the women's personal belongings. There was also an underlying concern that the belongings were a health hazard: some bags were filled with old food and insects.

swizzle stick perhaps, or a matchbook cover, and some objects that looked like nothing more than a rag, a bone, a hank of hair, but which were, in fact, tokens of some treasured secret.

Given the contents of their bags, boxes, and suitcases, it is not surprising that the women were fiercely protective and possessive of them, sometimes to the patronizing amusement of outsiders. The importance of clothing and toiletries is self-evident. Moreover, the women had to carry proof of their social existence with them. Without a home address, telephone number, or job as testimony to their existence, they needed their birth certificates and other documents to prove that they existed as legal persons with rights to assert and claims to make on society.

Many of the personal things—the letters, the religious materials, the photographs, and the mementos of people, relationships, and experiences—looked back to earlier, presumably happier times. In effect, the women carried their life histories with them. To lose one's stuff, or to have to jettison some of it, was to lose connections to one's past if not the past itself. Thus, for women who had only the one or two slender boxes they may have been allowed to store in the shelter, along with what they may have carried with them, their more personal belongings tended to be strongly oriented toward the past.[8]

Many other women, however, mainly recent arrivals to homelessness or those with a car or other resources, often had far more belongings than they could carry or store in the shelters. These belongings were typically stored in their cars, public storage warehouses, a church basement, a fellow Alcoholics Anonymous member's garage, or even a garage or attic in the house of a friend or relative.

Most of the time, these nonportable possessions looked forward, not backward. They were things that were being saved for the future rather than remembrances of things past. Here, in the automobiles and the public and private storage spaces, the women kept not only clothing but pots and pans and linens and silverware, lamps and chairs, hat boxes and electric typewriters, and sometimes rugs and other heavy, major household furnishings as well. Sara regularly visited her storage unit to fondle her carefully wrapped crystal and linens. "That sustains her," said Samantha.

Clearly, the main value of these furnishings lay not in sentiment but in the hope, if not the prospect, that they would all be needed tomorrow or next week or next month when the woman would once again set up housekeeping in her own place. So long as she continued to own pots and pans and linens and things, she could remain, in her own mind at least, a temporarily dispossessed homemaker whose return to homemaking was imminent. For the woman who had to give up these furnishings, however, the prospect of returning to homemaking receded into uncertainty and she was plunged deeper into the reality of homelessness.

Past and future, then, and even one's self, were embedded in one's belongings. When Louise could no longer pay for storage and lost her belongings to auction, she was surprised at her own reaction to the loss. Her belongings had been so much a part of her, she said, that now that she's lost them, she's not sure who she is.[9]

Great sacrifices were made to store belongings, and the ever-present threat of losing them was a major source of anxiety and stress. The smallest and cheapest spaces in public storage warehouses were 5' × 5' and rented for $37.50 to $42.50 a month, which meant that some of the women on public assistance spent about 25 percent of their income for storage alone. Others spent much more. During her first couple of years of homelessness, while she still had money from her divorce settlement (her share of the proceeds from sale of the house), Louise paid $156 a month to store her household goods. Kim maintained a storage space in her hometown as well as one in the shelter area. Together, these cost her about $90 a month.

For many women, it was much too easy to fall behind in storage payments, and the penalties built up quickly. The "late charge," invoked one day after the monthly due date, was $10. After 10 days, management put their own lock on the storage bin, denying access to the renter until all due monies had been paid. After 30 days, the stored contents were subject to public auction.

Fierce attachment to belongings meant that many women, storing their things on a month-to-month basis and not knowing how long they would have to continue, ended up making monthly storage payments that totaled many times the original or replacement cost of what was stored. Shirley's experience was a case in point. Shirley had been behind in her storage payments for several months but had managed to stave off the loss of her things to public auction each month by last-minute fund-raising heroics. Eventually, however, she missed another deadline. Suspecting that the auction hammer had come down on the contents of her locker, Shirley and I drove to the storage facility. Yes, the auction had been held, the manager told her, but her stuff was still recoverable because no one had seen fit to bid even $5 for the contents of her $42.50-per-month locker. Shirley was dismayed. This news was probably worse than learning that someone had bought them. "The footlocker alone is worth $50," she protested. "And the chair. Isn't that a nice chair?"

To lighten the financial burden, two or even three women sometimes shared a space, but in a 5' × 5' area, the only way to accommodate additional items was to pile them ever higher. This made for a variety of storage and retrieval problems requiring a strenuous and time-consuming reorganization for each use, especially if—as when June and Peggy doubled up—big or fragile items were involved (a sofa up on end, an old, heavy IBM Selectric typewriter, several lamps, a rug, books, dishes, and more).

So important was secure and adequate storage that women sometimes allowed it to be a determining factor in important life choices. Kim turned down a new job at a much higher salary because her current job allowed her to store her belongings in a locked attic at her place of employment. The higher salary would have more than covered the cost of public storage, but Kim decided the extra money was not worth the loss of convenience and easy access to belongings stored on the job. Elsie planned to prepay six months storage costs when she thought (incorrectly) that she was getting an $800 income tax refund.

Jeanette stored her household furnishings in her 1974 Datsun B-210 station wagon. The car broke down and was towed away by police before Jeanette could assemble the money to repair it. Distraught, Jeanette traced the car to the county's Abandoned Auto Lot. We drove there to salvage some of her smaller, more valued possessions. The lot attendant told Jeanette that the next auction would be the following Friday and that she could probably buy back her car (and everything in it) for

$25 or so, the going rate for junk autos. Successful bidders, he told her, would have three days in which to remove their purchases from the lot.

But Jeanette's station wagon had three flat tires, a dead battery, dead license plates, and surely a string of invisible problems as well. The cost of repurchasing the car, having it towed off the lot, and making even minimal repairs would be many times the value of the car, but Jeanette was determined to buy it back. Not for transportation, she explained, but as the only way she could retrieve and afford to keep her belongings. For her, the car had become, purely and simply, a storeroom.[10]

ENDNOTES

1. "Almost" is crucial because the issue is life and death. Some homeless people are killed by hopelessness. Some die quietly and others die violent deaths. Some die from untreated disease or injury, some freeze to death, and still others lose digits or limbs. Here is the sworn testimony of a doctor who treated homeless patients in several Washington, D.C., shelters: "During the winter of 1987/1988, I have personal knowledge that approximately 30 homeless persons . . . had one or more fingers, toes, feet, or legs amputated as a result of gangrene following frostbite. . . . I have been informed that during the winter of 1987/1988, at least 10 homeless persons froze to death." Janelle Goetcheus, MD, *Affidavit (W) in Support of Plaintiff's Memorandum*. . . .

In mild-wintered San Francisco in 1988, the death rate for homeless persons was 58% higher than that for the general population. National Coalition for the Homeless, *Safety Network* 8, no. 2 (February 1989), p. 1.

2. It was from the women that I learned to juxtapose good little things and bad little things in this way. It puts "little things" in a fresh perspective and supports Otto Jesperson's observation that the world is made up of little things; what is important is to see them largely. Cited by Geoffrey K. Pullum, *The Great Eskimo Vocabulary Hoax and Other Irreverent Essays on the Study of Language*, p. 68.

3. Contrary to popular belief, homeless persons do not have secret, ingenious, and sometimes easy ways of getting along. In fact, homeless people on the street have precisely those terrible problems that one would guess them to have. Kathleen Dockett, in her interview study of street homeless persons in Washington, D.C., reports that "a lack of access to bathing (68%) and laundry facilities were the most difficult needs to satisfy. The . . . need for sufficient sleep (63%) and safety in terms of finding a safe place to sleep (58%) were the second most difficult needs to satisfy. . . . There was a strong consensus . . . that shelters were unhealthy, dangerous, stressful." Dockett, *Street Homeless People in the District of Columbia: Characteristics and Service Needs*, pp. viii, ix. When one realizes that many homeless persons—mostly men—often choose street life over shelter life, one begins to get a sense of just how "unhealthy, dangerous, stressful" some shelters can be.

4. The chapter-by-chapter discussion of these needs is not meant to imply a hierarchy.

5. Elderly persons who live alone sometimes resort to much the same strategy of make-work, a sort of remembering to forget. In the morning, a woman goes to the supermarket and buys, say, a carton of milk and a loaf of bread. Later the same morning, she says, "Oh, I forgot to get eggs," and returns to the store. Still later, "I forgot to get potatoes," or "I forgot to go to the post office," and so on through the day, thereby filling it up with things to do.

6. I helped June to move to Mount Carmel, a women's shelter in downtown D.C., and one of the most preferred shelters in the city. She moved in with seven bags, boxes, and suitcases. The sister in charge explained, almost apologetically, that June would be allowed to store only two such items in the shelter. June went through her things. She threw some of them out and stored the remainder at the Catholic church she used to attend.

7. Of course not all bag ladies were forced into that status. Some women were or had become bag ladies for less obviously rational reasons, but they were a minority. If affordable, accessible, and secure storage space were available, surely many bag ladies would disappear.

8. In this discussion of storage, I have attempted to exclude hoarders—those women who hold on to things because they cannot let go of them. It is useful to keep in mind, however, that the storage problems of the occasional hoarder, even if self-inflicted, are as great or greater than everyone else's.

9. "To lose a home or the sum of one's belongings is to lose evidence as to who one is and where one belongs in this world." Kai T. Erikson, *Everything in Its Path: Destruction of Community in the Buffalo Creek Flood,* p. 177. See the section "The Furniture of Self" in this beautiful book for additional insights into the meanings embedded in one's house and personal possessions.

10. Jeanette did, in fact, buy back her car for $25, and she found "a Christian gas station owner" who agreed to tow it to his lot and wait for the money. The car never again moved under its own power, but Jeanette was able to keep her things there until, six weeks later, the minister of the church she attended found a church member who allowed her to store her things in his garage.

CHAPTER 12

As Rich-Poor Gap Widens in the U.S., Class Mobility Stalls

DAVID WESSEL

The notion that the U.S is a special place where any child can grow up to be president, a meritocracy where smarts and ambition matter more than parenthood and class, dates to Benjamin Franklin. The 15th child of a candle-and-soap maker, Franklin started out as a penniless printer's apprentice and rose to wealth so great that he retired to a life of politics and diplomacy at age 42.

The promise that a child born in poverty isn't trapped there remains a staple of America's self-portrait. President Bush, though a riches-to-riches story himself, revels in the humble origins of some in his cabinet. He says his attorney general "grew up in a two-bedroom house," the son of "migrant workers who never finished elementary school." He notes that his Cuban-born commerce secretary's first job for Kellogg Corp. was driving a truck; his last was chief executive.

But the reality of mobility in America is more complicated than the myth. As the gap between rich and poor has widened since 1970, the odds that a child born in poverty will climb to wealth—or a rich child will fall into the middle class—remain stuck. Despite the spread of affirmative action, the expansion of community colleges and the other social change designed to give people of all classes a shot at success, Americans are no more or less likely to rise above, or fall below, their parents' economic class than they were 35 years ago.

Although Americans still think of their land as a place of exceptional opportunity—in contrast to class-bound Europe—the evidence suggests otherwise. And scholars have, over the past decade, come to see America as a less mobile society than they once believed.

As recently as the late 1980s, economists argued that not much advantage passed from parent to child, perhaps as little as 20%. By that measure, a rich man's grandchild would have barely any edge over a poor man's grandchild.

"Almost all the earnings advantages or disadvantages of ancestors are wiped out in three generations," wrote Gary Becker, the University of Chicago economist and Nobel laureate, in 1986. "Poverty would not seem to be a 'culture' that persists for several generations."

But over the last 10 years, better data and more number-crunching have led economists and sociologists to a new consensus: The escalators of mobility move much more slowly. A substantial body of research finds that at least 45% of parents' advantage in income is passed along to their children, and perhaps as much as 60%. With the higher estimate, it's not only how much money your parents have that matters—even your great-great grandfather's wealth might give you a noticeable edge today.

Many Americans believe their country remains a land of unbounded opportunity. That perception explains why Americans, much more than Europeans, have tolerated the widening inequality in recent years. It is OK to have ever-greater differences between rich and poor, they seem to believe, as long as their children have a good chance of grasping the brass ring.

Family Fortune

Where men fall on the scale as adults when their fathers were in the...

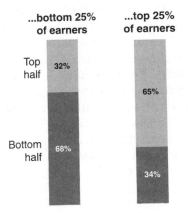

FIGURE 12.1   Family Fortunes

Note: 1995–98 wages for sons born between 1963–68. Figures don't add up to 100% due to rounding.

Source: Bhashkar Mazumder, Chicago Federal Reserve Bank.

This continuing belief shapes American politics and economic policy. Technology, globalization and unfettered markets tend to erode wages at the bottom and lift wages at the top. But Americans have elected politicians who oppose using the muscle of government to restrain the forces of widening inequality. These politicians argue that lifting the minimum wage or requiring employers to offer health insurance would do unacceptably large damage to economic growth.

Despite the widespread belief that the U.S. remains a more mobile society than Europe, economists and sociologists say that in recent decades the typical child starting out in poverty in continental Europe (or in Canada) has had a better chance at prosperity. Miles Corak, an economist for Canada's national statistical agency who edited a recent Cambridge University Press book on mobility in Europe and North America, tweaked dozens of studies of the U.S., Canada and European countries to make them comparable. "The U.S. and Britain appear to stand out as the least mobile societies among the rich countries studied," he finds. France and Germany are somewhat more mobile than the U.S.; Canada and the Nordic countries are much more so.

Even the University of Chicago's Prof. Becker is changing his mind, reluctantly. "I do believe that it's still true if you come from a modest background it's easier to move ahead in the U.S. than elsewhere," he says, "but the more data we get that doesn't show that, the more we have to accept the conclusions."

Still, the escalators of social mobility continue to move. Nearly a third of the freshmen at four-year colleges last fall said their parents hadn't gone beyond high school. And thanks to a growing economy that lifts everyone's living standards, the typical American is living with more than his or her parents did. People today enjoy services—cellphones, cancer treatment, the Internet—that their parents and grandparents never had.

Measuring precisely how much the prosperity of Americans depends on advantages conferred by their parents is difficult, since it requires linking income data across many decades. U.S. research relies almost entirely on a couple of long-running surveys. One began in 1968 at the University of Michigan and now tracks more than 7,000 families with more than 65,000 individuals; the other was started by the Labor Department in 1966.

One drawback of the surveys is that they don't capture the experiences of recent immigrants or their children, many of whom have seen extraordinary upward mobility. The University of California at Berkeley, for instance, says 52% of last year's undergraduates had two parents who weren't born in the U.S., and that's not counting the relatively few students whose families live abroad.

Nonetheless, those two surveys offer the best way to measure the degree to which Americans' economic success or failure depends on their parents. University of Michigan economist Gary Solon, an authority in the field, says one conclusion is clear: "Intergenerational mobility in the U.S. has not changed dramatically over the last two decades."

Bhashkar Mazumder, a Federal Reserve Bank of Chicago economist, recently combined the government survey with Social Security records for thousands of men born between 1963 and 1968 to see what they were earning when they reached their late 20s or 30s. Only 14% of the men born to fathers on the bottom 10% of the wage ladder made it to the top 30%. Only 17% of the men born to fathers on the top 10% fell to the bottom 30%.

LAND OF THE SELF-MADE MAN

Benjamin Franklin best exemplified and first publicized America as the land of the mobile society. "He is the prototype of the self-made man, and his life is the classic American success story—the story of a man rising from the most obscure of origins to wealth and international preeminence," one of his many biographers, Gordon S. Wood, wrote in 2004.

In 1828, a 14-year-old Irish immigrant named Thomas Mellon read Franklin's popular "Autobiography" and later described it as a turning point in his life. "Here was Franklin, poorer than myself, who by industry, thrift and frugality had become learned and wise, and elevated to wealth and fame," Mellon wrote in a memoir. The young Mellon left the family farm, became a successful lawyer and judge and later founded what became Pittsburgh's Mellon Bank. In front, he erected a statue of Franklin.

Even Karl Marx accepted the image of America as a land of boundless opportunity, citing this as an explanation for the lack of class consciousness in the U.S. "The position of wage laborer," he wrote in 1865, "is for a very large part of the American people but a probational state, which they are sure to leave within a longer or shorter term."

Self-made industrialist Andrew Carnegie, writing in the New York Tribune in 1890, catalogued the "captains of industry" who started as clerks and apprentices and were "trained in that sternest but most efficient of all schools—poverty."

The historical record suggests this widely shared belief about 19th-century America was more than myth. "You didn't need to be told. You lived it. And if you didn't, your neighbors did," says Joseph Ferrie, an economic historian at Northwestern University, who has combed through the U.S. and British census records that give the occupations of thousands of native-born father-and-son pairs who lived between 1850 and 1920. In all, more than 80% of the sons of unskilled men moved to higher-paying, higher-status occupations in the late 1800s in the U.S., but less than 60% in Britain did so.

The biggest factor, Mr. Ferrie says, is that young Americans could do something most British couldn't: climb the economic ladder quickly by moving from farm towns to thriving metropolises. In 1850, for instance, James Roberts was a 14-year-old son of a day laborer living in the western New York hamlet of Catharine. Handwritten census records reveal that 30 years later, Mr. Roberts was a bookkeeper—a much higher rung—and living in New York City at 2257 Third Ave. with his wife and four children.

As education became more important in the 20th century—first high school, later college—leaping up the ladder began to require something that only better-off parents could afford: allowing their children to stay in school instead of working. "Something quite fundamental changed in the U.S. economy in the years after 1910 and before the Great Depression," says Prof. Ferrie.

One reason that the once-sharp differences between social mobility in the U.S. and Britain narrowed in the 20th century, he argues, is that the regional economies of the U.S. grew more and more similar. It became much harder to leap several rungs of the economic ladder simply by moving.

The paucity of data makes it hard to say how mobility changed for much of the 20th century. Individual census records—the kind that Prof. Ferrie examines—are still under seal for most of the 20th century. Data from the two national surveys didn't start rolling in until the 1970s.

Whatever the facts, the Franklin-inspired notion of America as an exceptionally mobile society persisted through most of the 20th century, as living standards improved after World War II and the children and grandchildren of immigrants prospered. Jeremiads in the 1960s and 1970s warned of an intractable culture of poverty that trapped people at the bottom for generations, and African-Americans didn't enjoy the same progress as whites. But among large numbers of Americans, there was little doubt that their children would ride the escalator.

OLD WISDOM SHATTERS

In 1992, though, Mr. Solon, the Michigan economist, shattered the conventional academic wisdom, arguing in the American Economic Review that earlier studies relied on "error-ridden data, unrepresentative samples, or both" and misleadingly compared snapshots of a single year in the life of parent and child rather than looking over longer periods. There is "dramatically less mobility than suggested by earlier research," he said. Subsequent research work confirmed that.

As Mr. Mazumder, the Chicago Fed economist, put it in the title of a recent book chapter: "The apple falls even closer to the tree than we thought."

Why aren't the escalators working better? Figuring out how parents pass along economic status, apart from the obvious but limited factor of financial bequests, is tough. But education appears to play an important role. In contrast to the 1970s, a college diploma is increasingly valuable in today's job market. The tendency of college grads to marry other college grads and send their children to better elementary and high schools and on to college gives their children a lasting edge.

The notion that the offspring of smart, successful people are also smart and successful is appealing, and there is a link between parent and child IQ scores. But most research finds IQ isn't a very big factor in predicting economic success.

In the U.S., race appears to be a significant reason that children's economic success resembles their parents'. From 32 years of data on 6,273 families recorded by the University of Michigan's long-running survey, American University economist Tom Hertz calculates that 17% of whites born to the bottom 10% of families ranked by income remained there as adults, but 42% of the blacks did. Perhaps as a consequence, public-opinion surveys find African-Americans more likely to favor government redistribution programs than whites.

The tendency of well-off parents to have healthier children, or children more likely to get treated for health problems, may also play a role. "There is very powerful evidence that low-income kids suffer from more health problems, and childhood health does predict adult health and adult health does predict performance," observes Christopher Jencks, a noted Harvard sociologist.

Passing along personality traits to one's children may be a factor, too. Economist Melissa Osborne Groves of Maryland's Towson University looked at results of a psychological test for 195 father-son pairs in the government's long-running National Longitudinal Survey. She found similarities in attitudes about life accounted for 11% of the link between the income of a father and his son.

Nonetheless, Americans continue to cherish their self-image as a unique land where past and parentage puts no limits on opportunity, as they have for centuries. In his "Autobiography," Franklin wrote simply that he had "emerged from the poverty and obscurity in which I was born and bred to a state of affluence." But in a version that became the standard 19th-century text, his grandson, Temple, altered the words to underscore the enduring message: "I have *raised myself* to a state of affluence . . . "

PART FOUR

Racism

During the 1960s, the successful struggle for legislation to enforce equal opportunity for minorities—in jobs, housing, and education—created the hope that government action would effectively remove the most important barriers to racial equality in American society. This sense of optimism was enhanced by the expectation of an ever-expanding economy that seemed to promise there would be room for everyone to have a chance at the good life in America.

To some extent, these expectations were borne out—for a while. Blacks and other minorities made significant social and economic progress, particularly in the 1960s, as a result of civil rights protest, government action, and an expanding economy. But the urban riots of the 1960s also showed a more ominous side of the racial picture and revealed that some aspects of racial disadvantage in the United States were relatively impervious to both economic growth and the expansion of civil rights. And during the 1970s and early 1980s, some of the gains made by minorities in earlier years began to be reversed. Minority income fell behind as a proportion of white income, and minority poverty—especially in the inner cities—increased sharply. A combination of unfavorable economic trends, a less generous public policy, and a waning commitment to the vigorous enforcement of civil rights laws has taken its toll on minority progress in recent years. The depth of the disaster for many inner-city minorities was brutally revealed in the explosion of rioting in Los Angeles in 1992—the worst single urban civil disorder in America in this century.

Yet despite these troubling developments, some commentators have begun to argue that race is no longer very important in America. No one denies that minorities still suffer a variety of economic and social disadvantages. But it is now sometimes argued that these disadvantages no longer have much to do with outright racial discrimination—which, in this view, has greatly diminished over time. In this argument, the high rates of unemployment and poverty among black Americans, for example, are now mainly due to problems of culture or attitudes, rather than systematic barriers to economic opportunity.

The articles in this section, however, make it clear that this celebration of the end of racial discrimination is decidedly premature. Race still matters in the United

States, and it matters very much. In virtually every realm of American life, minorities must contend with a playing field that remains decidedly unequal.

How can this be true, when we have created so many laws and programs designed to level that field? One reason, as Michael K. Brown and his co-authors argue, is that for generations, the policies of both government and private employers worked in precisely the opposite direction—systematically providing advantages to white Americans that, though sometimes subtle, have shaped the country's racial situation ever since. Most Americans are unaware, for example, that black workers were largely excluded from both Social Security and unemployment compensation for decades—which helped trap them in poverty and economic insecurity and ensured that they fell farther behind whites on the income ladder. At the same time, the housing policies of both private banks and the federal government deliberately supported residential segregation in the cities, which effectively locked many African-Americans in impoverished, troubled neighborhoods and robbed them of one of the most important sources of personal wealth—the ownership of a valuable home. In these ways and others, the racial policies of an earlier era have left a legacy of inequality that we have yet to challenge successfully.

The effects of that inequality are disturbingly apparent in the criminal justice system—the site of some of the most dramatic, and divisive, racial disparities in the United States. A half century after the start of the Civil Rights movement, African Americans—especially young African Americans—are far more likely to spend time in jails and prisons than their white counterparts. As the report we reprint from the Sentencing Project notes, there are roughly nine times as many blacks behind bars than at the time of the famous *Brown v. Board of Education* court decision that ended the formal racial segregation of public schools. The reasons for that troubling increase, as the authors point out, are complex—ranging from stubbornly high crime rates to the unequal impact of the war on drugs. But the effects of this unprecedented level of imprisonment are felt in many ways, all of which should concern us. Today a stunning proportion of black children have at least one parent in jail during some part of their childhoods. About one in eight black men cannot vote because they have been convicted of a felony. More generally, the experience of jail or prison has come, in many communities, to seem like an "almost inevitable" aspect of growing up for young black Americans.

The persistence of racial disparities in housing, social benefits, and criminal justice is matched in other institutions as well, including education and jobs. Since the emergence of the civil rights movement in the 1950s and 1960s, there have been many attempts to tackle those inequalities and to promote racial equity and diversity.

One of the most important strategies to combat discrimination has been what is loosely called "affirmative action"—the requirement that institutions make special efforts to ensure a fair chance for historically underrepresented minorities. Many people wrongly believe that this means that colleges, businesses, and other institutions maintain "quotas" mandating that a certain percentage of their employees or students must be from minority groups. In fact, such quotas have been illegal since the 1970s. But universities and other institutions *have* been allowed to devise a variety of ways to increase racial and ethnic diversity.

Affirmative action has become one of most controversial social policies in the United States: many feel that it gives unfair preferences to minorities which have nothing to do with their merit or performance, while others believe that it is an essential tool to maintain a diverse community and to help redress the discriminatory policies of the past. However one feels about that issue in the abstract, it is important to put it in context. What is usually left out in the public debate over affirmative action is that many *other* groups besides minorities receive a variety of preferences in such things as admission to college, and have for a long time. Athletes, for example, have long been able to gain admission to exclusive colleges with lower grades and test scores than other applicants. And, as Daniel Golden shows, many universities now make special efforts to bend the standards in order to admit the children of wealthy parents. This is sometimes euphemistically called "development" admissions, but by whatever name, it is a kind of preference. The fact that, as one student puts it, "Everybody at Duke has something that got them in," helps to put the issue of affirmative action for minority students in better perspective.

Americans of Asian descent face complex forms of discrimination as well, as Ronald Takaki shows in "Asian Americans: The Myth of the Model Minority." According to the census, the "Asian or Pacific Islander" population is among the most rapidly increasing in the United States, and it is an extraordinarily diverse population—encompassing a wide range of groups from many different countries and very different traditions. The growth of the Asian-American population has been accompanied by many stereotypes, which, as Takaki shows, obscure the complexity of the Asian-American experience and hide continuing problems of discrimination and uneven opportunities. Part of the problem is that the very real educational and economic successes of some Asian American groups mask the difficulties faced by others—especially the growing Southeast Asian population—who face high rates of poverty, unemployment, school problems, and preventable diseases. Nor does the success of some Asian Americans mean that discrimination against them has disappeared. Despite considerable upward mobility, Asians often run into a "glass ceiling" in the job hierarchy—and sometimes face brutal, overt racism in the streets as well.

CHAPTER 13

The Roots of White Advantage

MICHAEL K. BROWN

MARTIN CARNOY

ELLIOTT CURRIE

TROY DUSTER

DAVID B. OPPENHEIMER

MARJORIE M. SHULTZ

DAVID WELLMAN

Almost forty years after the civil rights revolution ended, two questions bedevil most discussions of racial economic inequality: (1) Why has deep poverty endured in the black community alongside a burgeoning black middle class? (2) Why do large gaps remain in family income, wages, and employment between blacks and whites? For many people this is the paradox and the bane of the civil rights revolution. How is it, they ask, that civil rights laws ended racial discrimination and left behind an unruly black underclass and substantial racial inequality? . . .

THE ORIGINS OF MODERN STATE-SPONSORED RACIAL INEQUALITY

One need not go back three hundred years to find the antecedents of contemporary white advantage. The New Deal is the most recent benchmark for the accumulation of white privilege and the generation of black disadvantage. Franklin D.

Roosevelt's policies were instrumental to both the cause of racial equality and the perpetuation of racial inequality. New Deal agricultural policies paved the way for the mechanization of southern agriculture and precipitated black (and white) migration to the North and the entry of blacks into manufacturing jobs. The Wagner Act legalized unions; minimum wage laws put an economic floor under all workers; the Social Security Act gave workers a measure of security; and the Employment Act of 1946 codified the government's responsibility for aggregate employment and price levels. These policies, combined with postwar economic growth, undermined the prewar northern racial order, set in motion changes that would dismantle Jim Crow, and reduced black as well as white poverty.

African Americans benefited from New Deal policies. They gained from the growth of public employment and governmental transfers like social security and welfare. The Great Society went further, reducing racial inequality, ameliorating poverty among the black poor, and helping to build a new black middle class. But if federal social policy promoted racial equality, it also created and sustained racial hierarchies. Welfare states are as much instruments of stratification as they are of equality. The New Deal's class-based, or race-neutral, social policies did not affect blacks and whites in identical ways. Federal social policy contributed disproportionately to the prosperity of the white middle class from the 1940s on. Whites received more from the New Deal than old-age protection and insurance against the business cycle. Housing subsidies paved the way for a white exodus to the suburbs; federal tax breaks secured union-bargained health and pension benefits and lowered the cost to workers; veterans' benefits were an avenue of upward mobility for many white men. To assume that government policies benefited only blacks or were color-blind, as many white Americans commonly believe, is like looking at the world with one eye.

Three laws passed by Congress in the mid-1930s were instrumental in generating the pattern of racial stratification that emerged during the New Deal: the Social Security Act, the Wagner Act, and the Federal Housing Act. These laws contributed to the accumulation of wealth in white households, and they did more than any other combination of factors to sow and nurture the seeds of the future urban ghetto and produce a welfare system in which recipients would be disproportionately black. It is commonly assumed that the New Deal was based on broad and inclusive policies. While there is some truth to the claim that Roosevelt's New Deal was designed, as Jill Quadagno states it, to provide a "floor of protection for the industrial working class," it was riddled with discrimination. Brokered compromises over New Deal labor and social policies also reinforced racial segregation through social welfare programs, labor policy, and housing policy.[70] How and why did this happen?

Although the Social Security Act created a work-related social right to an old-age pension and unemployment compensation, Congress defied the Roosevelt administration and explicitly excluded domestic and agricultural workers from coverage. It also exempted public employees as well as workers in nonprofit, voluntary organizations. Only 53 percent of all workers, about 26 million people, were initially covered by the old-age insurance title of the Social Security Act, and less than half of all workers were covered by unemployment compensation. Congress subsequently excluded these exempt workers from the Wagner Act and the 1938 Fair Labor Standards Act as well.[71]

Congress's rejection of universal coverage was not a race-neutral decision undertaken because, as some people claimed at the time, it was difficult to collect payroll taxes from agricultural and domestic workers. As Charles Houston, Dean of the Howard University Law School, told the Senate Finance committee, "It [the Social Security bill] looks like a sieve with the holes just big enough for the majority of Negroes to fall through." Almost three-fifths of the black labor force was denied coverage. When self-employed black sharecroppers are added to the list of excluded workers, it is likely that three-quarters or more of African Americans were denied benefits and the protection of federal law. Black women, of whom 90 percent were domestic workers, were especially disadvantaged by these occupational exclusions.[72]

Agricultural and domestic workers were excluded largely because southern legislators refused to allow implementation of any national social welfare policies that included black workers. Roosevelt presided over a fragile coalition of northern industrial workers and southern whites bound to an agrarian economic order. Although blacks began to leave the party of Lincoln for the party of Roosevelt, three-quarters of the African American population still lived in the South, where they could not vote. Southerners feared that federal social policies would raise the pay of southern black workers and sharecroppers and that this in turn would undermine their system of racial apartheid. Black criticisms of the legislation were ignored as Roosevelt acquiesced to southern demands, believing he could not defy powerful southern committee chairmen and still pass needed social welfare legislation.

As black workers moved north into industrial jobs, they were eventually included under the Social Security Act, and Congress ultimately extended coverage of old-age insurance to agricultural workers in 1950 and 1954. Although the Social Security Administration made every effort to treat black and white workers equally, black workers were nevertheless severely disadvantaged by the work-related eligibility provisions of the Social Security Act. Both old-age insurance and unemployment compensation rewarded stable, long-term employment and penalized intermittent employment regardless of the reason. In the name of fiscal integrity, the architects of social insurance in the 1930s were adamant that malingerers, those on relief, or those weakly attached to the labor market be excluded from eligibility and their benefits limited. Due to labor market discrimination and the seasonal nature of agricultural labor, many blacks have not had stable, long-term employment records. Thus, they have had only limited eligibility for old-age and unemployment benefits.

The racial consequences of wage-related eligibility provisions were already apparent in the 1930s. Because labor market discrimination lowers the wages of black workers relative to white workers or denies them employment altogether, blacks receive lower benefits than whites from old-age insurance and unemployment compensation or are denied access at all. By 1939, for example, only 20 percent of white workers who worked in industries covered by social insurance and who paid payroll taxes for old-age insurance were uninsured, but more than twice as many black workers (42 percent) were uninsured.[73] From the outset, social security transferred income from African American workers to white workers. This disparity continues today. Even though most black workers are currently covered by social security, on average they still receive lower benefits than whites and pay a higher proportion of their income in social security taxes.[74] Like old-age insurance, there is little evidence of overt discrimination in unemployment compensation—eligible black workers are almost as likely as white workers are to receive benefits. But because states imposed strict eligibility requirements during the 1940s and 1950s, black workers were disproportionately excluded.[75] Social insurance is neither universal nor race-neutral.

In combination, labor market discrimination and work-related eligibility requirements excluded blacks from work and social insurance programs in the 1930s, forcing many to go on relief and later on welfare, Aid to Dependent Children (ADC). In fact, most black women were excluded from the unemployment compensation system until the late 1960s. This is because domestic workers were statutorily excluded from unemployment compensation, and as late as the 1950s more than half of all black women in the civilian labor force still worked as domestics. Unemployed black women typically had nowhere to turn but welfare, and this is exactly what they did. By 1960, African Americans accounted for two-fifths of all welfare recipients, a participation rate that did not change much even when the welfare rolls expanded in the 1960s. It is labor market discrimination and New Deal social policies, not welfare, as the conservatives believe, that has harmed black families. The problem cannot be explained by a pathological black family structure.[76]

Social insurance in the United States has operated much like a sieve, just as Charles Houston predicted, and blacks have fallen through the holes. The Wagner Act and the 1937 Housing Act compounded the problem, enlarging the holes in the sieve. Sometimes labeled the Magna Charta of the labor movement, the 1935 Wagner Act was, upon closer inspection, the Magna Charta of *white* labor. Black leaders tried to add an antidiscrimination amendment to the law, but the American Federation of Labor and the white southerners who controlled key congressional committees fought it. As a result, the final version excluded black workers. The law legalized the closed shop, which, as Roy Wilkins of the NAACP pointed out, would empower "organized labor to exclude from employment in any industry those who do not belong to a union." The law also outlawed strikebreaking, a weapon black workers had used successfully to force their way into northern industries. Preventing blacks from entering into newly protected labor unions meant that black workers were subject to the racist inclinations of white workers.[77] One of the consequences of the Wagner Act's failure to protect black workers was that union rules confined them to low-wage unskilled jobs. When these jobs were eliminated as businesses modernized after World War II, black unskilled workers were replaced by automated manufacturing technologies.[78] Thus, the current high levels of black unemployment can be traced directly to New Deal legislation that allowed white workers to deny job opportunities to blacks.

State-sponsored racial inequality was also augmented by a third set of New Deal policies: federal housing and urban renewal legislation. . . .

The mortgage loan programs of the Federal Housing Administration (FHA) and Veterans Administration (VA) were additional boons to white workers. These two federal programs financed more than one-third of all post–World War II mortgages, accounting for more than \$120 billion in new housing.[33] The FHA and VA insured home mortgages that allowed lenders to liberalize the terms and conditions of loans. VA mortgages also provided a direct subsidy to home buyers. Unlike the veterans' loans, FHA mortgages were redistributive, aiding working- and middle-class families. Both programs helped extend home ownership to millions of families who otherwise would have been unable to afford it. They also subsidized the development of postwar suburbs. Either the FHA or VA financed almost half of all suburban housing built in the 1950s and 1960s, a benefit that was typically reserved for whites.[34]

As we now know, FHA guidelines for lenders used racist criteria to assess the credit worthiness of loans. Housing expert Charles Abrams accurately concluded that the FHA policy "could well have been culled from the Nuremberg laws." Federal housing administrators were unwilling to insure mortgages in integrated neighborhoods, fearing that anything less than rigid segregation would undermine property values. The FHA underwriting manual warned lenders, "If a neighborhood is to retain stability, it is necessary that properties shall continue to be occupied by the same social and racial classes." Lenders were explicitly told to add restrictive covenants to contracts and deeds. As a consequence, FHA loans favored the suburbs. In a study of St. Louis County, Missouri, Kenneth Jackson compared how FHA loans were distributed in suburban towns with central cities in the same county. His study revealed enormous disparities between the treatment of central cities and suburban jurisdictions. St. Louis County, for example, received five times the number of mortgage loans and dollars as the city of St. Louis.[35] The upshot was that black families living in the city were denied mortgage insurance, and when they did receive a mortgage, the terms were less favorable.

African Americans received only 3 percent of all the home loans underwritten by FHA and VA in 1960, a total that amounted to just 30 percent of all black mortgages. White homeowners, on the other hand, were far more dependent on government-insured and subsidized mortgages: 42 percent of white mortgages in that year were paid for by FHA and VA loans. Black veterans fared somewhat better than black clients of the FHA (African American veterans received two-thirds of all government-sponsored mortgages held by blacks in 1960), but they lagged behind white veterans. By 1950, about 5 percent of black World War II veterans took advantage of a VA loan compared to 13 percent of white veterans.[36] But of course these mortgages could be used only to purchase segregate housing.

Using federal housing policies to sustain segregation is only the best-known instance of this practice. Until the 1960s federal social policy was also integral to propping up southern segregation. Southern states used federal subsidies for public works to reinforce the color line.[37] Veterans' hospitals, for example, were rigidly segregated. Most federal grants contained "nonintervention" clauses that prevented federal officials from supervising or controlling the construction of these buildings. The 1946 Hill-Burton Act contained an explicit exception allowing separate facilities for "separate population groups" if the plan made equitable provision for services of "like quality." Hill-Burton's separate but equal provision was declared unconstitutional in 1963, but by then southerners had used \$37 million in federal funds to build eighty-nine segregated medical facilities. In the process, many African Americans were denied medical care, while southern whites benefited from the best medical facilities the federal government could build.[38]

   These federal policies underwrote a new pattern of white accumulation and black disaccumulation throughout the country, but especially in the South and in northern cities. White families prospered as suburban developments were constructed, while black families were left holding a losing hand. After World War II, federal housing and urban renewal policies facilitated rigidly segregated neighborhoods and disinvestment in black communities. Blanket federal redlining signaled private investors to avoid making housing or business loans in black communities. One study of Chicago demonstrated that life insurance companies withdrew mortgage money from the city in the 1950s and 1960s for the same reasons the FHA refused to underwrite loans in black neighborhoods. The consequences were severe. As Douglas Massey and Nancy Denton write, "The lack of loan capital flowing into minority areas made it impossible for owners to sell their homes, leading to steep declines in property values and a pattern of disrepair, deterioration, vacancy, and abandonment." This meant that white-owned housing was more valuable than black-owned housing and that the value of white-owned housing largely depended on public policies that created and sustained residential segregation. Compounding these color-conscious, state-sponsored advantages, whites reaped all the benefits of home owning, which, in addition to being cheaper than renting, entitled them to America's major middle-class tax subsidy: the mortgage interest deduction.[39]

   The 1950s federal social policies guaranteed the members of an expanding white middle class that they would accumulate considerable wealth with government assistance. Consequently, whites today possess substantially more property and financial assets than black families. In 1993, the median net worth of white households was ten times that of black and Latino households. Blacks have less equity in their homes and fewer investments and Individual Retirement Accounts (IRAs, also known as Keogh accounts). While the ratio of black to white income is 62 percent, the ratio of black to white median net worth is just 8 percent. Perhaps more important, 61 percent of black households have no net financial assets whatsoever. In contrast, only 25 percent of white households find themselves in the same predicament. And even among households with equal incomes, blacks have substantially less wealth than whites.[40]

Editors' Note: *Notes for this reading can be found in the original source.*

CHAPTER 14

Schools and Prisons: Fifty Years after *Brown v. Board of Education*

SENTENCING PROJECT

OVERVIEW

The nation is currently celebrating the 50th anniversary of the historic *Brown v. Board of Education* decision that ordered the desegregation of public education. The decision in many ways marked the beginnings of the modern day Civil Rights Movement and during the ensuing half century there has been significant social and economic progress in American society. Much work needs to be done, but many institutions in society have become more diverse and responsive to the needs of African Americans and other people of color.

However, during this period no institution has changed more than the criminal justice system, and in ways that have had profound effects on the African American community. The unprecedented growth in the prison system has produced record numbers of Americans in prison and jail, and has had a disproportionate effect on African Americans. As seen in the figure . . . , there are now nine times as many African Americans in prison or jail as on the day of the *Brown* decision. An estimated 98,000 blacks were incarcerated in 1954, a figure that has risen to 884,500 today (See Figure 14.1).[1]

These absolute numbers translate into dramatic rates for black men in particular. One of every 21 adult black men is incarcerated on any given day. For black men in their late twenties, the figure is one in eight. There are now far more incarcerated black men in this age group (161,600) than the total number of *all* incarcerated African Americans in 1954 (98,000). Given current trends, one of every three (32%) black males born today can expect to go to prison in his lifetime.

The intersection between education and criminal justice is profound as well. In 1954, Chief Justice Warren noted, "In these days, it is doubtful that any child may

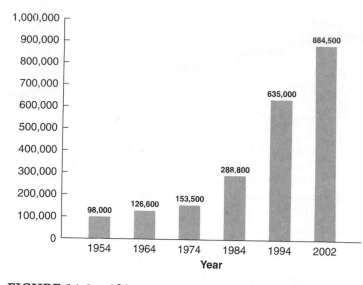

FIGURE 14.1   African Americans in Prison or Jail

reasonably be expected to succeed in life if he is denied the opportunity of an education."[2] In an era dominated by information technology where success is measured by one's specialized training, the fact that more than half (52%) of black men in their early 30s who are high school dropouts have a prison record underscores the nation's failure to heed Chief Justice Warren's warning.

While the incarceration rates for women are lower overall than for men, the racial disparities are equally dramatic. One of every 18 black females born today can expect to go to prison if current trends continue, or six times the rate for white women. These odds have increased dramatically in recent decades. Black women born today are five times more likely to go to prison in their lifetimes than black women born in 1974.

CAUSAL FACTORS

The factors contributing to the dramatic increase in the number of African Americans in prison and jail are complex, and involve dynamics both within and outside the criminal justice system. Overall, they represent a social policy that has emphasized a punitive response to the problem of crime at the expense of alternative approaches that focus on strengthening families and communities. These include the following:

Crime Rates.   Higher rates of involvement in some crimes explains part of the high rate of black imprisonment. For property offenses, blacks constituted 29.6% of arrests in 2002 and for violent offenses, 38%; these compare to the 12.3% black proportion of the total population. (Note that an arrest may not always be an accurate indicator of involvement in crime, but it often remains the best means of approximating this measure.) However, criminologist Alfred Blumstein, in a study on race and imprisonment, noted that higher arrest rates for drug crimes in particular were not correlated with higher rates of use in the general population. In short, drug arrest patterns were not a reliable indicator of drug offending, because African Americans are arrested more frequently than their rate of drug use would suggest.[3]

What appears to be a race-based relation for some offenses is in many respects one of social class. Youth surveys document that a significant proportion of teenage males of all races have engaged in serious crime. These rates drop much more sharply by the early 20s for whites than blacks, due to more ready access to adult roles—employment, college education, and stable relationships. Further, researchers have identified not just poverty, but *concentrated* poverty, as a significant contributor to crime rates due to the socioeconomic disadvantages it brings. Housing patterns in the U.S. often result in low-income African Americans living in concentrated poverty, but poor whites and other groups are rarely found in such situations.

Rising Imprisonment.   Much of the rising incarceration of Africa Americans mirrors the dramatic increases in imprisonment overall since 1970. From a combined prison and jail population of about 330,000, the nation's incarcerated population has now increased to 2.1 million. This increase is largely attributable to the adoption of "get tough" policies that emphasize harsher sentencing practices, rather than any significant increases in crime rates. An examination of the growth of the prison population from 1992 to 2001 found that the entire increase was explained not by crime rates, but by an increased likelihood that convicted offenders would be sentenced to prison and by longer prison terms.[4]

War on Drugs.   Two overlapping trends since 1980 have contributed to a substantial increase in the number of African Americans in prison. First, the inception of the war on drugs has resulted in a dramatic surge in the number of incarcerated persons, rising from about 40,000 persons awaiting trial or serving a sentence for a drug charge in 1980 to about 450,000 today. The current figure is only slightly less than the total number of incarcerated persons for *all* offenses in 1980.

Second, the prosecution of the drug war has disproportionately affected communities of color. Surveys conducted by the Department of Health and Human Services estimate that blacks constitute 13.3% of monthly drug users, yet blacks represent 32.5% of persons arrested for drug offenses.[5] Of all persons imprisoned for drug offenses, three fourths are black or Latino. These disparities result in large part through a two-tiered application of the drug war. In communities with substantial resources, drug abuse is primarily addressed as a public health problem utilizing prevention and treatment approaches. In low-income communities those resources are in short supply and drug problems are more likely to be addressed through the criminal justice system.

Crack/Cocaine Sentencing.   Federal legislation adopted in 1986 and 1988 provides for far harsher punishment of crack cocaine offenders than powder cocaine offenders, even though crack is a derivative of powder cocaine. Persons convicted of selling 500 grams of powder cocaine are subject to a mandatory five-year prison term; for crack cocaine, the same penalty is triggered by possession of just five grams of the drug. Enforcement of these laws has resulted in African Americans constituting 83% of crack defendants in 2001, despite the fact that approximately two-thirds of users in the general population are white. This represents a policy decision by agencies in the criminal justice system to pursue the "war on drugs" using tactics that have a detrimental impact on the African American community.

In addition, 14 states also maintain disparities in their sentencing differentials between crack and powder cocaine. Widespread concern about these disparities led the U.S. Sentencing Commission to recommend the elimination of the sentencing differential in 1995. This recommendation was overwhelmingly rejected by Congress and the Clinton Administration. A subsequent effort to revise the penalty structure in 2002 was opposed by the Bush Administration's Department of Justice.

"School Zone" Drug Laws. In recent years many states have adopted "school zone" drug enhancement laws that increase ties for drug crimes committed near a school. These laws, intended to deter drug-selling to school children, have in practice contributed to extreme racial/ethnic disparities, primarily due to housing patterns. In urban areas, large proportions of most cities are within the typical 1,000–1,500 foot range of these sanctions, whereas in suburban or rural communities, far fewer locations fall within this limit. Since African Americans disproportionately live in urban areas, any such crime (even a drug sale between consenting adults at 3 a.m. near a school) will produce these enhanced penalties. In one recent year, 99% of the juveniles automatically prosecuted as adults in Cook County (Chicago), Illinois under the school zone law were black and Latino.

"Three Strikes" and Habitual Offender Policies. Sentencing legislation that imposes harsher prison terms on offenders with prior convictions exerts a disproportionate effect on African Americans. Judges have always had the ability to impose lengthier term on repeat offenders, but this effect has been magnified through policies such as habitual offender laws and "three strikes and you're out" legislation. Whether one believes that African Americans are more likely to engage in crime or are subject to racial profiling and other discriminatory forms of decisionmaking, the result is that African Americans are more likely to have a prior criminal record than other groups. Therefore, policies that impose harsher penalties based on criminal history will have a disproportionate effect on African Americans. In California, for example, blacks constitute 29% of the prison population, but 44.7% of the persons serving a "three strikes" sentence.[6] These disparities take on added significance due to the extreme disparities created by such policies. A non-violent offense in California that might otherwise lead to no more than a few years in prison becomes a sentence of 25 years to Life when treated as a third strike offense.

Inadequate Defense Resources. Forty years after the historic *Gideon* decision guaranteeing right to counsel in criminal cases, the state of indigent defense remains highly inadequate in many areas of the country. An estimated 80% of criminal defendants are indigent and a 2000 report by the Department of Justice declared that public defense was in a "chronic state of crisis." In Virginia, for example, the maximum payment for attorneys representing a defendant in a felony case that can result in a life sentence is $1,096. In Lake Charles, Louisiana, the public defender office has only two investigators for the 2,500 new felony cases and 4,000 new misdemeanor cases assigned to the office each year. Since African Americans are disproportionately low-income, they are more likely to suffer the deficiencies produced by these dynamics.

Zero Tolerance Policies.   In response to the perceived problem of school violence, many states and school districts have enacted "zero tolerance" policies for violations of school regulations. Such policies result in automatic suspension or expulsion of students for infractions that in previous times might have been handled by school officials. While ostensibly targeted at gun violence and other serious crimes, in practice these policies have led to disciplinary action for behaviors such as bringing Advil or water pistols to school. Zero tolerance policies contribute to higher rates of suspension and expulsion, and ultimately to increased numbers of school dropouts. Children of color have been disproportionately affected by these policies. According to the Department of Education, 35% of African American children in grades 7–12 had been suspended or expelled at some point in their school careers, compared to rates of 20% for Hispanics and 15% for whites.[7] These figures in turn result in increased risk of involvement in the juvenile and adult criminal justice system.

IMPLICATIONS

At current rates of incarceration, one of every three black males born today can expect to be imprisoned at some point in his lifetime. Whether or not one believes that current crime control policies are "working" to reduce crime, such an outcome should be shocking to all Americans. Imposing a crime policy with such profound racial dynamics calls into question the nation's commitment to a free and democratic society.

Current imprisonment policies affect not only the nearly 900,000 African Americans in prison and jail, but increasingly, their families and communities as well. One of every 14 black children has a parent in prison on any given day; over the course of childhood, the figures would be much higher. Family formation, particularly in urban areas heavily affected by incarceration, is also affected by these trends. In the highest incarceration neighborhoods of Washington, D.C., the absence of black men has created a gender ratio of only 62 men for every 100 women.[8]

Community power is affected by felon disenfranchisement laws as well, which restrict voting rights while serving a felony sentence or in some cases permanently, depending on the state in which one lives. In the coming Presidential election, one of every eight black males (13%) will not be able to vote as a result of a current or previous felony conviction. These laws affect the political influence not only of people with a felony conviction, but of their communities as well. People in these neighborhoods who do not themselves have a felony conviction also have their political voices diluted since fewer residents representing their interests are able to participate in the electoral process.

None of these issues suggests that crime is not a problem for all Americans, or for African Americans in particular. But the approaches taken to address this problem over the past several decades have created a situation whereby imprisonment has come to be seen as an almost inevitable aspect of the maturing process for black men, and increasingly for black women. The social cost of these policies is substantial and growing larger each year. In this 50th anniversary of the *Brown* decision, it is time for the nation to reflect on progress in education, but also to assess how the overall status of the black community has been affected. The dynamics of criminal justice policy suggest that the nation has taken a giant step backward in this regard.

METHODOLOGY

Prison and jail custody data for Figure 14.1 were collected from various Bureau of Justice Statistics publications. Where possible, exact numbers were taken directly from the Bureau of Justice Statistics report. In the case of years in which exact prison or jail data were not available, the numbers were interpolated based on available information for contiguous years. These estimates were most commonly produced by taking the difference between the two points in time and assuming an average annual increase based on the number of years.

This briefing paper was written by Marc Mauer and Ryan Scott King, Assistant Director and Research Associate respectively, of The Sentencing Project.

ENDNOTES

1. See Methodology section for a description of the population estimates.
2. *Brown vs. Board of Education of Topeka*, 347 U.S. 483, 493. (1954).
3. Blumstein, Alfred. (1993). "Racial Disproportionality of U.S. Prison Populations Revisited," *University of Colorado Law Review*, Vol. 64, 743–760.
4. Karberg, Jennifer C. and Beck, Allen J. "Trends in U.S. Correctional Populations: Findings from the Bureau of Justice Statistics." Presented at the National Committee on Community Corrections Meeting, Washington, DC, April 16, 2004.
5. Substance Abuse and Mental Health Services Administration, Office of Applied Studies, *National Survey on Drug Use and Health, 2002*. Table 1.26A.
6. California Department of Corrections. *Second and Third Strikers in the Institution Population.* Sacramento, CA: Data Analysis Unit. (February 2004).
7. *Status and Trends in the Education of Blacks*, U.S. Department of Education, September 2003, p. 38.
8. Braman, Donald. (2002). "Families and Incarceration," in Mauer, Marc and Chesney-Lind, Meda, (Eds.), *Invisible Punishment: The Collateral Consequences of Mass Imprisonment.* New York: The New Press. P. 128.

CHAPTER 15

At Many Colleges, the Rich Kids Get Affirmative Action

DANIEL GOLDEN

Despite her boarding-school education and a personal tutor, Maude Bunn's SAT scores weren't high enough for a typical student to earn admission to Duke University.

But Ms. Bunn had something else going for her—coffeemakers. Her Bunn forebears built a fortune on them and, with Duke hoping to woo her wealthy parents as donors, she was admitted.

Afterward, her parents promptly became co-chairmen of a Duke fund-raising effort aimed at other Duke parents. "My child was given a gift, she got in, and now I'm giving back," says Maude's mother, Cissy Bunn, who declines to say how much the family has contributed to the university.

Most universities acknowledge favoring children of alumni who support their alma mater. But to attract prospective donors, colleges are also bending admissions standards to make space for children from rich or influential families that lack long-standing ties to the institutions. Through referrals and word-of-mouth, schools identify applicants from well-to-do families. Then, as soon as these students enroll, universities start soliciting gifts from their parents.

Duke says it has never traded an admission for a donation. "There's no quid pro quo, no bargains have been struck," says Peter Vaughn, director of development communications. While it won't comment on individual cases, the university notes that financial gifts from parents are used to update facilities and provide financial aid, among other things.

The formal practice of giving preference to students whose parents are wealthy—sometimes called "development admits"—has implications for the legal challenge to affirmative action, which the U.S. Supreme Court will hear April 1 [2003]. Special admissions treatment for the affluent has racial overtones, at least indirectly. Reflecting the distribution of wealth in America, the vast majority of major donors to higher education are white. Defenders of minority preference say such advantages for white applicants are precisely why affirmative action is still needed.

Top schools ranging from Stanford University to Emory University say they occasionally consider parental wealth in admission decisions. Other elite schools, such as Massachusetts Institute of Technology, say parental means don't influence them. "I understand why universities leverage parent contacts to enrich themselves," says Marilee Jones, dean of admissions at MIT. "If somebody's offering them a check, why not take it? But I honestly think it's out of control."

While children of the wealthy have long had advantages getting into colleges, a look at how "development" admissions works at Duke shows how institutionalized the process has become at some major universities.

Under-endowed compared with rivals such as Harvard, Princeton and Stanford, Duke has been particularly aggressive in snaring donors through admissions breaks. Widely considered one of the nation's top ten universities, Duke accepts 23% of its applicants and turns down more than 600 high-school valedictorians a year. Three-fourths of its students score above 1320 out of a perfect 1600 on the SATs.

Yet in recent years, Duke says it has relaxed these standards to admit 100 to 125 students annually as a result of family wealth or connections, up from about 20 a decade ago. These students aren't alumni children and were tentatively rejected, or wait-listed, in the regular admissions review. More than half of them enroll, constituting an estimated 3% to 5% of Duke's student body of 6,200.

The strategy appears to be paying off. For the last six years, Duke says it has led all universities nationwide in unrestricted gifts to its annual fund from non-alumni parents: about $3.1 million in 2001–2002. A university fund-raising campaign recently met its $2 billion goal. While 35% of alumni donate to Duke, 52% of parents of last year's freshman class contributed to the university—besides paying $35,000 in tuition and room and board.

Students admitted for development reasons graduate at a higher rate than the overall student body, Duke says, although their grades are slightly lower. These applicants are held to the same lesser standard as some top athletes; not whether they can excel, but whether they can graduate. "There's never been a case where I think the student can't be successful at Duke, and the student is admitted," says admissions director Christoph Guttentag.

Caroline Diemar, a Duke senior, says she favors maintaining minority preference for college admissions because she knows from experience that well-connected white students get a boost too. The daughter of an investment banker, she applied early to Duke despite an 1190 SAT score. Her candidacy was deferred to the spring.

She then buttressed her application with recommendations from two family friends who were Duke donors, and she was accepted. "I needed something to make me stand out," says Ms. Diemar, a sociology major with a 3.2 grade point average, below the 3.4 average of the senior class. "Everybody at Duke has something that got them in." The lesson she learned: "Networking is how you go about everything."

After she enrolled, Duke recruited Ms. Diemar's parents to serve as co-chairmen of a fund-raising effort. Her father, Robert Diemar, declined to say how much he has given to Duke. "We support all of our five children's schools," said Mr. Diemar, a Princeton alumnus. He said Duke accepted his daughter on merit.

The practice of giving preference to the children of potential donors has caused fissures on Duke's campus, with some worrying that it dilutes the student body's intellectual vitality and undermines racial and economic diversity. In November 2000, a report to the trustees by a university committee on admissions called for a one-third cut in applicants accepted for development reasons. Mr. Guttentag says he plans to reduce such admissions to about 65 this year to achieve "greater flexibility" in shaping next fall's freshman class.

Duke President Nannerl O. Keohane thinks the Supreme Court should uphold affirmative action because preferences for children of potential donors is "disproportionately favorable to white students. . . . The two are definitely linked, and it seems odd to me to allow one sort of preference, but not the other."

The University of Michigan, defendant in the affirmative action case before the Supreme Court, wants to continue to allow preferential treatment for minorities. It also gives preferential admissions treatment to children of potential donors—but only if they're white or Asian.

DISCRETIONARY POINTS

Under the 150-point "Selection Index" Michigan uses for undergraduate admissions, a review committee may award 20 "discretionary" points to children of donors, legislators, faculty members and other key supporters. Minorities underrepresented in higher education—Hispanics, African-Americans and Native Americans—qualify for an automatic 20 points, but they are ineligible for the discretionary points. The university says less than 1% of admitted students receive this edge.

The late Terry Sanford, Duke president from 1969 to 1985, practiced donor preference on a large scale. Mr. Sanford, a gregarious former North Carolina governor, used his wide circle of contacts in business, politics and the media to elevate Duke from a regional to a national university. According to Keith Brodie, Duke's president emeritus, Mr. Sanford would personally meet each year with the admissions and development directors to ensure special attention for 200 of these friends' children applying to Duke. More than 100 would ultimately enroll.

As president from 1985 to 1993, Dr. Brodie says, he removed himself from the admissions process, resisted lobbying by some trustees, and trimmed the number of underqualified students admitted due to donor preference to 20 a year. "A Duke education is too valuable an asset to squander," says Dr. Brodie, a professor of psychiatry, who was criticized as president for a lack of fund-raising zeal. "University presidents are under greater pressure than ever to raise money," he adds. "I suspect many of them have turned to admissions to help that process."

Harold Wingood, who was senior associate director of admissions under Dr. Brodie, recalls that 30 to 40 students per year were upgraded from "rejected" to "wait-list," or from "wait-list" to "admit" due to their family ties. "We'd take students in some

Under-represented minority

18%

North/South Carolina resident

15%

Children of alumni

12%

Recruited athlete

8%

Potential donor/development

3%–5%

**FIGURE 15.1   Study Break:
Proportion of the 1,654 Current Duke
University Freshmen Who Qualified
for Various Admission Preferences**

Note: Some students may have qualified for more
than one preference, or would have qualified for
admission on their academic records regardless
of preference.

Source: Duke admissions office.

cases with SAT scores 100 points below the mean, or just outside the top 15% of their
class," says Mr. Wingood, now dean of admissions at Clark University in Worcester,
Mass. "They weren't slugs, but they weren't strong enough to get in on their own."

The numbers have increased under Ms. Keohane, Duke's current president.
Duke says it admitted about 125 non-alumni children in 1998, and again in 1999,
who had been tentatively rejected or wait-listed prior to considering family connections. It accepted 99 such students in 2000. Similar data aren't available for 2001
or 2002, the school says.

Ms. Keohane says she didn't intentionally increase the number of wealthy
applicants given a leg up. She says "it is possible that the numbers drifted upward"
during the recent $2 billion-fund-raising campaign because "more people in devel-
opment expressed interest in candidates. But this was certainly not a policy direc-
tive, or even a conscious choice."

The system at Duke works this way: Through its own network and names supplied by trustees, alumni, donors and others, the development office identifies about 500 likely applicants with rich or powerful parents who are not alumni. (Children of major alumni donors are given similar preference in a separate process.) It cultivates them with campus tours and basic admissions advice; for instance, applying early increases their chances. It also relays the names to the admissions office, which returns word if any of the students forget to apply—so development can remind them.

The development office then winnows the initial 500 into at least 160 high-priority applicants. Although these names are flagged in the admissions-office computer, admissions readers evaluate them on merit, without regard to family means. About 30 to 40 are accepted, the others tentatively rejected or wait-listed. During an all-day meeting in March, Mr. Guttentag and John Piva Jr., senior vice president for development, debate these 120 cases, weighing their family's likely contribution against their academic shortcomings.

In her 2001 book, "Admissions Confidential," former Duke admissions officer Rachel Toor recalled that most admissions officers "hated to see these kids get in" because they were "the weakest part of our applicant pool." Nevertheless, most of the 120 students are admitted.

Once these children of privilege enroll, the development office enlists their parents as donors and fund raisers. According to Dr. Brodie, Duke's parent program originated as a forum for parent concerns about safety issues, but it has evolved into a fund-raising vehicle.

A committee of more than 200 non-alumni parents provides its volunteer army for the four classes currently at Duke. Committee members usually give at least $1,000 to Duke, and the eight co-chairmen and the national chairman much more—including at least two seven-figure gifts endowing faculty chairs.

Membership in the parents' committee is by invitation only and is overwhelmingly white. Lately, one affluent Chicago suburb—Lake Forest—has dominated its higher echelons. Lake Forest luminaries on the committee have included department-store heir Marshall Field V, who has given at least $100,000 to Duke; Paul Clark, chief executive of Icos Corp., a biotech firm; Robert DePree, chairman of corn-meal maker House-Autry Mills Inc.; and investment banker Willard Bunn III, Maude's father.

The Lake Forest couples are social friends, serve on many of the same Chicago-area boards and several sent their children to the same private elementary school, Lake Forest Country Day. They write recommendations to Duke for each other's children.

'PRETTY INTIMATE GROUP'

Susan DePree, Robert's wife, describes the Duke parents committee as a "pretty intimate group" but not "clubby." She declined to say how much she and her husband have contributed to Duke, but says they solicited at least one six-figure gift from a parent-committee member.

Maude Bunn, whose family lives in Lake Forest, attended an elite boarding school in Lawrenceville, N.J., where the Bunn Library opened in 1996. She says other Lake Forest parents recommended her to Duke.

Cissy Bunn acknowledges her daughter didn't fit the academic profile of a Duke student. "She's bright, she had good grades, but she doesn't meet the super-star status," Mrs. Bunn says. "Did my normal child take the place of somebody who could really make a difference in the world? Sure, yes, to an extent. But there are so many things you can lose sleep over. I'm happy for me and my child."

Maude Bunn says she initially felt very awkward at Duke because her admission "wasn't necessarily on my own merits." But these days, the sophomore says she is thriving. "The more time I've spent here, I feel more and more confident—they didn't have to take me if they didn't think I was equal to all the other students they are admitting," she says. "I'm doing just as well as everybody I know if not better." She is studying art history and wants a career in fashion.

Now her younger sister Meg, a high-school senior, is applying to Duke. Maude says the family likes Meg's chances. "The people my mother works with for fund raising told her, 'It's really hard to get the first child in,'" she says. "After that, sisters and brothers are easier." Duke says it, like many universities, gives some preference to siblings.

Mrs. Bunn says she's not twisting anyone's arm. "I told them, 'If she's qualified at all, that would be lovely,'" she says. "If she gets in, I'd be happy to stay on the parents' committee."

As college admission becomes increasingly competitive, parents try to help their children's chances in any way they can. Duke accepted Jane Hetherington in 2000, despite SAT scores in the mid-1200s and what she calls "average" grades in high school. She attributes her acceptance to a "wonderful recommendation" by Norman Christensen Jr., then dean of Duke's Nicholas School of the Environment and Earth Sciences, a graduate program. She got the recommendation after one meeting with him.

At the time, her father, John Hetherington, was vice president of Westvaco Corp., a paper-products firm that had donated to the school, sponsored research there and hired some of its graduates. Mr. Hetherington asked a family friend on the school's advisory board to have the dean interview Ms. Hetherington.

Mr. Christensen, a Duke professor, says he was impressed by Ms. Hetherington's devotion to environmental studies. The student's father later reciprocated by arranging a meeting between the school's new dean and Westvaco's chief executive officer, hoping the company would increase support for the school. Nothing came of it, says Mr. Hetherington. (Westvaco merged with Mead Corp. last year.)

"I don't feel we benefited from anything you would describe as the traditional white power structure network," says Mr. Hetherington, who is now a Republican state representative in Connecticut and favors a "sunset law" for affirmative action. He doesn't think his position affected his daughter's acceptance into college. "It worked out for some reason," he says. "In all candor, we got lucky."

CHAPTER 16

Asian Americans

The Myth of the Model Minority

RONALD TAKAKI

Today Asian Americans are celebrated as America's "model minority." In 1986, *NBC Nightly News* and the *McNeil/Lehrer Report* aired special news segments on Asian Americans and their success, and a year later, CBS's *60 Minutes* presented a glowing report on their stunning achievements in the academy. "Why are Asian Americans doing so exceptionally well in school?" Mike Wallace asked, and quickly added, "They must be doing something right. Let's bottle it." Meanwhile, *U.S. News & World Report* featured Asian-American advances in a cover story, and *Time* devoted an entire section on this meteoric minority in its special immigrants issue, "The Changing Face of America." Not to be outdone by its competitors, *Newsweek* titled the cover story of its college-campus magazine "Asian-Americans: The Drive to Excel" and a lead article of its weekly edition "Asian Americans: A 'Model Minority.'" *Fortune* went even further, applauding them as "America's Super Minority," and the *New Republic* extolled "The Triumph of Asian-Americans" as "America's greatest success story."

The celebration of Asian-American achievements in the press has been echoed in the political realm. Congratulations have come even from the White House. In a speech presented to Asian and Pacific Americans in the chief executive's mansion in 1984, President Ronald Reagan explained the significance of their success. America has a rich and diverse heritage, Reagan declared, and Americans are all descendants of immigrants in search of the "American dream." He praised Asian and Pacific Americans for helping to "preserve that dream by living up to the bedrock values" of America—the principles of "the sacred worth of human life, religious faith, community spirit, and the responsibility of parents and schools to be teachers of tolerance, hard work, fiscal responsibility, cooperation, and love." "It's no wonder," Reagan emphatically noted, "that the median incomes of Asian and Pacific-American families are much higher than the total American average." Hailing Asian and Pacific Americans as an example for all Americans, Reagan conveyed his gratitude to them: we need "your values, your hard work" expressed within "our political system."

But in their celebration of this "model minority," the pundits and the politicians have exaggerated Asian-American "success" and have created a new myth. Their comparisons of incomes between Asians and whites fail to recognize the regional location of the Asian-American population. Concentrated in California, Hawaii, and New York, Asian Americans reside largely in states with higher incomes but also higher costs of living than the national average: 59 percent of all Asian Americans lived in these three states in 1980, compared to only 19 percent of the general population. The use of "family incomes" by Reagan and others has been very misleading, for Asian-American families have more persons working per family than white families. In 1980, white nuclear families in California had only 1.6 workers per family, compared to 2.1 for Japanese, 2.0 for immigrant Chinese, 2.2 for immigrant Filipino, and 1.8 for immigrant Korean (this last figure is actually higher, for many Korean women are unpaid family workers). Thus the family incomes of Asian Americans indicate the presence of more workers in each family, rather than higher incomes.

Actually, in terms of personal incomes, Asian Americans have not reached equality. In 1980 the mean personal income for white men in California was $23,400. While Japanese men earned a comparable income, they did so only by acquiring more education (17.7 years compared to 16.8 years for white men twenty-five to forty-four years old) and by working more hours (2,160 hours compared to 2,120 hours for white men in the same age category). In reality, then, Japanese men were still behind Caucasian men. Income inequalities for other men were more evident: Korean men earned only $19,200, or 82 percent of the income of white men, Chinese men only $15,900 or 68 percent, and Filipino men only $14,500 or 62 percent. In New York the mean personal income for white men was $21,600, compared to only $18,900 or 88 percent for Korean men, $16,500 or 76 percent for Filipino men, and only $11,200 or 52 percent for Chinese men. In the San Francisco Bay Area, Chinese-immigrant men earned only 72 percent of what their white counterparts earned, Filipino-immigrant men 68 percent, Korean-immigrant men 69 percent, and Vietnamese-immigrant men 52 percent. The incomes of Asian-American men were close to and sometimes even below those of black men (68 percent) and Mexican-American men (71 percent).

The patterns of income inequality for Asian men reflect a structural problem: Asians tend to be located in the labor market's secondary sector, where wages are low and promotional prospects minimal. Asian men are clustered as janitors, machinists, postal clerks, technicians, waiters, cooks, gardeners, and computer programmers; they can also be found in the primary sector, but here they are found mostly in the lower-tier levels as architects, engineers, computer-systems analysts, pharmacists, and schoolteachers, rather than in the upper-tier levels of management and decision making. "Labor market segmentation and restricted mobility between sectors," observed social scientists Amado Cabezas and Gary Kawaguchi, "help promote the economic interest and privilege of those with capital or those in the primary sector, who mostly are white men."

This pattern of Asian absence from the higher levels of administration is characterized as "a glass ceiling"—a barrier through which top management positions can only be seen, but not reached, by Asian Americans. While they are increasing in numbers on university campuses as students, they are virtually nonexistent as administrators: at Berkeley's University of California campus where 25 percent of the students were Asian in 1987, only one out of 102 top-level administrators was an Asian. In the United States as a whole, only 8 percent of Asian Americans in 1988 were "officials" and "managers," as compared to 12 percent for all groups. Asian Americans are even more scarce in the upper strata of the corporate hierarchy: they constituted less than half of one percent of the 29,000 officers and directors of the nation's thousand largest companies. Though they are highly educated, Asian Americans are generally not present in positions of executive leadership and decision making. "Many Asian Americans hoping to climb the corporate ladder face an arduous ascent," the *Wall Street Journal* observed. "Ironically, the same companies that pursue them for technical jobs often shun them when filling managerial and executive positions."

Asian Americans complain that they are often stereotyped as passive and told they lack the aggressiveness required in administration. The problem is not whether their culture encourages a reserved manner, they argue, but whether they have opportunities for social activities that have traditionally been the exclusive preserve of elite white men. "How do you get invited to the cocktail party and talk to the chairman?" asked Landy Eng, a former assistant vice president of Citibank. "It's a lot easier if your father or your uncle or his friend puts his arm around you at the party and says, 'Landy, let me introduce you to Walt.'" Excluded from the "old boy" network, Asian Americans are also told they are inarticulate and have an accent. Edwin Wong, a junior manager at Acurex, said: "I was given the equivalent of an ultimatum: 'Either you improve your accent or your future in getting promoted to senior management is in jeopardy.'" The accent was a perceived problem at work. "I felt that just because I had an accent a lot of Caucasians thought I was stupid." But whites with German, French, or English accents do not seem to be similarly handicapped. Asian Americans are frequently viewed as technicians rather than administrators. Thomas Campbell, a general manager at Westinghouse Electric Corp., said that Asian Americans would be happier staying in technical fields and that few of them are adept at sorting through the complexities of large-scale business. This very image can produce a reinforcing pattern: Asian-American professionals often find they "top out," reaching a promotional ceiling early in their careers. "The only jobs we could get were based on merit," explained Kumar Patel, head of the material science division at AT&T. "That is why you find most [Asian-Indian] professionals in technical rather than administrative or managerial positions." Similarly an Asian-Indian engineer who had worked for Kaiser for some twenty years told a friend: "They [management] never ever give you [Asian Indians] an executive position in the company. You can only go up so high and no more."

Asian-American "success" has emerged as the new stereotype for this ethnic minority. While this image has led many teachers and employers to view Asians as intelligent and hardworking and has opened some opportunities, it has also been harmful. Asian Americans find their diversity as individuals denied: many feel forced to conform to the "model minority" mold and want more freedom to be their individual selves, to be "extravagant." Asian university students are concentrated in the sciences and technical fields, but many of them wish they had greater opportunities to major in the social sciences and humanities. "We are educating a generation of Asian technicians," observed an Asian-American professor at Berkeley, "but the communities also need their historians and poets." Asian Americans find themselves all lumped together and their diversity as groups overlooked. Groups that are not doing well, such as the unemployed Hmong, the Downtown Chinese, the elderly Japanese, the old Filipino farm laborers, and others, have been rendered invisible. To be out of sight is also to be without social services. Thinking Asian Americans have succeeded, government officials have sometimes denied funding for social service programs designed to help Asian Americans learn English and find employment. Failing to realize that there are poor Asian families, college administrators have sometimes excluded Asian-American students from Educational Opportunity Programs (EOP), which are intended for *all* students from low-income families. Asian Americans also find themselves pitted against and resented by other racial minorities and even whites. If Asian Americans can make it on their own, pundits are asking, why can't poor blacks and whites on welfare? Even middle-class whites, who are experiencing economic difficulties because of plant closures in a deindustrializing America and the expansion of low-wage service employment, have been urged to emulate the Asian-American "model minority" and to work harder.

Indeed, the story of the Asian-American triumph offers ideological affirmation of the American Dream in an era anxiously witnessing the decline of the United States in the international economy (due to its trade imbalance and its transformation from a creditor to a debtor nation), the emergence of a new black underclass (the percentage of black female-headed families having almost doubled from 22 percent in 1960 to 40 percent in 1980), and a collapsing white middle class (the percentage of households earning a "middle-class" income falling from 28.7 percent in 1967 to 23.2 percent in 1983). Intellectually, it has been used to explain "losing ground"—why the situation of the poor has deteriorated during the last two decades of expanded government social services. According to this view, advanced by pundits like Charles Murray, the interventionist federal state, operating on the "misguided wisdom" of the 1960s, made matters worse: it created a web of welfare dependency. But this analysis has overlooked the structural problems in society and our economy, and it has led to easy cultural explanations and quick-fix prescriptions. Our difficulties, we are sternly told, stem from our waywardness: Americans have strayed from the Puritan "errand into the wilderness." They have abandoned the old American "habits of the heart." Praise for Asian-American success is America's most recent jeremiad—a renewed commitment to make America number one again and a call for a rededication to the bedrock values of hard work, thrift, and industry. Like many congratulations, this one may veil a spirit of competition, even jealousy.

Significantly, Asian-American "success" has been accompanied by the rise of a new wave of anti-Asian sentiment. On college campuses, racial slurs have surfaced in conversations on the quad: "Look out for the Asian Invasion." "M.I.T. means Made in Taiwan." "U.C.L.A. stands for University of Caucasians Living among Asians." Nasty anti-Asian graffiti have suddenly appeared on the walls of college dormitories and in the elevators of classroom buildings: "Chink, chink, cheating chink!" "Stop the Yellow Hordes." "Stop the Chinese before they flunk you out." Ugly racial incidents have broken out on college campuses. At the University of Connecticut, for example, eight Asian-American students experienced a nightmare of abuse in 1987. Four couples had boarded a college bus to attend a dance. "The dance was a formal and so we were wearing gowns," said Marta Ho, recalling the horrible evening with tears. "The bus was packed, and there was a rowdy bunch of white guys in the back of the bus. Suddenly I felt this warm sticky stuff on my hair. They were spitting on us! My friend was sitting sidewise and got hit on her face and she started screaming. Our boy friends turned around, and one of the white guys, a football player, shouted: 'You want to make something out of this, you Oriental faggots!'"

Asian-American students at the University of Connecticut and other colleges are angry, arguing that there should be no place for racism on campus and that they have as much right as anyone else to be in the university. Many of them are children of recent immigrants who had been college-educated professionals in Asia. They see how their parents had to become greengrocers, restaurant operators, and storekeepers in America, and they want to have greater career choices for themselves. Hopeful a college education can help them overcome racial obstacles, they realize the need to be serious about their studies. But white college students complain: "Asian students are nerds." This very stereotype betrays nervousness—fears that Asian-American students are raising class grade curves. White parents, especially alumni, express concern about how Asian-American students are taking away "their" slots—admission places that should have gone to their children. "Legacy" admission slots reserved for children of alumni have come to function as a kind of invisible affirmative-action program for whites. A college education has always represented a valuable economic resource, credentialing individuals for high income and status employment, and the university has recently become a contested terrain of competition between whites and Asians. In paneled offices, university administrators meet to discuss the "problem" of Asian-American "overrepresentation" in enrollments.

Paralleling the complaint about the rising numbers of Asian-American students in the university is a growing worry that there are also "too many" immigrants coming from Asia. Recent efforts to "reform" the 1965 Immigration Act seem reminiscent of the nativism prevalent in the 1880s and the 1920s. Senator Alan K. Simpson of Wyoming, for example, noted how the great majority of the new immigrants were from Latin America and Asia, and how "a substantial portion" of them did not "integrate fully" into American society. "If language and cultural separatism rise above a certain level," he warned, "the unity and political stability of the Nation will—in time—be seriously eroded. Pluralism within a united American nation has been our greatest strength. The unity comes from a common language and a core public culture of certain shared values, beliefs, and customs, which make us distinctly 'Americans.'" In the view of many supporters of immigration reform, the post-1965 immigration from Asia and Latin America threatens the traditional unity and identity of the American people. "The immigration from the turn of the century was largely a continuation of immigration from previous years in that the European stock of Americans was being maintained," explained Steve Rosen, a member of an organization lobbying for changes in the current law. "Now, we are having a large influx of third-world people, which could be potentially disruptive of our whole Judeo-Christian heritage." Significantly, in March 1988, the Senate passed a bill that would limit the entry of family members and that would provide 55,000 new visas to be awarded to "independent immigrants" on the basis of education, work experience, occupations, and "English language skills."

Political concerns usually have cultural representations. The entertainment media have begun marketing Asian stereotypes again: where Hollywood had earlier portrayed Asians as Charlie Chan displaying his wit and wisdom in his fortune cookie Confucian quotes and as the evil Fu Manchu threatening white women, the film industry has recently been presenting images of comic Asians (in *Sixteen Candles*) and criminal Asian aliens (in *Year of the Dragon*). Hollywood has entered the realm of foreign affairs. *The Deer Hunter* explained why the United States lost the war in Vietnam. In this story, young American men are sent to fight in Vietnam, but they are not psychologically prepared for the utter cruelty of physically disfigured Viet Cong clad in black pajamas. Shocked and disoriented, they collapse morally into a world of corruption, drugs, gambling, and Russian roulette. There seems to be something sinister in Asia and the people there that is beyond the capability of civilized Americans to comprehend. Upset after seeing this movie, refugee Thu-Thuy Truong exclaimed: "We didn't play Russian roulette games in Saigon! The whole thing was made up." Similarly *Apocalypse Now* portrayed lost innocence: Americans enter the heart of darkness in Vietnam and become possessed by madness (in the persona played by Marlon Brando) but are saved in the end by their own technology and violence (represented by Martin Sheen). Finally, in movies celebrating the exploits of Rambo, Hollywood has allowed Americans to win in fantasy the Vietnam War they had lost in reality. "Do we get to win this time?" snarls Rambo, our modern Natty Bumppo, a hero of limited conversation and immense patriotic rage.

Meanwhile, anti-Asian feelings and misunderstandings have been exploding violently in communities across the country, from Philadelphia, Boston, and New York to Denver and Galveston, Seattle, Portland, Monterey, and San Francisco. In Jersey City, the home of 15,000 Asian Indians, a hate letter published in a local newspaper warned: "We will go to any extreme to get Indians to move out of Jersey City. If I'm walking down the street and I see a Hindu and the setting is right, I will just hit him or her. We plan some of our more extreme attacks such as breaking windows, breaking car windows and crashing family parties. We use the phone book and look up the name Patel. Have you seen how many there are?" The letter was reportedly written by the "Dotbusters," a cruel reference to the *bindi* some Indian women wear as a sign of sanctity. Actual attacks have taken place, ranging from verbal harassments and egg throwing to serious beatings. Outside a Hoboken restaurant on September 27, 1987, a gang of youths chanting "Hindu, Hindu" beat Navroz Mody to death. A grand jury has indicted four teenagers for the murder.

Five years earlier a similarly brutal incident occurred in Detroit. There, in July, Vincent Chin, a young Chinese American, and two friends went to a bar in the late afternoon to celebrate his upcoming wedding. Two white autoworkers, Ronald Ebens and Michael Nitz, called Chin a "Jap" and cursed: "It's because of you motherfuckers that we're out of work." A fistfight broke out, and Chin then quickly left the bar. But Ebens and Nitz took out a baseball bat from the trunk of their car and chased Chin through the streets. They finally cornered him in front of a McDonald's restaurant. Nitz held Chin while Ebens swung the bat across the victim's shins and then bludgeoned Chin to death by shattering his skull. Allowed to plead guilty to manslaughter, Ebens and Nitz were sentenced to three years' probation and fined $3,780 each. But they have not spent a single night in jail for their bloody deed. "Three thousand dollars can't even buy a good used car these days," snapped a Chinese American, "and this was the price of a life." "What kind of law is this? What kind of justice?" cried Mrs. Lily Chin, the slain man's mother. "This happened because my son is Chinese. If two Chinese killed a white person, they must go to jail, maybe for their whole lives. . . . Something is wrong with this country."

PART FIVE

Sexism

The 1960s were known as a decade of civil rights struggles, black militancy, anti-war protests, and campus disturbances. It seemed unlikely that yet another social movement could take hold and grow, but the consciousness of women's oppression could and did grow, with enormous impact over remarkably few years.

Black militancy, the student movement, the antiwar movement, youth militancy, and radicalism all affirmed freedom, equality, and liberation, but none of these was thought to be particularly necessary or applicable to women, especially by radical men. Ironically, it was political experience with radical men that led radical women to the consciousness of women as a distinctly oppressed group and, therefore, a group with distinctive interests.

The feminism that emerged in the 1970s was in fact both novel and part of a long and often painful series of movements for the liberation of women. Women's rights proposals were first heard more than a century ago. But the movement for the equality of women ground to a halt when the emergencies of the Depression and World War II pushed aside feminist concerns. With victory, both sexes gratefully resumed the middle-class dream of family, security, and upward mobility. These years of the late 1940s and early 1950s were the years of "The Feminine Mystique,"[1] when the *domestic* role of women dominated American culture.

When women began, in the 1970s, to once again reassert themselves and claimed to be able to be doctors and lawyers and bankers and pilots, they were met with derision. The "Long Amnesia" had taken hold and stereotyped women's roles into those of the 1940s and 1950s. People, especially men, had come to regard female domesticity almost as a natural phenomenon. Nevertheless, women persevered, and, in what was historically a brief period, it became inconceivable to see no female faces broadcasting the news, granting loans, and training to be jet pilots at the U.S. Air Force Academy.

By the twenty-first century most young women in American were growing up in a world so greatly changed from the 1950s that for many these battles seemed like pieces of a long-ago past. But the struggle for real equality between the sexes is hardly over, for reasons suggested by the readings in this part. Although the idea of male supremacy may be on the way out in most industrialized nations, there is still, in many respects, a long way to go.

How much this is true at the top of the economic scale is shown in the *Economist* magazine's discussion of the persistence of the "glass ceiling" that blocks women from anything like equal participation at the highest levels of American business. Women today in many countries, including the United States, are more likely to be corporate executives than they were a generation ago, but progress has stalled in recent years. Though women are almost half of the American work force, they still make up only about 8 percent of top managers in American business, and less than 1 percent of chief executive officers; and these proportions have barely changed at all over the past decade.

What accounts for the stubborn persistence of the "glass ceiling"? The *Economist* cites three key reasons: the exclusion of women from the informal social networks through which men have traditionally gotten influence and promotions, a pervasive stereotyping of women as less capable of leadership, and the lack of role models to guide women upward in the corporate hierarchy. The way these barriers work in practice is strikingly depicted in Liza Featherstone's account of the treatment of women at the nation's largest corporation, Wal-Mart stores. Though Wal-Mart hires great numbers of women, they have been overwhelmingly concentrated in low-level, poorly paying jobs—a situation that has resulted in a massive lawsuit against the company by women alleging sex discrimination. Women seeking to move up to better managerial positions were often derided by male executives, company meetings were sometimes held at strip clubs, a "boys club" culture often kept talented women out of the loop of important connections and kept them stuck in jobs that were below their capacity while less qualified men moved up the job ladder.

How, in a society supposedly committed to equality between the sexes, do such practices continue to flourish? Part of the problem is the stubborn persistence of sexist norms and expectations that, though often subtle, still shape the lives of men and women in very different ways. As Peggy Orenstein shows in "Learning Silence," these attitudes begin very early. Orenstein observed a California school that enjoys an exemplary curriculum. But she also found operating in the school a "hidden curriculum" that delivers unstated lessons—a "running subtext"—undermining girls' confidence in their ability to learn, especially in crucial subjects like science and math. Girls and boys are also given subtle but effective cues on how to behave in the classroom and where to locate themselves in the school's culture and social organization. Orenstein concludes that these faint but compelling lessons have the effect of teaching students their proper place in the status hierarchy of the larger society.

The early development of these gender expectations helps explain what the *Economist* calls the "glacially slow" pace of change in opportunities for women at the upper levels of the American economy. But change has been even slower when it comes to conditions in the lower-level jobs that are still disproportionately held by women—often women of color. As Pierrette Hondagneu-Sotelo shows in her description of domestic household workers in California, the women who do these jobs are typically immigrants as well. The conditions they frequently face on the job—low pay, long hours, isolation, and sometimes harsh treatment by employers—illustrate how traditional gender expectations linger even in the most modern of settings.

ENDNOTES

1. Betty Friedan, *The Feminine Mystique,* New York: Norton, 1963.

CHAPTER 17

The Conundrum
of the Glass Ceiling

THE ECONOMIST

WHY ARE WOMEN SO PERSISTENTLY ABSENT FROM TOP CORPORATE JOBS?

It is 20 years since the term "glass ceiling" was coined by the *Wall Street Journal* to describe the apparent barriers that prevent women from reaching the top of the corporate hierarchy; and it is ten years since the American government's specially appointed Glass Ceiling Commission published its recommendations. In 1995 the commission said that the barrier was continuing "to deny untold numbers of qualified people the opportunity to compete for and hold executive level positions in the private sector." It found that women had 45.7% of America's jobs and more than half of master's degrees being awarded. Yet 95% of senior managers were men, and female managers' earnings were on average a mere 68% of their male counterparts'.

Ten years on, women account for 46.5% of America's workforce and for less than 8% of its top managers, although at big *Fortune* 500 companies the figure is a bit higher. Female managers' earnings now average 72% of their male colleagues'. Booz Allen Hamilton, a consulting firm that monitors departing chief executives in America, found that 0.7% of them were women in 1998, and 0.7% of them were women in 2004. In between, the figure fluctuated. But the firm says that one thing is clear: the number is "very low and not getting higher."

In other countries the picture is similar. Not a single woman [was] featured in *Fortune* magazine's list this June of the 25 highest-paid CEOs in Europe. Although Laurence Parisot, the chief executive of Ifop, an opinion pollster, was chosen recently to head Medef, the French employers' association, she is a rare exception. Corinne Maier, an economist with EDF, a French energy group, gave a scathing description of French corporate life in last year's best-seller, "Bonjour Paresse." "Among the well-heeled battalions of executives," she wrote, "only 5% are women." Equality in the French workplace, claimed Ms. Maier, "is a far-off dream."

It is even farther off in Japan where, until 20–30 years ago, it was generally unacceptable for women to stay in the office after 5pm. One ambitious employee of a foreign multinational dared to hide in the ladies room until the men had left before returning to her desk to finish her work. There has been some progress since. This year two women have been appointed to head big Japanese companies. Fumiko Hayashi is now chairman and CEO of Daiei, a troubled supermarket chain; and Tomoyo Nonaka, a former newscaster, has been appointed boss of Sanyo Electric. Nissan has a general manager for "diversity development" who, when asked recently what has changed least in Japanese business in the past 20 years, replied: "The mindset of Japanese gentlemen."

In Britain, the number of female executive directors of FTSE100 companies rose from 11 in 2000 to 17 in 2004, according to Cranfield, a business school—17 women as against almost 400 men. A larger sample of British quoted companies found that 65% had no women on their board at all in 2003. No British woman has yet headed a big British company, although 44% of the workforce is female. Marjorie Scardino, CEO of Pearson, owner of the *Financial Times* which owns 50% of *The Economist,* is American, as is Laura Tyson, who heads the London Business School. Clara Furse, boss of London's stock exchange, was born in Canada.

It is progress of a sort—but of a glacially slow sort. The glass-ceiling phenomenon is proving peculiarly persistent. The top of the corporate ladder remains stubbornly male, and the few women who reach it are paid significantly less than the men that they join there.

This is despite the fact that companies are trying harder than ever to help women to climb higher. So-called "diversity programmes" (which are aimed at promoting minorities as well as women) are as common as diversity on the board is rare, and not just among service industries such as finance and retailing. No-nonsense formerly male clubs such as IBM (where two decades ago blue-suited identikit white men drove the company close to bankruptcy), GE (where the culture was not exactly female-friendly during the long rule of its legendary leader Jack Welch) and BP (where long hours at sea on windy oil rigs were a career booster), have appointed senior executives to be in charge of diversity. The three firms were the unlikely joint sponsors of a recent conference on "Women in Leadership."

DIVERSITY PAYS

Such companies no longer see the promotion of women solely as a moral issue of equal opportunity and equal pay. They have been persuaded of the business case for diversity. It has long been known that mixed groups are better at problem solving than like-minded ones. But the benefits of diversity are greater than this. Research by Catalyst, an American organisation that aims to expand "opportunities for women and business," found a strong correlation between the number of women in top executive positions and financial performance among *Fortune* 500 companies between 1996 and 2000.

For some companies the push towards greater diversity has come from their customers. Lou Gerstner, the man who turned around IBM partly by promoting diversity within the company, has said "we made diversity a market-based issue . . . it's about understanding our markets, which are diverse and multicultural." Lisa Bondesio, head of diversity in Britain for Deloitte, a big firm of accountants, says that diversity is "about how we differentiate ourselves in the marketplace."

Other companies surprisingly fail to reflect the diversity of their customers. Procter & Gamble (P&G), for example, the manufacturer of Pampers nappies, Max Factor and Tampax, boasts in its 2004 annual report that it was ranked "among the top companies for executive women" by the National Association for Female Executives. Yet it has only two women on its 16-person board, both of them non-executives, and out of the 45 people it lists as its top "corporate officers" only three are women—ie, 93% of them are men. P&G is an enormously successful company and its management programmes are widely admired. Its shareholders may wonder if it would do even better if the gender ratios at the top were less skewed.

Many companies have been motivated by a desire to broaden the pool of "talent" that their human-resources departments can fish in. They worry in general about the ageing populations of the developed world. But particular industries have other reasons for broadening their recruitment trawl. The big accounting firms, for example, had their reputations seriously dented by the demise of Enron and its auditor Arthur Andersen just before they had an unprecedented increase in business as a consequence of the extra duties imposed by the Sarbanes-Oxley act. They became the "employer of choice" for far fewer graduates at a time when they needed to attract far more. A consequence is that they have had to extend their recruitment and promotion efforts to more women.

The management-consulting business, where firms tend to follow the career strategy of "up or out," would like to hold on to many more of its women. But up or out can scarcely accommodate maternity leave, so it is no surprise that the industry loses twice as many women as men from the middle rungs of its career ladder.

Booz Allen Hamilton, a leading consulting firm, regularly wonders how to alter the fact that only 1–2% of its partners are women. Orit Gadiesh, the chairman of Bain, a rival, is a notable exception to the general exclusion of women from the top ranks. However, an earlier career in the Israeli army may have provided essential skills for her to reach the top.

Some firms' diversity programmes are working. At IBM, there are now seven women among its 40 top executives. GE says that 14% of its "senior executives" are now women, although none of them featured in the chief executive's recent reshuffle at the very top. The firm's six new business divisions are all headed by men.

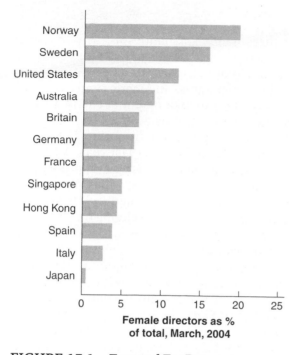

FIGURE 17.1   Few and Far Between

Source: Ethical Investment Research Service

By contrast, Alcan, a Canadian multinational metal manufacturer, has made extraordinary progress. Three out of its four main businesses are now headed by women (including the bauxite and alumina business). Steven Price, the company's HR director, says "it's been a long journey" to reach this point. Crucial has been "the tone at the top" and a determination to break down the perception that working long hours and wearing air miles like a "battle medal" are ways to get ahead in the company.

Why is it proving so difficult for women to reach the top of corporations? Are they simply less ambitious, less excited by the idea of limitless (albeit first-class) travel, late nights and the onerous responsibilities imposed by mounting regulation? A 2002 survey of top executives in American multinationals around the world did find them to be less ambitious, at least for the very top job: 19% of the men interviewed aspired to be CEO, whereas only 9% of the women did. At a slightly lower level there was less difference: 43% of women hoped to join a senior management committee, compared with 54% of the men. Catalyst, on the other hand, says that its research shows that women and men have equal desires to have the CEO job. "Ambition knows no gender," says Ilene Lang, the president of Catalyst and once a senior executive in Silicon Valley.

WHO'S IN THE CLUB?

Top businesswomen in America give three main explanations for why so few of them reach "C-level"—that group of executives who preface their titles with the word "chief." First comes the exclusion from informal networks. In many firms jock-talk and late-night boozing still oil the wheels of progress. In America and elsewhere it has become almost traditional for sales teams to take potential clients to strip clubs and the like. These activities specifically exclude most women.

Yasmin Jetha, a Muslim of Asian origin who made it to the board of Abbey, a British bank and a FTSE100 company until it was taken over last year by Spain's Banco Santander, says that although she neither drinks alcohol nor supports a rugby team, she made a point in her career of participating in industry-wide events where the opportunities for exclusion are less. More and more women in business are forming their own networks, which also help to counter male clubbishness.

The second hurdle is what Ms. Lang calls "pervasive stereotyping of women's capacity for leadership." Everyone is unconsciously biased and there is strong evidence that men are biased against promoting women inside companies. This was a central point in the landmark 1989 case in America of *Price Waterhouse v Hopkins,* where Ann Hopkins sued her employer when she was not given a partnership. She eventually won her case in the Supreme Court. Since then some companies have begun to take special steps to guard against bias. Deloitte, for example, carefully scrutinises its pay and promotion decisions for bias, especially its list of new partners announced annually in June.

The third hurdle is the lack of role models. There are too few women in top jobs to show how it is done. Helen Alexander, the chief executive of The Economist Group and one of very few female CEOs to have succeeded a female CEO (Ms. Scardino) says, however, that the role models that matter come earlier in life—at school or in the family. In addition, it seems to be important for many successful businesswomen to have had a supportive father.

Chris Bones, a senior human-resources executive with Cadbury Schweppes before he took over as head of Henley Management College at the beginning of this year, suggests another reason. The flattening of organisations in recent years, as layers of management have been stripped out, has meant that promotions now are far steeper steps than they used to be. This leaves fewer opportunities for people to reenter the workforce at higher levels. And many women inevitably need to take time off during their careers. In America, there is evidence to suggest that more women with children under the age of one are taking time off work than was the case some years ago.

More and more too are withdrawing to care for elderly parents at a time when they are on the cusp of the higher echelons. Ben Rosen, a professor at the Kenan-Flagler Business School in North Carolina who has done research on the topic, says that many women bail out of corporate life to become self-employed consultants and entrepreneurs, roles where they can have greater freedom and autonomy to manage the rest of their lives. This may be reinforcing companies' long-held belief that they should invest less in women's careers because they are unlikely to stay the course.

Ms. Maier's Gallic analysis of the issue is that French men spend more time at work than women, which "can be explained by their insatiable predatory instincts as well as by their casual approach to banal household chores." This leaves women with so much to do at home that they are more than twice as likely as men to work part-time, "which makes it all the more impossible to break the glass ceiling." In America a survey by the Centre for Work-Life Policy found that 40% of highly qualified women with spouses felt that their husbands did less work around the home than they created.

Another finding of the study was that qualified women leave work for a mixture of reasons—some pull them away (home and family life), and some push them away (the type of work, the people they are working with). In business, the push factors were found to be particularly powerful, "unlike, say, in medicine or teaching." The vast majority of women (93%) said they wanted to return to work, but found the options available to them "few and far between, and extremely costly." Across sectors, women lost 37% of their earning power when they spent three or more years out of the workforce.

Very few (5%) wanted to return to the companies they had left, claiming the work they had been doing there was not particularly satisfying. In Britain, women are increasingly dissatisfied with work. A recent study by the University of Bath of female workers between 1992 and 2003 showed an overall decline in their stated levels of job satisfaction. For full-time female managers the decline was an above-average 6%. For men, job satisfaction over the same period went up.

The only category of female workers with a significant rise in satisfaction (of 19%) was that of part-time craft workers. It has become a lot more rewarding to blow glass or design gardens than to strive forever in a vain bid to reach the boardroom.

CHANGE NEEDED

Will time alone erode the gap between men and women? The steep decline among women in the popularity of MBA degrees, the *sine qua non* (at least in America) of a fast-track corporate career, suggests not. What is more, women with MBAs are fast dropping out of the workforce. One study in America found that one out of every three such qualified women is not working full-time. For men, the comparable figure is one in 20.

What can be done to improve the gender balance at the top? In Norway, legislation has been passed decreeing that by the end of 2006 all companies must have at least two women on their boards. Norway already leads the world in the number of women on its company boards (see [Figure 17.1]).

In Britain a group of businesswomen has set up an organisation called WDOB, or Women Directors on Boards, whose aim is "to change the face of UK plc." Jacey Graham, its director, hopes to see the almost static percentage of female executive directors in Britain more than double (to 10%) by 2010.

Ms Graham says that such change "won't just happen." It needs specific intervention within companies—intervention that is led from the top. Opportunities for flexible working are particularly helpful in keeping women in the workforce. KPMG, one of the Big Four accounting firms, is aiming to double the percentage of its partners who are women (currently 13%). It says flexible working is a key measure to help it achieve this goal. Three-quarters of all requests for flexible working over the past 12 months have been from women.

Mentoring is also helpful. The WDOB has initiated a programme in which the chairmen and CEOs of 25 FTSE100 companies have agreed to mentor women who have been identified from other companies among the group as having boardroom potential. "The sad thing," says Ms. Graham, "is that some companies could not find a woman to put forward for mentoring." Women are enthusiastic mentors of each other. Colleen Arnold, the general manager of IBM Europe, Middle East and Africa, mentors 27 people formally and more than 100 informally. "Mentoring," she says, "is penalty-free."

Chief executives are appointed by sub-committees of companies' boards, often advised by headhunters. More of them will be women when more members of the sub-committees are women and when fewer headhunters are old white men. As Catalyst's Ms. Lang puts it "There are so many women qualified to be on boards who are out there, under the radar screen." Heidrick & Struggles, a firm of headhunters, says that boards may need to look beyond the top-management structures from which non-executive directors are usually drawn if they are "to increase markedly the ratio of female to male directors."

Some think the task is particularly urgent. Chris Clarke, the America-based CEO of Boyden, a firm of headhunters, and a visiting professor at Henley Management College in England, argues that women are superior to men at multi-tasking, team-building and communicating, which have become the essential skiffs for running a 21st-century corporation. Maria Wisniewska, who headed a Polish bank, Bank Pekao, and is an international adviser to the Conference Board, says: "The links between the rational and emotional parts of the brain are greater in women than in men. If so, and if leadership is about making links between emotion and intelligence, then maybe women are better at it than men."

CHAPTER 18

Selling Women Short

LIZA FEATHERSTONE

"It's not easy to have a family and a career," says the woman in the commercial earnestly. "But my company makes it a lot easier. My company takes family very seriously." The woman, "Margaret," is shown at home, spending relaxed quality time with her husband and children.

Beginning in mid-2003, American TV viewers were bombarded with advertisements like this one from a surprising source: Wal-Mart. The commercials were light on details—Margaret, a district manager for the retail chain, never says what Wal-Mart does, exactly, to help her balance motherhood with her demanding job—but their tone was inspiringly upbeat. In a similar ad, a middle-aged black woman talks about her successful career as a Wal-Mart department manager, smilingly pronouncing it a company of great "opportunity" for women. The woman says she is so pleased with her Wal-Mart career that she urged her daughter to apply for a job with the company. Now, both mother and daughter are enthusiastic members of the "Wal-Mart family."

Had the nation's favorite retailer shed its famously conservative, music-censoring image and embraced a women's-rights agenda? Not yet. These ads were part of a concerted attempt by the company to stave off a public relations disaster personified by a woman who looks a little like the happy, nameless department manager in the commercial but whose experience working for Wal-Mart was exactly the opposite.

That woman was Betty Dukes, a 54-year-old Wal-Mart worker in Pittsburg, California. Like her TV counterpart, she is African American, and she came to Wal-Mart hoping to get ahead. First hired by the company in 1994 as a $5-per-hour part-time cashier, Dukes was an eager employee with a sincere admiration for the "visionary spirit" of the chain's founder, Sam Walton. A year later, with excellent performance reviews, she was given a merit pay raise and a full-time job. Two years later, after being promoted to the position of customer-service manager—an hourly, not salaried, position, despite the "manager" designation—she began encountering harsh discrimination from her superiors: she was, she says, denied the training she needed in order to advance further; meanwhile, that training was given to male employees, many of whom were younger than Dukes and newer to the company.

When Dukes complained about this discrimination, managers got back at her by writing her up for minor offenses like returning late from breaks—offenses routinely committed by her white and male coworkers for which they were never punished, she says. When she kept complaining, she was denied a promotion and finally was demoted back to her cashier job. She went to the Wal-Mart district office to complain, but the company did nothing. Not only was the demotion humiliating, but the cashier job offered fewer hours and lower hourly pay, and being demoted disqualified Dukes from other promotions—a worker who has recently been disciplined can't be promoted. Even when she was once again eligible for promotion, four new management positions were filled by men. They hadn't been posted, which meant that other women besides Dukes were sidelined.

Before working for Wal-Mart, Dukes didn't know the meaning of the term "sex discrimination." She had long assumed it referred to something sexual—"like Bill Clinton, or Anita Hill"—and as a woman of traditional morality, figured it had nothing to do with her. "As a single person, I don't think much about sex or sexual activity," she explains.[1] "I didn't want to go around hollering 'sex'!" Of her treatment at Wal-Mart, she says, "I knew it was unfair." Until she heard that other women were bringing a lawsuit against the company, however, she didn't know it was illegal. She suspects she's not alone in her lack of sophistication about this issue: "A lot of women are being sex-discriminated against every day and don't know it."

Dukes, who still works full-time for Wal-Mart, is now a greeter rather than a cashier, which is not a promotion. "Greeters," as every Wal-Mart shopper knows, are the cheerful, friendly people—usually seniors—who welcome you as you walk in the door and, as you leave, thank you for shopping at Wal-Mart. Dukes's wages are still so low that in addition to her full-time Wal-Mart job she has had to take a second job working as a part-time house cleaner and companion to an elderly woman in exchange for rent. Without that arrangement Dukes would be unable to get by, even though she has no dependents and spends most of her free time in her Baptist church, where she is an associate minister.

In late spring 2000, Dukes filed a claim against the company. She soon learned that her experiences were not unique; they were shared by women all over the country. The following year she became the lead plaintiff in *Dukes v. Wal-Mart Stores, Inc.,* a would-be class-action suit representing 1.6 million women who are past and present employees of the company. Filed in the U.S. District Court in San Francisco in June 2001, the suit charges Wal-Mart with discriminating against women in promotions, pay, and job assignments, in violation of Title VII of the 1964 Civil Rights Act, which protects workers from discrimination on the basis of sex, race, religion, or national origin. Plaintiffs' attorneys filed a motion for class certification on April 28, 2003. Wal-Mart's guilt or innocence was not at issue at that stage. The question was, would the judge find enough evidence of possible systematic discrimination for the case to proceed as a class action. On June 22, 2004, the answer was a resounding yes: the judge certified the class, and *Dukes v. Wal-Mart* became the largest civil rights class-action suit in history. . . .

Rhonda Harper, a former vice president of marketing at Sam's Club, also gave provocative testimony about sexism in the corporate culture of Wal-Mart. Harper's salary was in the mid–200s, so hers was a more privileged perspective than that of most witnesses and plaintiffs, but one that offers great insight into the culture at the top and the attitudes of those who have the power to set the tone—and an example—for everyone else in the company. Harper was reluctant to testify because of an agreement she'd signed with the company, but the judge ruled that her obligation to obey a subpoena took precedence over her agreement with Wal-Mart. "The judge said I had to tell the truth, so here I am," she testified in her deposition.

Setting Wal-Mart in its context, Harper, who worked at headquarters, described Bentonville and the northwest Arkansas region as "a good ole boy environment. It is a culture that has been stable for many, many years. There hasn't been, as you would have in cosmopolitan areas, as much integration, diversity, differences expressed. Many of the people have lived there their entire lives." Many Wal-Mart officers "grew up together, went to school together, started out in the company together . . . which is one of the reasons why they're so successful, because it is a very close environment there."

Harper, who has an MBA from Emory University, is clearly sophisticated and well educated compared to many Wal-Mart executives, most of whom have not spent much time working in other companies or acquiring formal education. Harper and others have suggested that the company's rural, small-town northwest Arkansas roots may well contribute to the sexism in Wal-Mart's corporate culture. Yet the problem shouldn't be blamed on "the South," as many observers have been tempted to do. Gender disparities exist in Wal-Mart stores in every region. Besides, other southern companies have done relatively well in promoting women to the corporate level: according to Catalyst, an organization that tracks women's progress in the business world, 16.2 percent of the corporate officers in companies based in the South are women (the national average is 15.7 percent).

Rhonda Harper had tremendous promise, and Wal-Mart knew it. Before coming to Sam's Club she had worked in brand management at Kraft and in marketing at the American Red Cross, Nabisco, Vanity Fair Intimates, and other companies. Her name was known in the industry, and her award-winning work was widely recognized. She was recruited by Wal-Mart in 2000, and in March 2001, Wal-Mart's then CEO, Lee Scott, told her she was being groomed to become head of marketing for all of Wal-Mart within a few years.

In sharp contrast with many of the male executives at the company, Harper is articulate, her mind lively and critical. After a series of company-sponsored intelligence tests that was conducted by Personnel Decisions International (PDI), a Texas-based company, she was told she scored "in the top handful of [Wal-Mart] employees," including individuals at the highest levels--the CEO, for example—and was in the 99th percentile for people in any company holding a position similar to hers. After the PDI tests in late summer 2001, she says she was told by Dale

Thompson, the vice president of PDI, "You could be the one," meaning she could eventually become the CEO of Wal-Mart.

Despite Harper's obvious potential, she was never able to succeed at Wal-Mart. Eventually, after being repeatedly reprimanded and reminded of the importance of "fitting in better with the Wal-Mart culture," in late 2001 she had a meeting which she describes as "abrupt . . . I remember Tom Grimm [then president and CEO of Sam's Club] looking at me and saying, 'Rhonda, it's over.' . . . And I think that might have been the only thing he said." She was fired less than two months after the PDI consultant had said she might become the first female CEO of the company. (Since leaving Wal-Mart, she has moved to Marietta, Georgia, a suburb of Atlanta, and started her own marketing company, which made a profit in its very first year.)

Under questioning by plaintiffs' lawyers, Harper described behavior she witnessed at Wal-Mart. "In some cases it struck me as insensitive to individuals," she testified, particularly individuals who were women. "I found that somewhat ironic in a culture that was predicated on 'Respect for the Individual.' " Many hourly workers echoed Harper's observation. A black woman from Ohio who feels she suffered race and sex discrimination at Wal-Mart (she is not a plaintiff) said, "They always going on about respect for the individual. Where's it at?"

Wal-Mart's in-house training is overseen by the Walton Institute, based in Bentonville. Harper testified that in one training session at the Walton Institute she heard a store manager explain why there were no female managers in his store. Owing to child-care problems and the long hours required of managers, "He didn't think they would be able to perform the responsibilities Wal-Mart demanded." He thought that "they didn't fundamentally want it." As a mother with an extremely successful career, Harper found it unlikely that most women would be unable or unwilling to work management jobs simply because of child-care responsibilities.

Other attitudes Harper described were more ludicrous: "It wouldn't be abnormal" for senior management to refer to women working in the stores as "little Janie-Qs" and "girls."[4] She noted that "Janie-Q" was a "pet name for consumers as well as associates." Despite her objections, use of the term continued. Harper added dryly, "I believe . . . there would be some in the organization who would classify it as a term of endearment."

In a photo in a January 2001 issue of *Wally World,* the company newsletter, distributed to Wal-Mart workers, Jim Haworth, then the executive vice president of operations for Sam's Club, was shown sitting in a chair in the shape of a leopard-skin-covered spike heel. The photo was taken at a December 2000 holiday party for store employees, a party Harper remembered well. On another occasion, Harper saw Haworth onstage surrounded by women, some of whom were Wal-Mart associates, who were dancing and singing. Women were lining up to have their picture taken with Haworth—a ritual that was, according to Harper, very much part of company culture: "It was done year after year." (Haworth was promoted in July 2001 to executive vice president of operations for all of Wal-Mart.)

Harper also bristled at some of the recreation she was expected to take part in as a Wal-Mart executive, activities that she felt reflected the macho culture of Wal-Mart. One event she participated in was a quail-hunting expedition at the Walton family ranch in Texas, in February 2001. "Evidently that's the best time for quail," she remarked during her deposition. "Who knew?" Harper was one of only three women on the excursion, which was for about 30 of Wal-Mart's top officers.

The quail-hunting trip has been a cherished ritual in Wal-Mart culture since the company's founding. Sam Walton loved to hunt, and his family was accustomed to hosting Wal-Mart officers—many of whom hunted in northwest Arkansas—at the Texas ranch. "I thought it odd," Harper testified. "Actually, I thought it was a joke when they told me about it, quite frankly." During her fifteen months as a Wal-Mart officer, it was the company's only executive retreat. As she anticipated the excursion, "What went through my mind was, a ninety-thousand-acre ranch in Texas, you know, owned by the world's richest family, I'm thinking day spa." But just before they left, she realized her colleagues hadn't been kidding about the hunting. "They were serious, they were talking about snake guards . . . guns and shooting and all sorts of fun stuff." At the last minute, she went out and bought some hunting gear, realizing that "this isn't a corporate retreat. We're really going to go out there and kill things."

Julie Donovan, a *Dukes* witness, in an affidavit described a similarly macho culture at Wal-Mart headquarters. In 1996, when Donovan worked in the head office as a senior buyer, Ray Hobbs, a senior vice president, told Donovan that he was surprised that she, a woman, was in such a high position at Wal-Mart, and that it would be better if she were home raising children. During a performance evaluation during which they discussed her next move with the company, he "assured" her she shouldn't worry about trying to advance her career with Wal-Mart because "you aren't a part of the boy's club, and you should raise a family and stay in the kitchen." Hobbs also told her she did not play well with the "boys" at the company, and that because she didn't hunt or fish, she probably wouldn't advance any further. Informally—not through any written complaint or official use of the Open Door policy—she complained to her supervisor about the way she was being treated. He admonished her to "have a thick skin." Donovan also testified that in order to gain her male colleagues' respect, she had to focus conversations on hunting or sports.

"To be effective as an officer you need to be able to become part of the informal network," Rhonda Harper stated in her deposition, but this was difficult at Wal-Mart. "I didn't go fishing with them. I wondered if I had been able to do some of those things if I might have assimilated more quickly into the organization."

In 1995, Robert Reich, the Clinton administration's labor secretary, in the report of the Labor Department's Glass Ceiling Commission, *A Solid Investment Making Full Use of the Nation's Capital,* mentioned the lack of access to "informal networks of communication" as a major barrier to women's advancement in corporate America. As examples of this, he cited casual conversations conducted during hunting trips, golf games, and "other pursuits not usually undertaken by women and people of color." The camaraderie established through these kinds of activities "can give white males a commanding advantage." Even in the advertising industry, where women and gay men are plentiful, shooting weekends are not unknown. As recently as June 2001—the month Dukes filed her suit—the *New York Times,* in an article exploring barriers to women in corporate America, reported that women's exclusion from casual social and business relationships remained a problem and "the importance of male-bonding events, like golf, can't be overestimated" in solidifying males' advantages in the corporate world.[5] Golf remains controversial, as the fury over the Augusta Golf Club's sexist policies showed; part of the reason women's groups were so agitated by the Augusta Golf Club's exclusion of women is that golf is still a popular bonding activity for businesspeople.

Rhonda Harper testified that once, when she was traveling with a male officer, some store managers asked what it was like being his secretary. This was probably a misunderstanding and not a heinous act of sexism, but it indicates that a female Wal-Mart executive was highly unusual and, more disturbingly, for some in the company still unimaginable. On other business trips, Harper recalled, "I would be the only [woman] on the corporate jet. . . .The pilots would say, you know, 'Welcome gentlemen,' . . . I again don't know if you would classify that as sexist or not, but clearly there I was—I was sitting there." No one ever corrected the pilots or said, "We're not all gentlemen here." Harper recalls, "I would sometimes just go, 'And hello, ladies,' and there would be laughter, you know."

She described a sales conference, attended by thousands of store managers, with a football theme: "It was a very, in my opinion, traditionally male theme." She brought that up with her colleagues at headquarters, not because she thought it was sexist but because all that male bonding seemed like a distraction from focusing on the relationship with customers—the overwhelming majority of whom are women.

Of the particularly distasteful incidents at Wal-Mart—the "high heel thing"; Haworth's posing for pictures with a bevy of women; the airplane moment; the secretary comment; the references to Janie-Qs (all of which Harper discussed with her fellow officers)—Harper said she believed these incidents were "inappropriate or at the very least unusual," judging by her experience working for several other large corporations. It was "behavior that I would not anticipate existing in a corporate environment . . . I had never seen it before." She thought it was a real possibility that her Wal-Mart colleagues didn't know this kind of thing was inappropriate. "It is my nature to be very candid and direct," she testified. "I felt the need to bring [these concerns] forward because many of the folks who were at the officer level at Wal-Mart had never worked anywhere else."

Complaining about these incidents didn't help Harper make friends at Wal-Mart; neither did what many perceived as her haughty attitude. She just didn't fit in. Harper describes Wal-Mart headquarters as a cliquish atmosphere: "Either you're Wal-Mart, or you're everything else in the world." She attributes her problems at the company to the fact that she was an "outsider" who didn't conform to "the norm in the culture." The plaintiffs' lawyers asked Harper repeatedly whether her difficulties with Wal-Mart culture had to do with her gender; was she "different" because she was a woman? Harper was very careful not to exaggerate, not to blame her difficulties at the company solely on gender, and brought up examples of men who were also outsiders and had trouble fitting into Wal-Mart's insular culture. Eventually, however, she said, "I believe it has to do with who I am as a human being and one of my characteristics is that I am a woman." Her former boss, Celia Swanson, the Sam's Club executive vice president for membership, marketing, and administration—at that time the only woman among Wal-Mart's senior officers—

put it more bluntly, testifying in her deposition that Harper hadn't learned "how to work around and manage the male ego."

The atmosphere Rhonda Harper describes thrives in a much cruder form at Wal-Mart's middle-management level and in the stores. Many managers show an appalling lack of respect for women, which sends a clear message about their place in the company. Melissa Howard, a store manager in Decatur, Indiana, testified that at the annual meeting in Fayetteville, male managers would go out to strip clubs together and that it was "an accepted part of the culture." Once, when a group of district and store managers were making a 16-hour drive from Decatur to Bentonville for a meeting (typical of Wal-Mart's tightfistedness, the company wouldn't spring for plane tickets for this 700-mile journey), the men stopped the car to take a break in a strip club. Howard didn't want to go in, but it was nighttime and she didn't think it would be safe to sit in the parking lot alone. At one point, one of the strippers approached Howard, and Kevin Washburn, a district manager, offered the dancer $50 to go "out back" and have a "threesome" with himself and a shocked Howard. On the way home from Bentonville, the men stopped at two more strip clubs while Howard and the one other female manager sat in the back and repeatedly asked to be taken back to the motel.

Howard's district manager sometimes held lunch meetings at Hooters restaurants. Howard, the only female store manager in her district, was "forced to listen to lots of discussion among the male managers about the waitresses' breasts and butts and which sexual experiences they would like to have with them. While it was humiliating to be there, I was reluctant to complain."

Hooters is an Atlanta-based nationwide sports bar and restaurant chain in which the customers, 70 percent of whom are male, are waited on by attractive and scantily clad "Hooters Girls" who wear color-coordinated sporty outfits displaying porn-star cleavage and shorts that are as brief as shorts can be without being underwear. The company's website features aphorisms such as "Men have different faces so you can tell them apart," and boasts that since the company's founding, "the Hooters concept has undergone very little change . . . understandable given the tremendous success the Hooters concept has enjoyed." The Hooters "concept" is women with big breasts, wearing very little clothing, serving men.

Actually, the company argues that its "concept" is *feminist*. The company waxes eloquent on Hooters Girls' "right to use their natural female sex appeal to earn a living. . . .To Hooters, the women's rights movement is important because it guarantees women have the right to choose their own careers, be it a Supreme Court justice or Hooters Girl."

Hooters is quite right that women have a right to use their sexuality to earn a living. But it is preposterous for any other company to hold business meetings at the restaurant chain, and it is easy to imagine the mortification of a female manager attempting to be taken seriously by—or simply to fit in with—her male colleagues as they ogle Hooters Girls, watch sports on TV, and bask comfortably in a made-for-males environment.

Probably many companies employ middle-management goofballs who don't realize that this sort of thing isn't acceptable. But Wal-Mart's vice president for human resources should. When *Dukes* lawyers took Coleman Peterson's deposition and asked him what he thought of the practices Melissa Howard described, he was quick to insist that get-togethers at strip clubs on company time were not "something Wal-Mart culture would support and believe is okay." Asked about business meetings at Hooters, however, Peterson, the chief human resources officer of the world's largest workforce, reserved judgment. "It is conceivable in some small town that Hooters is kind of like the restaurant *du jour,* okay," he testified, "and that it is viewed as one of the most elegant and really one of the best places to meet and eat." In other words, it is perfectly okay to subject female employees to Hooters if it is the best restaurant in town. Joe Sellers later scoffed at this notion: "I don't even know if they serve food."

In Peterson's defense, Hooters does serve food. Indeed, one of its mottoes is "You can sell the sizzle, but you have to deliver the steak." Mike McNeil, a Hooters spokesman, did not think a Hooters restaurant would be an outlandish spot for an informal business meeting, although it has no conference or banquet rooms. But even McNeil seemed amused when told about Peterson's assertion that Hooters was sometimes the "most elegant and best place" around. "I was not aware of that [testimony]," he said, "but bless him whoever said that. We appreciate that. It's kinda like, in the eye of the beholder." Pausing to consider the possibilities, the flack said, "Wal-Mart is in a lot of small towns. So if you were in some place like Muskegon, Michigan, or Dothan, Alabama, that statement might actually be true."

The "knuckleheads" Melissa Howard worked with are hardly unique. At least the strippers she encountered weren't on store property. Angela Horton, a team leader in a Sam's Club in Onalaska, Wisconsin, testified that a company-sanctioned "Spirit Committee" hired a stripper to perform at her store's mandatory morning employee meeting, to celebrate a male store manager's birthday. The women who complained about this were called "a bunch of whiners."

In the stores, as at headquarters, "informal networks" pose obstacles to women's advancement. As an assistant manager in Indiana, Howard was often left to run the store by herself while the general manager went off and socialized with male employees—playing pool, going out to lunch, drinking together, and going to the race track. Other women have complained that managers play golf with male employees and don't befriend women or ask them to lunch. (Wal-Mart's anti-fraternization rules do prohibit managers from socializing with workers they supervise, but many workers say that this rule is often violated, to the advantage of men.) Numerous women have testified that an "old boy network" of friendships among men in the stores helps men to be promoted more quickly than women. . . .

One of Wal-Mart's own internal reports showed that stereotypes about women are pervasive in the company and have been a huge barrier for women seeking promotions. Many women at Wal-Mart have been told explicitly that they are not being promoted because they are women and that "women don't belong in management." When Tamara Zambrun applied for a job as a team lead (the hourly position that is frequently considered a feeder for salaried management) in Mountain Home, Idaho, her store manager, Skip Davis, said to her, "Being a female, what makes you more qualified for this job than a male employee?" Davis told her that her male coworkers might have trouble being supervised by a woman. "For over an hour," Zambrun testified in her class-member statement, "Mr. Davis required me to justify why he should give the promotion to a female instead of a male." Then he promoted a man instead.

Women describe an atmosphere of "hostility toward women in management." When Nancy Hom's director of operations called the Club he would ask to speak to a manager, even if she answered the phone. When Hom reminded him that she was a manager, rather than apologizing or admitting his mistake he'd ask her to have "one of the guys" return his call. A male assistant manager told her that the region was operated as "a good old boys club" and that he "wasn't complaining." Male managers hung out together and excluded female managers.

Working in a Cullman, Alabama, store in the early 1990s, Tammy Hall heard a male store manager tell a male assistant manager that women should be "at home with a bun in the oven" or "barefoot and pregnant." Many managers also believe that women who *are* pregnant or have children shouldn't be in management. The jewelry department head in Ohio says her manager, not wanting to promote her, constantly cited her family obligations. "It was always something. He said, 'I don't think you should go into management because you have small children.' I was like, 'don't make any decisions for me.'" Similarly, when Earwood was the personnel manager (an hourly position) in Urbana, Ohio, her store manager, Jim Phelps, asked her to add a curious stipulation to the support manager's job description. Since the support manager had to work evenings and weekends, he said, "It can't be anybody who has kids." Earwood, a single mother who had worked as a Wal-Mart support manager when her daughter was three years old, took offense.

Melissa Howard, the Bluffton, Indiana, store manager who had had to attend business meetings in the dignified environs of Hooters, was running a new Supercenter set to make a profit in its first year. In May, however, Kevin Washburn, the district manager who had invited Howard to step out for a threesome with an exotic dancer, was replaced by John Waters, who now asked her to step down and accept a demotion. The reason? A woman shouldn't be running a Wal-Mart store; Howard needed to be at home raising her daughter. Waters seemed to want to send a discouraging message to other women at the store, Howard observed in her class-member statement.

> He instructed me to step down "voluntarily" and to tell my employees at the morning meeting that having this new Supercenter was too stressful for a single parent and that I just needed to take a break. In other words, it was not enough for Mr. Waters to just get rid of me. I believe that he also wanted me to send a strong signal to other women that the job was not right for any mother. He told me to step down voluntarily, or he would have me out within four to six weeks—he would make my life "hell." I had no choice but to step down.

Another obstacle to women's advancement at Wal-Mart is the persistent segregation of departments. More than 90 percent of workers selling clothing at Wal-Mart are women, whereas less than 33 percent of those selling hardware or sporting goods are women. The gendered nature of different areas of the store is amusingly underscored by terminology like "hardlines" and "softlines." "Softlines" are clothing; "hardlines" are hardware, electronics, and other manly objects. Employees see the male-dominated departments as better stepping stones for promotion, but it's not clear that they are good stepping stones for women. According to Brad Seligman, they still don't have enough data to know. "Male" departments may just look like better routes to promotion because they have more men in them, and men are more likely than women to be promoted at Wal-Mart.

Aside from the stepping-stone issue, however, the departmental segregation often prevents women from getting experience that is often required for advancement. Dukes had been told that more floor experience was a prerequisite for promotion, but when she sought to gain additional experience she was denied the opportunity to work in "male" departments like hardware, despite having worked in hardware stores before she came to Wal-Mart. "I can mix a can of paint," she told reporters just after filing the suit in June 2001. "I want the chance to do it."[6] She shakes her head, still exasperated. "You don't have to have a man in those areas, by no means!"

And, as many plaintiffs have pointed out, segregation has a demoralizing, discouraging effect on women, sending the message that they are second-rate. Cleo Page was told by her manager that she needed to manage a bigger department before she could qualify for management training, and she hoped to manage the sporting goods department. But the manager discouraged her from applying, saying that "a man would feel more comfortable" buying sporting goods from a man. "She made it known in a store meeting not to apply if you are not a guy," says Page. "She didn't want a woman in there." That's when "I felt like I was just not going to make it."

Segregation of departments lets women know that they are not valued as much as men, and creates an environment that discourages them from seeking further promotions. In such a climate, says Dukes, "You are not going to run up to your district manager telling him you want to be promoted. You just don't have that zest and confidence." Sheila Hall asked repeatedly for a job in the hardware department of the Conway, Arkansas, store, and she finally got it when she pointed out that she'd already have it if she had "a penis between her legs"—yet as the only woman in the department she was taunted constantly by her coworkers and supervisors, who insisted that hardware was a "man's job." She eventually quit, feeling that in this environment she would never be promoted.

Editors' Note: *Notes for this reading can be found in the original source.*

CHAPTER 19

Learning Silence

PEGGY ORENSTEIN

Weston, California, sits at the far reaches of the San Francisco Bay Area. The drive from the city takes one through a series of bedroom communities, carefully planned idylls in which, as the miles roll by, the tax brackets leap upward, the politics swing right, and the people fade to white. But Weston is different: once an oddly matched blend of country folk and chemical plant workers, this is an old town, the kind of place where people still gather curbside under the bunting-swathed lampposts of Maple Street to watch the Fourth of July parade. Many of the businesses in Weston's center—doughnut shops, ladies' clothing stores, a few hard drinkers' bars, and picked-over antiquaries—haven't changed hands in over thirty years. There are a few fern bars and one café serving espresso here, but if people want high tone, they go to the city.

Not that Weston has remained suspended in time. The ramshackle houses downtown may still be populated by the families of mechanics, plant workers, and, in shoddy apartment complexes, a small community of working poor, but the hills that ring the town's edge have been gobbled up by tract homes where young professionals have hunkered down—a safe distance from urban ills—to raise their children. There's even a clean, modern supermarket by the freeway, built expressly for the new suburbanites, with a multiplex cinema across the street for their occasional evenings out.

The only place where Weston's two populations converge regularly is at Weston Middle School, a crumbling Spanish-style edifice just up the street from the post office, city hall, and, more important to the student body, a McDonald's. This is the town's sole middle school, and as such, it serves nearly nine hundred students a year from this disparate population. The bumper stickers on the cars dropping off the children reflect the mix: Toyota vans advertising the local NPR affiliate pull up behind rusty pickups that proclaim: "My wife said if I buy another gun she'll divorce me; God, I'll miss her!" There is also a staunch Christian population here—Mormons, Seventh-Day Adventists, and other, less austere sects whose cars remind other residents that "Jesus Loves You!"

In recent years, Weston Middle School has fulfilled its mandate well: the school entrance is draped with a "California Distinguished School" banner, earned last year by the students' estimable standardized test scores as well as the staff's exemplary performance. The teachers are an impressive, enthusiastic group who routinely seek methods of instruction that will inspire a little more engagement, a little more effort on the part of their pupils: an eighth-grade history teacher uses a karaoke microphone to juice up his lessons; an English teacher videotapes students performing original poems to bring literature to life; a science teacher offers extra credit to students who join him in cleaning up the banks of a local river. There is also some concern about gender issues in education: Weston's history teachers have embraced the new, more inclusive textbooks adopted by the state of California; in English, students write essays on their views about abortion and read, among other books, *Streams to the River, River to the Sea,* a historical novel which recasts Sacagawea as an intrepid female hero.

Yet the overt curriculum, as fine as it may be, is never the only force operating in a classroom. There is something else as well. The "hidden curriculum" comprises the unstated lessons that students learn in school: it is the running subtext through which teachers communicate behavioral norms and individual status in the school culture, the process of socialization that cues children into their place in the hierarchy of larger society. Once used to describe the ways in which the education system works to reproduce class systems in our culture, the "hidden curriculum" has recently been applied to the ways in which schools help reinforce gender roles, whether they intend to or not.

THE DAILY GRIND: LESSONS IN THE HIDDEN CURRICULUM

Amy Wilkinson has looked forward to being an eighth grader forever—at least for the last two years, which, when you're thirteen, seems like the same thing. By the second week of September she's settled comfortably into her role as one of the school's reigning elite. Each morning before class, she lounges with a group of about twenty other eighth-grade girls and boys in the most visible spot on campus: at the base of the schoolyard, between one of the portable classrooms that was constructed in the late 1970s and the old oak tree in the overflow parking lot. The group trades gossip, flirts, or simply stands around, basking in its own importance and killing time before the morning bell.

At 8:15 on Tuesday the crowd has already convened, and Amy is standing among a knot of girls, laughing. She is fuller-figured than she'd like to be, wide-hipped and heavy-limbed with curly, blond hair, cornflower-blue eyes, and a sharply up-turned nose. With the help of her mother, who is a drama coach, she has become the school's star actress: last year she played Eliza in Weston's production of *My Fair Lady.* Although she earns solid grades in all of her subjects—she'll make the honor roll this fall—drama is her passion, she says, because "I love entertaining people, and I love putting on characters."

Also, no doubt, because she loves the spotlight: this morning, when she mentions a boy I haven't met, Amy turns, puts her hands on her hips, anchors her feet shoulder width apart, and bellows across the schoolyard, "Greg! Get over here! You have to meet Peggy."

She smiles wryly as Greg, looking startled, begins to make his way across the schoolyard for an introduction. "I'm not exactly shy," she says, her hands still on her hips. "I'm *bold.*"

Amy is bold. And brassy, and strong-willed. Like any teenager, she tries on and discards different selves as if they were so many pairs of Girbaud jeans, searching ruthlessly for a perfect fit. During a morning chat just before the school year began, she told me that her parents tried to coach her on how to respond to my questions. "They told me to tell you that they want me to be my own person," she complained. "My mother *told* me to tell you that. I do want to be my own person, but it's like, you're interviewing me about who I am and she's telling me what to say—that's not my own person, is it?"

When the morning bell rings, Amy and her friends cut off their conversations, scoop up their books, and jostle toward the school's entrance. Inside, Weston's hallways smell chalky, papery, and a little sweaty from gym class. The wood-railed staircases at either end of the two-story main building are worn thin in the middle from the scuffle of hundreds of pairs of sneakers pounding them at forty-eight-minute intervals for nearly seventy-five years. Amy's mother, Sharon, and her grandmother both attended this school. So will her two younger sisters. Her father, a mechanic who works on big rigs, is a more recent Weston recruit: he grew up in Georgia and came here after he and Sharon were married.

Amy grabs my hand, pulling me along like a small child or a slightly addled new student: within three minutes we have threaded our way through the dull-yellow hallways to her locker and then upstairs to room 238, Mrs. Richter's math class.

The twenty two students that stream through the door with us run the gamut of physical maturity. Some of the boys are as small and compact as fourth graders, their legs sticking out of their shorts like pipe cleaners. A few are trapped in the agony of a growth spurt, and still others cultivate downy beards. The girls' physiques are less extreme: most are nearly their full height, and all but a few have already weathered the brunt of puberty. They wear topknots or ponytails, and their shirts are tucked neatly into their jeans.

Mrs. Richter, a ruddy, athletic woman with a powerful voice, has arranged the chairs in a three-sided square, two rows deep. Amy walks to the far side of the room and, as she takes her seat, falls into a typically feminine pose: she crosses her legs, folds her arms across her chest, and hunches forward toward her desk, seeming to shrink into herself. The sauciness of the playground disappears, and, in fact, she says hardly a word during class. Meanwhile, the boys, especially those who are more physically mature, sprawl in their chairs, stretching their legs long, expanding into the available space.

Nate, a gawky, sanguine boy who has shaved his head except for a small thatch that's hidden under an Oakland A's cap, leans his chair back on two legs and, although the bell has already rung, begins a noisy conversation with his friend Kyle.

Mrs. Richter turns to him, "What's all the discussion about, Nate?" she asks.

"*He's* talking to *me*," Nate answers, pointing to Kyle. Mrs. Richter writes Nate's name on the chalkboard as a warning toward detention and he yells out in protest. They begin to quibble over the justice of her decision, their first—but certainly not their last—power struggle of the day. As they argue, Allison, a tall, angular girl who once told me, "My goal is to be the best wife and mother I can be," raises her hand to ask a question. Mrs. Richter, finishing up with Nate, doesn't notice.

"Get your homework out, everyone!" the teacher booms, and walks among the students, checking to make sure no one has shirked on her or his assignment. Allison, who sits in the front row nearest both the blackboard and the teacher, waits patiently for another moment, then, realizing she's not getting results, puts her hand down. When Mrs. Richter walks toward her, Allison tries another tack, calling out her question. Still, she gets no response, so she gives up.

As a homework assignment, the students have divided their papers into one hundred squares, color-coding each square prime or composite—prime being those numbers which are divisible only by one and themselves, and composite being everything else. Mrs. Richter asks them to call out the prime numbers they've found, starting with the tens.

Nate is the first to shout, "Eleven!" The rest of the class chimes in a second later. As they move through the twenties and thirties, Nate, Kyle, and Kevin, who sit near one another at the back of the class, call out louder and louder, casually competing for both quickest response and the highest decibel level. Mrs. Richter lets the boys' behavior slide, although they are intimidating other students.

"Okay," Mrs. Richter says when they've reached one hundred. "Now, what do you think of one hundred and three? Prime or composite?"

Kyle, who is skinny and a little pop-eyed, yells out, "Prime!" but Mrs. Richter turns away from him to give someone else a turn. Unlike Allison, who gave up when she was ignored, Kyle isn't willing to cede his teacher's attention. He begins to bounce in his chair and chant, "*Prime! Prime! Prime!*" Then, when he turns out to be right, he rebukes the teacher, saying, "*See*, I told you."

When the girls in Mrs. Richter's class do speak, they follow the rules. When Allison has another question, she raises her hand again and waits her turn; this time, the teacher responds. When Amy volunteers her sole answer of the period, she raises her hand, too. She gives the wrong answer to an easy multiplication problem, turns crimson, and flips her head forward so her hair falls over her face.

Occasionally, the girls shout out answers, but generally they are to the easiest, lowest-risk questions, such as the factors of four or six. And their stabs at public recognition depend on the boys' largesse: when the girls venture responses to more complex questions the boys quickly become territorial, shouting them down with their own answers. Nate and Kyle are particularly adept at overpowering Renee, who, I've been told by the teacher, is the brightest girl in the class. (On a subsequent visit, I will see her lay her head on her desk when Nate overwhelms her and mutter, "I hate this class.")

Mrs. Richter doesn't say anything to condone the boys' aggressiveness, but she doesn't have to: they insist on—and receive—her attention even when she consciously tries to shift it elsewhere in order to make the class more equitable.

After the previous day's homework is corrected, Mrs. Richter begins a new lesson, on the use of exponents.

"What does three to the third power mean?" she asks the class.

"*I know!*" shouts Kyle.

Instead of calling on Kyle, who has already answered more than his share of questions, the teacher turns to Dawn, a somewhat more voluble girl who has plucked her eyebrows down to a few hairs.

"Do you know, Dawn?"

Dawn hesitates, and begins "Well, you count the number of threes and . . . "

"*But I know!*" interrupts Kyle. "*I know!*"

Mrs. Richter deliberately ignores him, but Dawn is rattled: she never finishes her sentence, she just stops.

"*I know! ME!*" Kyle shouts again, and then before Dawn recovers herself he blurts, "*It's three times three times three!*"

At this point, Mrs. Richter gives in. She turns away from Dawn, who is staring blankly, and nods at Kyle. "Yes," she says. "Three times three times three. Does everyone get it?"

"*YES!*" shouts Kyle; Dawn says nothing.

Mrs. Richter picks up the chalk. "Let's do some others," she says.

"Let me!" says Kyle.

"I'll pick on whoever raises their hand," she tells him.

Nate, Kyle, and two other boys immediately shoot up their hands, fingers squeezed tight and straight in what looks like a salute.

"Don't you want to wait and hear the problem first?" she asks, laughing.

They drop their hands briefly. She writes 8^4 on the board. "Okay, what would that look like written out?"

Although a third of the class raises their hands to answer—including a number of students who haven't yet said a word—she calls on Kyle anyway.

"Eight times eight times eight times eight," he says triumphantly, as the other students drop their hands.

When the bell rings, I ask Amy about the mistake she made in class and the embarrassment it caused her. She blushes again.

"Oh yeah," she says. "That's about the only time I ever talked in there. I'll never do that again."

BAD CHEMISTRY: "GUYS LIKE IT WHEN YOU ACT ALL HELPLESS"

It is another late-fall morning under the oak tree at Weston. Amy, Becca, and Evie huddle together slightly apart from the other students, the intimate turn to their shoulders making it clear that they're exchanging the juiciest gossip. A squadron of seventh-grade boys on bicycles zips by and the girls look up, annoyed, sidling to the left to avoid being hit.

A few seconds later, Becca, usually the most reserved of her friends, shrieks.

"Get that away from me!"

The bikers are forgotten as the girls scatter, screaming, their faces flushed, revealing Carl Ross, a boy from Evie's math class, whose feet are firmly planted where the girls once stood. An uncapped jar labeled "Felicia" dangles from his left hand. Until a minute ago, it held a large spider he'd captured for extra credit in science class. Felicia is currently hanging from a dead pine needle in his other hand, her legs tucked in and body contracted in fear.

Becca runs about ten feet and turns around. When she smiles, she reveals a mouth full of braces. "I'm *deathly* afraid of spiders," she says, her eyes shining as she looks back at her tormentor.

The other two girls run up to her. "God, me too!" Amy says breathlessly, clutching her friend's arms. "When I saw *Arachnophobia* my dad had to go check my room for me. He had to look under the bed!"

Evie's cheeks are pink and her dark hair is falling from its bun. She tucks the wayward wisps back in place as a second boy lets the bug drop from his finger by a lengthening strand of web. "Yuck, how disgusting," she says, widening her eyes. "I hope he doesn't come near me with that."

As a woman standing among these girls, I wasn't sure how to react. I desperately wanted them to stand up to the boys who increasingly joined in the game. I wanted them to be brave, to marvel at the spider's jewel-green body, to ask for a turn at holding it and watching it try to spin its escape. But I felt the pressure too: a real girl, a girl who wants a boy to like her, runs screaming from spiders. The more she likes a boy, the more she allows him to terrorize her, and the more helpless she pretends to be. Showing any real interest in spiders would've been imprudent for the girls, a denial of their newly important femininity. During my year at Weston, I saw girls run from spiders innumerable times; with each flight toward traditional femininity, I thought about who has permission, who has the right in our culture, to explore the natural world, to get dirty and muddy, to think spiders and worms and frogs are neat, to bring them in for extra credit in science. In fact, to be engaged in science at all.

"I'm not *really* afraid of that stuff, except snakes and blood," Amy admits later, after the hoopla. "But guys like it if you act all helpless and girly, so you do."

As with math, there is a circular relationship among girls' affection for science, their self-esteem, and their career plans. But unlike in math, the achievement gap between girls and boys in science is actually widening: the National Assessment of Educational Progress found that, for thirteen-year-olds, gender differences in all areas of science performance except biology actually increased during the 1980s, with boys' skills improving and girls' slipping during that time. This is particularly disturbing when one considers that today's young people are growing up in an era of rapid technological change; without a solid grounding in science, girls will not only be unable to participate in shaping that change, they will be helpless in the face of it.

Certainly, the culture outside the classroom discourages scientific competence in girls. Boys still have more casual exposure to science—whether it's light meters, chemistry sets, or, like Carl and his friends, spiders—and they're more likely to have computers at home. Science toys are still marketed almost exclusively toward boys, with boys featured on packages (or, worse still, girls *watching* boys) and the world of video games seems constructed with an entirely male audience in mind.

In school, girls opt out—or are pushed out—of science at every stage of advancement. In high school, boys and girls take introductory biology and chemistry in similar numbers, but far more boys go on to physics or advanced chemistry, while girls, if they take science at all, continue with biology. And although the numbers of women who pursue the sciences has skyrocketed, there were formerly so few that even huge jumps yield small results: for instance, the number of female engineers grew 131 percent during the 1980s, but women still make up only 8 percent of that field. In fact, a scant 16 percent of currently employed scientists are female, and that figure may well have peaked: by the late 1980s, the numbers of women pursuing degrees in science and engineering (excluding the social sciences) had leveled off and was dropping, especially in advanced physics and computer science.

Nonetheless, in spite of the achievement gap, today's girls believe that they can excel in science; the trouble is, boys (perhaps prejudiced by the overreaction to spiders and snakes) do not share that belief about their female classmates. Because of that disparity, science laboratory groups—in which boys grab equipment from girls, perform experiments for them, and ridicule girls' contributions—can become less an opportunity for partnership than a microcosm of unintended lessons about gender.

Amy's science class is taught by Mr. Sinclair, a mustachioed fellow with a receding hairline, who chose teaching as a profession during what he describes as his idealistic youth in the late 1960s. He periodically considers changing careers, mostly for financial reasons, but he enjoys his work too much to quit. Instead, he stays sharp by attending conferences on science instruction, subscribing to newsletters, seeking out new ways to teach. He tries hard to be creative because, he says, the kids tend not to like physical science very much. But judging from what happens in his classroom, it's really the girls who don't like it.

Like Mrs. Richter, Mr. Sinclair never intentionally discriminates against the girls in his class; both he and the other eighth-grade science teacher at Weston—who is also male—are quick to point out the few girls who do participate (although in further conversation I found that many of those girls felt neither affection nor affinity for the subject). What I saw instead, even more than in the math classes I observed, was a kind of passive resistance to participation by the girls that went unquestioned by the teacher. Call it gender bias by omission. When, week after week, boys raised their hands to ask or answer questions in far greater numbers than girls, when only boys shouted out responses, when boys enthusiastically offered up extra-credit demonstrations, the teacher simply didn't notice.

The very morning that Amy flees shrieking from Felicia the spider, Mr. Sinclair invites me to observe as her section of his physical science class performs an easy, fun experiment called "The Cartesian Diver." Each group of three students is given an empty dishwashing liquid bottle, an eyedropper, and a beaker of water. The idea is to fill the bottle with water, drop in the dropper, and, through some magical process that the students must determine (which turns out to be placing a little water in the dropper in advance, then squeezing the bottle to cause mass displacement), make the dropper sink and float at will.

In Amy's lab group there is another girl, Donna, and a boy, Liam, who sits between them. Liam performs the experiment as the two girls watch, occasionally offering encouragement, but no criticism. When he is successful, Amy squeals and pats him on the arm. Eventually Liam lets Donna and Amy each try the diver exactly once; then he recovers it and continues to play.

In another group of two girls and one boy directly behind Amy, Roger stands behind the girls, supervising . . . sort of.

"You're doing it wrong, ha-ha," he taunts in a singsong voice. Roger has a long rattail and a pierced ear; he wears an oversized tie-dyed T-shirt. The girls, who have styled their long blond hair identically, huddle together, trying to ignore him, and continue to attempt the experiment. Roger watches them a moment longer, then grabs the bottle from them, pours the water into the beaker and walks away with the dropper. The girls do not protest. When he comes back a few minutes later, the girls have refilled the bottle, but, still uncertain about how to proceed, have decided to empty it again and start over.

"Oh, smart," Roger says sarcastically. "*Real* smart." He grabs the bottle again. "*I'll* do it." He refills the bottle, puts the dropper in, and completes the experiment while the girls watch in silence.

I wander to the far corner of the room, where Allison, from Amy's math class, and Karla, a round-faced Latina girl with deep dimples and black hair pulled into a topknot, are having trouble with their diver. There are several girls sitting around them, yet they have asked a boy for help.

"I told him he could do it for us because he has man's hands," Karla, who once told me she wants to be an astronaut, tells me, smiling.

A second boy is watching the scene. When his friend completes the experiment, he pumps his fist in the air. "Yes!" he says. "A *man* had to do it!"

"But *how* did you do it?" Allison asks.

"I have magic hands," the first boy answers. "*Man* hands," and he laughs.

The girls laugh too—acting appropriately "helpless and girly"—but they never learn how to do the experiment. Instead, like the girls in the other groups, they have become outsiders in the learning process, passive observers rather than competent participants. In truth, "man hands" do complete most of the experiments in the room.

CHAPTER 20

Doméstica

PIERRETTE HONDAGNEU-SOTELO

Imagine that you are a young woman, newly arrived in the United States. You are penniless—no, hugely in debt from making the trip—you do not speak English, and you are without a passport or any other legitimizing documents. Vilified in political campaigns as an "illegal," or simply scorned as a "Mexican," you live as a fugitive. You know only a distant cousin, a childhood friend, or perhaps an older brother whose wife is determined to cut your stay in their already-crowded apartment to a minimum. What do you do? You take a live-in job; or as the women say, *te encierras.* You lock yourself up. . . .

Who are these women who come to the United States in search of jobs, and what are those jobs like? Domestic work is organized in different ways, and in this chapter I describe live-in, live-out, and housecleaning jobs and profile some of the Latina immigrants who do them and how they feel about their work. . . .

LIVE-IN NANNY/HOUSEKEEPER JOBS

For Maribel Centeno, newly arrived from Guatemala City in 1989 at age twenty-two and without supportive family and friends with whom to stay, taking a live-in job made a lot of sense. She knew that she wouldn't have to spend money on room and board, and that she could soon begin saving to pay off her debts. Getting a live-in job through an agency was easy. The *señora,* in her rudimentary Spanish, only asked where she was from, and if she had a husband and children. Chuckling, Maribel recalled her initial misunderstanding when the *señora,* using her index forger, had drawn an imaginary "2" and "3" in the palm of her hand. "I thought to myself, well, she must have two or three bedrooms, so I said, fine. 'No,' she said. 'Really, really big.' She started counting, 'One, two, three, four . . . two-three rooms.' It was twenty-three rooms! I thought, *huy!* On a piece of paper, she wrote '$80 a week,' and she said, 'You, child, and entire house.' So I thought, well, I have to do what I have to do, and I happily said, 'Yes.' "

"I arrived on Monday at dawn," she recalled, "and I went to the job on Wednesday evening." When the *señora* and the child spoke to her, Maribel remembered "just laughing and feeling useless. I couldn't understand anything." On that first evening, the *señora* put on classical music, which Maribel quickly identified. "I said, 'Beethoven.' She said, 'Yeah,' and began asking me in English, 'You like it?' I said 'Yes,' or perhaps I said, *'Sí,'* and she began playing other cassettes, CDs. They had Richard Clayderman and I recognized it, and when I said that, she stopped in her tracks, her jaw fell open, and she just stared at me. She must have been thinking, 'No schooling, no preparation, no English, how does she know this music?' " But the *señora*, perhaps because of the language difficulty, or perhaps because she felt upstaged by her live-in's knowledge of classical music, never did ask. Maribel desperately wanted the *señora* to respect her, to recognize that she was smart, educated, and cultivated in the arts. In spite of her best status-signaling efforts, "They treated me," she said, "the same as any other girl from the countryside." She never got the verbal recognition that she desired from the *señora*.

Maribel summed up her experiences with her first live-in job this way: "The pay was bad. The treatment was, how shall I say? It was cordial, a little, uh, not racist, but with very little consideration, very little respect." She liked caring for the little seven-year-old boy, but keeping after the cleaning of the twenty-three-room house, filled with marble floors and glass tables, proved physically impossible. She eventually quit not because of the polishing and scrubbing, but because being ignored devastated her socially.

Compared to many other Latina immigrants' first live-in jobs, Maribel Centeno's was relatively good. She was not on call during all her waking hours and throughout the night, the parents were engaged with the child, and she was not required to sleep in a child's bedroom or on a cot tucked away in the laundry room. But having a private room filled with amenities did not mean she had privacy or the ability to do simple things one might take for granted. "I had my own room, with my own television, VCR, my private bath, and closet, and a kind of sitting room—but everything in miniature, Thumbelina style," she said. "I had privacy in that respect. But I couldn't do many things. If I wanted to walk around in a T-shirt, or just feel like I was home, I couldn't do that. If I was hungry in the evening, I wouldn't come out to grab a banana because I'd have to walk through the family room, and then everybody's watching and having to smell the banana. I could never feel at home, never. Never, never, never! There's always something invisible that tells you this is not your house, you just work here."

It is the rare California home that offers separate maid's quarters, but that doesn't stop families from hiring live-ins; nor does it stop newly arrived Latina migrant workers from taking jobs they urgently need. When live-ins cannot even retreat to their own rooms, work seeps into their sleep and their dreams. There is no time off from the job, and they say they feel confined, trapped, imprisoned.

"I lose a lot of sleep," said Margarita Gutiérrez, a twenty-four-year-old Mexicana who worked as a live-in nanny/housekeeper. At her job in a modest-sized condominium in Pasadena, she slept in a corner of a three-year-old child's bedroom. Consequently, she found herself on call day and night with the child, who sometimes went several days without seeing her mother because of the latter's schedule at an insurance company. Margarita was obliged to be on her job twenty-four hours a day; and like other live-in nanny/housekeepers I interviewed, she claimed that she could scarcely find time to shower or brush her teeth. "I go to bed fine," she reported, "and then I wake up at two or three in the morning with the girl asking for water, or food." After the child went back to sleep, Margarita would lie awake, thinking about how to leave her job but finding it hard to even walk out into the kitchen. Live-in employees like Margarita literally have no space and no time they can claim as their own.

Working in a larger home or staying in plush, private quarters is no guarantee of privacy or refuge from the job. Forty-four-year-old Elvia Lucero worked as a live-in at a sprawling, canyon-side residence, where she was in charge of looking after twins, two five-year-old girls. On numerous occasions when I visited her there, I saw that she occupied her own bedroom, a beautifully decorated one outfitted with delicate antiques, plush white carpet, and a stenciled border of pink roses painstakingly painted on the wall by the employer. It looked serene and inviting, but it was only three steps away from the twins' room. Every night one of the twins crawled into bed with Elvia. Elvia disliked this, but said she couldn't break the girl of the habit. And the parents' room lay tucked away at the opposite end of the large (more than 3,000 square feet), L-shaped house.

Regardless of the size of the home and the splendor of the accommodations, the boundaries that we might normally take for granted disappear in live-in jobs. They have, as Evelyn Nakano Glenn has noted, "no clear line between work and non-work time," and the line between job space and private space is similarly blurred.[1] Live-in nanny/housekeepers are at once socially isolated and surrounded by other people's territory; during the hours they remain on the employers' premises, their space, like their time, belongs to another. The sensation of being among others while remaining invisible, unknown and apart, of never being able to leave the margins, makes many live-in employees sad, lonely, and depressed. Melancholy sets in and doesn't necessarily lift on the weekends.

Rules and regulations may extend around the clock. Some employers restrict the ability of their live-in employees to receive telephone calls, entertain friends, attend evening ESL classes, or see boyfriends during the workweek. Other employers do not impose these sorts of restrictions, but because their homes are located on remote hillsides, in suburban enclaves, or in gated communities, their live-in nanny/housekeepers are effectively kept away from anything resembling social life or public culture. A Spanish-language radio station, or maybe a *telenovela*, may serve as their only link to the outside world.

Food—the way some employers hoard it, waste it, deny it, or just simply do not even have any of it in their kitchens—is a frequent topic of discussion among Latina live-in nanny/housekeepers. These women are talking not about counting calories but about the social meaning of food on the job. Almost no one works with a written contract, but anyone taking a live-in job that includes "room and board" would assume that adequate meals will be included. But what constitutes an adequate meal? Everyone has a different idea, and using the subject like a secret handshake,

Latina domestic workers often greet one another by talking about the problems of managing food and meals on the job. Inevitably, food enters their conversations.

No one feels the indignities of food more deeply than do live-in employees, who may not leave the job for up to six days at a time. For them, the workplace necessarily becomes the place of daily sustenance. In some of the homes where they work, the employers are out all day. When these adults return home, they may only snack, keeping on hand little besides hot dogs, packets of macaroni and cheese, cereal, and peanut butter for the children. Such foods are considered neither nutritious nor appetizing by Latina immigrants, many of whom are accustomed to sitting down to meals prepared with fresh vegetables, rice, beans, and meat. In some employers' homes, the cupboards are literally bare. Gladys Villedas recalled that at one of her live-in jobs, the *señora* had graciously said, " 'Go ahead, help yourself to anything in the kitchen.' But at times," she recalled, "there was nothing, nothing in the refrigerator! There was nothing to eat!" Even in lavish kitchens outfitted with Sub-zero refrigerators and imported cabinetry, food may be scarce. A celebrity photographer of luxury homes that appear in posh magazines described to a reporter what he sees when he opens the doors of some of Beverly Hills' refrigerators: "Rows of cans of Diet Coke, and maybe a few remains of pizza."[2]

Further down the class ladder, some employers go to great lengths to economize on food bills. Margarita Gutiérrez claimed that at her live-in job, the husband did the weekly grocery shopping, but he bought things in small quantities—say, two potatoes that would be served in half portions, or a quarter of a watermelon to last a household of five all week. He rationed out the bottled water and warned her that milk would make her fat. Lately, she said, he was taking both her and the children to an upscale grocery market where they gave free samples of gourmet cheeses, breads, and dips, urging them all to fill up on the freebies. "I never thought," exclaimed Margarita, formerly a secretary in Mexico City, "that I would come to this country to experience hunger!"

Many women who work as live-ins are keenly aware of how food and meals underline the boundaries between them and the families for whom they work. "I never ate with them," recalled Maribel Centeno of her first live-in job. "First of all, she never said, 'Come and join us,' and secondly, I just avoided being around when they were about to eat." Why did she avoid mealtime? "I didn't feel I was part of that family. I knew they liked me, but only because of the good work I did, and because of the affection I showered on the boy; but apart from that, I was just like the gardener, like the pool man, just one more of their staff." Sitting down to share a meal symbolizes membership in a family, and Latina employees, for the most part, know they are not just like one of the family.

Food scarcity is not endemic to all of the households where these women work. In some homes, ample quantities of fresh fruits, cheeses, and chicken stock the kitchens. Some employer families readily share all of their food, but in other households, certain higher-quality, expensive food items may remain off-limits to the live-in employees, who are instructed to eat hot dogs with the children. One Latina live-in nanny/housekeeper told me that in her employers' substantial pantry, little "DO NOT TOUCH" signs signaled which food items were not available to her;

and another said that her employer was always defrosting freezer-burned leftovers for her to eat, some of it dating back nearly a decade.

Other women felt subtle pressure to remain unobtrusive, humble, and self-effacing, so they held back from eating even when they were hungry. They talked a lot about how these unspoken rules apply to fruit. "Look, if they [the employers] buy fruit, they buy three bananas, two apples, two pears. So if I eat one, who took it? It's me," one woman said, "they'll know it's me." Another nanny/housekeeper recalled: "They would bring home fruit, but without them having to say it, you just knew these were not intended for you. You understand this right away, you get it." Or as another put it, "*Las Americanas* have their apples counted out, one for each day of the week." Even fruits growing in the garden are sometimes contested. In Southern California's agriculture-friendly climate, many a residential home boasts fruit trees that hang heavy with oranges, plums, and peaches, and when the Latina women who work in these homes pick the fruit, they sometimes get in trouble.[3] Eventually, many of the women solve the food problem by buying and bringing in their own food; early on Monday mornings, you see them walking with their plastic grocery bags, carting, say, a sack of apples, some chicken, and maybe some prepared food in plastic containers.

The issue of food captures the essence of how Latina live-in domestic workers feel about their jobs. It symbolizes the extent to which the families they work for draw the boundaries of exclusion or inclusion, and it marks the degree to which those families recognize the live-in nanny/housekeepers as human beings who have basic human needs. When they first take their jobs, most live-in nanny/housekeepers do not anticipate spending any of their meager wages on food to eat while on the job, but in the end, most do—and sometimes the food they buy is eaten by members of the family for whom they work.

Although there is a wide range of pay, many Latina domestic workers in live-in jobs earn less than minimum wage for marathon hours: 93 percent of the live-in workers I surveyed in the mid-1990s were earning less than $5 an hour (79 percent of them below minimum wage, which was then $4.25), and they reported working an average of sixty-four hours a week.[4] Some of the most astoundingly low rates were paid for live-in jobs in the households of other working-class Latino immigrants, which provide some women their first job when they arrive in Los Angeles. Carmen Vasquez, for example, had spent several years working as a live-in for two Mexican families, earning only $50 a week. By comparison, her current salary of $170 a week, which she was earning as a live-in nanny/housekeeper in the hillside home of an attorney and a teacher, seemed a princely sum.

Many people assume that the rich pay more than do families of modest means, but working as a live-in in an exclusive, wealthy neighborhood, or in a twenty-three-room house, provides no guarantee of a high salary. Early one Monday morning in the fall of 1995, I was standing with a group of live-in nanny/housekeepers on a corner across the street from the Beverly Hills Hotel. As they were waiting to be picked up by their employers, a large Mercedes sedan with two women (a daughter and mother or mother-in-law?) approached, rolled down the windows, and asked if anyone was interested in a $150-a-week live-in job. A few women jotted down the phone number, and no one was shocked by the offer. Gore Vidal once commented that no one is allowed to fail within a two-mile radius of the Beverly Hills Hotel, but it turns out that plenty of women in that vicinity are failing in the salary department. In some of the most affluent Westside areas of Los Angeles—in Malibu, Pacific Palisades, and Bel Air—there are live-in nanny/housekeepers earning $150 a week. And in 1999, the *Los Angeles Times* Sunday classified ads still listed live-in nanny/housekeeper jobs with pay as low as $100 and $125.[5] Salaries for live-in jobs, however, do go considerably higher. The best-paid live-in employee whom I interviewed was Patricia Paredes, a Mexicana who spoke impeccable English and who had legal status, substantial experience, and references. She told me that she currently earned $450 a week at her live-in job. She had been promised a raise to $550, after a room remodel was finished, when she would assume weekend housecleaning in that same home. With such a relatively high weekly salary she felt compelled to stay in a live-in job during the week, away from her husband and three young daughters who remained on the east side of Los Angeles. The salary level required that sacrifice.

But once they experience it, most women are repelled by live-in jobs. The lack of privacy, the mandated separation from family and friends, the round-the-clock hours, the food issues, the low pay, and especially the constant loneliness prompt most Latina immigrants to seek other job arrangements. Some young, single women who learn to speak English fluently try to move up the ranks into higher-paying live-in jobs. As soon as they can, however, the majority attempt to leave live-in work altogether. Most live-in nanny/housekeepers have been in the United States for five years or less; among the live-in nanny/housekeepers I interviewed, only two (Carmen Vasquez and the relatively high-earning Patricia Paredes) had been in the United States for longer than that. Like African American women earlier in the century, who tired of what the historian Elizabeth Clark-Lewis has called "the soul-destroying hollowness of live-in domestic work,"[6] most Latina immigrants try to find other options.

Until the early 1900s, live-in jobs were the most common form of paid domestic work in the United States, but through the first half of the twentieth century they were gradually supplanted by domestic "day work."[7] Live-in work never completely disappeared, however, and in the last decades of the twentieth century, it revived with vigor, given new life by the needs of American families with working parents and young children—and, as we have seen, by the needs of newly arrived Latina immigrants, many of them unmarried and unattached to families. When these women try to move up from live-in domestic work, they see few job alternatives. Often, the best they can do is switch to another form of paid domestic work, either as a live-out nanny/housekeeper or as a weekly housecleaner. When they do such day work, they are better able to circumscribe their work hours, and they earn more money in less time.[8] . . .

JOB STRUCTURES

Live-in and live-out nanny/housekeepers find that the spatial and social isolation of the job intensifies their craving for personal contact. Typically they work for only one employer, and spend each day at the home of the same family. With the exception of those hired by very high income families who simultaneously employ several domestic workers, they generally have no co-workers with whom to speak. The job is, as one employer conceded, "a lonesome one." Nanny/housekeepers may be alone for most of the day, or they may spend the entire day with infants. If they are lucky, they may meet up for an hour or two with a group of nannies at a public park, or on arranged play dates.

Nanny/housekeepers with live-in jobs are the most isolated. They work long hours—on average, more than sixty hours a week—leaving the employer's home only on Saturday afternoons, when they retreat to a shared apartment or a rented room until Monday morning. During the rest of the week, they remain confined to their work site. Without anyone to speak with day after day, many of them become emotionally distraught and depressed. It is little wonder that they often seek more personalistic relations with the only adults they see, their employers.

Erlinda Castro, a middle-aged Guatemalan woman and mother of five, had spent three years working as a live-in housekeeper in three different households before finally establishing her route of weekly housecleaning jobs. In the first of her live-in jobs, she worked for a family whom she described as good employers, because they paid her what she had expected to earn and because they did not pile on an unreasonable number of duties. The school-age children were gone for most of the day, and her job tasks seemed fair and physically manageable. The employers did not criticize her work, and they never insulted or yelled at her. Unlike many other live-ins, she had her own room and there was food for her to eat. Yet Erlinda found her employers cold and impersonal, unresponsive to her attempts to engage them in conversation; and she told me that their aloofness drove her out of the job.

"I would greet the *señora*, 'Good morning, *señora* Judy,' " she recalled. "They spoke a little Spanish, but the *señor* never spoke. If I greeted him, maybe in between his teeth he would mutter, 'Heh,' just like that. That's how one is often treated, and it feels cruel. You leave your own home, leaving everything behind only to find hostility. You're useful to them only because you clean, wash, iron, cook—that's the only reason. There is no affection. There is nothing." She expected some warmth and affection, but instead she found a void. Erlinda Castro entered the home of these employers directly after leaving her home and five children in Guatemala. On weekends she visited with her husband, whom she had joined in Los Angeles. It was her first experience with paid domestic work, and although she was not put off by the pay, the job tasks, or the low status of the job, the impersonal treatment became intolerable. "I felt bad, really bad. I couldn't go on with that, with nothing more than, 'Good morning, *señora*' and, 'Good night, *señora*.' Nothing else. They would say nothing, nothing, absolutely nothing to me! They would only speak to me to give me orders." Erlinda stayed on that job for approximately one year, leaving it for another live-in job that a friend had told her about.

Being treated as though one is invisible is a complaint commonly voiced by domestic workers of color working for white employers. As the historian David Katzman has noted in his study of the occupation in the South, "One peculiar and most degrading aspect of domestic service was the requisite of invisibility. The ideal servant . . . would be invisible and silent[,] . . . sensitive to the moods and whims of those around them, but undemanding of family warmth, love or security."[9] In her early 1980s ethnographic research, for which she posed as a housecleaner, Judith Rollins revealed a telling moment: an employer and her teenage son conducted an entire conversation about personal issues in her presence. "This situation was," Rollins wrote in her field notes, "the most peculiar feeling of the day: being there and not being there."[10] At different times, African American, Japanese American, and Chicana domestic workers in the United States have had the same disturbing experience.[11]

Some domestic workers see personalism as the antidote to these indignities and humiliations. Verbal interaction affords them respect and recognition on the job. Elvira Areola, a Mexicana, had worked for eleven years for one family. I interviewed her several days after an acrimonious fight with her employer—a disagreement that became physical—had left her jobless and without an income. As a single mother, she found herself in a frightening position. Still, she expressed no regrets, partly because the almost completely nonverbal relationship that she had maintained for several years with the *patrona* had been so strained. Her female employer had not worked and was physically present in the home, yet they hardly interacted. "I would arrive [in the morning] and sometimes she wouldn't greet me until two in the afternoon. . . . I'd be in the kitchen, and she'd walk in but wouldn't say anything. She would ignore me, as if to say, 'I'm alone in my house and there's no one else here.' Sometimes she wouldn't speak to me the whole day . . . she'd act as if I was a chair, a table, as if her house was supposedly all clean without me being there." Her dissatisfaction with the lack of appreciation and verbal recognition was echoed in the accounts of many other women.

ENDNOTES

1. Glenn 1986:141.
2. Lacher 1997:E1.
3. One nanny/housekeeper told me that a *señora* had admonished her for picking a bag of fruit, and wanted to charge her for it; another claimed that her employer had said she would rather watch the fruit fall off the branches and rot than see her eat it.
4. Many Latina domestic workers do not know the amount of their hourly wages; and because the lines between their work and nonwork tend to blur, live-in nanny/housekeepers have particular difficulty calculating them. In the survey questionnaire I asked live-in nanny/housekeepers how many days a week they worked, what time they began their job, and what time they ended, and I asked them to estimate how many hours off they had during an average workday (39 percent said they had no time off, but 32 percent said they had a break of between one and three hours). Forty-seven percent of the women said they began their workday at 7 A.M. or earlier, with 62 percent ending their workday at 7 P.M. or later. With the majority of them (71 percent) working five days a week, their average workweek was sixty-four hours. This estimate may at first glance appear inflated; but consider a prototypical live-in nanny/housekeeper who works, say, five days a week, from 7 A.M. until 9 P.M., with one and a half hours off during the children's nap time (when she might take a break to lie down or

watch television). Her on-duty work hours would total sixty-four and a half hours per week. The weekly pay of live-in nanny/housekeepers surveyed ranged from $130 to $400, averaging $242. Dividing this figure by sixty-four yields an hourly wage of $3.80. None of the live-in nanny/housekeepers were charged for room and board—this practice is regulated by law—but 86 percent said they brought food with them to their jobs. The majority reported being paid in cash.

5. See, e.g., Employment Classified Section 2, *Los Angeles Times,* June 6, 1999, G9.

6. Clark-Lewis 1994:123. "After an average of seven years," she notes in her analysis of African American women who had migrated from the South to Washington, D.C., in the early twentieth century, "all of the migrant women grew to dread their live-in situation. They saw their occupation as harming all aspects of their life" (124). Nearly all of these women transitioned into day work in private homes. This pattern is being repeated by Latina immigrants in Los Angeles today, and it reflects local labor market opportunities and constraints. In Houston, Texas, where many Mayan Guatemalan immigrant women today work as live-ins, research by Jacqueline Maria Hagan (1998) points to the tremendous obstacles they face in leaving live-in work. In Houston, housecleaning is dominated by better-established immigrant women, by Chicanas and, more recently, by the commercial cleaning companies—so it is hard for the Maya to secure those jobs. Moreover, Hagan finds that over time, the Mayan women who take live-in jobs see their own social networks contract, further reducing their internal job mobility.

7. Several factors explain the shift to day work, including urbanization, interurban transportation systems, and smaller private residences. Historians have also credited the job preferences of African American domestic workers, who rejected the constraints of live-in work and chose to live with their own families and communities, with helping to promote this shift in the urban North after 1900 (Katzman 1981; Clark-Lewis 1994:129–35). In many urban regions of the United States, the shift to day work accelerated during World War I, so that live-out arrangements eventually became more prevalent (Katzman 1981; Palmer 1989). Elsewhere, and for different groups of domestic workers, these transitions happened later in the twentieth century. Evelyn Nakano Glenn (1986:143) notes that Japanese immigrant and Japanese American women employed in domestic work in the San Francisco Bay Area moved out of live-in jobs and into modernized day work in the years after World War II.

8. Katzman 1981; Glenn 1986.

9. Katzman 1981:188.

10. Rollins 1985:208.

11. Rollins 1985; Glenn 1986; Romero 1992; Dill 1994.

INSTITUTIONS
IN CRISIS

PART SIX

The Family

Is there a crisis in the American family? Certainly it is a time of change for the family, and for many families it is also a time of trouble. The "traditional" family, with the husband as the sole source of financial support and the wife as a full-time homebody, still exists, of course, but it is now a statistical minority. Increasingly large numbers of women, married or not, have entered the labor force. Others live in unconventional intimate arrangements and contribute to the increasing diversity of American family lifestyles. All of this diversity, this permissiveness, if you will, seems to many to be menacing the integrity and stability of the American family.

Still, the American family will doubtless remain with us for a long time. It may look less and less like the conventional family of suburbia in the 1950s—with its traditional male and female roles—but the family will nevertheless continue, with accompanying transformations, readjustments, and problems.

These changes do not, however, necessarily signal decline or decay. To conclude that the family is declining, one must point to a historical era when things were rosier. Certainly, the ideal of home, motherhood, and apple pie is part of our romantic mythology, but the myth did not always match the experience.

Nevertheless, many Americans—men and women, husbands and wives, parents and children—are experiencing marked uncertainties and anxieties. We have known deep changes in family life and in society. But our understanding of how to interpret these changes—and to deal with them—has been impaired by lack of knowledge about the relationship between family life and society, particularly about the impact of social forces upon the everyday workings of family life.

America has become a high-risk, high-stress society, and family life has been feeling the strain. Economic booms and recessions, the trade-offs between time spent at work and family time generate pressures for families and those living within them. This is especially true as economic inequality and homelessness have hardened into stubbornly persistent features of American life. But the middle-class family has also been hit uncommonly hard by economic decline. Layoffs among blue- and white-collar workers have resulted in downward social mobility for suburban as well as inner-city families, while others have prospered.

Sixteen years after the publication of her classic *Worlds of Pain,* Lillian B. Rubin undertook a new study of working-class families, which shows how the lack of a social safety net and the economic upheavals of the last two decades have undermined family life among "ordinary" Americans and, not so incidentally, have contributed to racial and ethnic antagonisms. In the selection we reprint here, Rubin describes how the pressures of time and the absence of child care and other supports have brought enormous stresses to working families—stresses that affect virtually every realm of family life, from sexuality to child rearing. "Time and money," Rubin concludes, are the "precious commodities in short supply."

As Rubin's research suggests, part of the problem for all too many American families is that we lack anything approaching a comprehensive national policy that could ease the strain between parenting and work. In the 1990s, some steps were taken to develop new national policies regarding family leaves and child care. But were these efforts adequate? Not if we compare the American approach with that of European countries.

In her article "More than Welcome," Brittany Shahmehri, an American journalist living in Sweden, gives us an in-depth description of that country's extensive supports for families, which are among the most generous in the world. The centerpiece of the Swedish approach is a guaranteed leave of absence from work for new parents when their children are born, which is not only far longer than our own brief parental leave, but is also paid. The generous parental leave, moreover, is only one of many "family-friendly" policies in Sweden, which provides an approach to nurturing families and children that contrasts conspicuously with the distinctly minimal efforts in the United States. The heart of the difference is that in Sweden, as in some other European countries, it is assumed that society as a whole has an interest in—and a responsibility for—the well-being of *all* children.

Families in poor inner-city neighborhoods face all the problems generally facing working-class families, and more. Elijah Anderson's continuing ethnographic study of an inner-city neighborhood in Philadelphia distinguishes between two family types, the "decent" and the "street" or "ghetto"—terms which residents themselves use in making judgments ascribing status to resident families. Anderson shows the difficulties and dilemmas faced by parents, and especially by single mothers, in maintaining "decent" values for their children in the face of an alienated and embittered "street" culture.

CHAPTER 21

Families on the Fault Line

LILLIAN B. RUBIN

It's hardly news that child care is an enormous headache and expense for all two-job families. In many professional middle-class families, where the child-care bill can be $1,500–2,000 a month, it competes with the mortgage payment as the biggest single monthly expenditure. Problematic as this may be, however, these families are the lucky ones when compared to working-class families, many of whom don't earn much more than the cost of child care in these upper middle-class families. Even the families in this study at the highest end of the earnings scale, those who earn $42,000 a year, can't dream of such costly arrangements.

For most working-class families, therefore, child care often is patched together in ways that leave parents anxious and children in jeopardy. "Care for the little ones, that's a real big problem," says Beverly Waldov, a thirty-year-old white mother of three children, the youngest two, products of a second marriage, under three years old. "My oldest girl is nine, so she's not such a problem. I hate the idea of her being a latchkey kid, but what can I do? We don't even have the money to put the little ones in one of those good day-care places, so I don't have any choice with her. She's just got to be able to take care of herself after school," she says, her words a contest between anxiety and hope.

"We have a kind of complicated arrangement for the little kids. Two days a week, my mom takes care of them. We pay her, but at least I don't have to worry when they're with her; I know it's fine. But she works the rest of the time, so the other days we take them to this woman's house. It's the best we can afford, but it's not great because she keeps too many kids, and I know they don't get good attention. Especially the little one; she's just a baby, you know." She pauses and looks away, anguished. "She's so clingy when I bring her home; she can't let go of me, like nobody's paid her any mind all day. But it's not like I have a choice. We barely make it now; if I stop working, we'd be in real trouble."

Even such makeshift solutions don't work for many families. Some speak of being unable to afford day care at all. "We couldn't pay our bills if we had to pay for somebody to take care of the kids."

Some say they're unwilling to leave the children in the care of strangers. "I just don't believe someone else should be raising our kids, that's all."

Some have tried a variety of child-care arrangements, only to have them fail in a moment of need. "We tried a whole bunch of things, and maybe they work for a little while," says Faye Ensey, a black twenty-eight-year-old office worker. "But what happens when your kid gets sick? Or when the baby sitter's kids get sick? I lost two jobs in a row because my kids kept getting sick and I couldn't go to work. Or else I couldn't take my little one to the baby sitter because her kids were sick. They finally fired me for absenteeism. I didn't really blame them, but it felt terrible anyway. It's such a hassle, I sometimes think I'd be glad to just stay home. But we can't afford for me not to work, so we had to figure out something else."

For such families, that "something else" is the decision to take jobs on different shifts—a decision made by one-fifth of the families in this study. With one working days and the other on swing or graveyard, one parent is home with the children at all times. "We were getting along okay before Daryl junior was born, because Shona, my daughter, was getting on. You know, she didn't need somebody with her all the time, so we could both work days," explains Daryl Adams, a black thirty-year-old postal clerk with a ten-year-old daughter and a nine-month-old son. "I used to work the early shift—seven to three—so I'd get home a little bit after she got here. It worked out okay. But then this here big surprise came along." He stops, smiles down fondly at his young son and runs his hand over his nearly bald head.

"Now between the two of us working, we don't make enough money to pay for child care and have anything left over, so this is the only way we can manage. Besides, both of us, Alesha and me, we think it's better for one of us to be here, not just for the baby, for my daughter, too. She's growing up and, you know, I think maybe they need even more watching than when they were younger. She's coming to the time when she could get into all kinds of trouble if we're not here to put the brakes on."

But the cost such arrangements exact on a marriage can be very high. When I asked these husbands and wives when they have time to talk, more often than not I got a look of annoyance at a question that, on its face, seemed stupid to them. "Talk? How can we talk when we hardly see each other?" "Talk? What's that?" "Talk? Ha, that's a joke."

Mostly, conversation is limited to the logistics that take place at shift-changing time when children and chores are handed off from one to the other. With children dancing around underfoot, the incoming parent gets a quick summary of the day's or night's events, a list of reminders about things to be done, perhaps about what's cooking in the pot on the stove. "Sometimes when I'm coming home and it's been a hard day, I think: Wouldn't it be wonderful if I could just sit down with Leon for half an hour and we could have a quiet beer together?" thirty-one-year-old Emma Guerrero, a Latina baker, says wistfully.

But it's not to be. If the arriving spouse gets home early enough, there may be an hour when both are there together. But with the pressures of the workday fresh for one and awaiting the other, and with children clamoring for parental attention, this isn't a promising moment for any serious conversation. "I usually get home about forty-five minutes or so before my wife has to leave for work," says Ralph Jo, a thirty-six-year-old Asian repairman whose children, ages three and five, are the product of a second marriage. "So we try to take a few minutes just to make contact. But it's hard with the kids and all. Most days the whole time gets spent with taking care of business—you know, who did what, what the kids need, what's for supper, what bill collector was hassling her while I was gone—all the damn garbage of living. It makes me nuts."

Most of the time even this brief hour isn't available. Then the ritual changing of the guard takes only a few minutes—a quick peck on the cheek in greeting, a few words, and it's over. "It's like we pass each other. He comes in; I go out; that's it."

Some of the luckier couples work different shifts on the same days, so they're home together on weekends. But even in these families there's so little time for normal family life that there's hardly any room for anyone or anything outside. There's so much to do when I get home that there's no time for anything but the chores and the kids," says Daryl's wife, Alesha Adams. "I never get to see anybody or do anything else anymore and, even so, I'm always feeling upset and guilty because there's not enough time for them. Daryl leaves a few minutes after I get home, and the rest of the night is like a blur—Shona's homework, getting the kids fed and down for the night, cleaning up, getting everything ready for tomorrow. I don't know; there's always something I'm running around doing. I sometimes feel like—What do you call them?—one of those whirling dervishes, rushing around all the time and never getting everything done.

"Then on the weekends, you sort of want to make things nice for the kids—and for us, too. It's the only time we're here together, like a real family, so we always eat with the kids. And we try to take them someplace nice one of the days, like to the park or something. But sometimes we're too tired, or there's too many other catch-up things you have to do. I don't even get to see my sister anymore. She's been working weekends for the last year or so, and I'm too busy week nights, so there's no time.

"I don't mean to complain; we're lucky in a lot of ways. We've got two great kids, and we're a pretty good team, Daryl and me. But I worry sometimes. When you live on this kind of schedule, communication's not so good."

For those whose days off don't match, the problems of sustaining both the couple relationship and family life are magnified enormously. "The last two years have been hell for us," says thirty-five-year-old Tina Mulvaney, a white mother of two teenagers. "My son got into bad company and had some trouble, so Mike and I decided one of us had to be home. But we can't make it without my check, so I can't quit.

"Mike drives a cab and I work in a hospital, so we figured one of us could transfer to nights. We talked it over and decided it would be best if I was here during the day and he was here at night. He controls the kids, especially my son, better than I do. When he lays down the law, they listen." She interrupts her narrative to reflect on the difficulty of raising children. "You know, when they were little, I used to think about how much easier it would be when they got older. But now I see it's not true; that's when you really have to begin to worry about them. This is when they need someone to be here all the time to make sure they stay out of trouble."

She stops again, this time fighting tears, then takes up where she led off. "So now Mike works days and I work graveyard. I hate it, but it's the only answer; at least this way somebody's here all the time. I get home about 8:30 in the morning. The kids and Mike are gone. It's the best time of the day because it's the only time I have a little quiet here. I clean up the house a little, do the shopping and the laundry and whatever, then I go to sleep for a couple of hours until the kids come home from school.

"Mike gets home at five; we eat; then he takes over for the night, and I go back to sleep for another couple of hours. I try to get up by 9 so we can all have a little time together, but I'm so tired that I don't make it a lot of times. And by 10, he's sleeping because he has to be up by 6 in the morning. So if I don't get up, we hardly see each other at all. Mike's here on weekends, but I'm not. Right now I have Tuesday and Wednesday off. I keep hoping for a Monday–Friday shift but it's what everybody wants, and I don't have the seniority yet. It's hard, very hard; there's no time to live or anything," she concludes with a listless sigh.

Even in families where wife and husband work the same shift, there's less time for leisure pursuits and social activities than ever before, not just because both parents work full-time but also because people work longer hours now than they did twenty years ago. Two decades ago, weekends saw occasional family outings, Friday-evening bowling, a Saturday trip to the shopping mall, a Sunday with extended family, once in a while an evening out without the children. In summer, when the children weren't in school, a week night might find the family paying a short visit to a friend, a relative, or a neighbor. Now almost everyone I speak with complains that it's hard to find time for even these occasional outings. Instead, most off-work hours are spent trying to catch up with the dozens of family and household tasks that were left undone during the regular work week. When they aren't doing chores, parents guiltily try to do in two days a week what usually takes seven— that is, to establish a sense of family life for themselves and their children.

"Leisure," snorts Peter Pittman, a twenty-eight-year-old African-American father of two, married six years. "With both of us working like we do, there's no time for anything. We got two little kids; I commute better than an hour each way to my job. Then we live here for half rent because I take care of the place for the landlord. So if somebody's got a complaint, I've got to take care of it, you know, fix it myself or get the landlord to get somebody out to do it if I can't. Most things I can do myself, but it takes time. I sometimes wonder what this life's all about, because this sure ain't what I call living. We don't go anyplace; we don't do anything; Christ, we hardly have time to go to the toilet. There's always some damn thing that's waiting that you've got to do."

Clearly, such complaints aren't unique to the working class. The pressures of time, the impoverishment of social life, the anxieties about child care, the fear that children will live in a world of increasing scarcity, the threat of divorce—all these are part of family life today, regardless of class. Nevertheless, there are important differences between those in the higher reaches of the class structure and the families of the working class. The simple fact that middle-class families have more discretionary income is enough to make a big difference in the quality of their social life. For they generally have enough money to pay for a baby-sitter once in a while so that parents can have some time to themselves; enough, too, for a family vacation, for tickets to a concert, a play, or a movie. At $7.50 a ticket in a New York or San Francisco movie house, a working-class couple will settle for a $3.00 rental that the whole family can watch together.

Finding time and energy for sex is also a problem, one that's obviously an issue for two-job families of any class. But it's harder to resolve in working-class families because they have so few resources with which to buy some time and privacy for themselves. Ask about their sex lives and you'll be met with an angry, "What's that?" or a wistful, "I wish." When it happens, it is, as one woman put it, "on the run"—a situation that's particularly unsatisfactory for most women. For them, the pleasure of sex is related to the whole of the interaction—to a sense of intimacy and connection, to at least a few relaxed, loving moments. When they can't have these, they're likely to avoid sex altogether—a situation the men find equally unsatisfactory.

"Sex?" asks Lisa Scranton, a white twenty-nine-year-old mother of three who feigns a puzzled frown, as if she doesn't quite know the meaning of the word. "Oh yeah, that; I remember now," she says, her lips smiling, her eyes sad. "At the beginning, when we first got together, it was WOW, real hot, great. But after a while it cools down, doesn't it? Right now, it's down the toilet. I wonder, does it happen to everybody like that?" she asks dejectedly.

"I guess the worst is when you work different shifts like we do and you get to see each other maybe six minutes a day. There's no time for sex. Sometimes we try to steal a few minutes for ourselves but, I don't know, I can't get into it that way. He can. You know how men are; they can do it any time. Give them two minutes, and they can get off. But it takes me time; I mean, I like to feel close, and you can't do that in three minutes. And there's the kids; they're right here all the time. I don't want to do it if it means being interrupted. Then he gets mad, so sometimes I do. But it's a problem, a real problem."

The men aren't content with these quick sexual exchanges either. But for them it's generally better than no sex at all, while for the women it's often the other way around. "You want to talk about sex, huh?" asks Lisa's husband, Chuck, his voice crackling with anger. "Yeah, I don't mind; it's fine, only I got nothing to talk about. Far as I'm concerned, that's one of the things I found out about marriage. You get married, you give up sex. We hardly ever do it anymore, and when we do, it's like she's doing me a favor."

"Christ, I know the way we've got to do things now isn't great," he protests, running a hand through his hair agitatedly. "We don't see each other but a few minutes a day, but I don't see why we can't take five and have a little fun in the sack. Sure, I like it better when we've got more time, too. But for her, if it can't be perfect, she gets all wound and uptight and it's like . . . " He stops, groping for words, then explodes, "It's like screwing a cold fish."

She isn't just a "cold fish," however. The problems they face are deeper than that. For once such conflicts arise, spontaneity takes flight and sex becomes a problem that needs attention rather than a time out for pleasure and renewal. Between times, therefore, he's busy calculating how much time has passed: "It's been over two weeks"; nursing his wounds: "I don't want to have to beg her"; feeling deprived and angry: "I don't know why I got married." When they finally do come together, he's disappointed. How could it be otherwise, given the mix of feelings he brings to the bed with him—the frustration and anger, the humiliation of feeling he has to beg her, the wounded sense of manhood.

Meanwhile, she, too, is preoccupied with sex, not with thoughts of pleasure but with figuring out how much time she has before, as she puts it, "he walks around with his mouth stuck out. I know I'm in real big trouble if we don't do it once a week. So I make sure we do, even if I don't want to." She doesn't say those words to him, of course. But he knows. And it's precisely this, the knowledge that she's servicing him rather than desiring him that's so hard for him to take.

The sexual arena is one of the most common places to find a "his and her" marriage—one marriage, two different sex lives. Each partner has a different story to tell; each is convinced that his or her version is the real one. A husband says mournfully, "I'm lucky if we get to make love once a week." His wife reports with irritation, "It's two, sometimes three times a week." It's impossible to know whose account is closest to the reality. And it's irrelevant. If that's what they were after, they could keep tabs and get it straight. But facts and feelings are often at war in family life. And nowhere does right or wrong, true or false count for less than in their sexual interactions. It isn't that people arbitrarily distort the truth. They simply report their experience, and it's feeling, not fact, that dominates that experience; feeling, not fact, that is their truth.

But it's also true that, especially for women, the difference in frequency of sexual desire can be a response—sometimes conscious, sometimes not—to other conflicts in the marriage. It isn't that men never withhold sex as a weapon in the family wars, only that they're much more likely than women to be able to split sex from emotion, to feel their anger and still experience sexual desire. For a man, too, a sexual connection with his wife can relieve the pressures and tensions of the day, can make him feel whole again, even if they've barely spoken a word to each other.

For a woman it's different. What happens—or, more likely, what doesn't happen—in the kitchen, the living room, and the laundry room profoundly affects what's possible in the bedroom. When she feels distant, unconnected, angry; when her pressured life leaves her feeling fragmented; when she hasn't had a real conversation with her husband for a couple of days, sex is very far from either her mind or her loins. "I run around busy all the time, and he just sits there, so by the time we go to bed, I'm too tired," explains Linda Bloodworth, a white thirty-one-year-old telephone operator.

"Do you think your lack of sexual response has something to do with your anger at your husband's refusal to participate more fully in the household?" I ask.

Her eyes smoldering, her voice tight, she snaps, "No, I'm just tired, that's all." Then noticing something in my response, she adds, "I know what you're thinking, I saw that look. But really, I don't think it's *because* I'm angry; I really am tired. I have to admit, though, that I tell him if he helped more, maybe I wouldn't be so tired all the time. And," she adds defiantly, "maybe I wouldn't be."

Some couples, of course, manage their sexual relationship with greater ease. Often that's because they have less conflict in other areas of living. But whether they accommodate well or poorly, for all two-job families, sex requires a level of attention and concern that leaves most people wanting much of the time. "It's a problem, and I tell you, it has to be well planned," explains thirty-four-year-old Dan Stolman, a black construction worker. "But we manage okay, we make dates or try to slip it in when the baby's asleep and my daughter's out with a friend or something. I don't mean things are great in that department. I'm not always satisfied and neither is Lorraine. But what can you do? We try to do the best we can. Sex isn't all there is to a marriage, you know. We get along really well, so that makes up for a lot.

"What I really miss is that we don't ever make love anymore. I mean, we have sex like I said, but we don't have the kind of time you need to make love. We talk about getting away for an overnight by ourselves once in a while. Lorraine's mother would come watch the kids if we asked her; the problem is we don't have any extra cash to spare right now."

Time and money—precious commodities in short supply. These are the twin plagues of family life, the missing ingredients that combine to create families that are both frantic and fragile. Yet there's no mystery about what would alleviate the crisis that now threatens to engulf them: A job that pays a living wage, quality child-care facilities at rates people can pay, health care for all, parental leave, flexible work schedules, decent and affordable housing, a shorter work week so that parents and children have time to spend together, tax breaks for those in need rather than for those in greed, to mention just a few. These are the policies we need to put in place if we're to have any hope of making our families stable and healthy.

CHAPTER 22

More Than Welcome

Families Come First in Sweden

BRITTANY SHAHMEHRI

Recently, my husband's laptop needed repair, and he called technical support to arrange for service. When he explained the problem, the phone representative at the multinational computer company said, "I'm going to recommend level-two support, but the technician will have to call you tomorrow to schedule an appointment. Today he's home with his sick kid."

When we still lived in the US, my husband might have wondered what a sick child had to do with his laptop. But last year we moved to Sweden, where parents not only are legally entitled to stay home with their sick children, but also get paid for doing so. Most amazing is that there's no shame in it. For fathers as well as mothers, it is assumed that when your child is sick, you are going to take care of him or her. That's more important than fixing someone's laptop on the spot. The computer company knows it and my husband's employer knows it. In almost every circumstance, the laptop can wait a day.

Even visiting tourists can see that Sweden has a child-friendly culture. A stroller logo is as common as the wheelchair logo in public restrooms and elevators. Buses accommodate strollers, and trains have places for children to play. (By the way, the children ride free.) Gas stations often have tiny working toilets as well as the standard toilets, as do zoos and other places that cater to children. "Amazing," I thought, the first time I visited.

But on closer examination, all of this is just window dressing. Sweden has one of the most generous parental leave policies in the world. Parents of each newborn or newly adopted child share 450 paid days to care for that child. The childcare system is of extremely high quality, offers a wide range of options, and is subsidized for all families. Parents are legally entitled to work reduced hours at their current jobs until their children reach the age of eight (when they formally enter school), and can take up to 60 paid days to take care of sick children. Toss in protected time to nurse a baby on the job and tuition-free universities, and to an American working parent, it sounds like utopia!

WHY SUCH WIDESPREAD SUPPORT?

According to Dr. Irene Wennemo, a Swedish family policy expert, the question of supporting families in Sweden is generally framed in terms of how the state should implement policies and what level of resources should be invested. "It's very accepted here that the state should be responsible for the living standard of children," Wennemo told me. "Children aren't a private thing; society has a responsibility for part of the cost."

Most of the reasons for this are self-evident. Children are members of society. It's not good for people, especially children, to live in poverty. Children should have equal opportunities. It's necessary for society that people have children, so it should be easy to combine working and having children. It's good for men and women to have equal access to both work and family.

"If you want a society in which it is accepted that both partners go out and work, then you have to take people's needs seriously," states Gunnar Andersson, a sociologist at Lund University. "Both school and child care must be really good, and there must be much more flexibility for all."[1]

"This is what our parents worked for," explains Anneli Elfwén, a Swedish midwife with two young sons. In the 1950s most Swedish women stayed home with the children. When women began to enter the workforce in the late 1960s, the need for stronger family policy became clear. The modern versions of parental leave policy and subsidized child care were implemented in the early 1970s and met with wide popular support. When I asked Elfwén why support for family policy was so widespread, she laughed, "Maybe we get it in the breastmilk. It's very natural for us."

HOW IT WORKS

When Elfwén's first son, Simon, was born in 1995, Elfwén was entitled to the same parental leave benefits that are offered to all Swedish families. She and her husband could share the 450 days of leave as they pleased, though one month was reserved for her, and one for her husband; and if either of them chose not to take their individual time, they would forfeit it.

One of the most unique aspects of Swedish parental leave is that it can be taken part time. Elfwén and her husband used the flexibility in their schedules to extend the time Simon spent at home with one of his parents. Between paid leave, flexible jobs, and the help of grandparents, the Elfwéns juggled a two-career, two-parent family. When their second son, Olle, was born in 1998, he, too, was entitled to 450 days of his parents' time. This made it possible for Elfwén to maintain the career that she loves, while keeping her children home until they were about three. The parental leave made all the difference.

Parents can continue to work reduced hours until their children reach the age of eight. This option was chosen by a couple I know, both schoolteachers. The mother took one day a week off, the father one day, and they staggered their hours on remaining days, so that their children spent less time in child care. Both parents were able to maintain professional lives while sharing the responsibility for raising their children.

CHOICES IN CHILD CARE

When it was time for the Elfwéns to decide on a preschool for Simon, they selected a Waldorf school with low student-teacher ratios and organic vegetarian meals. There are also traditional preschools, Christian schools, Montessori schools, co-operative schools, and even daycare centers that focus on gender equality. Families pay the county rather than the childcare center, and the amount depends on each family's household income. This means that, with few exceptions, parents can send their child to any childcare center without consideration to finances. So a single mother studying at university might pay $30.00 a month for her child to attend a school, while a family with three children and a household income of $40,000 would pay around $240 a month to have their three children in the same school. As of 2002, there will be a cap of $115 a month for the first child, ramping down according to income.

Of course, things are not perfect. It can be difficult to find a spot in the middle of the year, so it's necessary to plan ahead. The school we chose for my four year old did not suit him, so we kept him home while waiting for a place in a new school. In looking at the options, however, we were impressed with the low student-teacher ratios at all the preschools we visited, and the consistently high quality of care.

SEPARATE TAXATION AND CHILD ALLOWANCES

A few other odds and ends round out the package. People are taxed individually in Sweden, so a woman's income won't fall into a high tax bracket just because the household income is high. In addition, cash payments take the place of tax deductions for children. Each month, about $95.00 per child is deposited into the account of every family with a child, from the unemployed to the royal family. Families with more than two children receive a small bonus, so for my three children, we get a cash payment of $300 a month. Many families turn the money over to their children when they reach the age of 15 so they can learn to handle a checking account and manage their clothing and leisure purchases.

THE EMPLOYER'S ROLE

In Sweden, creating balance between work and family life is not left solely to the government and individual families. Section five of the Swedish Equal Opportunity Act reads, "An employer shall facilitate the combination of gainful employment and parenthood with respect to both female and male employees." Employers, in other words, are legally obligated to help employees combine parenthood and work. Employees who believe that an employer has directly violated this principle can take their case to the office of the Equal Opportunity Ombudsman (JämO).

Claes Lundkvist filed one of the eight cases registered with JämO last year regarding parenthood and employment. Lundkvist, a broadcast journalist for Swedish Radio, generally took his children to daycare each morning, and his wife, a physiotherapist with her own business, picked them up at the end of the day. But a new contract required Lundkvist to transfer to a branch more than an hour away. His working hours were inflexible as well. "My wife was very stressed taking all the responsibility," Lundkvist says. "It didn't work." After looking at JämO's Web page, he decided to pursue the issue.

The involvement of fathers as parents should be encouraged, according to JämO: "Employers may have an old-fashioned view of parenthood, or think that 'your wife can take care of that,' when the husband wants to be free to care for sick children or asks for more flexible working hours in order to combine work and family."[2] Changing the attitude of such employers is one of JämO's goals. JämO accepted Lundkvist's case, recognizing that without some adjustment in his new situation, his ability to combine work and family would be seriously impaired. The case initially met with resistance from Lundkvist's employers, and as he was a contract worker, JämO's power was limited. Lundkvist has since, however, negotiated a solution that does offer some flexibility.

With each case filed, the resulting publicity strengthens the public debate about men's rights and responsibilities as fathers. "It's hard to change gender roles," says Tommy Ferrarini, a PhD student at the Institute of Social Research in Stockholm who is currently doing research on family policy. But Ferrarini believes measures such as parental leave time allotted for the father shift social expectations: "It puts pressure on the employers when something becomes a right. It's all very individualized. . . . [This means] increased individual autonomy for the mother, the father, and the children. You give both parents the possibility of self-fulfillment."

WHAT FAMILY POLICY MEANS FOR WOMEN

Swedish mothers don't think they are doing it all, and they don't think the system is perfect. Some women have jobs that are more flexible than others; some are happier with their child care than others. While men are doing a larger share of the housework than in the past, couples still fight about who does the laundry. You'd be hard-pressed to find a Swedish mom who would call herself a superwoman.

Observing the situation, however, I see women who come pretty close to fulfilling the American "superwoman" myth. The vast majority of women have careers. With the help of their partners, they juggle children and work and birthday parties and still manage to make it to aerobics every week.

In the US, in contrast, the superwoman myth operates in a male-dominated corporate culture, and society views accepting help as a weakness. If you are granted a day off, you should be grateful. If your husband takes two unpaid weeks at the birth of a child, he should be grateful. If his company calls after a week and asks him to come back early (as my husband's company did), he should apologize when he says no, and then thank them for understanding.

In Sweden, you can certainly say "thank you" if you like, but no one has done you any favors. Among CEOs and entrepreneurs, you may see a more male-dominated culture, but even there, people are still likely to take a good portion of the five to eight weeks vacation they receive annually.

Swedish women face many of the same problems as their American counterparts. Their career advancement slows while children are young, and juggling everything can be very challenging. But women in Sweden do not have to do it alone. Families are supported by society, both financially and culturally. This means that women also give back to society, and not just in tax dollars—though even there, their contribution is substantial. Having women in the workplace changes the culture. Today, 43 percent of representatives in the Swedish Parliament and half of all State Ministers are women. In the long run, that will have an effect on the tone of the government as well as the laws that are passed.

CHILDREN ARE PEOPLE, TOO

Children in Sweden are not considered merely a lifestyle choice. They're members of society in their own right. Flexibility and support for families means that parents are better able to meet the needs of their children, something the children deserve. This approach offers myriad benefits to children, both emotionally and physically. Recent studies have suggested that "parental leave has favorable and possibly cost-effective impacts on pediatric health."[3] The same studies also indicate that with longer parental leaves, child and infant mortality rates go down.[4]

Respect for children is an important aspect of Swedish culture. Sweden has a Children's Ombudsman who represents children and young people in public debates, the ultimate goal being that young people can make their voices heard and gain respect for their views. In line with this, corporal punishment of any kind is illegal. Though controversial when it was first proposed, a Parliamentary Minister put the issue into context: "In a free democracy like our own, we use words as arguments, not blows. . . . If we can't convince our children with words, we will never convince them with violence."[5]

Children in Sweden are people, not property. Family policy is very much about creating a better situation for men and women who choose to have families, but at its core, family policy is all about children. A society that cherishes and respects children must make it possible for every child to be raised with certain minimal standards. Ensuring healthcare coverage, making sure children have enough to eat, and keeping children free of the risks that inevitably accompany poverty are a few modest goals. In Sweden, every child is entitled to be home with his or her parents for the first year of life. That is the minimum standard the society has chosen.

What that means is that any child you see on the street had access to her parents for the most important time in her development, and has access to free, high-quality medical and dental care. You know that she has enough food to eat, and that she likely attends a well-run preschool. That child has advocates in government and the support of society. Who will that child become? Right now it doesn't matter. The bottom line is that she lives in a society that values her just the way she is.

NOTES

1. Kristina Hultman, "A Step Away from a Childless Society?" *New Life: A Gender Equality Magazine for New Parents* (Stockholm: Swedish Government Division for Gender Equality, 2001): 10.

2. "What Is JämO?," a brochure published by the Equal Opportunity Ombudsman's office; see *www.jamombud.se.*

3. C. J. Ruhm, "Parental Leave and Child Health," *NBER Working Paper* no. W6554 (Cambridge, MA: National Bureau of Economic Research, 1998): 27.

4. Sheila Kamerman, "Parental Leave Policies: An Essential Ingredient in Early Childhood Education and Care Policies," *Social Policy Report 14,* no. 2 (2000): 10.

5. Louise Sylwander, "The Swedish Corporal Punishment Ban—More Than Twenty Years of Experience," Barnombudsmannen website, *www.bo.se* (choose the British flag for English).

For additional information about Sweden, see the following article in a past issue of *Mothering:* "Swedish Parents Don't Spank," no. 63.

CHAPTER 23

Decent and Street Families

ELIJAH ANDERSON

Almost everyone residing in poor inner-city neighborhoods is struggling financially and therefore feels a certain distance from the rest of America, but there are degrees of alienation, captured by the terms "decent" and "street" or "ghetto," suggesting social types. The decent family and the street family in a real sense represent two poles of value orientation, two contrasting conceptual categories. The labels "decent" and "street," which the residents themselves use, amount to evaluative judgments that confer status on local residents. The labeling is often the result of a social contest among individuals and families of the neighborhood. Individuals of either orientation may coexist in the same extended family. Moreover, decent residents may judge themselves to be so while judging others to be of the street, and street individuals often present themselves as decent, while drawing distinctions between themselves and still other people. There is also quite a bit of circumstantial behavior—that is, one person may at different times exhibit both decent and street orientations, depending on the circumstances. Although these designations result from much social jockeying, there do exist concrete features that define each conceptual category, forming a social typology.

The resulting labels are used by residents of inner-city communities to characterize themselves and one another, and understanding them is part of understanding life in the inner-city neighborhood. Most residents are decent or are trying to be. The same family is likely to have members who are strongly oriented toward decency and civility, whereas other members are oriented toward the street—and to all that it implies. There is also a great deal of "code-switching": a person may behave according to either set of rules, depending on the situation. Decent people, especially young people, often put a premium on the ability to code-switch. They share many of the middle-class values of the wider white society but know that the open display of such values carries little weight on the street: it doesn't provide the emblems that say, "I can take care of myself." Hence such people develop a repertoire of behaviors that do provide that security. Those strongly associated with the street, who have less exposure to the wider society, may have difficulty code-switching; imbued with the code of the street, they either don't know the rules for decent behavior or may see little value in displaying such knowledge.

At the extreme of the street-oriented group are those who make up the criminal element. People in this class are profound casualties of the social and economic system, and they tend to embrace the street code wholeheartedly. They tend to lack not only a decent education—though some are highly intelligent —but also an outlook that would allow them to see far beyond their immediate circumstances. Rather, many pride themselves on living the "thug life," actively defying not simply the wider social conventions but the law itself. They sometimes model themselves after successful local drug dealers and rap artists like Tupac Shakur and Snoop Doggy Dogg, and they take heart from professional athletes who confront the system and stand up for themselves. In their view, policemen, public officials, and corporate heads are unworthy of respect and hold little moral authority. Highly alienated and embittered, they exude generalized contempt for the wider scheme of things and for a system they are sure has nothing but contempt for them.

Members of this group are among the most desperate and most alienated people of the inner city. For them, people and situations are best approached both as objects of exploitation and as challenges possibly "having a trick to them," and in most situations their goal is to avoid being "caught up in the trick bag." Theirs is a cynical outlook, and trust of others is severely lacking, even trust of those they are close to. Consistently, they tend to approach all persons and situations as part of life's obstacles, as things to subdue or to "get over." To get over, individuals develop an effective "hustle" or "game plan," setting themselves up in a position to prevail by being "slick" and outsmarting others. In line with this, one must always be wary of one's counterparts, to assume that they are involved with you only for what they can get out of the situation.

Correspondingly, life in public often features an intense competition for scarce social goods in which "winners" totally dominate "losers" and in which losing can be a fate worse than death. So one must be on one's guard constantly. One is not always able to trust others fully, in part because so much is at stake socially, but also because everyone else is understood to be so deprived. In these circumstances, violence is quite prevalent—in families, in schools, and in the streets—becoming a way of public life that is effectively governed by the code of the street.

Decent and street families deal with the code of the street in various ways. An understanding of the dynamics of these families is thus critical to an understanding of the dynamics of the code. It is important to understand here that the family one emerges from is distinct from the "family" one finds in the streets. For street-oriented people especially, the family outside competes with blood relatives for an individual's loyalties and commitments. Nevertheless, blood relatives always come first. The folklore of the street says, in effect, that if I will fight and "take up for" my friend, then you know what I will do for my own brother, cousin, nephew, aunt, sister, or mother—and vice versa. Blood is thicker than mud.

DECENT FAMILIES

In decent families there is almost always a real concern with and a certain amount of hope for the future. Such attitudes are often expressed in a drive to work "to have something" or "to build a good life," while at the same time trying to "make do with what you have." This means working hard, saving money for material things, and raising children—any "child you touch"—to try to make something out of themselves. Decent families tend to accept mainstream values more fully than street families, and they attempt to instill them in their children. Probably the most meaningful description of the mission of the decent family, as seen by members and outsiders alike, is to instill "backbone" and a sense of responsibility in its younger members. In their efforts toward this goal, decent parents are much more able and willing than street-oriented ones to ally themselves with outside institutions such as schools and churches. They value hard work and self-reliance and are willing to sacrifice for their children: they harbor hopes for a better future for their children, if not for themselves. Rather than dwelling on the hardships and inequities facing them, many such decent people, particularly the increasing number of grandmothers raising grandchildren, often see their difficult situation as a test from God and derive great support from their faith and church community.

The role of the "man of the house" is significant. Working-class black families have traditionally placed a high value on male authority. Generally, the man is seen as the "head of household," with the woman as his partner and the children as their subjects. His role includes protecting the family from threats, at times literally putting his body in the line of fire on the street. In return he expects to rule his household and to get respect from the other members, and he encourages his sons to grow up with the same expectations. Being a breadwinner or good provider is often a moral issue, and a man unable to provide for a family invites disrespect from his partner. Many young men who lack the resources to do so often say, "I can't play house," and opt out of forming a family, perhaps leaving the woman and any children to fend for themselves.

Intact nuclear families, although in the minority in the impoverished inner city, provide powerful role models. Typically, husband and wife work at low-paying jobs, sometimes juggling more than one such job each. They may be aided financially by the contributions of a teenage child who works part-time. Such families, along with other such local families, are often vigilant in their desire to keep the children away from the streets.

In public such an intact family makes a striking picture as the man may take pains to show he is in complete control—with the woman and the children following his lead. On the inner-city streets this appearance helps him play his role as protector, and he may exhibit exaggerated concern for his family, particularly when other males are near. His actions and words, including loud and deep-voiced assertions to get his small children in line, let strangers know: "This is my family, and I am in charge." He signals that he is capable of protecting them and that his family is not to be messed with.

I witnessed such a display one Saturday afternoon at the Gallery, an indoor shopping mall with a primarily black, Hispanic, and working- to middle-class white clientele. Rasheed Taylor, his wife, Iisha, and their children, Rhonda, Jimmy, and Malika, wandered about the crowded food court looking for a place to sit down to eat. They finally found a table next to mine. Before sitting down, Mr. Taylor asked me if the seats were available, to which I replied they were. He then summoned his family, and they walked forward promptly and in an orderly way to take the seats. The three children sat on one side and the parents on the other. Mr. Taylor took food requests and with a stern look in his eye told the children to stay seated until he and his wife returned with the food. The children nodded attentively. After the adults left, the children seemed to relax, talking more freely and playing with one another. When the parents returned, the kids straightened up again, received their food, and began to eat, displaying quiet and gracious manners all the while. It was very clear to everybody looking on that Mr. Taylor was in charge of this family, with everyone showing him utter deference and respect.

Extremely aware of the problematic and often dangerous environment in which they reside, decent parents tend to be strict in their child-rearing practices, encouraging children to respect authority and walk a straight moral line. They sometimes display an almost obsessive concern about trouble of any kind and encourage their children to avoid people and situations that might lead to it. But this is very difficult, since the decent and the street families live in such close proximity. Marge, a slight, forty-three-year-old, married, decent parent of five who resides in such a neighborhood, relates her experience:

But you know what happens now? I have five children. Or I had five children—my oldest son got killed in a car accident. My children have always been different [decent]. And sometimes we have to act that way [street] that other people act to show them that you're not gonna be intimidated, that my child is gonna go to the store, they're gonna come out here and play, they're gonna go to school. You don't wanta do that, but you can't go to them and talk. 'Cause I've tried that. I've tried to go to people and say, "Listen. These are children. Let's try to make them get along." I remember years ago my sons had some expensive baseball mitts and bats that was given to them. I didn't buy them. They got them from Mr. Lee because he had the baseball team. And so he gave my sons some baseball bats and gloves. At that time the park at Twenty-seventh and Girard was Fred Jackson Stadium; they call it Ruth Bloom now. My sons played baseball there. So one little boy wanted to borrow some of the gloves and the bat. I told my children, "Don't let him hold [use] the gloves and the bat." But they let him hold them anyway. So he told them that when he finished with them he would put them on the porch. I told them they were never going to see them again, and they were never put on the porch. So I went to his mother, that was my neighbor, and I approached her very nicely and I said, "Johnny didn't bring Terry and Curtis's gloves and bat back." You know, she cursed me out! I was shocked. [She said,] "He doesn't have to take a so-and-so bat and a ball." And that woman really shocked me and hurt my feelings. I said, "Forget it. Just forget it." She was really ignorant. But I had to—even though I didn't get ignorant [get on her level] 'cause my son was there—but I had to say *some* negative things to her to let her know that I was just shocked. But I've been here [residing in this neighborhood] twenty-two years, and in twenty-two years I've had at least ten different, separate incidents that I had to go out and talk to somebody, to the point that I told my children, "No more." Somebody's gonna get hurt 'cause they don't know when to stop.

OK, my daughter, Annette, she went to Germantown High. So she was in about the ninth grade, had never had a fight in her life. She came from the store one day, and she told me about this girl that kept pickin' on her. She came up on the porch, and she said, "Mommy, come to the door. I want to show you this girl that keeps picking on me." Of course. Anybody that bothered them, I always wanted to see who it was in case I had to go see their parents or whatever. So I came and looked over the railing on the porch, and me and my daughter were lookin' down the street in that direction, not really at her [which could have been taken as offensive]. The girl came up and said, "Who the fuck are you lookin' at?" I said to my daughter, "Don't say anything." So I said to the girl, "You better go home. You better take your little butt home." OK. So she did go home. That afternoon, my daughter was sitting on the steps of the porch and reading a book—now this is a child who never had a fight, gets good grades. I think I raised her extremely well. She's a biochemist now. She's sitting on the step, reading her little book, and the girl came up to her, said something to her. I wasn't even out there, and so by the time my sons came to get me, my daughter and her were fighting. That was the first fight that she ever had in her life, and she was in the ninth grade. So I went out there and separated them. The girl went around the corner. When she came back, she had twenty different people with her. But I knew what was gonna happen. So—those same baseball bats I told you about—I told my son to get the baseball bats from the hallway. I said, "We're not gonna get off the porch, but if we have to, if they come up here, we're gonna have to do something." So they came back, and I had to actually coax them off like I was a little tough, like I'm not gonna take it. And I said to my sons, "If they come up here, we're gonna pay they ass back," and all that kind of stuff. And that's how I got them off us. I mean, it was about twenty of them, friends, family, neighbors.

As I indicated above, people who define themselves as decent tend themselves to be polite and considerate of others and teach their children to be the same way. But this is sometimes difficult, mainly because of the social environment in which they reside, and they often perceive a need to "get ignorant"—to act aggressively, even to threaten violence. For whether a certain child gets picked on may well depend not just on the reputation of the child but, equally important, on how "bad" the child's family is known to be. How many people the child can gather together for the purposes of defense or revenge often emerges as a critical issue. Thus social relations can become practical matters of personal defense. Violence can come at any time, and many persons feel a great need to be ready to defend themselves.

At home, at work, and in church, decent parents strive to maintain a positive mental attitude and a spirit of cooperation. When disciplining their children, they tend to use corporal punishment, but unlike street parents, who can often be observed lashing out at their children, they may explain the reason for the spanking. These parents express their care and love for teenage children by guarding against the appearance of any kind of "loose" behavior (violence, drug use, staying out very late) that might be associated with the streets. In this regard, they are vigilant, observing children's peers as well and sometimes embarrassing their own children by voicing value judgments in front of friends.

These same parents are aware, however, that the right material things as well as a certain amount of cash are essential to young people's survival on the street. So they may purchase expensive things for their children, even when money is tight, in order that the children will be less tempted to turn to the drug trade or other aspects of the underground economy for money.

THE DECENT SINGLE MOTHER

A single mother with children—the majority of decent families in the impoverished sections of the inner city are of this type—must work even harder to neutralize the draw of the street, and she does so mainly by being strict and by instilling decent values in her children. She may live with her mother or other relatives and friends, or she may simply receive help with child care from her extended family. In raising her children, she often must press others to defer to her authority; but without a strong man of the house, a figure boys in particular are prepared to respect, she is at some disadvantage with regard not only to her own sons and daughters but also to the young men of the streets. These men may test her ability to control her household by attempting to date her daughters or to draw her sons into the streets. A mother on her own often feels she must be constantly on guard and exhibit a great deal of determination.

Diane, a single mother of four sons, three of whom are grown, offers a case in point. Diane is forty-six years old, of average height, heavyset, and light-complexioned. One of her sons is a night watchman at the utility company, and another is a security guard at a downtown store. Diane herself works as an aide in a day care center. In describing her situation, she has this to say:

> It really is pretty bad around here. There's quite a few grandmothers taking care of kids. They mothers out here on crack. There's quite a few of 'em. The drugs are terrible. Now, I got a fifteen-year-old boy, and I do everything I can to keep him straight. 'Cause they [drug dealers and users] all on the corner. You can't say you not in it, 'cause we in a bad area. They be all on the corner. They be sittin' in front of apartments takin' the crack. And constantly, every day, I have to stay on 'em and make sure everything's OK. Which is real bad, I never seen it this bad. And I been around here since '81, and I never seen it this bad. At nights they be roamin' up and down the streets, and they be droppin' the caps [used crack vials] all in front of your door. And when the kids out there playin', you gotta like sweep 'em up. It's harder for me now to try to keep my fifteen-year-old under control. Right now, he likes to do auto mechanics, hook up radios in people's cars, and long as I keep 'im interested in that, I'm OK. But it's not a day that goes by that I'm not in fear. 'Cause right now he got friends that's sellin' it. They, you know, got a whole lot of money and stuff. And I get him to come and mop floors [she works part-time as a janitor], and I give him a few dollars. I say, "As long as you got a roof over yo' head, son, don't worry about nothin' else."

It's just a constant struggle tryin' to raise yo' kids in this time. It's very hard. They [boys on the street] say to him, "Man, why you got to go in the house?" And they keep sittin' right on my stoop. If he go somewhere, I got to know where he's at and who he's with. And they be tellin' him [come with us]. He say, "No, man, I got to stay on these steps. I don't want no problem with my mama!" Now, I been a single parent for fifteen years. So far, I don't have any problems. I have four sons. I got just the one that's not grown, the fifteen-year-old. Everyone else is grown. My oldest is thirty-five. I'm tryin'. Not that easy. I got just one more, now. Then I'll be all right. If I need help, the older ones'll help me. Most of the time, I keep track myself. I told him I'll kill him if I catch him out here sellin'. And I know most of the drug dealers. He better not. I'm gon' hurt him. They better not give him nothin'. He better not do nothin' for them. I tell him, "I know some of your friends are dealers. [You can] speak to 'em, but don't let me catch you hangin' on the corner. I done struggled too hard to try to take care of you. I'm not gon' let you throw your life away."

When me and my husband separated in '79, I figured I had to do it. He was out there drivin' trucks and never home. I had to teach my kids how to play ball and this and that. I said, "If I have to be a single parent, I'll do it." It used to be the gangs, and you fought 'em, and it was over. But now if you fight somebody, they may come back and kill you. It's a whole lot different now. You got to be street-smart to get along. My boy doesn't like to fight. I took him out of school, put him in a home course. The staff does what it wants to. [They] just work for a paycheck.

You tell the kid, now you can't pick their friends, so you do what you can. I try to tell mine, "You gon' be out there with the bad [street kids], you can't do what they do. You got to use your own mind." Every day, if I don't get up and say a prayer, I can't make it. I can't make it. I watch him closely. If he go somewhere, I have to know where he at. And when I leave him, or if he go to them girlfriends' houses, I tell the parents, "If you not responsible, he can't stay." I'm not gon' have no teenager making no baby.

These comments show how one decent inner-city parent makes sense of the breakdown in civility, order, and morality she sees occurring in her community and how she copes. When Diane was a child, and even when her older sons were growing up, gang fights were common, but they generally took the form of an air-clearing brawl. Today many community residents feel that if you run afoul of a gang or an individual, somebody may simply kill you. Note that the schools are included among the institutions seen to have abdicated their responsibilities, a widespread belief among many inner-city parents. . . .

The inner-city community is actually quite diverse economically; various people are doing fairly well, whereas others are very poor but decent and still others are utterly and profoundly suffering, alienated, and angry. Such is the social terrain the decent family must navigate and negotiate in order to remain whole as well as secure. This situation creates a major dilemma for decent families who are trying to raise their children to remain decent even though they must negotiate the streets. These parents want their children to value educations, jobs, and a future, but they also want them to get their fair share of respect and the props that go with it—and not to be dissed or attacked or shot.

PART SEVEN

The Environment

I t's sometimes said that in America today, everyone has become an environmentalist. If so, this represents a large change in a relatively short time. The environmental movement in the United States only took off in the 1960s and 1970s. Yet today many practices that seemed revolutionary in those days are now routine. School children learn about the virtues of recycling in the classroom; corporations run magazine advertisements urging the public to recognize their commitment to clean air and water. The vast majority of Americans, according to opinion polls, believe that maintaining a clean environment is worth whatever it costs.

These changes have been so pervasive and so rapid that some now insist that the battle against environmental destruction has been largely won and we can now relax our concern. Others think that we've already gone too far in the pursuit of environmental quality, to the point where cumbersome regulations are hobbling the economy and lowering our standard of living.

But as the articles in this part make clear, any complacency about the state of the environment is unwarranted. It's true that important gains have been made against some environmental problems. But for others, progress is slow at best, and at the same time, new and gravely threatening problems have emerged that were largely unforeseen only a few decades ago. One recent report, for example, estimates that nearly half the American population continues to breathe unhealthy levels of ozone, a toxic air pollutant that has been implicated in many kinds of respiratory disease.[1] Another tells us that there may no longer be *any* streams or rivers left in the United States that are free from chemical contamination.[2]

As James Gustave Speth makes clear, these are not isolated problems. They reflect a much larger and more fateful transformation of the relationship between human beings and the natural environment—one that has been going on for centuries, but has radically accelerated in recent years. Huge surges in population and economic activity, in particular, have made the "human footprint" much heavier than it was in the past, and this process can only continue in the coming years, especially as formerly poor nations push to become part of the developed industrial world. The great increases in population, production, and consumption around the world have dramatically increased older, familiar environmental problems—like industrial pollution and sewage—and also fostered new and, if anything, even more critical ones—like global climate change and the massive depletion of natural resources. In the long run, these may turn out to be the most formidable problems that human societies now confront.

Among the new threats to the environment, perhaps none is as troubling as the problem of global warming. In "The Heat Is On," Ross Gelbspan contends that, despite a concerted campaign to deny the seriousness of the threat of global warming, it is very real indeed. The extremes of weather experienced in the United States in recent years, he argues, are a forewarning of worse environmental disruptions in the future that could, in turn, bring unprecedented economic and social dislocations for generations to come.

Attacking global warming at the source—by, for example, reducing the burning of fossil fuels—may be the best way to avoid that scenario. But there has been considerable resistance to such steps by some corporations and governments, including our own, mainly on the ground that they would hurt the economy. As Gelbspan points out, however, the health of the economy ultimately depends on the state of the environment, not the other way around; and if we are not careful, the ongoing insult to the earth's atmosphere could bring economic as well as ecological havoc. Since this article was written, a flood of new scientific evidence has confirmed that climate change is indeed upon us—and is in fact proceeding faster than we had first thought, which makes the need for a concerted international effort even more urgent.

The adverse environmental trends described in these articles affect everyone on the planet, but it remains true that some people are affected more harshly, and more immediately, than others. Indeed, the concentration of some of the worst environmental problems among America's most disadvantaged people is one of the most troubling aspects of the growing inequality we've charted in previous sections of this book. Blacks, Hispanics, and Native Americans now carry much more than their share of the burden of environmental pollution. They are more likely to live near toxic waste dumps and other hazardous facilities, they breathe the most polluted air, and they suffer more often from lead poisoning and contaminated water supplies. Moreover, violations of pollution regulations are likely to be prosecuted much more zealously in white than in minority communities. In other words, the benefits of economic growth—jobs and income—go disproportionately to the affluent, while the toxic *costs* of growth are allotted to the poor, turning some poor communities into what the sociologist Robert Bullard[3] has called "sacrifice zones." Steve Lerner's harrowing description of the plight of the African American residents of Diamond, a small, poor community hard up against the "fenceline" of a massive Shell petrochemical complex in Louisiana, provides a compelling look at the human face of this widespread environmental injustice.

ENDNOTES

1. American Lung Association, *State of the Air: 2003*, New York, NY, May 2003.
2. John Heilprin, "Report Paints Gloomy U.S. Ecological Picture," Associated Press, September 25, 2002.
3. Robert Bullard, "Environmental Racism," in Jerome H. Skolnick and Elliott Currie, eds., *Crisis in American Institutions*, 12th edition, Boston, Allyn and Bacon, 2004, p. 241.

CHAPTER 24

A World of Wounds

JAMES GUSTAVE SPETH

crisis *1. Med. That change in a disease that indicates whether the result is to be recovery or death. 2. The decisive moment; turning point. 3. crucial time.*

We live in the twenty-first century, but we live with the twentieth century. The expansion of the human enterprise in the twentieth century, and especially after World War II, was phenomenal. It was in this century that human society truly left the moorings of its past and launched itself upon the planet in an unprecedented way.

Most familiar is the population explosion. It took all of human history for global population to expand by 1900 to a billion and a half people. But over the past century that many more people were added, on average, every thirty-three years. In the past twenty-five years, global population increased by 50 percent from four to six billion, with virtually all of this growth occurring in the developing world.[1]

Population may have increased fourfold in the past century, but world economic output increased twentyfold. From the dawn of history to 1950 the world economy grew to seven trillion dollars. It now grows by this amount every five to ten years. Since 1960 the size of the world economy has doubled and then doubled again.[2] Energy use moved in close step with economic expansion, rising at least sixteenfold in the twentieth century. One calculation suggests that more energy was consumed in those hundred years than in all of previous history.[3]

The twentieth century was thus a remarkable period of prodigious expansion in human populations and their production and consumption. Four consequences of these developments are important to note. *First,* while twentieth-century growth has brought enormous benefits in terms of health, education, and overall standards of living, these gains have been purchased at a huge cost to the environment. The enormous environmental deterioration is partly due to the greater scale of established insults: traditional pollution like soot, sulfur oxides, and sewage grew from modest quantities to huge ones. What were once strictly local impacts not only intensified locally but became regional and even global in scope.

Many previously unknown environmental risks also surfaced in the twentieth century. After World War II, the chemical and nuclear industries emerged, giving rise to a vast armada of new chemicals and radioactive substances, many highly biocidal in even the most minute quantities and some with the potential to accumulate in biological systems or in the atmosphere. Between 1950 and 1985 the U.S. chemical industry expanded its output tenfold. By 1985 the number of hazardous waste sites in the United States requiring clean-up was estimated to be between two thousand and ten thousand. The use of pesticides also skyrocketed during this period.[4] Today about six hundred pesticides are registered for use around the world, and five to six billion pounds of pesticides are released into the global environment each year.[5]

Turning from pollution to the world's natural resource base we find severe losses. From a third to a half of the world's forests are now gone, as are about half the mangroves and other wetlands.[6] Agricultural productivity of a fourth of allusable land has been significantly degraded due to overuse and mismanagement.[7] In 1960, 5 percent of marine fisheries were either fished to capacity or overfished; today 75 percent of marine fisheries are in this condition.[8] A crisis in the loss of biodiversity is fast upon us. A fourth of bird species are extinct, and another 12 percent are listed as threatened. Also threatened are 24 percent of mammals, 25 percent of reptiles, and 30 percent of fish species.[9] The rate of species extinction today is estimated to be a hundred to a thousand times the normal rate at which species disappear.[10]

Environmentalist Aldo Leopold wrote that "one of the penalties of an ecological education is that one lives alone in a world of wounds."[11] As is clear, there is a lot of bad news in the world of environmental affairs. Since Leopold wrote those words, alas, scientists have begun to study damage that he could not. Our world now suffers wounds beyond imagining at his death in 1948.

That said, in recent decades industrial countries have invested heavily in reducing a variety of well-known pollutants and in banning a number of severely risky substances such as leaded gasoline, DDT, and PCBs. Similarly, advances in agricultural productivity have reduced pressures to expand crop and grazing land into additional natural areas.

Second, the twentieth-century expansion is significant because it has pushed the human enterprise and its effects to planetary scale. This is the globalization of environmental impacts as well as economic activity. Human influences in the environment are everywhere, affecting all natural systems and cycles. Environmental writer Bill McKibben wrote in 1989 about what he called "the end of nature," by which he meant the end of the millennia in which humanity could view nature as a force independent of human beings.[12] Previously it was possible to think of nature as a place free of human control, an external and complex system sustaining life on earth, but the twentieth century brought us across a threshold to a new reality.

There are many measures of this new reality. Human activities have significantly depleted the earth's stratospheric ozone layer, thereby increasing the ultraviolet radiation that reaches the earth's surface and damaging both human health and ecosystems. Our use of fossil fuels—coal, oil, and natural gas—together with deforestation have increased the concentration of atmospheric carbon dioxide, a heat-trapping "greenhouse" gas, by about 32 percent and thus begun the process of man-made climate change.[13] Spring is arriving earlier, and species' ranges are shifting toward the poles.[14] Industrial processes such as the manufacture of fertilizers and other human activities now double the amount of nitrogen transferred from the atmosphere into biologically active forms,[15] with consequences that include the creation of at least fifty dead zones in the oceans, one the size of New Jersey in the Gulf of Mexico.[16] Each year human societies are appropriating, wasting, or destroying about 40 percent of nature's net photosynthetic product.[17] This output is the basic food supply for all organisms, so we are not leaving much for other species. Appropriation of freshwater supplies is similarly extensive, with widespread devastation of freshwater habitats.[18] More than 40 percent of the world's people live in river basins that suffer water stress.[19] By the mid-1990s, eighty countries with 40 percent of the world's population were experiencing serious water shortages.[20]

In terms of humans commandeering natural systems, our impact on the global climate machine is the most risky. In part because of fossil fuel use in the twentieth century, carbon dioxide in the atmosphere is now at its highest level in 420,000 years. While the public in the United States and especially abroad is increasingly aware of this issue, few Americans appreciate how close at hand is the widespread loss of the American landscape. The best current estimate is that, unless there is a major world correction, climate change projected for late this century will make it impossible for about half the American land to sustain the types of plants and animals now on that land.[21] A huge portion of America's protected areas—everything from wooded lands held by community conservancies to our national parks, forests, and wilderness—is threatened. In one projection, the much-loved maple-beech-birch forests of New England simply disappear off the U.S. map.[22] In another, the Southeast becomes a huge grassland savanna unable to support forests because it is too hot and dry.[23]

Ecologist Jane Lubchenco, in her 1998 address as president of the American Association for the Advancement of Science, made the following observation: "The conclusions . . . are inescapable: during the last few decades, humans have emerged as a new force of nature. We are modifying physical, chemical, and biological systems in new ways, at faster rates, and over larger spatial scales than ever recorded on Earth. Humans have unwittingly embarked upon a grand experiment with our planet. The outcome of this experiment is unknown, but has profound implications for all of life on Earth."[24]

A similar point was made in an eloquent plea released a decade ago by fifteen hundred of the world's top scientists, including a majority of Nobel scientists: "The earth is finite. Its ability to absorb wastes and destructive effluents is finite. Its ability to provide food and energy is finite. Its ability to provide for growing numbers of people is finite. And we are fast approaching many of the earth's limits. Current economic practices which damage the environment, in both developed and underdeveloped nations, cannot be continued without the risk that vital global systems will be damaged beyond repair.

"We must recognize the earth's limited capacity to provide, for us. We must recognize its fragility. We must no longer allow it to be ravaged. This ethic must motivate a great movement, convincing reluctant leaders and reluctant governments and reluctant peoples themselves to effect the needed changes."[25]

Third, the world economy's forward momentum is large. Economic growth will continue to expand dramatically in this century. With population poised to grow by 25 percent over the next twenty years, with people everywhere striving to better themselves, and with governments willing to go to extraordinary measures to sustain high levels of economic expansion, there is no reason to think that the world economy will not double and perhaps double again within the lifetimes of today's young people.

The next doubling of world economic activity will surely differ in some respects from the growth of the past. But there are good reasons to believe that that doubling could, from an environmental perspective, look a lot like the last. The pressures to persist with environmentally problematic technologies and practices are enormous. The U.S. Energy Information Agency projects that global emissions of carbon dioxide, the principal climate-altering gas, will increase by 60 percent between 2001 and 2025.[26] The Paris-based Organization for Economic Cooperation and Development estimates that its members' carbon dioxide emissions will go up by roughly a third between 1995 and 2020 if there is not major policy intervention,[27] while OECD motor vehicle use could rise by almost 40 percent.[28] During this same period, emissions of carbon dioxide outside the OECD are projected to go up 100 percent. Growing food demand is expected to increase the area under cultivation in Africa and Latin America, extending agriculture further into once-forested areas and onto fragile lands in semiarid zones. For this reason and others, countries outside the OECD are projected to lose another 15 percent of their forests by 2020.[29]

One area where growing populations and growing demands will come together to challenge us enormously is water—the supply of clean, fresh water. The United Nations' 2003 *World Water Development Report* concludes that twenty-five years of international conferences have yielded few solutions. A fifth of the world's people lack clean drinking water; 40 percent lack sanitary services. Between 1970 and 1990 water supplies per person decreased by a third globally and are likely to drop by a further third over the next twenty years absent a concerted international response.[30] Peter Aldhous, the chief news editor at *Nature*, puts the situation with water in perspective: "The water crisis is real. If action isn't taken, millions of people will be condemned to a premature death. . . . [P]opulation growth, pollution and climate change are conspiring to exacerbate the situation. Over the next two decades, the average supply of water per person will drop by a third. Heightened hunger and disease will follow. Humanity's demands for water also threaten natural ecosystems, and may bring nations into conflicts that—although they may not lead to war—will test diplomats' skills to the limit."[31] The U.N. report notes that to meet internationally agreed water supply and sanitation targets, 342,000 additional people will have to be provided with sanitation every day until 2015.[32]

Of course, economic growth can generate benefits for the environment, and has done so in many contexts. As people become wealthier, public support for a healthy environment and leisure activities based on nature increases. The press of the poor on the resource base can diminish as people live less close to the land. Governments of well-to-do countries tend to be more capable regulators and managers and can have more revenue for environmental, family planning, and other programs. There is no doubt that some important environmental indicators, such as sanitation, improve with rising incomes. But it is extraordinarily misguided to conclude from such considerations, as some do, that the world can simply grow out of its environmental problems. Were that true, the rich countries would have long ago solved their environmental challenges, and we would not have projections such as those just cited from the OECD and the United Nations. In developing countries undergoing rapid industrialization, new environmental problems (such as truly terrible urban air pollution and acid rain and smog over large regions) are replacing old ones. Collectively the environmental impacts of rich and poor have mounted as the world economy has grown, and we have not yet deployed the means to reduce the human footprint on the planet faster than the economy expands.[33]

The *fourth* and final observation about the economic expansion of the twentieth century follows from the preceding three: human society is in a radically new ethical position because it is now at the planetary controls. Scientist Peter Vitousek and his coauthors stated the matter forcefully in a 1997 article in *Science:* "Humanity's dominance of Earth means that we cannot escape responsibility for managing the planet. Our activities are causing rapid, novel, and substantial changes to Earth's ecosystems. Maintaining populations, species, and ecosystems in the face of those changes, and maintaining the flow of goods and services they provide humanity, will require active management for the foreseeable future."[34]

Scientists are a cautious lot, by and large, so when the most respected issue a plea for "active management of the planet," we should take careful notice. I do not think Vitousek and others who call for "planetary management" are suggesting that the uncontrolled planetary experiment we are now running can be made safe through flawless planning, more sophisticated human interventions, or large-scale engineering feats such as seeding the oceans with iron to draw more carbon dioxide out of the air. Rather, our responsibility is to manage ourselves and our impacts on nature in a way that minimizes our interference with the great life-support systems of the planet.

We know what is driving these global trends. The much-used "IPAT equation" sees environmental *Impact* as a product of the size of human *Populations,* our *Affluence* and consumption patterns, and the *Technology* we deploy to meet our perceived needs.[35] Each of these is an important driver of deterioration. However, what this useful IPAT formulation can obscure, in addition to the effects of poverty, is the vast and rapidly growing scale of the human enterprise.

Regarding this growth, here is what happened in just the past twenty years:[36]

Global population	up 35 percent.
World economic output	up 75 percent.
Global energy use	up 40 percent.
Global meat consumption	up 70 percent.
World auto production	up 45 percent.
Global paper use	up 90 percent.
Advertising globally	up 100 percent.

Today, the world economy is poised to quadruple in size again by midcentury, just as it did in the last half-century, perhaps reaching a staggering $180 trillion in annual global output. We probably could not stop this growth if we wanted to, and most of us would not stop it if we could. Close to half the world's people live on less than two dollars per day. They both need and deserve something better. Economic expansion at least offers the potential for better lives, though its benefits in recent decades have disproportionately favored the already well-to-do. Remember also that while growth is a serious complicating factor, even if we immediately stopped all growth in both population and economic activity, we would still bring about an appalling deterioration of our planetary habitat merely by continuing to do exactly what we are doing today.

The implications of all this are profound. We have entered the endgame in our traditional, historical relationship with the natural world. The current Nature Conservancy campaign has an appropriate name: they are seeking to protect the Last Great Places. We are in a race to the finish. Soon, metaphorically speaking, whatever is not protected will be paved. For biologists Pimm and Raven, the past loss of half the tropical forests will likely cost us 15 percent of the species there. Comparable rates of deforestation in the future would lead to much greater loss.[37] More generally, attacks on the environment of many types will likely be increasingly consequential. Whatever slack nature once cut us is gone.

Humans dominate the planet today as never before. We now live in a full world. An unprecedented responsibility for planetary management is now thrust upon us, whether we like it or not. This huge new burden, for which there is no precedent and little preparation, is the price of our economic success. We brought it upon ourselves, and we must turn to it with urgency and with even greater determination and political attention than has been brought to liberalizing trade and making the world safe for market capitalism. The risks of inaction extend beyond unprecedented environmental deterioration. Following closely in its wake would be widespread loss of livelihoods, social tensions and conflict, and huge economic costs.

Editors' Note: *Notes for this reading can be found in the original source.*

CHAPTER 25

The Heat Is On

ROSS GELBSPAN

After my lawn had burned away to straw last summer, and the local papers announced that the season had been one of the driest in the recorded history of New England, I found myself wondering how long we can go on pretending that nothing is amiss with the world's weather. It wasn't just the fifty ducks near my house that had died when falling water levels in a creek exposed them to botulism-infested mud, or the five hundred people dead in the Midwest from an unexpected heat wave that followed the season's second "one-hundred-year flood" in three years. It was also the news from New Orleans (overrun by an extraordinary number of cockroaches and termites after a fifth consecutive winter without a killing frost), from Spain (suffering a fourth year of drought in a region that ordinarily enjoys a rainfall of 84 inches a year), and from London (Britain's meteorological office reporting the driest summer since 1727 and the hottest since 1659).

The reports of changes in the world's climate have been with us for fifteen or twenty years, most urgently since 1988, when Dr. James Hansen, director of NASA's Goddard Institute for Space Studies, declared that the era of global warming was at hand. As a newspaper correspondent who had reported on the United Nations Conferences on the environment in Stockholm in 1972 and Rio in 1992, I understood something of the ill effects apt to result from the extravagant burning of oil and coal. New record-setting weather extremes seem to have become as commonplace as traffic accidents, and three simple facts have long been known: the distance from the surface of the earth to the far edge of the inner atmosphere is only twelve miles; the annual amount of carbon dioxide forced into that limited space is six billion tons; and the ten hottest years in recorded human history have all occurred since 1980. The facts beg a question that is as simple to ask as it is hard to answer. What do we do with what we know?

The question became more pointed in September, when the 2,500 climate scientists serving on the Intergovernmental Panel on Climate Change issued a new statement on the prospect of forthcoming catastrophe. Never before had the IPCC (called into existence in 1988) come to so unambiguous a conclusion. Always in years past there had been people saying that we didn't yet know enough, or that the evidence was problematical, or our system of computer simulation was subject to too many uncertainties. Not this year. The panel flatly announced that the earth had entered a period of climatic instability likely to cause "widespread economic, social and environmental dislocation over the next century." The continuing emission of greenhouse gases would create protracted, crop-destroying droughts in continental interiors, a host of new and recurring diseases, hurricanes of extraordinary malevolence, and rising sea levels that could inundate island nations and low-lying coastal rims on the continents.

I came across the report in the *New York Times* during the same week that the island of St. Thomas was blasted to shambles by one of thirteen hurricanes that roiled the Caribbean this fall. Scientists speak the language of probability. They prefer to avoid making statements that cannot be further corrected, reinterpreted, modified, or proven wrong. If its September announcement was uncharacteristically bold, possibly it was because the IPCC scientists understood that they were addressing their remarks to people profoundly unwilling to hear what they had to say.

That resistance is understandable, given the immensity of the stakes. The energy industries now constitute the largest single enterprise known to mankind. Moreover, they are indivisible from automobile, farming, shipping, air freight, and banking interests, as well as from the governments dependent on oil revenues for their very existence. With annual sales in excess of one trillion dollars and daily sales of more than two billion dollars, the oil industry alone supports the economies of the Middle East and large segments of the economies of Russia, Mexico, Venezuela, Nigeria, Indonesia, Norway, and Great Britain. Begin to enforce restriction on the consumption of oil and coal, and the effects on the global economy—unemployment, depression, social breakdown, and war—might lay waste to what we have come to call civilization. It is no wonder that for the last five or six years many of the world's politicians and most of the world's news media have been promoting the perception that the worries about the weather are overwrought. Ever since the IPCC first set out to devise strategies whereby the nations of the world might reduce their carbon dioxide emissions and thus ward off a rise in the average global temperature on the order of 4 or 5 degrees Celsius (roughly equal in magnitude to the difference between the last ice age and the current climate period), the energy industry has been conducting, not unreasonably, a ferocious public relations campaign meant to sell the notion that science, any science, is always a matter of uncertainty. Yet on reading the news from the IPCC, I wondered how the oil company publicists would confront the most recent series of geophysical events and scientific findings. To wit:

- A 48-by-22-mile chunk of the Larsen Ice Shelf in the Antarctic broke off last March, exposing rocks that had been buried for 200,000 years and prompting Rodolfo del Valle of the Argentine Antarctic Institute to tell the Associated Press, "Last November we predicted the [ice shelf] would crack in ten years, but it has happened in barely two months."
- In April, researchers discovered a 70 percent decline in the population of zooplankton off the coast of southern California, raising questions about the

survival of several species of that feed on it. Scientists have linked the change to 1 to 2 degree C increase in the surface water temperature over the last four decades.

- A recent series of articles in *The Lancet*, a British medical journal, linked changes in climate patterns to the spread of infectious diseases around the world. The *Aedes aegypti* mosquito, which spreads dengue fever and yellow fever, has traditionally been unable to survive at altitudes higher than 1,000 meters above sea level. But these mosquitoes are now being reported at 1,500 meters in Costa Rica and at 2,200 meters in Colombia. Ocean warming has triggered algae blooms linked to outbreaks of cholera in India, Bangladesh, and the Pacific coast of South America, where, in 1991, the disease infected more than 400,000 people.

- In a paper published in *Science* in April, David J. Thomson, of the AT&T Bell Laboratories, concluded that the .6 degree C warming of the average global temperature over the past century correlates directly with the buildup of atmospheric carbon dioxide. Separate findings by a team of scientists at the National Oceanic and Atmospheric Administration's National Climatic Data Center indicate that growing weather extremes in the United States are due, by a probability of 90 percent, to rising levels of greenhouse gases.

- Scientists previously believed that the transitions between ice ages and more moderate climatic periods occur gradually, over centuries. But researchers from the Woods Hole Oceanographic Institution, examining deep ocean sediment and ice core samples, found that these shifts, with their temperature changes of up to 7 degrees C, have occurred within three to four decades—a virtual nanosecond in geological time. Over the last 70,000 years, the earth's climate has snapped into radically different temperature regimes. "Our results suggest that the present climate system is very delicately poised," said researcher Scott Lehman. "Shifts could happen very rapidly if conditions are right, and we cannot predict when that will occur." His cautionary tone is underscored by findings that the end of the last ice age, some 8,000 years ago, was preceded by a series of extreme oscillations in which severe regional deep freezes alternated with warming spikes. As the North Atlantic warmed, Arctic snowmelts and increased rainfall diluted the salt content of the ocean, which, in turn, redirected the ocean's warming current from a northeasterly direction to one that ran nearly due east. Should such an episode occur today, say researchers, "the present climate of Britain and Norway would change suddenly to that of Greenland."

These items (and many like them) would seem to be alarming news—far more important than the candidacy of Colin Powell, or even whether Newt Gingrich believes the government should feed poor children—worthy of a national debate or the sustained attention of Congress. But the signs and portents have been largely ignored, relegated to the environmental press and the oddball margins of the mass media. More often than not, the news about the accelerating retreat of the world's glaciers or the heat- and insect-stressed Canadian forests comes qualified with the observation that the question of global warming never can be conclusively resolved. The confusion is intentional, expensively gift wrapped by the energy industries.

Capital keeps its nose to the wind. The people who run the world's oil and coal companies know that the march of science, and of political action, may be slowed by disinformation. In the last year and a half, one of the leading oil industry public relations outlets, the Global Climate Coalition, has spent more than a million dollars to downplay the threat of climate change. It expects to spend another $850,000 on the issue next year. Similarly, the National Coal Association spent more than $700,000 on the global climate issue in 1992 and 1993. In 1993 alone, the American Petroleum Institute, just one of fifty-four industry members of the GCC, paid $1.8 million to the public relations firm of Burson-Marsteller partly in an effort to defeat a proposed tax on fossil fuels. For perspective, this is only slightly less than the combined yearly expenditures on global warming of the five major environmental groups that focus on climate issues—about $2.1 million, according to officials of the Environmental Defense Fund, the Natural Resources Defense Council, the Sierra Club, the Union of Concerned Scientists, and the World Wildlife Fund.

For the most part the industry has relied on a small band of skeptics—Dr. Richard S. Lindzen, Dr. Pat Michaels, Dr. Robert Balling, Dr. Sherwood Idso, and Dr. S. Fred Singer, among others—who have proven extraordinarily adept at draining the issue of all sense of crisis. Through their frequent pronouncements in the press and on radio and television, they have helped to create the illusion that the question is hopelessly mired in unknowns. Most damaging has been their influence on decision makers; their contrarian views have allowed conservative Republicans such as Representative Dana Rohrabacher (R., Calif.) to dismiss legitimate research concerns as "liberal claptrap" and have provided the basis for the recent round of budget cuts to those government science programs designed to monitor the health of the planet.

Last May, Minnesota held hearings in St. Paul to determine the environmental cost of coal burning by state power plants. Three of the skeptics—Lindzen, Michaels, and Balling—were hired as expert witnesses to testify on behalf of Western Fuels Association, a $400 million consortium of coal suppliers and coal-fired utilities.[1]

An especially aggressive industry player, Western Fuels was quite candid about its strategy in two annual reports: "[T]here has been a close to universal impulse in the trade association community here in Washington to concede the scientific premise of global warming . . . while arguing over policy prescriptions that would be the least disruptive to our economy. . . . We have disagreed, and do disagree, with this strategy." "When [the climate change] controversy first erupted . . . scientists were found who are skeptical about much of what seemed generally accepted about the potential for climate change." Among them were Michaels, Balling, and S. Fred Singer.

Lindzen, a distinguished professor of meteorology at MIT, testified in St. Paul that the maximum probable warming of the atmosphere in the face of a doubling of carbon dioxide emissions over the next century would amount to no more than a negligible .3 degrees C. Michaels, who teaches climatology at the University of Virginia, stated that he foresaw no increase in the rate of sea level rise—another feared precursor of global warming. Balling, who works on climate issues at Arizona State University, declared that the increase in emissions would boost the average global temperature by no more than one degree.

At first glance, these attacks appear defensible, given their focus on the black holes of uncertainty that mark our current knowledge of the planet's exquisitely interrelated climate system. The skeptics emphasize the inadequacy of a major climate research tool known as a General Circulation Model, and our ignorance of carbon dioxide exchange between the oceans and the atmosphere and of the various roles of clouds. They have repeatedly pointed out that although the world's output of carbon dioxide has exploded since 1940, there has been no corresponding increase in the global temperature. The larger scientific community, by contrast, holds that this is due to the masking effect of low-level sulfur particulates, which exert a temporary cooling effect on the earth, and to a time lag in the oceans' absorption and release of carbon dioxide.

But while the skeptics portray themselves as besieged truth-seekers fending off irresponsible environmental doomsayers, their testimony in St. Paul and elsewhere revealed the source and scope of their funding for the first time. Michaels has received more than $115,000 over the last four years from coal and energy interests. *World Climate Review*, a quarterly he founded that routinely debunks climate concerns, was funded by Western Fuels. Over the last six years, either alone or with colleagues, Balling has received more than $200,000 from coal and oil interests in Great Britain, Germany, and elsewhere. Balling (along with Sherwood Idso) has also taken money from Cyprus Minerals, a mining company that has been a major funder of People for the West—a militantly anti-environmental "Wise Use" group. Lindzen, for his part, charges oil and coal interests $2,500 a day for his consulting services; his 1991 trip to testify before a Senate committee was paid for by Western Fuels, and a speech he wrote, entitled "Global Warming: the Origin and Nature of Alleged Scientific Consensus," was underwritten by OPEC. Singer, who last winter proposed a $95,000 publicity project to "stem the tide towards ever more onerous controls on energy use," has received consulting fees from Exxon, Shell, Unocal, Arco, and Sun Oil, and has warned them that they face the same threat as the chemical firms that produced chlorofluorocarbons (CFCs), a class of chemicals found to be depleting atmospheric ozone. "It took only five years to go from . . . a simple freeze of production [of CFCs]," Singer has written, ". . . to the 1992 decision of a complete production phase-out—all on the basis of quite insubstantial science."[2]

The skeptics assert flatly that their science is untainted by funding. Nevertheless, in this persistent and well-funded campaign of denial they have become interchangeable ornaments on the hood of a high-powered engine of disinformation. Their dissenting opinions are amplified beyond all proportion through the media while the concerns of the dominant majority of the world's scientific establishment are marginalized.[3] By keeping the discussion focused on whether there is a problem in the first place, they have effectively silenced the debate over what to do about it.

Last spring's IPCC conference in Berlin is a good example. Delegations from 170 nations met to negotiate targets and timetables for reducing the world's carbon dioxide emissions. The efforts of the conference ultimately foundered on foot-dragging by the United States and Japan and active resistance from the OPEC nations. Leading the fight for the most dramatic reductions—to 60 percent of 1990 levels—was a coalition of small island nations from the Caribbean and the Pacific that fear being flooded out of existence. They were supported by most western European governments, but China and India, with their vast coal resources, argued that until the United States significantly cuts its own emissions, their obligation to develop their own economies outranked their obligation to the global environment. In the end, OPEC, supported by the United States, Japan, Australia, Canada, and New Zealand, rejected calls to limit emissions, declaring emission limits premature.

As the natural crisis escalates, so will the forces of institutional and societal denial. If, at the cost of corporate pocket change, industrial giants can control the publicly perceived reality of the condition of the planet and the state of our scientific knowledge, what would they do if their survival were truly put at risk? Billions would be spent on the creation of information and the control of politicians. Glad-handing oil company ads on the op-ed page of the *New York Times* (from a quarter-page pronouncement by Mobil last September 28: "There's a lot of good news out there") would give way to a new stream of selective findings by privatized scientists. Long before the planet itself collapsed, democracy would break apart under the stress of "natural" disasters. It is not difficult to foresee that in an ecological state of emergency our political liberties would be the first casualties.

Thus, the question must be asked: can civilization change the way it operates? For 5,000 years, we have thought of ourselves as dependent children of the earth, flourishing or perishing according to the whims of nature. But with the explosion of the power of our technology and the size of our population, our activities have grown to the proportion of geological forces, affecting the major systems of the planet. Short of the Atlantic washing away half of Florida, the abstract notion that the old anomalies have become the new norm is difficult to grasp. Dr. James McCarthy of Harvard, who has supervised the work of climate scientists from sixty nations, puts it this way: "If the last 150 years had been marked by the kind of climate instability we are now seeing, the world would never have been able to support its present population of 5 billion people." We live in a world of man-size urgencies, measured in hours or days. What unfolds slowly is not, by our lights, urgent, and it will therefore take a collective act of imagination to understand the extremity of the situation we now confront. The lag time in our planet's ecological systems will undoubtedly delay these decisions, and even if the nations of the world were to agree tomorrow on a plan to phase out oil and coal and convert to renewable energies, an equivalent lag time in human affairs would delay its implementation for years. What too many people refuse to understand is that the global economy's existence depends upon the global environment, not the other way around. One cannot negotiate jobs, development, or rates of economic growth with nature.

What of the standard list of palliatives—carbon taxes, more energy-efficient buildings, a revival of public transportation? The ideas are attractive, but the thinking is too small. Even were the United States to halve its own carbon dioxide contribution, this cutback would soon be overwhelmed by the coming development of industry and housing and schools in China and India and Mexico for all their billions of citizens. No solution can work that does not provide ample energy resources for the development of all the world's nations.

So here is an informal proposal—at best a starting point for a conversation— from one man who is not an expert. What if we turned the deserts of the world into electricity farms? Let the Middle East countries keep their oil royalties as solar royalties. What if the world mobilized around a ten-year project to phase out all fossil fuels, to develop renewable energy technologies, to extend those technologies to every corner of the world? What if, to minimize the conflict of so massive a dislocation, the world's energy companies were put in charge of the transition—answering only to an international regulatory body and an enforceable timetable? Grant them the same profit margins for solar electricity and hydrogen fuel they now receive for petroleum and coal. Give them the licenses for all renewable energy technologies. Assure them the same relative position in the world's economy they now enjoy at the end of the project.

Are these ideas mere dreams? Perhaps, but there are historical reasons to have hope. Four years ago a significant fraction of humanity overturned its Communist system in a historical blink of an eye. Eight years ago the world's governments joined together in Montreal to regulate CFCs. Technology is not the issue. The atomic bomb was developed in two and a half years. Putting a man on the moon took eleven. Surely, given the same sense of urgency, we can develop new energy systems in ten years. Most of the technology is already available to us or soon will be. We have the knowledge, the energy, and the hunger for jobs to get it done. And we are different in one unmeasurable way from previous generations: ours is the first to be educated about the larger world by the global reach of electronic information.

The leaders of the oil and coal industry, along with their skeptical scientists, relentlessly accuse environmentalists of overstating the climatic threat to destroy capitalism. Must a transformation that is merely technological dislodge the keystone of the economic order? I don't know. But I do know that technology changes the way we conceive of the world. To transform our economy would oblige us to understand the limits of the planet. That understanding alone might seed the culture with a more organic concept of ourselves and our connectedness to the earth. And corporations, it is useful to remember, are not only obstacles on the road to the future. They are also crucibles of technology and organizing engines of production, the modern expression of mankind's drive for creativity. The industrialist is no less human than the poet, and both the climate scientist and the oil company operator inhabit the same planet, suffer the same short life span, harbor the same hopes for their children.

Each summer, our family walks the deep north Maine woods in search of adventure and a sense of renewal. The trip this year was different for me; I was visited by premonitions of the coming sickness of the forest, haunted by unwelcome and indescribably sad imaginings. They intruded at unexpected moments. One night while listening to a dialogue of loons on a black lake I suddenly experienced a momentary feeling of bottomless grief. Struck by the recognition of how fragile was the frame of the world, and how easily it could be shattered by our mutual distrust and confusion, I feared that the cause of survival would be lost to the greed and alienation and shortsightedness that dog our few last steps to the threshold of the millennium. My dream of reconfiguring the global economy was probably nothing more than the hopeless longing of a reporter, not a social thinker or macroeconomic engineer.

But I am also a husband and a father, a son, and a grandson. And someday perhaps a grandfather. Our history is rich with visionaries urging us to change our ways of thinking, asking questions about the meaning of the past and the shape of the future. Now the questions are being posed, in a language we don't yet fully understand, by the oceans. I have promised myself that next summer I will keep my lawn watered, at least as long as the water holds out.

ENDNOTES

1. In 1991, Western Fuels spent an estimated $250,000 to produce and distribute a video entitled "The Greening of Planet Earth," which was shown frequently inside the Bush White House as well as within the governments of OPEC. In near-evangelical tones, the video promises that a new age of agricultural abundance will result from increasing concentrations of carbon dioxide. It portrays a world where vast areas of desert are reclaimed by the carbon dioxide–forced growth of new grasslands, where the earth's diminishing forests are replenished by a nurturing atmosphere. Unfortunately, it overlooks the bugs. Experts note that even a minor elevation in temperature would trigger an explosion in the planet's insect population, leading to potentially significant disruptions in food supplies from crop damage as well as to a surge in insect-borne diseases. It appears that Western Fuels' video fails to tell people what the termites in New Orleans may be trying to tell them now.

2. Contrary to his assertion, however, virtually all relevant researchers say the link between CFCs and ozone depletion is based on unassailably solid scientific evidence. As if to underscore the point, in May the research director of the European Union Commission estimated that last winter's ozone loss will result in about 80,000 additional cases of skin cancer in Europe. This fall, the three scientists who discovered the CFC-ozone link won the Nobel Prize for Chemistry.

3. The industry's public relations arsenal, however, is made up of much more than a few sympathetic scientists. Last March, the Global Climate Coalition distributed a report by Accu-Weather Inc. that denied any significant increase in extreme weather events. The report flies in the face of contradictory evidence cited by officials of the insurance industry, which, during the 1980s, paid an average of $3 billion a year to victims of natural disasters—a figure that has jumped to $10 billion a year in this decade. A top official of a Swiss reinsurance firm told the World Watch Institute: "There is a significant body of scientific evidence indicating that [the recent] record insured loss from natural catastrophes was not a random occurrence." More succinctly, the president of the Reinsurance Association of America said climate change "could bankrupt the industry."

CHAPTER 26

Diamond

A Struggle for Environmental Justice in Louisiana's Chemical Corridor

STEVE LERNER

Josephine Bering, 87 years old,[1] can be found most days in her living room, sitting in a comfortable armchair next to her fish tank. She lives in Diamond, an African-American community 25 miles west of New Orleans on the banks of the Mississippi. Her house is located three streets from the fenceline with a Shell Chemical plant. The day I met her, she was wearing a white and green plaid dress and white socks. One of her many grandchildren slept on the couch while two others played in a back room. Outside and inside her home, the air was permeated with a smell that one would expect to encounter in a closed storage closet filled with industrial-strength cleansers.

Bering lived on the fenceline with the chemical plant for more than 60 years. Her late father polished floors and cut grass at the plant. A few years ago, in recognition of her father's long service, Shell officials helped Bering fix up her house. But when she suggested that it would be better to move her away from the fenceline and the health problems she associated with the fumes from their plants, Don Baker, a Shell official, replied "Repair is one thing; relocation is another."

That was not a good enough for Bering. "I want to get out of here for the sake of my health," she said. Her sister, also a resident of Diamond, died at 43 of what Bering describes as "phlegm on her lungs." The doctors told her that it came from living near the chemical plant and the refinery. "She suffered with that a long time," Bering remembered. Like her sister, Bering had respiratory problems and was "short-winded." Her asthma improved only when she left the area. She described the air around Diamond as smelling like ammonia or bleach. "It works on me terrible," she said. Asthma also afflicted one of her grandsons; when he stayed with her, she had to hook him up to "a breathing machine."

Then there were the unexplained allergies and skin problems that ran in the family. Bering attributed the cracked and discolored skin on her wrists to the chemicals coming from the adjacent Shell plant. To underscore the severity of this problem, she called in one of her granddaughters from the bedroom and told the gangly adolescent "Show the man your arms." Reluctantly, the 14-year-old girl stretched out her arms. "It is like that all over her body," volunteered Bering, whose sister was similarly afflicted.

"I don't have enough money to get out of here, so I have to just stay and suffer with it," Bering said. "All Shell has to do is buy people out and let them go. Just give us enough to get out of here. If they would move me out of here and relocate me, I would surely be happy." . . .

Diamond is not a place where most people would choose to live. Located in the heart of the "chemical corridor" between the mouth of the Mississippi River and Baton Rouge, the four streets of this subdivision are hard up against fencelines with a Shell Chemical plant and the huge Shell/Motiva oil refinery.[1] Residents here have long breathed the fumes from these two plants, suffered illnesses they attributed to toxic exposures, and mourned neighbors and friends killed by explosions at these facilities.

The view from the homes in Diamond is of heavy industry at work. There are catalytic cracking towers, stacks topped by flares burning off excess gas, huge oil and gasoline storage tanks, giant processing units where oil and its derivatives are turned into a wide variety of useful chemicals, and a Rube Goldberg maze of oversized pipes. The clanking and crashing of railroad cars coupling and uncoupling can be deafening, and the eerie sight of the superstructures of gargantuan oil tankers soundlessly moving up the Mississippi to dock and unload their crude oil completes the industrial landscape.

The streams of chemicals pouring out of the plants in the vast, sprawling Shell/Motiva Norco Complex are used in factories around the United States. Truly, these two mammoth plants are part of the front end of the system that has forged the American lifestyle by making products cheap and convenient. One cannot help but be in awe of the ingenuity, tenacity, and hard work that built these technological behemoths.

What seemed an incongruous sight, however, was a small residential community sandwiched between these two giant plants. The terrible cost of introducing heavy industry into a residential neighborhood soon became apparent. In the homes of Diamond residents there were many signs that this was not a healthy place to live. On many days the plant stank. Shell officials said that the smell was not dangerous and was caused by an organic digester unit that became backed up and gave off a rotten odor as millions of micro-organisms died. They were working on a solution to the problem, they said. But on some days the smell emanating from the plants had a toxic bouquet. Not infrequently, there was an acrid, metallic odor that caused headaches, sinus problems, and stinging eyes. There were even days, residents and visitors reported, when they could actually see a chemical fog swirling around their legs and seeping through the cracks into the houses.

And while it was notoriously difficult to prove that there existed a causal link between the toxic chemical released from the plant and the health of neighboring residents, inside the homes of Diamond residents were a disturbing number of children with asthma; young adults with severe respiratory, allergic, and unusual skin problems; and older people whose breathing had to be aided with oxygen tanks.

Then there was the history of periodic explosions. A 1973 explosion took the lives of two Diamond residents. A 1988 explosion that killed seven Shell workers blew out windows and doors and brought down sheetrock ceilings in many homes. Diamond was evacuated in the middle of the night. Many homes required extensive reconstruction.

If it was so poisonous and dangerous to live there, why didn't the residents of Diamond just move? The answer was that few of those who lived in Diamond stayed because they wanted to. Given an opportunity to sell their homes and move they would do so, but without getting decent prices for their homes they could not afford to leave. Living next to the Shell plants had not only been bad for their health, they said; it also had been lethal to property values. As the chemical and oil plants expanded to an area just across the street, residents who wanted to sell their homes and relocate could not find buyers who were foolish enough to want to purchase their homes. In other words, they were stuck: they could not bear living where they were because of the bad air, but they could not afford to move elsewhere. . . .

On a beautiful summer day in 1973, a Shell Chemical pipeline sprang a leak, eyewitnesses report. The pipe ran parallel to Washington Street in Diamond, which forms the fenceline between the industrial facility and the residential community. Diamond residents saw a white cloud of gas snake down the street. Dorothy Pedescleaux recalled telling some young men "You see that white stuff coming down the street? I bet it's going to be a fire." Just down the street, Leroy Jones, 16, was cutting grass at the home of Helen Washington, an elderly woman, who was indoors taking a nap. Jones had taken a break from his chore and was chatting with some friends who had stopped on their bike rounds of the neighborhood. After they left, Jones pulled the cord to start the lawnmower. A spark from the engine ignited the gas that had leaked out of the Shell pipeline, residents conjectured. The ensuing explosion scorched Leroy Jones and burned Helen Washington's house down. Badly burned, Jones stumbled around in shock, clutching his eyes. "When emergency workers arrived they wrapped (Jones's) blistered body in a baby quilt that a neighbor had hung out to dry," neighbors reported.[1] Jones died a few days later in the hospital. Helen Washington died immediately, burned up in her own home.

Larry Brown described the day Helen Washington and Leroy Jones died as one of the most traumatic in his life. He recalled a fog-like gas escaping from the Shell pipe and said he called out a warning to Leroy Jones not to start the lawnmower. "When he cranked it there was a big BOOM . . . a big flame . . . and I saw him crumple and claw his eyes," Brown recalled. Then one of the grandsons of Helen Washington ran into the burning house and pulled his grandmother out. "She was burned," Brown said. "I couldn't look at it. I just left. I'm trying to think how to put it: seeing someone burn . . . that is a horrible feeling to watch . . . another human being. I saw it, I smelled it, I still feel the stink of that flesh. . . . I ran for my life. I feel bad that I ran and didn't try to help. I didn't know what was going to happen [blow up] next."

Delwyn Smith, 51, remembered the bodies of Washington and Jones being carried to her mother's property: "They brought them over there and set them under mamma's oak tree right in the front yard."

Two boys on motorbikes had just passed when the explosion erupted. One of them was Devaliant Christopher Cole, 13 at the time. Cole remembered riding with a friend that day past a young man messing with a lawn-mower. When they were about two blocks past him there was a loud explosion. "I looked back and WHOOF . . . just like a big old fireball . . . and it kept burning for awhile," Cole recalled. "It looked like a flame-thrower. A big flame just shot across the street. It tore the house down . . . everything all at one time. . . . I never saw anything like that in my life."

The horror of death by fire rippled through the close-knit community. "I'm sorry in a way that I went over to see because it is forever etched in my memory. The fireball was like a rolling ball of fire through the street, and that lady and that little boy burned," said Audrey Eugene. Later Shell put a little sign up near the pipes saying that they were hazardous.

Ernestine Roberts, 52, was watching TV when the explosion occurred. She recalls: "We just started running. When we got there . . . the whole house was just flat. There was a lot of hollering and screaming going on because in a small town everyone knows everyone."

The fatal accident changed the way residents of Diamond viewed living next to Shell's facilities. "That [explosion] made quite a difference," recalled Lois Gales, who was in Diamond that day, pregnant with her first son. Suddenly she realized that accidents from the plant could reach out across the fenceline and take lives. It was at that moment that Gales realized "it was kind of dangerous living here."

Part of the fear this accident engendered had to do with the fact that no one was sure what was going to blow up next. "I just couldn't stop screaming," said Lois Parquet, who was afraid at the time that a pipeline near her house would burst next. "Who is to say what is under my property? . . . You don't know the danger that lies underground. . . . It was their time then, but it could be our time next. . . ."

Fear that there would be additional explosions continued to trouble some residents for years. "When the explosion happened I was under the line hanging up clothes," recalled 72-year-old Deloris Brown. "My nerves were just shattered when those people died. I went out in the street and looked at the flames and everything. . . . I was shook up. Other people got over it [the accident] right quick but I will never get over it." Jenny Taylor, 61, has the same problem: "After that fast big explosion you really haven't been yourself since because if trains hit too hard [coupling and uncoupling] you think one of them plants blowed up."

When asked how much the victims' families were paid in compensation, Shell officials say they have no record of it. But Diamond residents are unanimous in recalling that the relatives of Helen Washington were paid $3,000 for her burned house and land, and that Ruth Jones, Leroy's mother, was paid $500.[2] This compares poorly with a multi-million-dollar settlement Shell made with the families of two boys who were killed in a pipeline explosion in Canada.

Not only are there no records of the two fatalities that occurred in Diamond in 1973; there is also no mention of the event in Shell's Norco Museum. When questioned about the incident, curator Clarisse Webb did not know the details. Indeed, she asked if it had anything to do with Shell. Residents of Diamond, however, recall the incident well. "I think I heard they gave [Ruth Jones] $500, but, being elderly, she didn't know [that she deserved more], poor thing," Wendy Mashia said, adding that Shell had been "messing over people" for years. Gaynel Johnson also finds the minimal compensation for the deaths on Washington Street troubling: "You [Shell] could have given her [Ruth Jones] a check every month, and you could have bought her a home. But [instead] this lady was on rent until she died." Margie Richard goes even further, arguing that Shell should have offered to relocate the whole neighborhood after the explosion in 1973, when it became clear that living there was unsafe.

Monique Harden, formerly an attorney for the EarthJustice Legal Defense Fund, is also incensed about how Shell handled the deaths of Jones and Washington. "This horrendous tragedy in 1973 shows how little the lives of African-American residents in the Diamond community meant to Shell at the time. It is beyond an insult. The company doesn't feel sorry for what happened. It doesn't feel sorry for the loss of lives. It doesn't value the people and what they meant to the community or their families or survivors."

Providing some historical context for how it could have happened that the families of Leroy Jones and Helen Washington were compensated so minimally by Shell, Beverly Wright said: "It speaks, in the deep South, to the race issue and the extent to which African-Americans have been disenfranchised and have had no political power or support. That made it possible for people to devalue them and know that they were not going to be challenged."

While noting that there are no company records about what compensation was provided to victims of the accident in 1973, Shell spokesman David Brignac said he understands that the minimal compensation residents say was provided by Shell spoke powerfully to them about how their lives were valued by the company at the time. "We would do vastly differently today than what you describe people say we did back in 1973," he continued. "If [the minimal compensation] is a sore point and it is something that people are hanging onto, I agree that it is something we should do something about."

THE BIG BANG

The "big bang" in Diamond was not a cosmic event that occurred light years away; it was right next door. At 3:40 A.M. on May 4, 1988, a catalytic cracking unit at the Shell refinery blew up, killing seven Shell workers and injuring 48 other people (some workers, some residents). The explosion spewed 159 million pounds of toxic chemicals into the air, caused widespread property damage, and required the evacuation of 4,500 people.

Corrosion in a pipeline eight inches in diameter permitted 20,000 pounds of C-3 hydrocarbons to escape. A vapor cloud formed and then ignited. The explosion toppled a 16-story-tall fractionator. Debris from the explosion was found 5 miles away, and structural damage to homes and businesses radiated out a mile from the point of the explosion. The blast could be heard 25 miles away in New Orleans, where it set off burglar alarms. The east wall of the Norco Coop Supermarket on Fourth Street was blown off, and the ceiling of Bill's Dollar Store partially collapsed. After the explosion, a fire burned for 8 hours at the refinery before it was brought under control. A black film covered homes and cars in surrounding towns. The governor declared a state of emergency in Norco and St. Charles Parish.[3]

"The night the explosion happened. . . . I actually thought it was a nuclear bomb that had hit our area . . . that we were being invaded by another country," said Larry Brown, 51, as he sat in his house next to his parents' burned-out tavern. "At that particular time I was here with my parents. The explosion knocked me out of bed, and it scared the hell out of me because all I saw was flashes and everything falling down. . . . I ran outside, which was stupid, and I saw fire shooting 150 feet in the air. So I told my parents that it was time for us to go. At that time my father had both of his legs amputated because of poor circulation, so I got him and my mother together in the car and we got out. The police were in town with the mikes on their cars open telling everyone to evacuate. We went out through the spillway. . . . If the spillway had been full I hate to even think what would have happened, because it was real crowded on the road. It was a [traffic] jam with everyone trying to get out."

Brown had been a member of the crew Shell had hired to clean up after the explosion. One of the Shell workers killed was a friend of Brown's, and they found his foot about eight blocks away from the site of the explosion, Brown said. Brown quit the cleanup job when he was instructed to pick up material covered in asbestos. Told that there was no reason to believe the material was dangerous since it had not been tested, Brown said "I don't care if you tested it or not. I'm not going to be here." And he left. "They didn't have proper equipment to work with asbestos," he observed. Brown suspects that many residents were exposed to airborne asbestos when they returned home from the evacuation. "We later came to find that there was enough asbestos in the air that we shouldn't have been let back in for a week. . . . But you won't find that in their [Shell's] files," he charged.

Just as most people who were alive at the time remember where they were when Martin Luther King Jr. and John F. Kennedy were assassinated, everyone in Diamond remembers where he or she was when the catalytic cracking unit at the Shell refinery blew up. And each of them has a very personal way of describing the noise it made.

Delwyn Smith recalled that she had just gotten out of bed to get a glass of water and had returned to bed when the explosion hit. "BAAATUNG. . . . I thought it was a plane had crashed," recalled Smith, who noted that Diamond was in the flight path of nearby New Orleans Airport. All the windows in Smith's house were blown out, and the door was broken and hanging from the top hinge. Smith needed to buy gas to get out of town. "It was like chaos. . . . People were out there crying . . . like my aunt whose husband had just had open-heart surgery." The explosion made Smith realize that "it was not really safe here [in Diamond] at all."

Just how terrifying this explosion was to small children is best described by Ernestine Roberts, 52, who recalled lying in bed listening to Shell's industrial cacophony that night: "Shell had been roaring all night, but it was a different kind of roar. I could hear the difference and you knew something was going to happen. You could feel that something was going to happen. So I lay in bed and it was making this sound, making this sound, making this sound . . . and you get to know the sounds . . . but this was a different sound. I got up bedroom [sic] and headed for the kitchen and then all of a sudden BOOOOOM. It knocked me off my feet. I went running to the door, and all I could see was fire. I ran back in here to get my son. I was calling for him and he is not answering me. And all I could see was fire through the windows. And I am calling for him, I can't find him, I am looking in all the closets, I can't find him. . . . Now I am panicking. . . . I can't find him. Finally when I did find him he was under the bed. And I couldn't get him out because he was holding on to the box springs so I am telling him 'Come out, come out.' And he is not crying. He is just holding on and I cannot get him out. And I am pulling and trying to get him out. . . . And finally I pull him out and grab him up in a blanket. . . . And we just run. . . ."

Others were also terrified by the explosion. "That was just scary, scary, scary," say Deloris Brown, 72. "I just ran out through the back. . . . I just prayed I wouldn't cut my feet [on all the broken glass] . . . but I was running the wrong way. . . . The explosions worry me the most . . . and the odor. You hear a noise and you think: I wonder what is happening in Norco. I am afraid of the explosion and that anytime it might be something."

Many residents have not slept well since the explosion. "We slept in our clothes for a long time," said Jenny Taylor. "Tell you the truth I still have my clothes laid out on a chair so I can jump into them. . . . We don't know what they [the plants] are going to do, so you can't ever really be relaxed."

Many people decided to move out of Diamond. "It tore up the neighborhood so bad. You had people that rebuilt their house but you had a lot of people who didn't," recalled Devaliant Christopher Cole. Some just left. Boarded-up homes gave the community a damaged and bedraggled look and brought real estate values down.

Ever since 1988, Devaliant Cole has been waiting for the next accident. "Even now, with the train nearby and the train cars pushing and slamming, I jump up," he said. And when he drives home in the evening and sees smoke rising over Norco, he wonders what has happened.

After the explosion, some Diamond residents just wanted to get out of town. Audrey Eugene spoke with Shell officials about selling her home. "I was ready to leave. . . . You know when something like that happens you don't rest well. It is just too much. You sleep with your shoes right there by your bed, so while it happened in 1988 it didn't go away. . . . I don't have the means to just leave here without selling. . . . I didn't cause this problem. . . . If the land is important to them, let them have it as long as they compensate me what is fair," said Eugene.

Commenting on the safety record of the Shell/Motiva complex, Shell spokesman David Brignac said he was "confident that our safety record is going to improve and continue to improve." Shell had a strong safety program in place, not only for the benefit of the community but also for its own workers, he noted. Shell officials took the attitude that accidents don't just happen but rather have a preventable cause. A lot of time and money was spent on safety, he added. "Regrettably, we have had significant incidents," Brignac conceded, referring to the explosions in 1973 and 1988. The 1988 explosion was last major incident, and since then there have been improvements in safety procedures. Despite these improvements, Brignac is careful not to overpromise. "I can't tell residents that we will never have a big event [again]," he said. "So I don't know how to deal with that fear. I don't have a good answer."

"I FEEL LIKE I'M IN A HOLE"

"I made 80," said Janie Campbell when asked her age. She said it with no small amount of pride. Many of her friends who lived in the same heavily polluted neighborhood in Diamond died prematurely, she claimed. And, while she cannot prove it, Campbell attributes their early illnesses and deaths to fumes from the adjacent Shell petrochemical plants located just three short blocks from her front door. "Everybody that I knew they died of the cancer. And they all have their breathing machine. A lady died day before yesterday, and she had a big old breathing tank she had to travel with all the time because she couldn't breathe. Another young girl she died also," she said. Giving substance to Campbell's suspicions was a long history of air pollution violations by the neighboring refinery and chemical plant. The air in and outside her home had a biting metallic taste.

Forty years ago, Campbell moved to her home in Diamond, arriving in St. Charles Parish with a sick husband and seven children. She chose Diamond because she found a house there that cost $4,500 and buying it meant that she could own her own home instead of paying rent. The house was cheap because it was located right on the fenceline with Shell's chemical plant and refinery. Shortly after she arrived, her husband, a laborer for Louisiana Power and Gas, died from a stroke. To feed her family, Campbell took a job first as a janitor at Shell's refinery and later as a maid working in the home of a white family in Norco until age 70, when chronic health problems forced her to retire.

Born with poor eyesight, Campbell subsequently developed diabetes, an irregular heartbeat, and a cyst on her spine. She also has arthritis and is often short of breath. "Sometimes I can make do for myself and sometimes I can't," she explained. Though most of her children had left Diamond, one daughter, Mary, lived a few blocks away, that daughter checked on her mother, prepared her meals, did her shopping, and drove her to the doctor.

Explosions at the Shell plants in 1973 and 1988 left Campbell with a bad case of what she called "nerves." During the earlier incident she was sitting on her porch when, as she described it, "something blowed up at the chemical plant and it killed the old lady [Helen Washington] and the little boy [Leroy Jones] who was in the yard. It was like the fire [from the explosion] was coming over my house." Campbell became hysterical. "The funniest part is that every time the kids would start yelling and screaming I would tell them to shut up but then I would start screaming. But it wasn't really funny," she allowed. Hearing about the explosion, one of her sons-in-law came with a dump truck to evacuate her and the kids. The bed of the dump truck was so high that normally Campbell would have been unable to climb into it, but not this time. "I was so frightened that nothing was too high for me to get in," she said.

Campbell found that she did not get over her fright. The home she was working in as a maid had a squeaky faucet, and when the owner of the house turned it on Campbell thought there was another explosion: "I went running down the hall hollering and screaming that [the plant] blowed up again." It got so bad that her employer told her she had to see a doctor. Sent to a mental health clinic, Campbell told the doctor "My nerves are bad, but I don't think I'm crazy." "Janie," he said, "you aren't crazy. You just need some pills."

The 1988 explosion "picked my house off the pillars and dropped it back down," Janie Campbell recalled. "It was . . . just like going through hell. And since that time I don't sleep, I sleep light and if the house creaks I wake and if the trains hit connecting with each other I sit up in bed and say to myself 'Well, that is just the train.' So it is just scary and I have to live on nerve pills and I think that is just horrible to have to live on nerve pills to keep together at night. I just shake because there is too much pressure. I'm frightened."

Campbell is still worried that the refinery or the chemical plant might blow up again, and that she would be left behind in the confusion or the evacuation routes might be cut. She counts it a blessing that during the last big explosion the spillway was not full and Diamond residents were able to escape across it. But if the spillway is full during the next explosion she does not know how she will get out. She cannot drive or swim. "I feel like I am in a hole," she said. "Have you ever seen a hole way down and there is no way for you to come out? Well, I feel like I am in a hole. I'm in a hole with nowhere to go. I'm surrounded. The [railroad] track is there, the river is there, you don't know when an accident is going to happen and the spillway could be full of water. And I can't swim it and I can't walk it, and I can't go through it in a car because it [the water] is so high. . . . Where am I going to go? I just wish I could get away from here before I die so I could have peace of mind and sleep one night in peace without being afraid that the plant is going to blow up." Campbell was acutely aware of how close the plants are to her: "It is not like they are ten miles away. They are right here. And the odors. . . . It is just horrible. And now and then [the plants make loud noises like] VROOM, VROOM, like something they are trying to keep from blowing up. It [the gas] wants to blow up, and it is trying to escape from something. And when they have the flares coming out of the top, it makes a noise like something that is too full and it is trying to escape . . . the pressure. And you don't know if it is going to explode. You don't know what it is going to do. Nobody knows but the good Lord." Shell officials told her the plant was not going to blow up but, as she pointed out, they had not anticipated that the catalytic cracking plant would blow up in 1988. In fact, after the 1990 Clean Air Act required chemical companies to prepare a "worst-case scenario" map of vulnerable areas around their plants it became clear that Diamond was within three overlapping vulnerable zones.

Campbell prays to God that Shell officials will move her so she can have a few years of peace. "My [government] check is $525 a month," she noted. "You can't move on that, and nobody ain't going to buy here in Norco because everybody is afraid [of living near the plants]. I can't sell my house to nobody. Nobody don't want it."

Like many of her neighbors, Campbell would prefer to leave town rather than fight Shell. "I would go," she insisted, as long as Shell paid enough for her house that she could relocate in a safe area. "I'm not particular as long as it is a decent place. . . . I am not a picky person. . . . I just want to get away from here. I am looking just to get away. I just want to be gone. . . . People want to get away from here so bad. They are desperate because they know what they have been going through here and they don't want to raise up children here in this mess."

Editors' Note: *Notes for this reading can be found in the original source.*

PART EIGHT

Work and Welfare

Americans pride themselves on their commitment to the "work ethic." And despite predictions in the 1950s and 1960s that we were on the verge of becoming a "leisure" society, work remains central to the lives of most of us. It is how, as adults, we make a living, define our identities, and find our place in the scheme of things. Ideally, work is one of the most important ways in which we are enabled to participate in a larger human community.

But the reality of work, for all too many people, has always fallen short of the ideal. In the nineteenth century, many social theorists and social critics argued that for the great bulk of people in the emerging industrial societies, work had become a source of torment and exploitation rather than fulfillment. Karl Marx, one of the most influential of those critics, put it this way:

> What constitutes the alienation of labour? First, that the work is *external* to the worker, that it is not part of his nature; and that, consequently, he does not fulfill himself in his work but denies himself, has a feeling of misery rather than well-being, does not develop freely his mental and physical energies but is physically exhausted and mentally debased. The worker, therefore, feels himself at home only during his leisure time, whereas at work he feels homeless. His work is not voluntary but imposed, *forced labour*. It is not satisfaction of a need, but only a *means* for satisfying other needs. Its alien character is clearly shown by the fact that as soon as there is no physical or other compulsion it is avoided like the plague.[1]

Today, in the twenty-first century, the concerns of the nineteenth-century critics have become, if anything, more urgent. An array of rapid economic and technological changes has made the link between work and well-being more and more problematic. The increasingly competitive global economy has put new strains on the institution of work—radically reshaping the workplace, eliminating jobs, and lowering incomes and benefits for many of those who do work steadily. While these

changes have affected workers around the world, they have had an unusually destructive impact on *American* workers, who were once widely considered to be better off than their counterparts in Europe. Today the opposite is true. European
workers are typically paid more, have longer vacations and shorter workweeks, and
enjoy a much more generous set of social benefits.

That helps explain why, as we've seen earlier, poverty is both broader and
deeper in America than in most European countries. We are often told that the
United States has become a high-tech economy in which most jobs require considerable education and skill and are rewarded accordingly. But the reality is less
bright. Our economy has indeed produced many high-skill, high-wage jobs in recent years, but it has also produced a far greater number of low-level ones, paying
only the minimum wage or a little above it. This means increased stress and hardship for growing numbers of American workers and their families; beyond that, it
has undercut one of the basic tenets of the American ethos: the conviction that hard
work will lead to economic security and personal fulfillment. For more and more
Americans, that is only a dream.

Nowhere is this more true than for many of the immigrant workers who make
up a growing part of the American labor force—often doing the least attractive, but
crucial jobs on which the rest of the economy depends. We have exported many low-
level (and increasingly some higher-level) jobs to the developing world, but, as
David Shipler shows, we have also kept many of those jobs here at home, and "imported" many Third World workers to take them on. Some of those workers will
surely move upward out of those jobs, as many did in the past. But many will not,
because—as we've seen—upward mobility has become more difficult and less certain in today's economy. Meanwhile, along with their counterparts in other countries, they provide the steady flow of inexpensive goods and services that most
Americans have come to expect, but at the cost of long hours and sharply limited
opportunities.

If succeeding through work has become increasingly problematic for many of
the "working poor," it is even more so for those with no work at all. As far back as
the 1950s, many observers warned that the looming decline in manufacturing employment would have devastating consequences for the inner cities—already
wracked by crime, drugs, and family disruption—if we failed to develop alternative
ways to put people to work. For the most part, however, we didn't heed those warnings. The results, as William Julius Wilson's article shows, are exactly what was predicted. Deindustrialization has laid waste to job prospects in the inner cities, bringing
a corresponding—but hardly surprising—deepening of social problems in its wake.

It might seem logical that we would have responded to this massive loss of jobs
by creating new ones to take their place. For the most part, however, that is not what
we did. One reason for our reluctance to invest directly in new jobs was the widespread belief that the lack of jobs wasn't the real problem: that, as it was often said,
anybody could get a job if they really wanted one. Instead, many people blamed the
stubborn unemployment, poverty, and related ills of the cities on the personal or
cultural deficiencies of what has come to be called the "underclass." As Herbert
Gans argues, labeling many of the poor—especially the jobless poor—as an in-

tractable "underclass" serves to absolve the better-off from responsibility for their condition while emphasizing the moral and psychological failings of the poor themselves. Such labels, Gans suggests, may allow mainstream Americans to vent their anger and frustration at the poor, but they do not help us develop realistic ways of tackling the roots of poverty or joblessness.

The tendency to regard the problems of the jobless poor as, in effect, mainly their own fault has powerfully influenced our approach to providing support for the unemployed and marginally employed. Not only have we shied away from making a serious commitment to a strategy of full employment, but we have also been remarkably tightfisted in offering income benefits to those who cannot make a living through legitimate work. Indeed, by the 1980s it had become common to hear that the system we had established to help the casualties of economic insecurity—the welfare system—was itself the problem. Welfare, it was argued, caused joblessness and poverty by undermining the work ethic and encouraging people to become dependent on the "state" for survival. In fact, the provision of welfare in the United States had always been minimal by comparison with most other advanced industrial nations. But the belief that the welfare system was self-defeatingly generous has nevertheless prevailed in American social policy. In the 1990s, the nation embarked on a controversial welfare "reform" designed to get people off the welfare rolls and into jobs—without much concern about whether there were enough jobs available to accommodate them, at wages that could realistically support a family. But was the welfare system itself really the problem? Recent evidence on the effects of welfare reform suggests that though this policy did manage to move many people off of the welfare rolls, it was far less successful in moving them out of *poverty*. And despite the radical shrinking of the welfare system, the inner city problems described by Wilson remain very much with us.

That a great deal was, and is, wrong with our welfare system cannot be denied. But as Rosemary L. Bray shows in her autobiographical account of growing up on welfare, much of the fashionable view of welfare families held by more fortunate Americans is misleading and self-serving. Bray's mother, who scrambled to raise four children, send them to private schools, and ultimately turn them into "working, taxpaying adults," bears little resemblance to the stereotype of welfare women as lazy consumers of government handouts. Bray acknowledges that not all women on welfare are equally motivated. But her story of one family's successful use of the welfare system to help them move up from poverty should make us think twice about the idea that welfare's impact is uniformly negative.

ENDNOTE

1. Quoted in Shlomo Avineri, *The Social and Political Thought of Karl Marx* (Cambridge, Eng.: Cambridge University Press, 1971), p. 106.

CHAPTER 27

Importing the Third World

DAVID K. SHIPLER

Luxury is produced by humble hands. Not only in the squalid factories of "developing" countries but on American soil too, wealth and poverty intersect. Where immigrants have come seeking lives of plenty, they bring their deprivation with them, creating islands of hardship amid the surging tides of prosperity. For a paltry wage, albeit one far greater than at home, they feed and clothe and comfort the Americans they wish to emulate.

So it is in potato fields and sewing lofts, in cleaners and restaurants, and in the manicured gardens of suburban affluence. In Los Angeles, among shabby blocks around Spring and 8th, garments to be sold lucratively on Fifth Avenue and Wilshire Boulevard are sewn together by struggling Mexicans and Thais, Hondurans and Koreans. By the time the graceful dresses and tasteful blouses are pressed and hung on mannequins in glistening windows, all the stains of suffering have been erased.

A New Yorker can wander the sprawling expanse of Los Angeles searching in vain for a city. Vast stretches of low houses and warehouses, broad highways and scattered factories spread carelessly eastward from the Pacific as if land were an infinite resource. The garment district, however, is an exception; it has a taut urban feel. Structures are tall enough to cast shadows across streets, and streets are filled with a rainbow of complexions, a babel of tongues. Even without approaching the cluttered vibrancy of Manhattan's garment district, this neighborhood would make a New Yorker feel almost at home. Hand-pushed trolleys hung with clothing weave in and out of truck traffic among buildings exhausted from hard use. At lunchtime, creaky elevators traveling down from ten, twelve, thirteen stories disgorge the industrious, the slick, the honorable, the corrupt—in sum, a global population, the faces mostly Asian and Latino with smatterings of black and white. A couple of taco vans take up strategic positions in an alley and along a parking lot; workers and their bosses eat lunch quickly, then return to lofts crammed with sewing machines and bolts of fabric.

In her nine years since coming from Mexico, Candalaria worked here, moving from one to another sewing job as small companies appeared and evaporated like beads of sweat in the wind. She was quick, and she had better have been, because she was paid by the piece: three-quarters of a cent for each fly she sewed with a machine onto a pair of jeans. The arithmetic was coldly simple. "I have to do a hundred flies to get seventy-five cents," she noted. To make California's minimum wage, which was $5.75 at the time, that added up to 767 flies an hour, allowing her just under 5 seconds for each fly. "I'm pretty fast at this," she bragged, much faster than workers new to the industry. "I can do four cuts a day; each cut is twelve hundred to sixteen hundred pieces." At the highest end, that came out to about 86 an hour for an eight-hour day.

There was a catch, though. Her supervisor, a Vietnamese woman named Anh, kept track of the difference between Candalaria's piecework earnings and the minimum wage. If she didn't make the minimum wage on a certain day, Anh paid her anyway, and Candalaria owed her the difference. If she made more than the minimum wage, she owed Anh the excess. Even though this put a ceiling on her wage, it was a better deal than the below-minimum piecework pay that many garment workers received. Those who could not maintain the pace were fired.

Candalaria started work at 7 a.m., but Anh didn't let her punch in until 9 to make sure the records showed fewer hours. So quick and nimble were Candalaria's fingers that Anh accused her of fabricating tickets to exaggerate her production. The allegation led to arguments, and Candalaria once pulled out the notebook in which she had listed her hours. "The boss tried to take it from me," she remembered, "and tried to get me to sign something saying I'd faked the tickets." Constant chicanery gave the sewing loft the uncertainty of a dusty marketplace where no price was fixed and no bargaining power was had by the seller. Without immigration documents, Candalaria had no legal right to be in the United States or to sell what the American economy needed: cheap labor at the bottom rungs of production. So she had stayed in this sweatshop for a year and eight months. Was there a chance of finding a better job? She laughed at the silly question, and so did several men who were sitting with her. They worked at various sewing companies.

"When I put a label on a pair of pants, I get four cents," said Juan. This, after his nine years of experience in the garment district. "They pay a total of $2 to all the people who work on a pair of pants."

"I produce loops," said Jesus. "I get nine cents per pair of pants. Most of the factories don't pay minimum wage, but for people like Juan, he'll be able to reach that level. Someone who's new can't do that much." The inexperienced, those with less dexterity on the sewing machine, made as little as $3 an hour, he said.

Paying so little may seem like a boon for a boss, but he isn't always delighted. Low piecework wages reflect low productivity, and the sewing factories have deadlines to meet. Juan's employers, therefore, "expect workers to produce enough to reach the minimum wage," he explained, and they fire anyone who consistently falls short. When the state raises the minimum wage, the employer usually raises the required speed of production and leaves the rate per piece unchanged, workers' advocates report. That circumvents the law, of course—the law enacted by government, that is. More potent is the law of economics. Global manufacturing has put the five thousand sewing factories in Los Angeles in cruel competition with those in Honduras, Cambodia, and other Third World countries where living standards and labor costs are exceedingly low. Mexicans get about $4 a day for factory work; in Cambodia, where teachers earn $15 to $25 a month, Cambodians who sew garments get $30 to $45 a month, or 16 to 23 cents an hour. One response has been to import some features of the Third World into the United States.

Few American demonstrators against globalization and the World Trade Organization seem aware that if they want to protest sweatshops, they don't have to look for exploitation in poor nations; they can find more immediate targets by walking along 8th Street in L.A., where the bad publicity would surely provoke speedier results. Protesting globalization is like protesting the monsoon season. What's the point? The rain is going to come anyway, and it yields both hardship and benefit— destructive flooding that also produces enough water to grow rice. The best approach is to channel it, control it, prevent it from inundating the defenseless.

That is what several organizations in California have done since they formed a coalition called Sweatshop Watch[1] to lobby and litigate on behalf of garment workers. The organization has persuaded some laborers to overcome their fears of deportation and to expose both their direct employers—small sewing shops—and the larger, brand-name designers and manufacturers. Those big names often hire the abusive sewing contractors to do their dirty work by underpaying workers to assemble garments. In 2000 a Latino couple and their daughter, who were paid as little as $3 an hour, won a settlement of $134,000 from three manufacturers, John Paul Richard, Francine Browner, and BCBG Max Azria. The manufacturing firms had hired a private company to monitor conditions at the sewing contractors but did nothing when the monitor reported problems.

The most infamous case to date began in rural Thailand in the late 1980s, when Thai con artists recruited impoverished young people, most of them women, with promises of well-paid sewing jobs in the United States. Upon arrival, the workers were practically enslaved in a two-story apartment complex in El Monte, just east of Los Angeles. They ate, slept, and worked behind razor wire and windows covered with plywood. For seventeen or eighteen hours a day, they were forced to sew and assemble clothing for major American manufacturers, including Tomato, Clio, B.U.M., High Sierra, Axle, Cheetah, Anchor Blue, and Airtime. The apparel was sold at Sears, Target, May's, Nordstrom, Mervyn's, Miller's, and Montgomery Ward.[2] The workers' wages amounted to less than a dollar an hour, from which the Thai organizers subtracted the cost of groceries, inflated by a factor of four or five. Without medical care, the laborers suffered from various ailments; because of untreated gum disease, one had to pull out eight of his own teeth.

"They were told that if they tried to resist or escape, their homes in Thailand would be burned, their families murdered, and they would be beaten," writes Julie Su, one of their lawyers.[3] They were shown pictures of a man who had been badly battered after an escape attempt, and they were threatened with the dreaded Immigration and Naturalization Service if they complained—threats that came true, in a way. In 1995, seven years after the involuntary servitude began, and three years after the INS had received its first report on the problem, federal and state agents finally raided the place, "freeing" seventy-one hapless workers only to imprison them in a federal penitentiary pending deportation. The INS, bound by law to detain and deport illegal immigrants, thereby reinforced the intimidation commonly used by employers to enforce their workers' silence. The official toughness "could only serve to discourage workers from reporting labor law, civil rights, and human rights abuses, and push operations like El Monte further underground," Su argues. "The INS, we asserted, ought not conspire with exploitative employers." It took an entire week of vehement demonstrations by Sweatshop Watch members before the tormented Thai workers were released by the immigration agency.

In the end, their captors were jailed for two to seven years, and the workers won $4 million settling a civil suit. Most significantly, the manufacturers, who were two steps removed from the El Monte factory, did not escape responsibility. That was a breakthrough against high-rolling brand names that try not to sully their labels.

In the usual routine of the garment business, the manufacturer, or designer, draws the pattern and uses huge jigsaws, run either by hand or by computer, to cut thick stacks of fabric along the lines of the pattern. The cut pieces of clothing are then shipped to a contractor whose employees sew the pieces of each garment together, often on an assembly-line basis. It is at that level of assembly that most abuses occur. The contractor charges the manufacturer a per-garment price, and so is motivated to keep labor costs close to the bone. The manufacturer throws up his hands in a mock pretense of ignorance and helplessness over his contractor's relations with his employees. In the El Monte case, however, lawyers for the Thai workers argued successfully in court that the manufacturers could not plead such ignorance, having delivered cut pieces to a couple of small contractors in the garment district with demands for such a quick turnaround of finished apparel that they had to know the work would be farmed out to some larger operation—in El Monte, as it happened. The Thai laborers were joined in their lawsuit by the contractors' Latino employees, who were badly underpaid. It was a rare instance of inter-ethnic cooperation in Southern California, where workers' rights campaigns are usually organized into separate movements by Koreans, Latinos, Cambodians, and others.

Publicity over abuses led to state legislation in 1999 holding clothing manufacturers and retailers responsible for their sewing contractors' compliance with minimum wage and overtime laws. Enforcement has been less than thorough, however: A year after the law was enacted, state and federal investigations found that only one-third of the sewing contractors inspected in Los Angeles were observing labor laws, down from 39 percent the year before.[4]

The economics of the garment industry, like the market forces that govern much American enterprise, work against decent wages at the bottom, because competition is fierce, margins are razor thin, and many employers feel vulnerable. They don't think they could stay in business without hiring undocumented immigrants, but they risk prosecution and the confiscation of their stocks of clothing for doing so. Many small sewing contractors are recent immigrants themselves; a good number arrived from Hong Kong as the British colony was turned over to China. Some undoubtedly get rich on the backs of their Korean, Chinese, and Mexican workers, but others make considerably less than a fortune. "Many contractors are just able to cover their own paychecks," said an industry spokesman, Joe Rodriguez, who headed the Garment Contractors Association of Southern California. "One guy told me he was paying himself $36,000 a year. That's why things like health insurance are a pipe dream.". . .

It is mobility that has created the global reputation of the United States as a land of opportunity, and it is that impression that has generated the popular view of a society more open and less stratified than others. At the beginning of the twentieth century, the son of Polish immigrants could drop out of school after the eighth grade, work on the Jersey City docks for eight cents an hour, and rise to become president of Bethlehem Steel's steamship lines. That's what my grandfather did. Not today. Most modern American mobility is generated by economic growth, not by any absence of boundaries between races or classes. That economic expansion, rapid enough after World War II to open broad avenues of advancement, has slowed since the 1970s, leaving many workers behind, especially men and women with nothing more than high school diplomas. More mobility occurs between generations than within generations. It is a sad truth now that a young person with limited skills and education arriving on these shores—or entering the workforce from a background of poverty—will start on the bottom rung only to discover that the higher rungs are beyond his grasp. . . .

Nowhere is the stifling frustration more obvious than in the ethnic enclaves that serve America's economy. Formidable walls surround the subcultures of Koreans, Chinese, Vietnamese, Mexicans, Hondurans, Ethiopians, and others who populate the ranks of low-paid workers. Those who lack fluency in English, proper immigration papers, or advanced skills cannot easily scale those walls; they are imprisoned in an archipelago of scattered zones of cheap labor that promote the country's interests. They are not Americans, but they are an essential part of America. They sustain not only the garment industry, but also the restaurants, farms, parking garages, landscapers, painting contractors, builders, and other key contributors to American well-being.

"They treat 'em like shit," said Roxie Herbekian, a gangly, fast-talking union organizer and president of the Parking and Service Workers Union in Washington, D.C. She represented parking garage attendants in Washington, northern Virginia, and suburban Maryland, most of whom were Ethiopian immigrants, plus some West Africans, Latinos, and African-Americans. "People are routinely fired without good reason," she contended, "and there's a lot of racist division of work. It's very hard for people of color to get out of the garages into anything higher [such as] a supervisory position, a management position, accounting." Many workers "feel this wall of disrespect," she said. "A lot of the immigrants, particularly from Ethiopia, are professionals. There's a lot of lawyers, a lot of pharmacists, people that were highly trained . . . and then they're working these jobs, and some young white kid is the supervisor and treats 'em like they don't know anything."

Parking attendants get minimum wage—in the District of Columbia that is a dollar more than the federal minimum—but a lot of their time is off the clock, Herbekian complained. It may take a cashier twenty minutes after she punches out to complete forms and deposit receipts in the bank, but those minutes go unpaid. One big company had "forced breaks," she said. "They automatically deduct an hour and fifteen minutes for breaks—well, people don't get the break." They had to work right through most of it. Personal connections also count. If you have friends who can get you a late afternoon or evening shift parking cars downtown, you'll get up to $200 a week in tips from people retrieving their vehicles. But you need the contacts, and you need to be a man. Women are usually confined to the tipless position of cashier.

A fine-boned woman named Leti, fatigue and defeat etched in her ebony face, worked twelve hours a day as a cashier in a Washington garage. Although she spoke good English, she had never finished high school in Ethiopia, and her long hours and two children hadn't left her time to get her degree here. Seventeen years ago she arrived in the United States on a tourist visa, and two years later managed to get her green card, which signified her legal status as an immigrant. But neither the card nor her English nor her long time in the country opened doors. "I feel like I came last year," she said. "Nothing has changed."

In Los Angeles, "Nara" and her husband were also stuck. Her piercing eyes were bright with anger, her words bitter. For twelve hours a day six days a week, she worked as assistant cook in a Korean restaurant, where customers' tips were not shared with the staff in the hot kitchen. In the evenings, because her husband refused to cook for himself, she got home and had to prepare dinner for him and their son. "Cooking all day and then at home is like being in hell," she said angrily. During one of her many fights with her husband, she shouted at him, "Why did you make me come here?" He walked out and didn't return for ten days.

In 1991 he came from South Korea with $20,000; she arrived six months later with $15,000. Now their savings had dwindled to $5,000, and they had moved to a smaller, cheaper apartment where they slept in the living room, letting their boy of thirteen have the one bedroom. In Seoul, the husband ran an import-export business dealing mostly in sunglasses; in Los Angeles, he picked up odd jobs as a welder. She was a dress designer but without English couldn't get such work here, so she felt confined to the subculture of Korean restaurants in the "Koreatown" section of Los Angeles. "I went to a language institute for three months," Nara said through an interpreter, "but I forget very easily. I'm too old." She was forty-five. "I live in Koreatown; I can get along without English." She could get along, but she couldn't get out.

When they both had work their income didn't look bad on paper. She made between $1,700 and $1,800 a month, though her long days meant that the hourly rate barely reached California's minimum wage of $6.75 and omitted overtime, which the law required. He could earn $1,000 to $2,000 a month welding gates and fences, so together they may have taken in nearly $40,000 a year. That was a graphic illustration of the virtue of having two wage-earners and the hazards of being a single parent: At those low wages, single parenthood would have been a prescription for poverty.

Still, they felt pinched. Los Angeles was an expensive place to live. Public transportation was so bad that they had to own two vehicles, a truck and a car. Their jobs provided no health insurance, so they spent large sums on Korean doctors and dentists. As illegal immigrants, they got virtually no government benefits (which Nara insisted she would have refused in any case). Moreover, a psychological confinement imposed a mood of defeat. Marginalized, cloistered, and stagnant, Nara simply wanted to go back to South Korea; her husband wanted to stay.

Jung Hee Lee also felt trapped. A sinewy, diminutive woman with a wan smile, she arrived from South Korea with her husband in 1995; he was on a student visa to study computer science at UCLA. "We sold our house in Korea," she explained. "We had planned in Korea that if we sold the house, that's a lot of money, so we could come here and study for about three years comfortably. Both of us would study. We never imagined that I was going to work. It wasn't in the plan. But when we got here, that money ran out quickly, in a year." They were stunned by the cost of living. From a three-bedroom, two-bathroom house in Korea they descended to a one-bedroom apartment in Los Angeles. Their two children had beds; the parents slept on the floor.

She went from bank teller in Korea to waitress in Los Angeles, earning less than the minimum wage and spending hours delicately navigating the slippery floor tiles of a restaurant kitchen. One day, carrying a tray, she lost her footing and fell. Crockery crashed to the floor, and dreams shattered. Her back was injured so seriously that she could not work for a year. Desperate for money, her husband had to drop out of school and get a job—and the college degree was relegated to a distant hope. Jung's employer did not carry worker's compensation; she had found a lawyer who had agreed to take only a contingency fee if a lawsuit were successful, a process that was likely to run for at least five years.

Here again, the family's income was respectable enough, but the ambitions they brought with them to America had been extinguished. The husband, now a manager for a garment contractor, made about $2,000 a month, much better than most garment workers, and Jung was back waiting tables six nights a week in a Korean restaurant, where tips were often good enough to practically double her $800-a-month salary. Nevertheless, the money all disappeared, and they couldn't save. Without health insurance, their medical bills were huge. The tension in their life ground at their emotions. They would have returned home, but they felt ashamed to do so in defeat.

"If you look at the wages earned, it's not bad," she said. "But the problem is you work long hours. Most of the time you're at work, and who's going to take care of the children? So you end up spending about $500 a month for child care, and I don't have much time to spend with my family or husband. So it ends up, going to work, going home and sleeping, and coming out again. There's no time to cook so they always have to go out and eat," she said of her husband and children. That was expensive, and their diet and health suffered as a result.

"My husband is a salaried man, but he doesn't have any social life. He has friends, but he can't hang out with them. He has to come home and take care of the kids. So my husband and I have lots of trouble—arguments. He has no days off. . . . In Korea, we never argued. I've heard from other immigrants that the first five years of immigrant life you and your husband will argue, but if you can get past that you will be together."

But "together" was a relative term. Her husband was out of the apartment by 7:30 or 8 a.m. and back about 8:30 p.m., when she was still at work. "I walk in the door around twelve or one o'clock, I open up the door and my husband's snoring and everyone's asleep, and I feel like, why am I living? I get very depressed. In Korea, at least we spent evenings together so we'd have things to talk about. But right now we have nothing to talk about with each other. There's no time to talk, and there's no content to discuss." In one respect Korean immigrants are becoming assimilated into America: Their divorce rate is about 50 percent.

The salvation of immigrants to the United States has almost always been deferred to the subsequent generations. If the parents cannot speak English, the children can. If the parents are confined by long hours and low wages, the children are freed to find a way up along the path of higher skills and education. It's hard to make comparisons with earlier eras, but in today's ethnic enclaves the assumptions are not completely intact, the confidence is not entirely unshaken that the next generation will succeed, advance, emerge into the shared sunlight of the country's prosperity.

Indeed, when I asked Jung what she foresaw in her children's lives, she answered curiously; she described how active she had become in campaigning through the Korean Immigrant Workers Advocate to improve working conditions in Korean restaurants. That battle, if won, would make her children's lives better, she believed. So, I asked, she expected them to be working in restaurants? "There's no guarantee that they will not be working in a restaurant," she said sadly. "Of course, I would love to have my children go to Yale, Harvard, Columbia, New York University, and become a doctor, a lawyer, but—right now my sons dream is to become a police officer. My daughter's is to become a teacher in elementary school. But in looking at their future employment, who knows? They could end up working in the restaurants."

Editors' Note: *Notes for this reading can be found in the original source.*

CHAPTER 28

The Political Economy and Urban Racial Tensions

WILLIAM JULIUS WILSON

There is a new poverty in our nation's metropolises that has far ranging consequences for the quality of life in urban areas, including race relations. By the "new urban poverty," I mean poor segregated neighborhoods in which a substantial majority of individual adults are either unemployed or have dropped out of the labor force. For example, in 1990 only one in three adults (35%) ages 16 and over in the twelve Chicago community areas with poverty rates that exceeded 40 percent held a job.[1] Each of these community areas, located on the South and West sides of the city, is overwhelmingly black. We can add to these twelve high jobless areas three additional predominantly black community areas, with rates of poverty of 29, 30, and 36 percent respectively, where only four in ten (42%) adults worked in 1990. Thus, in these fifteen black community areas, representing a total population of 425,125, only 37 percent of all the adults were gainfully employed in 1990. By contrast, 54 percent of the adults in the seventeen other predominantly black community areas in Chicago, with a total population of 545,408, worked in 1990. This was close to the city-wide figure of 57 percent. Finally, except for one largely Asian community area with an employment rate of 46 percent, and one largely Latino community area with an employment rate of 49 percent, a majority of the adults held a job in each of the forty-five other community areas of Chicago.[2]

To repeat, the new urban poverty represents poor segregated neighborhoods in which a substantial majority of the adults are not working. To illustrate the magnitude of the changes that have occurred in inner-city ghetto neighborhoods in recent years, let me take the three Chicago community areas (Douglas, Grand Boulevard, and Washington Park) featured in St. Clair Drake and Horace Cayton's classic book entitled *Black Metropolis,* published in 1945. These three community areas, located on the South Side of the city of Chicago, represent the historic core of Chicago's black belt.

A majority of adults were gainfully employed in these three areas in 1950, five years after the publication of *Black Metropolis,* but by 1990 only four in ten in Douglas worked, one in three in Washington Park, and one in four in Grand Boulevard. In 1950, 69 percent of all males 14 and over worked in the Bronzeville neighborhoods of Douglas, Grand Boulevard, and Washington Park; by 1990 only 37 percent of all males 16 and over held jobs in these three neighborhoods.[3]

Upon the publication of the first edition of *Black Metropolis* in 1945, there was much greater class integration in the black community. As Drake and Cayton pointed out, Bronzeville residents had limited success in "sorting themselves out into broad community areas designated as 'lower class' and 'middle class.' . . . Instead of middle class areas, Bronzeville tends to have middle-class buildings in all areas, or a few middle-class blocks here and there" (pp. 658–660). Though they may have lived on different streets, blacks of all classes in inner-city areas such as Bronzeville lived in the same community and shopped at the same stores. Their children went to the same schools and played in the same parks. Although there was some class antagonism, their neighborhoods were more stable than the inner-city neighborhoods of today; in short, they featured higher levels of social organization.

By "social organization" I mean the extent to which the residents of a neighborhood are able to maintain effective social control and realize their common values. There are two major dimensions of neighborhood social organization: (1) the prevalence, strength, and interdependence of social networks; and (2) the extent of collective supervision that the residents direct and the personal responsibility they assume in addressing neighborhood problems (Sampson 1992).

Both formal institutions and informal networks reflect social organization. In other words, neighborhood social organization depends on the extent of local friendship ties, the degree of social cohesion, the level of resident participation in formal and informal voluntary associations, the density and stability of formal organizations, and the nature of informal social controls. Neighborhoods that integrate the adults by an extensive set of obligations, expectations, and social networks are in a better position to control and supervise the activities and behavior of children, and monitor developments—e.g., the breaking up of congregations of youth on street corners and the supervision of youth leisure time activities (Sampson 1992).

Neighborhoods plagued with high levels of joblessness are more likely to experience problems of social organization. The two go hand-in-hand. High rates of joblessness trigger other problems in the neighborhood that adversely affect social organization, ranging from crime, gang violence, and drug trafficking to family break-ups and problems in the organization of family life. Consider, for example, the problems of drug trafficking and violent crime. As many studies have revealed, the decline of legitimate employment opportunities among inner-city residents builds up incentives to sell drugs (Fagan 1993). The distribution of crack in a neighborhood attracts individuals involved in violence and other crimes. Violent persons in the crack marketplace help shape its social organization and its impact on the neighborhood. Neighborhoods plagued by high levels of joblessness, insufficient economic opportunities, and high residential mobility are unable to control the volatile drug market and the violent crimes related to it (Fagan 1993, Sampson 1986). As informal controls weaken in such areas, the social processes that regulate behavior change (Sampson 1988).

A more direct relationship between joblessness and violent crime is revealed in recent longitudinal research by Delbert Elliott (1992) of the University of Colorado, a study based on National Youth Survey data from 1976 to 1989, covering ages 11 to 30. As Elliott (1992) points out, the transition from adolescence to adulthood usually results in a sharp drop in most crimes, including serious violent behavior, as individuals take on new adult roles and responsibilities. "Participation in serious violent offending (aggravated assault, forcible rape, and robbery) increases from ages 11 to 12 to ages 15 and 16 then declines dramatically with advancing age" (Elliott 1992, p. 14). Although black and white males reveal similar age curves, "the negative slope of the age curve for blacks after age 20 is substantially less than that of whites" (p. 15).

The black–white differential in the percentage of males involved in serious violent crime, although almost even at age 11, increases to 3:2 over the remaining years of adolescence, and reaches a differential of nearly 4:1 during the late twenties. However, when Elliott (1992) only compared employed black and white males, he found no significant differences between the two groups in rates of suspension or termination of violent behavior by age 21. Employed black males experienced a precipitous decline in serious violent behavior following their adolescent period. Accordingly, a major reason for the substantial overall racial gap in the termination of violent behavior following the adolescent period is the large proportion of jobless black males, whose serious violent behavior was more likely to extend into adulthood.[4] The new poverty neighborhoods feature a high concentration of jobless males and, as a result, experience rates of violent criminal behavior that exceed those of other urban neighborhoods.

Also, consider the important relationship between joblessness and the organization of family life. Work is not simply a way to make a living and support one's family. It also constitutes the framework for daily behavior and patterns of interaction because of the disciplines and regularities it imposes. Thus in the absence of regular employment, what is lacking is not only a place in which to work and the receipt of regular income, but also a coherent organization of the present, that is, a system of concrete expectations and goals. Regular employment provides the anchor for the temporal and spatial aspects of daily life. In the absence of regular employment, life, including family life, becomes more incoherent. Persistent unemployment and irregular employment hinder rational planning in daily life, the necessary condition of adaptation to an industrial economy (Bourdieu 1965). This problem is most severe for a jobless family in a low employment neighborhood. The family's lack of rational planning is more likely to be shared and therefore reinforced by other families in the neighborhood. The problems of family organization and neighborhood social organization are mutually reinforcing.

FACTORS ASSOCIATED WITH THE INCREASE IN NEIGHBORHOOD JOBLESSNESS AND DECLINE OF SOCIAL ORGANIZATION

Although high jobless neighborhoods also feature concentrated poverty, high rates of neighborhood poverty are less likely to trigger problems of social organization if the residents are working. To repeat, in previous years the working poor stood out in neighborhoods like Bronzeville. Today the non-working poor predominate in such neighborhoods. What accounts for the rise in the proportion of jobless adults in inner-city communities such as Bronzeville?

An easy explanation is racial segregation. However, as we shall soon see, a race-specific argument is not sufficient to explain recent changes in neighborhoods like Bronzeville. After all, Bronzeville was just as segregated in 1950 as it is today, yet the level of employment was much higher back then.

Nonetheless, racial segregation does matter. If large segments of the African-American population had not been historically segregated in inner-city ghettos we would not be talking about the new urban poverty. The segregated ghetto is not the result of voluntary or positive decisions of the residents to live there. As Douglas Massey and Nancy Denton (1993) have carefully documented, the segregated ghetto is the product of systematic racial practices such as restrictive convenants, redlining by banks and insurance companies, zoning, panic peddling by real estate agents, and the creation of massive public housing projects in low-income areas. Moreover, urban renewal and forced migration uprooted many urban black communities. Freeway networks built through the hearts of many cities in the 1950s produced the most dramatic changes. Many viable low-income communities were destroyed. Furthermore, discrimination in employment and inferior educational opportunities further restricted black residential mobility.

Segregated ghettos are less conducive to employment and employment preparation than other areas of the city. Segregation in ghettos exacerbates employment problems because it embraces weak informal employment networks, contributes to the social isolation of individuals and families, and therefore reduces their chances of acquiring the human capital skills that facilitate mobility in a society. Since no other group in society experiences the degree of segregation, isolation, and poverty concentration as African-Americans, they are far more likely to be at a disadvantage when they have to compete with other groups in society, including other "discriminated against" groups, for resources and privileges.

But, to repeat, neighborhoods like Bronzeville were highly segregated decades ago when employment rates were much higher. Given the existence of segregation, one then has to account for the ways in which other changes in society interact with segregation to produce the recent escalating rates of joblessness and problems of social organization. Several factors stand out.

Prominent among these is the impact of changes in the economy, changes that have had an adverse effect on poor urban blacks, especially black males. In 1950, 69 percent of all males 14 and over worked in the Bronzeville neighborhoods of

Douglas, Grand Boulevard, and Washington Park, and in 1960, 64 percent of this group were employed. However, by 1990 only 37 percent of all males 16 and over held jobs in these three neighborhoods.[5]

Thirty and forty years ago, the overwhelming majority of black males were working. Many of them were poor, but they held regular jobs around which their daily family life was organized. When black males looked for work, employers considered whether they had strong backs because they would be working in a factory or in the back room of a shop doing heavy lifting and labor. They faced discrimination and a job ceiling, but they were working. The work was hard and they were hired. Now, economic restructuring has broken the figurative back of the black working population.

Data from our Urban Poverty and Family Life Study show that 57 percent of Chicago's employed inner-city black fathers (aged 15 and over and without bachelor degrees) who were born between 1950 and 1955 worked in manufacturing industries in 1974. By 1987 that figure fell to 27 percent. Of those born between 1956 and 1960, 52 percent worked in manufacturing industries as late as 1978. By 1987 that figure had declined to 28 percent.[6]

The loss of traditional manufacturing and other blue-collar jobs in Chicago has resulted in increased joblessness among inner-city black males and a concentration in low-wage, high-turnover laborer and service-sector jobs. Embedded in segregated ghetto neighborhoods that are not conducive to employment, inner-city black males fall further behind their white and their Hispanic male counterparts, especially when the labor market is slack. Hispanics "continue to funnel into manufacturing because employers prefer" them "over blacks, and they like to hire by referrals from current employees, which Hispanics can readily furnish, being already embedded in migration networks" (Krogh, p. 12). Inner-city black men grow bitter about and resent their employment prospects and often manifest or express these feelings in their harsh, often dehumanizing, low-wage work settings.

Their attitudes and actions create the widely shared perception that they are undesirable workers. The perception then becomes the basis for employer decisions to deny them employment, especially when the economy is weak and many workers are seeking jobs. The employment woes of inner-city black males gradually grow over the long term not only because employers are turning more to the expanding immigrant and female labor force, but also because the number of jobs that require contact with the public continues to climb. Because of the increasing shift to service industries, employers have a greater need for workers who can effectively serve and relate to the consumer. Our research reveals that they believe that such qualities are lacking among black males from segregated inner-city neighborhoods.

The position of inner-city black women in the labor market is also problematic. Their high degree of social isolation in poor segregated neighborhoods, as reflected in social networks, reduces their employment prospects. Although our research indicates that employers consider them more desirable as workers than the inner-city black men, their social isolation decreases their ability to develop language and other job-related skills necessary in an economy that rewards employees who can work and communicate effectively with the public.

The increase in the proportion of jobless adults in the inner city is also related to the outmigration of large numbers of employed adults from working and middle-class families. The declining proportion of non-poor families and increasing and prolonged joblessness in the new poverty neighborhoods make it considerably more difficult to sustain basic neighborhood institutions. In the face of increasing joblessness, stores, banks, credit institutions, restaurants, and professional services lose regular and potential patrons. Churches experience dwindling numbers of parishioners and shrinking resources; recreational facilities, block clubs, community groups, and other informal organizations also suffer. As these organizations decline, the means of formal and informal social control in the neighborhood become weaker. Levels of crime and street violence increase as a result, leading to further deterioration of the neighborhood.

As the neighborhood disintegrates, those who are able to leave do so, including many working and middle-class families. The lower population density created by the outmigration exacerbates the problem. Abandoned buildings increase and provide a haven for crack dens and criminal enterprises that establish footholds in the community. Precipitous declines in density also make it more difficult to sustain or develop a sense of community or for people to experience a feeling of safety in numbers (Jargowsky 1994, p. 18).

The neighborhoods with many black working families stand in sharp contrast to the new poverty areas. Research that we have conducted on the social organization of Chicago neighborhoods reveals that in addition to much lower levels of perceived unemployment than in the poor neighborhoods, black working and middle-class neighborhoods also have much higher levels of perceived social control and cohesion, organizational services, and social support.

The rise of new poverty neighborhoods represents a movement from what the historian Allan Spear (1967) has called an institutional ghetto—which duplicates the structure and activities of the larger society, as portrayed in Drake and Cayton's description of Bronzeville—to an unstable ghetto, which lacks the capability to provide basic opportunities, resources, and adequate social controls.

NEW POVERTY NEIGHBORHOODS AND URBAN RACIAL TENSIONS

The problems associated with the high joblessness and declining social organization (e.g., individual crime, hustling activities, gang violence) in inner-city ghetto neighborhoods often spill over into other parts of the city, including the ethnic enclaves. The result is not only hostile class antagonisms in the higher income black neighborhoods near these communities, but heightened levels of racial animosity, especially among lower income white ethnic and Latino groups whose communities border or are in proximity to the high jobless neighborhoods.

The problems in the new poverty neighborhoods have also created racial antagonisms among some of the higher income groups in the city. The new poverty in ghetto neighborhoods has sapped the vitality of local business and other institutions, and it has led to fewer and shabbier movie theaters, bowling alleys, restaurants, public parks and playgrounds, and other recreational facilities. Therefore residents of inner-city neighborhoods more often seek leisure activity in other areas of the city, where they come into brief contact with citizens of different racial, ethnic, or class backgrounds. Sharp differences in cultural style and patterns of interaction that reflect the social isolation of neighborhood networks often lead to clashes.

Some behavior of residents in socially isolated inner-city ghetto neighborhoods—e.g., the tendency to enjoy a movie in a communal spirit by carrying on a running conversation with friends and relatives during the movie or reacting in an unrestrained manner to what they see on the screen—offends the sensibilities of or is considered inappropriate by other groups, particularly the black and white middle classes. Their expression of disapproval, either overtly or with subtle hostile glances, tends to trigger belligerent responses from the inner-city ghetto residents who then purposefully intensify the behavior that is the source of middle-class concerns. The white, and even the black middle class, then exercise their option and exit, to use Albert Hirschman's (1970) term, by taking their patronage elsewhere, expressing resentment and experiencing intensified feelings of racial or class antagonisms as they depart.

The areas left behind then become the domain of the inner-city ghetto residents. The more expensive restaurants and other establishments that serve the higher income groups in these areas, having lost their regular patrons, soon close down and are replaced by fast-food chains and other local businesses that cater to the needs or reflect the economic and cultural resources of the new clientele. White and black middle-class citizens, in particular, complain bitterly about how certain conveniently located areas of the central city have changed following the influx of ghetto residents.

DEMAGOGIC MESSAGES

I want to make a final point about economic, political, and social situations that have contributed to the rise of racial antagonisms in urban areas. During periods of hard economic times, it is important that political leaders channel the frustrations of citizens in positive or constructive directions. However, for the last few years just the opposite frequently occurred. In a time of heightened economic insecurities, the negative racial rhetoric of some highly visible white and black spokespersons increased racial tensions and channeled frustrations in ways that severely divide the racial groups. During hard economic times people become more receptive to demagogic messages that deflect attention from the real source of their problems. Instead of associating their declining real incomes, increasing job insecurity, growing pessimism about the future with failed economic and political policies, these messages force them to turn on each other—race against race.

As the new urban poverty has sapped the vitality of many inner-city communities, many of these messages associate inner-city crime, family breakdown, and welfare receipt with individual shortcomings. Blame the victim arguments resonate with many urban Americans because of their very simplicity. They not only reinforce the salient belief that joblessness and poverty reflect individual inadequacies, but discourage support for new and stronger programs to combat inner-city social dislocations as well.

WHAT MUST BE DONE?

I have outlined some of the situations that inflate racial antagonisms in cities like Chicago—namely those that involve the interrelation of recent political policies and economic and social processes (including the emergence of the new urban poverty). Let me conclude . . . with some thoughts on social policy that build on this situational perspective.

I believe that it will be difficult to address racial tensions in our cities unless we tackle the problems of shrinking revenue and inadequate social services, and the gradual disappearance of work in certain neighborhoods. The city has become a less desirable place in which to live, and the economic and social gap between the cities and suburbs is growing. The groups left behind compete, often along racial lines, for the declining resources, including the remaining decent schools, housing, and neighborhoods. The rise of the new urban poverty neighborhoods exacerbates the problems. Their high rates of joblessness and social disorganization create problems that not only affect the residents in these neighborhoods but that spill over into other parts of the larger city as well. All of these factors aggravate race relations and elevate racial tensions.

Ideally it would be great if we could restore the federal contribution to the city budget that existed in 1980, and sharply increase the employment base. However, regardless of changes in federal urban policy, the fiscal crisis in the cities would be significantly eased if the employment base could be substantially increased. Indeed, the social dislocations caused by the steady disappearance of work have led to a wide range of urban social problems, including racial tensions. Increased employment would help stabilize the new poverty neighborhood, halt the precipitous decline in density, and ultimately enhance the quality of race relations in urban areas. The employment situation in inner-city ghetto neighborhoods would improve if the United States' economy, which is now experiencing an upturn, could produce low levels of unemployment over a long period of time.

I say this because in slack labor markets employers are—and indeed, can afford to be—more selective in recruiting and in granting promotions. They overemphasize job prerequisites and exaggerate experience. In such an economic climax, disadvantaged minorities suffer disproportionately and the level of employer discrimination rises. In contrast, in a tight labor market, job vacancies are numerous, unemployment is of short duration, and wages are higher. Moreover, in a tight labor market the labor force expands because increased job opportunities not only reduce unemployment but also draw into the labor force those workers who, in periods when the labor market is slack, respond to fading job prospects by dropping out of the labor force altogether. Accordingly, in a tight labor market the status of disadvantaged minorities improves because of lower unemployment, higher wages, and better jobs (Tobin 1965).

Moreover, affirmative action and other anti-bias programs are more successful in tight labor markets than in slack ones. Not only are sufficient positions available for many qualified workers, but also employers, facing a labor shortage, are not as resistant to affirmative action. Furthermore, a favorable economic climate encourages supporters of affirmative action to push such programs because they perceive greater chances for success. Finally, non-minority workers are less resistant to affirmative action when there are sufficient jobs available because they are less likely to see minorities as a threat to their own employment.

However, a rising tide does not necessarily lift all boats. Special additional steps to rescue many inner-city residents from the throes of joblessness should be considered, even if the economy remains healthy. Such steps might include the creation of job information data banks in the new poverty neighborhoods and subsidized car pools to increase access to suburban jobs. Training or apprenticeship programs that lead to stable employment should also be considered.

Nonetheless, because of their level of training and education, many of the jobs to which the inner-city poor have access are at or below the minimum wage and are not covered by health insurance. However, recent policies created and proposed by the Clinton Administration could make such jobs more attractive. By 1996, the expanded Earned Income Tax Credit will increase the earnings from a minimum-wage job to $7 an hour. If this benefit is paid on a monthly basis and is combined with health care, the condition of workers in the low-wage sector would improve significantly, and the rate of employment would rise.

Finally, given the situational basis of much of today's racial tensions, I think that there are some immediate and practical steps that the President of the United States can take to help create the atmosphere for serious efforts and programs to improve racial relations. I am referring to the need for strong political and moral leadership to help combat racial antagonisms. In particular, the need to create and strongly emphasize a message that unites, not divides, racial groups.

It is important to appreciate that the poor and the working classes of all racial groups struggle to make ends meet, and even the middle class has experienced a decline in its living standard. Indeed, Americans across racial and class boundaries worry about unemployment and job security, declining real wages, escalating medical and housing costs, child care programs, the sharp decline in the quality of public education, and crime and drug trafficking in their neighborhoods. Given these concerns, perhaps the President ought to advance a new public rhetoric that does two things: focuses on problems that afflict not only the poor, but the working and middle classes as well; and emphasizes integrative programs that contribute to the social and economic improvement of all groups in society, not just the truly disadvantaged segments of the population. In short a public rhetoric that reflects a vision of racial unity.

The President of the United States has the unique capacity to command nationwide attention from the media and the general public, the capacity to get them to consider seriously a vision of racial unity and of where we are and where we should go.

I am talking about a vision that promotes values of racial and inter-group harmony and unity; rejects the commonly held view that race is so divisive in this country that whites, blacks, Latinos, and other ethnic groups cannot work together in a common cause; recognizes that if a message from a political leader is tailored to a white audience, racial minorities draw back, just as whites draw back when a message is tailored to racial minority audiences; realizes that if the message emphasizes issues and programs that concern the families of all racial and ethnic groups, individuals of these various groups will see their mutual interests and join in a multi-racial coalition to move America forward; promotes the idea that Americans across racial and class boundaries have common interests and concerns including concerns about unemployment and job security, declining real wages, escalating medical and housing costs, child care programs, the sharp decline in the quality of public education, and crime and drug trafficking in neighborhoods; sees the application of programs to combat these problems as beneficial to all Americans, not just the truly disadvantaged among us; recognizes that since demographic shifts have decreased the urban white population and sharply increased the proportion of minorities in the cities, the divide between the suburbs and the central city is, in many respects, a racial divide and that it is vitally important, therefore, to emphasize city–suburban cooperation, not separation; and, finally, pushes the idea that all groups, including those in the throes of the new urban poverty, should be able to achieve full membership in society because the problems of economic and social marginality are associated with inequities in the larger society, not with group deficiencies.

If the President were to promote vigorously this vision, efforts designed to address both the causes and symptoms of racial tensions in cities like New York, Chicago, Philadelphia, Miami, and Los Angeles would have a greater chance for success.

ENDNOTES

1. The figures on adult employment presented in this paragraph are based on calculations from data provided by the 1990 U.S. Bureau of the Census and the *Local Community Fact Book for Chicago*, 1950. The adult employment rates represent the number of employed individuals (14 and over in 1950 and 16 over in 1990) among the total number of adults in a given area. Those who are not employed include both the individuals who are members of the labor force but are not working and those who have dropped out or are not part of the labor force. Those who are not in the labor force "consists mainly of students, housewives, retired workers, seasonal workers enumerated in an 'off' season who were not looking for work, inmates of institutions, disabled persons, and persons doing only incidental unpaid family work" (*The Chicago Fact Book Consortium*, 1984, p. xxv).

2. A community area is a statistical unit derived by urban sociologists at the University of Chicago for the 1930 census in order to analyze varying conditions within the city of Chicago. These delineations were originally drawn up on the basis of settlement and history of the area, local identification and trade patterns, local institutions, and natural and artificial barriers. Needless to say, there have been major shifts in population and land use since then. But these units remain useful to trace changes over time, and they continue to capture much of the contemporary reality of Chicago neighborhoods.

3. The figures on male employment are based on calculations from data provided by the 1990 U.S. Bureau of the Census and the *Local Community Fact Book for Chicago,* 1950.

4. In Elliott's study 75 percent of the black males who were employed between the ages of 18–20 had terminated their involvement in violent behavior by age 21, compared to only 52 percent of those who were unemployed between the ages of 18–20. Racial differences remained for persons who were not in a marriage/partner relationship or who were unemployed.

5. The figures on male employment are based on calculations from data provided by the 1990 U.S Bureau of the Census and the *Local Community Fact Book for Chicago,* 1950.

6. For a discussion of these findings, see Marilyn Krogh, "A Description of the Work Histories of Fathers Living in the Inner-City of Chicago." Working paper, Center for the Study of Urban Inequality, University of Chicago, 1993. *The Urban Poverty and Family Life Study* (UPFLS) includes a survey of 2,495 households in Chicago's inner-city neighborhoods conducted in 1987 and 1988; a second survey of a subsample of 175 respondents from the larger survey who were reinterviewed solely with open-ended questions on their perceptions of the opportunity structure and life chances; a survey of a stratified random sample of 185 employers, designed to reflect the distribution of employment across industry and firm size in the Chicago metropolitan area, conducted in 1988; and comprehensive ethnographic research, including participant observation research and life-history interviews conducted in 1987 and 1988 by ten research assistants in a representative sample of black, Hispanic, and white inner-city neighborhoods.

The UPFLS was supported by grants from the Ford Foundation, the Rockefeller Foundation, the Joyce Foundation, the Carnegie Corporation, the Lloyd A. Fry Foundation, the William T. Grant Foundation, the Spencer Foundation, the Woods Charitable Fund, the Chicago Community Trust, the Institute for Research on Poverty, and the U.S Department of Health and Human Services.

REFERENCES

Bell, Derrick. 1992. *Faces at the Bottom of the Well: The Permanence of Racism.* New York: Basic Books.

Caraley, Demetrios. 1992. "Washington Abandons the Cities," *Political Science Quarterly,* 107, Spring.

Drake, St. Clair and Horace Cayton. 1945. *Black Metropolis: A Study of Negro Life in a Northern City.* New York: Harcourt, Brace, Jovanovich, Inc.

Elliott, Delbert S. 1992. "Longitudinal Research in Criminology: Premise and Practice." Paper presented at the NATO Conference on Cross-National Longitudinal Research on Criminal Behavior, Frankfurt, Germany, July 19–25.

Fagan, Jeffrey. 1993. "Drug Selling and Licit Income in Distressed Neighborhoods: The Economic Lives of Street-Level Drug Users and Dealers," in *Drugs, Crime and Social Isolation* (edited by G. Peterson and A. Harold Washington). Urban Institute Press.

Hacker, Andrew. 1992. *Two Nations: Black and White, Separate, Hostile and Unequal.* New York: Charles Scribner's Sons.

Hirschman, Albert O. 1970. *Exit, Voice, and Loyalty: Responses to Decline in Firms, Organizations, and States.* Cambridge, Mass.: Harvard University Press.

Jargowsky, Paul A. 1994. "Ghetto Poverty Among Blacks in the 1980's," *Journal of Policy Analysis and Management,* Vol. 13, pp. 288–310.

Krogh, Marilyn. 1993. "A Description of the Work Histories of Fathers Living in the Inner-City of Chicago." *Working paper,* Center for the Study of Urban Inequality, University of Chicago.

Massey, Douglas S. and Nancy A. Denton. 1993. *American Apartheid: Segregation and the Making of the Underclass.* Cambridge, Mass.: Harvard University Press.

Rohter, Larry. 1993. "As Hispanic Presence Grows, So Does Black Anger." *New York Times,* June 20, p. 11.

Sampson, Robert J. 1986. "Crime in Cities: The Effects of Formal and Informal Social Control" in *Communities and Crime* (edited by Albert J. Reiss, Jr., and Michael Tonry) 271–310. Chicago: University of Chicago Press.

Sampson, Robert J. 1992. "Integrating Family and Community-Level Dimensions of Social Organization: Delinquency and Crime in the Inner-City of Chicago." Paper presented at the International Workshop: "Integrating Individual and Ecological Aspects on Crime." Stockholm, Sweden, August 31–September 5, 1992.

Sampson, Robert J. and William Julius Wilson. 1993. "Toward a Theory of Race, Crime, and Urban Inequality," in *Crime and Inequality* (edited by John Hagan and Ruth Peterson). Stanford University Press, in press.

Spear, Allan. 1967. *Black Chicago: The Making of a Negro Ghetto.* Chicago: University of Chicago Press.

Tobin, James. 1965. "On Improving the Economic Status of the Negro." *Daedalus,* 94, pp. 878–898.

Wacquant, Loïc J. D. and William Julius Wilson. 1989. "Poverty, Joblessness, and the Social Transformation of the Inner City" in *Welfare Policy for the 1990s* (edited by Phoebe Cottingham and David Ellwood), 70–102. Cambridge: Harvard University Press.

Weir, Margaret. 1993. "Race and Urban Poverty: Comparing Europe and America." Center for American Political Studies, Harvard University, Occasional Paper 93–9, March.

Wilson, William Julius. 1987. *The Truly Disadvantaged: The Inner City, the Underclass, and Public Policy.* Chicago: University of Chicago Press.

CHAPTER 29

The Underclass Label

HERBERT J. GANS

One of America's popular pejorative labels is "slum," which characterizes low-income dwellings and neighborhoods as harmful to their poor occupants and the rest of the community. In the nineteenth century, slums were openly faulted for turning the deserving poor into the undeserving poor, but in the twentieth century the causality was sometimes reversed, so that poor people with "slum-dweller hearts" were accused of destroying viable buildings and neighborhoods.

After World War II, "slum" and "slum dweller" as well as "blight" all became more or less official labels when the federal government, egged on by a variety of builder and realty pressure groups, started handing out sizeable sums for the "clearance" of low-income neighborhoods unfortunate enough to fit these terms as they were defined in the 1949 U.S. Housing Act. Although by and large only slums located in areas where private enterprise could build luxury and other profitable housing were torn down, more than a million poor households lost their homes in the next twenty years, with almost nothing done for the people displaced from them.

This chapter is written with that much-told history in mind, in order to suggest that the underclass label—as well as all but the most neutrally formulated behavioral term—can have dangerous effects for the poor and for antipoverty policy. While the emphasis will be on "underclass," the dangers of related labels will be discussed as well.

Labels may be only words, but they are judgmental or normative words, which can stir institutions and individuals to punitive actions. The dangers from such labels are many, but the danger common to all behavioral labels and terms is that they focus on behavior that hides the poverty causing it, and substitutes as its cause moral or cultural or genetic failures.

"THE UNDERCLASS" AS CODE WORD

The term "underclass" has developed an attention-getting power that constitutes its first danger. The word has a technical aura that enables it to serve as a euphemism or code word to be used for labeling. Users of the label can thus hide their disapproval of the poor behind an impressively academic term. "Underclass" has also become morally ambiguous, and as it is often left undefined, people can understand it in any way they choose, including as a label.

Because "underclass" is a code word that places some of the poor *under* society and implies that they are not or should not be *in* society, users of the term can therefore favor excluding them from the rest of society without saying so. Once whites thought of slaves, "primitives," and wartime enemies as the inhuman "other," but placing some people under society may not be altogether different.

A subtler yet in some ways more insidious version of the exclusionary mechanism is the use of "underclass" as a synonym for the poor, deserving and undeserving. While not excluding anyone from society, it increases the social distance of the poor from everyone else. This distance is increased further by the contemporary tendency of elected officials and journalists to rename and upgrade the working class as the lower middle class—or even the middle class.

Because "underclass" is also used as a racial and even ethnic code word, it is a convenient device for hiding antiblack or anti-Latino feelings. As such a code word, "underclass" accommodates contemporary taboos against overt prejudice, not to mention hate speech. Such taboos sometimes paper over—and even repress—racial antagonisms that people do not want to express openly.

Ironically, the racial code word also hides the existence of very poor whites who suffer from many of the same problems as poor blacks. When used as a racial term, "underclass" blurs the extent to which the troubles of whites and blacks alike are generated by the economy and by classism or class discrimination and require class-based as well as race-based solutions.

Like other code words, "underclass" may interfere with public discussion. Disapproval of the actions of others is part of democracy, but code words make covert what needs to be overt in order for the disapproval to be questioned and debated. If openly critical terms such as "bums" and "pauper" were still in use, and if umbrella terms such as "underclass" were replaced with specific ones such as "beggars" or "welfare dependents," upset citizens could indicate clearly the faults of which they want to accuse poor people. In that case, public discussion might be able to deal more openly with the feelings the more fortunate classes hold about the poor, the actual facts about the poor, and the policy issues having to do with poverty and poverty-related behavior.

THE FLEXIBILITY OF THE LABEL

Terms and labels undergo broadening in order to adapt them for use in varying conditions. Broadening also makes labels flexible so that they can be used to stigmatize new populations, or accuse already targeted ones of new failures.

One source of harm to such populations is flexible *meaning,* which stems from the vagueness of a new word, the lack of an agreed-upon definition for it. Since Oscar Lewis once identified nearly sixty-five "traits" for his culture of poverty, there is apt precedent for the flexibility of the underclass label that replaced Lewis's term. Flexibility becomes more harmful when pejorative prefixes can be added to otherwise descriptively used terms; for example, a female welfare recipient can also be described as a member of a permanent underclass, which suggests that she is incapable of ever escaping welfare. An underclass of young people becomes considerably more threatening when it is called "feral," and even worse is the idea of a biological underclass, which implies a genetic and thus permanent inferiority of a group of people whom public policy can render harmless only by sterilizing, imprisoning, or killing them.

Another serious danger follows from the flexibility of *subjects:* the freedom of anyone with labeling power to add further populations to the underclass, and to do so without being accountable to anyone. The poor cannot, after all, afford to bring libel and slander suits. If tenants of public housing are also assigned to the underclass, they are even more stigmatized than when they are coming from "the projects." Illegal immigrants who are refugees from a country not favored by the State Department or the Immigration and Naturalization Service are more likely candidates for public harassment or deportation if their native-born neighbors decide that their behavior marks them as members of the underclass. That they may be doing work that no one else will do or collecting entitlements for which they have paid their share of taxes becomes irrelevant once they have been assigned the label.

THE REIFICATION OF THE LABEL

A further source of danger is the reification of the label, which takes place when a definition is awarded the gift of life and label users believe there to be an actually existing and homogeneous underclass that is composed of whatever poor people are currently defined as underclass. Reification, which turns a definition into an actual set of people, hides the reality that the underclass is an imagined group that has been constructed in the minds of its definers. Once a stigmatized label is reified, however, visible signs to identify it are sure to be demanded sooner or later, and then invented, so that people bearing the signs can be harassed more easily.

Furthermore, once the signs are in place so that imagined groups can be made actual, the labels run the danger of being treated as causal mechanisms. As a result, the better-off classes may decide that being in the underclass is a cause of becoming homeless or turning to street crime. Homelessness then becomes a symptom of underclass membership, with the additional danger of the hidden policy implication: that the elimination of the underclass would end homelessness, thereby avoiding the need for affordable housing or for jobs and income grants for the homeless.

Even purely descriptive terms referring to actual people, such as "welfare recipients," can be reified and turned into causal labels. People may thus persuade themselves to believe that being on welfare is a cause of poverty, or of single-parent families. Once so persuaded, they can propose to eliminate both effects by ending welfare, and without appearing to be inhumane—which is what conservative politicians running for office, and the intellectuals supporting them, have been doing since the early 1990s. They ignore the fact that in the real world the causal arrow goes in the other direction, but they achieve their political aim, even if they also harm poor mothers and their children.

Since popular causal thinking is almost always moral as well as empirical, the reification of a label like "the underclass" usually leads to the assignment of *moral* causality. If the underclass is the cause of behavior that deviates from mainstream norms, the solution is moral condemnation, behavioral modification, or punishment by the elimination of financial aid. Thus people are blamed who are more often than not victims instead of perpetrators, which ignores the empirical causes, say, of street crime, and interferes with the development of effective anticrime policy. Blaming people may allow blamers to feel better by blowing off the steam of righteous (and in the case of crime, perfectly justified) indignation, but even justified blaming does not constitute or lead to policy for ending street crime.

A scholarly form of reification can be carried out with labels that are also scientific terms, so that the former are confused with the latter and thus obtain the legitimacy that accompanies scientific concepts. Conversely, the moral opprobrium placed on the labeled allows social scientists either to incorporate overt biases in their concepts or to relax their detachment and in the process turn scientific concepts into little more than operationalized labels.

A case in point is the operational definition of "the underclass" by Erol Ricketts and Isabel Sawhill, which has been widely used by government, scholars, and in simplified form even by popular writers. The two social scientists argue that the underclass consists of four populations: "high school dropouts," "prime-age males not regularly attached to the labor force," welfare recipients, and "female heads." Ricketts and Sawhill identify these populations as manifesting "underclass behaviors," or "dysfunctional behaviors," which they believe to be "at variance with those of mainstream populations."

The two authors indicate that they can "remain agnostic about the fundamental causes of these behaviors." Nonetheless, they actually adopt an implicit moral causality, because in defining the underclass as "people whose behavior departs from (mainstream) norms" and remaining silent about causality, they imply that the behaviors result from the violations of these values.

Ricketts and Sawhill provide no evidence, however, that the four behaviors in question are actually the result of norm violation. More important, their operational definition does not consider other causal explanations of the same behavior. No doubt some poor young people drop out of school because they reject mainstream norms for education, but Ricketts and Sawhill omit those who drop out because they have to go to work to support their families, or because they feel that their future in the job market is nil, as well as the youngsters who are forced out by school administrators and who should be called "pushouts."

Likewise, in addition to the "prime-age males" Ricketts and Sawhill believe to be jobless because they do not want to work, some of these men reject being targeted for a career of dead-end jobs, and others, most in fact, are jobless because there are no jobs for them. Indeed, the irony of the Ricketts-Sawhill definition is that when an employer goes out of business, workers who may previously have been praised as working poor but now cannot find other jobs are then banished to the underclass.

Poor mothers go on welfare for a variety of reasons. Some are working mothers who need Medicaid for their children and cannot get health benefits from their employers. Female family heads are often single because jobless men make poor breadwinners, not because they question the desirability of mainstream marriage norms.

If I read the two authors correctly, they are conducting essentially normative analyses of the four types of underclass people they have defined, even if they may not have intended to be normative. Thus, the measures they have chosen to operationalize their definitions bear some resemblance to popular pejorative labels that condemn rather than understand behavior. Conversely, Ricketts and Sawhill do not appear to consider the possibility that the failure of the mainstream economy is what prevents people from achieving the norms they are setting for the poor.

As a result, the two authors make no provision for data that measure the failures of the mainstream economy, and they do not include—or operationalize—a good deal of other information. For example, they could count home, school, and neighborhood conditions that interfere with or discourage learning, and the economic conditions that cause the disappearance of jobs and frustrate the desire for work. In addition, they might obtain information on job availability for jobless prime-age males, as well as for women on welfare—just to mention some of the relevant data that are publicly available. Until they include such data, their definition and operationalization of "underclass" are scientific only because and to the extent that their counting procedures observe the rules of science.

A different approach to the indiscriminate mixing of science and labeling, and to the reification of stereotypes, emerged in some proposals in the late 1980s to measure underclass status by poor people's answers to attitude questions: on their willingness to plan ahead, for example. Such attitude data could be found in the widely used Panel Survey of Income Dynamics. This type of question assumes not only that people should plan ahead, but that their failure to do so reflects their unwillingness, rather than their inability, to plan ahead, which has been documented in many empirical studies. Nonetheless, people whose poverty prevented them from planning ahead and who answered honestly that they did not so plan, would have been assigned a stigmatizing label—merely on the basis of their response to superficial and general questions. Fortunately this approach to "measuring" the underclass appears not to have been used so far by anyone in an influential position.

A final reification is spatial, an approach in which behavioral labels are applied to census tracts to produce "underclass areas." Such areas derive from statistical artifacts invented by the U.S. Bureau of the Census. The bureau developed the concept of "extreme poverty areas" for those places in which at least 40 percent of the people were poor. While this is inaccurate enough—especially for the 60 percent not poor—Ricketts and Sawhill subsequently identified "underclass areas," in which the proportion of people exhibiting all four of their behavioral indicators for being in the underclass was "one standard deviation above the mean *for the country as a whole*." The two authors did not explain why they chose this measure, even though poverty is not dispersed through the country as a whole but is concentrated in the cities of the northeast, midwest, and south, the latter being also the location of the most severe rural poverty.

Most people lack the methodological skills of social scientists, and do not see the assumptions that underlie the approaches to underclass counting. Once word gets out that social scientists have identified some areas as underclass areas, however, these neighborhoods can easily be stigmatized, the population labeled accordingly and accused of whatever local meanings the term "underclass" may have acquired.

When areas become known as underclass areas, local governments and commercial enterprises obtain legitimation to withdraw or not provide facilities and services that could ameliorate the poverty of the area's inhabitants. Labeling areas as underclass can also encourage governments to choose them as locations for excess numbers of homeless shelters, drug treatment centers, and other facilities that serve the very poor and that are therefore rejected by other neighborhoods.

In fact, "underclass areas" is basically a current version of the old label "slum," which also treated indicators of poverty as behavioral failures. In the affluent economy of the post–World War II era, similar defining and subsequent counting activities were used to justify "slum clearance," and the displacement of poor people for subsidized housing for the affluent. And as in all labeling, the poor people who are labeled are left to fend for themselves.

THE DANGERS OF THE UMBRELLA EFFECT

Since "underclass" is an umbrella label that can include in its definition all the various behavioral and moral faults that label-makers and users choose to associate with it, two further dangers accrue to those it labels.

The sheer breadth of the umbrella label seems to attract alarmist writers who magnify the many kinds of moral and behavioral harmfulness attributed to people it names. A correlate of the umbrella effect is amnesia on the part of writers about the extreme and usually persistent poverty of the labeled. Thus, the more widely people believe in the validity of the underclass label, and the broader its umbrella becomes, the more likely it is that political conditions will not allow for reinstituting effective antipoverty policy. If the underclass is dangerous, and dangerous in so many different ways, it follows that the government's responsibility is to beef up the police, increase the punishments courts can demand, and create other punitive agencies that try to protect the rest of society from this dangerous class.

Umbrella labels also do harm when they lump into a single term a variety of diverse people with different problems. This ignores the reality that the people who are assigned the underclass label have in common only that their actual or imagined behaviors upset the mainstream population, or the politicians who claim to speak in its name. Using this single characteristic to classify people under one label can be disastrous, especially if politicians and voters should ever start talking about comprehensive "underclass policies," or what Christopher Jencks has called "meta solutions." For one thing, many of the people who are tagged with the label have not even deviated from mainstream norms, and yet others have done nothing illegal. An underclass policy would thus be a drastic violation of civil rights and civil liberties.

At this writing, electioneering politicians as well as angry voters still remain content with policies that harm the people who bear specific labels, such as welfare recipients, illegal immigrants, and the homeless. In the past, however, the makers of earlier umbrella labels have proposed extremely drastic policies. In 1912, Henry Goddard suggested dealing with the feebleminded by "unsexing . . . removing, from the male and female, the necessary organs for procreation." Realizing that there would be strong popular opposition both to castration and ovariectomies, he proposed instead that the next best solution was "segregation and colonization" of the feebleminded. A few decades earlier, Charles Booth had offered the same solution for an equivalent category of poor people, and not long before he was forced to resign as vice president of the United States in 1974, Spiro Agnew suggested that poor people accused of behavioral shortcomings should be rehoused in rural new towns built far away from existing cities and suburbs.

Even a thoughtful underclass policy would be dangerous, because the people forced under the underclass umbrella suffer from different kinds of poverty and, in some cases, poverty-related problems, which may require different solutions. Reducing poverty for able-bodied workers requires labor market policy change; reducing it for people who cannot work calls for a humane income grant program. Enabling and encouraging young people to stay in school requires different policies than the elimination of homelessness, and ending substance abuse or street crime demands yet others. Labelers or experts who claim one policy can do it all are simply wrong.

THE HUMAN DANGERS OF LABELING

Most immediately, the underclass label poses a danger for poor people in that the agencies with which they must deal can hurt clients who are so labeled. For one thing, agencies for the poor sometimes build labels into their operating procedures and apply them to all of their clients. As a result, either evidence about actual clients is not collected, or the label is assumed to fit regardless of evidence to the contrary. Agencies responsible for public safety typically resort to this procedure as a crime prevention or deterrence measure, especially when those labeled have little legal or political power. For example, in 1993, the Denver police department compiled a roster of suspected gang members based on "clothing choices," "flashing of gang signals," or associating with known gang members. The list included two-thirds of the city's young black men, of whom only a small percentage were actual gang members.

Labeling also creates direct punitive effects of several kinds. Bruce Link's studies of people labeled as mentally ill have found that the labeling act itself can lead to depression and demoralization, which prevent those labeled from being at their best in job interviews and other competitive situations. Likewise, when poor youngsters who hang out on street corners are treated as "loiterers," they may end up with an arrest record that hurts them in later life—which is probably why middle-class teenagers who also hang out are rarely accused of loitering.

Some effects of labels are felt even earlier in children's lives. Teachers treat students differently if they think they come from broken homes. A long-term study of working-class London has found that labeling effects may even be intergenerational. Labeling of parents as delinquent makes it more likely that their children will also be labeled, adding to the numbers in both generations who are accused of delinquent or criminal behavior.

Sometimes the effect of labeling is more indirect: agencies cut off opportunities and the label turns into a self-fulfilling prophecy. When teachers label low-income or very dark-skinned students as unable to learn, they may reduce their efforts to teach them—often unintentionally, but even so students then become less able to learn. If poor youngsters accused of loitering are assumed to have grown up without the self-control thought to be supplied by male supervision, they may be harassed—sometimes to tease and entrap them into an angry response. The arrests and arrest records that inevitably follow may deprive youngsters from fatherless families of legal job opportunities, and help force them into delinquent ones. In all these cases, the self-fulfilling prophecy is used to declare the labeled guilty without evidence of misconduct.

Another variation of the entrapment process takes place in jails. John Irwin's study of San Francisco courts and jails reports that these sometimes punished defendants whether they were guilty or not, and adds that "the experience of harsh and unfairly delivered punishment frequently enrages or embitters defendants and makes it easier for them to reject the values of those who have dealt with them in this way." In this instance, as in many of the other instances when the labels are applied by penal institutions, the labeled are not necessarily "passive innocents," as Hagan and Palloni put it. Instead, labeling sometimes generates reactions, both on the part of the police and of those they arrest, that push both sides over the edge.

The direct and indirect effects of labeling even hurt the poor in seeking help, because when they evoke labels in the minds of service suppliers they may be given inferior service, the wrong service, or none at all. Services for the labeled are normally underfunded to begin with and service suppliers are frequently overworked, so that the agencies from which the poor seek help must operate under more or less permanent triage conditions. One way of deciding who will be sacrificed in triage decisions is to assume that most clients cheat, use every contact with them to determine whether they are cheating, and exclude those who can be suspected of cheating. Since clients are of lower status than service suppliers and lack any power or influence over them, the suppliers can also vent their own status frustrations on clients. An arbitrary denial of services to clients not only relieves such frustrations but also enables suppliers to make the needed triage choices. For that reason alone, poor clients who object to being mistreated are usually the first to be declared ineligible for help.

Labeling clients as cheaters encourages service suppliers to distrust them, and that distrust is increased if the suppliers fear revenge, particularly violent revenge, from these clients. Consequently, suppliers hug the rules more tightly, making no leeway in individual cases, and even punishing colleagues who bend the rules in trying to help clients. When clients, who presumably come with prejudices of their own about agency staffs, develop distrust of the staff, a spiraling effect of mutual distrust and fear is set up. This creates data to justify labeling on both sides. The mutual distrust also encourages the exchange of violence, or the preemptive strikes of staff members who fear violence from angry clients.

Admittedly, labeling of clients is only a small part of staff-client misunderstandings and client mistreatment. The previously noted lack of funds and staff, the stresses of operating in stigmatized agencies and with stigmatized clients, normal bureaucratic rules that always put the demands of the agency and its staff ahead of the needs of clients, as well as differences of class and race between staff and clients, wreak their own cumulative havoc.

The added role of labeling in reducing services is particularly serious for poor people who live at the edge of homelessness or starvation or ill health. Yet another cause for the reduction or ending of already minimal services may push them over the edge, into the streets or an emergency clinic, into chronic illness or permanent disability, or into street crime.

Nevertheless, agencies sometimes actively discourage labeled people from escaping their stigmatized status. Liebow reports a dramatic but typical incident from a women's shelter: two women were trying to escape homelessness by taking second jobs, which they were forced to give up in order to attend obligatory but aimless night meetings so as to retain their beds in the shelter. In unlabeled populations, taking second jobs would have been rewarded as upward mobility; among labeled ones it is identified as evasion of agency rules or flouting of service supplier authority, as well as evidence of the client troublemaking that is often associated with the label.

Consequently, one major ingredient in successful efforts to help the labeled poor is to remove the label. For example, scattered site housing studies suggest that such housing is successful in changing the lives of the rehoused when their origins and backgrounds are kept from their new neighbors, so that these cannot react to pejorative labels about slum dwellers.

The labels that have produced these effects are not created solely from overheated mainstream fears or imaginations. Like all stereotypes, such labels are built around a small core of truth, or apply "to a few bad apples," as lay psychology puts it. Labeling, however, punishes not only the bad apples but everybody in the population to whom the label is applied. By labeling poor young black males as potential street criminals, for example, the white and black populations fearful of being attacked may feel that they protect themselves, but at the cost of hurting and antagonizing the large majority of poor young black males who are innocent. Inevitably, however, a proportion of the innocent will react angrily to the label, and find ways of getting even with those who have labeled them. In the end, then, everyone loses, the label users as well as the labeled.

Nonetheless, labeling is only a by-product of a larger structural process that cannot be ignored. In any population that lacks enough legitimate opportunities, illegitimate ones will be created and someone will take them. When the jobs for which the poor are eligible pay such a low wage that even some of the employed will turn to drug selling or other crime to increase their incomes, the labeling process is set in motion that finally hurts many more people, poor and nonpoor, whether or not they are guilty or innocent. Still, the real guilt has to be laid at the door of the employers that pay insufficient wages and the market conditions that may give some of them little other choice.

THE INACCURACIES OF LABELS

Last but not least, labels are dangerous simply because they are inaccurate. "Underclass" is inaccurate if interpreted literally, because there can be no class that exists *under* society, as the class hierarchy extends from the top of society to its very bottom. Indeed, "underclass" is like "underworld," which is also part of society, and in fact could not long exist if it were not supplying demanded goods or services to an "overworld."

"Underclass" is also an inaccurate label because it so vague that there is no agreement on a single or simple definition. Several other labels, however, which have evolved from descriptive terms about which there is widespread consensus, offer good illustrations of how much the portraits of the labeled vary from data on actual people.

"Welfare dependent," "single-parent family," "teenage mother," and "the homeless" are relevant examples. "Welfare dependent" is a corruption of "welfare recipient," which assumes that recipients become dependent on the government by virtue of obtaining welfare. In fact, however, only 30 percent of all recipients who begin a period on welfare will stay on for more than two years, and only 7 percent will be on more than eight years, although some of those who leave it also return to it later. Further, about 20 percent of all welfare recipients report non-AFDC income, although if off-the-books employment is counted, nearly half of all recipients are working.

Some recipients would leave welfare and take their chances in the labor market if they could obtain medical insurance for their children. Still, many poor women clearly rely on AFDC and are thus dependent on the government program; what is noted less often is that often they are even more dependent on staying in the good graces of their welfare agency, which can decide to cut them off arbitrarily without a great deal of accountability.

Ironically enough, only welfare recipients are accused of being dependents; others who are subsidized by government without adding something to the economy in exchange for their subsidy are not so labeled. Students with government fellowships, home owners who receive federal tax and mortgage interest deductions, corporations that receive subsidies to stay in existence, as well as unproductive civil servants and the workers on superfluous military bases kept open to prevent the elimination of jobs, are not thought of as being dependent. Thus the economic dependency of welfare recipients is not the real issue, and the label is misnamed as well as partly inaccurate.

"Single-parent family," or at least the label, is also partly or wholly incorrect. For one thing, some families have a man in or near the household de facto if not de jure; more are embedded in an extended family in which mothers, grandmothers, and others share the parenting.

The notion that the children of such families are subject to undue school leaving, joblessness, and poverty, as well as crime and various pathologies, because they did not grow up in two-parent households is similarly incorrect. Since the modern family is not an economically productive institution, single-parenthood per se cannot logically cause poverty in the next generation, any more than growing up in a two-parent family can cause affluence. This helps to explain why well-off single parents are rarely accused of raising children who will grow up with economic or other problems. And since single-parent households are almost always poorer than other poor households, at least when their economic condition is measured properly, whatever economic effects children from such households suffer can be traced to their more extreme poverty or greater economic insecurity.

In addition, while the children of happy two-parent families are best off, all other things being equal, the children of single parents are sometimes emotionally and otherwise better off than the children of two parents who are in constant conflict. If parental conflict is more detrimental to children's well-being and performance than is single parenthood, it would explain the results of studies concluding that children of divorced parents are not uniformly worse off than those from intact families. Since the scarcity of money is a major cause of conflict—and spouse battering—among poor parents, this also helps to explain further the unwillingness of pregnant young women to marry their partners if they are jobless. None of this argues that poor single-parent families are desirable and should be encouraged, because if there is only one parent, the economic and other burdens on her and the children are often too great, and all may suffer. But the single-parent family structure and the burdens that come with it are usually the result of poverty.

The same conclusions apply to teenage pregnancy. Unmarried adolescents who bear children constitute about half of all adolescent mothers and 8 percent of all welfare recipients, although some adult welfare recipients also became mothers in adolescence. The younger among them may be reacting to school failures as well as family conflict, which can increase the urgency of the normal desire to feel useful to and loved by someone. More to the economic point, many scholars, beginning with Frank Furstenberg, Jr., have pointed out that the babies of such mothers will be in school when their occupational chances are better.

These observations are no argument for adolescent motherhood, especially since many of the babies are actually unwanted at time of conception, and may even be the product of a young woman's defeat by her sexual partner in a power struggle over wearing a condom, or over having sex at all. Unwanted fetuses, however, seem to turn into wanted babies, partly because of lack of access to abortion facilities but perhaps also because low-income families have traditionally welcomed new arrivals. Given the limited chances for upward mobility among the poor, additional babies do not represent the same obstacle to higher status that they sometimes do among the more affluent classes.

There is not even reliable evidence that poor women in their twenties are automatically better mothers than poor girls in their teens, especially if the teenagers have already been responsible for taking care of their younger siblings. Older mothers are probably more mature, but if adolescent mothers receive more help from their mothers and grandmothers than they would if they were older, then adolescence may sometimes be an advantage. It could also be an advantage on health grounds, if the hypothesis that poor mothers are healthier as teenagers than as adults turns out to be supported by sufficient evidence. Conversely, today's poor teenagers are in the unfortunate position of becoming mothers when America's culturally dominant female role models—upper-middle-class professional women—postpone motherhood as long as possible in order to put their careers on a secure footing. Thus what may be rational behavior for poor young women is decidedly irrational according to cultural norms these days. Teenage motherhood does not thereby become desirable, but once more, the fundamental problem is the poverty that helps to make it happen.

Finally, even the homeless label can be incorrect. For one thing, label users tend to combine panhandlers with the homeless, even though the former are frequently housed. Furthermore, homeless populations differ from community to community depending on the nature of the low-income labor and housing markets, and particularly of housing vacancy rates for poor nonwhites in these communities. Even the rates of mental illness and substance abuse vary.

More important, since the mentally ill and addicted homeless were poor to begin with, curing them would not by itself significantly increase their ability to find affordable housing, or jobs that would enable them to afford such housing. Most lack occupational skills and skin colors that are needed on the job market these days, the obvious virtues of mental health and freedom from addiction notwithstanding. Jencks argues that money spent on substance abuse could be used instead for shelter, but in most communities, it is both easier and cheaper to get hard drugs and alcohol than low-income housing. It is not yet even known how many homeless people turned to alcohol or drugs because of economic problems or familial ones—or just lack of family—and then became homeless, and how many became homeless first and addicts subsequently.

While dealing with mental illness and addiction are vital, homelessness is a disease of the housing market, just as being on welfare is a disease of the job market. The mentally ill and the addicted are the most vulnerable to both of these economic diseases, but as long as there are not enough dwelling units and jobs for the poor, someone will have to be homeless and on welfare. Whether intentionally or not, the most vulnerable are almost always "selected" for most deprivations, among other reasons because they are the least able to protest or to defend themselves.

Labels, whether applied to welfare recipients, the homeless, and other poor people, cannot ever describe the labeled, because labels mainly describe their imagined behavioral and moral deviations from an assumed mainstream. Justified or not, labels express the discontents of the mainstream and those speaking for it, not the characteristics and conditions of the labeled themselves. When label users are discontented and seek people on whom they can project their frustrations, the accuracy of the resultant labels is not a major consideration. In fact, accuracy may get in the way if frustrated people want to be enraged by poor people and thus able to blame them.

Ultimately, however, even accurate labels for the poor are dangerous because the labels cannot end poverty or the criminal and offending poverty-related behavior of some of the poor, or the fear, anger, and unhappiness of the labelers. In the long run, these latter may be the most dangerous effects of labels.

CHAPTER 30

So How Did I Get Here?

Growing Up on Welfare

ROSEMARY L. BRAY

Growing up on welfare was a story I had planned to tell a long time from now, when I had children of my own. My childhood on Aid to Families with Dependent Children (A.F.D.C.) was going to be one of those stories I would tell my kids about the bad old days, an urban legend equivalent to Abe Lincoln studying by firelight. But I know now I cannot wait, because in spite of a wealth of evidence about the true nature of welfare and poverty in America, the debate has turned ugly, vicious and racist. The "welfare question" has become the race question and the woman question in disguise, and so far the answers bode well for no one.

In both blunt and coded terms, comfortable Americans more and more often bemoan the waste of their tax money on lazy black women with a love of copulation, a horror of birth control and a lack of interest in marriage. Were it not for the experiences of half my life, were I not black and female and of a certain age, perhaps I would be like so many people who blindly accept the lies and distortions, half-truths and wrongheaded notions about welfare. But for better or worse, I do know better. I know more than I want to know about being poor. I know that the welfare system is designed to be inadequate, to leave its constituents on the edge of survival. I know because I've been there.

And finally, I know that perhaps even more dependent on welfare than its recipients are the large number of Americans who would rather accept this patchwork of economic horrors than fully address the real needs of real people.

My mother came to Chicago in 1947 with a fourth-grade education, cut short by working in the Mississippi fields. She pressed shirts in a laundry for a while and later waited tables in a restaurant, where she met my father. Mercurial and independent, with a sixth-grade education, my Arkansas-born father worked at whatever came to hand. He owned a lunch wagon for a time and prepared food for hours in our kitchen on the nights before he took the wagon out. Sometimes he hauled junk and sold it in the open-air markets of Maxwell Street on Sunday mornings. Eight years after they met—seven years after they married—I was born. My father made her quit her job; her work, he told her, was taking care of me. By the time I was 4, I had a sister, a brother and another brother on the way. My parents, like most other American couples of the 1950's, had their own American dream—a husband who worked, a wife who stayed home, a family of smiling children. But as was true for so many African-American couples, their American dream was an illusion.

The house on the corner of Berkeley Avenue and 45th Street is long gone. The other houses still stand, but today the neighborhood is an emptier, bleaker place. When we moved there, it was a street of old limestones with beveled glass windows, all falling into vague disrepair. Home was a four-room apartment on the first floor, in what must have been the public rooms of a formerly grand house. The rent was $110 a month. All of us kids slept in the big front room. Because I was the oldest, I had a bed of my own, near a big plate-glass window.

My mother and father had been married for several years before she realized he was a gambler who would never stay away from the track. By the time we moved to Berkeley Avenue, Daddy was spending more time gambling, and bringing home less and less money and more and more anger. Mama's simplest requests were met with rage. They fought once for hours when she asked for money to buy a tube of lipstick. It didn't help that I always seemed to need a doctor. I had allergies and bronchitis so severe that I nearly died one Sunday after church when I was about 3.

It was around this time that my mother decided to sign up for A.F.D.C. She explained to the caseworker that Daddy wasn't home much, and when he was he didn't have any money. Daddy was furious; Mama was adamant. "There were times when we hardly had a loaf of bread in here," she told me years later. "It was close. I wasn't going to let you all go hungry."

Going on welfare closed a door between my parents that never reopened. She joined the ranks of unskilled women who were forced to turn to the state for the security their men could not provide. In the sterile relationship between herself and the State of Illinois, Mama found an autonomy denied her by my father. It was she who could decide, at last, some part of her own fate and ours. A.F.D.C. relegated marginally productive men like my father to the ranks of failed patriarchs who no longer controlled the destiny of their families. Like so many of his peers, he could no longer afford the luxury of a woman who did as she was told because her economic life depended on it. Daddy became one of the shadow men who walked out back doors as caseworkers came in through the front. Why did he acquiesce? For all his anger, for all his frightening brutality, he loved us, so much that he swallowed his pride and periodically ceased to exist so that we might survive.

In 1960, the year my mother went on public aid, the poverty threshold for a family of five in the United States was $3,560 and the monthly payment to a family of five from the State of Illinois was $182.56, a total of $2,190.72 a year. Once the $110 rent was paid, Mama was left with $72.56 a month to take care of all the other expenses. By any standard, we were poor. All our lives were proscribed by the narrow line between not quite and just enough.

What did it take to live?

It took the kindness of friends as well as strangers, the charity of churches, low expectations, deprivation and patience. I can't begin to count the hours spent in long lines, long waits, long walks in pursuit of basic things. A visit to a local clinic (one housing doctors, a dentist and pharmacy in an incredibly crowded series of rooms) invariably took the better part of a day; I never saw the same doctor twice.

It took, as well, a turning of our collective backs on the letter of a law that required reporting even a small and important miracle like a present of $5. All families have their secrets, but I remember the weight of an extra burden. In a world where caseworkers were empowered to probe into every nook and cranny of our lives, silence became defense. Even now, there are things I will not publicly discuss because I cannot shake the fear that we might be hounded by the state, eager to prosecute us for the crime of survival.

All my memories of our years on A.F.D.C. are seasoned with unease. It's painful to remember how much every penny counted, how even a gap of 25 cents could make a difference in any given week. Few people understand how precarious life is from welfare check to welfare check, how the word "extra" has no meaning. Late mail, a bureaucratic mix-up . . . and a carefully planned method of survival lies in tatters.

What made our lives work as well as they did was my mother's genius at making do—worn into her by a childhood of rural poverty—along with her vivid imagination. She worked at home endlessly, shopped ruthlessly, bargained, cajoled, charmed. Her food store of choice was the one that stocked pork and beans, creamed corn, sardines, Vienna sausages and potted meat all at 10 cents a can. Clothing was the stuff of rummage sales, trips to Goodwill and bargain basements, where thin cotton and polyester reigned supreme. Our shoes came from a discount store that sold two pairs for $5.

It was an uphill climb, but there was no time for reflection; we were too busy with our everyday lives. Yet I remember how much it pained me to know that Mama, who recruited a neighbor to help her teach me how to read when I was 3, found herself left behind by her eldest daughter, then by each of us in turn. Her biggest worry was that we would grow up uneducated, so Mama enrolled us in parochial school.

When one caseworker angrily questioned how she could afford to send four children to St. Ambrose School, my mother, who emphatically declared "My kids need an education," told her it was none of her business. (In fact, the school had a volume discount of sorts; the price of tuition dropped with each child you sent. I still don't know quite how she managed it.) She organized our lives around church and school, including Mass every morning at 7:45. My brother was an altar boy; I laid out the vestments each afternoon for the next day's Mass. She volunteered as a chaperone for every class trip, sat with us as we did homework she did not understand herself. She and my father reminded us again and again and again that every book, every test, every page of homework was in fact a ticket out and away from the life we lived.

My life on welfare ended on June 4, 1976—a month after my 21st birthday, two weeks after I graduated from Yale. My father, eaten up with cancer and rage, lived just long enough to know the oldest two of us had graduated from college and were on our own. Before the decade ended, all of us had left the welfare rolls. The eldest of my brothers worked at the post office, assumed support of my mother (who also went to work, as a companion to an elderly woman) and earned his master's degree at night. My sister married and got a job at a bank. My baby brother parked cars and found a wife. Mama's biggest job was done at last; the investment made in our lives by the State of Illinois had come to fruition. Five people on welfare for 18 years had become five working, taxpaying adults. Three of us went to college, two of us finished; one of us has an advanced degree; all of us can take care of ourselves.

Ours was a best-case phenomenon, based on the synergy of church and state, the government and the private sector and the thousand points of light that we called friends and neighbors. But there was something more: What fueled our dreams and fired our belief that our lives could change for the better was the promise of the civil rights movement and the war on poverty—for millions of African-Americans the defining events of the 1960's. Caught up in the heady atmosphere of imminent change, our world was filled not only with issues and ideas but with amazing images of black people engaged in the struggle for long-denied rights and freedoms. We knew other people lived differently than we did, we knew we didn't have much, but we didn't mind, because we knew it wouldn't be long. My mother borrowed a phrase I had read to her once from Dick Gregory's autobiography: Not poor, just broke. She would repeat it often, as often as she sang hymns in the kitchen. She loved to sing a spiritual Mahalia Jackson had made famous: "Move On Up a Little Higher." Like so many others, Mama was singing about earth as well as heaven.

These are the things I remember every time I read another article outlining America's welfare crisis. The rage I feel about the welfare debate comes from listening to a host of lies, distortions and exaggerations—and taking them personally.

I am no fool. I know of few women—on welfare or off— with my mother's grace and courage and stamina. I know not all women on welfare are cut from the same cloth. Some are lazy; some are ground down. Some are too young; many are without husbands. A few have made welfare fraud a lucrative career; a great many more have pushed the rules on outside income to their very limits.

I also know that none of these things justify our making welfare a test of character and worthiness, rather than an acknowledgment of need. Near-sainthood should not be a requirement for financial and medical assistance.

But all manner of sociologists and policy gurus continue to equate issues that simply aren't equivalent—welfare, race, rates of poverty, crime, marriage and childbirth—and to reach conclusions that serve to demonize the poor. More than one social arbiter would have us believe that we have all been mistaken for the last 30 years—that the efforts to relieve the most severe effects of poverty have not only failed but have served instead to increase and expand the ranks of the poor. In keeping women, children and men from starvation, we are told, we have also kept them from self-sufficiency. In our zeal to do good, we have undermined the work ethic, the family and thus, by association, the country itself.

So how did I get here?

Despite attempts to misconstrue and discredit the social programs and policies that changed—even saved—my life, certain facts remain. Poverty was reduced by 39 percent between 1960 and 1990, according to the Census Bureau, from 22.2 percent to 13.5 percent of the nation's population. That is far too many poor people, but the rate is considerably lower than it might have been if we had thrown up our hands and reminded ourselves that the poor will always be with us. Of black women considered "highly dependent," that is, on welfare for more than seven years, 81 percent of their daughters grow up to live productive lives off the welfare rolls, a 1992 Congressional report stated; the 19 percent who become second-generation welfare recipients can hardly be said to constitute an epidemic of welfare dependency. The vast majority of African-Americans are now working or middle class, an achievement that occurred in the past 30 years, most specifically between 1960 and 1973, the years of expansion in the very same social programs that it is so popular now to savage. Those were the same years in which I changed from girl to woman, learned to read and think, graduated from high school and college, came to be a working woman, a taxpayer, a citizen.

In spite of all the successes we know of, in spite of the reality that the typical welfare recipient is a white woman with young children, ideologues have continued to fashion from whole cloth the specter of the mythical black welfare mother, complete with a prodigious reproductive capacity and a galling laziness, accompanied by the uncaring and equally lazy black man in her life who will not work, will not marry her and will not support his family.

Why has this myth been promoted by some of the best (and the worst) people in government, academia, journalism and industry? One explanation may be that the constant presence of poverty frustrates even the best-intentioned among us. It may also be because the myth allows for denial about who the poor in America really are and for denial about the depth and intransigence of racism regardless of economic status. And because getting tough on welfare is for some a first-class career move; what better way to win a position in the next administration than to trash those people least able to respond? And, finally, because it serves to assure white Americans that lazy black people aren't getting away with anything.

Many of these prescriptions for saving America from the welfare plague not only reflect an insistent, if sometimes unconscious, racism but rest on the bedrock of patriarchy. They are rooted in the fantasy of a male presence as a path to social and economic salvation and in its corollary—the image of woman as passive chattel, constitutionally so afflicted by her condition that the only recourse is to transfer her care from the hands of the state to the hands of a man with a job. The largely ineffectual plans to create jobs for men in communities ravaged by disinvestment, the state-sponsored dragnets for men who cannot or will not support their children, the exhortations for women on welfare to find themselves a man and get married, all are the institutional expressions of the same worn cultural illusion—that women and children without a man are fundamentally damaged goods. Men are such a boon, the reasoning goes, because they make more money than women do.

Were we truly serious about an end to poverty among women and children, we would take the logical next step. We would figure out how to make sure women who did a dollar's worth of work got a dollar's worth of pay. We would make sure that women could go to work with their minds at ease, knowing their children were well cared for. What women on welfare need, in large measure, are the things key to the life of every adult woman: economic security and autonomy. Women need the skills and the legitimate opportunity to earn a living for ourselves as well as for people who may rely on us; we need the freedom to make choices to improve our own lives and the lives of those dear to us.

"The real problem is not welfare," says Kathryn Edin, a professor of sociology at Rutgers University and a scholar in residence at the Russell Sage Foundation. "The real problem is the nature of low-wage work and lack of support for these workers—most of whom happen to be women raising their children alone."

Completing a five-year study of single mothers—some low-wage workers, some welfare recipients—Edin is quantifying what common sense and bitter experience have told millions of women who rotate off and on the welfare rolls: Women, particularly unskilled women with children, get the worst jobs available, with the least amount of health care, and are the most frequently laid off. "The workplace is not oriented toward people who have family responsibilities," she says. "Most jobs are set up assuming that someone else is minding the kids and doesn't need assistance."

But the writers and scholars and politicians who wax most rhapsodic about the need to replace welfare with work make their harsh judgments from the comfortable and supportive environs of offices and libraries and think tanks. If they need to go to the bathroom midsentence, there is no one timing their absence. If they take longer than a half-hour for lunch, there is no one waiting to dock their pay. If their baby sitter gets sick, there is no risk of someone having taken their place at work by the next morning. Yet these are conditions that low-wage women routinely face, which inevitably lead to the cyclical nature of their welfare histories. These are the realities that many of the most vocal and widely quoted critics of welfare routinely ignore. In his book "The End of Equality," for example, Mickey Kaus discusses social and economic inequity, referring to David Ellwood's study on long-term welfare dependency without ever mentioning that it counts anyone who uses the services for at least one month as having been on welfare for the entire year.

In the heated atmosphere of the welfare debate, the larger society is encouraged to believe that women on welfare have so violated the social contract that they have forfeited all rights common to those of us lucky enough not to be poor. In no area is this attitude more clearly demonstrated than in issues of sexuality and childbearing. Consider the following: A Philadelphia Inquirer editorial of Dec. 12, 1990, urges the use of Norplant contraceptive inserts for welfare recipients—in spite of repeated warnings from women's health groups of its dangerous side effects—in the belief that the drug "could be invaluable in breaking the cycle of inner-city poverty." (The newspaper apologized for the editorial after it met widespread criticism, both within and outside the paper.) A California judge orders a woman on welfare, convicted of abusing two of her four children, to use Norplant; the judge's decision was appealed. The Washington state legislature considers approving cash payments of up to $10,000 for women on welfare who agree to be sterilized. These and other proposals, all centering on women's reproductive capacities, were advanced in spite of evidence that welfare recipients have fewer children than those not on welfare.

The punitive energy behind these and so many other Draconian actions and proposals goes beyond the desire to decrease welfare costs; it cuts to the heart of the nation's racial and sexual hysteria. Generated neither by law nor by fully informed public debate, these actions amount to social control over "those people on welfare"—a control many Americans feel they have bought and paid for every April 15. The question is obvious: If citizens were really aware of who receives welfare in America, however inadequate it is, if they acknowledged that white women and children were welfare's primary beneficiaries, would most of these things be happening?

Welfare has become a code word now. One that enables white Americans to mask their sometimes malignant, sometimes benign racism behind false concerns about the suffering ghetto poor and their negative impact on the rest of us. It has become the vehicle many so-called tough thinkers use to undermine compassionate policy and engineer the reduction of social programs.

So how *did* I get here?

I kept my drawers up and my dress down, to quote my mother. I didn't end up pregnant because I had better things to do. I knew I did because my uneducated, Southern-born parents told me so. Their faith, their focus on our futures are a far cry from the thesis of Nicholas Lemann, whose widely acclaimed book *The Promised Land* perpetuates the myth of black Southern sharecropping society as a primary source of black urban malaise. Most important, my family and I had every reason to believe that I had better things to do and that when I got older I would be able to do them. I had a mission, a calling, work to do that only I could do. And that is knowledge transmitted not just by parents, or school, or churches. It is a palpable thing, available by osmosis from the culture of the neighborhood and the world at large.

Add to this formula a whopping dose of dumb luck. It was my sixth-grade teacher, Sister Maria Sarto, who identified in me the first signs of a stifling boredom and told my mother that I needed a tougher, more challenging curriculum than her school could provide. It was she who then tracked down the private Francis W. Parker School, which agreed to give me a scholarship if I passed the admissions test.

Had I been born a few years earlier, or a decade later, I might now be living on welfare in the Robert Taylor Homes or working as a hospital nurse's aide for $6.67 an hour. People who think such things could never have happened to me haven't met enough poor people to know better. The avenue of escape can be very narrow indeed. The hope and energy of the 1960's—fueled not only by a growing economy but by all the passions of a great national quest—is long gone. The sense of possibility I knew has been replaced with the popular cultural currency that money and those who have it are everything and those without are nothing.

Much has been made of the culture of the underclass, the culture of poverty, as though they were the free-floating illnesses of the African-American poor, rendering them immune to other influences: the widespread American culture of greed, for example, or of cynicism. It is a thinly veiled continuation of the endless projection of "dis-ease" onto black life, a convenient way to sidestep a more painful debate about the loss of meaning in American life that has made our entire nation depressed and dispirited. The malaise that has overtaken our country is hardly confined to African-Americans or the poor, and if both groups should disappear tomorrow, our nation would still find itself in crisis. To talk of the black "underclass threat" to the public sphere, as Mickey Kaus does, to demonize the poor among us and thus by association all of us—ultimately this does more damage to the body politic than a dozen welfare queens.

When I walk down the streets of my Harlem neighborhood, I see women like my mother, hustling, struggling, walking their children to school and walking them back home. And I also see women who have lost both energy and faith, talking loud, hanging out. I see the shadow men of a new generation, floating by with a few dollars and a toy, then drifting away to the shelters they call home. And I see, a dozen times a day, the little girls my sister and I used to be, the little boys my brothers once were.

Even the grudging, inadequate public help I once had is fading fast for them. The time and patience they will need to re-create themselves is vanishing under pressure for the big, quick fix and the crushing load of blame being heaped upon them. In the big cities and the small towns of America, we have let theory, ideology and mythology about welfare and poverty overtake these children and their parents.

PART NINE

Health and Medical Care

The social stratification of health and illness is one of the most devastating inequalities in American society. Despite our enormous wealth and technological potential, the United States still lags behind most other advanced industrial societies on many measures of health and access to health care. Americans have lower life expectancies and higher rates of infant death than citizens of many other developed countries; and some groups—including the urban and rural poor—still suffer shockingly high levels of preventable diseases and inadequate health care services. These problems are hardly new ones. In 1967, a National Advisory Commission on Health Manpower noted that the health statistics of the American poor "occasionally resemble the health statistics of a developing country."[1] Unfortunately, despite several decades of economic growth and stunning advances in medical technology, the same statement could still be made.

To be sure, for those who can afford it, the United States offers some of the best medical care in the world. Yet most Americans are less fortunate. One of the most striking differences between the United States and almost every other advanced society is our lack of any comprehensive system of national health insurance that makes adequate health care available to all citizens as a matter of right. Almost 42 million Americans—about 17 percent of the population—had no health insurance coverage at all during 2003. A recent study estimates that a much larger number—almost one out of three non-elderly Americans—go without health insurance at some point over the course of two years.[2] The proportions are even higher among some groups—notably the young, minorities, and the working poor. Many studies have shown that providing health insurance for everyone would not be hugely expensive, measured against the more than $1 trillion the United States now spends on health care. But we have not moved to make health care for all a reality, and in some respects have gone backwards in recent years, as health care "reforms" have led to ever more intensive efforts to cut costs and as pinched budgets have decimated the ability of states and counties to supply adequate care.

The human impact of the lack of accessible health care for all is compellingly illustrated in Susan Starr Sered and Rushika Fernandopulle's article on the health troubles of the uninsured. Health insurance, the authors point out, was once part of the package of benefits American workers could expect from their employers, like generous retirement plans. But as fewer and fewer jobs now provide insurance, increasing numbers of workers are left to fend with health problems without support. The result is a downward spiral in which workers who can't afford health care are forced to put off getting needed medical attention, which makes them sicker, which in turn makes them less able to get the kinds of jobs that could provide them with reliable health care—and the cycle continues, at great cost not only to the uninsured themselves but, ultimately, to the economy as a whole.

Why don't we have a system that provides health care to everyone? One reason is the American mistrust of government we've encountered already. We have, accordingly, left it up to the "market" to provide even the most basic care, except for the elderly and for those poor enough to be on welfare, whose medical care is partly subsidized by government. But our extreme reliance on the private market to deliver medical care sets us apart from virtually every other advanced society—including our northern neighbor, Canada. Many people have argued that Canada's much-praised universal health care system should be a model for the United States; others criticize it as a cumbersome example of heavy-handed government control. As the selection here by Pat Armstrong and Hugh Armstrong makes clear, Canada's system, while by no means perfect, isn't what some of its American opponents claim. It is not "socialized medicine": Most doctors work for themselves, not for the government, and Canadians can pick any doctor they choose. And it is *less* bureaucratic than the U.S. system, not more. Meanwhile, it has managed to keep Canadians' health costs relatively low compared with ours, while ensuring access to care for everyone. As a result, vast majorities of Canadians are deeply committed to their system, and wouldn't dream of replacing it with the one that prevails south of their border.

Our tendency to leave things to the mercies of the private "market" also extends to our treatment of the elderly. In "The Shame of Our Nursing Homes," Eric Bates describes in disturbing detail some of the realities of care for the nation's nursing home residents, who are subjects of what he calls "the nation's longest running experiment in privatization." Driven by the aim of maximizing their profits, many nursing home companies—part of a business worth over $87 billion a year in the late 1990s—have routinely skimped on patient care, with results that are often degrading and sometimes deadly. Why hasn't government moved more effectively to deal with these abuses—especially since the money that subsidizes the profits of these corporations comes from tax-supported programs like Medicaid and Medicare? In part, Bates suggests, because of the troubling political issue we examined in Part One: the nursing home companies have been big financial contributors to elected officials.

The final article, "Cater to the Children," charting the troubling history of the lead industry's effort to mislead the public about the dangers of lead paint, illustrates another way in which the pursuit of private gain can have devastating and enduring consequences for the health of Americans. As the authors point out, it is well known that lead is extremely dangerous, especially to children, and that exposure to lead paint has resulted in a public health disaster of tragic proportions. What is less well known is that the lead industry knew about the dangers of lead paint for decades, but promoted it anyway—using the image of fresh-faced children to sell its product and even going so far as to try to convince parents and others that lead paint was good for you. This history shows, in especially stark terms, how what may appear at first to be simply a medical problem turns out, on closer inspection, to be another example of the deleterious consequences of ignoring the public welfare in the interest of private profit.

ENDNOTES

1. Report of the National Advisory Commission on Health Manpower, quoted in R. M. Titmuss, "Ethics and Economics of Medical Care," in *Commitment to Welfare* (New York: Pantheon, 1968), p. 268.

2. Vicki Kemper, "Study finds more lack health insurance," *Los Angeles Times*, March 5, 2003.

CHAPTER 31

Sick Out of Luck

The Uninsured in America

SUSAN STARR SERED

RUSHIKA FERNANDOPULLE

Francine is one tough lady. She has spent her life doing hard physical labor—what she calls "men's work"—in the tobacco fields and factories of the Mississippi Delta. Today, she is one of the lucky ones: The factory she works in has not yet moved to Mexico or Indonesia, so she still has health coverage. Her sister, Carlene, on the other hand, is not so fortunate. Carlene works as a home healthcare aide, taking care of old people. Like many other African-American women in the region, and indeed many people all around the country whose work has moved from manufacturing to the service sector, Carlene cannot find a job that provides health insurance.

Carlene has multiple health problems, including a ferocious, persistent cough. Speaking on her diffident sister's behalf, Francine declares, "There should be a doctor somewhere so when you got no money, you can go to the doctor. There is no free clinic around here."

"So, what happens to uninsured people around here who don't have any money when they need to go to the doctor?" we ask her.

"They are shit out of luck."

During 2002–2003 we traveled to Texas, Mississippi, Idaho, Illinois, and Massachusetts, holding wide-ranging interviews with more than 120 uninsured Americans and approximately three dozen physicians, medical administrators, and health policy officials. In the course of our travels we met Americans who have seen loved ones die because they did not have medical coverage, Americans who have declared bankruptcy or were forced to sell their homes to pay for medical care, and Americans stuck in dead-end jobs because their health is too poor to allow them the career mobility available to Americans of earlier generations.

Unlike the health-care systems in most other Western countries, the core of America's health care is increasingly for-profit, employment-based, private insurance. This system flourished during the post-World War II era, when millions of blue-collar workers held long-term union contracts that guaranteed health-care benefits, and white-collar workers could expect to remain with—and rise up the ladder of—companies in which they built their careers.

In recent years, the connection between employment and health care has unraveled. As the nature of employment has changed globally, fewer people are able to stay in the same job for many years. As a result, jobs no longer serve as stable platforms for health-care arrangements. More than half of uninsured men and women work full-time throughout the year, and most of the others work part-time or for part of the year. They simply work at jobs without health benefits.

DOWN AND OUT IN DANVILLE

"When we find ourselves unable to provide for ourselves, and we've always been independent, it adds an emotional burden. You're trapped in a cycle you hate. I never in my life thought I would need this kind of help."

(Fran, Illinois)

Danville, Illinois, is a small city in the heart of the Midwestern Rust Belt. Like residents of manufacturing cities all over the country, Danville's citizens have had to learn a new vocabulary that includes terms like "corporate restructuring," "globalization of industry," "NAFTA and the WTO," "temp agencies," "outsourcing and downsizing," and "dislocated workers." As corporations such as General Motors have laid off American workers and moved their operations overseas, Danville has lost the jobs that had sustained this blue-collar community for many years.

The economic sea change that hit Danville has left its residents stunned, unsure where to assign blame—to themselves or to economic forces beyond their control. In Fran's words, "I had big plans, but circumstances kind of stepped in there for me and changed my plans. And I haven't been able to completely overcome the mindset. I was married for 28 years. I got divorced on Wednesday, lost my $18-an-hour job on Friday."

Fran, a petite, red-haired woman, had worked for seven years as an inventory-control supervisor at a large manufacturing plant. With three shifts of employees working for her, she had a job in which she felt accomplished and successful. She was caught by surprise when a foreign corporation purchased the plant. Like many other employees, she fell victim to general restructuring of the plant and to the new owners bringing in their own people from outside [central] Illinois.

"I was really making good money. I was up to almost $30,000 a year. And I have always taken care of myself. Even when I was married, I always worked full-time. We never, never took charity in any form. We always took care of ourselves.

"When I lost my job, I had no idea that was coming, blindsided there, and I kind of stepped back and said, what am I going to do now? I was 42 years old. I wasn't 20 anymore. I thought I would go back to junior college to get a degree. I was pretty excited at starting over fresh.

"I had plans for when I got out of school, I was studying local area networks on PCs. I was doing hardware parts, because I'd always done software and accounting-type work. And I was going to start my own business. I had a couple of people who were willing to back me. I wanted to go to college in a serious way. I started working part-time, and I went to school full-time."

Until 1992, when she was laid off and divorced, Fran had always had health insurance and had gone to the doctor for regular checkups. After that, "I paid for COBRA [a federally mandated insurance program offered to people leaving their jobs; COBRA allows them to continue their health insurance coverage, but at their own expense] for a while, but it was too expensive. I had never been sick; I was a really healthy and active person. So I figured it was a small gamble to go without insurance for two years while I went to college. I was getting along just fine until the middle of my second year when I was getting ready to graduate. That is when I started getting sick. "

Thinking she had a hangnail on her finger, she went to a local physician who told her to soak it and squeeze it, and to come back in three or four weeks if it didn't heal. "You'll have to bring $200 in cash, because we don't do surgery without insurance," they told her. But Fran did not have insurance, she did not have the cash, and she did not return.

"By about April, it got to the point where I could hardly make it to school. I was just exhausted. I found out I had diabetes. I had no clue, had never been sick in any way, shape, or form before that. And that not only affected me physically, it affected me, depression, you know. It's a hard thing to deal with all of a sudden. I had several operations on my hand, and I was sick."

A resourceful woman, Fran took advantage of the free health-care options available in her community. Thus, several months after the hangnail incident, she went to the County Health Department for a free Pap smear. The nurse there told her to go right over to the Vermillion Area Health Center, a small, nonprofit, mostly volunteer-run, part-time clinic. Gangrene had set into her finger at the site of the small injury. The gangrene was symptomatic of osteomyelitis (a deep infection of the bone) resulting from undiagnosed and untreated diabetes.

From a medical standpoint, Fran learned that for this sort of severe complication to set in—neuropathy and circulatory problems—she most probably had been diabetic for more than two years before it was diagnosed. Without standard medical screenings, the kind she had received regularly before the layoff, the disease progressed silently in her body. Fran also learned that if her diabetes is not controlled, she could end up blind, with an amputated leg, and with kidney failure, all fairly common complications from uncontrolled diabetes.

At this point, Fran is healthy enough and eager to work full-time. She has applied for many full-time jobs, but "with the economic situation being what it is, there's not a big call for a 55-year-old woman." The part-time and freelance bookkeeping jobs she has picked up over the past twelve years have paid enough for her to scrape by, but none has provided health insurance. Fran explains that she is caught in something of a catch-22: If she were to take a full-time, unskilled job outside her profession of bookkeeping and business management, she would probably earn too much to remain eligible for charity services at the Vermillion County Health Center. However, as an unskilled worker, she would not earn enough to pay for medical care out of pocket, and she would be unlikely to be given health insurance, especially a plan that would cover her preexisting condition. With diabetes and a history of osteomeylitis, she cannot take the risk of being without medical care. For Fran, the link between employment and health care has turned out to be sickening indeed.

A MINER'S TALE

"We have worked all of our lives, even went to work sick."

(Lenny, Idaho)

The son of an Idaho logger, Lenny began working to help support himself and his two brothers when he was 14. By age 18, he said, "I hit the road building houses for International Home." Not liking living out of a suitcase, he took a job working underground at Sunshine Mine at the age of 23, where he mined silver for 30 years.

"Sunshine had a terrible reputation for being the hottest mine, and it was hot! 1 worked in a place that the average was probably 90 degrees with humidity probably 98 percent. There was no protective equipment against the heat in those days. They just gave you a fan so you could blow the hot air around, but, yeah, that was hot. I lost weight, and I found out what cramps were, muscle cramps. Every muscle in your body had a charley horse that made your hands buckle backwards. Your legs would all wad up so you couldn't walk. Usually what we did is one guy would do part of the work, and the other guy would just kind of sit back so he could carry the other guy out at the end of the shift. He might not be able to get out otherwise, and we did that for six months of the year."

Despite the dreadful heat, taking a job at the mine was an easy decision for Lenny. "Benefits were the reason people went to the mines. Sunshine was a good mine as far as pay, it paid well, and they had the best insurance. They covered you, your wife, and all your kids 100 percent—dental, optical, everything." Shortly after he began working at Sunshine, his wife became pregnant. Soon after they had another child, and then a third, and Sunshine's benefits—a union-negotiated package of health and retirement benefits—looked better and better.

Then in 1972 a fire broke out in the mine. Lenny was one of the lucky ones—he survived. "What happened was we had a fire underground, and it's a hard rock mine. See, the railroads were put down and all this wood stuff for the railroads burned and the smoke had nowhere to go. The smoke was so concentrated that you could hardly see even if you had a lamp on your forehead. We made it out at about 1 p.m., and there was nobody outside the mine, and I thought, 'Man, everybody beat me out.'" In fact, few beat him out—91 of his fellow workers died in the fire.

After the fire, Lenny went back to work at the mine. The other local employment option, logging, rarely provided health benefits and seemed to Lenny even more dangerous than working underground. Moreover, in the wake of the fire, Sunshine had improved the ventilation system. Besides, Lenny had acquired some seniority at the mine.

In 1984, Lenny injured his back at work and underwent surgery. While the surgery helped some, his legs would give out from time to time. He managed to be reassigned to the less arduous position of shifter. As Lenny explains, "The shifter is the guy that goes underground. He takes a crew of 10 to 15 people down the mine shaft to a certain level, and he lines them all out. He also handles the motor, and he visits everybody at least once a day to make sure they are not hurt." After a few years as a shifter, he was made a mine foreman, which meant that he was in charge of the shifters and no longer had to go underground, a fortunate change because of his ongoing back troubles. "I didn't do this overnight. You know I spent 30 to 32 years there, so the last 10 years I had built up enough knowledge of the whole mine and all of the people that worked there that I was a natural for the position."

Things were better for a while, but then silver prices fell. In order to help save the mine and hold onto their jobs, the miners took cuts in pay and insurance and began paying part of their own premiums. For the first time in decades, they had to pay for their own optical care and for a variety of other medical treatments, though with the pay cuts few could afford it. Eventually, the price of silver fell below the cost of extracting it from the ground, and Sunshine closed for a year. When the mine reopened, management introduced more mechanization, took back only some of the employees, and decreased the benefits even further.

THE DEBTS PILE UP

In 2001, the mine closed permanently, and Lenny, along with his coworkers, lost his health insurance and other benefits. For thirty years at Sunshine—twenty years underground, often in stifling conditions—Lenny always felt that the trade-off was worthwhile. Good benefits and comprehensive health insurance for his family made up for the heat and danger. Now, still handicapped by the lingering effects of an injury on the job, Lenny found himself, at the age of 51, without health insurance.

Unemployment is high in northern Idaho, and finding another job was not easy. Calling on all his friends and relatives for help, he lined up a job installing telephone lines. "The job was okay, less money than the mines," and, as Lenny explains, "not the job that I spent 31 years learning. It is kind of hard, hanging upside down putting up the lines. It is hard to start at square one at my age. Some of the wires are underground, and you use a backhoe when you can. But when we get into where there are wires and stuff all together, you have to dig manually."

Still, he was relieved to find a job, and especially one that offered insurance. The rub was that it took 60 days on the job to get the insurance.

The luck that had made Lenny one of the survivors of the 1972 Sunshine fire had run out. Only 30 days after he began the job, he fell down on the pavement in full cardiac arrest. Paramedics flew him to Spokane, Washington, to a cardiac unit. Lenny's recovery was far better than anyone expected, but he was saddled with enormous medical bills. A year later, he was sent to the hospital for a bypass operation, angioplasty, and eventually open-heart surgery. The cardiologists saved his life, but Lenny is still suffering acute headaches as a result of falling to the pavement during the initial cardiac arrest. The cardiologist sent him to an ear, nose, and throat specialist, who then sent him to other specialists for treatments, none of which has eliminated his headaches.

The bill for his various surgeries, consultations, medications, and treatments is over $140,000—a sum that might as well be $1 billion, since Lenny will never be able to pay it. His sole income at this time is the $400 monthly pension he receives from Sunshine.

Lenny would like to go back to work, but he can no longer do the only kind of work he knows how to do—hard physical labor. After the injury to his head, he cannot climb telephone poles or bend over ditches; he is overcome by dizziness, which could be fatal from the top of a pole. "I can't get work, my doctor says I can't, so I have applied for Social Security [Disability]. But Social Security is one of those things, you know, it takes 10 years to get on it, so I don't know how that is going to work out."

According to the administrator of the Indigent Program in Shoshone County, Lenny is "emotionally at his wits end because Social Security is not being kind to him. He's a loose cannon."

Fortunately, the County Indigent Program and the state of Idaho have been able to provide Lenny with some assistance: They have paid most of his outstanding hospital bills. As the administrator explains, the "only" cost to Lenny is that Shoshone County has taken a $10,000 lien on his house.

FROM CLASS TO CASTE

Fran and Lenny represent the millions of Americans affected by a fundamental change taking place in our society. In the wake of changes to the economy and the structure of work, they have been transformed from proud members of the working class—a social category that connotes what one does, using one's hands in a more or less skilled capacity, to members of a new caste known as the working poor—a term used to describe who one is. Marginally employed as temps, subs, part-timers, or contracted or contingent laborers, members of this new caste are locked in employment situations that do not offer medical benefits. Without consistent and reliable access to health care, they find themselves situated outside of the traditionally fluid class structure of American society. We know, of course, that we are not writing about a caste system in the same sense as traditional Indian society. Rather, we have chosen to use the language of caste to describe a social arrangement that is emerging de facto from the political economy of our country at this time.

What makes Fran's and Lenny's situations castelike is the permanent effect that delayed, patchy, and second-rate health care has on their bodies: Even if economic conditions improve in Illinois or Idaho, they no longer will be healthy enough to rejoin the stratum of the labor market that provides health benefits. As the cost of health care in America has soared far beyond the costs of care in Canada, England, and other European countries, the millions who find themselves uninsured are now priced out of the health-care marketplace, potentially facing bankruptcy (of the record 1.57 million Americans who filed for personal bankruptcy in 2002, between one-third and one-half filed because of medical bills), and in substantially worse health than those who do have health insurance. Uninsured Americans receive less preventive care, poorer treatments for both minor and serious chronic and acute illnesses, and they often live shorter lives than members of comparable insured populations.

As in other caste systems, our new American caste system is characterized by outward markings on the body. Indeed, illness itself constitutes a physical marker: Rotten teeth, chronic coughs, bad skin, limps, sores that don't heal, obesity, hearing or vision deficits that are not corrected, addiction to pain medication—all these markings signal caste in very basic ways and often limit the employment opportunities available to those who have them. Several people we interviewed told of being promised a job over the telephone, rushing over to the personnel office, and then being told that the job was no longer available as soon as the hiring agent took a look at them.

Echoing the classical Indian caste system, membership in the American caste of the ill, infirm, and marginally employed carries a moral taint in addition to physical markings and occupational immobility. America has traditionally placed a moral value on productive work and good health. Work, of course, has long been construed as a moral virtue in America. We need only think of the generations of American women who embroidered samplers proclaiming that "idle fingers are the devil's playthings" and the moral disdain directed at so-called "welfare queens" for remaining outside the system of paid employment.

Uninsured Americans around the country spoke to us of the stigma of lacking health insurance—of medical providers who treated them like "losers" because they are uninsured. Similarly, the providers we spoke to emphasized the problem of "compliance" among the uninsured, complaining about "difficult" patients who do not follow through with their doctors' instructions. Sickness increasingly seems to be construed as a failure of ethical virtue, a failure to take care of oneself "properly," to eat the "right" foods or get "enough" exercise, to go for Pap smears; many construe it also as a genetic failure, a failure of will, a failure of commitment. The new media panic over obesity can only deepen caste-consciousness and exacerbate the stigma associated with having a body that has not been sculpted through high-priced gym memberships.

Speaking about what it means in her life to scrape by without health insurance, one of our respondents, a young college graduate in Massachusetts, said, "I just feel that the way the system is set up is like a bizarre version of natural selection, where the people who are poorest can't afford to keep themselves healthy, and so they die."

CHAPTER 32

Universal Health Care

What the United States Can Learn from the Canadian Experience

PAT ARMSTRONG

HUGH ARMSTRONG

with CLAUDIA FEGAN, M.D.

Ask any Canadian, "What is the difference between Canada and the United States?" Virtually every one of them will say "health care."

A remarkable 96 percent of Canadians prefer their health care system to the U.S. model.[1] And this support is not simply a reflection of Canadian nationalism in the face of a very large neighbor, although medicare certainly plays a central role as a "defining national characteristic."[2] Over the years, poll after poll has repeatedly demonstrated that health care is Canada's best-loved social program. An overwhelming majority of Canadians persistently say they want to keep their health care system.

In 1994, the Canadian government appointed a National Forum on Health to examine the current state and future possibilities of the health system. The focus groups and surveys conducted by the forum found that "the provision of health care services continues to receive strong and passionate support" among Canadians.[3] Similarly, the president of a major polling firm reported recently that among government programs "only the health care system received approval from a majority of Canadians." He went on to point out that the support even crosses social class lines. Otherwise strong differences in class values "don't occur to the same extent in the area of health care, perhaps because everyone can see themselves as becoming sick at some point."[4]

The current system is so popular that all Canadian politicians represent themselves as defenders of this sacred trust. Perhaps more surprisingly, so do many corporations in the private sector. Indeed, a major health insurance company has declared in a recent advertisement that it "believes strongly in the sanctity of Canadian medicare."[5]

The most important explanation for this support can be found in what are known as the five principles of the Canada Health Act. These are criteria for funding set out by the federal government, criteria the provinces* must follow in order to receive financial support for their health care services. Simply put, these principles require that core medical services be universal, portable, accessible, comprehensive, and publicly administered. In other words, all Canadians must have access to the medical services they require. These services must include all that is medically necessary, and must be provided regardless of age, prior condition, location, or employment. And they must be provided without regard to ability to pay. Canadian medicare was designed to allocate care on the basis of need, not individual finances.

And it worked. The system has delivered on the promised access to care. While "the number of uninsured Americans had risen to more than 40 million"[6] in 1995, virtually every Canadian is covered for essential care. This contrast in access to care can be traced to the basic philosophical approach used to fund services in Canada. As one 1981 task force put it, "Canadians are endeavouring to develop a health care system directed at health needs—not a competitive system to serve an illness market."[7]

This is made possible by the single-payer system. For the most part, health care in Canada is not *provided* by the government. It is *paid for* by governments. It is a public insurance system, a system in which governments at various levels pay for health services. Most of these services themselves are provided by nonprofit organizations or by doctors working on a fee-for-service basis. It is public payment for private practice and private provision.[8] This single-payer system has made care in Canada cheaper than in the United States, both because it significantly reduces administrative costs and because it allows for more coherent management of services.

Until medicare was introduced, Canadian health care costs were growing as fast as those in the United States. But "the period of the most rapid escalation *ended* with the establishment of universal coverage"[9] paid for from public funds. Even more startling is the fact that *public* spending on health care accounts for virtually the same proportion of each country's total economy. Yet, Canada covers the whole population and the United States covers only the elderly, the very poor, the military, and some of the disabled.

With the government as the main purchaser of services, health care is not only cheaper for individual taxpayers. It is also cheaper for employers, especially for those employers facing unions strong enough to successfully demand full health care coverage. In the United States, Chrysler pays more for health care than it pays

---

*Canada has a federal system with ten provinces and . . . [three] territories, each with its own health department. Although huge in size, the territories are tiny in population terms. Throughout this [chapter] "provinces" will be used to refer to both provinces and territories.

for steel.[10] In Canada, Chrysler does not have to pay for basic hospital or medical costs and therefore its employee costs are lower. Workers' compensation in Canada does not have to cover these basic costs either, and thus this protection too is cheaper for the Canadian employer.

With the single-payer scheme for many essential services, Canadians have a one-tier system. The rich and the poor go to the same hospitals and doctors. Neither receives a bill and the rich cannot buy quicker access, preferred status, or better facilities. What is covered by the public insurance system cannot be covered by a private insurer and doctors are not allowed to bill above the prescribed rate for services covered by the public insurance. Sharing facilities and services means that the entire population has a vested interest in maintaining the quality of care.

For more than a quarter century, Canada has been providing this comprehensive, accessible and high-quality care, without billing individuals for services or relating care to financial status. Equally important, it has done so more efficiently and at least as effectively as the competitive system serving an illness market in the United States. It is not surprising, then, that 96 percent of Canadians prefer their system to the American way. It is somewhat more surprising that a majority of Americans also prefer the Canadian system to that in the United States.[11] After all, health care services are very similar on both sides of the border.

In both countries, hospitals form the core of the system. And an operating room in one country looks much like one in the other. Hospitals in both countries offer high-tech services. On both sides of the border, most hospitals are owned by non-government organizations and function largely as independent entities. Hospitals in both countries vary in size and degree of specialization, although teaching hospitals across the continent tend to be large and diverse. Once in the door, it would be difficult to tell Toronto Hospital from the hospital in *Chicago Hope*.

Similarly, it would be difficult to identify which doctors are Canadian and which are American. Not only do both kinds wear white coats and stethoscopes, but the majority of doctors are paid on a fee-for-service basis. They are formally governed by agencies primarily made up of peers, intended to protect both patients and providers. Across North America, specialties are very similar and so are medical techniques. Indeed, research is freely shared and even jointly conducted across the border. Like hospitals, doctors' offices look virtually the same in Canada and the United States. Marcus Welby could be a Canadian.

Although doctors in both countries have fought hard to gain a monopoly over diagnosis and other medical practices, most of the actual patient care is provided by nurses of various kinds. Even the categories of nurses are basically the same on both sides of the border, as is their range of skills. Nurses are the main care providers both in and out of the hospital setting.

The settings where nurses and others provide care include long-term care facilities of various sorts. Homes for the elderly, nursing homes, and group homes are common everywhere in North America. And in both countries a great deal of care is provided in the home, often with assistance from home care nurses or other aides.

If health care is so similar in both countries, why is there such a strong preference for the Canadian system evident across the border as well as at home? Again, the explanation can be found mainly in the five principles on which Canadian health care delivery is based. And these in turn are related to the single-payer system and the insistence on one-tier delivery. They offer the most likely reasons for both Canadians and Americans preferring the Canadian approach. . . .

Is Canada's single-payer health care system perfect? Of course not. But it has been improved in a variety of ways since its inception, and the fact that it is paid for by public insurance makes it more sensitive to public opinion than are systems based on the profit motive. Problems remain, but they are not those commonly cited by media and other critics of public health insurance. It is to the problems, imagined and real, of Canadian medicare that we now turn.

WHAT THE PROBLEMS ARE NOT

I. Finances

Comparisons of public spending in Canada and other industrialized countries show two things. The Canadian level of public expenditure is in line with levels elsewhere, and it is very much under control. These conclusions hold, however public spending is measured.

Critics have argued that the Canadian public system spends both too much and too little on health care. At the height of the debt and deficit hysteria that swept through Canada, all social programs came under attack. These programs, including health care, were blamed for causing the debt through profligate overspending.

The charge did not stand up to careful scrutiny, however. In an analysis published by Statistics Canada's leading economic journal, two highly respected economists demonstrated that the growth in spending on all social programs, indeed on all programs, accounted for virtually none of the federal debt accumulated by the late 1980s. Rather, the debt was primarily attributable to a combination of reductions in corporate taxes and increases in real interest rates, or to the cost to the government (and others) of borrowing money.[12] Spending on social programs in general, and on health care in particular, is not the problem.

Some U.S. critics of the Canadian health care system have claimed that it is too expensive in light of the heavy tax burden it creates. Like health care spending, however, the level of taxes in Canada is about average in comparison with the levels in other industrialized countries. Both Canadian payroll taxes and fringe benefit costs are among the lowest, in large measure because of Canada's public, universal, and quite comprehensive health care system. Moreover, as the *World Competitiveness Report 1991* pointed out, publicly funded health care was a major factor placing Canada as high as fifth in its world competitiveness rankings.[13]

At the same time, some critics on both sides of the border have argued that on certain items Canada spends too little to provide adequate care. There is, however, little evidence that spending more would result in better or more accessible care. When public and private spending are combined, Canada spends much less on health care than the United States. Yet for less money, Canada provides more

TABLE 32.1   Public Spending on Health Care
Selected Industrialized Countries

Country	Percentage of GDP 1995	Percentage of all public spending, 1994*
Germany	8.2	18.4
France	7.7	13.6
Switzerland	7.1	18.6
Belgium	7.0	12.6
Canada	6.9	14.5
Iceland	6.9	17.7
Netherlands	6.8	12.2
United States	6.6	16.4

*The figure for Iceland's percentage of all public spending refers to 1995; for the United States it refers to 1993.

Source: Organisation for Economic Co-operation and Development, "OECD Health Data 97." http://www.oecd.org/statlist.htm (updated July 8, 1997), Health I Table.

hospital beds relative to population and the average lengths of stay in its hospitals are longer. The United States does have slightly more doctors, and many more of its doctors are specialists, but there is research to indicate that this represents excess capacity more than it represents what is needed for quality care.[14] In the midst of American plenty, moreover, there remain considerable shortages because the private system in the United States has greater difficulty distributing care equitably and efficiently. A 1996 study found that "problems in getting needed medical care affect about 17 million uninsured adults and 17 million insured adults in America."[15] This happens to very few Canadians.

There is no way to determine scientifically the appropriate amount to spend on health care. The allocation of society's resources is as much a matter of values as it is of evidence. For their part, Canadians have made it abundantly clear that they want to continue to devote a significant proportion of their tax dollars to health care. Canadians do not feel that they spend too much on their medicare system. Nor do they feel that they receive inadequate returns on their investment.

II. Waiting Lists

The rich cannot buy their way to the front of the line in the Canadian health care system. A few of them, and some U.S. critics, have as a result taken to complaining about the delays experienced before certain procedures are carried out. There are several aspects of the waiting list issue that merit consideration.

First, every society is almost certain to impose at least some waiting time for some health care procedures on at least some of its members. Every country in the world, including both Canada and the United States, does so now and always has.

To do otherwise would be possible, after enough providers were trained and facilities built, but it would be done at the cost of other priorities, including those that affect the social determinants of health. Just as one would not build the capacity of a mass transit system so that everyone has a comfortable seat during rush hour, so too with health care. The issue is not whether there should be rationing and waiting, but the principles that should govern the rationing and waiting.

Second, it should be made crystal clear that Canadians rarely wait for care that is required immediately. And, given that there are no financial costs to the individual at the point of receiving care, there is little incentive for patients to wait until their problems are severe. Most of the reports on waiting times that circulate widely refer to elective surgery, not to care that is required immediately.

Third, it should be remembered that Canadians have become so accustomed to readily accessible care that is portable throughout the country and that comes without cost to the individual that any waiting is considered intolerable. Surveys suggesting that waiting times have increased may thus leave a misleading impression. They may refer to increases in waiting times from a very low base, rather than the actual time people have to wait.

Fourth, we have scant comparative data in Canada, or in other countries, that would provide a solid basis for assessing the actual amounts of time people wait for care, or the consequences of their waits. How long, for example, do the "working poor" in the United States wait for diabetes diagnosis or for cataract surgery? In Canada, does waiting for elective surgery have long-term negative consequences? What are the consequences of waiting for different kinds of elective surgery? No discussion of waiting times can be adequate without such information.

Finally, and perhaps most importantly, the example of cardiac surgery in Ontario demonstrates that public systems are in a position to address waiting list problems when they are revealed. As the National Forum on Health explains,

> Experience . . . suggests that public health care can reduce waiting lists without increasing spending. The key is to ensure that waiting lists are structured and prioritized, and that incentives are in place to ensure that patients are served before their risk, or their degree of suffering, becomes unacceptably high. The solution is management, monitoring, and evaluation—not a bewildering array of public and private alternatives.[16]

III. Bureaucracy and Privacy

The beauty of the Canadian system lies in its simplicity. First, there were two short pieces of legislation, one on hospital insurance and then another on physician insurance. In 1984, these were consolidated and expanded into the Canada Health Act, another short and simple piece of legislation. Basically, the Canada Health Act lays down the five principles for the federal contribution to the funding of provincial health care programs. It therefore allows for diversity among and within provinces without creating enormous amounts of surveillance work. Health services have remained largely the way they were before medicare, except that now the bills are sent to a single payer in each province.

The consequence is less bureaucracy for both providers and patients. Because everyone belongs to the system, there is no need for fat files on each individual. Because the bills are paid from one source with little hassle, there is no need for detailed accounts of the supplies and services used by individuals, no need to hire collection agencies, and few resources spent on court battles over liability.

When Tommy Douglas first proposed to introduce public insurance coverage for doctors' services, one of the specters raised by his political opponents was that the confidentiality of individual health records would be lost. Public insurance was equated with government snooping into everyone's health file.

Ironically, however, personal health records and other personal records are much more likely to be invaded by private insurance companies competing to avoid high risks than by the public insurance agency. With everyone enrolled in a universal public scheme, there is no need to check individual medical histories or any other personal information to decide on program eligibility. And with everyone enrolled, there is also no reason to check on credit ratings, or on employment histories and status. Neither patients nor providers need to gain prior approval before undergoing tests or treatments, thus further reducing the situations in which outsiders demand personal health information. With hospitals operating under global budgets within a universal scheme, there is no need for financial administrators inside or outside the hospital to examine individual patient files.

All this contrasts sharply with private health insurance schemes. Private insurers have a financial incentive not only to enroll the best risks but also to specify as precisely as possible the services to be covered. A family history of cancer, a gay lifestyle, a clearly dangerous job or high job turnover could all mean a person is a risk. To make their enrollment and coverage decisions, private insurers need access to detailed personal medical, financial, and employment histories; to test results, and to physician and hospital practice patterns. Not incidently, they also need detailed reports on what individual physicians do, so their risk of incurring costs can be assessed. These requirements mean more bureaucracy and less privacy.

Drug prescription records may appear to provide an exception to the general rule that a public system protects privacy better. In Ontario, for example, the government has funded the establishment of a computer network that allows pharmacists to coordinate personal records on the filling of drug prescriptions. This integrated computer system enables pharmacists to watch out for drugs that may interact in harmful ways and for drugs that may be over-prescribed. The system could also enable the public insurance agency to monitor the prescribing patterns of individual doctors and the prescription drugs purchased by individual patients. It has been set up, however, on a voluntary basis, and the government and its public health insurance agency have no privileged access to individual prescription drug records.

What a public system does allow for is more information on, and more choice about, who has access to information on individual health files and on provider patterns. Again to use the example of Ontario, patient rights advocates have successfully pressed for legislation that severely restricts access to personal information on the diagnosis and treatment of mental illness. Not even parents and other relatives responsible for providing care, let alone insurance companies and governments, have access to the files without the permission of the adult patient.

IV. Choices and Abuses

Unlike the United States, which funds individuals who meet predetermined criteria, Canada has decided to fund services for everyone through a public system. As a result, Canadians have many more health care choices than do Americans. They are not prevented by predetermined criteria from qualifying for care. Individual Canadian patients and family physicians choose without outside interference who will be seen how often and by whom. On referral from a family physician, Canadian patients can go to any specialist or hospital, as frequently as medically appropriate and for as long as medically necessary.

Doctors too enjoy a wide range of choices, and freedom from supervision. There is little restriction on where they locate. In fact, a recent court decision in British Columbia struck down a provision in the fee schedule that penalized new entrants to medicine if they chose to set up their practices in heavily served urban areas. In this instance, the problem appears to be too much individual choice in the public system, not too little.[17] Physicians are guaranteed that their fees will be paid at the negotiated rate, and only very seldom are their activities scrutinized. Usually the monitoring of physicians' fees simply takes the form of letters sent to a random sample of patients inquiring whether they visited a specific physician on a specific date. The fee-for-service system under which nine out of ten Canadian doctors are paid allows them considerable choice about their hours of work and, ultimately, about how much income they will receive.

Like doctors, nurses and most other care providers in the public system must meet the health profession's standards of their province in order to practice in it. Most of the many female care providers are unionized, improving their choices in terms of pay, benefits, and working conditions.[18] The stability of a publicly financed system has been an important factor in this high rate of unionization.

The other side of choice is abuse. Within Canada, the claim is at times made that patients overuse their system, abusing their right to free choice and "free" care. This complaint is frequently combined with a call for user fees. The argument is advanced that such fees would simultaneously make people appreciate the benefits of the system more and make them be more careful about using it, thus ensuring more appropriate utilization.

There is very little evidence, however, of widespread abuse of access to care by Canadians. Nor is there evidence that user fees would prevent any of the abuse that does exist. One difficulty with attempting to collect such evidence concerns the definition of abuse. Those who use the system are unlikely to think that they are abusing it. Ask any patient waiting in a hospital emergency room, painfully or anxiously, whether *others* are there for frivolous reasons. Many will say that others do not look like they need immediate care. But they will be firmly convinced that their own visit is urgent and justified.

Furthermore, much of what might be defined as inappropriate use of the system would be so defined *after* diagnosis. Hindsight has 20/20 vision, as the saying goes. A mother may rush her screaming child to emergency only to discover that the problem is an earache that could have been dealt with by the family physician during regular office hours. But the earache could also have been an indication of a much more serious condition, and urgent care was sought precisely to find this out. When abuse is defined as use that is not medically necessary, the research that does exist has found very little abuse by patients.[19]

As a team of Canadian researchers has concluded from a thorough analysis of the uses of user fees,

> it is difficult to see how *patient*-initiated abuse *could* make up a large share of overall health care use and costs, because patients have little control over most of the decisions about the use of care. Call-back visits, referrals, hospital admissions and prescriptions, for example, all depend on the judgment and approval of a physician. No doubt there are some patients who "demand" a hospital procedure or a prescription, but the picture of patients eagerly requesting surgery or wanting to take medication just because the services are "free" makes even advocates of user charges laugh.[20]

At the same time, there is some evidence that the public insurance system encourages appropriate use in Canada. A study by Kevin Gorey published in a 1997 issue of the *American Journal of Public Health* found that "compared to their Detroit counterparts, poor women in Toronto have a survival rate for breast cancer that is 30 percent higher, for ovarian cancer that is 38 percent higher and for cervical cancer that is 48 percent higher." Moreover, "Toronto women have survival rates more than 50 percent above that of women in Detroit's poorest districts for lung, stomach and pancreatic cancer." Even after accounting for race and for the standards for measuring poverty, the differences remain.[21] The research suggests that Canadian medicare, with no user charges at the point of service, encourages appropriate and timely use, while user charges and other provisions that limit choice make the U.S. health care system less effective.

V. Quality, Technology, Research, and Innovation

Although it must be conceded that the Canadian system is more equitable than the U.S. alternative, it is on occasion argued that the quality of care is inferior in Canada, especially when it comes to advances related to research and technology. As we have seen, measuring quality is no simple task, and neither country is very good at it. Too much of the research on both sides of the border focuses on costs, measuring quality in terms of dollars spent and efficiency in terms of dollars saved. On both sides of the border, we know much more about expenditures per person than we do about whether these expenditures are worthwhile in terms of health outcomes.

As a result, researchers in both Canada and the United States have turned increasingly to the development of new and better ways to assess the quality of the care that is delivered. Especially for a country with a small population, Canada has a significant number of research organizations devoted to the assessment of quality in the delivery of health services. There are, for example, major centers at several universities in the provinces of British Columbia, Ontario, and Quebec that bring together multidisciplinary teams to examine health policy issues. The province of Manitoba has a Centre for Health Policy and Evaluation that maintains a database for hospital discharge information, enabling it to assess both the accessibility and the quality of care. Ontario's Institute for Clinical Evaluative Sciences (ICES) regularly produces a practice atlas that documents variations in practice patterns across the province, in an effort to prompt medical and other practitioners to evaluate whether they are following the most appropriate procedures. The Saskatchewan Health Services Utilization Review Commission (HSURC) has conducted and publicized a wide range of studies to help providers decide on the best approaches to care.

These and similar research organizations receive the bulk of their funding from the public purse. There are also national and provincial granting councils that provide financial support to individual researchers and teams of researchers based in hospitals and universities in every part of the country.[22] Lesser amounts come from a variety of charitable foundations. Partly as a result of this tax-supported investment in research, Canadians proportionately publish virtually as many articles in medical journals as do their U.S. counterparts.[23]

All this research activity leads to a number of conclusions. First, Canada devotes considerable time and resources to health-related research, and this research is frequently the basis for innovations in practice. Second, none of the research on quality reveals the existence of significant differences in the quality of health care in Canada and the United States. Although there is relatively more technology in the U.S., there is little evidence to show that all this technology is necessary or related to better quality care. There is, however, evidence that Canada distributes its technology more appropriately and equitably. Third, although neither country has developed very rigorous ways of measuring quality, the establishment of well-funded research centers in Canada with mandates to focus on evaluation and utilization concerns may bode well for the future.[24] The existence of a publicly administered health care system in Canada enhances the likelihood that research conducted there and abroad will be translated into improved care.

ENDNOTES

1. These results come from a 1993 Gallup poll cited in Nicole Nolan, "Bitter Medicine," *In These Times* (Jan. 20, 1997), p. 16.

2. National Forum on Health, "Values Working Group Synthesis Report," *Canada Health Action: Building on the Legacy,* Vol. II, *Synthesis Reports and Issues Papers* (Ottawa: Minister of Public Works and Government Services, 1997), p. 5.

3. National Forum on Health, "Values Working Group," p. 11.

4. Frank Graves, "Canadian Health Care—What Are the Facts? An Overview of Public Opinion in Canada," in *Access to Quality Health Care for All Canadians* (Ottawa: Canadian Medical Association, 1996), pp. 18–19.

5. In *Maclean's* (Dec. 2, 1996), pp. 50–51.

6. *UC Berkeley Wellness Newsletter* (May 1997).

7. Quoted in Malcolm G. Taylor, *Health Insurance and Canadian Public Policy: The Seven Decisions That Created the Canadian Health Insurance System and Their Consequences,* 2nd ed. (Kingston and Montreal: McGill–Queen's University Press, 1989), p. 433.

8. To borrow the titles from two books on Canadian approaches to the organization of social services: C. David Naylor, *Private Practices, Public Payment: Canadian Medicine and the Politics of Health Insurance 1911–1966* (Kingston: McGill–Queen's University Press, 1986); Josephine Rekart, *Public Funds, Private Provision* (Vancouver: University of British Columbia Press, 1994).

9. Robert Evans, "Health Care Reform: 'The Issue From Hell'," *Policy Options* (July–Aug. 1993), p. 37 (emphasis in original).

10. David U. Himmelstein and Steffie Woolhandler, *The National Health Program Book* (Monroe, ME: Common Courage Press, 1994), p. 40.

11. Robert J. Blendon and Humphrey Taylor, "Views on Health Care: Public Opinion in Three Nations," *Health Affairs* 8:1 (spring 1989), p. 152, where it is reported that 61 percent of Americans "would prefer the Canadian system of national health insurance" to the system they have now.

12. H. Mimoto and P. Cross, "The Growth of the Federal Debt," *Canadian Economic Observer* (June 1991), pp. 1–17.

13. World Economic Forum, *World Competitiveness Report 1991* (Lausanne, Switzerland: Institut pour l'étude des méthodes de direction de l'entreprise, 1992).

14. Tom Closson and Margaret Catt, "Funding System Incentives and the Restructuring of Health Care," *Canadian Journal of Public Health* 87:2 (March–April 1996), Table IV.

15. Reported in Robert Pear, "Health Costs Pose Problem for Millions, A Study Finds," *New York Times* (October 23, 1996), p. A4.

16. National Forum on Health, "Striking a Balance Working Group Synthesis Report," *Canada Health Action: Building on the Legacy,* Vol. II, *Synthesis Reports and Issues Papers* (Ottawa: Minister of Public Works and Government Services, 1997), p. 39.

17. Miro Cernetig and Robert Matas, "B.C. Can't Limit Where MDs Set Up Practices, Court Rules," Toronto *Globe and Mail* (Aug. 2, 1997), pp. A1, A7. Contrast this situation to that in the United States where, according to a recent report, at least 5 percent of new graduates in eleven of twenty-four specialties cannot find full-time positions anywhere, and "most job offers come from far-flung places, not urban areas." Leah Beth Ward, "Heartening Signs for Specialty M.D.'s," *New York Times* (Aug. 4, 1996), p. F8, reporting on a study in a March 1996 issue of the *Journal of the American Medical Association.*

18. Between 75 and 80 percent of registered nurses employed in the Canadian health care system are unionized, as against between 10 and 15 percent in the United States. Kit Costello, "Canadian Nurses—Our Northern Neighbors Fight Similar Battles," *California Nurse* 93:6 (June–July 1997), p. 12. Salaries for Canadian nurses averaged $US 39,161 for 37.5 hours work a week in 1992, as against $34,192 for 39.5 hours in the United States. Judith Shindul-Rothschild and Suzanne Gordon, "Single-Payer Versus Managed Competition: Implications for Nurses," *Journal of Nursing Education* 33:5 (May 1994), p. 204.

19. Greg L. Stoddart et al., "Why Not User Charges? The Real Issues," a discussion paper prepared for the [Ontario] Premier's Council on Health, Well-being and Social Justice (Sept. 1993), pp. 5–6.

20. Stoddart et al., "Why Not User Charges?," p. 5 (emphasis in original).

21. Jane Coutts, "Medicare Gives Poor a Better Chance," Toronto *Globe and Mail* (Aug. 1, 1997), p. A1.

22. See National Forum on Health, "Creating a Culture of Evidence-Based Decision-Making," *Canada Health Action: Building on the Legacy,* Vol. II, *Synthesis Reports and Issues Papers* (Ottawa: Minister of Public Works and Government Services, 1997), esp. pp. 21–23.

23. David U. Himmelstein and Steffie Woolhandler, *The National Health Program Book* (Monroe, ME: Common Courage Press, 1994), p. 109. In 1990, the U.S. figure was 526 articles per million population, while the Canadian figure was 520. Both were well behind Israel, Sweden, and the United Kingdom, but well ahead of Germany and Japan.

24. Noralou P. Roos et al., "Population Health and Health Care Use: An Information System for Policy Makers," *Milbank Quarterly* 74:1 (spring 1996), pp. 3–31.

CHAPTER 33

The Shame of Our Nursing Homes

ERIC BATES

The day before Kimberly Holdford left on a camping trip with her husband and twin girls in June of 1997, she stopped by a nursing home to visit her grandmother. It had been a month since Jewel Elizabeth Forester entered the Beverly Health and Rehabilitation Center in Jacksonville, Arkansas, to recover from a bout with the flu that had left her severely dehydrated. She hated the facility. Beverly aides seldom bathed her and often neglected to take her to the bathroom, leaving her caked in dried feces and sobbing in shame. Holdford didn't know what to do; Beverly was the only nearby nursing home with an available bed. "We're understaffed," she recalls an aide telling her. "We don't have enough people to do the job."

At 80, Forester remained feisty and sharp-witted, tackling crossword puzzles and reveling in the afternoon soaps. But on the day before the camping trip, Holdford found her groggy and disoriented. "What's wrong with my grandmother?" she asked the nursing staff. "She won't wake up." Assured that a doctor would be called, Holdford reluctantly left for the weekend.

But no one at Beverly called the doctor. The next day Forester was screaming in pain and moaning in her sleep. Aides tried to calm her down because she was disturbing other patients. On Monday a respiratory therapist found Forester nearly comatose. She was rushed to the hospital, where doctors found three times the maximum therapeutic level of a drug called digoxin in her system. The nursing home had administered an overdose of the drug, even though it had been warned that Forester had trouble tolerating the medication.

"What followed was nine days of the worst deathwatch you ever saw in your life," recalls Robert Holdford, Kimberly's husband. "She was screaming and moaning as her organs shut down from the overdose. She suffered an agonizing death because of Beverly."

Nor was Forester the only patient at the home to suffer from substandard care. With too small a staff to turn and feed them, some residents developed bone-deep wounds; one was hospitalized weighing only eighty-one pounds. Last September a 58-year-old man died after an untrained and unlicensed nurse punctured his stomach lining when she tried to reinsert a feeding tube.

Dan Springer, a vice president at Beverly, calls the facility "an aberration," but the company has acknowledged that things were seriously amiss. "We knew that we had some problems," a top executive told reporters after the home was finally shut down by the state. "It was horrible."

Such horror stories involving nursing homes have become almost commonplace. For three decades, federal and state investigations have repeatedly documented widespread understaffing, misuse of medication and restraints, even physical attacks on patients. Yet thousands of vulnerable citizens remain confined in depressing, debilitating—and often deadly—institutions like the one in Jacksonville. Last summer, a federal study found that nearly one-third of all nursing homes in California had been cited for violations that caused death or life-threatening harm to patients. Federal officials charged with policing dangerous homes "generally took a lenient stance," William Scanlon, director of health financing and systems issues for the US General Accounting Office (GAO), testified before a Senate panel in July. "Homes can repeatedly harm residents without facing sanctions."

Federal officials are promising to subject nursing homes to closer scrutiny. . . . President Clinton has ordered a crackdown on repeat offenders, the Justice Department is investigating charges of fraud and abuse, and Congress is poised to reshape Medicare and other programs that pay for long-term care. Yet such efforts focus more on cutting costs than improving care; they fail to recognize that standards remain lax and reforms fall short because of the very nature of nursing homes. Facilities that care for nearly 2 million elderly and disabled residents form a lucrative private industry that profits directly from pain—while taxpayers foot the bill. Nursing homes ring up $87 billion of business each year, and more than 75 cents of every dollar comes from public funds through Medicaid and Medicare. The less of that money homes spend on care, the more they pocket for themselves and their shareholders. To insure those profits, nursing homes are careful not to skimp when it comes to investing in politics: The industry gives millions in contributions to state and federal officials, insuring weak public oversight.

At a time when Republicans and Democrats alike are clamoring to let big business run everything from prisons to schools, nursing homes represent the nation's longest-running experiment in privatization—one that, after half a century, offers a graphic portrayal of what happens when private interests are permitted to monopolize public services. While the industry is currently struggling to adjust to new limits on Medicare spending, nursing homes still rely on a generous flow of public subsidies. Leading the for-profit field is Beverly Enterprises, which controls more nursing-home beds than any other firm in the nation. Founded in 1963 as privatization accelerated, the company now owns 561 homes like the one in Jacksonville, which is located just a few hours down the road from its corporate headquarters in Ft. Smith, Arkansas. Although Beverly posted a loss last year, it remains an industry giant. In 1997 the company enjoyed after-tax profits of $58.5 million on revenues of $3.2 billion.

The money did little to help elderly residents like Jewel Forester. "I trusted them not to let her come to harm," says Kimberly Holdford, looking at a photo of her grandmother. "Instead, this sweet little old woman who loved me all my life suffered a brutal death. Somebody has got to stop these big corporations from hurting our old people. They're supposed to be in the healthcare business, not the money-making business. All they care about is keeping profits up."

From colonial times, caring for the elderly poor has been a responsibility of government. At first, officials tried not only to pass the buck but to make a few as well. Until the 1820s villages and cities confronted with growing numbers of impoverished citizens routinely auctioned them off to families who provided squalid accommodations in return for grueling work. An observer at one Saturday-night auction at a village tavern noted that citizens "could speculate upon the bodily vigor and the probable capacity for hard labor of a half-witted boy, a forlorn-looking widow, or a halt and tottering old man." But as abuses—and profits—mounted, cities and counties began to operate their own poorhouses for the sick and aged. The expression "over the hill" comes from an 1871 ballad that depicts the plight of an old woman cast out by her children to live in a government-run workhouse.

As industrial mechanization eliminated jobs after World War I, the public began to protest overcrowding and illness in county poorhouses. Reformers often seemed less concerned about aiding the poor, however, than about keeping them away from the well-to-do. "Worthy people are thrown together with moral derelicts, with dope addicts, with prostitutes, bums, drunks—with whatever dregs of society happen to need the institution's shelter at the moment," the New York Commission on Old Age Security complained in a 1930 report. "People of culture and refinement," the commission noted, were forced to share services "with the crude and ignorant and feebleminded."

Spurred by scandals over conditions in public poorhouses, federal lawmakers decided to hand the elderly over to private industry. In 1935 Congress specifically framed the Social Security Act to prohibit cash payments to any "inmate of a public institution." Those over 65 received small monthly pensions, but none of the money could go to government-run homes for the aged. The massive transfer of tax dollars to private business fueled the creation of for-profit homes. Almost overnight, operators set up facilities to exploit pensioners. Sometimes little changed but the name. In Minnesota, private owners removed a large sign identifying "Dodge County Poor Farm," replacing it with one reading "Fairview Rest Home." The federal government soon began making direct payments to private nursing homes and providing low-interest loans for construction, insuring the fledgling industry a handsome profit. "So rapidly has the nursing home developed during the past 20 years," two observers noted in 1955, "that its history seems more like an eruption than an evolutionary development."

The eruption became volcanic in 1965, when Congress created Medicaid to assist the elderly poor and Medicare to provide health insurance for the aged. The two programs provided a huge profusion of public money into the nursing homes, with few strings attached. Most states limited the number of homes, thus insuring a supply of patients to fill the beds. They also reimbursed homes for all expenses, from mortgage and depreciation on the building to the staff and supplies inside—in essence, giving owners a blank check that virtually guaranteed them a healthy profit on their investment. Before long, global corporations like ITT rushed to cash in on the industry. With backing from Wall Street, the number of homes soared from 13,000 in 1967 to more than 23,000 in 1969.

"That was when nursing homes moved away from mom-and-pop operations to large, for-profit enterprises," says Charles Phillips, director of the Myers Research Institute in Beachwood, Ohio. "They were more interested in real estate transactions than healthcare. They shuffled properties back and forth between subsidiaries, jacking up property costs to increase reimbursement. Our current long-term-care system is fundamentally a creature of government policy. Those real estate ventures became the source of corporate empires."

Today those empires represent a booming business. With the number of elderly citizens needing long-term care expected to double over the next two decades, Wall Street sees a steady stream of customers for nursing homes—with a guaranteed flow of cash consisting almost entirely of public funds. "We believe nursing homes are well positioned to capitalize on this growing opportunity," the investment bank Hambrecht & Quist recently advised investors, predicting that corporate chains would boost profits by laying off staff members, cutting wages and doubling patient loads. With the help of large institutional investors like Goldman Sachs and Lazard Frères, nursing-home chains are also making shareholders happy by swallowing competitors at a record pace. Last year two of the largest chains in the country merged with two fellow giants, creating parent companies with annual revenues of about $3 billion each. Thanks to their big financial backers, seven chains now collect 20 cents of every dollar spent on nursing homes nationwide (see Box 33.1).

The oldest and largest chain is Beverly Enterprises. Founded by a California accountant at the outset of the federal bonanza, the company quickly earned him $10 million on his initial investment of $5,700. In the seventies, backed by the influential Arkansas brokerage house of Stephens, Inc., Beverly led the industry in a frenzied buying spree, adding nearly 1,000 nursing homes in less than a decade. "No other chain has been able to put together as successful an acquisition formula," reported a study by the Food and Allied Service Trades of the AFL-CIO.

For a time, Beverly found, bigger was better. For five years in the eighties the chain maintained an annual return on equity of 23 percent—the fifth-highest rate of any healthcare company nationwide. But unable to manage its far-flung network of nursing homes, Beverly lost $60 million in 1987 and began selling off facilities to avoid a hostile takeover. "We probably grew too fast," acknowledged David Banks, a former typewriter salesman and Stephens executive who now heads Beverly.

Led by Banks, the company also moved to Arkansas, where it enjoyed legal advice from a young attorney at the Rose Law Firm named Hillary Clinton and political support from her husband, Bill, in the governor's mansion. In one deal that demonstrated the kind of favoritism Beverly enjoyed, a state board approved $81 million in tax-free revenue bonds that would have given the company badly needed cash to pay its debts—without creating a single new job. Clinton, who appears to

B o x **33.1**

More Beds, More Money

Beverly Enterprises controls more than 60,000 nursing-home beds, more than any other company worldwide. But six other chains also enjoy significant shares of the industry, rapidly placing more patients in the hands of big conglomerates.

- Integrated Health Services (Owings Mills, Maryland). The chain moved into the front ranks of the industry when it acquired rival Horizon/CMS Healthcare for $1.2 billion. It now boasts 42,600 beds and revenues of $3 billion.
- Vencor (Louisville, Kentucky). The chain drew fire last year when it evicted low-income residents to make way for wealthier clientele. With 38,300 beds, it enjoys revenues of $3 billion.
- Sun Healthcare Group (Albuquerque, New Mexico). After a buying spree that brought it two smaller chains, Sun has vaulted into the big leagues with 44,000 beds and $3.2 billion in revenues.

- HCR Manor Care (Toledo, Ohio). A merger between two industry giants formed a new chain with 47,000 beds and revenues of $2.2 billion. Chairman Stewart Bainum Jr. immediately promised "future acquisitions, at the lowest cost of capital in the industry."
- Mariner Post-Acute Network (Atlanta, Georgia). Another member of the billion-dollar club, formed by the merger of Mariner Health Group and Paragon Health Network. Dogged by allegations of racketeering at a former nursing home in Tampa, the chain controls 48,100 beds and $2.7 billion in revenues.
- Genesis Health Ventures (Kennett Square, Pennsylvania). The company bought a pharmaceutical chain and sponsored a real estate investment trust for some of its 37,700 beds, boosting revenues to $1.4 billion.   E.B.

Source: All figures are from company officials; revenues are for the latest available twelve-month period.

have originally seen the deal as a way to help woo the company to Arkansas, backed away from it only after Steve Clark, his attorney general, revealed that a lobbyist had offered him $100,000 in campaign gifts if he supported the bond handout. "The only way this proposal can be described," Clark told a meeting of startled officials unused to hearing criticism of Beverly, "is one which is the product of the arrogance of wealth and the arrogance of power." Even Clinton was forced to concede that the deal went too far. "They were trying to milk this bond system," he said.

While Beverly executives and shareholders profited from the company's rapid growth during the eighties, many patients suffered. Across the nation, health officials filed reports on Beverly nursing homes documenting filthy living conditions, infected bedsores and painful deaths. The State of Washington banned the company from opening any new homes because of its poor track record. The chain bowed out of Maine after inspectors there cited it for substandard conditions. A Missouri grand jury investigated reports of Beverly patients with gaping wounds. Texas suspended Medicaid payments to twenty-four of the company's homes because of health hazards. California fined the firm $724,000 and put it on probation after accusing Beverly of contributing to the deaths of nine patients. At one home, inspectors found that ants had swarmed over the body of a woman, entering her respiratory system through a wound in her throat. "Something is very wrong at Beverly Enterprises," a deputy attorney general in California concluded. Beverly considered it business as usual. "We pretty much mirror the industry," said CEO Banks at the time of the California investigation.

Beverly certainly mirrors the industry in the way it cashes in on Medicaid and Medicare. To improve the bottom line, homes have funneled as much money as possible into property, administrative salaries and ancillary services like drugs and physical therapy, while cutting corners on patient care and staff wages. Many facilities have only one registered nurse on duty, relying on skeleton staffs of nurse's aides to provide almost all the hands-on care for dozens of patients. Most earn little more than the minimum wage and received only seventy-five hours of training for difficult jobs that require them to monitor and feed patients and move frail and disabled residents with little assistance. Annual turnover industrywide is nearly 100 percent.

"They're short-staffing," says an aide at a Beverly home in Center Point, Alabama. "If you have twenty residents, it means you can't spend as much time with them as you should. You don't give residents the kind of care they deserve."

In nursing homes, skimping on labor costs can be lethal. In Minnesota, investigators found that at least eight residents at Beverly homes died after receiving inadequate care and supervision between 1986 and 1988. Myrtle Schneuer, 83, choked to death after a nurse's aide gave her bacon and toast, despite a doctor's order to feed her only soft food because she had difficulty swallowing. Lucy Gralish, 79, suffered for three hours after a heart attack before the home called a doctor. Joy Scales, 65, died of a skull fracture after an aide left her unattended on the toilet, contrary to her doctor's orders. "So much of this goes right back to the question of staffing and corner-cutting," James Varpness, the Minnesota ombudsman for older residents at the time, told reporters. "Why are people being left unattended on toilets so that they fall off and fracture their skull? It's because the nursing staff has too much to do and something else that needs to get done."

In many homes there are still too few aides to do the job. In 1993 two dozen employees at a Beverly home in Yreka, California, signed a letter to David Banks, warning him that staffing was dangerously low. "We are jeopardizing the safety of our residents as well as our own," the employees wrote. "It is a matter of time before a tragedy occurs that may have been preventable." They were right. In 1995 a suit was filed alleging that Reba Gregory, a 69-year-old resident, had been dropped by a nursing aide who was trying to move her from her bed without assistance, fracturing her right hip and shoulder. Last March a jury awarded Gregory a record $95.1 million—later reduced by a judge to $3 million—after evidence showed that time sheets the company originally claimed were destroyed had in fact been doctored to reflect nonexistent staffing.

Beverly has also repeatedly broken the law to prevent its 65,000 employees from joining a union to improve staffing and conditions. Last August the National Labor Relations Board issued an unusual corporationwide "cease and desist" order against the company for 240 violations of labor laws in eighteen states including threats, coercion and surveillance of employees. A study of federal contractors by the GAO ranked Beverly among the fifteen worst violators of federal labor laws.

Beverly and others in the industry complain that Medicaid rates are simply too low to pay for decent staffing and adequate care. In Arkansas, where Beverly owns one of every six nursing-home beds, Medicaid reimburses the industry an average of $63.99 a day for each resident—only two-thirds the national average. But the low rates don't stop companies like Beverly from enjoying big profits. According to the latest available figures, Arkansas nursing homes rank second to last in the nation in median spending on direct care for patients and dead last in staffing levels. Such miserliness enables them to post the eighth-highest profit margin nationwide—nearly double the US average. Seven of the twenty most profitable homes in the state belong to Beverly.

Even when the company claims a loss, it still finds ways to make money. The home in Jacksonville, where Jewel Forester died of an overdose, reported a loss of $859,000 for fiscal 1998. . . . But cost reports filed with the state show that the "loss" included nearly $309,000 in "management fees and home office costs" that the home passed along to corporate headquarters. According to proxy statements, David Banks and two other Beverly executives topped $1 million in compensation for 1997.

When it comes to compensating nurse's aides, however, Beverly and other chains plead poverty. In Arkansas, where nursing homes pay half of their 25,000 employees only $5.15 an hour, the industry didn't want to use any of its profits to raise the minimum wage as mandated by Congress. So during the closing days of the 1997 state legislative session, lobbyists snuck an amendment into the budget requiring taxpayers to reimburse nursing homes for any increase in the minimum wage. Republican Governor Mike Huckabee vetoed the bill, but lawmakers easily overrode him. The measure could end up costing taxpayers more than $17 million.

Privatized nursing homes have other, less direct ways of raiding the public treasury. Until recently, the big money for conglomerates like Beverly has been in what are considered ancillary services—drugs, diapers, ventilators, speech therapy and other supplies and care that nursing-home patients often need. Medicare billings for physical and occupational therapy, for example, rose to $7 billion in 1996—double the 1993 rate and six times the 1990 rate. Such hefty reimbursements gave Beverly and other companies an incentive to create subsidiary firms to supply ancillary services to their own nursing homes. That way, they could bill taxpayers for the retail prices they pay their subsidiaries, rather than the lower costs the companies actually incur.

"These services typically are provided by outside contractors or through wholly-owned subsidiaries of nursing home companies that focused on maximizing revenues, not pursuing cost-effective care," Beverly notes in its latest annual report. Although the company says a new Medicare plan that caps some payments has prompted it to hire its own staff therapists, it acknowledges in the report that "there has been little incentive to reduce costs or pursue operating efficiencies, even though the result is higher costs for the government and other payors."

"Higher costs" for taxpayers means "higher profits" for Beverly. An internal company report on rehabilitative therapy shows the company has made much larger returns on ancillary services than cost reports for individual nursing homes indicate. In the first eleven months of 1994, according to the report, Beverly made revenues of $671 million on rehabilitative therapy—yet the services cost the company only $360 million. That's an annual return of 46 percent on revenues. In 1994 Beverly cleared more than $1 million on therapy every day—and almost all of it came from taxpayers.

"It's big money, and it's hidden money," says Elma Holder, founder of the National Citizens Coalition for Nursing Home Reform. "They have a set of books that show they're losing money on one side, and yet they're making money hand over fist on the other side."

Other internal documents show similar profit rates, even in homes where Beverly claims it has been unable to make money. In Texas, for example, the chain paid $100,000 to settle claims at a home where a resident's sore foot had been ignored for forty-three days until it rotted off her leg. In another case a judge awarded $55 million to the estate of a woman who died in 1994 from an infection caused by bedsores, including a bone-deep wound the size of a grapefruit at her tailbone. In 1997, calling the regulatory environment in Texas "punitive," Beverly sold its forty-nine nursing homes in that state to a company called Complete Care Services for $143 million in cash. But what Beverly claimed was a dry well looked more like a gusher to the new owners. According to internal documents, one investor who contributed $6 million expected to make $3.5 million in cash, management fees and interest in the first year—an immediate return of nearly 58 percent.

Nursing homes can enjoy even higher returns, of course, if they simply provide no services at all in return for government subsidies. A 1996 report by the GAO on Medicare payments to nursing homes found that "fraud and abusive billing practices are frequent and widespread." The federal government, the report added, allows homes to bill Medicare without confirming that "the care or items were necessary or were delivered as claimed." As a result, the program is highly vulnerable to exploitation.

A recent government audit showed that nursing homes billed Medicare for more than $3 billion in improper claims in 1996 and 1997. Another report estimated that taxpayers may be losing 15 cents of every Medicare dollar to fraud. In one case a Georgia company was certified to bill the insurance program for therapy services even though it had no salaried therapists. A clerical employee in a storefront office simply served as a shell company that subcontracted with two uncertified providers, adding a markup of 80 percent on every bill. Another company was a "paper organization" with no staff at all, enabling its "owner" to add $170,000 in administrative costs to Medicare bills over a six-month period.

[In July of 1998] Beverly announced that the Justice Department had launched an investigation into whether the company improperly billed Medicare for labor costs between 1990 and 1997. Two former Beverly employees have been called before a California grand jury, and Blue Cross of California is also reviewing its dealings with the company. Investors reacted angrily to the news. In October Beverly shareholders filed a class-action suit alleging that the company "engaged in a scheme to inflate billings to Medicare" by shifting labor costs at homes that weren't Medicare-certified to those that were.

Beverly says it is cooperating with investigators, but the company is quick to knock the government for its approach to inspections. "We believe the system that regulates nursing homes is punitive, subjective and inequitable," says vice-president Dan Springer. "Rather than the government finding problems, finding facilities and upsetting the lives of good people, why not flip the tables and work in partnership?" He adds that Beverly has devised a "report card" to evaluate its own operations. "There is no arguing that there are places where care needs to be improved. But there are instances where the process as it's implemented today doesn't recognize the positive things that go on in nursing homes."

It's no secret why companies like Beverly see "positive things" in nursing homes: With the number of elderly Americans requiring long-term care projected to reach 14 million by the year 2020, the industry is virtually guaranteed a profitable future. As with other public services that have been privatized, however, the question is: What is a reasonable profit, and how can taxpayers insure they're getting their money's worth? Congress has responded to the soaring costs of nursing homes by moving Medicare and other federal programs into managed care, which caps costs at set levels. But lowering costs doesn't automatically improve the quality of care. A new reimbursement plan that took effect on January 1 gives nursing homes a fixed amount for services, then allows them to spend the money however they see fit. "The less you spend, the more you make," says Elma Holder of the Citizens Coalition.

For its part, the industry knows how to use its political and financial clout to block any meaningful reform. In 1978, on a trip to Arkansas to testify about nursing-home abuses, Holder found herself being driven to the airport by an ambitious attorney general named Bill Clinton. "I remember him saying he would never take any money from corporations that ran nursing homes," she recalls. "I was quite impressed with this man, of course, that he would say that." In 1996 Clinton raised $1.1 million from nursing-home owners, including several who attended breakfasts at the White House. The following year, at the President's recommendation, Democrats named Alan Solomont, a Massachusetts nursing-home magnate who lobbied for weaker federal enforcement, the party's new finance chairman.

Beverly has contributed more than $100,000 to federal candidates and their parties since 1995, and its board of directors enjoys high-powered contacts on both sides of the aisle. Republicans on the board include Edith Holiday, the White House Cabinet liaison during the [George H. W.] Bush Administration, and Carolyne Davis, who served under President Reagan as administrator of the Health Care Financing Administration, the federal agency responsible for overseeing nursing homes.

Democrats include Beryl Anthony, a former US representative and chair of the Democratic Congressional Campaign Committee. The industry also uses its influence to block reforms at the state level. In Beverly's home state of Arkansas, an analysis of campaign contributions shows that nursing homes were the second-largest donor to state legislative candidates in 1994.

Given the political clout of companies like Beverly, it's hard to imagine lawmakers getting behind the reform proposals advocated for years by patients and their families. But with the cost of long-term care skyrocketing, some officials are starting to listen. Advocates say more money should be directed at keeping people out of nursing homes—by providing adult daycare, home health aides and other community-based programs that keep people healthy and independent. They also point to model facilities, like the nonprofit Hampton Woods in rural North Carolina or the state-run Benton Services Center in Arkansas, that invest in providing top-flight nursing care rather than maximizing profits.

The most promising reform efforts focus on the most direct and effective way to improve care: Require homes that rely on public funds to hire more nurses and aides. Advocates in sixteen states have convinced lawmakers to introduce measures that would raise minimum staffing levels, forcing homes to provide at least four hours of direct care each day. It's a seemingly simple idea, but it strikes at the heart of industry profits. Nursing homes would have to spend tax dollars directly on care rather than funneling money into lucrative sidelines. "It's the most serious issue we face," says Holder of the Citizens Coalition. "Common sense would tell you that you can't achieve good care if you don't have enough staffing, but no one wants to talk about it because of the cost involved."

Despite the cost—and opposition from nursing homes—staffing standards are gaining support from those traditionally supportive of the industry. In Arkansas, lawmakers are expected to vote . . . on a bill mandating that nursing homes hire more aides—and pay stiff penalties for understaffing. The measure's sponsor is State Senator John Brown, a conservative Republican who generally knocks government regulation in favor of "free enterprise." On a recent sunny afternoon Brown stands in a hallway of the state capitol in Little Rock, at the bottom of a marble staircase leading to the governor's office, and caucuses with patient advocates about how to pay for the increased staffing.

"We have to talk about where the money's going to come from," Brown says.

"How about profits?" suggests Virginia Vollmer, a member of Arkansas Advocates for Nursing Home Residents.

Brown surprises her by nodding in agreement. "But we've got to look behind their published numbers," he says. "Whether it's the way they report expenses or amortize interest, there are different accounting ploys that homes can use to make money. By and large they have a pretty good return. We're paying them hundreds of millions of dollars, but in too many cases they're endangering people rather than caring for them."

The advocates are encouraged, but they remain skeptical. "I don't know that any of the increased staffing will come out of the industry's pockets," says Jim Porter, whose mother died in a Beverly home in Little Rock last November. "It will probably all come out of the taxpayer's pocket. That's the shame of it." Like Senator Brown, Porter is hardly an antibusiness activist. The chairman of the Arkansas Entertainer's Hall of Fame and a Beverly investor, Porter called CEO David Banks personally after witnessing the inadequate care at his mother's nursing home. "I told him they weren't paying the salary they need to get and keep the help they need," Porter recalls. "He said he knew they were having problems and he'd get things in order. But he didn't."

Porter has a simple explanation for why care at Beverly and other nursing homes remains substandard. "Greed," he says. "They don't want to pay these nurse's aides more because it would be money out of their profits. It's as simple as that." He also has a simple idea of how to improve care: Return nursing homes to public control. Given the history of abuses at county homes and the current political climate, it's not a proposal that's likely to gain much ground. But it does suggest the depth of frustration with a privatized system that profits from pain—and the importance of remembering who ultimately pays the price.

"Perhaps nursing homes should be taken over by the state, county or city," Porter says. "Each one of them could be run for less by the government, because there wouldn't be an owner sitting there siphoning off hundreds of thousands of dollars. Imagine what kind of care we could provide with all those profits."

CHAPTER 34

Cater to the Children

GERALD MARKOWITZ

DAVID ROSNER

According to the Centers for Disease Control and Prevention, it is estimated that 1 of every 20 children in the United States suffers from subclinical lead poisoning,[1] and a recent article in *Science* argues that "paint appears to be the major source of childhood lead poisoning in the United States."[2] Yet it is only during the past 15 years that the history of this tragic situation has been addressed in any detail,[3-7] primarily through the documentation of childhood lead poisoning in the public health and medical literature of the first half of the 20th century. Here we analyze the role and influence of the lead industry in shaping popular and professional opinion about lead and lead paint products. Specifically, we discuss how the Lead Industries Association (LIA, the trade group representing lead pigment manufacturers) and its member companies sought to assuage growing public and professional concerns about the dangers to children of lead-based paint. Often employing the image of children themselves, the LIA and its members engaged in aggressive marketing and advertising campaigns to persuade the public of their product's appropriateness for indoor use. . . .

The continuing use of lead paint into and after the 1950s cannot be understood without an appreciation of the enormous resources the lead industry devoted to allaying public health concerns from the 1920s through the early 1950s. Whatever responsibility the public health community had for this tragedy pales in comparison with the power and determination of the industry in perpetuating the use of lead-based paint. The lead industry, as a sponsor of research and as a clearinghouse of information about lead, was positioned to be in the forefront of efforts to prevent lead exposure in children. Instead, the industry placed its own economic interests ahead of the welfare of the nation's children.

MEDICAL KNOWLEDGE OF THE DANGERS OF LEAD-BASED PAINT

Historians have shown that knowledge of the dangers of lead poisoning to workers and children can be traced back into the 19th century[8,9] and that in the first third of the 20th century a broad scientific literature on the subject accumulated in Australia, England, and the United States. Alice Hamilton and others documented lead hazards among American workers in the pigment manufacturing, battery, painting, plumbing, ceramics, pottery, and other industries.[10,11] In 1921 the president of the National Lead Company, Edward J. Cornish, wrote to David Edsall, the dean of Harvard Medical School, saying that lead manufacturers, as a result of "fifty to sixty years" experience, agreed that "lead is a poison when it enters the stomach of man—whether it comes directly from the ores and mines and smelting works" or from the ordinary forms of carbonate of lead, lead oxides, and sulfate and sulfide of lead.[12]

At the same time, others began to systematically document the dangers of lead to children. In 1904, J. Lockhart Gibson, an Australian, was among the first English-language authors to directly link lead-based paint to childhood lead poisoning, specifically noting the dangers to children from painted walls and verandas of houses.[13] A year later, he urged, "[T]he use of lead paint within the reach of children should be prohibited by law."[14(p753)] In 1908 another Australian, Jefferis Turner, delivered a presidential address to the Section of Diseases of Children of the Australasian Medical Congress in which he noted that lead poisoning was due to paint powder that stuck to children's fingers, which they then bit or sucked.[15] In 1914, Americans Henry Thomas and Kenneth Blackfan, the latter a physician at Johns Hopkins Department of Pediatrics in Baltimore, detailed the case of a boy from Baltimore who died of lead poisoning after ingesting white lead paint from the railing of his crib.[16] In 1917, Blackfan reviewed the English-language literature on lead poisoning in children, noting specifically cases of children who chewed the white paint from their cribs.[17] By the mid-1920s, there was strong and ample evidence of the toxicity of lead paint to children, to painters, and to others who worked with lead as studies detailed the harm caused by lead dust, the dangers of cumulative doses of lead, the special vulnerability of children, and the harm lead caused to the nervous system in particular.[18]

Outside the United States, the dangers represented by lead paint manufacturing and application led to many countries' enacting bans or restrictions on the use of white lead for interior paint: France, Belgium, and Austria in 1909; Tunisia and Greece in 1922; Czechoslovakia in 1924; Great Britain, Sweden, and Belgium in 1926; Poland in 1927; Spain and Yugoslavia in 1931; and Cuba in 1934.[19] In 1922, the Third International Labor Conference of the League of Nations recommended the banning of white lead for interior use.[20] In the United States and Canada, there were calls for the use of non–lead-based paints in interiors. As early as 1913, Alice Hamilton wrote that "the total prohibition for lead paint for use in interior work would do more than anything else to improve conditions in the painting trade."[21] By the early 1930s, a consensus developed among specialists that lead paint posed a hazard to children.[22–27] Robert Kehoe, medical director for the Ethyl Gasoline Corporation and director of the Kettering Laboratories of the University of Cincinnati, perhaps the nation's leading expert on lead poisoning, concluded that "strenuous efforts must be devoted to eliminating lead from [children's] environment,"[28] especially since safer alternatives to lead, specifically titanium- and zinc-based paints, existed throughout the late 19th and early 20th centuries. In 1914, the director of the scientific section of the Paint Manufacturers' Association noted with approval the development of "sanitary leadless" paints and predicted that "lead poisoning will be done away with almost entirely."[29]

Despite the accumulating evidence of lead paint's dangers to young children, the industry did nothing to discourage the use of lead paint on walls and woodwork or to warn the general public or public health authorities of the dangers inherent in the product. In fact, it did the opposite: it engaged in an energetic promotion of lead paint for both exterior and interior uses from the 1920s through the Second World War. For a portion of that period, white lead in paint was "the most important outlet for pig lead metal,"[30] according to the LIA, which was organized in 1928 to promote the use of lead.[31] A can of pure white lead paint was composed of huge amounts of lead, creating a large market for mining companies and pigment manufacturers.[32]

Within 6 months of the LIA's founding, its secretary, Felix Wormser, noted, "Of late the lead industries have been receiving much undesirable publicity regarding lead poisoning."[33] A year later, the *United States Daily,* a newspaper "Presenting the Official News of the Legislative, Executive and Judicial Branches of the Federal Government," ran a front-page story on lead poisoning and children: "Lead poisoning as a result of chewing paint from toys, cradles and woodwork is now regarded as a more frequent occurrence among children than formerly."[34]

The reaction of the lead industry to growing negative publicity was to assure the public as well as the public health community that such fears were unfounded and that there was no reason to suspect that toys were being painted with lead pigments. In 1933, Charles F. McKahnn and Edward C. Vogt, pediatricians at Harvard Medical School and Boston's Infants' and Children's Hospitals, published an article in the *Journal of the American Medical Association* in which they mentioned a personal communication from Felix Wormser that led them to believe that "the lead industry and the manufacturers of cribs and toys . . . have cooperated by substituting other types of pigments for the lead pigments formerly used."[35(p1131)] Two years later, a major toy company acknowledged that it had been assured that its toys were safe but had found that the toys had been painted with lead. On investigation, the company found that the paint manufacturers were "willing to sign an agreement that the paint furnished would be non-poisonous, but only a few agreed that they would furnish materials that were entirely free of lead."[36] Another company responded to an inquiry from the Children's Bureau by informing the bureau that "we found that lead in the form of Lead Chromate was being used extensively in colored finishes [of toys]."[37]

Throughout the 1930s and 1940s, continuing reports of poisoned children and workers caused heightened concern among the lead pigment manufacturers, despite the LIA's assurances to the public health community. At the annual meeting of LIA members in June 1935, Wormser noted, "Hardly a day goes by but what this subject receives some attention at the headquarters of the Association." The threat of negative publicity about the health problems associated with lead was so serious that Wormser told the members, "[I]f all other reasons for the establishment of a cooperative organization in the lead industries were to disappear, the health problem alone would be sufficient warrant for its establishment."[38,39] The LIA responded to the undesirable publicity by seeking to rebut research findings and other news of lead's toxicity, whether to children or adults.

Sometimes even major corporations were intimidated. In the early 1930s, the Metropolitan Life Insurance Company had reported on the potential hazards to children from lead, and shortly thereafter Louis Dublin, the respected statistician at the Metropolitan, wrote to the US Children's Bureau requesting that because of the "strong remonstrance by the Lead Industries Association" about the publicity resulting from the earlier article, the Bureau refrain from mentioning "[t]he Metropolitan, either directly or by inference, in connection with whatever releases you may make." The Metropolitan official explained that "you will readily understand that we wish to avoid any controversy with the lead people."[40]

In 1939, the National Paint, Varnish and Lacquer Association (NPVLA), a trade group representing pigment and paint manufacturers, among others, privately acknowledged its "responsibility to the public and the protection of the industry itself with respect to the use of toxic materials in the industry's products."[41] In a letter marked "CONFIDENTIAL Not for Publication," the association informed its members that "the vital factor concerning toxic materials is to intelligently safeguard the public." The letter said that manufacturers should apply "every precautionary measure in manufacturing, in selling and in use where toxic materials are likely to or do enter a product" and noted that "children's toys, equipment, furniture, etc. are not the only consideration." It warned NPVLA members that toxic materials "may enter the body through the lungs . . . through the skin, or through the mouth or stomach." The letter specifically pointed out that lead compounds such as white lead, red lead, litharge, and lead chromate "may be considered as toxic if they find their way into the stomach."

The NPVLA reproduced for its members a set of legal principles established by the Manufacturing Chemists' Association regarding the labeling of dangerous products. The first principle was "A manufacturer who puts out a dangerous article or substance without accompanying it with a warning as to its dangerous properties is ordinarily liable for any damage which results from such failure to warn." Even when a product was widely understood to be dangerous, the Manufacturing Chemists' Association suggested that warnings be included. Further, the legal principles stated, "The manufacturer must know the qualities of his product and cannot escape liability on the ground that he did not know it to be dangerous." The NPVLA letter concluded by calling on NPVLA members to make a "sincere effort in taking advantage of every possible precaution in the use of toxic materials in manufacturing, selling and in use."[42]

DO NOT FORGET THE CHILDREN

The lead pigment manufacturers did not act on the NPVLA's advice. Rather, they actively sought to promote the use of lead in general and the safety of lead for interior uses in particular. Sherwin-Williams' logo was a can of paint poured over the entire globe, with the slogan "Covers the Earth." The Dutch Boy logo of National Lead Company paints was a familiar symbol in the first half of the 20th century and was an essential part of the company's marketing strategy for white lead. In addition to appealing to master painters, homeowners, wives, and mothers, National Lead sought to influence generations of owners by marketing directly to children. In fact, children were a prime target of the company's advertising campaign from early on, even before the LIA was founded. In a promotion to paint distributors, the company advised store owners, "Do Not Forget the Children."[43] In the 1920s, National Lead produced "A Paint Book for Girls and Boys" titled *The Dutch Boy's Lead Party.* Its cover showed the Dutch Boy, bucket and brush in hand, looking at lead soldiers, light bulbs, shoe soles, and other members of the "lead family."[44] The Dutch Boy also promoted the use of lead paint in schoolrooms, suggesting that summer was the best time to "get after the school trustees to have each room repainted" with "flat paint made of Dutch Boy white-lead and flatting oil."[45]

By the late 1920s and into the Depression, as information about lead paint's danger to children continued to accumulate—and after the LIA had acknowledged the inappropriateness of using lead paint on children's toys and furniture—the National Lead Company used the Dutch Boy to promote the use of lead in children's rooms. In one of its several paint books for children, National Lead suggested that its paint "conquers Old Man Gloom":

> The girl and boy felt very blue
> Their toys were old and shabby too,
> They couldn't play in such a place,
> The room was really a disgrace.

> This famous Dutch Boy Lead of mine
> Can make this playroom fairly shine
> Let's start our painting right away
> You'll find the work is only play.

The booklet shows the Dutch Boy mixing white lead with colors and painting walls and furniture.[46]

To emphasize the benign qualities of lead paint, a National Lead Company's advertisement depicted a child in a bathtub scrubbing himself with a brush. His Dutch Boy cap, clothes, and shoes were slung on a chair, and a can of Dutch Boy All-Purpose Soft Paste and paintbrush sat on the floor next to him. The caption read, "Takes a Scrubbing with a Smile."[47] Another promotion showed a crawling infant touching a painted wall. The caption proclaimed, "There is no cause for worry when fingerprint smudges or dirt spots appear on a wall painted with Dutch Boy white-lead."[48] The explicit message was that it was easy to clean the wall; the implicit message was that it was safe for toddlers to touch woodwork and walls covered with lead paint. The theme of children painting appeared in numerous advertisements and articles.[49,50(p77)]

Even in 1949, National Lead remained particularly proud of its marketing campaign directed at children.

> souvenir figures [of the Dutch Boy Painter] in the form of paper weights, statuettes, etc. The appeal was particularly strong to children and the company has never overlooked the opportunity to plant the trademark image in young and receptive minds. One of the most successful promotions for many years was a child's paint book containing paper chips of paint from which the pictures (including, of course, several Dutch Boys) could be colored. . . . The company still will loan a Dutch Boy costume—cap, wig, shirt, overalls and wooden shoes—to any person who writes in and asks for it for any reasonable purpose, and the little painter has graced thousands of parades and masquerades.[51]

This marketing of the Dutch Boy image was seen as an essential element of National Lead Company's increasing profitability; the company's sales rose from $80 million in 1939 to more than $320 million in 1948. The continuing use of the Dutch Boy image was understood by the broader marketing industry as a clever method of improving the image of National Lead. In 1949, one marketing journal noted that "putting the boy, with his wooden keg and brush, in the attitude of a house painter, gave animation to the subject, tied him up with the product and suggested that the quality of the paint was so good that even a child could use it."[52]

In addition to portraying children in its advertisements, the pigment industry emphasized lead paint's "healthful" qualities. As early as 1923, National Lead advertisements in *National Geographic Magazine* promoted the idea that "lead helps to guard your health."[53] Throughout the 1920s, National Lead advertisements in *The Modern Hospital* called the company's tinted paint "the doctor's assistant" because of its cheerful color and the fact that it could be washed with soap and water. The ads assured readers that walls covered with National Lead paint "do not chip, peel or scale."[54] In 1930 the ads suggested, "Every room in a modern hospital deserves a Dutch Boy quality painting job."[55]

In the early 1930s the LIA produced a book, *Useful Information About Lead,* that suggested that the "prospective paint user" would be well advised to use paints containing a high percentage of lead, "the higher the better." A section called "White Lead in Paint" stated that "well painted buildings, both inside and out, go hand in hand with improved sanitation." The book included no warnings about the dangers of lead, despite the fact that the book was produced "to disseminate accurate information regarding lead products and how they best may be used." It included pictures of home and hotel interiors with captions such as "White lead paint is widely used for home interiors."[56] The theme of safety continued to be used to promote lead paint through the early war years. In 1943 Eagle Picher advertisements in *National Painters Magazine* urged professional painters to use "four arguments with prospects—you'll find they really sell paint jobs." The fourth argument was that

"Eagle White Lead is just about the purest, safest, most fool-proof paint you or anybody else can use."[57]

THE WHITE LEAD PROMOTION CAMPAIGN

In addition to specific companies' ads, in 1938 the lead industry as a whole, through the LIA, began its White Lead Promotion Campaign, the single largest activity undertaken by the LIA up until that date. The purpose of the campaign was to increase interest in white lead in paint because the LIA recognized that "white lead is also constantly subject to attack from the health standpoint."[58] The LIA thought that there was a "morale problem" and that advertising would help "to offset the stigma attached to lead because of attacks made upon it by consumer organizations." The association believed the campaign would "help to dispel fear or apprehension about its use."[59]

Early in the promotion campaign, LIA secretary Felix Wormser made it clear that white lead was being promoted for use in interiors.[60] In a 1938 article, the LIA's *Lead* magazine produced an elaborate economic rationale for using lead paint in residential housing, specifically in low-cost construction.[61] The magazine continued to promote white lead for interiors of low-cost homes in its July 1939 issue. In an article on decorating plywood structures, the magazine showed pictures of a recreation room and a kitchen painted with white lead.[62]

Two representatives of the LIA, Seldon Brown and W. L. Frazee, traveled throughout the country visiting officials of public and private institutions in efforts to convince them to use white lead. The LIA specifically targeted markets in urban areas. In mid-October 1940 the LIA reported, "In the course of his work with government officials in the neighborhoods of New York City, our representative also conducted a survey of painting practices of 36 real estate developments. A separate report of this survey has been sent to interested members."[63] Brown reported his success with the Brooklyn Brewcourt Management Company: "Through a demonstration of the true costs of white lead as compared with mixed paint for interiors, Mr. Kilman plans to use white lead on several jobs and probably all future works."[64]

In 1940 the campaign was expanded to include municipal, state, and county institutions. Brown specifically marketed white lead paint for public schools, noting in reports to the association whether institutions he visited used mixed paint or white lead on both exterior and interior walls. The LIA claimed that Brown made a total of 427 calls in his first 2 years on the job, of which 380 were to state, county, and miscellaneous institutions. Brown was particularly insistent on pushing white lead for interior use. When he visited one superintendent of maintenance for Seattle's public school system, Brown initially met with resistance. The superintendent, he reported was "completely sold on white lead for exteriors, but can't see the value of white lead for interiors and [I] was not able to convince him. It was suggested that a demonstration of white lead and flat wall paint be [run] for this department by a lead salesman."[65] Brown also reported on his ability to sell the virtues of white lead to those who knew little about it.[66–69] In Flint, Mich, the superintendent of maintenance for the Board of Education was "very interested in our description of the qualities of interior white lead. [He] said that he thought that white lead was going out because he has heard so little about it. [He knew] nothing about white lead for interiors. [But he] plans to run comparative tests between white lead and present mixed paint used on interiors."[70,71]

In addition to selling to schools, the LIA marketed lead paint to cities, hotels, and even health departments. Frazee reported that he had visited Little Rock, Ark, where he convinced a local hotel manager to have "his entire hotel, inside and out, done with lead and lead reducing oil."[72,73] In Pierce County, Washington, the LIA representative visited the county health department, where he "explained properties of interior white lead paint, stressing sanitary aspects of a highly desirable and washable surface."[74]

In addition, the White Lead Promotion Campaign comprised an advertising campaign, the placement of articles promoting the use of white lead in trade and popular journals, and mailings. In 1939, *Dutch Boy Painter* magazine announced a "big, new, cooperative advertising effort in behalf of white-lead. . . . A series of large-size advertisements in such widely read magazines as the *Saturday Evening Post, Colliers, American Home, Country Gentleman,* and *Better Homes and Gardens* will bring the white-lead story to the public in general and to home-owners in particular." The magazine campaign would produce "67,570,526 separate messages that will be carried in the publications named."[75,76]

In 1940, the secretary of the LIA praised the campaign's success in countering concerns about lead's effect on human health:

> One beneficial result of our campaign is the good will it is building up for lead in general. I have always felt that the cultivation of good will for our metal and publicity about the indispensable work it does for mankind is something that lead needs more than other common metals because lead in many forms is constantly under attack on account of its toxic qualities. Our campaign helps to meet this issue.[77]

The LIA saw its promotional campaign as an important antidote to the negative publicity that lead was receiving in the national press: "[I]n the long run [the campaign] will share in dispelling anxiety about [lead's] use. In any event the problem remains serious for our industry. Hardly a day passes but what this office has to devote some attention to lead poisoning," said Wormser in 1941.[78]

THE DANGERS OF LEAD PAINT BECOME NATIONAL NEWS

In December 1943 the issue of lead poisoning from paint among children, already familiar to those in the industry and to some pediatricians and public health professionals, became national news. *Time* magazine reported on an article by pediatricians Randolph Byers and Elizabeth Lord in the *American Journal of Diseases of Children.* The *Time* article noted that parents' lack of understanding of the dangers of lead-based paint led many to use this toxic material on toys, cribs, and window-sills. When children chewed the painted surfaces, a variety of physical and nervous disorders resulted. "All but one child, Dr. Lord discovered, were school failures. Only five had normal I.Q.s, and four of the five were so erratic that they could not learn easily."[79] The reaction of the LIA secretary was to deny the reliability of Byers and Lord's data; he went so far as to pay a personal visit to Byers in Boston. In a preliminary report on the *Time* piece, the LIA maintained that the assumption regarding the relationship between lead poisoning in early infancy and later mental retardation had not been proven and that many of the cases of lead poisoning had "never been conclusively proven."[80]

The LIA's denials of the dangers posed by lead paint came despite detailed warnings from Robert Kehoe that the association's position was indefensible. Shortly after publication of the Byers and Lord article and the *Time* article, Robert Kehoe wrote to Wormser, "I am disposed to agree with the conclusions arrived at by the authors, and to believe that their evidence, if not entirely adequate, is worthy of very serious consideration." He informed the head of the LIA that in his own work he had seen "serious mental retardation in children that have recovered from lead poisoning."[81] Kehoe left no doubt that he would be willing to assist the board of LIA, but he objected to Wormser's denial of the importance of paint in causing lead poisoning in children. Kehoe argued that the position of the LIA was insupportable. "Unfortunately for Wormser's thesis, comparable results have been obtained in almost every other area of the United States where there have been facilities that enable accurate investigation of this type to be made."[82] "Small children crawl about on the floor and contaminate themselves pretty generally with every kind of dust or dirt that is within their environment. Eventually everything they get on their hands goes into their mouths, and therefore considerably greater opportunities exist for the dangerous exposure of small children of a variety of materials."[83,84]

But the LIA refused to accept the mounting research and evidence of lead poisoning. In December 1945, the association proposed a campaign to counteract the "medical and public misinformation usually amounting to actual prejudice against lead, because of its toxic qualities, [and which] is a subject of vital importance to all the lead industries in the United States." The LIA complained, "If anything, the problem has become even more serious in the last five years than ever before, owing primarily to the spread of considerable anti-lead propaganda and also to occasional faulty medical research which has penetrated deep into medical annals and caused many physicians and hospitals to assume erroneous positions on the question of lead poisoning." The LIA believed that the issue was "so fundamental" to the future welfare of the lead industries and the continued manufacture and use of many important lead products, such as white lead, red lead, litharge, sheet lead, and pipe lead, that unless immediate attention were paid to the problem "the opposing forces may grow strong enough to do us injury which it would take years of work to correct." As a result, the LIA outlined a safety and hygiene program, one purpose of which was to address the existing literature saying that lead represented a health hazard to the worker and the consumer.[85]

In 1946 the problem intensified: Wormser reported to the LIA that

attention to the serious problem faced by all the lead industries because of the toxic nature of our metal is occupying a growing rather than a diminishing amount of the Association's time. This is largely owing to attacks upon lead that cannot be ignored for,
if unchallenged, they may very easily lead to the sponsoring of totally unwarranted State
and Federal legislation of a regulatory or prohibitive character. . . . Suffice it to say here
that this is an unending battle from which we can only withdraw at our peril.[86]

In general, Wormser continued to argue that the danger to the public was minimal.[87]

As late as 1952, the LIA continued to promote the usefulness of white lead in
both interior and exterior coverings. In its book *Lead in Modern Industry,* the LIA
noted that "white lead adds more desirable qualities to paint than any other white
pigment and has practically no undesirable qualities to nullify its advantages." The
book continued, "the profitable application of white lead is not confined to exterior
use. Pure white lead paints can be utilized to advantage for interior decoration, particularly in public and traditional buildings where elaborate decoration is used and
it is very expensive and inconvenient to repaint often."[88]

In summaries of his activities in 1952, the director of health and safety of the
LIA, Manfred Bowditch, called childhood lead poisoning "a major 'headache' and
a source of much adverse publicity." He counted 197 reports of lead poisoning in
9 cities, of which 40 cases were fatal, although he noted that this was an "incomplete"
estimate, especially for New York City.[89] In New York, 44 cases were reported, of
which 14 were fatal. Between 1951 and 1953, according to George M. Wheatly of the
American Pediatrics Association, "there were 94 deaths and 165 cases of childhood
lead poisoning . . . in New York, Chicago, Cincinnati, St. Louis, and Baltimore."[90]

Reports from health departments, publicized in the popular press, were
demonstrating the widespread nature of the lead paint hazard. In 1952 the LIA collected "nearly 500 newspaper clippings featuring lead poisoning, often in sizable
headlines."[91] In 1956 the LIA noted that a headline in the New York *Daily News,*
"Lead Poisoning Killed 10 Kids in Brooklyn in '55, Highest Toll in the City," was
"based largely on data from the Health Department."[92] In addition to "the common
run of newspaper studies on childhood and other types of plumbism," the LIA
noted 2 "items of adverse publicity transcending [them] in importance." In July
1956 *Parade* magazine, which reached more than 7 million readers of 50 newspapers across the country, ran an article titled "Don't Let YOUR Child Get Lead Poisoning," and the CBS television network carried a broadcast on childhood lead
poisoning.[93]

BLAMING THE VICTIMS

The LIA recognized as early as 1952 that to continue fighting a rearguard action attacking the extent of the lead poisoning problem would be "prohibitively expensive
and time-consuming."[94] But the association continued to deflect responsibility for

this tragedy away from the industry itself, placing the blame on poverty, not on the lead industry: "The major source of trouble is the flaking of lead paint in the ancient slum dwellings of our older cities, [and] the problem of lead poisoning in children will be with us for as long as there are slums."[95] Bowditch acknowledged "that the overwhelmingly major source of lead poisoning in children is from structural lead paints chewed from painted surfaces, picked up or off in the form of flakes, or adhering to bits of plaster and subsequently ingested." But who was responsible for this condition? According to Bowditch and the LIA, "Childhood lead poisoning is essentially a problem of slum dwellings and relatively ignorant parents." He maintained that lead poisoning was "almost wholly confined to the older cities of the eastern third of the country" and that "until we can find means to (a) get rid of our slums and (b) educate the relatively ineducable parent, the problem will continue to plague us."[96]

The president of the NPVLA, Joseph F. Battley, elaborated on this theme but used contemporary psychological explanations to rationalize away corporate responsibility for the pollution of children's environments. There might be dietary deficiencies, he said, but even "a well-fed child may still be emotionally hungry because he does not receive as much loving attention as he needs. Another may suffer from a sense of insecurity. To gain the comfort and reassurance they crave, they often place inedible objects [i.e., flaking paint] in their mouths."[97] As late as 1959, lead poisoning was still "a headache" for the industry.[98]

In the 1940s and early 1950s, state and local health departments sought to warn consumers about the dangers lead paint presented to children and others. The industry organized to oppose these efforts. Early labeling regulations in California in 1945 and Maryland in 1949 were opposed by the LIA and NPVLA, and the LIA took credit for the repeal of Maryland's statute.[99] Confronted with pressure in a number of localities and states for increased regulation, the NPVLA's counsel suggested that "the best course to pursue from the standpoint of the industries interested in the use of lead as a pigment and otherwise is to launch a campaign of education directed at the legislatures to forestall any further unnecessary legislation."[100]

In May 1954, the New York City Health Department proposed a sanitary code provision that would have banned the sale in the city of paints containing more than 1% lead and would have required lead paint to be labeled as poisonous and not for interior use.[101] This was consistent with the recommendations of the American Medical Association, which suggested labels saying "WARNING: This paint contains an amount of lead which may be POISONOUS and should not be used to paint children's toys or furniture or interior surfaces in dwelling units which might be chewed by children."[102] Both the NPVLA and the LIA opposed such wording. They supported and helped to develop the standard adopted in 1955 by the voluntary American Standards Association, which did not require the use of the word "poison."[103] New York City's regulation limited the amount of lead in interior paints to 1% but did not include the more explicit warning, and the industry adopted the same voluntary standard. Even in 1958, the LIA continued to oppose "any legislation of a prohibitory nature."[104]

Although the industry claimed that it had stopped using lead in interior paints in the 1940s, and it is clear that other pigments increasingly replaced lead during that time, lead continued to be present in paints sold for interior use well into the 1950s. In one survey commissioned by the US Department of Housing and Urban Development, "about one third of [Pittsburgh's] dwelling units built in [1940–1959] had surfaces with high (2 mg/cm^2 or more) concentrations of lead and nearly 10 per cent of the rooms tested had such lead levels."[105] In 1970, federal legislation prohibited the use of lead paint in federally financed and subsidized housing, and the Consumer Products Safety Commission prohibited the use of all lead paint after February 27, 1978. Yet in 1971, the New York City Health Department tested 76 paints and "found eight of them with amounts of lead ranging from 2.6 to 10.8 percent."[106]

A TERRIBLE LEGACY

Despite the medical evidence concerning the dangers to children of lead-based paint, the reports from Baltimore and other cities of lead poisoning of children, occasional articles in the popular press concerning the dangers of lead-based paint, and internal correspondence from leading lead authorities around the country acknowledging that lead paint was a serious hazard, the industry neither removed lead from paint nor warned consumers of its danger until very late in the game. In fact, at critical moments during this long history, the lead industry actually misled the public health community, assuring it that lead paint was not being used on toys, interior surfaces, or cribs. The industry also consciously used children in its advertising and promotion campaigns in ways that aggravated the public health crisis. By employing children in its marketing strategies, the industry reinforced the public's perception that lead paint was safe, thereby countering the increasing medical, public health, and popular literature documenting lead paint's dangers. This terrible legacy still haunts us today, as more and more cities become aware of the enormous intellectual, physical, emotional, and economic costs of the decades during which an entire industry ignored the growing evidence of lead's impact on children's health and shaped Americans' understanding of the dangers posed by lead.

Editors' Note: *Notes for this reading can be found in the original source.*

PART TEN

The Schools

Hardly a year goes by without another dire report on the sad state of America's public schools. Although they are often reasonably satisfied with the schools their own children attend, many Americans believe that the schools in *general* are falling apart. Bad schools are routinely blamed for a host of our national problems, from uneven economic growth to youth violence.

As many commentators have pointed out, the popular image of the schools is more than a little misleading. *Overall,* the public schools are not as bad as they are often said to be. They are educating more children, from a wider range of backgrounds—and often with more difficult problems—than ever before. Scores on achievement tests, which fell disturbingly in the 1970s, aren't falling any more. More American students go on to college than those of most other industrial countries—and our system of higher education remains one of the best in the world, drawing students from every part of the globe.

Nevertheless, there are a number of serious problems with American schools, and the articles in this part help us to separate the real ones from those that are mostly mythical.

Perhaps the most fundamental of those problems is the persistence of deep inequalities in schooling that continue to divide America's schoolchildren into educational haves and have-nots. At their best, schools—both private and public—offer students high-quality teaching, substantial resources, and excellent facilities. But at their worst, American schools can be astonishingly bad—offering dilapidated and aging classrooms, few resources, and an educational experience that cannot possibly prepare the young for a productive role in society. Unsurprisingly, these "savage inequalities," in the words of the writer Jonathan Kozol, fall along lines of income and race.

Michael Johnston, a young teacher fresh out of Yale, went to teach in a troubled, largely black high school in Greenville, Mississippi, which embodied all of these problems. In the selection from his book about that experience that we reprint here, Johnston describes one of the ways in which such schools shortchange their students, with results that are not only wasteful but, as in this case, can be tragic. Unwilling or unable to deal seriously with one student's academic deficiencies, the school system keeps promoting him anyway—which only increases his inability to do the work the schools require, and deepens his frustration and anger. When this neglect ultimately leads to violence, it surprises no one.

The problems that Johnston describes in one Mississippi high school are part of a broader pattern in which educational resources, like others, are increasingly distributed in markedly unequal ways. Earlier sections have charted a shift upward in wealth and income, as well as political influence, in the United States. But these aren't the only realms in which that upward tilt has taken place. Education is another. We have always prided ourselves on the inclusiveness of our system of public education, as a symbol and embodiment of fundamental American values. What has traditionally made college, for example, a way of moving upward for generations of lower-income Americans was that a college education could be had for free, or nearly so—meaning that the opportunity to gain a higher education was separated from one's ability to pay. But as Ellen Mutari and Melaku Lakew show, going to college today, even at many public universities, increasingly means long hours of outside work, the burden of taking on heavy student loans, or "maxing out" credit cards—a reality that may not be news to many readers of this book. As college becomes less and less affordable, it becomes that much harder for working people to achieve the American Dream through their own efforts.

In "Reading, Writing, and . . . Buying?," the editors of *Consumer Reports* magazine point to another growing problem in the schools—the increasing penetration of commercial advertising into the classroom. Schoolchildren represent a vast potential market for a wide variety of consumer goods; a market that, until recently, has been largely untapped. But many corporations have been moving aggressively to find ways of selling their products to the captive school audience, including everything from commercial-laden "news" channels on TV to cafeteria menus advertising brand-name foods. As the authors point out, all of this represents a troubling breakdown of the distinction between education and sales, between the quest for learning and the quest for profit: and it could profoundly alter the purpose of education in the United States.

Jennifer Washburn's discussion of the growing links between universities and private industry illustrates another aspect of that blurring of the boundaries between education and the pursuit of profit. Traditionally, universities have been committed to the disinterested search for knowledge. But like many other institutions in America, they have become increasingly subject to the influence of private corporations, and the line between objective research and corporate public relations is now sometimes difficult to draw. Corporations not only fund important research, but often help to shape its conclusions. And in some areas—such as research on the safety and effectiveness of new drugs—the consequences are both unethical and dangerous.

CHAPTER 35

In the Deep Heart's Core

MICHAEL JOHNSTON

Two months after school began a new student entered my second-block class. When he first appeared at my door in the middle of my second block, I suspected that he was a troublemaker looking for a good prank. As he continued knocking on the door I could no longer ignore him. Months of being fooled by tricksters had taught me to demand a copy of his schedule before I let him cross my room's threshold. Much to my surprise, he pulled a crumpled schedule from his pocket. I scanned the page for my name: "English II: Johnston, 227. Jevon Jenkins." He stood barely six feet tall, but was the heaviest student I had seen on campus. Jevon was dark-skinned but his face was splotched with patches of brighter skin, as if he'd been severely burned. His arms were covered from wrist to biceps with tattoos; two I recognized as familiar gang emblems, the Deuces and CCP—the Carver Circle Posse. His vacant stare implied that he was incapable of humor or affection, cold enough that a visible show of disinterest might take some serious conjuring.

He did not seem to know anyone in the classroom, and after I approved his schedule he walked to the opposite corner of the room without instruction. He sat in one of the three wide rectangular desks I had placed along the back wall. He was too large to fit in one of the regular desks. Emmanuel, one of the student band directors, had already taken the large desk on the other side of the room, so I couldn't contest Jevon's seat choice. My biggest trouble with Emmanuel was that I would often find him at his desk composing classical music rather than working on the current assignment.

Jevon carried no accessories whatsoever—no backpack, jacket, pen, notebook; nothing. Sadly, this was rather common at Greenville High School; it was in part a protest because locker privileges had been revoked two years earlier due to security concerns. Students had to transport all their belongings and all their books, and setting them down even for a minute meant exposure to theft or vandalism. For some students, their refusal to acquire school supplies articulated their attitudes toward school in general: They would agree to show up each day as the law and their parents mandated, and they would sometimes agree not to keep others from learning, but this did not mean they had to expend their own time and energy to help the process run more smoothly. I guessed that even Jevon's pockets were empty, except for perhaps a lighter and a crumpled up cigarette.

Jevon acted much like the rest of the students on their first day: passive, restrained, calculating. After his comfort level grew, he made casual acquaintance with a few of the marginal characters who occupied the back of the room. One of them, Bryant, who generally was in school only two days a week, had taken a liking to Jevon, mostly due to a common interest in obtaining cigarettes and drug paraphernalia during the day. Toward the end of his second week, Jevon asked to go to the bathroom, saying his stomach hurt horribly and he had been sick all morning. Since this was his first request, I granted it. Naturally I continued the class, but some thirty minutes later I noticed that Jevon's desk was still empty. As the rest of the class was making sporadic efforts at some independent work, I ventured out into the hallway to search for Jevon. Much to my surprise, when I stepped into the hallway he was but a few feet away.

"Where have you been for the last thirty minutes?"

"I've been in the bathroom. Sick. I don't feel so good." He looked at the floor, deferential but not penitent. He was lying and he didn't care that I knew.

Perhaps he was curious to see how I'd handle an obvious lie that I could not prove. He still looked at the ground and shifted his feet like a boy. I looked at his tattoos; there was one on each forearm that I could not decipher, each set off by long scars that ran down his arms. In this moment when he was caught, his idiosyncrasies were still boyish, but I could feel them evolving into more worrisome habits. I chose to handle the situation by straddling a line of discipline, assuring him he couldn't expect bathroom privileges in the future. He nodded indifferently and passed back into the room. In the back of the room his surly partner, Bryant, looked up, and as he did I saw a wide smile spread across Jevon's face—the first I had ever seen. I realized then that I had erred on the side of leniency, and the effect would become obvious.

Jevon soon missed three days while the class was at work on group projects, and he returned on the day before the project's culmination. I had almost forgotten about him when the tardy bell rang for second block. As the crowd cleared, dispersing with haste into their various rooms, a solitary figure was revealed lumbering down the hall. Jevon was late, had missed a number of days, and was about to miss the test grade that the next day's projects represented.

When he reached the doorway, I told him that he had fallen behind on an assignment that was due the following day, and that he needed to work hard that day in order to receive a passing grade. He looked straight through me. Whatever he had seen in the three days of his absence, its intensity had made human figures inconsequential. I handed him a copy of the presentation topics and told him to get started right away. Without looking at it, he collected it the way a truck collects an insect on its windshield. He did not greet the small cadre of boys with whom he had grown familiar, nor did he acknowledge the rest of his classmates. Slightly disturbed by his manner, I watched him all the way to his seat. Noticing my attention, the students grew anxious themselves. I chose to disregard Jevon, and to do my best to proceed with the business of class.

Once I had gotten the students started on their work, I returned my attention to Jevon. Though I hadn't studied him closely during my instructions, I did notice that he was working on something, and I was moderately pleased. Perhaps his new disposition was in fact a wake-up call to the urgency of his own situation.

But as I started back toward Jevon's desk, I soon saw the fruits of his labor: On his desk he had spread out hundreds of shreds from the paper I had handed him. I told him that he must clean up the shredded paper and obtain a copy of the assignment from someone else before the class was over. He looked up and, with his eyes trained on me, swept the shreds off his desk and watched them sprinkle to the ground. Then he propped his big elbow on the desk and extended his pudgy middle finger directly at me.

I sent him to the principal's office.

The next occurrence was less than two weeks later. I was down in the annex during my conference period when I noticed Mr. Taylor, the history teacher, marching his class out into the open field behind the annex. I saw Jevon in the back of the group. Somehow Jevon noticed me up in the second-floor window, and when Mr. Taylor looked the other way, Jevon held his giant arm aloft and once again shot me the middle finger. Not wanting to engage in a disciplinary struggle with a student in someone else's class, I walked away from the window and thought for a minute. While running errands, I found myself in the downstairs annex ten minutes later when Mr. Taylor's class came filing in from the field. Jevon was again at the end of the line. Knowing he was coming I waited outside the door to see if he would acknowledge his earlier gesture. He swaggered toward me, smiling. He stared at me with a wry grin and then suddenly threw both of his hands toward me in a defiant gesture that mimicked rap stars.

"What you gonna do, huh?" he sneered. "What you gonna do?"

He continued staring at me as he passed close enough to threaten a punch, and certainly close enough to deliver one. Then he curled his hand into a gun, pointed it at the lockers and fired, releasing a guttural boom as his arm kicked back from the explosion. He turned toward me as he continued walking, holding his phony smoking gun aloft as he watched imaginary gunpowder swirl off the barrel.

As he reached the end of the hallway, he pointed his makeshift gun directly at me and said, "See that! That's what happens if I fail!"

He turned away and with a wide enticing smile he let his pudgy brown hand relax. I looked at my watch; in twenty-two minutes Jevon would be arriving in my room for second block.

I decided to turn to Mr. Hudson, the assistant principal, for advice. Mr. Hudson and Mr. Amos together made up the entire administration of Greenville High School. Mr. Hudson spent the entire day dealing with discipline. Every time a teacher "wrote up" a student—filled out a disciplinary referral form—the student was sent to Mr. Hudson's office. Mr. Hudson hollered at kids when they needed to be hollered at, and told them to shut their traps when they needed to shut them. The only complaint I ever heard about Mr. Hudson was that he too readily believed in the inherent goodness of the students he disciplined. He was blessed with the patience of a father and the devotion of a preacher.

There was a similarity between the entrance to Mr. Hudson's office and the local street corner on a Friday night: Both were bustling with riffraff waiting for something to happen. For repeat offenders this area became a reliable and often enjoyable hangout spot, a perch from which they could heckle any passersby, knowing they were already in trouble. For predominantly good kids who took pride in their reputation as decent students, being spotted on the wall outside Mr. Hudson's office was Greenville High's version of the Puritan stocks, an obvious social stigma. On this particular morning, business was a bit quieter than usual, since the penitent outnumbered the proud.

Like a seasoned FBI agent, Mr. Hudson responded to my mention of Jevon Jenkins with the wistful frustration over the one that kept getting away.

"Yeah, we've been tracking him now for some time. What we got to do is get enough of a paper trail on him that we can take him to a hearing."

The hearing was the school district's highest court. It was a small and sundry court, presided over by the school board, where the defendant was present and the plaintiff—the school's representative (usually Mr. Hudson) or a slighted teacher—brought forth testimony and witnesses to bear upon the defendant's guilt. This elaborate legal process was necessary because the school board could hand out the severest form of disciplinary punishment—it could either dismiss students or refer them to alternative settings, in our case Garrett Hall, the alternative school.

Mr. Hudson raised his head from his papers to give me my assignment: "Document everything you got. Each event on a separate referral form, and bring them all to me, and we'll get this started. For now we'll see if we can get you a parent conference. Ms. Coris has been having some trouble with him too."

I returned to my room and began to write up the events, waiting for the toll of the bell. I had just begun the second referral when the bell rang and the first of my second-block students filtered through the door. Mr. Taylor's class was only two doors down from mine, so Jevon was always one of the first to arrive. I did not go to the doorway to look for him. Instead, I stayed in the room and conversed with the two students who had already arrived. A moment later Jevon arrived without salutation and proceeded disinterestedly to his place in the corner. We were a good deal of the way through class before I heard from Jevon again. As before, he had been occupied with some labor at his desk. I didn't suspect that it was the assignment the rest of the class was working on, but he seemed to be doing some writing of his own kind: harmless enough. He raised his hand to call me back to his desk.

He had a blank notebook sitting squarely on his desk and I wondered what had happened to the fruits of his labor. He asked plainly if he could go to the bathroom. Without pleading he told me that he would not take long and I could watch him from the doorway if I liked. The boys' bathroom was in direct sight of my doorway. With my monitoring, his trip could not last long enough to commit either of the most common bathroom offenses: gambling and smoking. I conceded, more out of curiosity than courtesy, anxious to see if he was trying to get himself into trouble or steer clear of it. I granted his request and returned to the front of the room. As I did so, out of the corner of my eye I caught Jevon flashing a toothy smile at his partner, Bryant. I watched Jevon raise his considerable body from his desk and stand in front of Bryant, and watched Bryant reach into his backpack and pull something out, placing it furtively in Jevon's hands. Bryant smiled sheepishly at me and quickly returned his eyes to his blank paper. Jevon also put his head down and moved slowly but steadily towards the door.

I stepped in front of the door. "You need to give me whatever's in that hand."

"What? There ain't nothing."

"Give it to me, Jevon, or you go back to your seat."

By now Jevon and I had taken center stage; the entire class looked up from their papers to see how this would be resolved. Jevon no longer wished to deny that there was something in his hand; he simply refused to turn it over. I looked at the thickness of his hand and I knew that any attempt to force it from him would be futile, but I refused to let him out of my supervision with it.

"I'm just going to the bathroom. Just let me go to the bathroom, you already said I could." His eyes did not once raise to meet mine.

"It comes to me or you go to your seat, Jevon. It's that simple."

He thought for a minute, shuffling one foot and raising his head a little to look back toward the class. I moved slightly from the doorway, in part because I believed he had made his decision to return to his seat, and in part because I feared he was on the verge of snapping and barging out the door. He turned without comment or ceremony and returned to his desk. The class shifted in their seats and mumbled a few comments. Some minutes later I was leaning over a student's desk proofreading an essay when I heard a chair squeak. I raised my eyes to see Jevon, backpack in hand, rising from his desk and walking, without urgency, toward the door. He made no show of defiance or disrespect, but simply chose to leave. I knew that to call to him with any urgency would only weaken my already debilitated position.

He had made up his mind, and that decision included disregarding consequences. I knew it would be worthless to threaten him with them now.

"I'll see you in the office, Jevon," I called after him. Disconcerted, I looked back over to his desk. A muffled laughter erupted from the two boys who sat closest to Jevon. I walked over to get a better look.

In the middle of the desk, in permanent black marker, Jevon had drawn an incredibly graphic picture of a man and woman having sex. The drawing itself was about the size of a notebook pad, and it was placed so perfectly in the center of the desk that it seemed almost like a place mat awaiting future visitors. I sent all my referrals to Mr. Hudson that afternoon, including the new one, and three days later I had a parent conference scheduled with Jevon's mother.

I had forgotten about the conference, and was busy preparing for my second block, when Jevon's mother poked her head in my doorway.

"Hello, are you Mr. Johnston?"

A bit surprised, I told her I was.

"I am Jevon Jenkins's mother. I'm here for a conference." Julie Coris, Jevon's French teacher, entered the room right behind her. The three of us sat down, Jevon's mother and I obviously unfamiliar with what should happen next.

Julie started by telling Jevon's mother that the source of his problems in her class were not his fault. Jevon had been placed in her French II class, though he had never taken French I. Julie told her that she had gone to the counselor several times to request a schedule change. However, the counselors said that since Jevon had arrived a month and a half late, all other classes were full and they wanted to leave him there and "see how he does." Julie concluded with a clear prognosis: "There is no way Jevon will pass."

"Yes," Jevon's mother said, "that's what I'm wondering, is does he have any chance to pass at all? If he starts doing all his work and he gets some makeup work?"

My fantasy of Jevon completing makeup work was snuffed by Julie's abrupt response: "No, there is just no way."

His mother then turned to make me the same offer; I glanced through the grade book at the string of zeros and naked boxes where grades were meant to be, wincing like a salesman offered a low price. For a moment I thought of Corelle's heroic makeup efforts.

"He seems capable of doing the work, that doesn't seem to be the problem. But he's very far behind in many of the basic skills, and I am not sure he would be able to catch up with the rest of the kids," I told her. I watched her eyes, and I glanced back toward Jevon's cave in the back of the room. I imagined him as a student rather than a menace, and I couldn't let this offer slip away. "But as far as the numbers go, if he worked hard for the rest of the year, and made up all the assignments that he has missed . . . yes, he could still pass."

She was visually pleased and sensed that it was her turn to speak.

"Well, see, this has all gone back so far, but when we finally brought him to Greenville High they had told me that he was all on grade level, but then he got in trouble so fast that we had to send him back to that military school again, and so we've never even gotten to figure out where he's really at."

Julie and I sensed that we had happened upon a clue to the riddle we had both been studying for weeks, and we pressed her to tell us Jevon's story from the beginning. It was so unbelievable, and so obvious, that I scratched down notes as quickly as I could, hoping to find some ledge in the wall of Jevon's past, a place where he and I could perhaps find a foothold and begin to climb again. By the time the story was over, I could see all the little places along the way where she had lost the small but invaluable battles, and the moment when she finally gave up, handing her boy over to God, unaware that often it is not God who comes first to claim those who have been left to him.

She said that Jevon was born in Jackson and spent his first three years of school there. He presented such discipline problems in the second grade that she and his teachers decided to send him to an "alternative school" for a year. I had never heard of a third grader being sent to alternative school, but if it resembled the alternative schools at the high school level then it must have been an eye-opening experience for a seven-year-old. As most teachers will acknowledge, a good portion of disciplinary problems arises from the defense mechanisms of students who feel insecure about their ability to do the work. Even Jevon's mother acknowledged that the situation was no different for Jevon; part of his problem, she said, stemmed from the fact that he wasn't as "quick" as the rest of the kids. After the year at the alternative school, Jevon was returned to fourth grade at his old school. If Jevon had not left for alternative school, he would have been retained in the second grade, based on his academic ability. Instead, he was sent to the alternative school for disciplinary reasons and after one year returned as a fourth grader.

This kind of mistake is notorious in public schools. In the Delta it has grown so common that many families use it as a strategy for promotion: If a child is failing a grade, send him to stay with an aunt in a neighboring county, where he will be enrolled in a grade based on his age. After a few months, return that child to the old school system where he will again be placed in a grade level according to his age, thereby executing a promotion without any work.

Jevon continued to exhibit the same behavior when he returned to the public elementary school in Jackson, so before Christmas he was sent back to the alternative school for another year. He returned a year later and was admitted to the fifth grade. As is common, the alternative school had made some inroads at curtailing his insolence, but had not seriously addressed his academic deficiencies; as a result, Jevon failed the fifth grade two years in a row. Since Jevon was then thirteen years old and already weighed more than two hundred pounds, the principal thought it emotionally unhealthy to retain Jevon for another year in the elementary school. The principal was at a loss: He couldn't in good faith promote a student who did not have the necessary skills, but neither could he retain a student who was so socially and emotionally removed from his peers that interaction was likely to be unhealthy for both parties. The answer with Jevon always seemed to be, "Send him to someone else." With some assistance from the principal, Jevon's mother decided to send him to Boys' Town in Memphis, a much larger, better resourced, privately run school for troubled boys. He spent two years at Boys' Town. Convinced that Jevon had made some progress, his mother and he moved to Greenville. Now fifteen years old, with his last formal school experience having been in the fifth grade, Jevon enrolled as a freshman at Greenville High School.

To no one's surprise, Jevon was well behind his classmates academically, and was socially uncomfortable because he had not been in a normal school environment since the fifth grade. He was unsuccessful in two tries at that level. Also to no one's surprise, his anxiety manifested itself in a continual display of discipline problems. Before he had the chance to illustrate that he was failing due to inadequate academic preparation, Jevon was removed from Greenville High School before Thanksgiving for fighting, and placed in Garrett Hall. The alternative school obtained a record of Jevon's past, and informed him that if he could successfully complete what it outlined as the skill requirements for sixth, seventh, and eighth grades during the eight months that he was there, he could return to the ninth grade.

Apparently Jevon worked diligently over those months, and he was reinstated to the ninth grade at Greenville High School the following year. But again his disciplinary problems persisted, and his academic preparation was inadequate; again he was removed before the semester was over. This time he was sent to the Dogwood School. The Dogwood School was both more militaristic and more evangelical than any of the others, believing that enough exposure to regimentation and to the Bible could cure anyone. Unfortunately, Dogwood ran on a different schedule from Greenville High, so it was not until October that he was released from Dogwood and enrolled in Greenville High School as a tenth grader.

This is why Jevon arrived two months late to English II, French II, world history, and algebra II. He was expected to outrace his peers to compensate for the missed lessons, although the last time he had successfully passed a course in school was ten years earlier, in the second grade. Counselors placed him in French II and English II, despite the fact that he had never taken—never mind passed—English I or French I. As his mother finished her story I sat enraged, wanting to burn public education to the ground and start again just for Jevon. I glanced over her shoulder at the calendar: It was almost Thanksgiving, and Jevon was right on schedule.

To his credit, Jevon lasted until Christmas. He failed my class with a sixty, despite some marked improvements. One day the following semester, I picked up the newspaper as I waited for a faculty meeting to begin, and recognized Jevon's photograph on the front page. I wanted not to read it, already knowing what it would say. Jevon had been arrested and convicted of three different offenses. Two instances of armed robbery did not surprise me; it was the third that broke my heart. Jevon had also been convicted of sexually assaulting a seven-year-old girl. A coldness opened inside me, and I turned to the teacher next to me, who had young children.
    "How old is a child when he's in second grade?"
    "Seven."
    "That's what I was afraid of."

kid moved around, emotional disorder mom / ~~the~~ school officials effects on kids who don't fit in/fail. Who's problem is the ~~school~~ kid, parents, school, government!?

CHAPTER 36

Class Conflict

The Rising Costs of College

ELLEN MUTARI

MELAKU LAKEW

Brigit M. just graduated from a public college in southern New Jersey with a 4.0 GPA. Putting herself through college with a full course load, she worked 25 to 30 hours a week off campus as a waitress, plus 8 to 12 hours a week on campus as a writing and economics tutor. She had a scholarship, but, as she says, "You think a full scholarship is great, but it doesn't cover books, transportation, and health care costs." She was lucky to have a flexible employer who was willing to accommodate her course schedule. But the time juggle was still difficult: "It was hard to come home from work at 11:00 P.M. and still have to write a paper that was due for an 8:30 A.M. class."

Brigit is one of almost six million working students in the United States. Many of these students do much more than put in a few hours in the school cafeteria or library. They cannot afford a college education without working long hours at one or more off-campus jobs, taking on heavy student loans, and using credit cards to fill in the gaps. The costs of college have skyrocketed, increasing faster than inflation, family incomes, and taxpayer funding of public institutions and financial aid programs. Full-time annual tuition now ranges from an average of $1,627 for a public community college to $15,380 on average for a private college or university. Total costs—including books and fees—are much higher. The total cost of attending a public community college on a full-time basis averages $7,265 a year, while a four-year public university averages $10,889, and a private college or university typically costs $19,443. Today's college students face tremendous monetary pressures.

Many Americans believe in education as a way of ensuring economic opportunity. Politicians and business leaders trumpet college education as means out of poverty, a by-your-own-bootstraps way of attaining the American Dream. Yet college is becoming less and less affordable, especially for students from lower-income families. Tuition at public and private institutions is rising faster than most families' incomes, according to a 2002 study by the National Center for Public Policy and Higher Education. Consequently, families paying college tuition today are shelling out much larger percentages of their incomes than families did twenty years ago. In 1980, the poorest one-fifth, or quintile, of Americans could pay tuition at a public two-year college with only 6% of their family income. By 2000, this percentage had doubled to 12% of family income. Four-year colleges and universities, including public-sector ones, take an even bigger bite out of tight family budgets. Tuition at a private college represents 25% of the annual income of the poorest quintile of families—up from 13% in 1980. It is not only the poorest families that are losing ground. Middle-class incomes have also failed to keep pace with rising tuition. Only the wealthiest families, those in the top income quintile—who since the 1980s have benefited from inflated stock prices, as well as tax cuts and other economic policies skewed toward the rich—have soaring incomes to match escalating tuition costs.

Why is tuition rising so fast? One reason is that colleges and universities are receiving less funding of other kinds; tuition is replacing other revenue sources such as donations, grants, contracts, and perhaps most significantly, state government appropriations to public-sector institutions. In fact, state appropriations to public two-year colleges, four-year undergraduate schools with some graduate programs, and research universities actually fell between the 1988–89 and 1997–98 academic years, and stayed level for four-year bachelor's institutions. The anti-tax, anti-government, anti-public services rhetoric and policies of the past few decades have undermined states' financial support for public institutions of higher learning. Yet these are the institutions with the explicit mission of making college accessible to all. The short-sighted mentality of "tax cuts today" has eroded our nation's public investment in human capital, much as it has our public infrastructure of roads, schools, and bridges.

STUDENTS WORKING OVERTIME

The gap between total costs and aid for full-time students is significant, averaging $5,631 a year at public community colleges and $6,904 at public four-year institutions. For students attending private colleges and universities, the gap is over $10,000.

More and more, students make up this shortfall with paid work. Almost three-fourths of all full-time college students work while attending school, reports the U.S. Department of Education in its 1999–2000 National Postsecondary Student Aid Survey (NPSAS). This figure is up four percentage points since the 1995–96 survey, and accounts for both on- and off-campus jobs, as well as work-study positions. While we might expect to see older, non-traditional students working, the U.S. Bureau of Labor Statistics reports high rates of employment even among traditional-age college students (those between 16 and 24 years old). These are the students we would most expect to receive parental support so that they could focus on classes

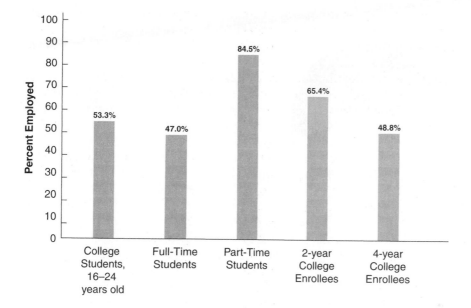

FIGURE 36.1 Rates of Employment among College Students 16–24 Years Old, October 2001

Source: U.S. Bureau of Labor Statistics, "College Enrollment and Work Activity of 2001 High School Graduates," News Release USDL 02-288.

and social life. But over half of these college students were holding down jobs (see Figure 36.1). Even young people who are full-time students and those enrolled in four-year colleges are employed at high rates, 47.0% and 48.8% respectively. For part-time students, employment rates are substantially higher, at 84.5%. Is this because working people choose to attend college on a part-time basis? Or because the costs of college require so many work hours that students cannot take a full-time course load?

Students' work hours indicate that they are paying for more than an occasional pizza in the dorm. Some 71% of full-time students who work are putting in more than the 15 hours per week one might expect of an on-campus work-study job, according to a summary of the NPSAS findings by the State Public Interest Research Groups' (PIRGs) Higher Education Project (see Figure 36.2). One out of five of these students working over 15 hours per week holds down the equivalent of a full-time job—balancing 35 or more weekly hours of paid work against a full-time course load.

Horace K. is a senior majoring in business, a member of the Student Senate, and a prominent student leader on campus. He works 14 hours a week between Sunday and Wednesday at his campus Student Development office. He has another 15- to 20-hour job at the local mall on Fridays, Saturdays, and Sundays. Saturday he is at the mall all day, then Sunday he follows his shift at the mall with a night shift at his on-campus job. Horace points out, "If I don't work, there's no way to buy books, food, and things of that nature." He feels lucky to have these jobs. After his

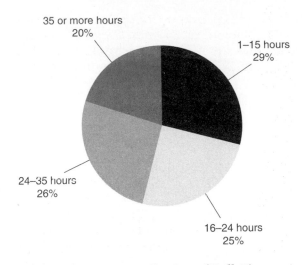

**35 or more hours
20%**

**1–15 hours
29%**

**24–35 hours
26%**

**16–24 hours
25%**

FIGURE 36.2   Distribution of Full-Time Students Who Work, by Hours Worked per Week, 1999–2000

Source: Tracey King and Ellynne Bannon, *At What Cost? The Price That Working Students Pay For A College Education,* The State PIRGs' Higher Education Project, 2002.

first year, he was told he no longer qualified for work-study jobs because his father earned "too much." He could not find an on-campus job, there was no bus to the mall, and he did not have a car. His summer jobs paid for a car so he could commute to the mall.

While many students report educational benefits from their experiences in the work world, they also say that working has negative impacts on their grades, library access, class choices, and ability to get help with course work. For example, Auliya A., a first-year student, was told she had to attend an all-day orientation for her new job at an Atlantic City casino, forcing her to choose between employment and a quiz in one of her classes. Persistence in college studies, especially rates of completion, tend to be lower among students working full-time. One out of five first-year students working 35 or more weekly hours did not finish the school year, compared with only one out of 17 students working fewer than 15 hours per week. According to the PIRG study, the longer a student's weekly work hours, the lower the benefits and the higher the drawbacks they report. The conclusion of the PIRG findings seems to be that a moderate amount of paid work (less than 16 hours per week) yields a positive engagement with the world, but that long work hours harm academic achievement and students' overall college experience.

Of course, students from families with annual incomes of less than $20,000 are more likely to work, and to work longer hours, than those with family incomes of $100,000 or more. These students cite necessities such as tuition, fees, or living expenses as the primary reason for working, while well-off students work for spending money and job experience. According to the PIRG report, half of low-income students who work indicate that they could not afford to continue their studies without a job. Almost one-third (32%) of students from low-income families said that their grades suffered because of their paid jobs, while 23% of students from wealthy families voiced the same concern.

INCREASING DEBT BURDEN

The same students who are working long hours to pay their rising tuition bills are likely to rely on financial aid. Indeed, seven out of ten full-time students receive financial aid. Unfortunately, financial aid does not help as much as it once did. Pell grants are the most important needs-based aid program for low-income college students. Growing out of the War on Poverty and Great Society initiatives of the 1960s, federal Pell grants were created in 1972 as the core program for low-income and working-class college students. Grant aid per student, though, has not kept pace with the rate of tuition increases. Consider how far a Pell grant stretches. The maximum Pell grant of $4,000 represents only 39% of the average cost of attending a four-year public institution. Back in 1975–76, by contrast, the maximum Pell grant was equivalent to 84% of that cost. Grant aid programs originally reflected a vision that higher education should be accessible to all students, but today Congress is undermining that vision by allowing funding to erode.

As grant programs have become stingier, student loans (including federally guaranteed loans) have come to comprise a greater portion of financial aid. Because she worked so many hours, Brigit managed to graduate with only around $5,000 of debt. But this is far less than average. Various studies estimate that average student debt upon completion of a four-year degree falls between $12,000 and $19,000, depending on research methodology. Students are graduating from college shouldering more than a gown: their monthly debt payments typically amount to $150 to $200, and last for 10 years.

At least student loans have reasonable interest rates. That makes them quite different from the high-interest credit card debts many students pile up. Credit card companies aggressively market their wares to college students they know are struggling to make ends meet. Issuers customize their standards for college students, lowering or eliminating experience ratings and income requirements. "When you're a freshman," explains Horace, "you apply and you can get any kind of credit you want." Concern about aggressive marketing to students who may not understand the implications of carrying debt has led some universities to put limits on how their students can be solicited. Nonetheless, approximately two-thirds of college students have at least one credit card; these students carry an average balance of $2,748, according to one study reported by the General Accounting Office. Approximately 15% of students with cards have balances over $1,000. The degree to which students use their cards for direct college costs is hard to pin down. The GAO found studies indicating that as many as 21% of card users paid tuition with their cards and 7% used them for room and board.

Horace's story is instructive. He is graduating with $17,000 in debt from a series of government-subsidized and unsubsidized loans. None of his financial aid was grant aid. At one time, he also had $6,000 in credit card debt. During his first year, he says, he would "walk down the hallways, sign up for a card, and get free t-shirts." Enticed by the aggressive marketing, he wound up with six cards that he used to pay for tuition and books until he found steady employment. He has gradually paid off four of the cards, but still owes $2,000 between two of them.

SOCIETY'S COSTS AND BENEFITS

There is a silver lining for students who struggle with course work and paid work, tuition bills and credit card bills. A college education brings tremendous benefits—both tangible economic gains and personal growth. College, as most students today recognize, is an "investment good," and the economic returns are substantial. The U.S. Census Bureau found that in 2000, college graduates earned 80% more than people with a high school diploma. As the U.S. economy has shifted from a manufacturing base, where jobs requiring only a high school diploma were plentiful, to a high-tech, "information-based" service economy, the demand for college graduates has escalated. Of course, the service economy also involves plenty of jobs in sectors like retail and food service. But even when a college degree is unnecessary for explicit job content, employers increasingly use it as a screening device to identify workers who they think will be hard-working and obedient.

So going to college is a little like buying a house: those who can afford the up-front costs reap great financial rewards later. This economic reality has boosted college enrollments despite the financial difficulties. The college enrollment rate of graduating high school students has risen for several decades, peaking in 1997 at 67%. There was a slight reversal as the rate fell to 63% for the high school class of 2000.

The market, however, now has the upper hand in determining who will have access to higher education. Both the federal government and the states have been shifting their responsibility for providing adequate resources for higher education to the private sector and students themselves. Markets allow the well-to-do to pay for tutors, college preparatory courses, and private college education for their children, who go on to keep the so-called "family tradition," while working-class and poorer students are more likely to be excluded from educational opportunities that can transform their lives.

Treating higher education like any other commodity to be distributed by market forces is a dangerous approach. Even the most narrow-minded economists agree that improving access to education generates benefits for society as a whole—it produces what economists call "positive externalities." Better access to education creates higher levels of skill and knowledge in the workforce, for instance. It also allows for the fuller use of one of our most valuable economic resources—our youth.

But restricting access to higher education is wrong for reasons much deeper than the fact that it "underutilizes" people. Education offers people an opportunity to expand their interests, understand human relationships, and develop a moral compass—it is not just job training, but a basis of human development. As Stanford education professor and feminist economist Myra Strober notes, economic theory is "ill suited to convey the complex and transformational goals" of education. It also fails to identify what is really wrong with leaving access to the market: education and development should be for everyone, not just those who can pay.

Viewed from this perspective, access to education should be considered a basic social right due to all people, like health care, child care, and adequate income. In most other highly-industrialized countries, people expect their government to guarantee the opportunities and material support needed to live decently: it is part of government's public purpose to provide for social rights. Access to an affordable education is one of those rights—but one that is now threatened as rising costs collide with declining aid.

CHAPTER 37

Reading, Writing, and . . . Buying?

CONSUMER REPORTS

Gavin Wahl of Palisade, Colo., arrived home from first grade last year toting free book covers with ads for Frosted Flakes, Lay's potato chips, and deodorant. Then 6-year-old Gavin proclaimed Pizza Hut as his favorite pizza. "We don't even go to Pizza Hut," says George Wahl, Gavin's father. He attributes his son's comment to the school's Pizza Hut reading program, which rewards children with pizza coupons.

Gavin also told his parents about a school movie on tooth care. "I'm supposed to brush with Sparkle Crest," he said.

That was the last straw for his father. "He told me what to buy," George Wahl says in disgust. "Now the school is going to be a conduit for this kind of thing."

Advertising to kids is nothing new. But these days, there's a disturbing difference in the quantity and quality of such ads:

- This has become the "decade of sponsored schools and commercialized classrooms," according to a new study that tracked increased media reports of commercialism in the schools by the University of Wisconsin at Milwaukee's Center for the Analysis of Commercialism in Education. The center is a nonprofit research group that receives support from Consumer's Union.
- Not only is advertising in schools pervasive, but some sponsored classroom materials give a biased view of public-policy issues. Workbooks that address global warming, for example, subtly steer class lessons in directions advantageous to the sponsor.
- Outside of school, marketers are milking the "nag factor." They're pitching to kids traditionally "adult" purchases such as cars, vacations, and telephone lines—and are even feeding kids arguments they can make—hoping parents will cave in to their kids' requests.

THE IMPACT

No matter what parents may think of these practices, one thing is clear: Advertisers are winning. Spending by youngsters ages 4 to 12 has tripled in the 1990s, rising to $24.4 billion [in 1997], according to a leading market researchrer, James U. McNeal of Texas A&M University. Moreover, [in 1997] children influenced purchases totalling nearly eight times that amount, McNeal says.

At a minimum, ads take power away from parents, says Diane Levin, a professor of education at Boston's Wheelock College who has studied how children respond to toy advertising. "The industry says parents need to decide what's appropriate," she says, "but then they go about using every marketing ploy they can to make it harder for parents to assert their authority." One example she cites: the gift registry at Toys 'R' Us, in which a child generates a list of favored toys by pointing at them with an electronic wand. The message to kids, she says, is that "anything that's out there I can want and nag to get."

Commercial messages in schools also undermine the authority and credibility of teachers and principals. In schools that bolster their budgets by granting exclusive contracts to soft-drink companies, how seriously can students be expected to follow admonitions to limit soda in favor of healthful snacks? Who can forget the headlines from March, when a high school principal suspended an Evans, Ga., student for wearing a Pepsi shirt on the school's "Coke in Education Day"?

As for today's marketers, "These are kids who grew up with advertising. They don't see a problem," says Ellen Wartella, dean of the University of Texas College of Communication. Wartella's research dates back to the 1970s, when she demonstrated that young children have difficulty telling the difference between advertising and other programming.

"I'm not sure we can go back to an age when children weren't commercialized," Wartella adds. "But we certainly have to have standards that say not everything goes."

As of now, we don't. The Federal Trade Commission, the government agency that has done the most recently to protect children, has focused on cases of fraud and deception, not fairness. Watchdog groups such as the Center for Media Education (202 628-2620; *www.cme.org*) have taken it upon themselves to alert the public to marketplace excesses.

Parents themselves don't like advertising's effect on children, according to a 1997 survey by Roper Starch Worldwide. Nearly 80 percent of adults said that marketing and advertising exploit kids by convincing them to buy things that are bad for them or that they don't need.

George Wahl is in this majority. The idea that Gavin will be "a Pepsi drinker for life, and this is something that was planted in his head when he was a toddler, to me that's offensive," he says.

AD CAMPAIGNS

Market researchers probe virtually every aspect of kids' lives, going beyond how kids shop to sample their most intimate thoughts and feelings.

Last year, according to the child-marketing newsletter Selling to Kids, Roper Starch Worldwide and Just Kids Inc. studied kids' daydreams and fantasies, so that these could be incorporated into marketing and advertising programs. They found that 80 percent of U.S. kids daydream about helping people and 24 percent about protecting the environment. Such data, the newsletter says, can provide dividends for companies savvy enough to form the right strategic alliances with environmental groups.

Researchers even try to gauge how effectively kids nag their parents. Recently, Selling to Kids described a study by Western International Media, "The Nag Factor," which found that 3- to 8-year-olds were 14 percent more likely to get parents to buy a toy if they emphasized that the toy was important to them. "It's not just getting kids to whine, it's giving them a specific reason to ask for the product," a Western International official says in the newsletter.

Marketers also play on kids' emotional needs. Gene Del Vecchio, a senior partner at advertising agency Ogilvy & Mather Worldwide, regales attendees at child-marketing conferences with techniques featured from his recent book "Creating Ever-Cool: A Marketer's Guide to a Kid's Heart." Del Vecchio's key principle for making a product cool: "Satisfy a kid's timeless emotional need(s) but routinely dress it up in a current fad or trend." These needs include empowerment (because kids are lowest in society's power structure), peer approval, gender identification, and the desire to be a couple of years older.

How do marketers view children? Brochures from industry conferences refer to goals such as "successful ways of reaching kids and their gatekeepers in schools." Other brochures say:

- "Today's savvy kids are tomorrow's loyal customers. It's not enough to throw crayons and a placemat at a child and expect any kind of loyalty. Kids need more sophisticated and challenging ways to learn about your product or service—and to remember you fondly for years to come."
- "Kids are intensely concerned about the environment. . . . Find out how you can put these findings to work for you in giving the 'cool' factor to your marketing strategy."
- "We will explore creating an intimate relationship with teens—one based on an intimate understanding of their lives and instincts, and reflecting them back in advertising."

SCHOOLS ON THE BLOCK

It's easy to understand why marketers focus on schools. Sponsoring educational programs achieves several goals: It builds good community relations by associating a company with a good cause; it penetrates a six-hour time period—9 a.m. to 3 p.m.—that's been traditionally off-limits to advertisers; and it gains priceless credibility for a company through association with trusted teachers.

Educators themselves have not yet come to terms with the issues raised by commercialism in schools. The University of Wisconsin study found little discussion of these issues in publications by and for educators.

The University of Wisconsin media analysis followed several types of school-house commercialism: sponsorship of school events; exclusive sales of products like soft drinks; incentive programs such as collecting product labels; appropriation of space such as walls and bulletin boards; sponsored educational materials; and provision of electronic equipment or programming in return for the right to advertise. (The report is posted at *www.uwm.edu/Dept/CACE.*)

Here are some ways kids now receive commercial messages in school:

- Eight million students are required to watch Channel One, a news broadcast that includes commercials.
- More than half of American classrooms—25 million students—receive advertising-laden book covers, and 6 million schoolchildren receive advertising-filled cafeteria menus.
- Scholastic Inc., a respected educational publisher, continues to trade on its reputation by producing sponsored educational material for a variety of marketers under the Scholastic name, some of it thinly veiled promotions for Hollywood blockbusters.

Some school materials engage in subtle politicking. Teacher and student guides for Chevron's free school video on the Greenhouse effect contain valid information about global warming, but they also steer students in the industry's direction (one of the biggest man-made causes of these gases is automobile emissions). For example, most scientists now agree that global warming is occurring. But the guide repeatedly stresses disagreements among scientists over the issue. One exercise encourages students to discuss "What, if anything, can be done to safeguard the public against errors in judgment by policymakers, who may be reacting to political pressures?"

In another activity, students must decide whether certain scenarios promote or reduce atmospheric greenhouse gases. An obvious contributor to the problem—the single-driver automobile trip -isn't mentioned.

The value of influencing teachers has also not been lost on a group of oil, chemical, pharmaceutical, and other companies who fund the Keystone Science School in Keystone, Colo., a division of the nonprofit Keystone Center. In the school's annual Key Issues program, companies committed to "changing and enhancing the way science and environmental issues are taught in classrooms"—companies such as Dow Chemical, DuPont, and Union Carbide—sponsor hundreds of teachers. The stated mission is to help teachers understand various viewpoints; to be sure, the corporate viewpoint is among them. A liaison from the sponsoring company can help teachers maintain their corporate relationship through the years.

THE HOME FRONT

Even in the home, where television ads aimed at kids have been standard fare for decades, marketers are finding ways to increase their presence.

For example, parents who leave their set tuned to the Public Broadcasting System, confident that their kids are getting a break from advertising, are in for a rude surprise. "Barney & Friends," "Arthur," and other favorite shows feature ads for Chuck E. Cheese's, McDonald's, and Kellogg's Frosted Flakes. Donna Williams, a PBS spokeswoman, called them "enhanced underwriting credits," and some do offer positive educational messages. But the likes of Ronald McDonald asking, "Did somebody say McDonald's?" on PBS member station WNET in New York breaches the station's sponsorship guidelines, which prohibit the appearance of company mascots. The ad was deemed appropriate because, overall, it's noncommercial and promotes "using your imagination," says Katherine Schultheis of WNET.

Marketers are also running child-oriented ads for whole categories of products—such as cars and vacations—traditionally associated with adults. Last year, kids ages 4 to 12 influenced $188 billion in purchases—$17.7 billion in car sales alone, according to market researcher McNeal. It's no wonder, then, that Chevrolet ran a two-page spread for its Venture minivan in Sports Illustrated for Kids, with appealing scrapbook photos of Mom, Dad, the kids, and the family dog.

Now that many families have embraced the home computer, millions of children surf the World Wide Web, a trend marketers have quickly picked up on. The web has become a gold mine for companies that practice database marketing—using mailing lists of children to target them with advertising. Here's how it works: Companies use eye-catching graphics, interactive games, and chat rooms to attract children, then collect their name, address, and other information, often without a parent's knowledge. In a report to Congress this June, the FTC noted that 89 percent of the children's web sites it surveyed collect personal information from children, while less than 10 percent provide for parental control, such as the ability to review, correct, or delete information. The commission recommended that Congress pass legislation to let parents take control back from marketers.

Marketing and issue messages on the web are no less useful than sponsored school materials for shaping kids' views on public-policy issues. On Shell's G-Whiz Kids site (*www.shellus.com/whizkid*), for example, kids earn a "Certificate of Advanced Energy Studies" by teaching others about Shell's reasons why "gasoline is fueling America's future." Chevron's kids' site (*www.chevroncars.com*) teaches children that America's security and way of life depend on oil, "the fuel that makes our country go."

CHAPTER 38

Hired Education

JENNIFER WASHBURN

Michael Wolfe, a gastroenterologist at Boston University, admits he was duped by the Pharmacia Corporation, the manufacturer of the blockbuster arthritis drug Celebrex. (In 2003, the company was purchased by Pfizer.) In the summer of 2000, *The Journal of the American Medical Association* asked Wolfe to write a review of a study showing that Celebrex was associated with lower rates of stomach and intestinal ulcers and other complications than two older arthritis medications, diclofenac and ibuprofen. Wolfe found the study, tracking 8,000 patients over a six-month period, persuasive, and penned a favorable review, which helped to drive up Celebrex sales.

But early the next year, while serving on the Food and Drug Administration's (FDA) arthritis advisory committee, Wolfe had occasion to review the same drug trial again, and was flabbergasted by what he saw. Pharmacia's study had run for one year, not six months, as the company had originally led both Wolfe and the *Journal* to believe. When the complete data was considered, most of Celebrex's advantages disappeared because the ulcer complications that occurred during the second half of the study were disproportionately found in patients taking Celebrex.

"I am furious," Wolfe told *The Washington Post* in 2001. "I looked like a fool. But . . . all I had available to me was the data presented in the article." Remarkably, none of the *Journal* study's 16 authors, including eight university professors, had spoken out publicly about this egregious suppression of negative data. All the authors were either employees of Pharmacia or paid consultants of the company.

Celebrex, an anti-inflammatory drug similar to Vioxx, is once again in the news due to concerns that it may be associated with the same cardiovascular risks that caused Vioxx to get yanked from the market. In recent months, we've heard a great deal about conflicts of interest at both the FDA, the agency that approves drugs for public safety, and the National Institutes of Health, where publicly funded scientists moonlight as consultants for the very companies that manufactured the drugs they are testing. Still largely ignored, however, is the role played by the once-autonomous ivory tower and the university scientists who, either knowingly or unknowingly, facilitate the pharmaceutical industry's manipulation of drug testing by lending it an aura of objectivity.

Today, market forces are dictating what is happening in the world of higher education as never before, causing universities to look and behave more and more like business enterprises. Instead of honoring their traditional commitment to teaching, disinterested research, and the broad dissemination of knowledge, universities are aggressively striving to become research arms of private industry. Faced with declining government funding, they are avidly seeking to enhance their role as "engines" of economic growth, promising state legislators and governors that they will help drive regional economic development by pumping out commercially valuable inventions.

This radical redefinition of the university's mission can be traced back to the economic stagnation of the 1970s. Propelled by heightened competition from Germany and Japan, Congress passed landmark legislation in 1980 that allowed universities to automatically retain the rights to intellectual property stemming from taxpayer-financed research. The intent of the legislation, popularly known as the Bayh-Dole Act (its sponsors were Senators Birch Bayh and Bob Dole), was to stimulate innovation and speed the transfer of federally financed research to industry. What it accomplished in the process was the introduction of a dangerous new profit motive into the heart of the university.

As a result, schools now routinely operate expensive patenting and licensing operations to market their faculty's inventions, extracting royalty income and other fees in return. They invest their endowment money in risky startup firms founded by their professors. They run their own industrial parks and venture capital funds. They publish newsletters encouraging faculty members to commercialize new research by launching independent, faculty-owned companies. Star professors consult for, or hold equity in, the same firms that manufacture the drugs they are studying, while also often accepting generous fees to join corporate advisory boards and speakers' bureaus. Sometimes these professors even hold the patent to the drug or device being tested. In a study of 800 scientific papers published in leading journals of medicine and molecular biology, Sheldon Krimsky, a professor of public policy at Tufts University, found that slightly more than a third of the lead authors based at research institutions in Massachusetts had a significant financial interest in their own reports. So pervasive are such ties that journal editors now frequently complain that they can no longer find academic experts who do not have a financial interest in a drug or therapy the journal would like to review.

Research suggests that publicly funded science, most of it performed at universities, was a critical contributor to the discovery of nearly all of the 25 most important breakthrough drugs introduced between 1970 and 1995. If university scientists lose their independence, who will perform this pathbreaking research and objectively evaluate the safety and effectiveness of drugs already on the market? Conflicts of interest are more than an academic concern. When it comes to health policy, they pose a serious threat to public health.

With the possible exception of business schools, the nation's medical schools have been more infiltrated by industry than any other sector of the university. Pharmaceutical companies sponsor daily lunches for medical students at which they market their latest drugs; they ply professors with fancy dinners, gifts, luxurious trips, and free prescriptions designed to influence medical decisions and prescribing habits. The drug industry also spends millions of dollars financing clinical drug research at the academy, but increasingly this money comes with many more strings attached. After conducting a thorough review of the medical literature for *The New England Journal of Medicine* in 2000, Thomas Bodenheimer, an internist at the University of California, San Francisco, concluded that academic investigators were rapidly ceding to industry control over nearly every stage of the clinical research process.

In the past, for example, it was common for university scientists to initiate the research protocol. Now, studies are frequently conceived and designed in the company's own pharmacological and marketing departments, thus removing this formative stage of the research from academic hands almost entirely. The company then shops the study around to various academic institutions (and a growing number of competing for-profit subcontractors that run clinical trials) in search of investigators to conduct the research. As university medical schools have grown more dependent on industry grants to sustain their operations, their professors have become increasingly willing to accept an industry-initiated protocol without modification, even though the study may be largely designed to secure a company's market position. Should a professor reject the study or insist on changes, another university scientist will very likely be more solicitous.

Industry also encourages the use of ghostwriters on scientific papers. This means an article or review bylined by a prominent academic might in fact have been written by a medical-communications company working for the drugmaker, with the "author" paid an honorarium to attach his or her name to it. When Wyeth-Ayerst sought to boost market demand for Redux, one part of the once highly popular "fen-phen" diet-drug combination, the company hired a company called Excerpta Medica to help draft the manuscripts and pay doctors to review and sign the articles. One of the many doctors who signed Excerpta's papers was Richard Atkinson, a renowned obesity expert at the University of Wisconsin-Madison. Atkinson denied having any knowledge of Excerpta's connection to Wyeth, but as an independent academic, he nonetheless agreed to lend his name to a company he apparently knew little about. (Excerpta maintains that all its authors were told of the company's association with the manufacturer.) In a deposition on January 15, 1999, Wyeth-Ayerst executive Jo Alene Dolan admitted that her company had written the article for Atkinson, stressing that all drug companies ghostwrite articles. Shortly before the article could be published, Redux was pulled from the market because of its association with serious heart and lung problems.

Scientists who perform industry-sponsored research are also asked routinely to sign legal contracts requiring them to keep both the methods and the results of their work secret for a period of time. Research conducted by David Blumenthal and Eric Campbell, health-policy researchers at Harvard University, suggests that data withholding and publication delays have become far more common over the last 25 years, particularly in molecular biology, medicine, and other life-science disciplines, where commercial relationships have grown dramatically in recent years. In a survey of 2,167 life-science faculty, Blumenthal found that nearly one in five of them had delayed publication for more than six months to protect proprietary information.

Industry also manipulates academic research by suppressing negative studies altogether. Recently, it came to light that a whole class of popular antidepressants—including such heavily prescribed drugs as Paxil, Zoloft, and Prozac—are largely ineffectual in treating childhood depression and actually increase the risk of suicide. One of the main reasons this information was not available to doctors and the broader public, it turns out, is that the academic investigators who led these studies either allowed industry to bury their research or were complicit in downplaying negative findings in their own published papers. How prevalent is such corporate meddling? The question has received surprisingly little scholarly attention, but what research does exist is not encouraging. One survey of major university-industry research centers in the field of engineering, for example, found that 35 percent would allow corporate sponsors to delete information from papers prior to publication.

But all the blame for the eroding objectivity of university researchers does not rest with industry. Universities themselves are complicit: They are so financially invested in their professors' research through patents, equity, and other financial holdings that their disinterested pursuit of knowledge has been gravely compromised. For instance, when the Harvard Center for Risk Analysis' longtime director, Professor John D. Graham, was nominated by President George W. Bush to become the government's "regulatory czar" at the Office of Information and Regulatory Affairs (part of the Office of Management and Budget), it helped to expose just how extensive Harvard's financial conflicts really were. Congressional hearings revealed that Graham's center solicited tobacco money and worked with the tobacco industry to disparage the risks of secondhand smoke. (Harvey Fineberg, a dean at the Harvard School of Public Health, demanded that one check from Philip Morris be returned. In response, Graham wrote to the company asking if it might send the $25,000 back to the Harvard center via the Philip Morris subsidiary Kraft Foods instead.) Graham's center also argued that cell-phone use by drivers should not be restricted, even though its own research, which was funded by AT&T Wireless Communications, showed that such use could lead to a thousand additional highway deaths a year. As a member of the Environmental Protection Agency's scientific advisory board subcommittee on dioxin, a known human carcinogen, Graham argued that reducing dioxin levels might "do more harm . . . than good." His Harvard center, meanwhile, was heavily funded by dioxin producers.

Worse yet, the universities' loyalties are now so conflicted that schools are increasingly willing to cave in to narrow Commercial demands rather than defend their own professors' academic freedom or the public interest. When researchers at the University of Utah discovered an important human gene responsible for hereditary breast cancer, for example, they didn't make it freely available to other scientists, even though we—the U.S. taxpayers—paid $4.6 million to finance the research. The university raced to patent it, then granted the monopoly rights to Myriad Genetics

Inc., a startup company founded by a University of Utah professor, which proceeded to hoard the gene and prevent other academic scientists from using it.

Professors, too, are increasingly driven by the bottom line. More and more, they not only accept industry grants to support their research but also hold stock in or have other financial ties to the companies funding them. Many experts fear this skewing of professors' research toward short-term commercial goals will impede long-term scientific and technological innovation. Financial entanglements between researchers and corporations have grown so common that the Securities and Exchange Commission (SEC) has investigated numerous academic researchers suspected of engaging in insider trading. In a case filed in Pennsylvania, the SEC charged Dale J. Lange, a Columbia University neurologist, with pocketing $26,000 in profits after Lange bought stock in a company that was about to release promising new findings concerning a drug to treat Lou Gehrig's disease. Lange had good reason to expect the stock to soar because he had conducted the confidential clinical trials himself. In 2000, an investigation by *USA Today* found that more than half the experts hired to advise the U.S. government on the safety and effectiveness of drugs—a large number of whom are academics—now have financial links to companies that will be affected by their conclusions.

When Wyeth-Ayerst was trying to get its diet drug, Redux, approved for sale in the United States, for example, it faced a serious hurdle: Patients in Europe who had taken a drug virtually identical to Redux had an increased chance of getting a rare, life-threatening lung ailment known as pulmonary hypertension. To combat this negative health profile, the company packed an FDA hearing room with a who's who list of the nation's top academic obesity experts, all of whom were *also* paid consultants to Wyeth-Ayerst or other companies involved in the sale of Redux. In addition, the company recruited expert "opinion leaders," such as George Blackburn, a renowned obesity expert at Harvard, to testify before the Medical Society of Massachusetts for approval of the drug. Blackburn and other academic luminaries further participated in the company's "Visiting Important Professors Program" and were paid thousands of dollars in honoraria to fly to fancy resorts and promote Redux at medical conferences. Not surprisingly, the drug handily won market approval, and prescriptions in the United States began to soar.

Soon, however, evidence of the drug's association with lung damage surfaced once again, and the company turned to leading university scientists to do damage control. In the summer of 1996, an internal company memo revealed that the company was planning to spend $5.8 million to pay for more university-based studies, noting that that money was needed to "establish and maintain relationships with opinion leaders at the local and national level to communicate to their colleagues the benefits of Redux and to encourage its use." Among the many doctors willing to heed the company's call was Atkinson, the obesity expert at the University of Wisconsin, whose name appeared on a company-authored article. "Let me congratulate you and your writer,"wrote Atkinson in a thank-you letter to the ghostwriting firm that was one of numerous company documents that became public during subsequent legal proceedings. "Perhaps I can get you to write all my papers for me!"

So how does this growing web of academic-industry ties affect research outcomes? A vast body of work suggests that industry-funded research is far from impartial. In 1996, Stanford researcher Mildred Cho co-authored a study in the *Annals of Internal Medicine* that found that 98 percent of papers based on industry-sponsored research reflected favorably on the drugs being examined, compared with 79 percent of papers based on research not funded by industry. An analysis published in *The Journal of the American Medical Association* in 1999 found that studies of cancer drugs funded by the pharmaceutical industry were nearly eight times less likely to reach unfavorable conclusions than similar studies funded by non-profit organizations. More recently, a systematic review of 1,140 clinical trial studies, published by researchers at Yale in 2003, concluded that, from cancer to arthritis to cholesterol, the evidence is overwhelming that when research is industry-sponsored, it is "significantly more likely to reach conclusions that [are] favorable to the sponsor" than non–industry-funded research.

In the area of health and drug research, of course, the results of such manipulation can be deadly. Running down the list of drugs recently pulled from the market or subject to increased health warnings—Rezulin, the diabetes drug; Redux (or fen-phen), the diet drug; Retin-A, the anti-wrinkle cream; Neurontin, the epilepsy drug; Paxil, Zoloft, and the many other antidepressants now deemed ineffective for children—one finds that a remarkable number of prominent university professors with close financial ties to the manufacturers played a central role in lobbying for these drugs to be approved, recommending them to other doctors, and, in many cases, urging that they remain on the market long after the problems or lack of effectiveness became known. Not infrequently, the university scientists who shill for the drug companies most aggressively are also the biggest-name professors in their fields.

Universities have gone out of their way to assure the public that their clinical trials meet the highest standards of "scientific excellence" and "academic rigor." But over the last 20 years, public dismay over the growing financial entanglements in clinical research has prompted the federal government to impose tougher conflict-of-interest regulations, only to encounter fierce university opposition. In 1995, the federal government finally succeeded in pushing through rules that would apply to all academic researchers funded by the Department of Health and Human Services (HHS) or the National Science Foundation (NSF). But the rules, which remain in place today, were not tough enough to be effective. Although they mandate that serious conflicts of interest must be managed and/or eliminated, they leave the determination of what action is to be taken, if any, entirely up to the university. The policy also doesn't provide any guidance on which conflicts warrant serious attention, nor does it impose any prohibitions, such as banning financial conflicts outright in the area of human-subject research. Significantly, the policy also says nothing about institutional conflicts of interest.

The result, not surprisingly, is that university conflict-of-interest rules vary widely. One comprehensive 2000 survey of the written policies at 100 academic institutions found that only 55 percent of schools required disclosure of conflicts of interest from all faculty, and only 19 percent specified any limits on researchers' financial ties to corporate sponsors. Worse yet, under this fragmented system, there is enormous pressure on universities to keep their policies lax. Schools with tighter restrictions run the risk of losing talented faculty to competing schools with more permissive policies, where the financial rewards and commercial prospects are likely to be greater.

Another conspicuous problem with the HHS/NSF policy is that it does not require universities to make any of the information they compile on faculty financial conflicts available to the public. Many academic journals do require their authors to disclose corporate financial ties. But in practice, reporting is astonishingly poor. In a 2001 study, Tufts' Krimsky found that a mere 0.5 percent of the 61,134 papers appearing in 181 peer-reviewed journals contained statements about the authors' financial ties. More recent studies have found similarly low levels of reporting.

In some respects, the whole debate reflects how far the academic world remains from dealing seriously with the issue; disclosure of potential conflicts of interest is, after all, a far cry from eliminating them outright, as many professions not only recommend but also require. In the legal profession, for example, attorneys are prohibited from taking on cases in which they have a financial interest or other explicit conflicts that might be seen to compromise their professional integrity. The same is true of judges. But when it comes to academia, neither the medical community nor the government (whether through Congress or the regulatory agencies) has taken up the task, instead proceeding under the assumption that universities can be trusted to manage these commercial interactions themselves. It's a nice idea. But are academic institutions really capable of performing this function? There is good reason to be skeptical: Far from being independent watchdogs capable of dispassionate inquiry, universities are increasingly joined at the hip to the very market forces the public has entrusted them to check, creating problems that extend far beyond the research lab.

PART ELEVEN

Crime and Justice

In recent years, crime has often been perceived by the public as America's number one social problem. Violent crime has made many Americans afraid to walk their streets at night, and has greatly diminished the quality of life in many parts of the United States. And though levels of violent crime are not as high as they were at their peak in the early 1990s, they remain higher than those of other advanced industrial societies—despite dramatic increases in the number of people who have been put behind bars.

Many Americans believe that we have been shockingly lenient with criminals. In the excerpt we reprint here, Elliott Currie argues that this is a myth, and examines the factual underpinnings of this myth—as well as the belief that our investments in prisons are cost effective and efficacious. The reality is that we tend to be quite punitive with those "street" criminals we actually catch—considerably more so than most other countries. And, with more than two million people in our jails and prisons on any given day, we are becoming more so all the time.

Politicians, however, looking for quick fixes to the crime problem, have passed a variety of even more punitive measures in recent years—including so-called three strikes and you're out laws, mandating 25-year to life sentences for criminals convicted of three felonies. In California, the third felony may be a relatively minor offense, such as stealing a bicycle or possessing a small amount of drugs. Despite the harshness of this law, it has been recently upheld by the U.S. Supreme Court, which ruled in 2003 that a sentence of 25 years to life for stealing three golf clubs did not constitute the "cruel and unusual punishment" prohibited by our constitution.

These laws are surely "tough," but are they effective? Jerome H. Skolnick calls California's three-strikes law a "wild pitch"—arguing that the law is too rigid and will result in a vast and costly expansion of the prison system into a home for aged and low-level offenders. In response, John J. DiIulio maintains that, as a nation, we are actually soft on criminals, allowing some of the most dangerous to bargain their way into lesser charges at the front end of the system, while releasing them early to parole and community supervision at the back. In his reply, Skolnick says that Di-Iulio's generalizations are inaccurate, and offers data to show why.

As of 2004, there were more than 7,500 inmates in California prisons sentenced to 25 years to life as "third strikers," and another 32,500 "second strikers." One result of locking up so many prisoners for such long terms will be the aging of the state's prison population: it's estimated that there will be more than 30,000 inmates over the age of 60 by the year 2020, whose need for extra care will cost the state's taxpayers roughly a billion dollars a year.[1] (This did not prevent the state's voters from defeating, in 2004, a modest proposal to soften the law's harsh provisions.) The law has also generated sharp racial disparities: at last count, only 28 percent of second and third strike inmates were white, while fully 72 percent were black or Hispanic.[2]

California is hardly alone in this respect: as we've seen, one of the most striking, and disturbing, developments in American criminal justice has been the great increase in the number of minority offenders—especially young offenders—behind bars. The article by Philippe Bourgois puts a human face on such statistics. Bourgois, an anthropologist, spent several years "hanging out" with a group of young drug dealers in New York City. He concluded that drugs in the inner city are a symptom of a profound "social marginalization and alienation" and that the underground economy of drug dealing has become the fastest-growing "equal opportunity employer" for poor young men. For though selling drugs actually brings in a relatively meager "salary" for the majority of dealers, it compares favorably with the low-wage, dead-end jobs that are the only legitimate work most of them have ever experienced. It is young men like these who increasingly make up our swollen prison population.

At the other end of the scale is another kind of criminal—the affluent offenders, often corporate executives, who commit so-called "white collar" crimes. The term was coined by an American criminologist, Edwin Sutherland, in the 1930s to mean crimes committed by otherwise "respectable" people in the course of their business. It has long been understood that these "respectable" offenders are treated very differently by the criminal justice system than the ones who appear in the articles by Bourgois and Skolnick. They are far less likely to ever see the inside of a prison or jail, and unlikely, on the whole, to stay long if they do. But the article here by Ken Silverstein shows something more: that even companies that are repeat offenders, whose crimes kill and injure people and who may receive substantial fines as a result, are often rewarded by billions of dollars in government contracts. Indeed, some of the biggest government contractors in America are also among the worst and most persistent violators of federal environmental and health and safety laws. In this case, if in few others, we are indeed lenient in our treatment of criminals.

ENDNOTES

1. Sandra Kobrin, "Dying on Our Dime," *Los Angeles Times Magazine,* June 26, 2005.
2. California Department of Corrections, *Second and Third Strikers in the Institution Population,* Sacramento, CA, December 2004.

CHAPTER 39

The Myth of Leniency

ELLIOTT CURRIE

Many Americans believe that the main reason we remain a frighteningly violent country is that we are shockingly lenient with criminals. That would seem, at first glance, a difficult position to maintain in the country that boasts the developed world's highest imprisonment rate. And, in fact, the idea that serious, violent criminals are treated leniently in the United States *is* a myth. But it is a myth that is deeply entrenched in the public imagination. How is it possible to maintain that America is "soft" on criminals in the face of the enormous increases in punishment in recent years?

One way to make this case is simply to downplay the magnitude of our recent increases in incarceration. Thus James Q. Wilson speaks of our "inching up" the costs of offending in recent years, a jarringly peculiar way to describe the quintupling of the prison population. Others simply sidestep the extraordinary growth of imprisonment and argue that misguided liberal policies allow most offenders to go unpunished and vast numbers of "known violent predators," in the phrase of the conservative Council on Crime in America, to run loose. William Bennett, John J. Di-Iulio, and James P. Walters, the authors of the leading recent conservative tract on crime, put it this way in the course of arguing for "more incarceration":

> Today and every day the "justice" system permits known, convicted, violent and re-peat criminals, adult and juvenile, to get away with murder and mayhem on the streets. Criminals who have repeatedly violated the life, liberty, and property of others are routinely set free to do it all over again.

The myth of leniency is propped up by several "facts" that have been recycled repeatedly in popular and academic publications across the country in recent years. It is common to read, for example, that the overwhelming majority of violent criminals are let off without punishment, and that indeed "only 1 in 100" violent crimes results in a prison sentence; that in the rare cases when offenders are punished, the sentences they receive, even for heinous crimes, are shockingly, even ludicrously, short and that most violent criminals are not put in prison at all but are "community-based"—that is, on pretrial release, probation, or parole—an arrangement that allows them to commit further heinous crimes. All of these "facts" carry the same basic message: the heart of our crime problem lies in misguided leniency—"the failure to restrain known violent offenders," as the Council on Crime in America puts it. Contrary to what the figures on the swollen prisons would seem to tell us, the reality is that we are letting most criminals off with little or no punishment—and they are repaying us by murdering, raping, and robbing with impunity.

The prescription that follows from this diagnosis is short on specifics, but its general direction is clear. "Our view," writes the Council,

> is that America needs to put more violent and repeat criminals, adult and juvenile, behind bars longer, to see to it that truth-in-sentencing and such kindred laws as are presently on the books are fully and faithfully executed, and to begin reinventing probation and parole agencies in ways that will enable them to supervise their charges, enforce the law, and enhance public safety.

It is important to be clear: no one denies that serious offenders are sometimes let off lightly, or that we should do all we can to prevent such miscarriages of justice. But these critics are saying something more: that lenient sentencing and "revolving-door justice" are the norm in America and are responsible for America's continuing crime problem. What do we make of this argument? How do we square this picture of dramatic leniency with the reality of bursting prisons?

We can't. All of these claims are at best disingenuous, at worst painfully transparent distortions of the way criminal justice in America really works.

Consider first the statement, repeated over and over again by John DiIulio and the Council and picked up by opinion-page editors around the country, that "only 1 in 100 violent crimes results in a prison sentence." The figure itself is technically correct. In 1992, for example, there were over 10 million crimes of violence recorded in the annual survey of criminal victimization carried out by the U.S. Bureau of Justice Statistics; and, as Bennett, DiIulio, and Walters put it, "only about 100,000 persons convicted of a violent crime went to state prison." But do the numbers really tell us that "revolving-door justice" lets the wicked off with a slap on the wrist, or less?

Not at all. To begin with, it is important to understand that the majority of violent crimes are not serious ones. Thus, in 1995, 6.2 million were "simple assaults"; almost 5 million—more than half of all violent crimes—"simple assaults without injury." We are talking here about schoolyard fights or minor barroom altercations, which few would argue should result in a state prison sentence. (Most assaults, too, are "attempted" or "threatened," not "completed.") Another bit of sleight of hand is that the figure of 100,000 sent to state prison conveniently leaves out those who go to local jails, federal prisons, or juvenile institutions—implying that not going to state prison means that the offender is set free, which distorts the picture considerably.

But there is a much more fundamental problem. It is indeed true that most crimes—including many very serious ones—don't result in punishment. As every serious student of crime knows, however, that isn't primarily because the justice system is lenient with offenders; it is because the vast majority of crimes do not enter the criminal justice system at all. The Council on Crime in America provides the basic figures itself: of the more than 10 million violent crimes picked up in the national victim survey in 1992, only a little over 4 million were even *reported* to police. To be sure, more serious crimes of violence (as well as crimes like auto theft, which are reported in order to collect insurance) are more often reported. But even for robbery and assault the percentages are relatively low, and they are lower still for rape and domestic violence (more than 9 in 10 motor vehicle thefts, but only two-thirds of robberies, half of aggravated assaults, and one third of rapes are reported to the police, according to the victim surveys). And of those violent crimes that *are* reported, other than homicide, the majority do not result in an arrest (are not "cleared," in the language of criminal justice). Of those 10 million violent victimizations, just 641,000 led to an arrest at all. Hence, that "1 in 100" figure has already been transformed beyond recognition—for only 6 in 100 even enter the system. And once in the system, more offenses are dropped for lack of evidence, or otherwise dismissed, or the defendant is acquitted. The result is that the 10 million crimes are followed by only about 165,000 *convictions*—meaning that most offenses never arrive at the stage of sentencing at all.

A recent analysis, conducted by the *Los Angeles Times*, of 32 homicides that took place in the course of one week in the summer of 1994 in Los Angeles County illustrates how difficult it can be to bring a crime to the sentencing stage—even for a crime that is among those *most* likely to result in arrest and conviction. Nearly half of the 32 murder cases in that week did not result in an arrest; of those that did, a fifth were dismissed, or the suspects released or acquitted. A look at the circumstances of these cases shows some of the reasons why:

> Francisco Robert Vasquez, 20, is shot numerous times in an East Los Angeles alley. Vasquez may have been killed by fellow gang members, police say. Empty shell casings are found at the scene. But no gun is found and no suspects are arrested.

> Near MacArthur Park, at a drug sales corner controlled by 18th Street gang members, Louie Herrera, 27, is killed in a burst of gunfire. A suspect is identified, but charges are dropped after a witness becomes uncooperative, then disappears.

As these cases show, homicides that take place in the murky world of urban gangs and drugs are hard to solve. And the difficulty of achieving solid arrests and convictions is even greater for most other serious offenses. It follows that if we can improve our ability to make good arrests, and to convict those arrested, we might be able to make significant inroads against violent crime—an issue to which we'll return (indeed, the proportion of violent-crime cases that result in convictions has already increased in recent years). But it is *not* true that the gap between the large number of violent crimes committed and the much smaller number that are punished results from our leniency toward convicted offenders—from the fact that, as DiIulio puts it, "our criminal justice system is not handing down sentences to fit the crimes."

If our concern is whether we are encouraging crime by failing to punish known offenders, the real question is how many of those who are actually caught and convicted are then put behind bars. And here the evidence is unequivocal. We've already seen that the chances of incarceration for violent offenses have risen sharply in recent years in the United States; as a result, the probability that a convicted violent offender will go behind bars is very high indeed, and for repeat offenders a virtual certainty. In 1994, 77 percent of offenders convicted of felony robbery went to prison; another 11 percent went to jail, making the total incarcerated almost 9 in 10. Similarly, 88 percent of felons convicted of rape were incarcerated, four out of five of them in prison. Keep in mind that these are *averages* that lump together first-time offenders with repeaters, and less serious versions of these crimes with more serious ones. The kinds of offenders that critics like DiIulio say are now allowed to roam free—serious, violent repeaters—have been going behind bars routinely for many years, and the proportion has risen substantially since the 1970s.

But what about the *severity* of their sentences? Isn't it true that even those we do send to prison get out after a laughably short time—thus both subverting justice and encouraging predators? Here too the myth of leniency is widespread. Many Americans believe that we generally let convicted criminals off with a slap on the wrist, even those guilty of heinous offenses; John DiIulio insists that "hard time for hardened criminals is rare." Once again, that view would seem hard to reconcile with the enormous increases in imprisonment over the past twenty-five years. How is it possible to make this argument? What evidence is offered in its support?

Here is one example. In 1993 Senator Phil Gramm, later to run for president, wrote an op-ed piece in the *New York Times* entitled "Don't Let Judges Set Crooks Free." Gramm wrote that America was "deluged by a tidal wave of crime," and he identified the "main culprit" as "a criminal justice system in which the cost of committing crimes is so shamelessly cheap that it fails to deter potential criminals." Years of "soft sentencing" had brought "a dramatic decline in the cost of committing a crime and a dramatic increase in crime." As evidence, Gramm pointed to a study by an economist named Morgan Reynolds, of Texas A&M University, which has been widely cited by proponents of the myth of leniency. Reynolds's study purported to estimate the amount of time offenders committing various kinds of crimes could "expect to serve" in prison as of 1990. And the calculations are indeed startling. According to Gramm, a murderer can "expect" to spend just 1.8 years in prison. A rape earns 60 days. A robbery, according to these "findings," results in 23 days behind bars, and a car theft just a day and a half. Proof positive, according to Gramm, that a "soft" justice system is responsible for the tidal wave of crime.

The figures have been used over and over again to demonstrate the extraordinary leniency of the American justice system. And were the implications drawn from them even remotely true it would indeed be a scandal. If judges were in fact sentencing rapists to just two months behind bars and letting robbers free in less than a month, we would have a bizarre justice system indeed. But anyone who has ever followed a serious criminal trial, or known anyone who was actually sentenced to prison, knows instantly that there is something very wrong with these figures.

The standard data on the length of sentences for various crimes are published by the U.S. Bureau of Justice Statistics on the basis of periodic surveys of prison systems across the country. There are complexities involved in measuring the length of the time prisoners actually serve; it makes a considerable difference, for example, whether we try to measure it by looking at average time served by prisoners who are *released* or by estimating the time that will be served by offenders now going *into* prison. The figures on time served by released prisoners reflect the sentencing and parole policies in force some years before, when they were sentenced, while the expected time to be served for new admissions is what a convicted offender can *now* expect—which, under current conditions, will be longer. But however we measure it, the average time serious offenders spend behind bars bears no resemblance to the numbers cited by Gramm.

Among offenders sentenced in 1994—the most recent year available—the estimated time to be served in prison for murder was 127 months, or about 10 years. That figure, it should be noted, markedly understates the penalties for murder, for two reasons. First, it includes what in most states is called "nonnegligent manslaughter," a lesser offense that carries a far lower sentence than murder, and thus brings down the average. Even more importantly, the figure of 10 years does *not* include the roughly 27 percent of murderers who are sentenced to life imprisonment or death, which reduces the average far more. But even with these sentences excluded, the current penalty for murder is still many times higher than the figure Gramm provides. The same disparity holds true for the other crimes as well. The average expected time to be served for a convicted rapist in 1994 was not 60 days but 85 *months*, or just over 7 years. For robbery it was not 23 days but 51 *months*, or well over 4 years.

These figures on expected time to be served also put into perspective the frequent complaint that because of parole and "good time" provisions, most prisoners serve only a fraction of the sentence handed down in court—another sign of leniency run wild. In 1994, the Justice Department estimated that offenders sentenced for violent crimes would serve on average about 46 percent of their sentences, 54 percent for rape. But whether this is an indication of leniency obviously depends on the length of the original sentence. If all first-time robbers were sentenced to fifty-year terms, the fact that they wound up serving just half of that sentence would probably not trouble even the most punitive among us. The United States, as we've seen, generally imposes very harsh sentences by international standards; the widespread use of sentence reductions serves only to bring our average time served for serious violent crimes roughly into line with some (but not all) other advanced industrial countries. Robbers sentenced in 1994 received an average term of not quite 10 years, of which they would probably serve 4 years and 3 months. Rapists received over 13 years on average and could expect to serve over 7.

Note too that the time that offenders are likely to serve behind bars for some offenses has risen with stunning rapidity in recent years, as sentences have gotten harsher and as parole and "good time" provisions have increasingly come under siege. In just four years, from 1990 to 1994, the estimated time to be served in state prison for murder went up by two years and for rape by eleven months. Among newly committed state prison inmates generally, the estimated minimum time to be served rose from an average of thirty-one months in 1985 to forty-three months in 1995.

It is sometimes claimed that average prison sentences have *decreased* in recent years—proof, again, that we have in fact become "softer," not harder, on criminals.

The U.S. Bureau of Justice Statistics, during the Bush administration, released statistics purporting to show that "there is no evidence that the time served in prison, prior to the first release on a sentence, has been increasing"—that indeed the median time served by state prison inmates had dropped from 17 months in 1981 to 13 months in 1988. The implication was that despite the "get tough" campaigns of the 1970s and 1980s we were, oddly enough, more lenient at the end of the period than at the beginning. That was highly unlikely on the face of it, and the bureau's own chart showed that time served had risen for robbery and sexual assault and stayed level for homicide—while falling for lesser crimes, notably drug offenses and larceny. And there lies the key to the overall drop in the average time served in prison. Drug offenders were 8 percent of the inmate population in 1980 and 26 percent by 1993; violent offenders fell from 57 to 45 percent of the total. Since, with some important exceptions, drug offenders were being sentenced to shorter terms, that meant a flood of inmates with less severe sentences entering the persons, bringing down the average. Think of what happens when a river floods: say the usual depth of the river is twenty feet. The flood submerges hundreds of square miles of surrounding countryside under five feet of water. The *average* depth of the water has accordingly fallen considerably—small comfort, of course, to those whose homes and farms are now underwater.

Now, reasonable people may disagree about whether the existing sentences for violent crimes are appropriate. Some may feel that an average of seven years in prison for a rape is too little. But these actual sentence lengths are light-years away from the figures cited by Gramm (and others) to demonstrate that "soft sentencing" has flooded the nation with crime. What accounts for this wide disparity? Where did Reynolds get his numbers? The trick, again (as with the "1 in 100" figure) is that the numbers have very little to do with how "toughly" or "leniently" we are treating offenders in the courts—with "soft sentencing"—but primarily with the low rates of *arrest* for most offenses. Reynolds's figure of 23 days for robbery is derived by dividing the average time served by the robbers who are arrested and convicted *by the total number of robberies committed*, whether anyone is ever caught or not, much less convicted. It is true that, by this calculation, the "average cost" of a robbery is low—but that is because the average robbery isn't followed by an arrest, much less a conviction. Thus in 1994 about 1.3 million robberies took place, of which about 619,000 were reported to the police. But there were fewer than 46,000 adult felony convictions for robbery, of which almost all—more than 40,000—resulted in some incarceration in a jail or prison; and as we've seen, robbers who went to prison could expect to stay for well over 4 years. Again, if we could improve our ability to catch robbers in the first place, we might substantially increase the "average cost" of robberies. But it is pure sleight of hand to argue, as Gramm and others do, that weak *sentencing* practices account for the numbers, or that we treat the robbers we catch with shocking leniency.

Indeed, what the figures on the relatively low percentage of crime resulting in punishment really add up to is a profound argument for a greater emphasis on crime *prevention*—as opposed to punishment after the fact. For even if we assume that we could boost our capacity to apprehend robbers, no one seriously argues that we will ever arrive at the point where most robberies result in an arrest; and therefore no amount of increasing punishment will make as much difference as its proponents hope. That is surely not the conclusion that the purveyors of the "1 in 100" figure intended. But it is the only one that stands the test of hard scrutiny.

The fact that we already give relatively lengthy sentences to violent criminals—especially repeaters—helps explain why the rash of "three strikes and you're out" laws passed in recent years have in practice had much less impact than many people expected. Critics of these laws thought states would go broke trying to accommodate a flood of new prisoners; supporters thought large drops in violent crime were sure to come as huge numbers of violent predators roaming the streets finally got their just desserts. What has actually happened confounds both expectations, especially in those jurisdictions—which include most of the states as well as the federal government—where three-strikes laws are aimed solely at violent repeat offenders. As a study by the Campaign for an Effective Crime Policy has shown, none of those states has put many violent offenders away under their new laws. That is surely not because prosecutors are unwilling to charge offenders under the "tough" statutes. It may be in part because some judges, in some jurisdictions, are still managing to sentence offenders in ways that circumvent the harshest provisions of these laws. But it is *mainly* because most repeat violent offenders who come before the courts in these states would have been sentenced to "hard" time under the laws that already existed.

In California, where the three-strikes law was broadly drawn to target relatively low-level property and drug offenders as well as violent repeaters (any felony can trigger a third strike, leading to a mandatory sentence of twenty-five years to life), the number of people sentenced under the law has, unsurprisingly, been higher. But the proportion of *violent* offenders sentenced has still been relatively low. As of 1995, more people had been sentenced under California's three-strikes law for simple marijuana possession than for murder, rape, and kidnapping combined, and more for drug possession generally than for *all* violent offenses. Even in that state, where legislators led a stampede to pass the three-strikes law by arguing that hordes of violent repeaters were roaming the streets unpunished, the number of offenders given third *or second* "strikes" for a violent offense was fewer than 3,000 over the first two years of the law. And most of those violent offenders would have gone to prison *without* the new law. Before the passage of the three-strikes law, California already had on the books a mandatory five-year "enhancement" for the second conviction for many felonies, as well as a "habitual offender" statute providing for life imprisonment (with a minimum of twenty years before parole) for violent offenders who had caused "great bodily harm" to victims and had already served two prison sentences for similar offenses. In short, California's prisons have not been flooded with repeat violent offenders by the three-strikes law, mainly because such offenders were already being sentenced to relatively "tough" terms *before* the new law.

Again, no one denies that truly dangerous people sometimes slip out of the system. But to acknowledge that mistakes do occur is not the same as believing that the system as a whole is "soft" on serious violent criminals. And ironically, the wholesale return of genuinely "bad apples" to the streets has sometimes happened precisely because of unreflective efforts to "get tough," notably in states where dangerous criminals have been released to make room in overcrowded prisons for far less serious offenders incarcerated under mandatory sentences. The most studied case is Florida, where—despite the addition of 25,000 new prison beds—a huge influx of drug offenders during the 1980s resulted in massive prison overcrowding, forcing the state to establish an early-release program, which deposited tens of thousands of offenders who did *not* have mandatory sentences onto the streets. That number included a great many violent criminals, even robbers and rapists, most of whom received little serious supervision once in the community. (The state legislature has recently shifted its policy, to target incarceration on violent offenders and seek out alternatives for the nonviolent.)

With occasional exceptions, then, it remains true that serious, violent criminals, especially if they are repeaters, are likely to do hard time if caught and convicted. But what about the fact that so many violent criminals are out on bail, or on probation or parole? Doesn't that show that we are shockingly "soft"? Wouldn't cracking down on such people by abolishing parole altogether—and putting many of those now on probation behind bars—have a dramatic effect on the crime rate?

Probably not. Here the problems are more genuine. But they are more complicated, and more difficult to solve, than critics like the Council on Crime in America would have us believe. Their argument begins with the undisputed observation that, at any given point, more people who have committed crimes are under some form of "community" supervision than in prison and that the number of "community-based" offenders has grown along with the rise in the prison population. (Between 1980 and 1994, the number of prison inmates increased at an annual average of 8.4 percent, the parole population by 8.5 percent, and the probation population by 7.2 percent.) But it is not apparent why this should be taken as evidence of a "weak" justice system. John DiIulio, for example, argues that the fact that in 1991, 590,000 people who had been convicted of a violent crime were "residing in our communities" on parole or probation, while only 372,000 were in prison, represents "another sobering example of how the scales are tipping" toward the criminal. But that conclusion doesn't follow. Unless we believe that everyone accused of a crime ought to be detained until trial, that everyone convicted of an offense—no matter how minor—should be sent to jail or prison, and that all of those sent to prison should stay there for the rest of their lives, it is not clear why the sheer fact of growth in the number of people on pretrial release, probation, or parole is a sign of either leniency or bad policy.

The real issue is whether we are allowing the *wrong* people to remain free—whether large numbers of "known violent predators" who ought to be behind bars are being released into the community. The Council on Crime in America insists that they are, and points to statistics showing that large proportions of violent crimes (up to a third, depending on the jurisdiction and the offense) are committed by offenders who are on probation, parole, or pretrial release. Many Americans likewise believe that large numbers of predators are routinely released to community supervision, and their belief is fed by sensational media anecdotes about horrible crimes committed by parolees and offenders released on bail. Again, no one denies that such tragedies happen, or that we should do all we can to prevent them. But do these figures really tell us that we are typically lenient with "known, violent predators"?

No. To begin with, the numbers, though (usually) technically correct, are, once again, misleadingly presented. The Washington-based Sentencing Project offers this useful example: suppose in a given county there are a thousand offenders under pretrial release. There are also three murders, one of which was committed by an offender under pretrial supervision. Thus the *proportion of murders* accounted for by pretrial releasees is a substantial one-third. But the other side of the coin is that *only one in one thousand* pretrial releasees committed a murder—which suggests that trying to prevent that murder by incarcerating all the offenders we now release before trial would be extraordinarily expensive and indeed, for practical purposes, probably impossible.

There is another, even more fundamental, problem with the assertion that we are letting hordes of violent offenders go free even though we *know* they are dangerous characters. Consider this example. A young man is arrested in a big, crime-ridden city for a minor drug deal. Because he has no prior arrests and no known history of violence, he is given a year's probation. While on probation he kills an acquaintance in a fight. Is it meaningful to say the murder resulted from the "failure to restrain" a known violent offender? Not really, because it is hard to conceive of a reasonable argument that would have justified putting him in prison for a long time on the strength of what was known about him. Could we improve our capacity to *predict* which among the vast pool of minor offenders who come into the courts are truly dangerous—thus ensuring that the violent do not elude our control? Maybe. But it is important to remember that our criminal justice systems *already* try to do just that, and many have adopted elaborate risk-assessment procedures, backed by considerable research and experience, to guide those decisions. Hence, realistically, our ability to get *much* better at predicting which of those offenders poses a high enough risk to justify lengthy incarceration is limited.

What holds for probation also applies to parole. Many people believe that if we abolished parole altogether, we could sharply reduce violent crime, and that belief is based in part on the reality that heinous crimes are sometimes committed by people on parole. But unless we believe that everyone convicted of a crime of violence—of whatever seriousness—should stay in prison for the rest of their lives, most *will* at some point be released to the community—and it is not clear why it would be better for them to be in the community *without* supervision than with it. The real question, for both probation and parole, is whether we can do a better job than we now do of monitoring and supervising offenders in the community and thereby reduce the risks that they will do harm. And here the answer is certainly yes. Many probation and parole agencies in the United States, especially in the big cities, are stretched well past the point of effectiveness, their ability to provide meaningful supervision of offenders drastically eroded by years of fiscal starvation and caseloads that can run into the hundreds. The Council on Crime in America, to their credit, reject the idea that all offenders necessarily belong behind bars and suggest that improving the capacity of parole and probation agencies to supervise them outside prison walls makes eminent sense. What they do *not* say, however, is that one of the main reasons why the effectiveness of the probation and parole systems has been so badly compromised is that we have systematically disparaged what they do as "soft" on crime while diverting the money we could have used to improve them into the prisons. We desperately need better community supervision of offenders. But we are unlikely to get it unless we rein in the rush toward indiscriminate incarceration.

As importantly, if we want to prevent crimes committed by "community-based" offenders, we will need to invest more in programs to provide those we *do* incarcerate with a better chance of succeeding on the outside when they are released, as nearly all of them will be. But it should be obvious that if we make no effort to improve the capacity of ex-offenders to live and work productively outside prison walls, we shouldn't profess great surprise when many of them fail—especially if they are also returning to communities with few and perhaps diminishing opportunities for success. And we should not blame that failure on the leniency of the justice system.

CHAPTER 40

Wild Pitch

"Three Strikes, You're Out" and Other Bad Calls on Crime

JEROME H. SKOLNICK

A ccording to the pundits, the polls, and the politicians, violent crime is now America's number one problem. If the problems were properly defined and the lessons of past efforts were fully absorbed, this could be an opportunity to set national crime policy on a positive course. Instead, it is a dangerous moment. Intuition is driving the country toward desperate and ineffectual responses that will drive up prison costs, divert tax dollars from other vital purposes, and leave the public as insecure and dissatisfied as ever.

The pressures pushing federal and state politicians to vie for the distinction of being toughest on crime do not come only from apprehensive voters and the tabloid press. Some of the leading organs of elite opinion, notably the *Wall Street Journal*, have celebrated gut-level, impulsive reactions. In one *Journal* column ("Crime Solution: Lock 'em Up"), Ben J. Wattenberg writes that criminologists don't know what works.

What works is what everyone intuitively knows: "A thug in prison cannot shoot your sister." In another *Journal* column ("The People Want Revenge"), the conservative intellectual Paul Johnson argues that government is failing ordinary people by ignoring their retributive wishes. Ordinary people, he writes, want neither to understand criminals nor to reform them. "They want them punished as severely and cheaply as possible."

Johnson is partly right and mostly wrong. Ordinary people want more than anything to walk the streets safely and to protect their families and their homes. Intuitively, like Wattenberg, many believe that more prisons and longer sentences offer safety along with punishment. But, especially in dealing with crime, intuition isn't always a sound basis for judgment.

The United States already has the highest rate of imprisonment of any major nation. The prisons have expanded enormously in recent years in part because of get-tough measures sending low-level drug offenders to jail. Intuitions were wrong: the available evidence does not suggest that imprisoning those offenders has made the public safer.

The current symbol of the intuitive lock-'em-up response is "three strikes and you're out"—life sentences for criminals convicted of three violent or serious felonies. The catchy slogan appears to have mesmerized politicians from one coast to the other and across party lines. Three-strikes fever began in the fall of 1993 in the wake of the intense media coverage of the abduction and murder of a 12-year-old California girl, Polly Klaas, who was the victim, according to police, of a criminal with a long and violent record. California's Republican Governor Pete Wilson took up the call for three strikes, and on March 7 the California legislature overwhelmingly approved the proposal. Even New York Governor Mario Cuomo endorsed a three strikes measure. The U.S. Senate has passed a crime bill that adopts three strikes as well as a major expansion of the federal role in financing state prisons and stiffening state sentencing policy. In his 1994 State of the Union address, President Clinton singled out the Senate legislation and three strikes for praise.

But will three strikes work? Teenagers and young men in their twenties commit the vast majority of violent offenses. The National Youth Survey, conducted by Colorado criminologist Delbert S. Elliott, found that serious violent offenses (aggravated-assault, rape, and robbery involving some injury or weapon) peak at age 17. The rate is half as much at age 24 and declines significantly as offenders mature into their thirties.

If we impose life sentences on serious violent offenders on their third conviction —after they have served two sentences—we will generally do so in the twilight of their criminal careers. Three strikes laws will eventually fill our prisons with geriatric offenders, whose care will be increasingly expensive when their propensities to commit crime are at the lowest.

Take the case of "Albert," described in the *New York Times* not long ago by Mimi Silbert, president of the Delancey Street Foundation in San Francisco. At age 10, Albert was the youngest member of a barrio gang. By the time he was sent to San Quentin at the age of 19, he had committed 27 armed robberies and fathered two children. Now 36, he is a plumber and substitute teacher who has for years been crime-free, drug-free, and violence-free. According to Silbert, the Delancey Street program has turned around the lives of more than 10,000 Alberts in the past 23 years.

To imprison the Alberts of the world for life makes sense if the purpose is retribution. But if life imprisonment is supposed to increase public safety, we will be disappointed with the results. To achieve that purpose, we need to focus on preventing violent crimes committed by high-risk youths. That is where the real problem lies.

The best that can be said of some three-strikes proposals is that they would be drawn so narrowly that they would have little effect. The impact depends on which felonies count as strikes. Richard H. Girgenti, director of the New York State Division of Criminal Justice Services, says that the measure supported by Governor

Cuomo would affect only 300 people a year and be coupled with the release of non-violent prisoners. President Clinton is also supporting a version of three strikes that is more narrowly drawn than California's. Proposals like California's, however, will result in incarcerating thousands of convicts into middle and old age.

REGRESSING TO THE MEAN

Before Governor Wilson signed the most draconian of the three-strikes bill introduced in the legislature, district attorneys across the state assailed the measure, arguing that it would clog courts, cost too much money, and result in disproportionate sentences for nonviolent offenders. So potent is the political crime panic in California that the pleas of the prosecutors were rebuffed.

The prospect in California is ominous. Even without three-strikes legislation, California is already the nation's biggest jailer, with one out of eight American prisoners occupying its cells. During the past 16 years, its prison population has grown 600 percent, while violent crime in the state has increased 40 percent. As Franklin E. Zimring and Gordon Hawkins demonstrate in a recent issue of the *British Journal of Criminology*, correctional growth in California was "in a class by itself" during the 1980s. The three next largest state prison systems (New York, Texas, and Florida) experienced half the growth of California, and western European systems about a quarter.

To pay for a five-fold increase in the corrections budget since 1980, Californians have had to sacrifice other services. Education especially has suffered. Ten years ago, California devoted 14 percent of its state budget to higher education and 4 percent to prisons. Today it devotes 9 percent to both.

The balance is now expected to shift sharply in favor of prisons. To pay for three strikes, California expects to spend $10.5 billion by the year 2001. The California Department of Corrections has estimated that three strikes will require the state to add 20 more prisons to the existing 28 and the 12 already on the drawing board. By 2001, there will be 109,000 more prisoners behind bars serving life sentences. A total of 275,621 more people are expected to be imprisoned over the next 30 years—the equivalent of building an electric fence around the city of Anaheim. By the year 2027 the cost of housing extra inmates is projected to hit $5.7 billion a year.

But will California be better off in 2027—indeed, will it have less crime—if it has 20 more prisons for aging offenders instead of 20 more college campuses for the young?

Of course, Wilson and other politicians are worrying about the next elections, not the next century. By the time the twice-convicted get out of prison, commit a third major offense, and are convicted and sentenced to life terms, Wilson and the others supporting three strikes will be out—that is, out of office, leaving future generations a legacy of an ineffectual and costly crime policy. To avoid that result, political leaders need to stop trying to out-tough one another and start trying to out-reason each other.

THE LIMITS OF INTUITION

H. L. A. Hart, the noted legal philosopher, once observed that the Enlightenment made the form and severity of punishment "a matter to be *thought* about, to be *reasoned* about, and *argued,* and not merely a matter to be left to feelings and sentiment." Those aspirations ought still to be our guide.

The current push to enact three strikes proposals is reminiscent of the movement in the 1970s to enact mandatory sentencing laws, another effort to get tough, reduce judicial discretion, and appease the public furies. But mandatory sentencing has not yielded any discernible reduction in crime. Indeed, the result has been mainly to shift discretionary decision-making upstream in the criminal justice system since the laws have continued to allow great latitude in bringing charges and plea bargaining.

Ironically, mandatory sentencing allowed the serial freedom of Richard Allen Davis, the accused murderer of Polly Klaas. Before 1977, California had a system of indeterminate prison sentencing for felony offenders. For such felonies as second-degree murder, robbery, rape, and kidnapping, a convict might receive a sentence of 1 to 25 years, or even one year to life. The objective was to tailor sentences to behavior, to confine the most dangerous convicts longer, and to provide incentives for self-improvement. However, in 1977, declaring that the goal of imprisonment was punishment rather than rehabilitation, the state adopted supposedly tougher mandatory sentences. Richard Allen Davis benefited from two mandated sentence reductions, despite the prescient pre-sentencing report of a county probation officer who warned of Davis's "accelerating potential for violence" after his second major conviction. Under indeterminate sentencing, someone with Davis's personality and criminal history would likely have been imprisoned far longer than the mandated six years for his first set of offenses.

Most criminologists and policy analysts do not support the reliance on expanded prisons and the rigidities of habitual offender laws. Some, like David Rothman, have apologized for their naiveté joining the movement to establish determinate sentencing in the 1970s and now recognize that it has been a failure.

Others, like John J. DiIulio, Jr., take a harder line, although the hardness of DiIulio's line seems to depend on his forum. In a January 1994 column appearing—where else?—in the *Wall Street Journal,* DiIulio supported the superficially toughest provisions of the Senate crime bill. (The *Journal*'s headline writers called the column "Let 'em Rot," a title that DiIulio later protested, though his own text was scarcely less draconian.) But writing in *The American Prospect* in the fall of 1990 ("Getting Prisons Straight") and with Anne Thomson Piehl in the fall of 1991 for the *Brookings Review,* DiIulio's message was more tempered.

The Brookings article reviews the debate over the cost-effectiveness of prisons. Imprisonment costs between $20,000 to $50,000 per prisoner per year. But is that price worth the benefit of limiting the crimes that could have been committed by prisoners if they were on the street? "Based on existing statistical evidence," write DiIulio and Piehl, "the relationship between crime rates and imprisonment is ambiguous." This is hardly a mandate for "letting 'em rot." DiIulio and Piehl recognize that the certainty of punishment is more effective than the length and that "even if we find that 'prison pays' at the margin, it would not mean that every convicted criminal deserves prison; it would not mean that it is cost effective to imprison every convicted felon." I agree and so do most criminologists. Does DiIulio read DiIulio?

THE RISE OF IMPRISONMENT

Two trends are responsible for the increase in imprisonment. First, the courts are imposing longer sentences for such nonviolent felonies as larceny, theft, and motor vehicle theft. In 1992 these accounted for 60.9 percent of crime in America, according to the Federal Bureau of Investigation's Uniform Crime Reports.

Second, drugs have become the driving force of crime. More than half of all violent offenders are under the influence of alcohol or drugs (most often alcohol) when they commit their crimes. The National Institute of Justice has shown that in 23 American cities, the percentage of arrested and booked males testing positive for any of ten illegal drugs ranged from a low of 48 percent in Omaha to 79 percent in Philadelphia. The median cities, Fort Lauderdale and Miami, checked out at 62 percent.

There has been an explosion of arrests and convictions and increasingly longer sentences for possessing and selling drugs. A Justice Department study, completed last summer but withheld from the public until February this year, found that of the 90,000 federal prison inmates, one-fifth are low-level drug offenders with no current or prior violence or previous prison time. They are jamming the prisons.

The federal prison population, through mandated and determinate sentences, has tripled in the past decade. Under current policy, it will rise by 50 percent by the century's turn, with drug offenders accounting for 60 percent of the additional prisoners. Three-strikes legislation will doubtless solidify our already singular position as the top jailer of the civilized world.

THE FEAR FACTOR

The lock-'em-up approach plays to people's fear of crime, which is rising, while actual crime rates are stabilizing or declining. This is by no means to argue that fear of crime is unjustified. Crime has risen enormously in the United States in the last quarter-century, but it is no more serious in 1994 than it was in 1991. The FBI's crime index declined 4 percent from 1991 to 1992.

In California, a legislative report released in January indicates that the overall crime rate per 100,000 people declined slightly from 1991 to 1992, dropping from 3,503.3 to 3,491.5. Violent crimes—homicide, forcible rape, robbery, and aggravated assault—rose slightly, from 1,079.8 to 1,103.9. Early figures for 1993 show a small decline.

On the other coast, New York City reported a slight decline in homicides, 1,960 in 1993, compared with 1,995 in 1992, and they are clustered in 12 of the city's 75 police districts, places like East New York and the South Bronx. "On the east side of

Manhattan," writes Matthew Purdy in the *New York Times,* "in the neighborhood of United Nations diplomats and quiet streets of exclusive apartments, the gunfire might as well be in a distant city."

So why, when crime rates are flat, has crime become America's number one problem in the polls? Part of the answer is that fear of crime rises with publicity, especially on television. Polly Klaas's murder, the killing of tourists in Florida, the roadside murder of the father of former basketball star Michael Jordan, and the killing of commuters on a Long Island Railroad train sent a scary message to the majority of Americans who do not reside in the inner cities. The message seemed to be that random violence is everywhere and you are no longer safe—not in your suburban home, commuter train, or automobile—and the police and the courts cannot or will not protect you.

A recent and as yet unpublished study by Zimring and Hawkins argues that America's problem is not crime per se but random violence. They compare Los Angeles and Sydney, Australia. Both cities have a population of 3.6 million, and both are multicultural (although Sydney is less so). Crime in Sydney is a serious annoyance but not a major threat. My wife and I, like other tourists, walked through Sydney at night last spring with no fear of being assaulted.

Sydney's crime pattern explains the difference. Its burglary rate is actually 10 percent higher than L.A.'s, and its theft rate is 73 percent of L.A.'s. But its robbery and homicide rates are strikingly lower, with only 12.5 percent of L.A.'s robbery rate and only 7.3 percent of L.A.'s homicide rate.

Americans and Australians don't like any kind of crime, but most auto thefts and many burglaries are annoying rather than terrifying. It is random violent crime, like a shooting in a fast-food restaurant, that is driving fear.

Violent crime, as I suggested earlier, is chiefly the work of young men between the ages of 15 and 24. The magnitude of teenage male involvement in violent crime is frightening. "At the peak age (17)," Delbert Elliott writes, "36 percent of African-American (black) males and 25 percent of non-Hispanic (white) males report one or more serious violent offenses." Nor are young women free of violence. One in five African-American females and one in ten white females report having committed a serious violent offense.

Blacks are more likely than whites to continue their violence into their adult years. Elliott considers this finding to be an important insight into the high arrest and incarceration rates of young adult black males. As teenagers, black and white males are roughly comparable in their disposition to violence. "Yet," Elliott writes, "once involved in a lifestyle that includes serious forms of violence, theft, and substance use, persons from disadvantaged families and neighborhoods find it very difficult to escape. They have fewer opportunities for conventional adult roles, and they are more deeply embedded in and dependent upon the gangs and the illicit economy that flourish in their neighborhoods."

The key to reformation, Elliott argues, is the capacity to make the transition into conventional adult work and family roles. His data show that those who successfully make the change give up their involvement in violence. Confinement in what will surely be overcrowded prisons can scarcely facilitate that transition, while community-based programs like Delancey Street have proven successful.

Just as violent crime is concentrated among the young, so is drug use. Drug treatment must be a key feature of crime prevention both in prisons and outside. There is some good news here. In early 1994, President Clinton and a half-dozen cabinet members visited a Maryland prison that boasts a model drug-treatment program to announce a national drug strategy that sharply increases spending for drug treatment and rehabilitation. Although the major share of the anti-drug budget, 59 percent, is still allocated to law enforcement, the change is in the right direction. A number of jurisdictions across the country have developed promising court-ordered rehabilitation programs that seem to be succeeding in reducing both drug use and the criminality of drug-using offenders.

Drugs are one area where get-tough policies to disrupt supply have been a signal failure, both internationally and domestically. Interdiction and efforts to suppress drug agriculture and manufacture within such countries as Peru and Colombia have run up against what I have called "the Darwinian Trafficker Dilemma." Such efforts undercut the marginally efficient traffickers, while the fittest—the most efficient, the best organized, the most ruthless, the most corrupting of police and judges—survive. Cocaine prices, the best measure of success or failure, dropped precipitously in the late 1980s. They have recovered somewhat, but likely more from monopolistic pricing than government interference.

Domestically, get-tough intuitions have inspired us to threaten drug kingpins with long prison terms or death. Partly, we wish to punish and incapacitate them, but mostly we wish to deter others from following in their felonious paths. Unfortunately, such policies are undermined by the "Felix Mitchell Dilemma," which I named in honor of the West Coast's once notorious kingpin, who received a life sentence in the 1980s, albeit a short one since he was murdered in federal prison. Mitchell's sentence and early demise did not deter drug sellers in the Bay Area. On the contrary, drug sales continued and, with Mitchell's monopolistic pricing eliminated, competition reduced the price of crack. The main effect of Mitchell's imprisonment was to destabilize the market, lower drug prices, and increase violence as rival gang members challenged each other for market share. Drug-related drive-by shootings, street homicides, and felonious assaults increased.

Recently, two of Mitchell's successors, Timothy Bluitt and Marvin Johnson, were arrested and sent to prison. So will peace finally come to the streets? "When a guy like Bluitt goes down, someone takes his place and gets an even bigger slice of the pie," an anonymous federal agent told the *San Francisco Chronicle* this past January. "The whole process is about consolidating turf and power."

Youngsters who sell drugs in Oakland, Denver, Detroit, South Central Los Angeles, Atlanta, and New York are part of generations who have learned to see crime as economic opportunity. This does not excuse their behavior, but it does intensify our need to break the cycle of poverty, abuse, and violence that dominates their lives. Prisons do not deter criminals partly because the Mitchells and Bluitts do not rationally calculate choices with the same points of reference that legislators employ. Drug dealers already face the death penalty on the streets.

History reminds us that gang violence is not novel, but it has not always been so lethal. The benchmark sociological study of the urban gang is Frederick Thrasher's research on 1,313 Chicago gangs published in 1927. The disorder and violence of these gangs appalled Thrasher, who observed that they were beyond the ordinary controls of police and other social agencies. He described gang youth, of which only 7.2 percent were "Negro," as "lawless, godless, wild." Why didn't more of them kill each other? They fought with fists and knives, not assault weapons.

PREVENTING VIOLENT CRIME

If violent crime prevention is our strategic aim, we need to test tactics. We need to go beyond the Brady Bill and introduce a tight regulatory system on weapons and ammunition, and we need more research and analysis to figure out what control system would be most effective. Successful gun and ammunition control would do far more to stem the tide of life-threatening violence than expensive prisons with mandated sentences.

The Senate crime bill, however, promises to increase the nation's rate of imprisonment. Besides its three strikes provisions, the legislation incorporates Senator Robert Byrd's $3 billion regional prison proposal. If enacted, states can apply to house their prisoners in 10 regional prisons, each with a capacity of 2,500 inmates.

To qualify, states must adopt "truth in sentencing" laws mandating that offenders convicted of violent crimes serve "at least 80 percent of the sentence ordered," the current average served by federal offenders. They also must approve pretrial detention laws similar to those in the federal system. And the states must ensure that four categories of crime—murder, firearms offenses resulting in death or serious bodily injury, sex offenses broadly defined, and child abuse—are punished as severely as they are under federal law. In effect, the Senate crime bill federalizes sentencing policy.

According to H. Scott Wallace of the National Legal Aid and Defender's Association, the mandate will add about 12,000 prisoners to the average state's correctional population but will offer only about 3 percent of the space needed to house them.

The most costly provision of the Senate crime bill—$9 billion worth—is its proposal for 100,000 more police, a measure endorsed by the administration. Its potential value in reducing crime is unclear. We need more research on constructive policing, including community policing, which can be either an effective approach or merely a fashionable buzzword. We need to address the deficiencies of police culture revealed in the corruption uncovered by New York City's Mollen Commission and the excessive force revealed on the Rodney King beating videotape. More police may help in some places but not much in others. And they are very expensive.

A leading police researcher, David H. Bayley, has explained the ten-for-one rule of police visibility: ten cops must be hired to put one officer on the street. Only about two-thirds of police are uniformed patrol officers. They work three shifts, take vacation and sick leave, and require periodic retraining. Consequently 100,000 new officers will mean only about 10,000 on the street for any one shift for the entire United States.

Even if we were to have more and better police, there is no guarantee they will deter crime. Criminologists have found no marginal effect on crime rates from putting more cops on the street. Indeed, Congress and the president need look no farther than down their own streets to discover that simply increasing police doesn't necessarily make the streets safe. Washington, D.C., boasts the highest police-per-resident ratio in the nation with one cop for every 150 civilians. It is also America's homicide capital.

We might get more bang for the patrolling buck by investing in para-police, or the police corps, or private police, rather than by paying for more fully sworn and expensive officers. Under the leadership of former Chief Raymond Davis, Santa Ana, California, had the most effective community-oriented policing department in the nation. Davis, who faced a weak police union, could innovate with community- and service-oriented civilians who wore blue uniforms but carried no guns—a new and cost-effective blue line.

The crime bill allocates approximately $3 billion for boot camps, another get-tough favorite. Criminologist Doris MacKenzie has found, contrary to intuition, no significant difference between camp graduates and former prison inmates in the rate at which they return to prison. Similarly, a General Accounting Office report concluded that there is no evidence that boot camps reduce recidivism.

If the public wants boot camps primarily for retribution, it doesn't matter whether they work. Under the Eighth Amendment's bar on cruel and unusual punishment, we're not permitted to impose corporal punishment with whips and clubs. In boot camps, however, we can require painful exercises and hard and demeaning labor to teach these miscreant youth a message of retribution. But if correctional boot camps are intended to resocialize youth and to prepare for them noncriminal civilian life, the camps are inadequate.

We need to experiment with boot camps plus—the "plus" including skills training, education, jobs, community reconstruction. Conservatives who stress moral revitalization and family values as an antidote to youth crime have the right idea. Yet they rarely if ever, consider how important are the structural underpinnings—education, opportunity, employment, family functioning, community support—for developing such values.

Eventually, we are going to have to choose between our retributive urges and the possibilities of crime prevention. We cannot fool ourselves into thinking they are the same. One punishment meted out by criminal law is a blunt and largely ineffectual instrument of public protection. It deters some, it incapacitates others, and it does send a limited moral message. But if we want primarily to enhance public safety by preventing crime, we need to mistrust our intuitions and adopt strategies and tactics that have been researched, tested, and critically evaluated. In short, we need to embrace the values of the enlightenment over those of the dark ages.

Instant Replay

Three Strikes Was the Right Call

John J. DiIulio Jr.

Jerome H. Skolnick's essay on crime policy ("Wild Pitch: 'Three Strikes, You're Out' and Other Bad Calls on Crime," Spring 1994), omitted some important facts and ignored several valid arguments.

Echoing the anti-incarceration consensus within criminology, Skolnick asserts that life without parole for thrice-convicted violent felons is a bad policy idea, a "wild pitch." Actually, it's more of an underhanded lob to career criminals, most of whom would hardly be affected by it. In 1991 there were about 35,000 new court commitments to federal prisons. Less than 6 percent of federal prisoners were sentenced for violent crimes. About 30 percent of the 142,000 persons committed to state prisons were sentenced for violent crimes. If 10 percent of all prisoners sentenced for violent crimes were on their "third strike," then the law would have affected some 4,500 persons in a corrections population of nearly 4.5 million. Love it or hate it, "three strikes" would have little impact on the size of prison populations, and would do nothing to plug the worm's hole of phoney "mandatory minimum" laws. These laws have put about three-quarters of all convicts—over 3 million criminals—on the streets under "supervision" that in most cases means a monthly chat with an overworked, underpaid probation or parole agent.

Millions of crimes are committed each year by convicted offenders whom the system didn't keep behind bars. Within three years of their release, persons convicted of property crimes are about as likely to commit a violent crime as persons convicted of violent crimes in the first place. And please, no more nonsense about "intermediate sanctions." Recent studies show that fully half of all probationers don't even comply with the basic terms of their sentences (pay fines, do community service, accept drug treatment) before being released from custody, and only one-fifth of the violators are ever disciplined in any way. Meanwhile, repeat criminals who beat the system inflict hundreds of billions of dollars in damages on their victims and society each year.

Skolnick may think the Polly Klaas tragedy is mere sensationalism, but all the data show that the system routinely permits known predatory criminals to plea bargain their way to lesser charges at the front end, only to give them numerous get-out-of-jail-free cards at the back end. In 1991 thirty-four states released more than 325,000 prisoners combined, 90 percent of them to community-based supervision. About half of these offenders had served *a year or less* in prison before their releases. On average, they served 35 percent of their time in confinement. This average held pretty well for all types of offenders. Thus, murderers received a maximum sentence of 20 years but served under 8 years (below 40 percent of their sentences) in prison, while drug traffickers (organized traffickers, *not* mere possessors) received an average of 4 years and served about 14 months (35 percent of their sentence) before release. The state-level data paint the same bleak picture in finer detail. In New Jersey, for example, the typical prisoner had 9 arrests, and 6 convictions, committed over a dozen serious crimes (excluding *all* drug crimes) in the year prior to his incarceration, had about a 50–50 chance of victimizing again after his release, and was most likely to victimize poor and minority citizens.

No Americans suffer more from permissive penal practices than the law-abiding minority citizens of inner city neighborhoods. Middle-class and affluent Americans are spending record amounts on private security devices, rent-a-cops, and other measures intended to make the environments in which they live relatively impervious to crime. That spending, in conjunction with now commonplace danger-avoidance behaviors (don't walk alone or ride the subway at night, don't drive through "bad neighborhoods"), help explain the recent decrease in crime rates nationally. But poor folks can't afford private security measures. Instead, they rely mainly on a "justice system" that virtually invites the criminally deviant to prey upon the truly disadvantaged.

Like most criminologists, Skolnick obscures the public protection value of imprisonment behind criminologically *de rigueur* rhetoric about the steep increase in the rate of incarceration, the U.S. having the highest incarceration rate in the world, etc. But he doesn't mention that the rate increase in community-based supervision has been even steeper. Nor does he note that only 6 percent of state prisoners are nonviolent first-time offenders. The federal system, in which prisoners must serve at least 85 percent of their time behind bars, consists largely of "non-violent" drug dealers with multiple convictions. My Princeton colleague, Ethan Nadelmann, has made a number of powerful arguments for decriminalizing drugs. He's persuaded me on some points, but not all, and not on the bottom line of legalization. But most criminologists who balk at mandatory prison terms for drug merchants lack the courage of their criminological convictions. Rather than asserting that we're locking up too many harmless people for too long, criminologists ought to get specific—identify these people, and tell us, on a jurisdiction-by-jurisdiction basis, precisely what classes of criminals they would like to let out sooner.

I agree with Skolnick that it is irrational to wait until career criminals are drifting into their less crime-prone years before slapping them with long sentences. James Q. Wilson and others made that case years ago. But there are at least four other considerations. First, the differences among the criminal classes in prison today are not that wide. We're not talking about criminals—we're talking about plea-bargain-gorged *convicted and imprisoned criminals*—the vast majority of whom carry a criminal portfolio featuring multiple property crimes, multiple violent crimes, or both.

Second, it's true that older criminals commit fewer and less serious crimes than do younger criminals. But less crime isn't no crime and we don't have any reliable way of predicting which prisoners are harmless "geriatric inmates" and which are still dangerous. (Ask the Massachusetts authorities who recently got burnt by a 61-year-old released prisoner who murdered again.)

Third, if we're really so concerned about waiting too long before hammering repeat criminals with heavy sentences, why not support "two strikes" laws that incarcerate them while they're hot—if not for life, then for 15- to 20-years with no good time and no parole? California and dozens of other states are moving in this direction. Godspeed to them. Of course, when pressed most criminologists want only "violent" crimes to count as a "strike"—major drug felonies, carjacking at knife-point, etc., aren't supposed to count. These folks have to stop decriminalizing things without admitting it, and without telling the rest of us why. This goes especially for all their hypocritical cheers for gun control. New Jersey, like many states, has dozens of tough gun laws. But the penalties for gun law violations aren't strictly enforced. Would those who want more restrictions on guns also favor making serious gun-law violations a "strike"? I would.

Fourth, society has a right not only to protect itself from convicted criminals but to express its moral outrage at their acts by, among other things, keeping them behind bars. For example, what is the right moral posture when it comes to cases like the 73-year-old man recently sentenced to life without parole for the 1963 murder of civil rights worker Medgar Evers? In my view, the public and their elected leaders have a better grasp of the moral *and* empirical issues at stake than do most of our country's criminologists.

Skolnick and most other criminologists are sure that prison is not the answer. But what, precisely, is the question? If the question's how to solve America's crime problem, plus all the rest of its urban problems, then prison is no answer. But if the question is what can protect the public from violent and repeat criminals, then prison is a very good answer indeed. Professionally, criminologists should not ignore the data on how little time most violent and repeat criminals spend behind bars. Morally they should not ignore the pleas of a majority of Americans of every demographic description. Nor should they belittle the lived experiences of the Klaas family and others that, like my own, have suffered the murder of a loved one at the hands of a released repeat criminal, or had their lives and property trifled with or ruined by thugs whom the system let loose. We can forgive the public, which has become so frustrated with America's revolving door justice that it applauds Singapore's institutionalized canings.

As Skolnick noted, the "100,000 cops" provision of the crime bill would actually mean about 10,000 around-the-clock cops distributed by Congress among hundreds of jurisdictions. The federal bucks are just seed dollars that will dry up in a half-decade, leaving the states and cities to bite the bullet. Still, with artful administration by the Office of Justice Programs (read: not the 1970s saga of the Law Enforcement Assistance Administration revisited), there is still the chance that the community policing provisions of the bill could be married to its manpower provisions. At least that's what the academics (including David Bayley, author of the 10-for-1 rule cited by Skolnick) and government officials who joined me at Brookings for a session with the Justice Department hope will happen.

In the 1980s Skolnick and other criminologists made excellent arguments for community policing. But community policing was oversold as a do-more-with-less strategy. You can't just retrain cops and put more of them on foot patrol. Many big city police forces have contracted. The thin blue line is stretched too thin, especially in the underserved inner city where crime is out of control. Community policing should be embraced for what it is—a do-better-with-more strategy. The cheap talk's over, the bill's due, and it includes more money for more cops. The public is willing to pay; criminologists should belly up to the bar, too, and endorse more police.

Skolnick has cited my January 1994 op-ed on crime for the *Wall Street Journal,* which had also recently run pieces on crime by syndicated columnist Ben Wattenberg, historian Paul Johnson, and several others. In that op-ed, I supported what President Clinton said on crime in his State of the Union address, and condemned Attorney General Reno and other liberal elites who respond with doublespeak to the public's legitimate calls for tougher anti-crime measures. Skolnick compares this op-ed to a 1990 article I published in *The American Prospect,* and a 1991 article I co-authored for the *Brookings Review.* Finding my "message" to be "more tempered" in these essays than it was in the op-ed, he writes that the "hardness of DiIulio's line seems to depend on his forum." He concludes by asking, "Does DiIulio read DiIulio?"

For the record, my *TAP* article was mainly about prison rehabilitation programs, including drug treatment. I have continued to write on that issue, done what I could to encourage Senate Republicans and others not to throw the drug treatment baby out with the crime bill bath water, and accepted a public tribute on that score from Democratic Congressman Charles Schumer of New York. I'm for more prisons, stiffer and enforced sentences, and whatever rehabilitation programs work to cut costs and reduce recidivism. But there's no need to genuflect at the prisoner rehabilitation altar in an op-ed that calls for tougher sentencing.

Whether or not imprisoning Peter keeps Paul honest, with Peter locked up, society saves itself from the crimes he might have continued to commit. And by keeping him behind bars for all or most of his term, society spares itself the crimes that might have followed his early release. For example, between 1987 and 1991 Florida parolees committed some 25,000 new crimes, including 5,000 violent crimes and 346 murders. The *Brookings Review* article referenced by Skolnick was a cost-benefit analysis of imprisonment based on official criminal records and prisoner self-report data, which revealed that in the year prior to incarceration, the typical prisoner committed about a dozen serious offenses, excluding all drug crimes. The study found that for most prisoners "prison pays" (i.e., the social benefits of incarceration are nearly 1.4 times the social costs).

Last year I completed another major prisoner self-report survey. The results, which will be published this year, indicate that the benefits of imprisonment are even greater than reported in the *Brookings* study. Still, as I wrote in the first study, "the relationship between imprisonment rates and crime rates is ambiguous." Finding that prison pays at the margin does "not mean that it is cost-effective to imprison every convicted felon."

Amazingly, however, Skolnick and other criminologists have repeatedly cited those obvious cautions and ignored the major finding of the study—namely, that contrary to all their assertions, *prison pays.* Incarcerating a greater fraction of convicted felons would yield positive social benefits, and quite dramatic ones if we factored in even a small deterrence benefit and included even a tiny fraction of all drug crimes.

Skolnick notes that the *Journal* tagged my January 1994 article "Let 'em Rot." As I made clear in my blistering top-of-the-letters-page response, the *Journal* editors' title has everything to do with the casual callousness of some conservative elites and nothing to do with either the public's concerns about crime or my views, backed by extensive research, on the practical attainability and moral necessity of humane (not luxurious) prison administration. Still, Skolnick asserted that my "message" in the piece was as "draconian" as the title.

If criminologists like Skolnick think it's "draconian" to want most violent and repeat criminals to spend most of their time behind bars, to be fed up with fake get-tough measures, to condemn liberal elites who just don't get it, and to want what majorities of every demographic group in America wants in the way of effective justice, then so be it. That says more about the perversity of the criminologists' message (prisons are teeming with petty criminals, Americans are a punitive people, voters are fools, politicians are weathervanes, drugs ought to be decriminalized, and the "experts" always know best) than it does about any venue-sensitive changes in my writing. And since Skolnick liked tarring me with a title against which I had publicly protested, let me note that last November I wrote an op-ed for, if I may imitate Skolnick—where else?—*The New York Times.* My loud, clear, and on-the-record "message" on prisons (more!) was exactly the same there as in the criminologically incorrect *Journal* piece. But the *Times* billed the article "Save the Children."

Jerome H. Skolnick Replies

John DiIulio's response is shot through with overheated generalizations. His first paragraph contains his first big—no, colossal—error, namely that three strikes "would have little impact on the size of prison populations." That's not true in California, the nation's most populous state, where three strikes is currently on the books.

DiIulio assumes that only "violent" felonies count as "strikes," but the California law itemizes "serious" felonies as well. Consequently, California is expected to imprison an additional 3,850 as a result of the Three Strikes law next year.

DiIulio estimates that three strikes will affect a total of only 4,500 felons in all state prisons in a given year based on 1991 estimates of prison population. Subtract 3,850 from 4,500 and you have only 650 additional felons incarcerated for life, in a given year, as a result of the three strikes laws impending in other states. That's not believable.

DiIulio's point would be better made as follows: the impact of three strikes laws on the size of prison populations will depend on how legislatures define third offenses that count as "strikes." DiIulio himself doesn't see much difference between property offenders and violent offenders. He mistrusts intermediate sanctions as well, although he fails to mention how starved parole and probation services are in comparison to prisons. DiIulio disavows "Let 'em rot" as his maxim, but "Lock 'em up" seems to be advised.

California's legislature has plenty of DiIulio-like thinkers. Consequently, the Department of Corrections expects significant increases in prison population as a result of three strikes, and so will other states if they follow California's lead. Moreover, since these are life sentences, their impact on prison population increases with time.

Even before three strikes legislation passed in California, the Department of Corrections predicted that its 1999 population would be more than seven times what it was in 1980. The CDC now predicts that three strikes will enlarge this number by more than half again.

The CDC estimates that three strikes will require at least 20 new prisons, in addition to the dozen already under construction. Eventually, in 2027–28, California is expected to incarcerate 272,438 criminals—the equivalent of building an electric fence around the city of Anaheim.

Interestingly, nobody, including three strikes supporters such as Governor Pete Wilson, disputes these figures. What they warrant instead is that prisons save money.

In New Jersey, where the Senate unanimously approved a three strikes law on May 12, Louis F. Kosco, the bill's sponsor, echoed this theme to a *New York Times* reporter who questioned how cash-strapped governments will cover the cost of booming prison populations. "Each time they go through the revolving door, repeat offenders cost the state a great deal in legal and parole expenses," he said. "And we must take into account the economic and social costs. . . ." George Romero, Chief Economist of the California Governor's Office of Planning and Research, issued a report in late February which estimates the amount of these savings. The average criminal, he says, hits the rest of us up for around $200,000 a year.

Consequently, although Californians will spend $383 million to imprison an estimated additional 3,580 under the three strikes law now in effect, the state will save, Romero computes, $716 million. California will really strike it rich in 2027, when the state can count on imprisoning 272,438 at a whopping savings of $54 billion compared to a measly $6.3 billion in prison costs. But three false assumptions undermine the report's conclusions:

First, the report assumes a finite group of criminals. If we keep them locked up for life or close to it, crime, the report assumes, will tumble significantly. The fallacy is this: serious violent crime is committed primarily by 15–24 year old males. The rate declines when they move into their thirties, as DiIulio acknowledges.

As Gottfredson and Hirschi assert convincingly in their recent *A General Theory of Crime,* the serious, predatory offenses said to be associated with career criminals are actually committed by young people "some of whom go on committing them for awhile, but most of whom spend their . . . late twenties running afoul of the authorities over alcohol, drugs and family squabbles." Even Sheldon and Eleanor Glueck, after a lifetime of research, report a substantial reduction in serious criminality in the 25–31 age range. If we lock them up for life as three strikes demands, they will be replaced by younger criminals. Geriatric cases will fill the prisons, while offenders will remain youthful. In the end, the public is no safer.

Second, there is no such animal as "the average criminal" or an "average murderer." The eight-year figure supplied by DiIulio includes premeditated murderers, and those who kill accidentally while driving under the influence. Both deserve punishment, but criminal law sensibly distinguishes their respective moral culpability. Sensible public policy should not penalize all felons, even violent felons, with equal, mandated, discretionless severity. Three strikes laws, and Romero's analysis, tend to treat all felons equally. This is neither morally justified nor fiscally sound.

Finally, prison costs are certain while savings are speculative. While shelling out for the five-fold increase in corrections since 1980, Californians have had to sacrifice other services in education, health, and welfare. California's public schools, which once ranked near the top, now rank near the bottom, close to Mississippi's. Its higher education system has been ravaged by the need to offer a generous retirement package to many of its most distinguished faculty because it can no longer afford to pay them without firing twice as many junior faculty.

Three strikes will shift the budget balance sharply in favor of prisons and away from educational and social services, in the absence of which teenage crime will flourish. Vast "savings" from expanded prisons are the 1994 crime control version of voodoo economics.

Even without three strikes legislation, California is already the nation's biggest jailer, with one out of eight American prisoners occupying its cells. California's prison system has grown twice as much as the systems in the next three largest states (New York, Texas, and Florida) and four times as much as Western Europe's.

If high rates of imprisonment (recall DiIulio wants "more prisons, stiffer and enforced sentences") lead to feelings of public safety, Californians should feel twice as safe as New Yorkers, Texans, and Floridians and four times as safe as citizens of France. They don't. As Joan Petersilia and Peter Reuter conclude in their RAND book *Urban America: Policy Choices for Los Angeles and the Nation,* California locks up too many people, often for the wrong offenses (drug offenders accounted for 26 percent of California prisoners in 1990, up from 11 percent in 1980) and has too little to show for it in enhanced public safety.

As reports of these facts are filtering through, the public and the press are beginning to reconsider. For example, a 70-year-old San Francisco woman refused to testify against an addict-burglar who had broken into her car. She didn't think he deserved a life sentence and called the Three Strikes law "a holocaust for the poor" in a local newspaper.

Even the Klaas family has come out against the current law, saying they were bamboozled into supporting it in a time of grief. They support a more moderate bill that eliminates household burglaries as strikes. The California three strikes law is tough and dumb, and anyone remotely familiar with the criminal justice system understands that.

According to DiIulio, I and other criminologists are out of touch with the concerns of middle class Americans. This is hyperbolic nonsense. Granted, most criminologists are skeptical that expanding imprisonment by mandating life sentences is a solution to America's crime problem. But we are skeptical for the very reason that DiIulio is: "If the question's how to solve America's crime problem . . . then prison is no answer." If we starve education and social services to pay for excessively long prison sentences, if we concentrate on building prisons at the expense of schools, crime will increase and public safety will suffer.

The criminal sanction is both an expression of moral outrage and a method of controlling crime. Unfortunately, the two goals are not always in sync. The call for long, mandated prison sentences is a response to moral outrage. Some criminals should be locked up for decades, even for life, to protect the public. For that goal we need more, rather than less, discretion from judges and parole boards.

Likewise, it makes no sense to mandate five-year sentences for an 18-year-old caught selling drugs, unless we simply want to express moral outrage. Someone else will almost certainly take his place. (See Daniel Feldman, "Imprisoner's Dilemma," *TAP* Summer 1993.)

Yes, time served for violent felonies has decreased in the last ten years. Two trends are responsible. We've been sending more nonviolent offenders to state prison because local jails are overcrowded, and we've been locking up parolees who flunk their drug tests. The latter account for about 25 percent of California's prison population.

DiIulio's rantings about criminologists as "elitists" belie a central truth. Criminologists are deeply concerned with controlling crime, especially in communities of disadvantage. I didn't write, as DiIulio claims, that the Polly Klaas tragedy is "mere sensationalism." I did say that had supposedly "soft-on-crime" indeterminate sentencing been in effect, Richard Allen Davis would not have been released.

I also tried to account for the fact that at a time when crime rates are flat or declining in California (and the nation), crime has become America's number one concern. Klaas's murder, plus a number of other highly publicized crimes, I wrote, "have sent a scary message to the majority of Americans who do not live in the inner city." Polly was an especially lovely, vivacious girl with a winning smile. And she was white and became "America's daughter." But the fact remains, a teenager's chances of being murdered in east Oakland or southeast Washington D.C. are considerably higher than in Petaluma, a bucolic northern California suburb.

What most criminologists question are policies directing funds away from crime prevention measures in disadvantaged communities and toward the expensive financing of mandated life sentences, especially for those convicted of nonviolent felonies. If crime control is the issue, criminologists have a lot to contribute. If moral outrage is what it's all about, the ranters and ravers will win the day.

Nor are criminologists opposed to appropriate, just, and effective incapacitation. When thoughtfully applied, it can protect the public against repeatedly violent criminals. True, we will make mistakes. The answer, however, is not to eliminate discretion, but to use it wisely, as is done in Minnesota's widely acclaimed sentencing guideline system.

Even DiIulio agrees imprisoning criminals for decades when they are beyond their high crime years makes no sense. He wants to hammer them while they're hot. The issue then becomes what does it mean to hammer, for which offenses, and how hot?

I agree that prosecutors will soften the impact of three strikes in California and other states. Prosecutors are the most powerful actors in the criminal justice system. They can and will bargain, no matter what the legislation says. Even so, California and other states that follow its model will experience a vast expansion of imprisonment.

Let me conclude on a personal note. This business of argument by "elite" name calling (including Janet Reno in that category, no less) scarcely advances the debate. Besides, how can a Princeton professor and contributor to the *Brookings Review* and *The American Prospect* classify others as elites and himself as an ordinary working stiff? C'mon, let's be real. If the cultural revolution were to come to America, John DiIulio and I would be sentenced to plow the fields together side by side.

CHAPTER 41

Workaday World, Crack Economy

PHILIPPE BOURGOIS

I was forced into crack against my will. When I first moved to East Harlem—"El Barrio"—as a newlywed in the spring of 1985, I was looking for an inexpensive New York City apartment from which I could write about the experience of poverty and ethnic segregation in the heart of one of the most expensive cities in the world. I was interested in the political economy of inner-city street culture. I wanted to probe the Achilles' heel of the richest industrialized nation in the world by documenting how it imposes racial segregation and economic marginalization on so many of its Latino/a and African-American citizens.

My original subject was the entire underground (untaxed) economy, from curbside car repairing and baby-sitting to unlicensed off-track betting and drug dealing. I had never even heard of crack when I first arrived in the neighborhood—no one knew about this particular substance yet, because this brittle compound of cocaine and baking soda processed into efficiently smokable pellets was not yet available as a mass-marketed product. By the end of the year, however, most of my friends, neighbors and acquaintances had been swept into the multibillion-dollar crack cyclone: selling it, smoking it, fretting over it. I followed them, and I watched the murder rate in the projects opposite my crumbling tenement apartment spiral into one of the highest in Manhattan.

But this essay is not about crack, or drugs, per se. Substance abuse in the inner city is merely a symptom—and a vivid symbol—of deeper dynamics of social marginalization and alienation. Of course, on an immediately visible personal level, addiction and substance abuse are among the most immediate, brutal facts shaping daily life on the street. Most important, however, the two dozen street dealers and their families that I befriended were not interested in talking primarily about drugs. On the contrary, they wanted me to learn all about their daily struggles for subsistence and dignity at the poverty line.

Through the 1980s and 1990s, slightly more than one in three families in El Barrio have received public assistance. Female heads of these impoverished households have to supplement their meager checks in order to keep their children alive. Many are mothers who make extra money by baby-sitting their neighbors' children, or by housekeeping for a paying boarder. Others may bartend at one of the half-dozen social clubs and after-hours dancing spots scattered throughout the neighborhood. Some work "off the books" in their living rooms as seamstresses for garment contractors. Finally, many also find themselves obliged to establish amorous relationships with men who are willing to make cash contributions to their household expenses.

Male income-generating strategies in the underground economy are more publicly visible. Some men repair cars on the curb; others wait on stoops for unlicensed construction subcontractors to pick them up for fly-by-night demolition jobs or window renovation projects. Many sell "numbers"—the street's version of off-track betting. The most visible cohorts hawk "nickels and dimes" of one illegal drug or another. They are part of the most robust, multibillion-dollar sector of the booming underground economy. Cocaine and crack, in particular during the mid-1980s and through the early 1990s, followed by heroin in the mid-1990s, have become the fastest-growing—if not the only—equal-opportunity employers of men in Harlem. Retail drug sales easily outcompete other income-generating opportunities, whether legal or illegal.

Why should these young men and women take the subway to work minimum-wage jobs—or even double-minimum-wage jobs—in downtown offices when they can usually earn more, at least in the short run, by selling drugs on the street corner in front of their apartment or schoolyard? In fact, I am always surprised that so many inner-city men and women remain in the legal economy and work nine-to-five plus overtime, barely making ends meet. According to the 1990 Census of East Harlem, 48 percent of all males and 35 percent of females over 16 were employed in officially reported jobs, compared with a citywide average of 64 percent for men and 49 percent for women. In the census tracts surrounding my apartment, 53 percent of all men over 16 years of age (1,923 out of 3,647) and 28 percent of all women over 16 (1,307 out of 4,626) were working legally in officially censused jobs. An additional 17 percent of the civilian labor force was unemployed but actively looking for work, compared with 16 percent for El Barrio as a whole, and 9 percent for all of New York City.

"IF I WAS WORKING LEGAL . . ."

Street dealers tend to brag to outsiders and to themselves about how much money they make each night. In fact, their income is almost never as consistently high as they report it to be. Most street sellers, like my friend Primo (who, along with other friends and co-workers, allowed me to tape hundreds of hours of conversation with him over five years), are paid on a piece-rate commission basis. When converted into an hourly wage, this is often a relatively paltry sum. According to my calculations, the workers in the Game Room crackhouse, for example, averaged slightly less than double the legal minimum wage—between 7 and 8 dollars an hour. There were plenty of exceptional nights, however, when they made up to ten times minimum wage—and these are the nights they remember when they reminisce. They forget about all the other shifts when they were unable to work because of police raids, and they certainly do not count as forfeited working hours the nights they spent in jail.

This was brought home to me symbolically one night as Primo and his co-worker Caesar were shutting down the Game Room. Caesar unscrewed the fuses in the electrical box to disconnect the video games. Primo had finished stashing the leftover bundles of crack vials inside a hollowed-out live electrical socket and was counting the night's thick wad of receipts. I was struck by how thin the handful of bills was that he separated out and folded neatly into his personal billfold. Primo and Caesar then eagerly lowered the iron riot gates over the Game Room's windows and snapped shut the heavy Yale padlocks. They were moving with the smooth, hurried gestures of workers preparing to go home after an honest day's hard labor. Marveling at the universality in the body language of workers rushing at closing time, I felt an urge to compare the wages paid by this alternative economy. I grabbed Primo's wallet out of his back pocket, carefully giving a wide berth to the fatter wad in his front pocket that represented Ray's share of the night's income—and that could cost Primo his life if it were waylaid. Unexpectedly, I pulled out fifteen dollars' worth of food stamps along with two $20 bills. After an embarrassed giggle, Primo stammered that his mother had added him to her food-stamp allotment.

> *Primo:* I gave my girl, Maria, half of it. I said, "Here take it, use it if you need it for whatever." And then the other half I still got it in my wallet for emergencies.
>
> Like that, we always got a couple of dollars here and there, to survive with. Because tonight, straight cash, I only got garbage. Forty dollars! Do you believe that?

At the same time that wages can be relatively low in the crack economy, working conditions are often inferior to those in the legal economy. Aside from the obvious dangers of being shot, or of going to prison, the physical work space of most crackhouses is usually unpleasant. The infrastructure of the Game Room, for example, was much worse than that of any legal retail outfit in East Harlem: There was no bathroom, no running water, no telephone, no heat in the winter and no air conditioning in the summer. Primo occasionally complained:

> Everything that you see here [sweeping his arm at the scratched and dented video games, the walls with peeling paint, the floor slippery with litter, the filthy windows pasted over with ripped movie posters] is fucked up. It sucks, man [pointing at the red 40-watt bare bulb hanging from an exposed fixture in the middle of the room and exuding a sickly twilight].

Indeed, the only furnishings besides the video games were a few grimy milk crates and bent aluminum stools. Worse yet, a smell of urine and vomit usually permeated the locale. For a few months Primo was able to maintain a rudimentary sound system, but it was eventually beaten to a pulp during one of Caesar's drunken rages. Of course, the deficient infrastructure was only one part of the depressing working conditions.

> *Primo:* Plus I don't like to see people fucked up [handing over three vials to a nervously pacing customer]. This is fucked-up shit. I don't like this crack dealing. Word up.
>   [gunshots in the distance] Hear that?

In private, especially in the last few years of my residence, Primo admitted that he wanted to go back to the legal economy.

> *Primo:* I just fuck up the money here. I rather be legal.
>   *Philippe:* But you wouldn't be the head man on the block with so many girlfriends.
>   *Primo:* I might have women on my dick right now but I would be much cooler if I was working legal. I wouldn't be drinking and the coke wouldn't be there every night.
>   Plus if I was working legally I would have women on my dick too, because I would have money.
>   *Philippe:* But you make more money here than you could ever make working legit.
>   *Primo:* O.K. So you want the money but you really don't want to do the job.
>   I really hate it, man. Hate it! I hate the people! I hate the environment! I hate the whole shit, man! But it's like you get caught up with it. You do it, and you say, "Ay, fuck it today!" Another day, another dollar. [pointing at an emaciated customer who was just entering] But I don't really, really think that I would have hoped that I can say I'm gonna be richer one day. I can't say that. I think about it, but I'm just living day to day.
>   If I was working legal, I wouldn't be hanging out so much. I wouldn't be treating you. [pointing to the 16-ounce can of Colt 45 in my hand] In a job, you know, my environment would change . . . totally. Cause I'd have different friends. Right after work I'd go out with a co-worker, for lunch, for dinner. After work I may go home; I'm too tired for hanging out—I know I gotta work tomorrow.
>   After working a legal job, I'm pretty sure I'd be good.

BURNED IN THE FIRE ECONOMY

The problem is that Primo's good intentions do not lead anywhere when the only legal jobs he can compete for fail to provide him with a livable wage. None of the crack dealers were explicitly conscious of the links between their limited options in the legal economy, their addiction to drugs and their dependence on the crack economy for economic survival and personal dignity. Nevertheless, all of Primo's colleagues and employees told stories of rejecting what they considered to be intolerable working conditions at entry-level jobs.

Most entered the legal labor market at exceptionally young ages. By the time they were 12, they were bagging and delivering groceries at the supermarket for tips, stocking beer off the books in local bodegas or running errands. Before reaching 21, however, virtually none had fulfilled their early childhood dreams of finding stable, well-paid legal work.

The problem is structural: From the 1950s through the 1980s second-generation inner-city Puerto Ricans were trapped in the most vulnerable niche of a factory-based economy that was rapidly being replaced by service industries. Between 1950 and 1990, the proportion of factory jobs in New York City decreased approximately threefold at the same time that service-sector jobs doubled. The Department of City Planning calculates that more than 800,000 industrial jobs were lost from the 1960s through the early 1990s, while the total number of jobs of all categories remained more or less constant at 3.5 million.

Few scholars have noted the cultural dislocations of the new service economy. These cultural clashes have been most pronounced in the office-work service jobs that have multiplied because of the dramatic expansion of the finance, real estate and insurance (FIRE) sector in New York City. Service work in professional offices is the most dynamic place for ambitious inner-city youths to find entry-level jobs if they aspire to upward mobility. Employment as mailroom clerks, photocopiers and messengers in the highrise office corridors of the financial district propels many into a wrenching cultural confrontation with the upper-middle-class white world. Obedience to the norms of highrise, office-corridor culture is in direct contradiction to street culture's definitions of personal dignity especially for males who are socialized not to accept public subordination.

Most of the dealers have not completely withdrawn from the legal economy. On the contrary—they are precariously perched on its edge. Their poverty remains their only constant as they alternate between street-level crack dealing and just-above-minimum-wage legal employment. The working-class jobs they manage to find are objectively recognized to be among the least desirable in U.S. society; hence the following list of just a few of the jobs held by some of the Game Room regulars during the years I knew them: unlicensed asbestos remover, home attendant, street-corner flier distributor, deep-fat fry cook and night-shift security guard on the violent ward at the municipal hospital for the criminally insane.

The stable factory-worker incomes that might have allowed Caesar and Primo to support families have largely disappeared from the inner city. Perhaps if their social network had not been confined to the weakest sector of manufacturing in a period of rapid job loss, their teenage working-class dreams might have stabilized them for long enough to enable them to adapt to the restructuring of the local economy. Instead, they find themselves propelled headlong into an explosive confrontation between their sense of cultural dignity versus the humiliating interpersonal subordination of service work.

Workers like Caesar and Primo appear inarticulate to their professional supervisors when they try to imitate the language of power in the workplace; they stumble pathetically over the enunciation of unfamiliar words. They cannot decipher the hastily scribbled instructions—rife with mysterious abbreviations—that are left for them by harried office managers on diminutive Post-its. The "common sense" of white-collar work is foreign to them; they do not, for example, understand the logic in filing triplicate copies of memos or for postdating invoices. When they attempt to improvise or show initiative, they fail miserably and instead appear inefficient—or even hostile—for failing to follow "clearly specified" instructions.

In the highrise office buildings of midtown Manhattan or Wall Street, newly employed inner-city high school dropouts suddenly realize they look like idiotic buffoons to the men and women for whom they work. But people like Primo and Caesar have not passively accepted their structural victimization. On the contrary, by embroiling themselves in the underground economy and proudly embracing street culture, they are seeking an alternative to their social marginalization. In the process, on a daily level, they become the actual agents administering their own destruction and their community's suffering.

Both Primo and Caesar experienced deep humiliation and insecurity in their attempts to penetrate the foreign, hostile world of highrise office corridors. Primo had bitter memories of being the mailroom clerk and errand boy at a now-defunct professional trade magazine. The only time he explicitly admitted to having experienced racism was when he described how he was treated at that particular work setting.

> *Primo:* I had a prejudiced boss. . . . When she was talking to people she would say, "He's illiterate," as if I was really that stupid that I couldn't understand what she was talking about.
>
> So what I did one day—you see they had this big dictionary right there on the desk, a big heavy motherfucker—so what I just did was open up the dictionary, and I just looked up the word, "illiterate." And that's when I saw what she was calling me.
>
> So she's saying that I'm stupid or something. I'm stupid! [pointing to himself with both thumbs and making a hulking face] "He doesn't know shit."

In contrast, in the underground economy Primo never had to risk this kind of threat to his self-worth.

> *Primo:* Ray would never disrespect me that way; he wouldn't tell me that because he's illiterate too, plus I've got more education than him. I almost got a G.E.D.

The contemporary street sensitivity to being dissed immediately emerges in these memories of office humiliation. The machismo of street culture exacerbates the sense of insult experienced by men because the majority of office supervisors at the entry level are women. In the lowest recesses of New York City's FIRE sector, tens of thousands of messengers, photocopy machine operators and security guards serving the Fortune 500 companies are brusquely ordered about by young white executives—often female—who sometimes make bimonthly salaries superior to their underlings' yearly wages. The extraordinary wealth of Manhattan's financial district exacerbates the sense of sexist-racist insult associated with performing just-above-minimum-wage labor.

"I DON'T EVEN GOT A DRESS SHIRT"

Several months earlier, I had watched Primo drop out of a "motivational training" employment program in the basement of his mother's housing project, run by former heroin addicts who had just received a multimillion-dollar private sector grant for their innovative approach to training the "unemployable." Primo felt profoundly disrespected by the program, and he focused his discontent on the humiliation he faced because of his inappropriate wardrobe. The fundamental philosophy of such motivational job-training programs is that "these people have an attitude problem." They take a boot-camp approach to their unemployed clients, ripping their self-esteem apart during the first week in order to build them back up with an epiphanic realization that they want to find jobs as security guards, messengers and data-input clerks in just-above-minimum-wage service-sector positions. The program's highest success rate had been with middle-aged African-American women who wanted to terminate their relationship to welfare once their children leave home.

I originally had a "bad attitude" toward the premise of psychologically motivating and manipulating people to accept boring, poorly paid jobs. At the same time, however, the violence and self-destruction I was witnessing at the Game Room was convincing me that it is better to be exploited at work than to be outside the legal labor market. In any case, I persuaded Primo and a half-dozen of his Game Room associates to sign up for the program. Even Caesar was tempted to join.

None of the crack dealers lasted for more than three sessions. Primo was the first to drop out, after the first day. For several weeks he avoided talking about the experience. I repeatedly pressed him to explain why he "just didn't show up" at the sessions. Only after repeated badgering on my part did he finally express the deep sense of shame and vulnerability he experienced whenever he attempted to venture into the legal labor market.

> *Philippe:* Yo Primo, listen to me. I worry that there's something taking place that you're not aware of, in terms of yourself. Like the coke that you be sniffing all the time; it's like every night.
>
> *Primo:* What do you mean?
>
> *Philippe:* Like not showing up at the job training. You say it's just procrastination, but I'm scared that it's something deeper that you're not dealing with. . . .
>
> *Primo:* The truth though—listen Felipe—my biggest worry was the dress code, 'cause my gear is limited. I don't even got a dress shirt, I only got one pair of shoes, and you can't wear sneakers at that program. They wear ties too—don't they? Well, I ain't even got ties—I only got the one you lent me.
>
> I would've been there three weeks in the same gear: T-shirt and jeans. *Estoy jodido como un bón!* [I'm all fucked up like a bum!]
>
> *Philippe:* What the fuck kinda bullshit excuse are you talking about? Don't tell me you were thinking that shit. No one notices how people are dressed.
>
> *Primo:* Yo, Felipe, this is for real! Listen to me! I was thinking about that shit hard. Hell yeah!
>
> Hell, yes, they would notice if somebody's wearing a fucked-up tie and shirt.
>
> I don't want to be in a program all *abochornado* [bumlike]. I probably won't even concentrate, getting dished, like . . . and being looked at like a sucker. Dirty jeans . . . or like old jeans, because I would have to wear jeans, 'cause I only got one slack. Word though! I only got two dress shirts and one of them is missing buttons.
>
> I didn't want to tell you about that because it's like a poor excuse, but that was the only shit I was really thinking about. At the time I just said, "Well, I just don't show up."

And Felipe, I'm a stupid [very] skinny nigga'. So I have to be careful how I dress, otherwise people will think I be on the stem [a crack addict who smokes out of a glass-stem pipe].

Philippe: [nervously] Oh shit. I'm even skinnier than you. People must think I'm a total drug addict.

Primo: Don't worry. You're white.

CHAPTER 42

Unjust Rewards

KEN SILVERSTEIN

In 1989, an explosion ripped through a Phillips Petroleum chemical plant in Pasadena, Texas, killing 23 workers and injuring more than 100. Federal officials fined the company $4 million, citing "clear evidence that the explosion was avoidable had recognized safety practices been followed." In 1999 and 2000, two more explosions at the plant left another 3 workers dead and 73 injured. Phillips was hit with an additional $2.3 million in fines for ignoring safety hazards.

In 1994, a worker was killed in an explosion at an Arizona factory run by TRW, the nation's leading maker of air bags. The company, which had a record of violating workplace laws at the plant, settled criminal charges in the case for $1.7 million. Officials later discovered that TRW, in a move "clearly approved by management," was illegally dumping chemical waste from the plant at landfills in three states. Last year, the company paid a record $24 million in civil and criminal penalties.

In 1999, a jury found Koch Industries guilty of negligence in the deaths of two teenagers killed in a fire caused by a corroded pipeline. The following year, the Kansas-based energy giant paid $30 million—the largest civil penalty in the history of the Clean Water Act—for illegally discharging 3 million gallons of crude oil in six states. Last year, Koch paid $25 million to settle charges that it lied about how much oil it was pumping out of federal lands, cheating the government in nearly 25,000 separate transactions.

Phillips, TRW, and Koch have more in common than a history of repeatedly violating workplace and environmental laws. They also rank among the nation's largest government contractors. Between 1995 and 2000, the three corporations received a combined total of $10.4 billion in federal business—at the same time that regulatory agencies and federal courts were citing the companies for jeopardizing the safety of their employees, polluting the nation's air and water, and even defrauding the government.

That's not supposed to happen. Federal contracting officers are charged with reviewing the record of companies that do business with the government and barring those that fail to demonstrate "a satisfactory record of integrity and business ethics." But officials are given no guidelines to follow in making such decisions, and there's no centralized system they can consult to inform them of corporate wrongdoing. As a result, a government report concluded in 2000, those responsible for awarding federal contracts are "extremely reluctant" to take action, even when they are aware of violations. And in the rare instances when the rule is enforced, it is almost always employed against small companies with little clout in Washington.

Shortly before leaving office, President Clinton issued a new order to provide clear guidelines for deciding which firms share in the roughly $200 billion in federal contracts awarded each year. The new "contractor responsibility rule"— championed by Vice President Al Gore and developed after two years of congressional testimony and public hearings—specified that federal officials should weigh "evidence of repeated, pervasive, or significant violations of the law." Officials were told to consider whether a company has cheated on prior contracts or violated laws involving the environment, workplace safety, labor rights, consumer protection, or antitrust activities.

The measure was never implemented. In one of his first acts as president, George W. Bush put the rule on hold after only 11 days in office, saying the issue needed further study. With big business suing to block the new guidelines, Bush revoked the rule 11 months later.

Some 80,000 contractors do at least $25,000 in business with the federal government each year, and the great majority comply with the law. But a six-month investigation by *Mother Jones* of the nation's 200 largest contractors found that the government continues to award lucrative contracts to dozens of companies that it has repeatedly cited for serious violations of workplace and environmental laws. The government's own database of contractors was matched with lists of the worst violations documented by the Environmental Protection Agency (EPA) and the Occupational Safety and Health Administration (OSHA) between 1995 and 2000. Among the findings:

- Forty-six of the biggest contractors were prosecuted by the Justice Department and ordered to pay cleanup costs after they refused to take responsibility for dumping hazardous waste and other environmental violations. General Electric—which received nearly $9.8 billion from the government, making it the nation's 10th-largest contractor—topped the list with 27 cases of pollution for which it was held solely or jointly liable.
- Fifty-five of the top contractors were cited for a total of 1,375 violations of workplace safety law that posed a risk of death or serious physical harm to workers. Ford Motor, which ranks 177th among contractors with $442 million in federal business, led the OSHA list with 292 violations deemed "serious" by federal officials. In 1999, six workers were killed and dozens injured when a boiler exploded at Ford's River Rouge Complex in Dearborn, Michigan. The company was hit with a $1.5 million fine after an internal memo revealed that Ford had decided not to replace safety equipment on the aging boilers because it would then have to fully upgrade them to meet "all present safety standards."

TABLE 42.1   The Dirty Dozen: Federal Contractors with Both EPA and OSHA Violations, Ranked by Penalties (1995–2000)

	Contracts (in millions)	Rank as Contractor	EPA Violations	OSHA Violations	Total Penalties
Ford Motor	$442	177	12	292	$6,082,271
TRW	10,267	9	3	79	5,745,234
Archer Daniels Midland	471	168	4	93	1,676,850
ExxonMobil	2,173	43	20	5	1,481,400
E.J. DuPont de Nemours	446	175	17	23	956,700
Avondale Industries	1,347	66	1	73	759,100
General Motors	4,854	18	21	14	418,393
General Electric	9,777	10	27	48	369,363
Olin Corp.	1,310	68	7	4	168,500
Atlantic Richfield	675	138	10	1	150,600
DaimlerChrysler	1,575	54	7	166	130,121
Textron	5,507	17	4	78	111,215

ABOUT THE DATA

The "contractor responsibility rule" revoked by President Bush required officials to review a company's recent history of violating federal laws. To determine which contractors have the worst records in two significant areas covered by the rule—the environment and workplace safety—*Mother Jones* compiled a list of 200 corporations that did the most business with the government between 1995 and 2000. The list was then matched to two federal databases: a list of companies prosecuted by the Justice Department and found liable for environmental violations, and a list of firms cited by the Occupational Safety and Health Administration for posing a serious risk of injury or death to workers. Database work was conducted by Ron Nixon of Investigative Reporters and Editors, a nonprofit organization based in Columbia, Missouri. Additional reporting was provided by George Sanchez, with documentation from the Project on Government Oversight, a research group based in Washington, D.C. A complete list of violations committed by the top 200 contractors is available online at *www.motherjones.com*.

• Thirty-four leading contractors were penalized for violating both environmental and workplace safety rules. The firms were hit with a total of $12.6 million in EPA penalties and $5.9 million in OSHA fines—costs more than covered by the $229 billion in federal contracts they were awarded during the same period.

"It is clear that, in many cases, the government continues to do business with contractors who violate laws, sometimes repeatedly," concludes a 2000 report by the Federal Acquisition Regulatory Council, the agency that oversees federal contractors. Others put it more bluntly. "Government should not do business with crooks," says Rep. George Miller (D-Calif.), who has demanded that the White House make public any closed-door meetings it had with corporate lobbyists to discuss killing the contractor responsibility rule. Bush's decision, Miller says, "sends a message to contractors that the government doesn't care if you underpay your workers, or expose them to toxic hazards, or destroy the public lands—the government will do business with you anyway."

During Bill Clinton's second term in office, a coalition of labor, civil rights, and consumer groups lobbied the government to crack down on contractor misconduct. Backed by Miller and other congressional allies, they pointed to numerous studies documenting the extent of the problem. A 1995 report by the Government Accounting Office revealed that 80 major federal contractors had violated the National Labor Relations Act by seeking to suppress unions. Another GAO report found that in 1994 alone, OSHA imposed fines of $15,000 or more on each of 261 companies that had received a combined $38 billion in federal contracts. Noting that some contractors place workers "at substantial risk of injury or illness," the report added that the "prospect of debarment or suspension can provide impetus for a contractor to undertake remedial measures to improve working conditions."

In July 1999, Clinton declared his support for the reform coalition and announced plans to revise the rule. What emerged ever the next two years was a set of specific guidelines for federal contracting officers to follow in determining a company's eligibility. The new rule created a hierarchy of violations to be considered, topped by convictions for contract fraud. It stipulated that only repeated and serious wrongdoing, not administrative complaints, should be weighed. And it acknowledged a need for flexibility, noting that companies with serious violations might continue to receive contracts if they "correct the conditions that led to the misconduct."

"We view this fundamentally as empowering the government to do what every business in the world does, which is not to be forced to do business with people it doesn't trust," said Joshua Gotbaum, who helped draft the rule as controller of the Office of Management and Budget.

Clinton's move generated a fast and furious reaction from business and industry. The Business Roundtable, the U.S. Chamber of Commerce, and the National Association of Manufacturers launched a fierce lobbying campaign against the new rule. Despite a provision stating that only a pattern of "pervasive" and "significant" abuses would be considered, business opponents argued that the guidelines gave contracting officers excessive discretion to arbitrarily torpedo a contractor. "The proposed rules would allow contract officers to blacklist firms without regard to the number, nature, or severity of violations," said the National Center for Policy Analysis, a business-backed think tank. "Suspicions raised by rivals or disgruntled employees could cost firms millions, if not billions, of dollars."

To fight the measure, the business coalition hired Linda Fuselier of the Capitol Group, a high-powered lobbyist who had previously helped insurance firms avoid cleanup costs at Superfund waste sites. Opponents flooded officials with hundreds of comments opposing the guidelines. And when Clinton formally issued the new rule in December 2000, they went to federal court seeking to get the provision thrown out.

The court never had to decide the issue. A month later, when Bush took office, he immediately moved to postpone the rule. On January 31, 2001, federal agencies were quietly ordered to delay implementing it for six months—without issuing a public notice or soliciting comment. The Congressional Research Service issued an opinion concluding that the secret suspension of the rule was probably illegal, but the move went virtually unreported in the media. When Bush finally revoked the rule while vacationing at his Texas ranch last December, corporate executives and their allies in Congress hailed the decision. "There was never any rational basis or need for additional standards, since existing regulations already ensure the government does not do business with unethical companies," declared Rep. Thomas Davis III, a Republican from Virginia.

In reality, the government makes little effort to review contractors' records—and even the most diligent contracting officer would find it almost impossible to do so. The government does not maintain a central database to store information on contractors' records of compliance with the law. The EPA and OSHA maintain their own lists of corporate violations, but parent companies are not linked to their subsidiaries, which can number in the hundreds. OSHA makes some of its records available online, but the EPA and many other agencies do not. "There's no process built into the review system," says Gary Bass, executive director of OMB Watch, a Washington-based advocate of government accountability. "Just finding the right information is complicated and time-consuming."

As a result, even contractors that commit the most obvious violations are never suspended or debarred. One GAO study found that the government continues to award business to defense contractors that have committed fraud on prior contracts. General Dynamics, the nation's fifth-largest contractor, paid the government nearly $2 million in 1995 to resolve charges that it falsified employee time cards to bill the Pentagon for thousands of hours that were never worked on a contract for testing F-16 fighters. Northrop Grumman, the nation's fourth-largest contractor, paid nearly $6.7 million in 2000 to settle two separate cases in which it was charged with inflating the costs of parts and materials for warplanes. Yet the two defense giants continue to receive federal contracts, collecting a combined total of $38 billion between 1995 and 2000.

Opponents argue that the government already has the power to force contractors to clean up their act, without cutting them off from federal business. In addition, some contractors can be difficult to replace. The Pentagon, for example, maintains that it cannot afford to ban large defense contractors who provide specialized services and products, and the government is reluctant to take away contracts from nursing homes that commit Medicare fraud, fearing that patients will be hurt. "Debarment and suspension isn't practical," says Steven Schooner, a lawyer in the Office of Federal Procurement Policy under Clinton. "If the government needs the goods they produce, it's the only one that loses."

But while big contractors are all but immune from scrutiny, the government has no qualms about denying business to smaller operations that violate the law. Some 24,000 contractors are currently barred from government work, and almost all are small firms or individuals like Kenneth Hansen, a Kansas dentist banned from receiving federal funds to provide care for low-income patients because he defaulted on $164,800 in student loans. "We never take down the big guys," concedes Schooner, now a government-contracts law professor at George Washington University.

The review of environmental and workplace violations by *Mother Jones* reveals that many big contractors could have been forced to forfeit federal business had Bush not interceded on their behalf. Consider the record of ExxonMobil, which became the nation's 43rd-largest contractor when the two oil giants merged in 1999. Between 1995 and 2000, the firms received a total of $2.2 billion from the government for everything from renting fuel storage space to the Pentagon to selling oil to the Commerce Department. At the same time, they were openly disregarding the law. ExxonMobil has been held liable, either on its own or with other companies, in 20 cases in which it refused to clean up Superfund sites or take responsibility for air and water violations. The company is a partner in Colonial Pipeline, an Atlanta-based firm that the Justice Department sued in 2000 for multiple spills in nine states. In one incident, a pipeline rupture poured 950,000 gallons of diesel fuel into the Reedy River in South Carolina, killing 35,000 fish and other wildlife. In 1995, Mobil was hit with a $98,500 fine for its failure to inspect equipment at a refinery in Torrance, California, where 28 workers were injured in an explosion. In 1999, authorities discovered that Exxon had knowingly contaminated water supplies near a refinery in Benicia, California, with benzene and toluene, both of which cause cancer and birth defects.

One of the federal contractors with the worst record of workplace violations is Avondale Industries, which builds ships for the Navy. Between 1990 and 1996, nine workers died at Avondale's shipyard outside New Orleans, a death rate nearly three times that at other Navy shipyards. In 1999, OSHA inspectors uncovered hundreds of violations of safety and health standards, including Avondale's failure to provide safe scaffolding or training for employees who work at dangerous heights. OSHA hit the company with $717,000 in fines, among the largest ever imposed on a shipbuilder. "The stiff penalties are warranted," said then-Secretary of Labor Alexis Herman. "Workers should not have to risk their lives for their livelihood."

Yet just a month after the fines, the government awarded Avondale $22 million to work on amphibious assault ships at the New Orleans yard. The following year, three more workers were killed in accidents at the Avondale yard. One of the victims, 33-year-old Faustino Mendoza, died of head injuries when he fell 80 feet from scaffolding that lacked required safety features—the same problem that had been found during the most recent inspection. OSHA fined Avondale $49,000 for the "repeat" violation, but the penalty amounted to a tiny fraction of the $1.3 billion the firm received in federal business between 1995 and 2000. (Last year, Avondale became a subsidiary of Northrop Grumman.)

Another contractor with a pattern of workplace abuses is Tyson Foods, which received more than $163 million between 1995 and 2000, mostly for supplying poultry to government agencies. In 1999, seven workers died at plants run by Tyson or its independent operators. One of the victims was a 15-year-old boy—hired in violation of child-labor laws—who was electrocuted at a Tyson plant in Arkansas. The company has also attempted to buy influence with federal officials. In 1997, Tyson pleaded guilty to giving former Agriculture Secretary Michael Espy more than $12,000 in "gratuities" while the firm had issues before his department.

Even though the current federal rule requires contractors like Tyson, Avondale, and ExxonMobil to demonstrate "integrity and business ethics," they are in no danger of being barred from receiving federal business under the current standard. Indeed, the government continues to award major contracts to companies that have both defrauded the government *and* violated environmental and workplace laws.

TRW, the nation's ninth-largest contractor, supplies the government with everything from military satellites and spacecraft to auto parts and hand tools. Yet the company's subsidiaries have been cited for cheating the government on defense contracts, and last year it settled two cases in which it forced its employees to work off the clock and mishandled pension payments. In 1997, TRW was also listed in a "rogues' gallery" of OSHA violators in a study by *Business and Management Practices.* In just two years, the magazine found, the company racked up 67 violations and $113,202 in fines. In a single inspection in December 1999, OSHA cited TRW for 43 serious and repeat violations at an auto-parts plant in Michigan.

Some of TRW's most egregious offenses took place at two air-bag plants that lie at the foot of the Superstition Mountains near Mesa, Arizona. Within two years after they opened in 1989, the factories had experienced dozens of fires and explosions, and were the target of at least six investigations by state regulators. "There were explosions so big that they felt like earthquakes," says Bunny Bertleson, who lives less than two miles from one of the plants. "Then clouds would come blowing out of the stacks."

The cause of the blasts was sodium azide, a highly volatile chemical that triggers the explosion that inflates air bags upon impact. Sodium azide is also highly toxic. It can damage the heart, kidneys, and nervous system if it is inhaled or comes into contact with the skin or eyes. Acute exposure can cause death.

A string of injuries suffered by workers at the Mesa plants drew the attention of state regulators. Employees frequently reported feeling queasy and dizzy, a condition they dubbed the "azide buzz," but say the company failed to address the problem. "There was constant pressure to get the production numbers up," recalls Felipe Chavez, a former employee. "That was the only priority." TRW insists that such exposure is rare, and that employee safety is "our highest priority." But in 1994, a spark detonated a small quantity of sodium azide, killing one worker and injuring six. The following year, the Mesa fire chief shut down one of the plants for two days, calling it an "imminent threat to both life and property."

The Arizona attorney general's office had already taken TRW to court and won consent orders requiring it to halt the fires, which were releasing sodium azide into the air, and to properly manage hazardous waste at the plants. In 1995, after the company failed to take safety steps it had promised to make to settle prior charges, a state superior court ordered TRW to pay $1.7 million—the largest corporate criminal consent judgment in state history.

But neither court-ordered fines nor injuries to workers prompted TRW to clean up its act. In 1997, an anonymous caller informed a state environmental agency that TRW was illegally storing wastewater laced with sodium azide at one of its Mesa plants. Following up on the tip, state investigators discovered that the company had illegally disposed of hundreds of thousands of gallons of chemical wastewater at landfills in Arizona, Utah, and California. The Arizona attorney general's office determined that the dumping was not "the work of low-level employees" but involved the "approval or acquiescence" of management.

Given the scope of the illegal dumping and TRW's history of breaking its promises, the state pressed criminal charges against the company. In a statement, TRW said that "the errors that occurred did not result in harm to the environment, local residents, or our employees." But last year, the company agreed to pay $24 million to the government for the illegal dumping—the largest such consent agreement in history.

Yet the company's pattern of lawbreaking has not harmed its ability to do business with the government. Between 1995 and 2000, when most of the illegal dumping and other abuses took place, TRW received nearly $10.3 billion in federal contracts—more than 400 times the amount it agreed to pay for its environmental crimes. After the company was caught dumping sodium azide, federal officials reviewed its violations and decided that it should remain eligible to work for the government. Last year, TRW received another $2.5 billion in federal contracts.

PART TWELVE

America in the World

The terrorist attacks on September 11, 2001, drove home for Americans the reality that we are part of a global community that is connected, for better or worse, in multiple and intricate ways—and that what happens in our own country cannot be divorced from what happens in the rest of the world. To an important extent, of course, that has always been true. America has never existed in pristine isolation from the rest of the globe. We are, for one thing, a nation of immigrants, and we cannot understand our history without understanding the importance of the international slave trade in the eighteenth and nineteenth centuries, for example, or the impact of social changes in countries as diverse as Ireland, Poland, and Mexico on our development as a society.

But the world is even more tightly connected today than in the past, with the increasing speed of transportation and communication and the continued movement of vast numbers of people across nations and continents because of war, oppression, or economic insecurity. More than ever, it is impossible to think about many social problems in America without setting them in the context of the changes that are reshaping the wider world. In this section, we introduce some of the most important of them.

We begin with a wide-ranging discussion by Moises Naim, editor of the journal *Foreign Policy,* of five global social problems—the international trade in drugs, arms, intellectual property, people, and money. Our efforts to deal with these problems, Naim argues, have been badly flawed, in part because we have tried to deal with them as if they were merely problems of law enforcement, when in fact they have become something much larger and more complex. We are probably most familiar with the drug trade, which, after decades of efforts at control, now amounts to a business worth an estimated $400 billion a year, roughly equivalent to the entire economic output of Spain. But we have also made little headway against the trade in small arms, which accounts for 1,000 deaths a *day* around the world. These global businesses, nimble, decentralized, and hugely profitable, have easily outmaneuvered resource-poor governments. If we want to have a greater impact on them, Naim argues, we will need, among other things, to invest more in international agencies to control them. Today, for example, Interpol, the main international police agency, has an annual budget that is less than the cost of one of the more advanced boats or airplanes now used by international drug traffickers.

Naim's analysis suggests that these problems are partly of our own making—a reflection of our own global policies. But our policies toward other countries are hardly random: from the beginning, they have been influenced by complex and shifting economic and political interests. As Michael Klare shows, one of the most important motives behind America's foreign policy (and that of many other countries) has been the desire to ensure a steady supply of energy—which, in our petroleum-driven economy, prominently includes oil. Concern over securing oil supplies helped to shape the political landscape of the contemporary Middle East, with all its volatility and tragedy; helped precipitate World War II; and, more recently, has been a backdrop for our two wars with Iraq. And as oil reserves inevitably dwindle, Klare points out, conflict over them is likely to increase.

In the excerpt from his book *Blowback,* Chalmers Johnson extends this point, arguing that the spread of American power around the world has bred a host of troubling, unforeseen consequences. We do not always recognize those consequences as being the results of our own intervention, of course—but, Johnson argues, they often are. American economic policies, for example, imposed partly through international agencies such as the International Monetary Fund, can undermine economies halfway around the world: when this happens, it is often assumed to be the natural effect of an abstract process of "globalization." Johnson argues that we have created a global "empire" based on extending American military and economic power "to every corner of the world." But we have paid far too little attention to the consequences—especially the effect on how we are viewed by the people around the world whose lives are being shaped by these policies. We may, as a result, be breeding a global crisis of massive proportions. The growth of international terrorism, Johnson argues, is only the most dramatic expression of that crisis.

Blowback was written before the events of September 11, 2001, but they only confirm the importance of his disturbing analysis. The report of the national commission launched to study the lessons of those events, part of which we reprint here, concludes that if we want to prevent terrorism in the future, we will need to adopt a more thoughtful and more socially aware approach to our relations with the world beyond our borders. Combating terrorism is not, they insist, just a military or political problem: It will require serious efforts to change the way America operates and is perceived in the rest of the world. Perhaps most importantly, it must include what the Commission calls an "agenda of opportunity"—a commitment to increasing educational and economic options in vulnerable countries, especially for the young. No one can guarantee that such a strategy will succeed in reducing the threat of global terrorism—but *not* tackling those issues virtually guarantees that we will fail.

CHAPTER 43

Five Wars We're Losing

MOISES NAIM

T he persistence of al Qaeda underscores how hard it is for governments to stamp out stateless, decentralized networks that move freely, quickly, and stealthily across national borders to engage in terror. The intense media coverage devoted to the war on terrorism, however, obscures five other similar global wars that pit governments against agile, well-financed networks of highly dedicated individuals. These are the fights against the illegal international trade in drugs, arms, intellectual property, people, and money. Religious zeal or political goals drive terrorists, but the promise of enormous financial gain motivates those who battle governments in these five wars. Tragically, profit is no less a motivator for murder, mayhem, and global insecurity than religious fanaticism.

In one form or another, governments have been fighting these five wars for centuries. And losing them. Indeed, thanks to the changes spurred by globalization over the last decade, their losing streak has become even more pronounced. To be sure, nation-states have benefited from the information revolution, stronger political and economic linkages, and the shrinking importance of geographic distance. Unfortunately, criminal networks have benefited even more. Never fettered by the niceties of sovereignty, they are now increasingly free of geographic constraints. Moreover, globalization has not only expanded illegal markets and boosted the size and the resources of criminal networks, it has also imposed more burdens on governments: Tighter public budgets, decentralization, privatization, deregulation, and a more open environment for international trade and investment all make the task of fighting global criminals more difficult. Governments are made up of cumbersome bureaucracies that generally cooperate with difficulty, but drug traffickers, arms dealers, alien smugglers, counterfeiters, and money launderers have refined networking to a high science, entering into complex and improbable strategic alliances that span cultures and continents.

Defeating these foes may prove impossible. But the first steps to reversing their recent dramatic gains must be to recognize the fundamental similarities among the five wars and to treat these conflicts not as law enforcement problems but as a new global trend that shapes the world as much as confrontations between nation-states did in the past. Customs officials, police officers, lawyers, and judges alone will never win these wars. Governments must recruit and deploy more spies, soldiers, diplomats, and economists who understand how to use incentives and regulations to steer markets away from bad social outcomes. But changing the skill set of government combatants alone will not end these wars. Their doctrines and institutions also need a major overhaul.

THE FIVE WARS

Pick up any newspaper anywhere in the world, any day, and you will find news about illegal migrants, drug busts, smuggled weapons, laundered money, or counterfeit goods. The global nature of these five wars was unimaginable just a decade ago. The resources—financial, human, institutional, technological—deployed by the combatants have reached unfathomable orders of magnitude. So have the numbers of victims. The tactics and tricks of both sides boggle the mind. Yet if you cut through the fog of daily headlines and orchestrated photo ops, one inescapable truth emerges: The world's governments are fighting a qualitatively new phenomenon with obsolete tools, inadequate laws, inefficient bureaucratic arrangements, and ineffective strategies. Not surprisingly, the evidence shows that governments are losing.

Drugs

The best known of the five wars is, of course, the war on drugs. In 1999, the United Nations' "Human Development Report" calculated the annual trade in illicit drugs at $400 billion, roughly the size of the Spanish economy and about 8 percent of world trade. Many countries are reporting an increase in drug use. Feeding this habit is a global supply chain that uses everything from passenger jets that can carry shipments of cocaine worth $500 million in a single trip to custom-built submarines that ply the waters between Colombia and Puerto Rico. To foil eavesdroppers, drug smugglers use "cloned" cell phones and broadband radio receivers while also relying on complex financial structures that blend legitimate and illegitimate enterprises with elaborate fronts and structures of cross-ownership.

The United States spends between $35 billion and $40 billion each year on the war on drugs; most of this money is spent on interdiction and intelligence. But the creativity and boldness of drug cartels has routinely outstripped steady increases in government resources. Responding to tighter security at the U.S.-Mexican border, drug smugglers built a tunnel to move tons of drugs and billions of dollars in cash until authorities discovered it in March 2002. Over the last decade, the success of the Bolivian and Peruvian governments in eradicating coca plantations has shifted production to Colombia. Now, the U.S.-supported Plan Colombia is displacing coca production and processing labs back to other Andean countries. Despite the heroic efforts of these Andean countries and the massive financial and technical support of the United States, the total acreage of coca plantations in Peru,

Colombia, and Bolivia has increased in the last decade from 206,200 hectares in 1991 to 210,939 in 2001. Between 1990 and 2000, according to economist Jeff DeSimone, the median price of a gram of cocaine in the United States fell from $152 to $112.

Even when top leaders of drug cartels are captured or killed, former rivals take their place. Authorities have acknowledged, for example, that the recent arrest of Benjamin Arellano Felix, accused of running Mexico's most ruthless drug cartel, has done little to stop the flow of drugs to the United States. As Arellano said in a recent interview from jail, "They talk about a war against the Arellano brothers. They haven't won. I'm here, and nothing has changed."

Arms Trafficking

Drugs and arms often go together. In 1999, the Peruvian military parachuted 10,000 AK-47s to the Revolutionary Armed Forces of Colombia, a guerrilla group closely allied to drug growers and traffickers. The group purchased the weapons in Jordan. Most of the roughly 80 million AK-47s in circulation today are in the wrong hands. According to the United Nations, only 18 million (or about 3 percent) of the 550 million small arms and light weapons in circulation today are used by government, military, or police forces. Illicit trade accounts for almost 20 percent of the total small arms trade and generates more than $1 billion a year. Small arms helped fuel 46 of the 49 largest conflicts of the last decade and in 2001 were estimated to be responsible for 1,000 deaths a day; more than 80 percent of those victims were women and children.

Small arms are just a small part of the problem. The illegal market for munitions encompasses top-of-the-line tanks, radar systems that detect Stealth aircraft, and the makings of the deadliest weapons of mass destruction. The International Atomic Energy Agency has confirmed more than a dozen cases of smuggled nuclear-weapons-usable material, and hundreds more cases have been reported and investigated over the last decade. The actual supply of stolen nuclear-, biological-, or chemical-weapons materials and technology may still be small. But the potential demand is strong and growing from both would-be nuclear powers and terrorists. Constrained supply and increasing demand cause prices to rise and create enormous incentives for illegal activities. More than one fifth of the 120,000 workers in Russia's former "nuclear cities"—where more than half of all employees earn less than $50 a month—say they would be willing to work in the military complex of another country.

Governments have been largely ineffective in curbing either supply or demand. In recent years, two countries, Pakistan and India, joined the declared nuclear power club. A U.N. arms embargo failed to prevent the reported sale to Iraq of jet fighter engine parts from Yugoslavia and the Kolchuga anti-Stealth radar system from Ukraine. Multilateral efforts to curb the manufacture and distribution of weapons are faltering, not least because some powers are unwilling to accept curbs on their own activities. In 2001, for example, the United States blocked a legally binding global treaty to control small arms in part because it worried about restrictions on its own citizens' rights to own guns. In the absence of effective international legislation and enforcement, the laws of economics dictate the sale of more weapons at cheaper prices: In 1986, an AK-47 in Kolowa, Kenya, cost 15 cows. Today, it costs just four.

Intellectual Property

In 2001, two days after recording the voice track of a movie in Hollywood, actor Dennis Hopper was in Shanghai where a street vendor sold him an excellent pirated copy of the movie with his voice already on it. "I don't know how they got my voice into the country before I got here," he wondered. Hopper's experience is one tiny slice of an illicit trade that cost the United States an estimated $9.4 billion in 2001. The piracy rate of business software in Japan and France is 40 percent, in Greece and South Korea it is about 60 percent, and in Germany and Britain it hovers around 30 percent. Forty percent of Procter & Gamble shampoos and 60 percent of Honda motorbikes sold in China in 2001 were pirated. Up to 50 percent of medical drugs in Nigeria and Thailand are bootleg copies. This problem is not limited to consumer products: Italian makers of industrial valves worry that their $2 billion a year export market is eroded by counterfeit Chinese valves sold in world markets at prices that are 40 percent cheaper.

The drivers of this bootlegging boom are complex. Technology is obviously boosting both the demand and the supply of illegally copied products. Users of Napster, the now defunct Internet company that allowed anyone, anywhere to download and reproduce copyrighted music for free, grew from zero to 20 million in just one year. Some 500,000 film files are traded daily through file-sharing services such as Kazaa and Morpheus; and in late 2002, some 900 million music files could be downloaded for free on the Internet—that is, almost two and a half times more files than those available when Napster reached its peak in February 2001.

Global marketing and branding are also playing a part, as more people are attracted to products bearing a well-known brand like Prada or Cartier. And thanks to the rapid growth and integration into the global economy of countries, such as China, with weak central governments and ineffective laws, producing and exporting near perfect knockoffs are both less expensive and less risky. In the words of the CEO of one of the best known Swiss watchmakers: "We now compete with a product manufactured by Chinese prisoners. The business is run by the Chinese military, their families and friends, using roughly the same machines we have, which they purchased at the same industrial fairs we go to. The way we have rationalized this problem is by assuming that their customers and ours are different. The person that buys a pirated copy of one of our $5,000 watches for less than $100 is not a client we are losing. Perhaps it is a future client that some day will want to own the real thing instead of a fake. We may be wrong and we do spend money to fight the piracy of our products. But given that our efforts do not seem to protect us much, we close our eyes and hope for the better." This posture stands in contrast to that of companies that sell cheaper products such as garments, music, or videos, whose revenues are directly affected by piracy.

Governments have attempted to protect intellectual property rights through various means, most notably the World Trade Organization's Agreement on Trade-Related Aspects of Intellectual Property Rights (TRIPS). Several other organizations such as the World Intellectual Property Organization, the World Customs Union, and Interpol are also involved. Yet the large and growing volume of this trade, or a simple stroll in the streets of Manhattan or Madrid, show that governments are far from winning this fight.

Alien Smuggling

The man or woman who sells a bogus Hermes scarf or a Rolex watch in the streets of Milan is likely to be an illegal alien. Just as likely, he or she was transported across several continents by a trafficking network allied with another network that specializes in the illegal copying, manufacturing, and distributing of high-end, brand-name products.

Alien smuggling is a $7 billion a year enterprise and according to the United Nations is the fastest growing business of organized crime. Roughly 500,000 people enter the United States illegally each year—about the same number as illegally enter the European Union, and part of the approximately 150 million who live outside their countries of origin. Many of these backdoor travelers are voluntary migrants who pay smugglers up to $35,000, the top-dollar fee for passage from China to New York. Others, instead, are trafficked—that is, bought and sold internationally—as commodities. The U.S. Congressional Research Service reckons that each year between 1 million and 2 million people are trafficked across borders, the majority of whom are women and children. A woman can be "bought" in Timisoara, Romania, for between $50 and $200 and "resold" in Western Europe for 10 times that price. The United Nations Children's Fund estimates that cross-border smugglers in Central and Western Africa enslave 200,000 children a year. Traffickers initially tempt victims with job offers or, in the case of children, with offers of adoption in wealthier countries, and then keep the victims in subservience through physical violence, debt bondage, passport confiscation, and threats of arrest, deportation, or violence against their families back home.

Governments everywhere are enacting tougher immigration laws and devoting more time, money, and technology to fight the flow of illegal aliens. But the plight of the United Kingdom's government illustrates how tough that fight is. The British government throws money at the problem, plans to use the Royal Navy and Royal Air Force to intercept illegal immigrants, and imposes large fines on truck drivers who (generally unwittingly) transport stowaways. Still, 42,000 of the 50,000 refugees who have passed through the Sangatte camp (a main entry point for illegal immigration to the United Kingdom) over the last three years have made it to Britain. At current rates, it will take 43 years for Britain to clear its asylum backlog. And that country is an island. Continental nations such as Spain, Italy, or the United States face an even greater challenge as immigration pressures overwhelm their ability to control the inflow of illegal aliens.

Money Laundering

The Cayman Islands has a population of 36,000. It also has more than 2,200 mutual funds, 500 insurance companies, 60,000 businesses, and 600 banks and trust companies with almost $800 billion in assets. Not surprisingly, it figures prominently in any discussion of money laundering. So does the United States, several of whose major banks have been caught up in investigations of money laundering, tax evasion, and fraud. Few, if any, countries can claim to be free of the practice of helping individuals and companies hide funds from governments, creditors, business partners, or even family members, including the proceeds of tax evasion, gambling, and other crimes. Estimates of the volume of global money laundering range between 2 and 5 percent of the world's annual gross national product, or between $800 billion and $2 trillion.

Smuggling money, gold coins, and other valuables is an ancient trade. Yet in the last two decades, new political and economic trends coincided with technological changes to make this ancient trade easier, cheaper, and less risky. Political changes led to the deregulation of financial markets that now facilitate cross-border money transfers, and technological changes made distance less of a factor and money less "physical." Suitcases full of banknotes are still a key tool for money launderers, but computers, the Internet, and complex financial schemes that combine legal and illegal practices and institutions are more common. The sophistication of technology, the complex web of financial institutions that crisscross the globe, and the ease with which "dirty" funds can be electronically morphed into legitimate assets make the regulation of international flows of money a daunting task. In Russia, for example, it is estimated that by the mid-1990s organized crime groups had set up 700 legal and financial institutions to launder their money.

Faced with this growing tide, governments have stepped up their efforts to clamp down on rogue international banking, tax havens, and money laundering. The imminent, large-scale introduction of e-money—cards with microchips that can store large amounts of money and thus can be easily transported outside regular channels or simply exchanged among individuals—will only magnify this challenge.

WHY GOVERNMENTS CAN'T WIN

The fundamental changes that have given the five wars new intensity over the last decade are likely to persist. Technology will continue to spread widely; criminal networks will be able to exploit these technologies more quickly than governments that must cope with tight budgets, bureaucracies, media scrutiny, and electorates. International trade will continue to grow, providing more cover for the expansion of illicit trade. International migration will likewise grow, with much the same effect, offering ethnically based gangs an ever growing supply of recruits and victims. The spread of democracy may also help criminal cartels, which can manipulate weak public institutions by corrupting police officers or tempting politicians with offers of cash for their increasingly expensive election campaigns. And ironically, even the spread of international law—with its growing web of embargoes, sanctions, and conventions—will offer criminals new opportunities for providing forbidden goods to those on the wrong side of the international community.

These changes may affect each of the five wars in different ways, but these conflicts will continue to share four common characteristics:

They are not bound by geography. Some forms of crime have always had an international component: The Mafia was born in Sicily and exported to the United States, and smuggling has always been by definition international. But the five wars are truly global. Where is the theater or front line of the war on drugs? Is it Colombia or Miami? Myanmar (Burma) or Milan? Where are the battles against money launderers being fought? In Nauru or in London? Is China the main theater in the war against the infringement of intellectual property, or are the trenches of that war on the Internet?

They defy traditional notions of sovereignty. Al Qaeda's members have passports and nationalities—and often more than one—but they are truly stateless. Their allegiance is to their cause, not to any nation. The same is also true of the criminal networks engaged in the five wars. The same, however, is patently *not* true of government employees—police officers, customs agents, and judges—who fight them. This asymmetry is a crippling disadvantage for governments waging these wars. Highly paid, hypermotivated, and resource-rich combatants on one side of the wars (the criminal gangs) can seek refuge in and take advantage of national borders, but combatants of the other side (the governments) have fewer resources and are hampered by traditional notions of sovereignty. A former senior CIA official reported that international criminal gangs are able to move people, money, and weapons globally faster than he can move resources inside his own agency, let alone worldwide. Coordination and information sharing among government agencies in different countries has certainly improved, especially after September 11. Yet these tactics fall short of what is needed to combat agile organizations that can exploit every nook and cranny of an evolving but imperfect body of international law and multilateral treaties.

They pit governments against market forces. In each of the five wars, one or more government bureaucracies fight to contain the disparate, uncoordinated actions of thousands of independent, stateless organizations. These groups are motivated by large profits obtained by exploiting international price differentials, an unsatisfied demand, or the cost advantages produced by theft. Hourly wages for a Chinese cook are far higher in Manhattan than in Fujian. A gram of cocaine in Kansas City is 17,000 percent more expensive than in Bogotá. Fake Italian valves are 40 percent cheaper because counterfeiters don't have to cover the costs of developing the product. A well-funded guerrilla group will pay anything to get the weapons it needs. In each of these five wars, the incentives to successfully overcome government-imposed limits to trade are simply enormous.

They pit bureaucracies against networks.   The same network that smuggles East European women to Berlin may be involved in distributing opium there. The proceeds of the latter fund the purchase of counterfeit Bulgari watches made in China and often sold on the streets of Manhattan by illegal African immigrants. Colombian drug cartels make deals with Ukrainian arms traffickers, while Wall Street brokers controlled by the U.S.-based Mafia have been known to front for Russian money launderers. These highly decentralized groups and individuals are bound by strong ties of loyalty and common purpose and organized around semiautonomous clusters or "nodes" capable of operating swiftly and flexibly. John Arquilla and David Ronfeldt, two of the best known experts on these types of organizations, observe that networks often lack central leadership, command, or headquarters, thus "no precise heart or head that can be targeted. The network as a whole (but not necessarily each node) has little to no hierarchy; there may be multiple leaders. . . . Thus the [organization's] design may sometimes appear acephalous (headless), and at other times polycephalous (Hydra-headed)." Typically, governments respond to these challenges by forming interagency task forces or creating new bureaucracies. Consider the creation of the new Department of Homeland Security in the United States, which encompasses 22 former federal agencies and their 170,000 employees and is responsible for, among other things, fighting the war on drugs.

RETHINKING THE PROBLEM

Governments may never be able to completely eradicate the kind of international trade involved in the five wars. But they can and should do better. There are at least four areas where efforts can yield better ideas on how to tackle the problems posed by these wars:

Develop more flexible notions of sovereignty.   Governments need to recognize that restricting the scope of multilateral action for the sake of protecting their sovereignty is often a moot point. Their sovereignty is compromised daily, not by nation-states but by stateless networks that break laws and cross borders in pursuit of trade. In May 1999, for example, the Venezuelan government denied U.S. planes authorization to fly over Venezuelan territory to monitor air routes commonly used by narcotraffickers. Venezuelan authorities placed more importance on the symbolic value of asserting sovereignty over air space than on the fact that drug traffickers' planes regularly violate Venezuelan territory. Without new forms of codifying and "managing" sovereignty, governments will continue to face a large disadvantage while fighting the five wars.

Strengthen existing multilateral institutions.   The global nature of these wars means no government, regardless of its economic, political, or military power, will make much progress acting alone. If this seems obvious, then why does Interpol, the multilateral agency in charge of fighting international crime, have a staff of 384, only 112 of whom are police officers, and an annual budget of $28 million, less than the price of some boats or planes used by drug traffickers? Similarly, Europol, Europe's Interpol equivalent, has a staff of 240 and a budget of $51 million.

One reason Interpol is poorly funded and staffed is because its 181 member governments don't trust each other. Many assume, and perhaps rightly so, that the criminal networks they are fighting have penetrated the police departments of other countries and that sharing information with such compromised officials would not be prudent. Others fear today's allies will become tomorrow's enemies. Still others face legal impediments to sharing intelligence with fellow nation-states or have intelligence services and law enforcement agencies with organizational cultures that make effective collaboration almost impossible. Progress will only be made if the world's governments unite behind stronger, more effective multilateral organizations.

Devise new mechanisms and institutions. These five wars stretch and even render obsolete many of the existing institutions, legal frameworks, military doctrines, weapons systems, and law enforcement techniques on which governments have relied for years. Analysts need to rethink the concept of war "fronts" defined by geography and the definition of "combatants" according to the Geneva Convention. The functions of intelligence agents, soldiers, police officers, customs agents, or immigration officers need rethinking and adaptation to the new realities. Policymakers also need to reconsider the notion that ownership is essentially a physical reality and not a "virtual" one or that only sovereign nations can issue money when thinking about ways to fight the five wars.

Move from repression to regulation. Beating market forces is next to impossible. In some cases, this reality may force governments to move from repressing the market to regulating it. In others, creating market incentives may be better than using bureaucracies to curb the excesses of these markets. Technology can often accomplish more than government policies can. For example, powerful encryption techniques can better protect software or CDs from being copied in Ukraine than would making the country enforce patents and copyrights and trademarks.

In all of the five wars, government agencies fight against networks motivated by the enormous profit opportunities created by other government agencies. In all cases, these profits can be traced to some form of government intervention that creates a major imbalance between demand and supply and makes prices and profit margins skyrocket. In some cases, these government interventions are often justified and it would be imprudent to eliminate them—governments can't simply walk away from the fight against trafficking in heroin, human beings, or weapons of mass destruction. But society can better deal with other segments of these kinds of illegal trade through regulation, not prohibition. Policymakers must focus on opportunities where market regulation can ameliorate problems that have defied approaches based on prohibition and armed interdiction of international trade.

Ultimately, governments, politicians, and voters need to realize that the way in which the world is conducting these five wars is doomed to fail—not for lack of effort, resources, or political will but because the collective thinking that guides government strategies in the five wars is rooted in wrong ideas, false assumptions, and obsolete institutions. Recognizing that governments have no chance of winning unless they change the ways they wage these wars is an indispensable first step in the search for solutions.

CHAPTER 44

Oil, Geography, and War

MICHAEL T. KLARE

Of all the resources discussed in this book, none is more likely to provoke conflict between states in the twenty-first century than oil. Petroleum stands out from other materials—water, minerals, timber, and so on—because of its pivotal role in the global economy and its capacity to ignite large-scale combat. No highly industrialized society can survive at present without substantial supplies of oil, and so any significant threat to the continued availability of this resource will prove a cause of crisis and, in extreme cases, provoke the use of military force. Action of this sort could occur in any of the major oil-producing areas, including the Middle East and the Caspian basin. Lesser conflicts over petroleum are also likely, as states fight to gain or retain control over resource-rich border areas and offshore economic zones. Big or small, conflicts over oil will constitute a significant feature of the global security environment in the decades to come.

Petroleum has, of course, been a recurring source of conflict in the past. Many of the key battles of World War II, for example, were triggered by the Axis Powers' attempts to gain control over petroleum supplies located in areas controlled by their adversaries. The pursuit of greater oil revenues also prompted Iraq's 1990 invasion of Kuwait, and this, in turn, provoked a massive American military response. But combat over petroleum is not simply a phenomenon of the past; given the world's ever-increasing demand for energy and the continuing possibility of supply interruptions, the outbreak of a conflict over oil is just as likely to occur in the future.

The likelihood of future combat over oil is suggested, first of all, by the growing buildup of military forces in the Middle East and other oil-producing areas. Until recently, the greatest concentration of military power was found along the East-West divide in Europe and at other sites of superpower competition. Since 1990, however, these concentrations have largely disappeared, while troop levels in the major oil zones have been increased. The United States, for example, has established a permanent military infrastructure in the Persian Gulf area and has "prepositioned" sufficient war matériel there to sustain a major campaign. Russia, meanwhile, has shifted more of its forces to the North Caucasus and the Caspian Sea basin, while China has expanded its naval presence in the South China Sea. Other countries have also bolstered their presence in these areas and other sites of possible conflict over oil.

Geology and geography also add to the risk of conflict. While relatively abundant at present, natural petroleum does not exist in unlimited quantities; it is a finite, nonrenewable substance. At some point in the future, available supplies will prove inadequate to satisfy soaring demand, and the world will encounter significant shortages. Unless some plentiful new source of energy has been discovered by that point, competition over the remaining supplies of petroleum will prove increasingly fierce. In such circumstances, any prolonged interruption in the global flow of oil will be viewed by import-dependent states as a mortal threat to their security—and thus as a matter that may legitimately be resolved through the use of military force. Growing scarcity will also result in higher prices for oil, producing enormous hardship for those without the means to absorb added costs; in consequence, widespread internal disorder may occur.

Geography enters the picture because many of the world's leading sources of oil are located in contested border zones or in areas of recurring crisis and violence. The distribution of petroleum is more concentrated than other raw materials, with the bulk of global supplies found in a few key producing areas. Some of these areas— the North Slope of Alaska and the American Southwest, for example—are located within the borders of a single country and are relatively free of disorder; others, however, are spread across several countries—which may or may not agree on their common borders—and/or are located in areas of perennial unrest. To reach global markets, moreover, petroleum must often travel (by ship or by pipeline) through other areas of instability. Because turmoil in these areas can easily disrupt the global flow of oil, any outbreak of conflict, however minor, will automatically generate a risk of outside intervention.

That conflict over oil will erupt in the years ahead is almost a foregone conclusion. Just how much violence, at what levels of intensity, and at which locations, cannot be determined. Ultimately, the frequency and character of warfare will depend on the relative weight and the interplay of three key factors: (1) the political and strategic environment in which decisions over resource issues are made; (2) the future relationship between demand and supply; and (3) the geography of oil production and distribution.

THE POLITICS OF OIL SECURITY

Many resources are needed to sustain a modern industrial society, but only those that are viewed as being vital to national security are likely to provoke the use of military force when access to key supplies is placed in jeopardy.* There is no question

---

*In 1998, the U.S. National Security Council defined "vital interests" as those interests "of broad, overriding importance to the survival, safety, and vitality of our nation. Among these are the physical security of our territory and that of our allies, the safety of our citizens, our economic well-being, and the protection of our critical infrastructures. We will do what we must to defend these interests, including—when necessary—using our military might unilaterally and decisively" (*A National Security Strategy for a New Century*, October 1998).

that oil has enjoyed this distinctive status in the past. Ever since the introduction of oil-powered warships at the beginning of the twentieth century, petroleum has been viewed as essential for success in war. Before that time, petroleum had largely been used to provide illumination, most commonly in the form of kerosene. (Indeed, many of the major oil companies of today, including Exxon, Mobil, and Royal Dutch/Shell, were initially established in the nineteenth century to produce and market kerosene to the growing urban populations of Europe and North America.) The critical turning point came in 1912, when the British Admiralty—then led by First Lord of the Admiralty Winston Churchill—decided to convert its combat vessels from coal to oil propulsion.[1]

The transition from coal to oil provided British ships with a significant advantage in speed and endurance over the coal-powered vessels of its adversaries, especially Germany. But it also presented London with a significant dilemma: while rich in coal, Britain possessed few domestic sources of petroleum and so was vitally dependent on imported supplies. With a war about to begin, and the reliability of overseas suppliers in question, the cabinet decided—on a strict national security basis—to endow the government with direct responsibility for the delivery of oil. On June 17, 1914, Parliament voted to approve the government's acquisition of a majority stake in the Anglo-Persian Oil Company (APOC), a London-based firm that had recently discovered petroleum in southwestern Persia. With this vote, it became British policy to protect APOC's oil concession area in Persia—thus, for the first time, making the security of overseas petroleum supplies a major state responsibility.[2]

The link between oil and military policy was made even more substantial during World War I itself, when all of the major belligerents employed oil-driven vehicles for combat, reconnaissance, and logistics. The airplane and the tank—oil-powered machines that were to revolutionize the conduct of warfare—were introduced during the conflict. Scarcely less important was the widespread use of motor vehicles to carry troops and supplies to the battlefield: over the course of the war, the British army's fleet of trucks grew from 10,000 to 60,000; the American Expeditionary Force brought with it another 50,000 motor vehicles.[3] It is with this in mind that Lord Curzon, former viceroy of India and soon-to-be foreign secretary, told a group of government and industry officials in London that the Allies had "floated to victory upon a wave of oil."[4]

This perception continued to influence strategic thinking after World War I and in the years leading up to World War II. Believing that the next major conflict would see an even greater reliance on oil-powered weapons than the last, many governments followed the British example by creating state-owned oil companies and by seeking control over foreign sources of petroleum. Britain, for its part, expanded its oil interests in the Persian Gulf area and strengthened its dominant position in Iran (the new name for Persia). France established a state-owned firm, the Compagnie Française des Pétroles, and obtained concessions in the Mosul area of northwest Iraq. Germany and Japan—both of which lacked domestic sources of petroleum—laid plans to acquire their supplies from Romania and the Dutch East Indies, respectively.[5]

Once war broke out, the competitive pursuit of oil by all sides had a significant impact on the tempo and trajectory of battle. In the Pacific, Japanese efforts to gain control over the petroleum supplies of the Dutch East Indies produced mounting alarm in Washington and led, in 1941, to the imposition of a U.S. embargo on oil exports to Japan. This, in turn, persuaded Japanese officials that a war with the United States was inevitable, propelling them to seek an initial advantage through a surprise attack on the U.S. naval base at Pearl Harbor. In the European theater, Germany's desperate need for oil helped trigger its 1941 invasion of Russia. Along with Moscow and Leningrad, a major target of the invasion was the Soviet oil center at Baku (in what is now Azerbaijan). Both efforts ended in failure: the Japanese plan to import East Indian oil was foiled by American air and submarine attacks on tanker ships, while the German drive on Baku was thwarted by stubborn Soviet resistance. With their supplies of oil becoming increasingly scarce, Japan and Germany were unable to mount effective resistance to Allied offensives and so were eventually forced to concede defeat.[6]

After the war, petroleum continued to be seen by military planners as a vital combat necessity. With military organizations placing even greater emphasis on the role of airpower and armored forces, the need for reliable oil supplies became more critical than ever. This influenced the strategic thinking not only of the European powers, which had long been dependent on imported supplies, but also of the United States, which for the first time began to acquire significant supplies of petroleum from outside the country. Fearing that the Soviet Union would seek control over the Persian Gulf area—rapidly becoming the leading source of Western oil imports—Washington established a modest military presence in the region and sought to integrate Iran, Iraq, Saudi Arabia, and other key oil-producing states into the Western alliance. Both the Truman Doctrine (1947) and the Eisenhower Doctrine (1957) included promises of U.S. military aid to any state in the region that came under attack from Soviet or Soviet-backed forces.[7]

Initially, American moves in the Middle East were governed by classical military considerations: to prevent a hostile power from gaining control over a vital resource needed for the effective prosecution of war. With the outbreak of the October 1973 Arab-Israeli conflict, however, the perception of oil as a strategic commodity took on an entirely new meaning. To punish Washington for its support of Israel and to build worldwide pressure for an acceptable outcome to the conflict, the Arab states cut off all petroleum deliveries to the United States and imposed rolling cutbacks on deliveries to other countries. At the same time, the Organization of Petroleum-Exporting Countries (OPEC) announced a fourfold increase in the price of oil. Occurring at a time when petroleum supplies were already under pressure from rapidly growing demand, the oil embargo and OPEC price increase sent a powerful shock wave through the global economy: oil shortages developed in many areas, industrial output declined, and the world plunged into a prolonged economic recession. From this time on, oil was seen not only as an essential military commodity but also as a prerequisite for global economic stability.[8]

The Arab oil embargo was rescinded in March 1974, and the economic crisis gradually receded. Nevertheless, the events of 1973–74 left a profound and lasting impact on the perceived link between oil and the national security of the major industrialized powers. Worried that significant supply disruptions could occur again, the oil-importing countries sought to minimize their vulnerability by searching for new petroleum deposits in more secure locations (the North Sea and the North Slope of Alaska, for example) and by storing large quantities of oil in special reservoirs. The United States, for its part, stored hundreds of millions of barrels of oil in its newly established Strategic Petroleum Reserve.

The American response to the "oil shocks" of 1973–74 was not limited to defensive measures. For the first time, senior officials began talking of using force to protect vital petroleum supplies in peacetime, to guarantee the health of the economy. Specifically, policy makers began to consider American military intervention in the Middle East to prevent any interruption in the flow of Persian Gulf oil. Initially private, these deliberations became public in 1975 when Henry Kissinger, then secretary of state, told the editors of *Business Week* that the United States was prepared to go to war over oil. Although reluctant to employ force in a dispute over prices alone, he stated, Washington would have no such hesitation "where there's some actual strangulation of the industrialized world."[9]

This formulation of Western security interests has governed American military planning ever since. When, in 1979, the shah of Iran was overthrown by militant Islamic forces and the world experienced a second major "oil shock," President Carter was quick to threaten the use of force against any adversary that might seek to impede the flow of oil from the Persian Gulf area. On January 23, 1980, Carter declared that any attempt by a hostile power to constrict the flow of oil in the Gulf "will be repelled by any means necessary, including military force."[10] In line with this principle, known since as the Carter Doctrine, the United States commenced a military buildup in the Persian Gulf area that has continued to this day. This principle has, moreover, periodically been put to the test. During the Iran-Iraq war of 1980–00, when the Iranians stepped up their attacks on oil shipping in the Gulf (presumably to punish Kuwait and Saudi Arabia for their financial support of Iraq), the United States agreed to "reflag" Kuwaiti tankers with American flags and provide them with a U.S. naval escort.[11]

The Carter Doctrine was next invoked in August 1990, when Iraqi forces occupied Kuwait and positioned themselves for an assault on Saudi Arabia. Concluding that Iraqi control of both Kuwaiti and Saudi oil fields would pose an intolerable threat to Western economic security, President Bush quickly decided on a tough military response—dispatching large numbers of American forces to defend Saudi Arabia and, if need be, to drive the Iraqis out of Kuwait. "Our country now imports nearly half the oil it consumes and could face a major threat to its economic independence," he told the nation on August 7. Hence, "the sovereign independence of Saudi Arabia is of vital interest to the United States."[12] A number of other concerns, including Iraq's burgeoning weapons capabilities, also figured in the U.S. decision to employ force in the Gulf, but senior administration officials always placed particular emphasis on the threat to Western oil supplies and the continued health of the American economy.[13]

Since Desert Storm, American leaders have continued to stress the importance of unhindered oil deliveries to the health and stability of the global economy. "America's vital interests in the [Persian Gulf] region are compelling," General J. H.

Binford Peay III, commander in chief of the U.S. Central Command (CENTCOM), declared in 1997. "The unrestricted flow of petroleum resources from friendly Gulf states to refineries and processing facilities around the world drives the global economic engine."[14] In accordance with this outlook, the United States has beefed up its forces in the Gulf and taken other steps to protect friendly powers in the area. At the same time, Washington has enhanced its capacity to intervene in the Caspian Sea region and in other areas holding large supplies of oil.

A similar perspective regarding the role of oil in maintaining economic stability also governs the security policies of other states, including China and Japan. Both of these countries have bolstered their capacity to protect vital petroleum supplies: China has tightened its hold on Xinjiang (a potential source of oil and the site of a rebellion by members of the Muslim Uighur ethnic group) and the islands of the South China Sea (another potential source of oil); Japan has extended the reach of its air and naval forces to better protect its sealanes.

For oil-importing countries, the safe delivery of oil is the basis of their economic security. For oil exporters, however, the *possession* of oil dominates economic thinking. Even at the depressed prices of the late 1990s, the sale of oil was enormously lucrative for those countries; as demand grows and prices rise, the monetary value of oil reserves will climb even higher. In 1997, for instance, the U.S. Department of State placed the value of untapped Caspian Sea oil supplies at a staggering $4 trillion—and oil prices were then considerably lower than they are today.[15] It is therefore not surprising that any state possessing some piece of this latent wealth will view its protection as a vital aspect of national and economic security. . . .

THE INESCAPABLE CONSTRAINTS OF GEOGRAPHY

As older fields are depleted, the global competition for oil will focus increasingly on those few areas of the world that still contain significant supplies of petroleum. These areas will automatically acquire increased strategic importance, as will the transit routes used for carrying oil to distant markets. Clearly, any instability or disorder in these critical areas could impede the continued flow of oil, thus provoking outside intervention. The relative likelihood of conflict is therefore closely related to the geography of oil distribution and to the political environment in key producing and transit regions.

The most significant fact about petroleum, from a world security point of view, is that so much of it is concentrated in a few major producing areas. As shown by Table 44.1, fourteen countries—Saudi Arabia, Iraq, the United Arab Emirates (UAE), Kuwait, Iran, Venezuela, Russia, Mexico, the United States, Libya, China, Nigeria, Norway, and the United Kingdom—jointly possess all but 10 percent of the known world supply. Among these fourteen, the possession of oil is even more highly concentrated, with the five leading producers—Saudi Arabia, Iraq, the UAE, Kuwait, and Iran—together holding nearly two-thirds of global reserves.

The high concentration of petroleum in a handful of major producing areas means that the global availability of oil is closely tied to political and socioeconomic

TABLE 44.1 Global Reserves and Production of Petroleum (as calculated in 1999)

Producer (in order by reserves)	Estimated Reserves (bbl)	Percent of World Reserves	Production, 1998 (mbd)
Saudi Arabia	261.5	24.8	9.2
Iraq	112.5	10.7	2.2
United Arab Emirates	97.8	9.3	2.7
Kuwait	96.5	9.2	2.2
Iran	89.7	8.5	3.8
Venezuela	72.6	6.9	3.3
Russia	48.6	4.6	6.2
Mexico	47.8	4.5	3.5
United States	30.5	2.9	8.0
Libya	29.5	2.8	1.4
China	24.0	2.3	3.2
Nigeria	22.5	2.1	2.2
Norway/United Kingdom (North Sea)	16.1	1.5	6.0
Total	949.6	90.1	53.9

Source: BP Amoco, *Statistical Review of World Energy 1999.*

bbl = billion barrels
mbd = million barrels per day

conditions within a relatively small group of countries. When war or political turmoil erupts in these countries, and the global flow of oil is subsequently disrupted, the rest of the world is likely to experience significant economic hardship.[16] This was made painfully evident in 1973–74, when the Arab oil embargo produced widespread fuel shortages and triggered a prolonged economic recession; the same message was delivered again in 1979–80, following the revolution in Iran. A close look at Table 44.1 suggests, moreover, that such traumas can occur again in the future: a majority of the countries listed in this group have experienced war or revolution during the past ten to twenty years, and many continue to face internal or external challenges.

The epicenter of all this disorder is, of course, the Middle East. That so many of the world's leading oil producers are located in this fractious region has long been a matter of grave concern for leaders of the major importing nations. Even before the discovery of oil, the states in this region were torn by internal divisions along ethnic and political lines, and by the historic rift between Sunni and Shiite Muslims. Once the flow of petroleum began, these divisions were further strained by disputes over the ownership of oil fields and the distribution of oil revenues. This fiery cauldron has been further heated in recent years by the rise of Islamic fundamentalism, the endurance of authoritarian regimes, and deep frustration (among many Arabs) over Israel's treatment of the Palestinians.[17]

Because the Middle East has so often been convulsed by social and political unrest, the major consuming nations have sought to reduce their dependence on Persian Gulf oil by developing alternative sources elsewhere. This is the impulse that led to the rapid development of North Sea and North Slope reserves in the 1970s and, more recently, to the establishment of new production areas in Africa, Latin America, and the Caspian region. "We are undergoing a fundamental shift away from reliance on Middle East oil," the National Security Council optimistically reported in 1998. "Venezuela [has become] our number one foreign supplier and Africa supplies 15 percent of our imported oil."[18]

But while shifting production to these other areas may diminish the importers' reliance on the Middle East, this does not guarantee that the new sources of petroleum will be any less free of disorder and conflict. Colombia and Nigeria, for example, have experienced considerable internal violence over the past few years, while Venezuela is going through a painful and potentially disruptive political transition. Nor is the Caspian Sea area likely to prove any less unstable than the Persian Gulf.

It is true that the development of multiple producing areas allows consuming nations to switch from one source of oil to another when a crisis erupts in any individual area, but the number of such sources are few, and those among them that are entirely free of conflict (or the risk of conflict) are fewer still.

It is clear, then, that a strategy of diversification can succeed for only so long. Ultimately, the oil-importing countries will be forced to rely on the same group of unreliable suppliers in the Persian Gulf, the Caspian, Latin America, and Africa. Like it or not, major importing countries will have to pay close attention to political developments in key producing areas and will have to intervene—in one way or another—whenever local and regional turmoil threatens to disrupt the flow of petroleum.

NOTES

1. For background on the decision to switch from coal to oil, see Geoffrey Jones, *The State and the Emergence of the British Oil Industry* (London: MacMillan, 1981), pp. 9–31.

2. For background and discussion, see ibid., pp. 129–76.

3. Ibid., p. 177. See also Daniel Yergin, *The Prize* (New York: Touchstone, Simon and Schuster, 1993), pp. 167–83.

4. This was said to a celebratory meeting of the Inter-Allied Petroleum Council in London on November 21, 1918. Cited in Yergin, *The Prize*, p. 183.

5. For background on this period, see Jones, *The State and the Emergence of the British Oil Industry*, pp. 208–44; Yergin, *The Prize*, pp. 184–206, 260–308.

6. See Yergin, *The Prize*, pp. 308–88.

7. For background on these endeavors, see David S. Painter, *Oil and the American Century* (Baltimore: Johns Hopkins University Press, 1986), and Michael B. Stoff, *Oil, War, and American Security* (New Haven: Yale University Press, 1980). On the Nixon Doctrine, see James H. Noyes, *The Clouded Lens* (Stanford, Calif.: Hoover Institution Press, 1979), and U.S. Congress, House, Committee on Foreign Affairs, Subcommittee on the Near East and South

Asia, *New Perspectives on the Persian Gulf,* Hearings, 93rd Congress, 1st session (Washington, D.C.: Government Printing Office, 1973).

8.   For background on these events, see Yergin, *The Prize,* pp. 588–632.

9.   Interview in *Business Week,* January 13, 1975, p. 69.

10.   From the transcript of Carter's address in *The New York Times,* January 24, 1980.

11.   For background on this episode, see Anthony H. Cordesman and Abraham R. Wagner, *The Lessons of Modern War,* volume II, *The Iran-Iraq War* (Boulder: Westview Press, 1990), pp. 277–80, 295–302, 317, 329.

12.   From the transcript of Bush's speech in *The New York Times,* August 8, 1997.

13.   Alluding to Kissinger's earlier comments, Defense Secretary Richard Cheney told the Senate Armed Services Committee in September 1990 that Washington could not allow Saddam Hussein to acquire "a stranglehold on our economy." U.S. Congress, Senate, Committee on Armed Services, *Crisis in the Persian Gulf Region: U.S. Policy Options and Implications,* Hearings, 101st Congress, 2d Session (1990), pp. 10–11. These hearings represent one of the best sources for information on U.S. security thinking at the time.

14.   U.S. Central Command (CENTCOM), *1997 Posture Statement* (MacDill Air Force Base, Fla.: CENTCOM, n.d.), p. 1.

15.   U.S. Department of State, *Caspian Region Energy Development Report,* p. 3.

16.   For further discussion of this point, see Edward R. Fried and Philip H. Trezise, *Oil Security: Retrospect and Prospect* (Washington, D.C.: Brookings Institution, 1993).

17.   For discussion, see the essays in Gary G. Sick and Lawrence G. Potter, eds., *The Persian Gulf at the Millennium* (New York: St. Martin's Press, 1997).

18.   U.S. National Security Council, *A National Security Strategy for a New Century* (Washington, D.C.: White House, October 1998), p. 32.

CHAPTER 45

Blowback

CHALMERS JOHNSON

Northern Italian communities had, for years, complained about low-flying American military aircraft. In February 1998, the inevitable happened. A Marine Corps EA-6B Prowler with a crew of four, one of scores of advanced American jet fighters and bombers stationed at places like Aviano, Cervia, Brindisi, and Sigonella, sliced through a ski-lift cable near the resort town of Cavalese and plunged twenty people riding in a single gondola to their deaths on the snowy slopes several hundred feet below. Although marine pilots are required to maintain an altitude of at least one thousand feet (two thousand, according to the Italian government), the plane had cut the cable at a height of 360 feet. It was traveling at 621 miles per hour when 517 miles per hour was considered the upper limit. The pilot had been performing low-level acrobatics while his copilot took pictures on videotape (which he later destroyed).

In response to outrage in Italy and calls for vigorous prosecution of those responsible, the marine pilots argued that their charts were inaccurate, that their altimeter had not worked, and that they had not consulted U.S. Air Force units permanently based in the area about local hazards. A court-martial held not in Italy but in Camp Lejeune, North Carolina, exonerated everyone involved, calling it a "training accident." Soon after, President Bill Clinton apologized and promised financial compensation to the victims, but on May 14, 1999, Congress dropped the provision for aid to the families because of opposition in the House of Representatives and from the Pentagon.[1]

This was hardly the only such incident in which American service personnel victimized foreign civilians in the post–Cold War world. From Germany and Turkey to Okinawa and South Korea, similar incidents have been common—as has been their usual denouement. The United States government never holds politicians or higher-ranking military officers responsible and seldom finds that more should be done beyond offering pro forma apologies and perhaps financial compensation of some, often minimal sort.

On rare occasions, as with the Italian cable cutting, when such a local tragedy rises to the level of global news, what often seems strangest to Americans is the level of national outrage elsewhere over what the U.S. media portray as, at worst, an apparently isolated incident, however tragic to those involved. Certainly, the one subject beyond discussion at such moments is the fact that, a decade after the end of the Cold War, hundreds of thousands of American troops, supplied with the world's most advanced weaponry, sometimes including nuclear arms, are stationed on over sixty-one base complexes in nineteen countries worldwide, using the Department of Defense's narrowest definition of a "major installation"; if one included every kind of installation that houses representatives of the American military, the number would rise to over eight hundred.[2] There are, of course, no Italian air bases on American soil. Such a thought would be ridiculous. Nor, for that matter, are there German, Indonesian, Russian, Greek, or Japanese troops stationed on Italian soil. Italy is, moreover, a close ally of the United States, and no conceivable enemy nation endangers its shores.

All this is almost too obvious to state—and so is almost never said. It is simply not a matter for discussion, much less of debate in the land of the last imperial power. Perhaps similar thinking is second nature to any imperium. Perhaps the Romans did not find it strange to have their troops in Gaul, nor the British in South Africa. But what is unspoken is no less real, nor does it lack consequences just because it is not part of any ongoing domestic discussion.

I believe it is past time for such a discussion to begin, for Americans to consider why we have created an empire—a word from which we shy away—and what the consequences of our imperial stance may be for the rest of the world and for ourselves. Not so long ago, the way we garrisoned the world could be discussed far more openly and comfortably because the explanation seemed to lie at hand—in the very existence of the Soviet Union and of communism. Had the Italian disaster occurred two decades earlier, it would have seemed no less a tragedy, but many Americans would have argued that, given the Cold War, such incidents were an unavoidable cost of protecting democracies like Italy against the menace of Soviet totalitarianism. With the disappearance of any military threat faintly comparable to that posed by the former Soviet Union, such "costs" have become easily avoidable. American military forces could have been withdrawn from Italy, as well as from other foreign bases, long ago. That they were not and that Washington instead is doing everything in its considerable powers to perpetuate Cold War structures, even without the Cold War's justification, places such overseas deployments in a new light. They have become striking evidence, for those who care to look, of an imperial project that the Cold War obscured. The by-products of this project are likely to build up reservoirs of resentment against all Americans—tourists, students, and businessmen, as well as members of the armed forces—that can have lethal results.

For any empire, including an unacknowledged one, there is a kind of balance sheet that builds up over time. Military crimes, accidents, and atrocities make up only one category on the debit side of the balance sheet that the United States has been accumulating, especially since the Cold War ended. To take an example of quite a different kind of debit, consider South Korea, a longtime ally. On Christmas Eve 1997, it declared itself financially bankrupt and put its economy under the guidance of the International Monetary Fund, which is basically an institutional surrogate of the United States government. Most Americans were surprised by the economic disasters that overtook Thailand, South Korea, Malaysia, and Indonesia in 1997 and that then spread around the world, crippling the Russian and Brazilian economies. They could hardly imagine that the U.S. government might have had a hand in causing them, even though various American pundits and economists expressed open delight in these disasters, which threw millions of people, who had previously had hopes of achieving economic prosperity and security, into the most abysmal poverty. At worst, Americans took the economic meltdown of places like Indonesia and Brazil to mean that beneficial American-supported policies of "globalization" were working—that we were effectively helping restructure various economies around the world so that they would look and work more like ours.

Above all, the economic crisis of 1997 was taken as evidence that our main doctrinal competitors—the high-growth capitalist economies of East Asia—were hardly either as competitive or as successful as they imagined. In a New Year's commentary, the columnist Charles Krauthammer mused, "Our success is the success of the American capitalist model, which lies closer to the free market vision of Adam Smith than any other. Much closer, certainly, than Asia's paternalistic crony capitalism that so seduced critics of the American system during Asia's now-burst bubble."[3]

As the global crisis deepened, the thing our government most seemed to fear was that contracts to buy our weapons might now not be honored. That winter, Secretary of Defense William Cohen made special trips to Jakarta, Bangkok, and Seoul to cajole the governments of those countries to use increasingly scarce foreign exchange funds to pay for the American fighter jets, missiles, warships, and other hardware the Pentagon had sold them before the economic collapse. He also stopped in Tokyo to urge on a worried Japanese government a big sale not yet agreed to. He wanted Japan to invest in the theater missile defense system, or TMD, antimissile missiles that the Pentagon has been trying to get the Japanese to buy for a decade. No one knew then or knows now whether the TMD will even work—in fifteen years of intercept attempts only a few missiles in essentially doctored tests have hit their targets—but it is unquestionably expensive, and arms sales, both domestic and foreign, have become one of the Pentagon's most important missions.

I believe the profligate waste of our resources on irrelevant weapons systems and the Asian economic meltdown, as well as the continuous trail of military "accidents" and of terrorist attacks on American installations and embassies, are all portents of a twenty-first-century crisis in America's informal empire, an empire based on the projection of military power to every corner of the world and on the use of American capital and markets to force global economic integration on our terms, at whatever costs to others. To predict the future is an undertaking no thoughtful person would rush to embrace. What form our imperial crisis is likely to take years or even decades from now is, of course, impossible to know. But history indicates that, sooner or later, empires do reach such moments, and it seems reasonable to assume that we will not miraculously escape that fate.

What we have freed ourselves of, however, is any genuine consciousness of how we might look to others on this globe. Most Americans are probably unaware of how Washington exercises its global hegemony, since so much of this activity takes place either in relative secrecy or under comforting rubrics. Many may, as a start, find it hard to believe that our place in the world even adds up to an empire. But only when we come to see our country as both profiting from and trapped within the structures of an empire of its own making will it be possible for us to explain many elements of the world that otherwise perplex us. Without good explanations, we cannot possibly produce policies that will bring us sustained peace and prosperity in a post–Cold War world. What has gone wrong in Japan after half a century of government-guided growth under U.S. protection? Why should the emergence of a strong China be to anyone's disadvantage? Why do American policies toward human rights, weapons proliferation, terrorism, drug cartels, and the environment strike so many foreigners as the essence of hypocrisy? Should American-owned and -managed multinational firms be instruments, beneficiaries, or adversaries of United States foreign policy? Is the free flow of capital really as valuable as free trade in commodities and manufactured goods? These kinds of questions can only be answered once we begin to grasp what the United States really is.

If Washington is the headquarters of a global military-economic dominion, the answers will be very different than if we think of the United States as simply one among many sovereign nations. There is a logic to empire that differs from the logic of a nation, and acts committed in service to an empire but never acknowledged as such have a tendency to haunt the future.

The term "blowback," which officials of the Central Intelligence Agency first invented for their own internal use, is starting to circulate among students of international relations. It refers to the unintended consequences of policies that were kept secret from the American people. What the daily press reports as the malign acts of "terrorists" or "drug lords" or "rogue states" or "illegal arms merchants" often turn out to be blowback from earlier American operations.

It is now widely recognized, for example, that the 1988 bombing of Pan Am flight 103 over Lockerbie, Scotland, which resulted in the deaths of 259 passengers and 11 people on the ground, was retaliation for a 1986 Reagan administration aerial raid on Libya that killed President Muammar Khadaffi's stepdaughter. Some in the United States have suspected that other events can also be explained as blowback from imperial acts. For example, the epidemic of cocaine and heroin use that has afflicted American cities during the past two decades was probably fueled in part by Central and South American military officers or corrupt politicians whom the CIA or the Pentagon once trained or supported and then installed in key government positions. For example, in Nicaragua in the 1980s, the U.S. government organized a massive campaign against the socialist-oriented Sandinista government. American agents then looked the other way when the Contras, the military insurgents they had trained, made deals to sell cocaine in American cities in order to buy arms and supplies.[4] . . .

Needless to say, blowback is not exclusively a problem faced by Americans. One has only to look at Russia and its former satellites today to see exactly how devastating imperial blowback can be. The hostage crisis of 1996–97 at the Japanese embassy in Lima, in which a handful of Peruvian revolutionaries took virtually the entire diplomatic corps hostage, was probably blowback from Japan's support for the antiguerrilla policies of President Alberto Fujimori and for the operations of Japanese multinational corporations in Peru. Israel's greatest single political problem is the daily threat of blowback from the Palestinian people and their Islamic allies because of Israeli policies of displacing Palestinians from their lands and repressing those that remain under their jurisdiction. The United States, however, is the world's most prominent target for blowback, being the world's lone imperial power, the primary source of the sort of secret and semisecret operations that shore up repressive regimes, and by far the largest seller of weapons generally.

It is typical of an imperial people to have a short memory for its less pleasant imperial acts, but for those on the receiving end, memory can be long indeed. Among the enduring sources of blowback, for instance, are the genocidal cruelties some nations have perpetrated during wartime. Japan to this day is trying to come to grips with the consequences of its actions in China during World War II. Japanese reactionaries are still reluctant to face atrocities committed in China and Korea: the rape of Nanking, conscription of conquered women to serve as prostitutes for frontline troops, and gruesome medical experimentation on prisoners of war are but the better known of these. But given the passage of time and some payment of compensation, many Chinese would probably accept a sincere apology for these events. However, Japanese armies also terrorized and radicalized an essentially conservative peasant population and thereby helped bring the Chinese Communist Party to power, leading to thirty million deaths during the Great Leap Forward and savaging Chinese civilization during the Cultural Revolution. There are many educated Chinese who can never forgive Japan for contributing to this outcome.

Today, we know of several similar cases. In pursuing the war in Vietnam in the early 1970s, President Richard Nixon and his national security adviser Henry Kissinger ordered more bombs dropped on rural Cambodia than had been dropped on Japan during all of World War II, killing at least three-quarters of a million Cambodian peasants and helping legitimize the murderous Khmer Rouge movement under Pol Pot. In his subsequent pursuit of revenge and ideological purity Pol Pot ensured that another million and a half Cambodians, this time mainly urban dwellers, were murdered.

Americans generally think of Pol Pot as some kind of unique, self-generated monster and his "killing fields" as an inexplicable atavism totally divorced from civilization. But without the United States government's Vietnam-era savagery, he could never have come to power in a culture like Cambodia's, just as Mao's uneducated peasant radicals would never have gained legitimacy in a normal Chinese context without the disruption and depravity of the Japanese war. Significantly, in its calls for an international tribunal to try the remaining leaders of the Khmer Rouge for war crimes, the United States has demanded that such a court restrict its efforts to the period from 1975 to 1979—that is, after the years of carpet bombing were over and before the U.S. government began to collaborate with the Khmer Rouge against the Vietnamese Communists, who invaded Cambodia in 1978, drove the Khmer Rouge from power, and were trying to bring some stability to the country.

Even an empire cannot control the long-term effects of its policies. That is the essence of blowback. Take the civil war in Afghanistan in the 1980s, in which Soviet forces directly intervened on the government side and the CIA armed and supported any and all groups willing to face the Soviet armies. Over the years the fighting turned Kabul, once a major center of Islamic culture, into a facsimile of Hiroshima after the bomb. American policies helped ensure that the Soviet Union would suffer the same kind of debilitating defeat in Afghanistan as the United States had in Vietnam. In fact, the defeat so destabilized the Soviet regime that at the end of the 1980s it collapsed. But in Afghanistan the United States also helped bring to power the Taliban, a fundamentalist Islamic movement whose policies toward women, education, justice, and economic well-being resemble not so much those of Ayatollah Khomeini's Iran as those of Pol Pot's Cambodia. A group of these mujahideen, who only a few years earlier the United States had armed with ground-to-air Stinger missiles, grew bitter over American acts and policies in the Gulf War and vis-à-vis Israel. In 1993, they bombed the World Trade Center in New York and assassinated several CIA employees as they waited at a traffic light in Langley, Virginia. Four years later, on November 12, 1997, after the Virginia killer had been convicted by an American court, unknown assailants shot and killed four American accountants, unrelated in any way to the CIA, in their car in Karachi, Pakistan, in retaliation.

It is likely that U.S. covert policies have helped create similar conditions in the Congo, Guatemala, and Turkey, and that we are simply waiting for the blowback to occur. Guatemala is a particularly striking example of American imperial policies in its own "backyard." In 1954, the Eisenhower administration planned and the CIA organized and funded a military coup that overthrew a Guatemalan president whose modest land reform policies were considered a threat to American corporations. Blowback from this led to a Marxist guerrilla insurgency in the 1980s and so to CIA- and Pentagon-supported genocide against Mayan peasants. In the spring of 1999, a report on the Guatemalan civil war from the U.N.-sponsored Commission for Historical Clarification made clear that "the American training of the officer corps in counterinsurgency techniques" was a "key factor" in the "genocide. . . . Entire Mayan villages were attacked and burned and their inhabitants were slaughtered in an effort to deny the guerrillas protection."[5] According to the commission, between 1981 and 1983 the military government of Guatemala—financed and supported by the U.S. government—destroyed some four hundred Mayan villages in a campaign of genocide in which approximately two hundred thousand peasants were killed. José Pertierra, an attorney representing Jennifer Harbury, an American lawyer who spent years trying to find out what happened to her "disappeared" Guatemalan husband and supporter of the guerrillas, Efraín Bámaca Velásquez, writes that the Guatemalan military officer who arrested, tortured, and murdered Bámaca was a CIA "asset" and was paid $44,000 for the information he obtained from him.[6]

Visiting Guatemala in March 1999, soon after the report's release, President Clinton said, "It is important that I state clearly that support for military forces and intelligence units which engaged in violence and widespread repression was wrong, and the United States must not repeat that mistake. . . . The United States will no longer take part in campaigns of repression."[7] But on virtually the day that the president was swearing off "dirty tricks" in other people's countries, his government was reasserting its support for Turkey in its war of repression against its Kurdish minority.

The Kurds constitute fifteen million people in a Turkish population estimated at fifty-eight million. Another five million Kurds live largely within reach of Turkey's borders in Iraq, Iran, and Syria. The Turks have discriminated against the Kurds for the past seventy years and have conducted an intense genocidal campaign against them since 1992, in the process destroying some three thousand Kurdish villages and hamlets in the backward southeastern part of the country. Former American ambassador to Croatia Peter W. Galbraith comments that "Turkey routinely jails Kurdish politicians for activities that would be protected speech in democratic countries."[8] The Europeans have so far barred Turkey from the European Union because of its treatment of the Kurds. Because of its strategic location on the border of the former Soviet Union, however, Turkey was a valued American ally and NATO member during the Cold War, and the United States maintains the relationship unchanged even though the USSR has disappeared.

After Israel and Egypt, Turkey is the third-highest recipient of American military assistance. Between 1991 and 1995, the United States supplied four-fifths of Turkey's military imports, which were among the largest in the world. The U.S. government, in turn, depends on the NATO base at Incirlik, Turkey, to carry out Operation Provide Comfort, set up after the Gulf War to supply and protect Iraqi Kurds from repression by Saddam Hussein—at the same time that the United States acquiesces in Turkish mistreatment of its far larger Kurdish population. One obvious reason is that communities like Stratford and Bridgeport, Connecticut, where Black Hawk and Comanche helicopters are made, depend for their economic health on continued large-scale arms sales to countries like Turkey. At the time of the Gulf War, a senior adviser to the Turkish prime minister said to John Shattuck, assistant secretary of state for human rights, "If you want to stop human rights abuses do two things—stop IMF credits and cut off aid from the Pentagon. But don't sell the weapons and give aid and then complain about the Kurdish issue. Don't tell us about human rights while you're selling these weapons."[9]

The capture in February 1999 of the Kurdish guerrilla leader Abdullah Ocalan exposed the nature of American involvement with Turkey, in this case via a CIA gambit that holds promise as a rich source of future blowback. The CIA term for this policy is "disruption," by which it means the harassment of terrorists around the world. The point is to flush them out of hiding so that cooperative police forces or secret services can then arrest and imprison them. According to John Diamond of the Associated Press, "The CIA keeps its role secret, and the foreign countries that actually crack down on the suspects carefully hide the U.S. role, lest they stir up trouble for themselves." There are no safeguards at all against misidentifying "suspects," and "the CIA sends no formal notice to Congress." Disruption is said to be a preemptive, offensive form of counterterrorism. Richard Clarke, President Clinton's antiterrorism czar, likes it because he can avoid "the cumbersome Congressional reporting requirements that go with CIA-directed covert operations" and because "human rights organizations would have no way of identifying a CIA role." The CIA has carried out disruption operations in at least ten countries since September 1998. In the case of Ocalan's capture, the United States "provided Turkey with critical information about Ocalan's whereabouts." This was the first time some of the details of a "disruption" campaign were made public.[10]

In a sense, blowback is simply another way of saying that a nation reaps what it sows. Although people usually know what they have sown, our national experience of blowback is seldom imagined in such terms because so much of what the managers of the American empire have sown has been kept secret. As a concept, blowback is obviously most easy to grasp in its most straightforward manifestation. The unintended consequences of American policies and acts in country X are a bomb at an American embassy in country Y or a dead American in country Z. Certainly any number of Americans have been killed in that fashion, from Catholic nuns in El Salvador to tourists in Uganda who just happened to wander into hidden imperial scenarios about which they knew nothing. But blowback, as demonstrated in this [reading], is hardly restricted to such reasonably straightforward examples.

From the hollowing out of key American industries due to Japan's export-led economic policies to refugee flows across our southern borders from countries where U.S.-supported repression has created genocidal conditions or where U.S.-supported economic policies have led to unbearable misery, blowback can hit in less obvious and more subtle ways and over long periods of time. It can also manifest itself domestically in ways that are often not evident, even to those who created or carried out the initial imperial policies.

Because we live in an increasingly interconnected international system, we are all, in a sense, living in a blowback world. Although the term originally applied only to the unintended consequences for Americans of American policies, there is every reason to widen its meaning. Whether, for example, any unintended consequences of the American policies that fostered and then heightened the economic collapse of Indonesia in 1997 ever blow back to the United States, the unintended consequences for Indonesians have been staggering levels of suffering, poverty, and loss of hope. Similarly, the unintended consequences of American-supported coups and bombing in Cambodia in the early 1970s were unimaginable chaos, disruption, and death for Cambodians later in the decade.

Our role in the military coup in Chile in 1973, for example, produced little blowback onto the United States itself but had lethal consequences for liberals, socialists, and innocent bystanders in Chile and elsewhere. On the nature of American policies in Chile, journalist Jon Lee Anderson reports, "The plan, according to declassified United States government documents, was to make Chile ungovernable under [elected socialist president Salvador] Allende, provoke social chaos, and bring about a military coup. . . . A CIA cable outlined the objectives clearly to the station chief in Santiago: 'It is firm and continuing policy that Allende be overthrown by a coup. . . . We are to continue to generate maximum pressure toward this end utilizing every appropriate resource. It is imperative that these actions be implemented clandestinely and securely so that United States Government and American hand be well hidden.' "[11]

No ordinary citizen of the United States knew anything about these machinations. The coup d'état took place on September 11, 1973, resulting in the suicide of

Allende and the seizure of power by General Augusto Pinochet, whose military and civilian supporters in their seventeen years in power tortured, killed, or "disappeared" some four thousand people. Pinochet was an active collaborator in Operation Condor, a joint mission with the Argentine militarists to murder exiled dissidents in the United States, Spain, Italy, and elsewhere. This is why, when Pinochet traveled to England in the autumn of 1998 for medical treatment, Spain tried to extradite him to stand trial for genocide, torture, and state terrorism against Spanish citizens. On October 16, 1998, the British police arrested Pinochet in London and held him pending his possible extradition.

Although few Americans were affected by this covert operation, people around the world now know of the American involvement and were deeply cynical when Secretary of State Madeleine Albright opposed Pinochet's extradition, claiming that countries like Chile undertaking a "transition to democracy" must be allowed to guarantee immunity from prosecution to past human rights offenders in order to "move forward."[12] America's "dirty hands" make even the most well-intentioned statement about human rights or terrorism seem hypocritical in such circumstances. Even when blowback mostly strikes other peoples, it has its corrosive effects on the United States by debasing political discourse and making citizens feel duped if they should happen to take seriously what their political leaders say. This is an inevitable consequence not just of blowback but of empire itself.

NOTES

1. "Some Aid Canceled for Gondola Deaths," *Los Angeles Times*, May 15, 1999.

2. Department of Defense, "U.S. Military Installations" (updated to July 17, 1998), *DefenseLINK*, on-line at http://www.defenselink.mil/pubs/installations/foreignsummary.htm; and John Lindsay-Poland and Nick Morgan, "Overseas Military Bases and Environment," *Foreign Policy in Focus* 3.15 (June 1998), on-line at http://www.foreignpolicy-infocus.org/briefs/vol13/v3n15mil.html. According to one report, when the Soviet Union collapsed in 1991, the United States had 375 military bases scattered around the globe staffed by more than a half million personnel. Joel Brinkley, "U.S. Looking for a New Path as Superpower Conflict Ends," *New York Times*, February 2, 1992.

3. Charles Krauthammer, "What Caused Our Economic Boom?" *San Diego Union-Tribune*, January 5, 1998.

4. For documentary evidence, including Oliver North's notebooks, see "The Contras, Cocaine, and Covert Operations," *National Security Archive Electronic Briefing Book*, no. 2, on-line at http://www.seas.gwu.edu/nsarchive. Also see James Risen, "C.I.A. Said to Ignore Charges of Contra Drug Dealing in '80's," *New York Times*, October 10, 1998.

5. Mireya Navarro, "Guatemala Study Accuses the Army and Cites U.S. Role," *New York Times*, February 26, 1999; Larry Rohter, "Searing Indictment," *New York Times*, February 27, 1999; Michael Shifter, "Can Genocide End in Forgiveness?" *Los Angeles Times*, March 7, 1999; "Coming Clean on Guatemala," editorial, *Los Angeles Times*, March 10, 1999; and Michael Stetz, "Clinton's Words on Guatemala Called 'Too Little, Too Late,'" *San Diego Union-Tribune*, March 16, 1999.

6. José Pertierra, "For Guatemala, Words Are Not Enough," *San Diego Union-Tribune*, March 5, 1999.

7. John M. Broder, "Clinton Offers His Apologies to Guatemala," *New York Times*, March 11, 1999. Also see Broder, "Clinton Visit in Honduras Dramatizes New Attitude," *New York Times*, March 10, 1999; and Francisco Goldman, "Murder Comes for the Bishop," *New Yorker*, March 15, 1999.

8. Peter W. Galbraith, "How the Turks Helped Their Enemies," *New York Times*, February 20, 1999.

9. John Tirman, *Spoils of War: The Human Cost of America's Arms Trade* (New York: Free Press, 1997), p. 236.

10. John Diamond, "CIA Thwarts Terrorists with 'Disruption'; It's Prevention by Proxy," *San Diego Union-Tribune*, March 5, 1999; and Tim Weiner, "U.S. Helped Turkey Find and Capture Kurd Rebel," *New York Times*, February 20, 1999.

11. Jon Lee Anderson, "The Dictator," *New Yorker*, October 19, 1998; Peter Kronbluth, "Chile and the United States: Declassified Documents Relating to the Military Coup," *National Security Archive Electronic Briefing Book*, no. 8, on-line at http://www.seas.gwu.edu/nsarchive; and Philip Shenon, "U.S. Releases Files on Abuses in Pinochet Era," *New York Times*, July 1, 1999.

12. Michael Ratner, "The Pinochet Precedent," *Progressive Response* 3.3 (January 28, 1999).

CHAPTER **46**

What to Do?

A Global Strategy against Terrorism

THE 9/11 COMMISSION

REFLECTING ON
A GENERATIONAL CHALLENGE

Three years after 9/11, Americans are still thinking and talking about how to protect our nation in this new era. The national debate continues.

Countering terrorism has become, beyond any doubt, the top national security priority for the United States. This shift has occurred with the full support of the Congress, both major political parties, the media, and the American people.

The nation has committed enormous resources to national security and to countering terrorism. Between fiscal year 2001, the last budget adopted before 9/11, and the . . . fiscal year 2004, total federal spending on defense (including expenditures on both Iraq and Afghanistan), homeland security, and international affairs rose more than 50 percent, from $354 billion to about $547 billion. The United States has not experienced such a rapid surge in national security spending since the Korean War.[1]

This pattern has occurred before in American history. The United States faces a sudden crisis and summons a tremendous exertion of national energy. Then, as that surge transforms the landscape, comes a time for reflection and reevaluation. Some programs and even agencies are discarded; others are invented or redesigned. Private firms and engaged citizens redefine their relationships with government, working through the processes of the American republic.

Now is the time for that reflection and reevaluation.The United States should consider *what to do*—the shape and objectives of a strategy. Americans should also consider *how to do it*—organizing their government in a different way.

Defining the Threat

In the post–9/11 world, threats are defined more by the fault lines within societies than by the territorial boundaries between them. From terrorism to global disease or environmental degradation, the challenges have become transnational rather than international. That is the defining quality of world politics in the twenty-first century.

National security used to be considered by studying foreign frontiers, weighing opposing groups of states, and measuring industrial might. To be dangerous, an enemy had to muster large armies. Threats emerged slowly, often visibly, as weapons were forged, armies conscripted, and units trained and moved into place. Because large states were more powerful, they also had more to lose. They could be deterred.

Now threats can emerge quickly. An organization like al Qaeda, headquartered in a country on the other side of the earth, in a region so poor that electricity or telephones were scarce, could nonetheless scheme to wield weapons of unprecedented destructive power in the largest cities of the United States.

In this sense, 9/11 has taught us that terrorism against American interests "over there" should be regarded just as we regard terrorism against America "over here." In this same sense, the American homeland is the planet. . . .

Engage the Struggle of Ideas

The United States is heavily engaged in the Muslim world and will be for many years to come. This American engagement is resented. Polls in 2002 found that among America's friends, like Egypt—the recipient of more U.S. aid for the past 20 years than any other Muslim country—only 15 percent of the population had a favorable opinion of the United States. In Saudi Arabia the number was 12 percent. And two-thirds of those surveyed in 2003 in countries from Indonesia to Turkey (a NATO ally) were very or somewhat fearful that the United States may attack them.[23]

Support for the United States has plummeted. Polls taken in Islamic countries after 9/11 suggested that many or most people thought the United States was doing the right thing in its fight against terrorism; few people saw popular support for al Qaeda; half of those surveyed said that ordinary people had a favorable view of the United States. By 2003, polls showed that "the bottom has fallen out of support for America in most of the Muslim world. Negative views of the U.S. among Muslims, which had been largely limited to countries in the Middle East, have spread. . . . Since last summer, favorable ratings for the U.S. have fallen from 61% to 15% in Indonesia and from 71% to 38% among Muslims in Nigeria."[24]

Many of these views are at best uninformed about the United States and, at worst, informed by cartoonish stereotypes, the coarse expression of a fashionable "Occidentalism" among intellectuals who caricature U.S. values and policies. Local newspapers and the few influential satellite broadcasters—like al Jazeera—often reinforce the jihadist theme that portrays the United States as anti-Muslim.[25]

The small percentage of Muslims who are fully committed to Usama Bin Ladin's version of Islam are impervious to persuasion. It is among the large majority of Arabs and Muslims that we must encourage reform, freedom, democracy, and opportunity, even though our own promotion of these messages is limited in its effectiveness simply because we are its carriers. Muslims themselves will have to reflect upon such basic issues as the concept of jihad, the position of women, and the place of non-Muslim minorities. The United States can promote moderation, but cannot ensure its ascendancy. Only Muslims can do this.

The setting is difficult. The combined gross domestic product of the 22 countries in the Arab League is less than the GDP of Spain. Forty percent of adult Arabs arc illiterate, two-thirds of them women. One-third of the broader Middle East lives on less than two dollars a day. Less than 2 percent of the population has access to the Internet. The majority of older Arab youths have expressed a desire to emigrate to other countries, particularly those in Europe.[26]

In short, the United States has to help defeat an ideology, not just a group of people, and we must do so under difficult circumstances. How can the United States and its friends help moderate Muslims combat the extremist ideas?

Recommendation: The U.S. government must define what the message is, what it stands for. We should offer an example of moral leadership in the world, committed to treat people humanely, abide by the rule of law, and be generous and caring to our neighbors. America and Muslim friends can agree on respect for human dignity and opportunity. To Muslim parents, terrorists like Bin Ladin have nothing to offer their children but visions of violence and death. America and its friends have a crucial advantage—we can offer these parents a vision that might give their children a better future. If we heed the views of thoughtful leaders in the Arab and Muslim world, a moderate consensus can be found.

That vision of the future should stress life over death: individual education and economic opportunity. This vision includes widespread political participation and contempt for indiscriminate violence. It includes respect for the rule of law, openness in discussing differences, and tolerance for opposing points of view.

Recommendation: Where Muslim governments, even those who are friends, do not respect these principles, the United States must stand for a better future. One of the lessons of the long Cold War was that short-term gains in cooperating with the most repressive and brutal governments were too often outweighed by long-term setbacks for America's stature and interests.

American foreign policy is part of the message. America's policy choices have consequences. Right or wrong, it is simply a fact that American policy regarding the Israeli-Palestinian conflict and American actions in Iraq are dominant staples of popular commentary across the Arab and Muslim world. That does not mean U.S. choices have been wrong. It means those choices must be integrated with America's message of opportunity to the Arab and Muslim world. Neither Israel nor the new Iraq will be safer if worldwide Islamist terrorism grows stronger.

The United States must do more to communicate its message. Reflecting on Bin Ladin's success in reaching Muslim audiences, Richard Holbrooke wondered, "How can a man in a cave outcommunicate the world's leading communications society?" Deputy Secretary of State Richard Armitage worried to us that Americans have been "exporting our fears and our anger," not our vision of opportunity and hope.[27]

Recommendation: Just as we did in the Cold War, we need to defend our ideals abroad vigorously. America does stand up for its values. The United States defended, and still defends, Muslims against tyrants and criminals in Somalia, Bosnia, Kosovo, Afghanistan, and Iraq. If the United States does not act aggressively to define itself in the Islamic world, the extremists will gladly do the job for us.

- Recognizing that Arab and Muslim audiences rely on satellite television and radio, the government has begun some promising initiatives in television and radio broadcasting to the Arab world, Iran, and Afghanistan. These efforts are beginning to reach large audiences. The Broadcasting Board of Governors has asked for much larger resources. It should get them.
- The United States should rebuild the scholarship, exchange, and library programs that reach out to young people and offer them knowledge and hope. Where such assistance is provided, it should be identified as coming from the citizens of the United States.

An Agenda of Opportunity

The United States and its friends can stress educational and economic opportunity. The United Nations has rightly equated "literacy as freedom."

- The international community is moving toward setting a concrete goal—to cut the Middle East region's illiteracy rate in half by 2010, targeting women and girls and supporting programs for adult literary.
- Unglamorous help is needed to support the basics, such as textbooks that translate more of the world's knowledge into local languages and libraries to house such materials. Education about the outside world, or other cultures, is weak.
- More vocational education is needed, too, in trades and business skills. The Middle East can also benefit from some of the programs to bridge the digital divide and increase Internet access that have already been developed for other regions of the world.

Education that teaches tolerance, the dignity and value of each individual, and respect for different beliefs is a key element in any global strategy to eliminate Islamist terrorism.

Recommendation: The U.S. government should offer to join with other nations in generously supporting a new International Youth Opportunity Fund. Funds will be spent directly for building and operating primary and secondary schools in those Muslim states that commit to sensibly investing their own money in public education.

Economic openness is essential. Terrorism is not caused by poverty. Indeed, many terrorists come from relatively well-off families. Yet when people lose hope, when societies break down, when countries fragment, the breeding grounds for terrorism are created. Backward economic policies and repressive political regimes slip into societies that are without hope, where ambition and passions have no constructive outlet.

The policies that support economic development and reform also have political implications. Economic and political liberties tend to be linked. Commerce, especially international commerce, requires ongoing cooperation and compromise, the exchange of ideas across cultures, and the peaceful resolution of differences through negotiation or the rule of law. Economic growth expands the middle class, a constituency for further reform. Successful economies rely on vibrant private sectors, which have an interest in curbing indiscriminate government power. Those who develop the practice of controlling their own economic destiny soon desire a voice in their communities and political societies.

The U.S. government has announced the goal of working toward a Middle East Free Trade Area, or MEFTA, by 2013. The United States has been seeking comprehensive free trade agreements (FTAs) with the Middle Eastern nations most firmly on the path to reform. The U.S.-Israeli FTA was enacted in 1985, and Congress implemented an FTA with Jordan in 2001. Both agreements have expanded trade and investment, thereby supporting domestic economic reform. In 2004, new FTAs were signed with Morocco and Bahrain, and are awaiting congressional approval. These models are drawing the interest of their neighbors. Muslim countries can become full participants in the rules-based global trading system, as the United States considers lowering its trade barriers with the poorest Arab nations.

Recommendation: A comprehensive U.S. strategy to counter terrorism should include economic policies that encourage development, more open societies, and opportunities for people to improve the lives of their families and to enhance prospects for their children's future.

Turning a National Strategy into a Coalition Strategy

Practically every aspect of U.S. counterterrorism strategy relies on international cooperation. Since 9/11, these contacts concerning military, law enforcement, intelligence, travel and customs, and financial matters have expanded so dramatically, and often in an ad hoc way, that it is difficult to track these efforts, much less integrate them.

Recommendation: The United States should engage other nations in developing a comprehensive coalition strategy against Islamist terrorism. There are several multilateral institutions in which such issues should be addressed. But the most important policies should be discussed and coordinated in a flexible contact group of leading coalition governments. This is a good place, for example, to develop joint strategies for targeting terrorist travel, or for hammering out a common strategy for the places where terrorists may be finding sanctuary.

Presently the Muslim and Arab states meet with each other, in organizations such as the Islamic Conference and the Arab League. The Western states meet with each other in organizations such as NATO and the Group of Eight summit of leading industrial nations. A recent G-8 summit initiative to begin a dialogue about reform may be a start toward finding a place where leading Muslim states can discuss—and be seen to discuss—critical policy issues with the leading Western powers committed to the future of the Arab and Muslim world.

These new international efforts can create durable habits of visible cooperation, as states willing to step up to their responsibilities join together in constructive efforts to direct assistance and coordinate action.

Coalition warfare also requires coalition policies on what to do with enemy captives. Allegations that the United States abused prisoners in its custody make it harder to build the diplomatic, political, and military alliances the government will need. The United States should work with friends to develop mutually agreed-on principles for the detention and humane treatment of captured international terrorists who are not being held under a particular country's criminal laws. Countries such as Britain, Australia, and Muslim friends, are committed to fighting terrorists. America should be able to reconcile its views on how to balance humanity and security with our nation's commitment to these same goals.

The United States and some of its allies do not accept the application of full Geneva Convention treatment of prisoners of war to captured terrorists. Those Conventions establish a minimum set of standards for prisoners in internal conflicts. Since the international struggle against Islamist terrorism is not internal, those provisions do not formally apply, but they are commonly accepted as basic standards for humane treatment.

Recommendation: The United States should engage its friends to develop a common coalition approach toward the detention and humane treatment of captured terrorists. New principles might draw upon Article 3 of the Geneva Conventions on the law of armed conflict. That article was specifically designed for those cases in which the usual laws of war did not apply. Its minimum standards are generally accepted throughout the world as customary international law.

Proliferation of Weapons of Mass Destruction

The greatest danger of another catastrophic attack in the United States will materialize if the world's most dangerous terrorists acquire the world's most dangerous weapons. . . . [A]l Qaeda has tried to acquire or make nuclear weapons for at least ten years. . . . [O]fficials worriedly discuss[ed], in 1998, reports that Bin Ladin's associates thought their leader was intent on carrying out a "Hiroshima."

These ambitions continue. In the public portion of his February 2004 worldwide threat assessment to Congress, DCI Tenet noted that Bin Ladin considered the acquisition of weapons of mass destruction to be a "religious obligation." He warned that al Qaeda "continues to pursue its strategic goal of obtaining a nuclear capability." Tenet added that "more than two dozen other terrorist groups are pursuing CBRN [chemical, biological, radiological, and nuclear] materials."[28]

A nuclear bomb can be built with a relatively small amount of nuclear material. A trained nuclear engineer with an amount of highly enriched uranium or plutonium about the size of a grapefruit or an orange, together with commercially available material, could fashion a nuclear device that would fit in a van like the one Ramzi Yousef parked in the garage of the World Trade Center in 1993. Such a bomb would level Lower Manhattan.[29]

The coalition strategies we have discussed to combat Islamist terrorism should therefore be combined with a parallel, vital effort to prevent and counter the proliferation of weapons of mass destruction (WMD). We recommend several initiatives in this area.

Strengthen Counterproliferation Efforts.   While efforts to shut down Libya's illegal nuclear program have been generally successful, Pakistan's illicit trade and the nuclear smuggling networks of Pakistani scientist A. Q. Khan have revealed that the spread of nuclear weapons is a problem of global dimensions. Attempts to deal with Iran's nuclear program are still underway. Therefore, the United States should work with the international community to develop laws and an international legal regime with universal jurisdiction to enable the capture, interdiction, and prosecution of such smugglers by any state in the world where they do not disclose their activities.

Expand the Proliferation Security Initiative.   In May 2003, the Bush administration announced the Proliferation Security Initiative (PSI): nations in a willing partnership combining their national capabilities to use military, economic, and diplomatic tools to interdict threatening shipments of WMD and missile-related technology.

The PSI can be more effective if it uses intelligence and planning resources of the NATO alliance. Moreover, PSI membership should be open to non-NATO countries. Russia and China should be encouraged to participate.

Support the Cooperative Threat Reduction Program.   Outside experts are deeply worried about the U.S. government's commitment and approach to securing the weapons and highly dangerous materials still scattered in Russia and other countries of the Soviet Union. The government's main instrument in this area, the Cooperative Threat Reduction Program (usually referred to as "Nunn-Lugar," after the senators who sponsored the legislation in 1991), is now in need of expansion, improvement, and resources. The U.S. government has recently redoubled its international commitments to support this program, and we recommend that the United States do all it can, if Russia and other countries will do their part. The government should weigh the value of this investment against the catastrophic cost America would face should such weapons find their way to the terrorists who are so anxious to acquire them.

Editors' Note: *Notes for this reading can be found in the original source.*

Credits

pp. 20–26: "Take the Rich off Welfare" by Mark Zepezauer from *Take the Rich off Welfare,* pp. 1, 82–89. Reprinted by permission of South End Press.

pp. 27–32: "Tax Cheats and Their Enablers" by Robert S. McIntyre, Citizens for Tax Justice, 2005. Reprinted by permission.

pp. 33–43: "The Cost of Money" from *Selling Out* by Mark Green. Copyright © 2002 by Mark Green. Reprinted by permission of HarperCollins Publishers.

pp. 44–49: "Water for Profit" by John Luoma from *Mother Jones,* November/December 2002. Copyright © 2002, Foundation for National Progress. Reprinted by permission.

pp. 53–64: "Nickel-and-Dimed: On (Not) Getting by in America" by Barbara Ehrenreich from *Harper's,* January 1999. Copyright © 1999 by Barbara Ehrenreich. Reprinted by permission of International Creative Management, Inc.

pp. 65–74: "Generation Broke" by Tamara Draut and Javier Silva. Reprinted by permission of Demos.

pp. 75–81: "Retirement's Unraveling Safety Net" by Dale Russakoff from *Washington Post,* May 15, 2005. Copyright © 2005, The Washington Post, reprinted with permission.

pp. 82–92: "The Limits of Markets" by Robert Kuttner from *The American Prospect,* March/April. Reprinted by permission.

pp. 95–103: From *Top Heavy: The Increasing Inequality of Wealth in America and What Can Be Done about It,* by Edward Wolff,

pp. 104–111: "Doing Poorly: The Real Income of American Children in Comparative Perspective" by Lee Rainwater and Timothy M. Smeeding. Reprinted by permission.

pp. 112–120: Reprinted with the permission of The Free Press, a division of Simon & Schuster Adult Publishing Group, from *Tell Them Who I Am: The Lives of Homeless Women* by Elliot Liebow. Copyright © 1993 by Elliot Liebow.

pp. 121–126: "As Rich-Poor Gap Widens in the U.S., Class Mobility Stalls" by David Wessel from *The Wall Street Journal,* May 13, 2005. Copyright © 2005 Dow Jones & Co. Reprinted by permission of Dow Jones & Co. via Copyright Clearance Center.

pp. 130–135: "The Roots of White Advantage" by Michael K. Brown from *Whitewashing Race,* pp. 66, 77–79, 26–30. Copyright The University of California Press. Reprinted by permission of The University of California Press via Copyright Clearance Center.

pp. 136–141: "Schools and Prisons: Fifty Years after *Brown v. Board of Education.*" Reprinted by permission of The Sentencing Project.

pp. 142–147: "At Many Colleges, the Rich Kids Get Affirmative Action" by Daniel Golden from *The Wall Street Journal,* February 20, 2003. Copyright © 2003 Dow Jones & Co. Reprinted by permission of Dow Jones & Co. via Copyright Clearance Center.